WITHDRAWN
HARVARD LIBRARY
WITHDRAWN

The Sermons of
Henry King (1592–1669),
Bishop of Chichester

Portrait of Henry King, Bishop of Chichester, in the council chamber, Council House, Chichester. (Photo by Ken Clinch, reproduced by permission of Chichester City Council.)

The Sermons of Henry King (1592–1669), Bishop of Chichester

Edited with an Introduction and Commentary
by Mary Hobbs

Rutherford • Madison • Teaneck
Fairleigh Dickinson University Press

Scolar Press

© 1992 by Associated University Presses, Inc.

All rights reserved. Authorization to photocopy items for internal or personal use, or the internal or personal use of specific clients, is granted by the copyright owner, provided that a base fee of $10.00, plus eight cents per page, per copy is paid directly to the Copyright Clearance Center, 27 Congress Street, Salem, Massachusetts 01970. [0-8386-3390-0/92 $10.00+8¢ pp, pc.]

Associated University Presses
440 Forsgate Drive
Cranbury, NJ 08512

The paper used in this publication meets the requirements of the American National Standard for Permanence of Paper for Printed Library Materials Z39.48-1984.

Library of Congress Cataloging-in-Publication Data

King, Henry, 1592–1669.
 [Sermons]
 The sermons of Henry King (1592–1669), Bishop of Chichester / edited with an introduction and commentary by Mary Hobbs.
  p. cm.
 Includes bibliographical references and indexes.
 ISBN 0-8386-3390-0 (alk. paper)
 1. Church of England—Sermons. 2. Anglican Communion—Sermons. 3. Sermons, English. I. Hobbs, Mary. II. Title.
 BX5133.K47S44 1992
 252'.03—dc20   89-46292
                                              CIP

Published in Great Britain in 1992 by
Scolar Press
Gower House
Croft Road
Aldershot
Hants GU11 3HR
England

British Library Cataloguing-in-Publication Data
King, Henry 1592–1669
 The sermons of Henry King (1592–1669), Bishop of Chichester.
 1. Church of England. Sermons
 I. Title II. Hobbs, Mary
 252.03

ISBN 0-85967-839-3

PRINTED IN THE UNITED STATES OF AMERICA

Contents

Abbreviations   8
Preface   9

1. Introduction   15
    The Life   15
        Before the Civil Wars   15
        Civil Wars and Interregnum   22
        The Restoration   25
    An Adventurer in a Middle Way   31
    The Sermons   40
        King as Preacher   40
        Structure   41
        Style   44
        Imagery   47
        King and Donne   48
    Henry King's Reading   50
    Notes to the Introduction   53

2. Editorial Principles   59
    The Sermons: Abbreviations   60

3. The Sermons to 1627   63
    1621   63
    Act   82
    Spital   95
    Lent 1   115
    Lent 2   125

4. An Exposition upon the Lord's Prayer   135
    I. An Exposition upon the Lord's Prayer   135
    II. Our Father which art in Heaven   143
    III. Hallowed be thy Name   151
    IV. Thy Kingdome come   159
    V. Thy will bee done in Earth, etc.   166
    VI. Give us this day our daily Bread   175
    VII. And forgive us our Debts   184
    VIII. As wee forgive our Debtors   191
    IX. And leade us not into Temptation   196
    X. But deliver us from Evill   203
    XI. For thine is the Kingdome, etc.   210

5. The Sermons to 1669   219
    1640   219
    1661   232
    Duppa   241
    Visitation   252
    Commemoration of Charles I, King and Martyr   263

CONTENTS

Explanatory Notes	277
Appendix 1: Index of Sources Used by King	301
Appendix 2: A Chronology of King's Life	310
Glossary	315
Bibliography	320
Index to the Sermons	323
General Index	332

Abbreviations

Ath. Oxon.	*Athenae Oxonienses*
BL	British Library, London
Bod.	Bodleian Library, Oxford
OED	*Oxford English Dictionary*
PRO	Public Record Office, London
SAC	*Sussex Archaeological Collections*
SRS	Sussex Record Society

Also see THE SERMONS: ABBREVIATIONS, pp. 60–62.

Preface

The poems of Henry King, friend of John Donne and executor of his will, were edited in 1967 by Margaret Crum, but his sermons have not been reprinted since the seventeenth century. Modern historians, literary scholars, and theologians have not yet discovered the quality and value of his prose. Nor are they aware of King's historical significance as a representative figure from the true "middle" of the seventeenth-century Church of England (however that broad middle ground may have moved over the period). My first consideration, therefore, has been to make available to the widest modern audience, in accessible form, the text of Henry King's prose. Only by that availability will the unfortunate accidents of history that have led to his neglect be overcome.

A sensitive reading of the sermons, which have a much wider range of interest than sermons of today, suggests their importance on their own merits as fine examples of seventeenth-century prose. Like metaphysical poetry, they cry out to be read aloud. At times, they startle with a beauty of rhythm and phrase comparable to that of Thomas Browne, or of Donne himself at his most melodious. King cannot be shown to have Donne's compelling vigour and density of thought, or the sudden ingenuity of some of his analogies and imagery. Nor has he the elliptical staccato force of Lancelot Andrewes, or Joseph Hall's homely vigour of image and hearty courtier's bonhomie. At King's quite frequent best, however, in grace of structure, sweetness of sound, elegiac intensity of mood, and occasional dry wit, he has few equals. Most readers of Donne's prose encounter his finer anthologised passages only, but in his 160 extant sermons, his editor Evelyn Simpson was the first to admit how much was "dull and tedious."[1]

Of the many sermons King must have preached, only ten, with a further eleven collected and published as *An Exposition upon the Lord's Prayer* in 1628, survive today, spanning his long life as a cleric, from the reign of James I to that of Charles II. In comparison with Donne, therefore, we possess a correspondingly high proportion of his more carefully wrought and polished writing, with inspired meditative passages, fascinating byways of learning, and many contemporary insights. Thomas Fuller was convinced that King's "printed Sermons on the Lords-prayer, and others which he preached, remaining fresh in the minds of his Auditors will report him to all posterity."[2] But it was not to be.

My introduction and notes, lengthy as they may seem, are necessarily a skeleton (from which indeed some of the bones may still be missing). It has been assembled in order that specialists from other disciplines besides the literary may be encouraged to join in reconstructing the whole. The difficulties facing an editor today in presenting King, or any other seventeenth-century preacher, without a lifetime of studying the subjects that were part of his thorough education in (for instance) literature, ancient history, philosophy, and theology, can be paralleled in another modern context. Speaking on Italian Renaissance academies, that great polymath Frances Yates still had to admit, "Our urgent need is that a Greek scholar who is a specialist in late Byzantine history and also in fifteenth-century Italy should turn his attention to these problems."[3] The inevitable incompleteness of my work is, however, no good reason for not beginning the preliminary task—that is, to present King's sermons in more easily accessible context for the modern reader than their present seventeenth-century dress.

Much about King's life can be read elsewhere, but so far it has not adequately been set within its background. Already, in the introduction that follows, a new picture is presented, from the sermons and elsewhere, of King's role at the time the Laudian canons were drawn up in 1640 and as one of the few active bishops who remained in England during the Interregnum. His will, however, and the material found in various account books, ecclesiastical registers, and his Restoration correspondence with Archbishop Sheldon need further investigation. I have also pointed towards literary areas that would repay more specialised study (such as the relationship of the sermons to those of Joseph Hall and John Donne, and to the work of Richard Hooker).

The keen interest of historians today in the Church of this period has brought a growing realisation of the importance of the beleaguered and largely unexplored middle position between the well-served Puritan and Arminian extremes, as a norm for defining them. Because the sermon was a major forum for ideas in that age, Henry King's writings play a part here. Since he was not a notably original thinker, he was a thoroughly representative moderate Calvinist (though, like others who started from that position, he was forced nearer as the century progressed to what might be termed moderate Arminianism). His comments on contemporary issues, therefore, provide a touchstone for the truth of scholars' deductions from new information brought to light by recent specialist studies of early seventeenth-century records. A fuller picture of King's career also highlights the need for more detailed investigation than previously afforded of those bishops who remained in England during the long twenty years of wars and interregnum. Moreover, many of the issues that faced the seventeenth-century church are once more present today, both from within and without, particularly over church discipline and government.

King has an added strength over most other sermon writers of the period with similar views. As a poet and a lover of music, he used language rhythmically and picturesquely, without a fierce straining of conceits, so that he is both readable and memorable.

In the literary field, King's prose is important not only for itself but also for a fuller understanding of his poetry. At times it supports, at others it suggests the need for a reappraisal of the evidence for the dating and canon of his poems, his methods of composition, and his reading. Some would argue today that such considerations are not relevant, any more than is the biography of a poet, in approaching poetry. The tortured speculations about meaning, however, in reputable modern academic writings on seventeenth-century literature and on John Donne's poetry in particular, show that knowledge of a writer's personal and contemporary background and of the changed usage of words is still necessary to solve "problems" that are sometimes of a critic's own making.

Since Margaret Crum's edition of King's poems, which has established itself as the foundation of modern King studies, significant new material has come to light. She based her work on three major authoritative manuscripts. Three other similarly authoritative manuscripts are now known, and I have found a catalogue in Chichester Cathedral Library listing many of the books King owned. Some of these are still on the shelves, marked at passages quoted in his writings, and at least fifteen more titles appear in this catalogue from John Donne's library than Sir Geoffrey Keynes recorded at Chichester in his bibliography of Donne. Moreover, two of King's sermons bear an important, hitherto-unnoted relationship to two of Donne's, of interest to the study of both writers; Richard Hooker's influence can be detected—as one might expect, remembering Henry King's temporary possession of the manuscript of the last three books of the *Laws of Ecclesiastical Polity*—in some unnoticed areas of King's thought. Other intriguing literary connections, for instance with George Herbert, suggest further areas for investigation, while the generally accepted view of Henry King's close friendship with Izaak Walton needs revising.[4]

The extraordinary modern disregard of King can be traced in the first place to unkind accidents of chance, the wars that deprived him of his manuscripts, and the absence of a biographer or printed funeral sermon from which literary historians might quote. His neglect in this century is no doubt the result of a cavalier dismissal of him as a "kind of pale imitation of Donne" in Fraser Mitchell's *English Pulpit Oratory* (1932), an influential study of seventeenth-century preaching, written in the wake of T. S. Eliot's 1930s revival of interest in seventeenth-century poetry and prose. There has been no subsequent, firsthand appraisal of the complete canon of King's prose. Not surprisingly, therefore, More and Cross omitted him from *Anglicanism* (1937), their equally influential anthology of "authoritative" seventeenth-century religious literature.[5]

Purists will regret, as I do myself, the discreet modernisation of punctuation for the sake of clarity, the omission of longer Latin and Greek quotations where King has expressed their meaning in his own words, and the transliteration of the short Greek quotations, chiefly biblical, that remain (see *Editorial Principles*). Relatively few students of seventeenth-century literature, history, or even theology nowadays know Greek or have the necessary perseverance to read attentively through a text too much broken up by such quotations. The lines from classical poets have been retained, however, since King clearly used them not so much to display his learning as because of his sheer love of old schooltexts as familiar to his audience as to himself.

The only full set of the original sermons available is that in the Bodleian Library at Oxford, to which I am indebted for my copytext of all but the *Exposition upon the Lord's Prayer*. Those wishing to investigate the physical similarity suggested in the introduction between the printed text of the early sermons and King's printed poems (which reflect his carefully supervised manuscripts)[6] will need to consult the originals. One day, when King is better known, a facsimile reproduction of them would of course do him greater justice.

Fortunately, the late Sir Geoffrey Keynes gave a full bibliographical account of King's prose in *A Bibliography of Henry King D. D. Bishop of Chichester* (1977): the appropriate references to this work will be found in the notes to each sermon.

I wish to thank Dr. Andrew Foster for his firm belief in Henry King's importance to modern historical studies (to which he introduced me), and his unfailing help and encouragement, as well as Miss Ursula Bickersteth for her sustaining support. Dr. Peter Beal, the Reverend Dr. Richard Bowyer, the Reverend Jeremy Haselock, the Reverend Canon Professor Roy Porter, Mrs. Mary Holtby, the late Miss Joan Hopkins, Mr. Hilton Kelliher, the Reverend Gavin Kirk, the Right Reverend Edward Knapp-Fisher, Mrs. Katherine Lippiett, and Mr. Jeremy Potter all have given invaluable help of one kind or another. I must thank Mr. John Creasey and Mrs. Josephine Barnes of Dr. Williams's Library in particular for far-reaching and cheerful assistance, which I also received from several fellow cathedral librarians: Mr. Bernard Barr of York Minster, Miss Penelope Morgan of Hereford, and Mrs. Enid Nixon of Westminster Abbey. I am grateful in addition to the staff of the Bodleian Library, the British Library, the University of London Library and that of its Institute of Classical Studies, and of the libraries of Trinity College, Dublin, and the Warburg Institute. I hope Professor Henry Chadwick, K.B.E., will not mind my recording his important role, together with that of the late Dame Helen Gardner, in putting me on the right road. Finally, I thank those who typed transcripts of the sermons, Mrs. Jillie Appleforth, Mrs. Jennie Paterson, and Miss Marjorie Preston, as well as my patient husband Keith, who has had to share me for so many years with Henry King.

Notes

1. "He is the most uneven of writers" (Donne, *Sermons* 6.15–16); and see 7.1: "in even the greatest sermons, there are frequent passages in which we descend from the heights to the lower plane of bitter controversy or of over-subtle exposition."
2. Fuller, *Worthies*, 133.
3. Frances Yates, *Collected Essays*, vol. 2 (London: Routledge, and Kegan Paul, 1983), p. 9.
4. Poems by Herbert undoubtedly seem echoed by King; see notes to *ELP I*. They were exact contemporaries at Westminster, though they went to different universities and there is no external evidence of friendship other than their mutual friendship with Donne. When King was writing, however, Herbert's poems were unprinted and never in general circulation in manuscript verse anthologies. Izaak Walton is not mentioned among the few friends named in King's will in 1653, which, taken with King's address "Honest Isaac!" in the

letter prefacing the life of Hooker in 1664, suggests that the "closeness" of their friendship could be as fictitious as Shakespeare's meetings with Ben Jonson at the Mermaid; though see Crum, *Poems,* 13 and note.

5. Horton Davies's recent study of metaphysical preachers *Like Angels from a Cloud* follows Mitchell Fraser's biased critical assessment and is seriously inaccurate in King's biographical details.

6. See Crum, *Poems,* 54 and the fuller discussion of King's manuscripts in Hobbs, "Stoughton Manuscript" 81–102.

The Sermons of
Henry King (1592–1669),
Bishop of Chichester

1
Introduction

THE LIFE

It is now over twenty years since Margaret Crum wrote her scholarly life of Henry King to introduce his poems, and the time has come for another assessment. Like all who succeeded John Hannah, Crum built on his pioneer edition of 1843, which in its thorough, Victorian way recorded much of the family documentation then still available, including wills, memorial inscriptions, letters, and genealogies—not only of Henry King, but of his ancestors and immediate descendants. In addition, she correlated and corrected the more recent work of Lawrence Mason and Percy Simpson,[1] and examined hitherto unnoted manuscript sources in the Bodleian, particularly among the Fell papers (Bod. MSS Rawlinson D.317, 398, and 1092), John Walker's papers for his *Sufferings of the Clergy* (Bod. MSS J. Walker), the University archives, and William Fulman's manuscripts, now at Corpus Christi College. Earlier modern editors—George Saintsbury, John Sparrow, James Baker—were less concerned with King's life than his poems, but there was a useful, though rather selective, study of his place in seventeenth-century thought by Ronald Berman, and some valuable *obiter dicta* are to be found in Sir Geoffrey Keynes's bibliography of King.

The bare facts are these: Henry King (1592–1669), the eldest of the five sons of Dr. John King—Bishop of London from 1611 until his death in 1621—was born at Worminghall in Oxfordshire, and educated first at Thame, and then with his next brother John at Westminster and Christ Church. At Oxford, they together took the degrees of bachelor of arts and master of arts in 1611 and 1614, in 1624 both were made canons of Christ Church, and in 1625, bachelor of divinity and doctor of divinity. In the absence of any record, it seems likely Henry was ordained by 23 January 1616, when he was made a prebendary of St. Paul's in London. University statutes did not allow Fellows to be married, so after only three years as a don, Henry King had to leave Oxford in 1617 (in which year he also became archdeacon of Colchester) when he married Anne Berkeley, an heiress, about nine years his junior. He was a royal chaplain to James I and Charles I, but gained no other preferment until 1639 when he was made Dean of Rochester; and in 1642 (the day after a bill in Parliament to deprive bishops of their place in the House of Lords) he became Bishop of Chichester. Within a year, he was ejected from his see after the siege of that city. He remained in England, withdrawn but active, until the Restoration. Like Bishop Duppa of Salisbury and a very few others, he secretly continued to ordain men to the ministry according to the Prayer Book ordinal. He was one of two bishops chosen to cross the Channel and consecrate new ones, but Charles II was recalled before this was effected. At the age of sixty-eight, King returned to Chichester without preferment, where he died nine years later and was buried in his cathedral. Had this been all, his perhaps would be considered an unremarkable career; but closer examination reveals a very different picture.

BEFORE THE CIVIL WARS

Henry King was a poet and the friend of musicians and poets, notably of John Donne until his death in 1631. In 1615, his father ordained Donne, then a lawyer, only a year before Henry's own ordination, though Donne was twenty years his senior. During his lifetime, Henry King was a popular preacher. His sermon on his father's death immediately went into three editions, and *An Exposition upon the Lord's Prayer* (1628) was revised and reprinted in 1634 and reached a second impression the same year. His 1661 sermon for Charles II's birthday, with its remarks on hereditary kingship, was reprinted after his death, in 1713, when the question of the Hanoverian succession seemed likely to produce a similar political crisis to the civil war he described. There have been no further editions of his prose, however. King's poems, written for the most part in the 1620s and 1630s, circulated in manuscript, some quite widely, and were first published in 1657, preceded in 1651 by his verse translation of the Psalms.

Scattered records are gradually filling out details of King's life. The Deans' Books of St. Paul's give information on the layout of "Vicaridge House" near St. Paul's Churchyard, in which he lived when Archdeacon of Colchester: he succeeded in transferring it to his son Henry's name on the eve of the Civil War. I am indebted to Dr. Peter Beal for an entry in George Aungier's account books (sold at Sothebys, 26 June 1984) that shows that as early as 1634 King paid rent for a house near Albury, Surrey. King's will and the 1646 draft Chancery petition drawn up by the mathematician, William Oughtred, Rector of Albury, about King's son John's seduction of Oughtred's youngest daughter,[2] reveal that King, his sister Elizabeth Holt, and their families were living in that area from 1643 to 1646.

A hitherto unnoted entry in the Lincoln's Inn admissions book shows that Henry King was made an honorary member of that Inn on 6 June 1619, with his uncle Philip King, Auditor of St. Paul's and of Christ Church, as one of his sponsors.[3] This is significant, for King's use of legal imagery is greater than usual for anyone other than a lawyer, even for that litigious age. He was executor of his uncle's will in 1636 and evidently was very close to him. He may refer to having contemplated a legal career himself when he says in his 1621 sermon that his father, Bishop John King, had "dedicated (in his desire) all his Sonnes . . . to the Ministery of this Church, and by no means willing to heare of any other course (though otherwise invited by *gracious offers for some of them in particular*" (italics mine). His membership of the Inn may also explain how he obtained access to manuscript versions of Donne's sermons circulating in the 1620s chiefly among the Inns of Court and why some of his rarely copied poems are found in verse commonplace books from the same source.[4] Moreover, his 1626 Whitehall sermon answers Donne's Valediction sermon preached at Lincoln's Inn, on the same text from Ecclesiastes: "Remember now thy Creator in the days of thy youth."[5]

On 5 November 1617, Henry King preached his first public sermon, at Paul's Cross, for the anniversary of the Gunpowder Plot. Chamberlain's unkind comment, quoted by Margaret Crum, about so young a man beginning "in such a place and such a time" suggests some personal dislike of him or his father since, as Millar Maclure points out, promising young men who had left the university frequently made their debut there.[6] His first printed sermon was also preached there in 1621, a defence of his father (who had died on 30 March) against a Roman Catholic claim that he had been converted on his deathbed. The rumours were published in *The English Protestant's Plea* some time after 19 September, the date of its imprimatur by Matthew Kellison, president of the English College at Douai. King James directed Henry to preach in reply, which he did on 25 November, three days after Donne was installed as Dean of St. Paul's. The sermon was registered at Stationers' Hall on 14 December and ran to three editions before 25 March, the next two carrying the retraction of the libeller, in "The Examination of Thomas Preston," dated 20 December.[7] In apologising to the reader at the end for thus checking the rumours "on the sudden," "till haply some more deliberate pen" could answer with a less "hastily formed" birth, Henry reveals that "those calumnious tongues gave out my Revolt also as well as my Father's," and that his brother John "also had his share in this lewd imputation."

Despite the personal provocation, King's attack on papists and the Pope is less vehement or scurrilous than is common among contemporary writers. The lyric poet is never far absent from the sermon writer; the Pope, for instance, will "lessen himselfe, and contract his greatnesse into short titles, (as the Snake hides her length by folding her selfe up into many gyres, and doubles) . . . even when he means to *build his nest in the Starres;* when he aims not at Rome's alone, but the worlds *supremacy.*" In the 1621 sermon, King discourses for the first time on two of his recurrent themes; the necessity of order in the natural world and in its microcosm, the world of men, and the nature of memory. He also makes his first attack in print on unlettered Puritan preachers, "Lay Mechanicke Presbiters of both sexes," who "torment a Text" as if they were trying to become journeymen to the pulpit as well as their trades. "A little lesse preaching, and some more praying would doe well," he remarks tartly. When he comes to the possibilities of any converter approaching the Bishop's bed unseen, he wittily reduces the whole thing to absurdity. The detailed account of this good man's death, evidently from cancer, attended not only by his family but by senior bishops of the English Church deserves to be better known.

Henry King's most popular poem "An Exequy" was written about the death of his young wife Anne in January 1624. Like his elegy on his father,[8] however, the poem was not necessarily (as has been assumed) composed at the actual time of her death. There are passages about sorrow, mutability, and loss, surmounted by triumphant hope, that show close similarity not only to the tone, but to the wording of the poem, in the two Lent sermons of 1626 and 1627 and also in the undated sermon that forms the fourth section, "Thy Will be Done," in *The Lord's Prayer.* This suggests that they and the poem all may have been written about the same, slightly later, period. His determined attempt to come to Christian terms with the loss of his wife issued in the sermons in a great hope and confidence in the Resurrection, at a time when many preachers were turning inwards, wracked by doubts of their salvation.

In the year following Anne's death, Henry and John King received their divinity degrees together at Oxford; a week later, the King and Parliament moved there to avoid the worsening plague. The proclamation ordering the Vice-Chancellor and Heads of Houses to clear the University was received on the day after the two brothers preached the sermons for the Act or degree-giving at Morning and Evening Prayer in the University Church of St. Mary the Virgin. Henry's is one of two of his sermons that bear a strong resemblance to, though not through plagiarising, sermons of Donne's.

The Act sermon was preached (if Evelyn Simpson's deduction is correct) in the same year, on the same text, as one in Donne's series on the thirty-second Psalm.[9] Both preachers deal with repentance and confession. They quote many of the same authors, but it is King who identifies the exact location of his quotations in his margins. In addition, there are resemblances in both sermons to Hooker's treatise on confession, printed during the Civil War as the sixth book of *Ecclesiastical Polity.* The manuscript, as we learn from King's letter to Izaak Walton prefixed to the *Life* of Hooker, was almost certainly at that time in Henry King's possession; though later it was demanded from him by Archbishop Abbot. The resemblances are closer than would result merely from King and Donne's independent use of the same commentators on their text, or a closeness in position to Hooker, that great cartographer of the Anglican via media. Nevertheless, they develop their theme in different ways; one would guess that they discussed both Hooker's views and those further points and illustrations that they shared. Evelyn Simpson notes that during his later years, Donne "learned to depend on the younger friends and scholars who looked up to him with admiration. . . . [George] Herbert and Henry King are the most eminent of these and Donne had warm affection for both of them."[10]

Donne's sermon follows Hooker in relating private confession not only to auricular confession as practised by the Roman Catholic Church, but to public confession and to satisfaction for sin; neither point was touched on by King. On the other hand, King follows Hooker in two detailed attacks on the Roman Catholic position, which Donne merely glances at in passing. Their treatment of the Roman Church differs: Henry on the whole attacks with facts, though not with the long historical background found in Hooker's more leisurely treatise. The worst indictment King makes is that the successors of Peter have attempted to sit "as God . . . to condemn or to absolve like him . . . a Riot not lesse then Lucifer's; and their aspiring violence must expect a Præcipitation as violent and deepe as his." Donne, the still-sensitive convert, is vitriolic in comparison, with comments such as: "in the Romane Church, they poysoned God, (when they had made their Breadgod they poysoned the Emperour with that bread)."[11]

Two of King's sections in particular resemble Donne's sermon verbally—that on David's repentance and the speed of God's forgiveness, and that on the uses of adversity (topics both share with Hooker). Elsewhere, however, there are constant, brief, verbal resemblances, similar to the echoes of Shakespeare's plays in others of King's sermons, as though he might be writing in the context of Donne's words. At so close a date, it seems likely that if King's sermon is the later, Donne himself (in the absence of any known manuscript copies of his sermon) was King's source.

Henry's discourse is primarily pastoral, on the need for repentance for wrongdoing and God's mercy in forgiving. Notwithstanding, the carefully reasoned arguments are couched (presumably with his Oxford audience in mind) in a style quite different from his other sermons, using the terms of academic or legal disputation: "Nay, we find . . . But Eckius and others answer. . . . Well then, grant . . . and it shall appear. . . ." His clear statement of the position of *central* Anglicans on confession at that period (which also follows Hooker) is particularly valuable: Donne touches on this subject only in passing. The Church of England's unquestioning acceptance of the word "absolve"—"we refuse not private confession made to God, nay, sometimes, a *private Confession* to our ghostly Father the Minister, who hath authoritie . . . to pronounce an *Absolution* upon our hearty *Repentance*"—is sometimes conveniently forgotten in controversy today.

To lead into his beautiful final prayer, King ends, as so often in the prewar sermons, with a "devout exstasie." (White Kennett, referring to him in his *Register* with approval as a "most admirable and florid Preacher in his younger days," clearly had such passages in mind.) "I am at my farthest, even lost and confounded in the vast subject of God's mercy; which like *a deepe sea* through which I cannot wade, stops my passage; so that here I can onely stand upon the banck, and cry with S. Paul, *O altitudo, O the depth of his mercy.*"[12]

The plague of 1625 was the worst of the century before the Great Plague of 1665. As a result, the marriage of Charles I and his French queen Henrietta Maria was delayed till February 1626, and Henry King's first Whitehall sermon of the new reign, in Lent (an occasion that puts him in the same bracket as famous preachers like Lancelot Andrewes, Joseph Hall, and Donne) followed almost immediately afterwards on 3 March. It was the one that took the same text as Donne's Valediction sermon (probably familiar in manuscript to many of his hearers). Beautiful writing is found in all King's sermons, but this and the one preached for the following Lent of 1627 are the finest in their entirety of all King's prose: essay-sermons (King knew Montaigne and quotes him in the second edition of *The Lord's Prayer*) overlaid with an elegiac melancholy, which anticipates the harmonies of Thomas Browne in the next decade. The meditations, perhaps inspired by school or university "themes," on youth and age, on mutability, on God's Book of Creatures, or on the symbolism of the dove in the Psalms, are clearly the work of one who, as Fuller later described him, "delighted in the studies of *Musick* and *Poetry.*"[13] The two sermons are alike, too, in their natural style, light use of Latin and Greek, echoes of Shakespeare, and more generalised references to learned sources: "a Father" or "the Philosopher."

Also in 1626, King was chosen to preach in the prestigious Easter sermon-marathon held annually before the Lord Mayor, the Aldermen, and Common Councillors of the City of London. From Easter Monday to Wednesday, these sermons were delivered from an open-air pulpit near the Spital, the old Bedlam Hospital of St. Mary outside Bishopsgate, and by custom were particularly long.[14] Henry, who preached for the most part for the conventional contemporary "hour's stay" to which he invites his audience at the beginning of his funeral sermon for Bishop Duppa, overcomes the difficulty by virtually preaching three sermons in a row, on the literal, historical, and moral aspects of his text of "deliverance" from the ninety-first Psalm. His sermon is seventy-seven pages long in quarto, as compared with his average forty pages. He shows an awareness of his audience in his praise and blame of the City fathers' conduct of their affairs (in innocuously general terms, except for the practice of imprisoning debtors). Moneylending and fair dealing are recurrent themes, from the 1621 sermon to passages in *The Lord's Prayer* that are similar enough to suggest they may be contemporary with their dated counterparts.

After Old and New Testament examples of God's direct intervention in history, he cites examples from English history, popular at the time chiefly with ecclesiastical writers older than himself: the Armada, blown by the storms "till at last the Rockes became their Monument, and the fierce Northerne Sea their Grave," the Gunpowder Plot, and, he adds with interesting contemporary detail, the recently ended plague. Donne's sermon on 15 January to his parishioners at St. Dunstan's on the same theme is prophetic and macabre: "Every puff of wind within these walls, may blow the father into the son's eys, or the wife into her husband's. . . . Every grain of dust that flies here, is a piece of a Christian." Joseph Hall (shortly to become Bishop of Exeter), though he presents gruesome dramatic evocations like "Neither might the corpses be allowed to lie single in their earthen beds, but are piled up like faggots," is hectically joyful in his conviction that the danger is now past: "O how soon is our fasting and mourning turned into laughter and joy!"[15] Henry King is altogether more realistic. He also recalls vivid details, like the red cross marked on the door of sealed houses; but he cautiously warns against overconfidence: "In bedding or garments infected there is . . . a lurking, residuous contagion, able to cause a Relapse no lesse fearfull then the late Disease."

This is a carefully wrought sermon, more full of conceits than his later work, with a long, lively meditation on Christ's passion, death, descent into Hell, and resurrection, in terms of the contest between Christ and the Devil, which at times echo *Piers Plowman,* the mystery plays, or the mediaeval sermon. He compares sacred matters with classical legend more freely here than elsewhere, bringing in Perseus and the Gorgon, for instance, and the Trojan horse. There is immense vigour in the extended metaphor of the Devil's hunting after Christ from his birth, with the Jews as his pack of hounds tearing him to pieces. There are many memorable phrases, such as those referring to the fallen angels—"Those collapsed Spirits, like dying Stars, vanish't into sulphur and darkness"—and the plague, which "like a tempestuous *Autumne* . . . shakes us by heaps into our Graves."

Each of the residential prebendaries was required to preach in St. Paul's, though probably no more than twice a year,[16] and it seems King by 1626 had already preached the first seven of the sermons that make up the *The Lord's Prayer* (1628), for he starts the eighth, "As we Forgive our Debtors" (which tackles once more, as the 1621 and Spital sermons had done, his citizen and property-owning audience's business dealings), with a reference to the same "Contagion which lately dispersed us." This caused a gap in his sermon-course and may have been the occasion of his revising and deciding to print the series. In fact, from his references at the beginning of the fourth sermon to the return of Prince Charles from the Spanish expedition in October 1623, the first three may have predated even that event, and all four certainly were preached before the death of King James in March 1625. "This our Evening Sacrifice," at the end of the first sermon, suggests a course at Evensong—the Lord's Prayer was among the acceptable subjects laid down in August 1622 by James I's decree concerning afternoon sermons.

The Exposition upon the Lord's Prayer is the fullest account we have of King's theology and of his preaching method, and shows his prose style becoming more flexible and varied, in parallel with the dated sermons—the last two sections are far more relaxed, even gently humorous (as in the fear and terror that appear on all sides at the beginning of Sermon X: "*Temptation* (like Egypt) at our heeles, in the preceding Petition; and *Evill* (like the Canaanite) in This"). The book as a whole is a fascinating mixture of practical devotion, of scholastic theology, of polemical attacks against the two jarring extremes of Catholicism and Puritanism, and of serendipitous matters such as numerology, names, volcanoes, astronomy, and astrology. Much of it is in the meditative essay style of the 1626 and 1627 Whitehall sermons, with which several sections of *The Lord's Prayer* must have been contemporary. There is a resemblance to the style of Joseph Hall's meditations and earlier sermons in such measured phrases as "It was a wise meditation of a philosopher," or "One saith," and so on. There are once more set "themes"—man and the universe, the seven deadly sins, loss and decay.

It is true, the weighty theological and philosophical discourses on sin and forgiveness, backed up with evidence from the Fathers (in sermons seven and eight particularly, perhaps because these were prepared at leisure during the plague), and the legal imagery of debt, crime, and punishment, beloved of his period but alien to us, may daunt the modern reader a little. At the same time, King is, even today, a useful guide to understanding such complicated matters as God's will and his being, and (such is his instinct for teaching) the heaviest sermons are also those with the most delightful illustrations and colloquialisms. One simply must accept these less palatable passages as part of King's method to "unveil the sense" of the prayer for his untrained audience by making accessible to them—with analogies that for us are more attractive than the matters they illustrate—the great tradition of writings about it, not only in the early Church Fathers but in the Schoolmen and in contemporary theologians, both Catholic and Reformed.

Nevertheless, King keeps in sight a more important end, as in all his preaching and "thorowout this whole Tract upon Christ's Prayer" (as he points out before the final "Amen"): to "prepare your Meditations, by kindling a Religious zeale in you," with prayer, with gratitude to God for salvation, and by accepting life's hardships in sure hope of the glory to come. Each sermon is illuminated by passages rooted in the poetical books of the Old and New Testaments, and King's prose leaves a lasting impression of the brightness of eternity. His summary of the power of the prayer in the second section is unforgettable: "So that in this short Prayer, as in a little Orbe, the Sonne of righteousnesse moves. From hence doth every Starre, every faithful servant and Confessor of Christ (for they are Incarnate Starres), borrow a ray of light, to illuminate and sanctifie the body of his meditations."

Though he apparently at this time wrote no poetry, the years during which these sermons were preached and the book was prepared for publication represent his finest prose. It was a period when he moved in London musical and literary circles and knew people such as the antiquarian Henry Spelman who gave him a copy of his *Glossarium* on 27 June 1628 (now in Chichester Cathedral Library, with Henry's proud note of the gift on the front endpaper). It was far from the "arid period" after his wife's death suggested by Margaret Crum.[17]

When Donne died in 1631, his two executors, Henry King and John Mountfort, another residentiary canon of St. Paul's, were directed to sell his books for the estate, with the exception of a schedule of benefactions, now lost. One of these, Donne's Bellarmine, was left, according to Walton, to "a most dear Friend." This friend was evidently Henry King, for it, too, appears in Chichester Cathedral Library, in a binding that shows that Donne received it originally from Sir Thomas Roe.[18] An old catalogue at Chichester of the books inherited by Henry King's son John from his father and bequeathed to the Cathedral in 1672 suggests that after Donne died, Henry chose a number of small volumes for himself before selling the rest to booksellers (such as the one in Duck Lane, noted on the flyleaf of a Paracelsus from Donne's library). At least fifteen more than the six signed titles listed at Chichester by Sir Geoffrey Keynes in his bibliography show Donne's characteristic marginal markings.[19] In 1633, Donne's poems were printed. Their system of punctuation, to which Dame Helen Gardner drew attention,[20] as careful as the punctuation of Henry King's poetry manuscripts, makes it probable that King, and not Izaak Walton as some have thought, edited them in that year for publication.

In the thirties William Laud was in power, and Henry King apparently was out of favour (he ceased to sit on the Court of High Commission from 1633, the year Laud became Archbishop of Canterbury). He revised and in 1634 twice reprinted *The Lord's Prayer* and must have supervised the reprinting of his father's *Lectures upon Jonas* in the same year. A number of his lyrics and occasional poems also date from this period, but it is regrettable, when one considers the quantity of any preacher's regular output of sermons, that (like Joseph Hall and many others not in sympathy with Laud) he seems not to have been asked to preach at Court;[21] and we have no printed sermons from that decade. His sermon manuscripts presumably were lost, along with "my own Private Papers, which had bene the moniments of my course in study through all my life,"[22] at the siege of Chichester in 1642.

One other very important sermon remains from before the Civil Wars, preached at Paul's Cross on the anniversary of the King's accession in 1640. That year, Laud became increasingly unpopular for his insensitive approach to the liturgical reform of parish churches and clearly was searching for friends outside his own circle; in December, he was imprisoned in the Tower. It was no longer strictly possible to be a "moderate" Calvinist: the Arminians, from the time they were in the ascendant, had gradually forced Calvinist reformers into a position of open opposition they had not needed to assume under King James. King had been installed Dean of Rochester the previous year. As a senior ecclesiastic, still regarded as Calvinist in theology but devoted (like the Arminians) to the monarchy, he may have been set up by Laud, as acceptable to other moderates, to bolster the fading power of the King and the Church: the Paul's Cross sermons, which were long and weighty and preached before important personages in church and state, were used regularly to promote an official viewpoint. Joseph Hall, less of a moderate than King in both theology and style, was asked in the same year to write *Episcopacy by Divine Right* (though Laud insisted on a number of alterations before he would allow it to be printed).

Ronald Berman used King's sermon extensively to demonstrate his political thinking,[23] but even he overlooked the most significant fact about it. It was preached on 27 March, yet its first thirty-eight pages closely echo the wording of the first of the notorious Laudian Canons promulgated on 30 May[24]—that "Concerning the regal power," and also the King's prefatory letter to the published canons. The Convocation of Clergy convened to draw up the canons met on 13 April at the opening of the Short Parliament. The sermon was not entered at Stationer's Hall until 29 April (in itself perhaps a significant choice of date, since the canons were promulgated the next day), but substantial rewriting for publication by King is unlikely, since his text is one of those "express texts both of the Old and New Testaments" quoted in the first canon, which "clearly established" the Divine Right of Kings as "being the ordinance of God himself." He may have been shown a preliminary draft of what Laud intended to put forward. The sermon was licensed for the press by a former chaplain of Laud's, Dr. John Wykes.

In the sermon King defends monarchy further than Hooker would have done, as nearest God's own pattern of rule in the natural order. Nevertheless, as a good Shakespearean, he recognises that God may give, direct, or permit the title to rule by various routes, which (he says) the Romans saw as "Birth or Conquest, Election or Usurpation," the first and last of which God has allowed in English history. King's arguments challenge three writers in particular, notorious representatives of the chief contemporary forms of opposition to the doctrine that a ruler's authority derived directly from God. He refutes them from their own "Fathers": "Let the Allegations I have produced out of their owne Books testifie for me, that I slander them not." The Spanish Jesuit Mariana and the papalists claimed for the Pope the power to choose and remove temporal rulers. "Junius Brutus" (a pseudonym of Theodore Beza) in *Vindiciae contra Tyrannos* (1579) expressed the Huguenot Calvinist view that the power of choice lay with the people of God sitting in commission with God, while James I's Scottish Presbyterian tutor George Buchanan claimed for the people alone the choice and limitation of a ruler, as a matter of natural law (so helping to prepare the way not only for the civil wars but for later theories of social contract).

By 1640, Henry King is no longer defending monarchy in theory only, with examples from the Continent or from Elizabeth's reign. He is forced to define his views more specifically against the English Parliament's demand that Charles I should be financially and judicially subject to them, instead of exercising his own capricious and autocratic discretionary powers. King tries to win the sympathy of his hearers by his long references (with unmistakeable Shakespearean echoes) to "the disquiet, the frequent toyle and daily disturbance to which a King is submitted," and his picture of the monarch as the shepherd of his people echoes the first speech of James I (the anniversary of whose death he also commemorates in the sermon) to his Parliament in 1603.[25] The monarch, as "Christ's image and Deputy," is the guardian of both civil and ecclesiastical laws; so for the Calvinists in his audience King demonstrates how well Charles I may be said to have fulfilled the role of a Godly Prince. On the one hand, he has preserved the reformed Church of England from further schism and shown an outstanding example of piety in his own life, besides restoring St. Paul's, the nation's mother-church. On the other, he has administered justice fairly but firmly at home, leaving his people "free to the exercise of true Religion, and quietly enjoying every man his own"—more like James Shirley's masque *The Triumphs of Peace* (1639) than the harsh reality. At the same time, by the unpopular Ship Money, he has built up a strong navy as a peaceful and necessary protection against threats from foreign powers.

King's style henceforth is for the most part terser and more businesslike than in the earlier sermons, and he is on the whole more interesting in content than in eloquence. For the benefit of Puritan listeners, his Old Testament references include more of the historical books, with the prophetic visions of Daniel and Ezekiel, and his New Testament ones also include those favoured by them—St. Paul's Epistle to the Romans and the Book of Revelation. All references are carefully (though not always accurately) identified in the margins. King's account of the reaction of continental Protestant leaders to the reformed Church of England and to King Edward VI's Prayer Book is of particular interest to the modern reader, as is his admiring firsthand portrait of Charles I's character and achievements in the second half of the sermon, nine years before such an attitude became general among Royalists in the wake of the King's execution. The irony of the metaphorical language, so early in the struggle between Charles I and Parliament, is apparent today: King is indignant that critics of monarchy "have presumed to set the people on the Bench, and place the King at the Barre," and bids them thank God for their settled kingdom, in which "barbarous Rapes and horrid Massacres" are "cries wherewith your eares have never been acquainted." His final prayer is "that for our sins God deprive us not too soone of so rich a Blessing by Taking Him Away. . . . And when the sad Day comes wherein He must exchange This Kingdome for a Better, Let His Crown of Gold be changed into a *Crown of Glory*."

Presumably the appointment of Henry King to a bishopric at last, in October 1641, was not only to please the moderate and reasonable Puritans, but was in the nature of a reward for this sermon.

CIVIL WARS AND INTERREGNUM

For the period from the civil wars to the Restoration, serious work on the surviving records really has begun only in the last two decades, often within narrowly defined geographical, chronological, or thematic limits.[26] Two things bedevil the task of assessment: the paucity and sporadic nature of surviving records, and the rarity of any one scholar's possessing sufficient knowledge not to be tempted to fill gaps by unwarranted assumptions, which may be invalidated by fresh documentary discoveries or (as in the case of Henry King) evidence from other fields. A third factor, an invidious one, is that in the absence of primary documents, even the most recent scholars turn to seventeenth-century writers who recorded contemporary happenings many years after the events. Their accounts are partial in both senses of the word: the full facts were not available to them, and certainly John Walker, Edmund Calamy, and Clarendon had ulterior purposes. Biographers and diarists such as Antony Wood, Izaak Walton, Pepys, and Evelyn naturally wrote from their own differing affinities and experiences. In the neglected sermons of higher clergy like Henry King, however, there remains valuable *contemporary* evidence, of prime importance both in supporting recent findings and correcting false assumptions.

One assumption now increasingly seen as inaccurate is that bishops like King who remained in England during the Interregnum were "content" with their retirement. On the contrary, it seems that furious underground activity among the clergy involved many more bishops than previously supposed.[27] R. S. Bosher is the only historian so far, however, to use Henry King's first-hand statements about the Interregnum Church in his funeral sermon for Bishop Brian Duppa. Even Bosher does not enquire further into his activities over a span of time that, as with "the Middle Ages," covers in reality several quite distinct periods: he states that from the time of the Civil War and Commonwealth, "King of Chichester [is chiefly remembered] for his slender output of romantic verse."[28] His romantic poetry was all written by the mid-1630s, however; only a handful of elegies and the psalm translations came later.

When Chichester surrendered to Sir William Waller on 29 December 1642, Henry King, its bishop, fled to Petworth,[29] and then made his way to Shere, near Guildford, where he already was renting a house near his cousin George Duncombe at Albury. His sister Elizabeth Holt, with her family, evidently kept house for him and his son John, for he mentions in his will "the tyme I sojourned under her roofe." He left the district in the year of Duncombe's death, 1646. While a residentiary canon of St. Paul's he was associated with his cousin in various legal transactions over Chapter property and also over property in the Guildford area.

It seems clear that he was a keen businessman, for besides other scattered leases for property (including some in his archdeaconry of Colchester), his will mentions sums he had lent, including one thousand pounds to Richard, Earl of Dorset, who had died without repaying him, and a bond with his parliamentarian neighbour at Petworth, the Earl of Northumberland, "whereof my Sister [Anne] Dutton knows." Perhaps this last loan and the loan of three thousand pounds made by him and Prebendary John Mountford, his co-executor of Donne's will, to the Earl of Arundel, another Sussex neighbour, were made on the eve of the Civil War (as was his placing the St. Paul's dwelling in his son Henry's name) to divest himself of some of his capital and to prevent assets falling into Parliamentary hands. Useful interest on the last-named sum was repaid through a Dr. Lawrence from 1642 to 1648, when the principal was also repaid.[30] (King and Mountfort may not have been alone among the higher clergy in taking such steps; this area is worth further investigation.)

King was one of the fourteen bishops harshly sequestered in March 1643—he enjoyed his see for only ten months before losing not only his income, but his palace, his goods, his library, and his papers. His will claims "that greater Fortune discending from my famous Ancestors melted and miscarried," and with all he had accrued later "in my matche and other course of life, were allmost totally consumed [by] Publick calamitie or private injurie"—evidently from the two local men against whom he petitioned at the Restoration, the regicides William Cawley and John Downes.[31] From this first period of the wars, no doubt, come the vivid glimpses in the sermon of 30 January 1664/5, commemorating the execution of Charles I, King and Martyr, of the Parliamentary woman captain parading her female troop each morning "with drums beating and colours flying" through the streets of Chichester (an incident recorded nowhere else); of clergy turned out with their families (as was Bruno Ryves, briefly Chichester's dean) into foul weather; of young boys marching up and down, while old men "who needed a Staff to under prop them, Ty'd to their Swords, with feeble Knees knocking one against the other faster than the Drum beat . . . went tottering about the Streets." From this period also comes the sorry episode of King's son John's seduction of William Oughtred's daughter and his own inexplicable decision, after his first stern reaction, to defend his son. This undoubtedly contributed to his moving, early in 1646, to his nephew John's home at Blakesware, in Hertfordshire.[32]

By 1647, possibly after the summer, when it became clear that the hoped-for agreement between Charles I and the Army would not take place, King must have set up the "college" described by Izaak Walton in his notes for a life of John Hales, at Richings Park "near Eton,"[33] home of Lady Salter, widow of Sir William and niece of Bishop Duppa. At the end of this period he seems to have moved to the village of Langley, about a mile away, where his sister Dorothy Hubert and her husband lived, making his home with them (at least before her death in 1658); and with his brother Philip, in the next-door parish of Hitcham, until the Restoration. During this second period of retirement, therefore, King was less than six miles from Windsor when on 8 February 1649 Charles

I's body was brought from Whitehall to the Castle for burial; Henry King's elegy for his dead master, "From my sad Retirement March 11, 1648[/9]," first published anonymously about 1659,[34] seems to show some detailed knowledge of this event.

The year 1653, in which King wrote his will, may mark the beginning of a third period—his insufficiently explored involvement with Bishop Brian Duppa of Salisbury in schemes for preserving the ordained priesthood. Both are named together by Bosher, with Ralph Brownrigg, Joseph Hall, and three Irish bishops, as ordaining according to the Prayer Book ordinal in the 1650s, and both ordained East Anglian candidates after the death of Brownrigg, who had retired near to Cambridge.[35] This gives a possible reason for the so-far unexplained making of King's will at a time when he was apparently in good health. He would have been in real danger of imprisonment and perhaps death if discovered, and the will probably was intended to safeguard his heirs' inheritance.

One section of the will, the disposition of his books, particularly relates to the sermons. Many of the titles noted in their margins from his wide reading reappear in an *Old Catalogue of Books to 1737* which I have found in Chichester Cathedral Library. This almost certainly lists the books acquired at King's death by his son John and bequeathed by him at his own death to the Cathedral.[36] The sermons and this catalogue (of which only three hundred of the one thousand volumes recorded remain) together provide a valuable record of the reading of an early seventeenth-century moderate Calvinist divine trained at Oxford.

According to King's will, the Chichester siege was responsible for the loss of all but "a small remainder of a large Library taken from me at Chichester, contrary to the condicōn and contracte of the Generall and Counsell of Warre." Nevertheless, the catalogue reveals that this cannot have been the final situation. Some of his father's and brothers' books, at least twenty titles from John Donne's library, and books marked in graphite by King at passages used in prewar sermons, such as his 1555 edition of St. Augustine and George Buchanan's *De Iure Regni apud Scotos,* were evidently with him at the time of his death and are now in Chichester Cathedral Library. He may have recovered them, perhaps from William Cawley's son John, whom he ordained. Perhaps he even managed to carry some books with him when he escaped.

About July 1653, when the will was made, Brian Duppa, as the foremost active bishop still in England, summoned the rest to his home in Richmond to see if together they could agree on a legal temporary dispensation from the use of the Book of Common Prayer. The majority of the bishops expected Cromwell would soon lift his ban on the book, however, and nothing was done; though in the event, fresh Royalist uprisings made Cromwell more, not less strict on the continuing Church of England. Duppa was at this time in close contact with Charles II (whose tutor he had been) at the Hague, through one of the King's messengers to England, Eleazor Duncon, a canon of York.

When Duppa died as Bishop of Winchester in 1662, Henry King, speaking as one who had "heartily Lov'd, and from the converse of many younger years Valued" him, preached his funeral sermon at Westminster Abbey. He reveals that he himself was involved not only in ordinations and deliberations, but in an even more important undertaking (which a letter from Eleazor Duncon to the future Earl of Clarendon as early as 1655 confirms).[37] By 1658, only eleven of the twenty-six English bishops, of an average age of seventy-three, were still alive, and the Church of England was in danger of losing, merely by default, the apostolic succession it proudly claimed to have preserved at the Reformation. Charles II wanted this pressing matter resolved. A plan was made, known only to five bishops, of whom Henry King was one, for himself and another, probably Accepted Frewen, Bishop of Lichfield and Coventry, to cross the channel and consecrate new bishops from among able younger churchmen, some of them in exile with Charles. Owing (King says) to the "great Age and greater Infirmity" of his partner, nothing was done, though the succession was in fact saved by the Restoration. Bosher, again, is the only historian to use King's account in the sermon of these discussions,[38] but he fails to perceive the significance of one statement: "how industrious he [i.e., Duppa] was, some who yet live know, and none better than My self, *who was His only associate* in several travels undertaken to bring it to effect" (italics mine).

One reason why modern historians give all the credit to Duppa[39] is that Henry King was not one of the indefatigable band of polemicists pounding into print in the 1650s, nor even (as an erstwhile diocesan administrator rather than an academic) involved, like many of them, in learned projects such as Brian Walton's Polyglot Bible. King himself, perhaps wistfully, recognises this in the letter accompanying a copy of his translation of the Psalms for Archbishop Ussher in 1651: "Thus whilst your Grace, and other Champions of the Church (the Chariots and Horsemen of Israel) engage against the publick Adversaries of Truth, I come behind with the Carriages and humbly in the Temple's Porch fit the Songs of *Sion* to celebrate the Triumphs of your Pens."[40] It is not surprising, therefore, that King, like Sheldon, is omitted from the Presbyterian Robert Baillie's list of the contemporary leaders of the Church of England and their "writes."[41] This is ironic, since very much the same kind of defence of the Church of England and its tenets that Baillie notes from Hammond and others at this period is anticipated, though of course not so systematically, in King's arguments against the extremes of both Papistry and Puritanism in his 1620s sermons and in that splendid book *The Lord's Prayer,* briefly alluded to once only by Berman, and by others before Horton Davies totally ignored.

In fact, from the funeral sermon, it seems that Henry King's role during the Interregnum had been essentially as Duppa's man. He is not mentioned in the correspondence between the most energetic organisers of the continuing episcopal Church, Gilbert Sheldon and Henry Hammond, unless under a so-far-unbroken alias, though William Dillingham told Sancroft in 1657 that King was his neighbour and he had visited him. Nor is he mentioned in the correspondence between Duppa himself and Justinian Isham, but there is ample evidence in his letters of Duppa's caution over censorship and fear of discovery: he only once names Sheldon, with whom he was certainly in close touch.[42] The example of King (whose role, from the fragmentary but conclusive evidence that remains, was far greater than has been allowed) illustrates how incomplete a picture of the Church of England during the Interregnum historians have thus far been able to provide.

THE RESTORATION

A significant fact about Henry King, rediscovered by Ronald Berman from a nineteenth-century article, is his nomination as Archbishop of York at the Restoration, of which historians say nothing. Wood, perhaps, hints at this in his comment that "not being removed to a better see, [he] became discontented . . . and a favourer thereupon of the Presbyterians in his diocese."[43] No appointment for York had been suggested in any of the confidential lists prepared by Edward Nicholas or Edward Hyde by the time of the Restoration. The evidence that King was eventually put forward comes in a letter from Edward Burton, the aggrieved rector of Broadwater, near Worthing, who expected to succeed him at Chichester. He speaks of the Bishop's having "treated with diverse noblemen and gentlemen about renewing of leases, and with the two chaplains to goe with him into the North. The Bishop told me himselfe he was to remove, hearing that I was to be his successor." Burton notes "the same was stronge, both in court and city, for a fortnight." His explanation for King's not having been promoted is that "after all this, he withdrew himselfe into the country, and, through his negligence and carelessness in not following it up as he ought to have done, Dr. Frewen, the Bishop of Coventry and Litchfield, got it from him."[44]

Burton may be right. His undated letter must have been written between June and 2 September, when Frewen's appointment was announced—probably in the first half of August, when King relinquished his stall at St. Paul's to his brother Philip and when pressure was on Charles II to appoint to the remaining bishoprics. I. M. Green's passing references to the diocese of Chichester, though he makes no mention of Henry King, build up a picture of its unusually speedy reorganisation of church goverment, being among the first to appoint archdeacons and a vicar general, to reconstitute its cathedral chapter, to ordain and make institutions—all of which were the work of its bishop who withdrew to Chichester during much of August for that purpose.[45]

Two other factors, however, may have contributed to Henry King's not being promoted. Pepys heard him preach before Charles II on 8 July 1660, "a great flattering sermon, which I did not like that clergy should meddle with matters of state."[46] This may be no more than the reaction of a loyal Cromwellian brought up, under the Commonwealth, to criticise the previous regime. But King's post-Restoration sermons not unnaturally show greater personal vehemence against the Puritans than those from before the wars, and unlike King's Whitehall sermon of the following May 1661, this one was not printed by royal command, or indeed at all, nor was he chosen as a Lent preacher that year. Charles may well have been embarrassed by an indiscreet remark. He was anxious at the first to establish as comprehensive a church as possible and reconcile Nonconformists with Anglicans. He had diplomatically been too tired to attend an Anglican service of thanksgiving at Westminster Abbey on the evening of his return—Henry King was one of the four bishops who arranged it.

The other factor in King's failure to obtain preferment lies in the nature of those first promoted. I. M. Green criticises Bosher for grouping together the most influential Church leaders in the Restoration settlements as "Laudians"[47] but does not note that there was a significant link between them nevertheless, including the three bishops advanced. They had been connected personally either with Charles II himself—Duppa as his tutor, Juxon at his father's execution—or, in the case of Frewen (and many of the lesser clergy promoted), with members of the intellectual group that gathered before the wars at Great Tew, near Oxford, the home of Lucius Carey, Viscount Falkland. Among these were Edward Hyde, later Earl of Clarendon, the strongest single influence with the King in the first years of the Restoration; Henry Hammond (though he died as Parliament made its decision to recall the King); Hammond's friend and colleague from the Interregnum, Gilbert Sheldon, who as Bishop of London and then Archbishop of Canterbury was indeed the architect of the Restoration Church settlements; and George Morley and John Earle, who had been with the King in exile and were both administratively involved with clergy appointments in the first months of the Restoration. There was great competition for posts at the time. Accepted Frewen, though older than King and possibly ailing (if he was the bishop unable to accompany him abroad), consecrated bishop later than him and a comparative cypher, was President of Magdalen College, Oxford, the college of which Hammond was a Fellow, at the same time that Sheldon was Warden of All Souls', and he indeed had been responsible for conveying the colleges' plate to Charles I in 1642.[48] Henry King had put himself outside such close academic circles when he married and became a church administrator.

Frewen and his immediate successor as archbishop normally would have taken the oath at their enthronement on the York Gospels, but these had been lost during the civil wars. In the circumstances, it is intriguing to discover that at the time of the Restoration, they may have been with Henry King at Chichester, since they were returned thence to York, but only in 1678, nine years after his death, by order of his executors.[49] It may also be relevant that King's later correspondence with Sheldon, who presumably engineered Frewen's appointment, is decidedly stiff.

King nevertheless appears to have been very active at Court in the first two years of the new reign, as well as in his diocese.[50] He was commanded to preach at Whitehall in 1661 on 29 May, which was not only the King's birthday and his Accession Day, but the very first official commemoration of both events.[51] The continuity of Henry King's belief in the Divine Right of Kings is emphasised in the sermon by his use, over a long passage, of many of the same authors (and some of the same quotations) as in his prewar 1640 sermon, though with significant differences that suggest that his immediate source lay in a manuscript commonplace book as well as in the earlier sermon.[52] His attitude is more uncompromising now, however. He reiterates the word "Right," which found no place in 1640: "This is the *Magna Charta* for Princes, the *Great Charter* by which Kings hold the Right to their Kingdoms: *By Me Kings Rule*. It is *God who sets up and pulls down.*"

King's mind was not unaffected by recent political thinking. He has come to agree with the opponents of monarchy that the crown may be lawfully achieved in the first instance by an elective, as well as a hereditary, right: he takes pleasure in proving that Charles II can lay claim to both. Like Hooker, however, he believed that the ruling power, once removed from a bad ruler, reverts "into his hand who first gave it"—"the Right [is] so firm that it can never be Reversed or Reassumed by Those who first conferr'd it."

With the memory of the Interregnum still fresh in his mind, he emphasises—for those of his hearers who like Charles II have spent the last ten years abroad—the sufferings of loyal subjects who remained: there are several covert side swipes at Parliamentarian turncoats in his audience. The press and the pulpit have become a heavier target with him than were ever the Pope or the Genevan Consistory, but King retains his dry sense of humour: for example, "Twas fit that such men who had before understood the use of the Hammer and the Ax should be employ'd, when Churches were to be demolished."

He is less enthusiastic in this sermon over the character of Charles II than over that of Charles I. He puts before the King the Aristotelian qualities of a good ruler, which he had so fervently commended in Charles I in the 1640 sermon, in the hope rather than the assurance that he will live up to them; and there is a new formality in phrases like "that Royal Person whom God hath set over us." Though Henry King's style is still vigorous in his Restoration sermons, and there are touches of the old poetry, there are also perhaps signs of age, in lengthy, apparently irrelevant biblical, linguistic, and theological commentaries—for instance the long digression on heredity in this sermon.[53] (It was probably this passage, as much as the vivid evocation of the miseries of civil war, that gave rise to a new edition of it, the only one of King's sermons to receive posthumous recognition, in 1713, when the Hanoverian succession was endangered by Tory support for the Pretender, and Harley's lassitude seemed likely to bring about a new civil war.)

Almost exactly a year later, on 24 April 1662, King was preaching Duppa's funeral sermon in Westminster Abbey (from which we learn that in the previous year, at the time of the Coronation, he also had given the official Garter Day sermon in Duppa's place, during his sickness, though this sermon does not survive). King was a natural choice for the task. Although three years younger than Duppa, the two men were similarly educated at Westminster and Christ Church: they had both been chaplains to Richard, third Earl of Dorset; King had contributed to Duppa's collection of elegies for Ben Jonson, *Jonsonus Virbius* (1631); he succeeded Duppa as Bishop of Chichester; and they had been closely connected during the Interregnum. In this, his first funeral sermon,[54] King follows very closely the patristic form of funeral oration—he quotes Gregory Nazianzen's *Orationis Laudem Patris*. Such sermons were common at this time, in particular the twofold division, first into a lofty philosophical discourse and then a biography (often of great value to the modern historian) of the subject of the sermon. Many were expanded for publication (like Dr. Nicholas Bernard's sermon for Ussher) into full-length works, complete with dedications (like Joseph Hall's) and, in some cases, commendatory verses. King evidently published his text much as he preached it, since its forty-four pages would have taken no more time than the customary hour he mentions.

He begins with a long philosophical preamble on death, aided, one feels, by his commonplace book entries on the subject. It is an excellent example of its genre. What is less customary are the moments of sheer poetry that make this the closest in tone to his prewar sermons. There is a traditional literary personification of Death, cruel and rapacious, and extended metaphysical images, like the comparison of the world to an old man or a falling building: and there is the serene and lovely passage beginning "He who is lodg'd in Earth lies in an *Inner Chamber* which Noises cannot disturb"—an old man's view of his approaching end, which compares interestingly with the earlier passage on death at the close of the Spital sermon. There are unusually few learned references—perhaps King had not yet regained his Chichester books (another possible reason for the reappearance of so many of his prewar references in the previous sermon). The long academic digression on funeral rites again suggests a lessening of stylistic judgment in old age, and there are some quite savage attacks on individual Puritans and their behaviour when in power, a constant feature of the postwar sermons. Indeed, as in the verse elegy on Charles I King polished for publication on the eve of the Restoration, he shows some sympathy for those who cannot understand why God witholds his vengeance from the perpetrators of the recent wars—God's ways, he concludes, are not our ways: there are subtler forms of punishment than those we see, and the Royalists who suffered will receive their reward in heaven. Nevertheless, he warns his hearers that the regicides are not alone to blame; the ultimate responsibility for the past carnage may be "chargd upon the Heads of every one of us who survive," a theme he develops in 1665, at the close of the sermon commemorating Charles, King and Martyr.

The significant additions to our knowledge of King's and Duppa's activities during the Interregnum already have been noted. Duppa's life is well documented, and his correspondence reveals his character fully; but King adds some interesting details of his career, in particular at Westminster School and (in the only passage where he shows some warmth towards Charles II) regarding the monarch's concern for his dying tutor.

In March 1662, Convocation composed a book of articles for the statutory visitations of the clergy by the bishops; it was given to Archbishop Juxon for approval, but the aging prelate put it aside until, in the autumn, many of them decided to act on their own initiative. In October, Bishop King conducted the first Chichester Visitation since his consecration in 1642, based on these articles. It came at a particularly delicate stage in the relations between the official Church and those sectarian ministers who had looked after parishes between 1642 and 1660: on 24 August 1662, the new Act of Uniformity had come into force, whereby those who refused to subscribe to the official form of church goverment were ejected, forcibly if needed, from those benefices for which, in some cases, they had cared pastorally and well. King's sermon, preached at Lewes on 8 October, evidently impressed the vicar of Horsted Keynes, Giles Moore, for he wrote in his journal "There was a Visitation at Lewis by the Bishop of Chichester who There Himselfe at St Michaels preached in person."[55] Despite Wood's suggestion that King had been "a favourer of Presbyterians in his Diocese," the sermon, which shows a fervent desire to persuade the "jarring factions" among his clergy to unity by "the laying controversies asleep, and silencing Disputes" as an example to their flocks, remains firm on essentials. He would hear of no conditional reordination, such as more liberal bishops like Bramhall were willing to contemplate, or of the blurring of distinction between the ordained ministry and the laity implied in the joint Presbyterian and Church of England ordinations held by Bishops Gauden and Reynolds. The Book of Common Prayer had been reinstated, only slightly revised, earlier in 1662 (on 19 May), and King to the end insisted on full ordination for all clergy in his diocese according to its ordinal, one of the traditional formularies of the Church of England.

This is a most interesting sermon, not only as historical evidence of the difficulties of settlement but also for King's revealing comments on contemporary preaching styles. It is outstanding for its balance between firmness and sweet reasonableness tempered with humour. His primary concern is not with church government but with the pastoral role of the clergy and of bishops—he includes himself in his exhortations—which the disputes of the past years have hindered. (Sentences like "How many in seeking to solve unnecessary scruples, have raised doubts, and tied knots in many a Conscience, which they are not able to untie again?" have an uncomfortably modern ring.) After the political struggles of the past years, he sees the life of the Church needs to be deepened and renewed. The clergy must lead by their example and by their sermons—he shows a Calvinist's faith in the necessity of preaching and the power of the spoken word—and preachers must teach sound doctrine attractively and fearlessly. King's opening paragraphs are most tender of the consciences of those who will be antagonistic to instruction from a member of the established Church. He describes his discourse as "a short View of the Priest's Duty," in which the ability to preach well stands to the fore. His remarks on preaching styles anticipate the eighteenth century, with its love of "decorum." He quotes in both Greek and Latin, to emphasise the importance of learning to those who "are so Umbragious to boggle at anything which is not presented to them in their Mother-Tongue," and from a wide range of early Church Fathers as well as the by-then generally accepted Authorised Version of the Bible.

There is a difference in style: many of his paragraphs are a single sentence, unlike the long periods of previous sermons, a concession to the new fashion for terseness (if not merely a printing device), and give an appearance of jerkiness to the pages, though his words are as melodious and well chosen as ever. The sermon was published in London rather than in Chichester, which possibly argues a desire to influence national thinking at this time—the sermon of his surrogate Malachy Conant at a later Visitation was printed locally.

Subscription books and scattered records show King ordaining many of the old intruded Presbyterian and Independent incumbents during the next years. White Kennett describes his attempt to persuade one of them, Richard Stretton, curate of Petworth, to conform by offering him one hundred pounds of his own money and the choice of a canonry in the cathedral. His concern is also shown in his recommendations for ships' chaplains: the one for Sam Oakes reads "He was once a Parlamentarian, but recommended formerly to the L[ord] B[isho]p by y[e] D[uke]. of Glouc[este]r, and is a convert conformist and of good parts."[56] His large diocese, which then as now embraced the whole length of East and West Sussex, was one of the most notoriously nonconforming, however, as his letters to Sheldon indicate; and some of his clergy, like Francis Challoner, who took his complaints to the Archbishop, were not to be won over.[57]

Pepys heard "a good and eloquent sermon," never printed, by King at Whitehall on the words "they that sow in sorrow shall reap in joy," on 9 March 1663. In 1665, King was invited to deliver another significant Whitehall sermon on 30 January, the official commemoration of Charles I's execution. This time, the republican Pepys found it "much cried up—but methinks but a mean sermon."[58] The choice of Henry King possibly was suggested by the appearance of a second edition of his poems in November of the previous year: its four additions included the elegy for King Charles mentioned above, and another for Sir Charles Lucas and Sir George Lisle, executed at Colchester in 1648. Both poems were obviously in his mind while writing the sermon, for it shares several of their literary and historical references. He must have known two other works also. His first words seem a deliberate echo of the beginning of Nicholas Bernard's celebrated funeral sermon for Archbishop Ussher: "The text is . . . hung throughout in mourning," and King probably intends a further parallel in his repeated use, like Bernard, of the formula "May I not?" King's sermon seems to have set the vehement style of sorrow on 30 January for many succeeding years; for in January 1721, Francis Atterbury was still beginning: "This is a *Day of Trouble, of Rebuke, and Blasphemy,* distinguished by . . . the sad Sufferings of an excellent Prince, who fell a Sacrifice to the Rage of his Rebellious Subjects; and, by his fall, derived Infamy, Misery, and Guilt, on them, and their sinful Posterity."[59]

The other work that one would guess King referred to may so have irritated him that he set out to expose in some measure its shortcomings. *The Subject's Sorrow, or Lamentations on the Death of Britain's Josiah, King Charles* originally was printed anonymously in 1649 and reissued (without date) after the Restoration, when the author was identified by its editor as Robert Brown, vicar of Sligo. It is divided equally into a disquisition on the Divine Right of Kings (possibly owing something to Henry King's own 1640 sermon) and a catalogue of Charles's virtues (as in that sermon) according to those required by Aristotle in a just ruler. The sermon shows devoted loyalty but no inside knowledge. Where Henry King, as one of the few royal chaplains still alive who experienced the events alluded to, picks up this model in his own sermon, he emphasises constantly "I speak upon knowledge" or "My selfe knew." Like Brown, he draws an extended parallel between Charles and the Old Testament King Josiah, and he may well look directly at this sermon (though Charles's execution produced a number of such effusions) when he says, "I speak not in the custom of those who in their funeral Sermons ofttimes bely the Dead, attributing Vertues to them whereof, whilest they liv'd, they were not guilty. But my own knowledge, confirm'd by an attendance upon him for many years, makes me confidently rise to this Superlative."

Historically, this is perhaps the most important of all King's sermons. Some of its details already have been quoted above. Some (like the words of the protagonists in Charles's trial, at which King could not have been present) derive from the eyewitness account published daily by Gilbert Mabbott, *A Perfect Narrative of the Proceedings of the High Court of Justice in the Tryal of the King,* but there are many more touches that argue personal experience, and some tantalising references to events and characters found recorded nowhere else. King also eloquently revives the favourite contemporary Royalist comparison of Charles's sufferings and execution with those of Christ in his Passion.

It is sad that King's attack on Milton is so violent, but he knew him only as an enemy pamphleteer, Latin Secretary to Cromwell: *Paradise Lost,* written in Milton's seclusion, was still three years from publication.[60] It was Milton's *Iconoclastes,* attacking the little volume purporting to be Charles I's meditations before his death, *Eikon Basilike,*[61] that drew down Henry King's wrath, and it is worth looking carefully at King's words about that volume. At the Restoration, John Gauden, Dean of Worcester, claimed to have written it with Charles's knowledge and assistance. It is curious, however, that if his involvement were more than merely editorial, we really have only his own word for it (though he managed to persuade the Duke of York, who was a young boy at the time of the execution, and through him other influential people) until 1692, when Anthony Walker defended him in *A True Account of the Author,* claiming that Duppa—whom one would expect Henry King to have spoken with about it—wrote two of the chapters. Sheldon, moreover, who like Gauden had waited on Charles in his imprisonment, disliked him strongly. Since Henry King, one of the few survivors from the court of Charles I who also knew Gauden (to whose collection on the death of Lady Stanhope he contributed a poem), was nevertheless convinced it could have been written by no other pen than Charles's, the attribution to Gauden may not be as certain as some modern scholars assume.

Once again, there are long academic digressions in this sermon, of biblical textual exegesis, on mourning customs in antiquity, and on funeral music. When King reaches the character of Charles I and the account of his trial and death, on the other hand, his style is as vigorous as ever, crisply ironic and dramatic, remarkable for a seventy-three-year-old at that time of shorter lifespan. It is noticeable that his final conventional good wishes to the reigning monarch are perceptibly cooler than in his 1661 sermon and end with the hope that as he inherited Charles I's kingdoms, "so *He may Inherit his Vertues too*"—a wish that, by that fifth year of Charles II's reign, it had become obvious was made in vain.

A list of Lent preachers at Court for 1666 shows that the Bishop of Chichester preached on Sunday, 4 March of that year. Giles Moore records two further Visitation sermons, never printed, in 1666 and 1669, the latter only three weeks before King's death.[63] In the same year, he had been invited once more to preach at Whitehall in Lent, on 28 February 1669. His letter accepting Sheldon's invitation exists, and the sermon, again never printed, was heard by John Evelyn, who recorded in his diary only that it was on the very characteristic earlier theme "of the preciousness of time etc."[64] So King's sermons, though comparatively few survive, spanned his long life as a priest, from his ordination in 1616/7 to his death at the ripe age of 77.

He died on 30 September 1669 at Chichester, one of only two bishops in the seventeenth century who did not pass through that impoverished diocese on the way to more desirable sees. It seems there was no one left who knew him well enough to write his life or to publish his sermons, despite the significance of his earlier role in the Church of England. His last wishes were disregarded. Like his father,[65] he asked in his will for a plain tombstone (with the words "Deposita redditurae animae"—"All that is left of a soul returned home"). He asked to lie in the choir at Chichester. Today, his ornate and fulsome memorial, recut by a descendant in the eighteenth century and twice moved since, now stands in the north transept of his cathedral, though it looks up at the library that his books helped to refound. His real monument is his poetry and this handful of well-wrought printed sermons.

AN ADVENTURER IN A MIDDLE WAY

Thomas Fuller (himself worth closer study as the historian of the middle way) names Henry King among those bishops he considers "moderates," in contrast to Arminian or Calvinist, at the beginning of the civil wars, along with Prideaux, Winiffe, and Brownrigg.[66] All of these individuals have been virtually ignored by historical theologians, who have concentrated instead on "the more authoritative and better-known writings of the period" (as More and Cross called them), representing "what was clearly the dominant teaching of the Anglican Church in that age."[67] *Anglicanism*—More and Cross's anthology of such writings, which has understandably influenced all subsequent studies—claimed to draw its examples from the whole century, from Richard Hooker and Lancelot Andrewes to the Nonjurors. In practice, however, it was almost entirely confined to those theologians whose works had been reprinted in the nineteenth century. Because its thematic arrangement took little account of variety of viewpoint or of chronology, this work has provided a distorted and and incomplete picture.

The sermons of Henry King, "an adventurer in a middle-way," as he called himself in another context,[68] are significant in that they help to redress this, by highlighting characteristic tenets of the central Church of England, which found little place in More and Cross. That "mean," which George Herbert called the "praise and glory" of the British Church (difficult to define, then as now, but manifesting surprisingly little change throughout King's long life as a churchman, from King James I to the Restoration), is an aspect that is still neglected by recent writers, as well as by More and Cross.

It is important to realise that King's primary purpose in preaching is not to expound systematic theology. He sees instead, like Robert Sanderson and Jeremy Taylor later (and indeed like the more Calvinist Jacobean and Caroline bishops, amongst whom were his own father and Joseph Hall), the great need for a "practical divinity" to aid Christians in their daily life and prayer. His theological views, chiefly expressed in *The Lord's Prayer* and in the sermons contemporary with it in the period from 1621 to 1628, are elicited in response to particular Roman Catholic and Puritan dogmas and practices that he considers have departed from those of the primitive Church.

King's primary intention, to increase his hearer's devotion and strengthen their faith by the help of received wisdom in palatable form, remains uppermost. In *The Lord's Prayer,* for instance, after a brief catalogue of comments on the phrase "In heaven as in earth" from the early Fathers, St. Paul, and the gospels, he remarks "I stand not to amplify this point: only to repeat the several Interpretations which learned Men give of *Coelum* and *Terra* in this place is a sufficient morall and Application." Moreover, King brings to the translation of his authorities the same felicity of phrase as in his more lyrical meditations and perorations, so that St. Augustine, St. Chrysostom, and the rest speak with his voice. His method of citing all his authorities in his margins might appear to suggest that he harbours the "preposterous conceit" so deplored by John Hales, "that learning consists rather in variety of turning and quoting of sundry authors, than in soundly discovering and laying down truth of things."[69] Only very occasionally, however, in complicated theological exposition, are his sermons weighted with too much learning.

King would have made no claim of originality in his thinking. Influenced in the first place by his strict Calvinist father—but with men like Neile and Laud, already moving towards the dominant position ecclesiastical power gave them in the 1630s, putting forward in his university days an undeniably more attractive, tolerant attitude towards election and grace—it would not be surprising if his "adventuring" in the middle way left him somewhat confused about exactly where he stood. His themes, illustrations, and sources mirror the common thinking of his time and are paralleled in other preachers like John Donne and Joseph Hall. Those central doctrines he regards as conformable to the faith of the Church of England he is content to accept in their traditional form rather than, like philosophers from John Hales to the Cambridge Platonists, searching out fresh interpretations in the light of modern experience. Nor has he Donne's restless, scientific lawyer's curiosity, which speculates on such matters as the nature of the afterlife, of angels, or of chaos. It is characteristic that he never tackles, in the extant sermons, the burning contemporary question of the nature of God's presence in the Eucharist. King's attitude to theological enquiry, that of many ordinary divines in the sixteenth and early seventeenth centuries, is made explicit in *The Lord's Prayer* under the clause "Thy will be done": "oure taske . . is not so much to Dispute of his Will as to Doe it."

As all Calvinists would agree, that "Will" can best be understood from its reflection in the Scriptures, but King is not using those for theological polemic: "Thus looking on it, we shall bee able to satisfie our selves in so much as becomes Christians, *not over-curious to understand*" (italics mine). Later in that same work, King rates "every new Opinion or strange doctrine wherewith our Times, like over-ranke soiles, abound" as amongst the most dangerous temptations of his day, since "our Religion is planted betwixt two extremes, both which have but one End, leading us by different pathes to destruction": the Papists, who (he says) think man can earn his salvation by his own efforts, and the strict Calvinists, who "preach *Moses* not *Christ* . . . never well but when they are busied in arguments of Judgement and Reprobation." "Let not then a misgovern'd curiositie thrust thee into any impertinent searches, or suspicious thoughts of God."

By the Restoration, his experience of the bitter conflicts of war and interregnum led him to conclude even more strongly at his Visitation: "I have lived, and shall die in this Opinion, That there can be no greater danger to a setled Church, than Liberty to dispute and call in question the Points and Articles of an Established Religion."

He constantly withdraws from theological or philosophical argument, taking his hearers with him to meditate on the truths that lie behind the debate and gaze with adoration on God's mercy and glory. He is not concerned with self-analysis, like the Puritans, nor with methods of meditation. At the beginning of *The Lord's Prayer,* he calls meditation "an Art we can no where else learne, but from Him who hath . . . the *Keyes of David.*" He probably nevertheless knew Joseph Hall's *Arte of Divine Meditation* (1606) and certainly had on his shelves the works of such continental mystical writers as Luis of Granada and Jean Gerson, alongside Dionysius the Areopagite and Saint Augustine. Where other preachers (such as Lancelot Andrewes and Mark Frank) seem to relate more easily to the Incarnation, it is the Resurrection that inspires King. He exclaims in a memorable passage of the Spital sermon: "O that this happy Meditation might so incorporate with our thoughts, that our sleeps and our wakings, our dayes and our nights, our studies and whole discourse might be nothing else but *Resurrection!*" One cannot help but wonder how far the loss of his wife created in him this attitude of firm trust and hope in the Resurrection, as a positive way of coping with death, until which time (as he concludes *The Exequy*):

> I am content to live
> Divided, with but half a heart,
> Till we shall meet and never part.

Reason increasingly predominated over faith in religion as the century progressed. King, preaching in the 1620s, places it on a lower level, however. Man has dominion over the creatures, as he says in *The Lord's Prayer XI,* "Reason over Him, Faith over Reason, and God over Faith." Reason may help man to choose between good and evil, but it is only "the Light of Nature," and not "the True Light, *Christ Jesus*" *(The Lord's Prayer VIII).*

King was one of a new kind of bishops consecrated between 1640 and 1643. Charles I said he appointed them "to satisfie the tymes" and please the Puritans, when Secretary Nicholas was urging him to find men "of whom there is not the least suspicion of favouring the Popish partie." John Morrill says "all of them were strict Calvinists in the mould of Grindal and Abbott."[70] These two were strict predestinarians, as were Thomas Morton, Arthur Lake, and Nicholas Felton, friends present, like Abbot, at the deathbed of Henry's father, Bishop John King. Indeed John King himself was the man upon whom in many respects Henry modelled his own theology and practice. But English Calvinism, like English Arminianism, was a native adaptation, and the conflicts within it were less a matter of theology than of church government. Indeed, the Church of England has never (until perhaps today) regarded its theology as separate from that of the rest of the universal Catholic church, though its distinctive attitude to that theology suffered far-reaching changes in the course of the seventeenth century. James I's representatives at the Synod of Dort in 1619 (who included initially Joseph Hall) assented to the five Calvinist canons it eventually passed. But Henry King, like many of the more intelligent Church of England clergy who could not be identified as Arminians in a political sense, "bid John Calvin good-night," in John Hales's picturesque phrase, over the uncompromisingly rigid first and second canons. These stated that God had eternally decreed some men to election and others to reprobation and that Christ died for the elect only.

King's discussion of these matters, the theology of grace with its central questions of freewill, election, predestination, and whether the elect can fall from grace, are elicited by his consideration in *The Lord's Prayer* of the need for prayer, and particularly of the clauses "Thy will be done" and "Lead us not into temptation." They were topical questions at the time King was preaching: Richard Montague's attack on Calvinists and their theology in *A New Gagg for an Old Goose* actually was debated in Parliament in 1624.

King regards the election of the faithful by God before Creation as a view nevertheless consonant with the doctrines of universal salvation and prevenient grace that were an essential part of Arminian theology. When God created humankind as a microcosm of the universe, "that Act of his Will was accompanied with a Mercie greater and more ancient than the other, whereby he did Preelect *Mankind* to Salvation . . . long before the foundations of the greater World were layed" (italics mine).[71] He considers it open to all men—the lowest and meanest included and not merely a privileged "elect"—to accept the election God offers and also their subsequent redemption by Christ from the consequences of Adam's fall: this acceptance consists solely of repenting for sin and leading a new life. The only reprobates, for King and more moderate Calvinists like him, are those who voluntarily reject God, "men of prophane lips and perverse life that hate to be reformed": only such men are outside the Church. He quotes Cyprian via Augustine: "The Church prayes not onely for constancy and perfection of Faith in the Elect, but the Inchoation of it in those that are yet Unbeleevers." And he goes further (with a glance at contemporary colonisation): "whilst there is a World layed open to our discovery which hath not discovered Christ, not heard of Him," his Kingdom is not fully come.

King's view of justification, the extent of one's role in one's own redemption, also differs from the Papists and from extremists like John Cosin and Richard Montague: Redemption was a mercy to which God "was not perswaded upon Conditions, either . . . (as the Arminian holds) a prevision or fore sight of Faith, or . . . any forestalled Merit, or for Good workes which Hee foresaw at our Election (as some of the Papists flatter themselves)." King appears to agree with that most influential of English Calvinists William Perkins and the voluntarists that, since Christ has restored fallen humanity (for the voluntarists, of course, "the elect" only) to a state of grace again, "it is in a Man's owne Will and choice whether he will do any foule fact, perpetrate an Ill." He sums up the opposing views and his own middle position neatly: "a man is not good against his Will, nor is there any Necessity of sinning layed upon him." And he points out, "It was more Glory to leave him to the libertie of his Election, and more Honour for Man to have the *Power to resist Temptation,* than to have been guarded with such a privilege, as that he *Could not bee tempted at all.*"

King nevertheless has also a firm (one might say again, Arminian) belief in the existence of original sin, and he ventures further from the Calvinist position, in holding that the elect may subsequently fall from grace. Adam's fall "did disinherit him, and us in him," and "Though the Heart of Man be never so well manured by Grace . . . for all that, Original sinne will send up those ranke weedes, those wild tares to grow amongst our best Harvests," so that "Though it be in [man's] Election to act no mischiefe, 'tis more than he can undertake to doe any Good; yea, or to thinke well, without the assistance of God." King's cavalier dismissal in the Spital sermon of scientific explanations for natural phenomena, and the part played by doctors and medicine in ending the plague may derive from a similar view to Calvin's "soli Deo gloria"—glory is not due to earthly agents. However, though people cannot earn salvation by works, they still must not, as stricter Calvinists advocate, wait passively for God to do all. "Religion and Faith are but aiery emptie sounds, if we possesse nothing of them beyond the words. The fruit of either consists in their Application." "It is no speculative, but a practick memory Christ lookes for; and to remember his words is to practise them." And again, "he hath left some part of thine election to bee made up by thy selfe . . . God will not save thee if thou implore Him not . . . we must pray for the supply of our wants, but not only pray; we must join our own endeavours to our prayers." In all this, as usual, he says no more than other moderates such as Joseph Hall, who while accepting that the grace to do well comes only from God, yet exhorts his hearers to live always as though their own efforts *were* necessary.

Strict Calvinist preaching on predestination, postulating humanity's total depravity after the Fall, but the irresistibility of grace for the "elect," resulted in an inward turning to estimate one's own worthiness, a gloomy awareness of guilt, and the fear of damnation. Temperament is as important an element as theology in directing people towards the middle way. King's merciful God does not merely (as he says in the Act sermon) "*remit the punishment* of the sinne and reteine the *Guilt,* treasuring up that . . . to presse against us in the last day: but he *forgives* that too." The love and gratitude that overflow the endings of the 1620s sermons, full of words like *rejoice, happy,* and *fruition,* show that a negative Calvinism is ultimately foreign to his nature. The contemplation of God's superlative mercies will always move him to an exstasy of glory, from his "O altitudo" in the Act sermon to his fine panegyric on mercy in *The Lord's Prayer XI* and his rhapsody on light in the Restoration sermon on Duppa's death.

Puritan is a word King never uses in the sermons, although at the early date of 1621, he records it and its derisive Court origin, in his poem on a Christ Church play before King James (Crum, *Poems* 67). The performance, he says, would have been more successful.

> Had there appear'd some sharp, cross-garter'd man,
> Whome their loud laugh might nickname Puritan,
> Cas'd up in factious breeches, and small ruff,
> That hates the Surplis, and defyes the Cuff.

Nevertheless, in moral theology at any rate, if not wholly in doctrine, many of King's strictures on contemporary behaviour would popularly be considered Puritan and one can see why Wood's informant thought he had been "made a bishop to please that party."[72] He preaches against swearing, which wounds Christ afresh, against gluttony, and drunkenness (the "fashionable vice," as he calls it), in which since James I's reign, the Court had given the lead—though of course, Catholic spiritual teachers on the continent were making similar criticisms.

He defends the "precious memory" of those begetters of the Reformation, Wyclif, Hus, and Luther in *The Lord's Prayer,* and in the 1640 sermon King cites Calvin's and Bucer's recommendations of the English Church and its Prayer Book. Like most Calvinists of his time, he is strongly anti-Papist, but this was as much on political as on religious grounds. England had found to her cost, ever since Elizabeth's reign, that "Twas never well with Christendome, since the Romish Clergy left Divinity and studied Politics." King's fiercest strictures against the Pope are for his claiming universal temporal as well as spiritual authority. His other target is scheming Jesuits, "Meere pit-falls strewed with Religion, as Coffins with flowers, to cover the ruins of many a State swallowed up by their policy"—as he calls them in *The Lord's Prayer III.* However, his images are frequently, as in this instance, poetic, and though he certainly implies that the Pope is Antichrist (on which some Arminians like Cosin more temperately cast doubt), he does not indulge in unpleasant abuse like some of his contemporaries (such as Joseph Hall, with his "Jesuit in a Popish dame's chamber", John Donne's coarse railings against the Pope, and even the eirenic James Ussher, who called him "a man of Sin, a harlot").[73] King prefers good-tempered ridicule, as in his delightful picture of the Pope in his 1640 sermon, "if he list to play at Foot-ball with Crownes, spurning them into what Gole he pleases." In the eighth section of *The Lord's Prayer,* taking issue with the English Jesuit Stapleton, who was "willing to quarrel with the Truth if *Calvin* spake it," King continues "Yet I will not wreake the injury upon *Stapleton,* wee are upon a Theme of Forgiveness."

Like other moderates among the Calvinists and not merely those clergy labelled by their contemporaries "Arminians," King assumes that his own "best Reformed Church of England" has been satisfactorily purified from the mediaeval Church's accretions to the teaching and practice of the early Church. It alone, in fact, retains untainted the marks of true Catholicism, while the continental reformers have swept them all away and the Papists still wander in error. He attacks lucrative Catholic practices such as pilgrimages, indulgences, or (at the end of the second section of *The Lord's Prayer*) delivering our prayers "to the hand of any officious busie Saint that would intercept them" (with a nice comparison with the ancient Roman tutelar deities who, like mediaeval saints, presided over every aspect of daily life).[74] Under "Deliver us from Evil," he surveys at some length the mediaeval doctrine of Purgatory, "a fine Tale for a *Romanza,* but a ridiculous History to bee brought into a Church," wittily suggesting that those who sought to localise it on earth might have placed it in Tierra del Fuego, had it only been discovered in time. He does not understand the religious life (his "cloystered frailty" parallels Milton's dislike of a "fugitive and cloistered virtue"). In the Act sermon, he censures the Roman practice of auricular confession, but because it is "constrained," not voluntary like the "*private Confession* to our ghostly Father, the Minister" allowed by the Prayer Book to the Church of England, for "the happy discharge of a troubled soule." He argues against the distinction between mortal sins and venial ones, "that separate not from the grace of God" and "need not so much trouble a man's conscience," to which Cosin and others more extreme subscribed.[75] His picturesque example reminds his hearers that "hee that Robs a Cottage, though hee take little, nay though he take nothing, is in as much danger of an Arraienement as he that robs a Palace." In these criticisms, however, King is again saying no more than Donne or Hall, or some contemporary Catholic writers. King's father's erstwhile friend Archbishop de Dominis, for instance (who, when he arrived in England in 1617, may have influenced the newly ordained King to take a tolerant, more ecumenical view of religion) held similar views on Purgatory, which he, too, considered only an abuse and not an integral, unreformable part of the Roman Church's belief, as strict Calvinists would see it.

It is important to note that King's "middle" temperament is repelled by as many Puritan characteristics as Papist. There are many digs at separatists such as the Anabaptists, the Brownists, and the Family of Love. He is no strict Sabbatarian. He dislikes Puritan hypocrisy over such matters as christening children "with Propositions and wholsome Sentences": in his disquisition on names under "Hallowed be thy Name," he instances "*Sin defy: Fight the good fight of faith,* and the like. But I should neither much blame or censure them, did they not doe it out of grosse affectation, and insolent opposition to the customes used by us." As a residentiary canon of St. Paul's he would have been involved, like his Dean, with stiff-necked Puritans such as the city merchant Humphrey Smith, who with his whole household refused to kneel for the sacrament or to take off his hat to pray, causing such irritation to Donne that he burst out, in one sermon, "does God stand there and wilt thou sit, sir, and never kneele?"[76]

This points to the reason for King's reaction: that such men, "in [God's] owne peculiar, his proper place, the Church . . . scarce honour Him with a bended knee or an uncovered head—cheap low-rated complements, which they passe upon all other occasions . . . as if the outward worship of God had past away with the old abolished ceremonies, and with them were now extinct." He speaks out against another Puritan custom, extempory prayer, for the same reason: that it is bad manners "to tender [God] a raw unseasoned meditation that cost no paines nor studie in the shaping of it." He earlier called the Puritan preachers' omission of the Lord's Prayer before the sermon "a contempt, you know, contrary to the Canon *or good manners*" [italics mine].

Moreover (in this, which is perhaps a matter of intelligence, his stricter Calvinist father is like him) King does not bar from his writings the Apocryphal wisdom literature or its quaint illustrations, though most Puritans considered that compilation a corrupt later accretion, as was the tradition of the Descent into Hell that King dramatises so vividly in the Spital sermon. He happily quotes Greek and Latin secular literature as well as the more acceptable historians, criticising Puritan anti-intellectuals, in his Visitation sermon, . . . "who account Ignorance a mark of the Spirit, and none so fit for the Ministery as those who never took Degree in the Schools."

In King's attack on extempory prayer in the first section of *The Lord's Prayer,* there are further pointers of significance in understanding his "middle" position. The first is that there, as elsewhere, his real target is not the thing itself, providing it is capable of good use, but rather the abuse or extreme. He continues: "I [do not] disallow extemporall *Prayers,* when need or occasion shall require. Seasonably used they are the fruits of a ripe, well-tun'd Devotion." And when he attacks the sermons of "Lay Mechanicke Presbiters" in the 1621 sermon, like Joseph Hall in his "Holy Panegyric,"[77] he observes that the regular preachers were "never more, nor better . . . *I onely strike at the abuse*" [italics mine]. Similarly, in the Act sermon, when condemning the Roman Church's use of auricular confession as "the *Master-key* to open into all the secrets of Christendom," he adds, "There had been no Controversie about this point of Confession, had not some ignorant and importunate Physitians corrupted this wholesome Medicine with their drugges of Tradition."

King's admiring reference to "our Liturgie" is also significant, for he shares with other "middle" preachers like Brownrigg[78]—compared with the Puritan extreme especially—an unshakeable devotion to the Book of Common Prayer. It is the repository of "our setled Liturgie," expressly commended by Calvin, Peter Martyr, and Bucer as "a work beyond Exception, every way consonant to the Word of God," from which we have in no significant way departed since the Reformation, as he claims in *1640.* The rhythms of the Prayer Book are everywhere in King's sermons, even in concealed allusions, like that to the marriage service that creeps into the Visitation sermon: "The Ministery was not an Office Rashly Instituted, Therefore ought not to be Unadvisedly Undertaken."

If King's support of the use of the cross in baptism appears an acceptance of "Arminian" rites and ceremonies, his reason, one he shares with other "middle" men, is that it is prescribed in the Prayer Book. The practice is abominated by Puritans, however, whose "umbrageous Phantasies startle now at anything of Decency and Order—As if Popery were obtruded in that *Sign,* which hath no other meaning but to signify to the world that *we are not ashamed of the Cross of Christ crucified,*" as he remarks acidly in the funeral sermon for Duppa. There is nowhere an indication that King wanted to bring back the "old abolished ceremonies," or that he approved of other

Arminian practices, such as placing the altar at the east end of the church and railing in the holy table. In the 1620s when most of his extant sermons were preached, these were not yet matters of unavoidable confrontation, but it would not be surprising if he came to accept them in the 1630s as matters of good order, just as kneeling and removing one's hat were of good manners.

Order—one of King's, as well as Donne's and Hall's, favourite themes—the universal chain of being in a hierarchy that sustains the world, he regards as the stabilising influence both of the microcosmic world and the macrocosmic universe. "God is a God of Order," he says, both in *The Lord's Prayer* and in *1640* where (like Hooker)[79] he finds "good naturall reason for it," for the natural law expresses itself in order, and the universe is subject to God rather than to science. "There is nothing so much sets out the Universe as *Order*, to see how subordinate causes depend of their Superiors, and this sublunary Globe of the Celestiall." His many strictures against "those two jarring extremes of Papacy and Presbytery" result from the way they disturb order. He delightfully reassures his hearers in the Spital sermon that after the indiscriminate burials of the 1625 plague, "We shall *Arise in Order*. That confused tumultous kind of Death shall not disguise us from the knowledge of our Maker, who will distinguish each Bone, and give it to the right Owner."

In the 1621 sermon, King argues the natural necessity for inequality, which produced the mediaeval political ecclesiastical hierarchies: "Looke up to Heaven and reade over that bright booke, you shall see an inequality of light in those celestiall bodies . . . as in heaven, so in earth hath he ordained greater lights and higher powers, to goe before his people." He does not, like the Laudian Arminians in the 1630s and 1640s, claim a distinct level in the natural hierarchy for the Church but (like Archbishop de Dominis) he certainly considered it a "historically perpetuated vehicle of spiritual 'ordo'."[80] It was not for him, as for those ardent for further reform, merely a convenient method of ecclesiastical government, but a body "whereof Christ is head." Moreover, "as wee are all parts of that mysticall body, so are we also of a Politicall. Of which body . . . the King is the Head" *(The Lord's Prayer VI)*.

It is because "nothing so demonstrates the God of order" as monarchy (a subject on which Donne, of all his 160 sermons, preached only one) that King supports the Divine Right of Kings. Joseph Hall, emphatically no Arminian, voiced the same view in 'A Holy Panegyric': "Monarchy is the best of governments; and likest to His rule, that sits in the assembly of Gods."[81] It is important to look carefully at how King expresses it, however. Rulers indeed are selected by God (and like guardian angels, each nation must have its own—King is concerned to reject the universal authority claimed by the Pope). Thereafter, however (as he said in *1621*), "*Lord* or *Master* are not onely stiles of preeminence, but of care." In the sermons of the 1620s, the frequent image of the king as head or heart of a commonwealth is Tudor (and Shakespearean, with echoes of the historical plays) rather than Stuart. Like Claudius in *Hamlet*, Henry King believes the monarch "beares that awful Motto of safety written about his sacred Person, *Touch not mine anointed*" *(The Lord's Prayer IV)*. But though, in the order of things, he is "the Glasse thorow which we may behold God: He is his Picture" yet he "resembles Him no neerer than dead Colours doe the Life." For kings are subject to mutability, "Kingdomes expire like the Kings, and they like us," and cares, "like a wreath of thorns, impale their heads and swarm within the circle of a crown." Moreover, under "The Power and the Glory," he states, "The highest evidence of Earthly Power is the Power of *Making Lawes*, and the tying up of factious dispositions in an Obedience of doing whatsoever they command. But unto what height is this Power elevated in God, who is the universal Law-giver, ruling them which rule us?" Other more Calvinist Royalists than King, like Thomas Morton or Tobie Matthews, subscribed to this view of divine right.

Indeed, though he may begin to seem more Arminian, King still, when Laud comes to power, follows a middle way. He would have found it difficult to assent to at least two of the articles put forward by Bishop Juxon for the clergy of diocese of London in 1635.[82] The seventh states that "The order of bishops is by the law of God," an episcopal form of Divine Right, which in practice produced a prelatical elite. King's attitude to bishops again results from his concept of natural order: as the Lords Spiritual, they are a necessary link in the chain of being, alongside Lords Temporal, Privy Councillors, magistrates, and all those set in authority. But unlike Laud, he sees this as a matter of degree rather than of separate order. Within the same natural order, he sees that each minister is in turn "a kind of Bishop, set over the soules committed to his charge."

King, like the older English Calvinists, regards bishops primarily as godly pastors, rather than governors and princes with temporal as well as spiritual powers. As with kings, he stresses the duties above the privileges of the office. To his puritanical diocesan clergy in the Visitation sermon of 1662, he instances St. Paul's bishop Titus, "advanced to that high place of Government in the Church," commenting with St. Augustine: "Think not that because we are Bishops we cannot do amiss, or are exempted from receiving their Advise, who fairly admonish us of our Duties." In the 1621 sermon, he quotes with approval Theophylact: "when Christ made his Apostles Bishops and Superintendants of his Church, he appoynted them not so much to *Lord* the flocke, as to *feed* it." He relates this to the example of his father John King's "unwearied industrie," which showed the world that "they which for gaine, or ease, or for ambition aimed at Bishopricks, mistooke that waighty calling." As Bishop of London, John King had visited "each Pulpit within your City (some of them oftner), & not onely taught within it, but . . . in all the adjoining villages where hee lived, never allowing his numerous affaires so much as a Sabbath or Sundaye's rest whilest he was able." Henry King inherits another ideal cultivated by the Jacobean bishops: St. Paul's dictum that "a bishop must be given to hospitality"; he praises Duppa's "generous way of living, to His owne, and the Honour of His whole Order."

The bishop at his consecration is also appointed a guardian of the Church's faith (a role King lived out to his cost during the Interregnum). One recognised mark of episcopacy was the bishop's authority, handed down from the apostles and the early Church, to ordain men to the Church's ministry. Again, King's doctrine of ordination is derived from the Prayer Book, whose ordinal was designed by the Reformers to reflect the Church of England's continuing membership of the one catholic and apostolic Church. "We are perswaded," he says in the Visitation sermon, "that in the Lawful Ordination in our Church, the *Spirit of God* is imparted in those words, *Receive the Holy Ghost*. Nor must we judge them Ministers who want those Seals of Ordination to their patent." Ordination certainly set the clergy apart from the laity. King casually remarks in the final section of *The Lord's Prayer*: "I deny not, that in the Church the Priest's Prayers are more acceptable than the congregation's, because he is the Mediator betwixt God and the People: Yet I will never beleeve but the Congregation's *Amen* is more obligatory, more effectuall than the Priest's." It is a difference of function, here particularly for the liturgy, within the same Body of Christ. To him, the difference is ordained by God, however, not laid down by man. The minister is God's chosen arrow, King says at his Visitation: "How disordered then must their motion needs be, who leap out of the Quiver, and fly without their Mission." With such a belief in the catholicity of the Church of England, he could never have conformed to Cromwell's liberal Interregnum Church, though few were as loyal or as stubborn as he.

The second point at which he would have disagreed with the London diocesan articles would have been the fifth, which states "That ministerial power in forgiving sins is not merely declaratory." King quite clearly affirms more than once (especially in the Act sermon) that the power given by Christ to the apostles as his representatives, and from thence to "his *Priests*" at their ordination, "of *Binding and loosing*—that is, *of shewing men to be bound, or loosed*"—from their sins, was "not a *Judiciary* power (as the Church of Rome unwarrantably assumes)," but "a *Ministeriall*, a *Declaratory* power" in the name of the whole Church. On the other hand, this insistence on the minister's authority to pronounce absolution on behalf of the Church shows that he views confession as something deeper than merely a psychologically beneficial exercise. Nevertheless, he does not accept it as a full sacrament, like Baptism and the Eucharist, the two ordained by Christ in the gospels; and he by no means takes up the full English Arminian position, of Overall, Andrewes, and later Laud, who thought confession always desirable before taking communion. His interest in the subject may have been more than academic. He had succeeded to the prebend of St. Pancras in St. Paul's, which carried with it the ancient office of Confessor to the Cathedral, revived by Lancelot Andrews when he held the same prebend.

In considering Laudian Arminianism as reflected in Bishop Juxon, T. A. Mason notes further aspects of episcopacy, the political and the juridical. He sees these as distinguishable by a preoccupation with such matters of church government as the necessity of enforcing tithes, the restitution of church lands, and the iniquity of enclosure. King's forceful verse translation of "The Woes of Esay"[83] shows sympathy with the latter view and indeed as early as 1626, in his Spital sermon, he inveighs against all three: "But one foot of *Church-land* taken into your estate, like the King's Waste, may alter your Tenure in God's blessings and bring your whole fortune into Wardship.... The least defraudation of God is *Sacriledge* ... the wilful deteining [of tithes] may exasperate *Him*." If these are really Arminian attitudes, they were common to all contemporary higher clergy, particularly those such as archdeacons concerned with the administration of church property.

King shows himself interestingly egalitarian, in theory at least. It was, perhaps surprisingly, the Arminians who criticised "ranked" pews in churches, though the Puritans were noisy social levellers. King twice quotes "God is a God of the valleyes as well as the hils" in *The Lord's Prayer,* to show that "our Prayers do not ascend in their ranks." In the second section he warns his hearers that even the meanest "have God for their Father, as well as themselves."

So far, King's "middle way" veers towards both moderate Calvinism and moderate Arminianism; the latter position, it is probably fair to say, was chiefly a result of the built-in apostolicity of the Book of Common Prayer. His desire for "middleness," however, can be incontrovertibly demonstrated from the most fundamental of all disputes between the two extremes, the relative importance to be afforded to the Bible and preaching as against the sacraments. By their bias towards one or other of these, it is possible to distinguish the strict Calvinist reformer (who looks to the early Church) and the Laudian Arminian (who looks in addition towards mediaeval Church tradition). Early in *The Lord's Prayer,* King's own position is stated unequivocally. As a means of grace, the Bible and the sacrament of the Eucharist are equal partners.

Certainly the Bible, William Chillingworth's "Religion of Protestants," is "that sacred Booke, which we beleeve, contains all that may conduce to our salvation." Like all his contemporaries, even textual scholars like Henry Hammond, King reads the Bible literally and goes to some lengths to reconcile apparently contradictory texts. But in his commentary on "Give us this day our daily bread," after commending the word of God as "our Soules food," he immediately couples it with the bread in the Sacrament, which is "the bait or provision to strengthen the Soule in her journey," for the sacraments are "the visible Seales of [God's] grace and favour." On the one hand, "Receive the Holy Sacrament so often as thou canst prepare thy selfe ... S. Bernard allowes it thee every day, if thou darest allow it thy selfe" (a comparatively rare position at this time); on the other, "Heare the Word of God preached in abundance ... so much as is sufficient—or if that bee too little, as much as thou listest." And he warns, "take heed the frequent reception of the one do not make thee loath and undervalue thy Lord's Supper, nor the plentifull hearing of God's Word make thy devotion surfet." In the 1621 sermon, however, his fiercest criticism is reserved for those who "lay all Churches where there is any suspicion of a Sermon ... to satisfie that wanton itch of hearing, which like a Tetter, the more it is rubbed, the more it spreads." And from his reference to the Sacrament as "the Sacred representation of his Body and Blood" and "these holy Mysteries," and his quoting with approval (in the same section of *The Lord's Prayer*) the mediaeval description "Angel's food and Bread from Heaven," it seems clear that he regards the Sacrament as more than a sign in the Zwinglian sense.

Again, of the Bible's place in relation to tradition, he is in no doubt. It neither must be "wrested to make Heresie authenticall," in the sectarian manner, "nor abased so low as to make Tradition Judge of it," like the Papists, with whom "man's stupid Traditions [are] valued above God's Scripture." He thanks God (with a sarcastic dig at the unintelligible Latinate English of the current Roman translation from Rheims) that the Bible (thanks to the Reformation) is "free and open for us to Heare in all Churches of this Land" *(The Lord's Prayer IV)*. Once more, however, a middleness of temperament makes him censure the overzealous Puritan even more strongly: " 'tis not enough to know the Bible, or bee able to repeat the severall volumes of [God's] Will, unless a practise be joyned to this speculative science of Christianity."

This pragmatic but lyrical preacher faithfully reflects the voice of moderation, the "middle way" of many unsung clergy and laity of his age, with all its complexities and contradictions, hemmed in, as it must have seemed, by both extremes, and during the Interregnum seemingly lost forever—though at the Restoration it too was after all restored; the English as a race are fundamentally moderates by temperament. King, in his passionate love of order and fear of fanatical extremes, anticipates the eighteenth century and even the Latitudinarians. But his love for the Church of England and her liturgy, and for his king, however, is wholly of his age.

THE SERMONS

KING AS PREACHER

Henry King's preaching was much esteemed in his own day. White Kennett, (writing in 1728) relates that King's Restoration funeral sermon for Brian Duppa was preached "to the great content of the Auditory," and Margaret Crum quotes Abraham Wright's contemporary admiration for his preaching manner: "a modest and mowrnfull tone, especially the last part."[84] The real criterion, however, is that Pepys, that highly critical sermon taster who liked "oratory without affectation or study," "a good and moral sermon," thought King's unprinted 1668 sermon "good and eloquent." This is high commendation, for Pepys frequently censures what he hears as "a flat dead sermon, both from matter and manner of delivery," "dull drowzy," "long and sad," or "a poor dry sermon."[85] If King could please him, he therefore must have been neither a "witty" preacher (in the derogatory sense of overfull of wordplay and farfetched imagery), nor prolix and overweighted with learning.

Why did Fraser Mitchell dismiss King so disastrously? It is worth looking at his comments in detail.[86] In the first place, he offers little to support his censure. In the second, in spite of himself, in some passing remarks he actually praises King's prose, though he insists that he "cannot be pronounced of the first rank." On the one hand, he compares him unfavourably with Cosin, Hacket, Brownrigg (with all of whom I would suggest King deserves a rather more than equal place), and with Mark Frank, who better merits Mitchell's estimate.[87] On the other, he quotes approvingly H. J. Massingham's judgement of King's poetry, which he admits is equally true of his prose: "a kind of resigned, subdued and melancholy Donne, without the greater poet's fine madness on the one hand or his abstruseness on the other . . . a quietist of the deepest feeling, who knew how to express it in a grave diction . . . and a soberly rich imagery to which it is exquisitely appropriate."[88] John Sparrow's warm commendation of the poems, in his introduction to the Nonesuch edition, might also be applied equally to King's prose: he comments on "the supreme felicity of phrase and the pointed diction sometimes achieved by King . . . his felicity of technique enabled him to describe the religious experiences of his mind in words of beauty, even if those experiences are common to very many."[89]

Mitchell apparently based his view on only two of King's sermons, the Act and the Spital, almost the earliest; he therefore does not take into account some of King's finest prose, which is found in *The Lord's Prayer*. His example of King's "imitation" of Donne does not withstand close examination: he compares a passage from the Act sermon with Donne, *Sermons* 5.266.

> Thinkest thou, by drawing a Curtaine about thy Bed, or by putting out a candle in thy Chamber, to hide thine incontinencie from God, or darken his knowledge? Foole thou canst not! Thou bearest a Lampe in thine own brest, thy conscience; . . . *a watching Candle,* that burnes at midnight, and will light the Judge to descry thee. Or if that taper burne dimmely, if it have wasted into a snuffe, so that thou hast no Conscience, or but a seared one, which lies smothering in the socket, and can onely glimmer, not shine; why yet, God is (as Basil saith) . . . *all eye,* to survey thee.

> That that God, who hath often looked upon me in my foulest uncleannesse, and when I had shut out the eye of the day, the Sunne, and the eye of the night, the Taper, and the eyes of all the world, with curtaines and windowes and doores, did yet see me, and see me in mercy . . . should so turne himself from me. . . .

The verbal similarities are confined to curtains and tapers and God's observance despite concealment: the theme and development of the two sermons is quite different.

It is a pity Mitchell did not notice that another of Donne's sermons closely resembled the Act sermon.[90] Indeed, he praises that sermon for achieving "the passionate, almost 'physical' note of Donne's contemplation of the Passion of Christ,"[91] commending King's not following slavishly the usual traditions or patristic sources that might have influenced him. He finds "an intensity of feeling due to the strength of the preacher's imagination about King's treatment which distinguishes him from the other 'witty' preachers, and brings him into the same relationship with Donne which the others owed to Andrewes."[92] Mitchell continues (in no way substantiating his judgement), "unfortunately, however, King's average style falls considerably short of the distinction attained [there]"—no one who had read more of King could make such a comment. He concludes, "King may be regarded as a minor 'metaphysical', and a preacher whose personal tastes and attainments rather than his participation in the common interests and characteristics of his school[93] entitle him to more than passing notice." Later, however, in praising Mark Frank, Mitchell cites King as the *only* other seventeenth-century "imitator of Andrewes *[sic]* who succeeded in pouring the old wine of patristic allusion and fanciful 'wit' into the new bottles of a connected literary medium, without suffering the flavour of the wine to be lost in the transference."[94] On balance, therefore, one must conclude that Mitchell estimated King quite highly.

In his actual section on King, nevertheless, Mitchell damned him with faint praise. This seems to have determined the attitude of subsequent influential writers on seventeenth-century prose. George Williamson, for instance, ignores King's sermons altogether in his *Senecan Amble,* and Douglas Bush in the *Oxford History of English Literature* does not mention them in his account of King. Ronald Berman is concerned to study King in his historical context, though he includes a masterly summary of the development of King's prose style. Not unnaturally, he regards the sermons chiefly as a source of ideas—he refers throughout to "the Bishop of Chichester" (even when speaking of the 1620s), or "the irrascible Bishop," as though the bitterness engendered by the civil wars was a feature of King's prose from the start. Millar Maclure's work on the Paul's Cross sermons naturally deals with King's theological position. The only recent critic to consider King's sermons as literature, Horton Davies, makes an arbitrary judgment, explicitly based on Mitchell, about the inferiority of this "Prince of Wails" and his "lugubrious" style (a charge which, unlike the pun, he makes no attempt to substantiate). He too, however, elsewhere in his work, admits that King's style is worthy of note, for he uses a high proportion of illustrations from *The Lord's Prayer* as good examples when discussing characteristic metaphysical themes and qualities.[95]

STRUCTURE

An introduction to a specific author is not the place to consider fully the different rhetorical structures and figures employed in seventeenth-century sermons and their lineage. Both have in any case been exhaustively treated in works on the preaching, rhetoric, and prose of the period.[96] However, King's practice must be located within that tradition.

In the first place, he lays out the division of his text within his prewar sermons in numbered points (unlike Donne, who usually indicates divisions in his printed texts in the margins only). Thereafter, however, King's plan is worked gracefully into the shape of the argument. In the second Lent sermon, he gradually rebuilds his text by recapitulating each time the words considered so far, before continuing with those he is to use next. Often he provides some witty context, such as that after the clause dealing with man's earthly wants in *The Lord's Prayer,* "Give us this day our daily Bread": "Thus you see, like men set on shore for refreshment and provision of some necessaries for their voyage, we are cal'd aboord againe." Though he may begin (as Joseph Hall often does) *in medias res,* as in the Lent sermons—"I wonder why Tertullian was so stiff and peremptory in that assertion of his," and "I know some Writers interpret this Psalme in a Mysticall sense"—after a sentence or two of exordium, he states his plan. His occasional use of Latin marginal terms like *introductio, divisio,* and the careful numbering of points shows him following (though loosely only) the kind of classical development of themes and orations, Ciceronian in origin, used at the time in schools and universities.

His sentences are rarely in the long, intricately structured, complex Ciceronian style, however; though that style sometimes leads up to the fine climaxes of his perorations. Nor are they short, clipped sentences and phrases in the extreme Senecan style, typified by much of Lancelot Andrewes's writing and by Joseph Hall's later sermons. King uses a natural and skillful blend of long and short, probably instinctive in one who was both lyric poet and musician. His short sentences provide an effective contrast to long compound ones—"They shall rest softer upon that cold pillow of earth than a Bed of downe" (at the end of the second Lent sermon), or (to the man who expects mercy because he has committed no grave crime), "Surely I hope so too." Sometimes, however, he interrupts his sentence structure altogether when passion or devotion overcomes him, resuming further on with a repetition of the word of departure: "the Popes . . . the Popes, I say . . ." or "did he . . . did he all this? . . ." Occasionally, he piles similar adverbial clauses in a great heap to prepare the way for a final, triumphant monosyllable like "there beginne but never end." Long lists of examples, which are a regular part of the style of his father, of John Donne, and of Joseph Hall, do not occur in his work.

Like Andrewes, King tends to divide his text word by word and, as Joseph Hall did, to deal with what he calls the "temporal [or secular] considerations" behind each word as it stands (for instance he examines Puritan "names" and contemporary "kingdoms" in *The Lord's Prayer*), as well as contemplating the text as a whole in its spiritual sense. Everywhere, however, his usage is flexible: if common sense dictates, two or three words are grouped together, to avoid the nonsensical "crumbling of a text into small parts" objected to by George Herbert.[97] "I take the words in that Method wherein they ly," he says at the beginning of the 1661 sermon, and in Duppa's funeral sermon, "I trouble you not with any Curious but a Plain Division." This "division," reminiscent of the Ciceronian fivefold one, is in the manner also of the more humanist Protestant sermon manuals, like that of Bartholomew Keckermann, whose *Rhetoricae Ecclesiae* (Geneva 1614) is still among King's books. It is a method followed most explicitly in the fourth and fifth sermons of *The Lord's Prayer.*

Next, King "opens the sense" of his passage, with the help of modern as well as traditional commentators. Frequently, he names them in the text as well as in the marginal references, but on ten occasions, he adds in the margin (presumably when preparing for publication) works not referred to in the text. Sometimes, particularly in sections of *The Lord's Prayer* probably revised some time after he preached them, however, his marginal references are general, to authors only rather than to a precise work.

From time to time, like a good Calvinist, King claims his independence of allegory: "My discourse runs not by that compass; I take it literally." Or he speaks of "the literal meaning and temporal [contemporary] acception" of his text. Nevertheless, the poet in him was undoubtedly attracted to the quaint mystical interpretations he found in his favourite Fathers such as Augustine and Ambrose, on which he tends to linger before righteously dismissing them. The typological interpretation of Old Testament figures and events as foreshadowing Christ and the New Testament—"Christ . . . was figured in Salomon," "Egypt was figuratively the Captivitie of Sinne"—or even of contemporary seventeenth-century figures was more acceptable to Calvinists, because it was Bible based. When King appears to be carried away, by enthusiasm or indignation or sheer weight of theological fact, into abandoning his text altogether, this is intentional. He returns disarmingly to the point, as in the Spital sermon, with remarks like "But I lose my selfe in this vast subject of God's mercy. . . . Let me carry you backe once more." Such digression, not surprisingly, frequently helps to fill out the long St. Paul's Cross and Spital sermons.

King next amplifies his theme. Usually, he works from Old Testament to New Testament examples, though he may add classical illustrations, chiefly (but not, like more Calvinist preachers, exclusively) from the historians Tacitus, Herodotus, Livy, Plutarch, Suetonius, Valerius Maximus, and others less well known. He also happily mingles classical, legendary characters with the sacred: in *The Lord's Prayer V,* good men must "like Atlas stand, not lie under their burthens," and in *The Lord's Prayer XI,* though Ulysses "fainingly" had the winds in a bag, it is Christ who rules over them. In the earlier sermons, there are also illustrations from "unnatural" natural history, from Pliny via Conrad Gesner (possibly as adapted into English by Edward Topsell in *A Historie of Foure-Footed Beastes*).

The text is then applied, sometimes to a modern controversy like papal authority over national rulers, or auricular confession, but always to a moral interpretation, to guide his hearers in their daily living, like the contemplation of hellfire in "Deliver us from Evil": "Nothing but the breath of Prayer can coole, nothing but the Teares of contrition and Penitence quench this fire." King's final perorations also aim to kindle his hearers' devotion and "bring all heaven before their eyes," and indeed, many of his meditations take wing, like the conclusion of the first Lent sermon:

> Wee beseech Almightie God to feather us with the wings of the morning, that wee may begin our flight to him betimes. . . . What then though our Lifes short Taper be wasted to a snuffe, and almost burnt out . . . if it will but serve to light us fairely towards our graves, wee shall not then feare to goe unto our last beds in the darke. Our Bodies will sleepe in their dust without a candle, and for our Soules they will need none, being translated into that region of light, where there is *no need of a candle,* but the brightnesse of God's face holds on the day everlastingly.

It is rash indeed to contrast this with Donne's famous "one equall light . . . one equall musick" passage, yet to juxtapose them highlights a significant difference between the two preachers. Donne's meditation is splendidly mindstretching to the very end:

> Keepe us Lord so awake in the duties of our Callings, that we may thus sleepe in thy Peace, and wake in thy glory, and change that infallibility which thou affordest us here, to an Actuall and undeterminable possession of that Kingdome which thy Sonne our Saviour Christ Jesus hath purchased for us, with the inestimable price of his incorruptible Blood.[98]

King leaves thought aside, rapt in contemplation of that final glory.

The length of the sermons, an average of forty quarto pages, leaves little room in the customary hour's duration for much addition or alteration to have occurred to the texts before printing. The dedicatory epistle to the two Lent sermons bears this out: King offers Charles I "this cold service" of what he already had heard, to "practise part of that trouble upon your Eye, which hath already exercised your Eare." In the 1621 Paul's Cross sermon, King speaks, in his address to the reader at the end, of the interim nature of his defence of his father, indicating that (for speed in this instance) the printed sermon closely followed the spoken one.[99] He also reveals the precise nature of his additions for publication: "explicating some remarkable *circumstances,* which better become a Margin then a speech"—marginal quotations like those from Thomas Preston's book and, no doubt, marginal glosses such as the details of those present at Bishop John King's bedside.

The same kinds of addition are found in the revised edition (1634) of *An Exposition Upon the Lord's Prayer,* though of its seven extra pages, most are due to each section or sermon beginning on a new page. There is only what amounts to about one page of fresh material, chiefly in the third section on names. However, there are lengthy new marginal quotations, particularly in Greek from Chrysostom (without reference to him in the text), and in the eighth section a textual reference to "Ambrose" is now authenticated in the margin by the Latin relevant passage. Occasionally, the sense of a passage is clarified by the addition of a single word; and references are made more precise. Sometimes, however, King's source still eluded him, and he retained forms such as "Nay (saith another)," or "one saith." Where he has translated into English or paraphrased Greek and Latin quotations of any length, his sentences are sometimes complete before the addition of the original quotation, suggesting that it, too, was added for publication (some clear examples of quotations intruding upon the syntax are indicated in the explanatory notes). Short Latin or Greek tags, on the other hand, are usually an integral part of the sentence, and his quotations from the classical poets would be familiar to most of his audience and expected even by those who did not understand them, as showing their preacher was suitably learned. His first three printed sermons contain more short Greek as well as Latin quotations than any others. *The Lord's Prayer,* however, though it has longer theological passages in both languages, has fewer such brief quotations. The length of the individual sections is similar to that of the separately printed sermons, suggesting that they were expanded little for publication.

Since the printed sermons are therefore presumably much as they were when delivered, and we fortunately have the texts King himself published, rather than a pirated version or even an official posthumous one (like Ussher's printed sermons) from someone else's notes, it is relevant to enquire what the texts reveal of his writing methods. In most cases, he must have overseen the printing himself. The frequent "dramatic" punctuation preserved resembles that of his many authoritative poetry manuscripts, particularly in the use of capital letters and italics, and is unlike that found in the printed sermons of Donne, Hall, or other contemporary preachers. It may seem at first sight "capricious,"[100] but on closer observation, it can be seen to imply the natural emphases of speech, and suggests a rhetorical intention (such as was present in contemporary play texts). For instance, the first line of the *Act* passage quoted by Mitchell (for comparison with Donne, see above), emphasising "*Curtaine,*" "*Bed,*" and "*Chamber,*" prescribes a subtle pace for reading aloud. Such an intention is more clearly present in King's carefully supervised poetry manuscripts, some unusual characteristic spellings of which reappear in the printed text of 1657. Some of the same spellings are found in the early printed sermons,[101] surely indicating that the originals were copied for King by the same amanuenses. The authoritative poetry manuscripts (which are a rarity in the history of seventeenth-century literature) already approximate the appearance of printed texts in their beautiful italic, with catchwords at the foot of each quarto page. Sermons similarly laid out would be an easily read *aide-mémoire* for a preacher. Everything suggests that King's carefully modulated sentences and well-placed quotations and instances would be read or memorised as they stood for the pulpit. Donne's practice of speaking only from notes and writing up his sermons later, for friends or for publication, was apparently unusual in the early part of the century. Joseph Hall's admission is more characteristic, and his method was almost certainly that used by King:

> Never durst I climb into the pulpit to preach any sermon, whereof I had not before in my poor and plain fashion, penned every word in the same order, wherin I hoped to deliver it; although, in the expression, I listed not to be a slave to syllables.[102]

STYLE

King's vocabulary, like his sentence structure, generally is direct and natural, even in moments of heightened rhythm and majesty. In satirical passages, however, in keeping with literary tradition, he uses forceful, homely words such as "rove and bangle," or speaks colloquially, for instance of those whose wealth persuades them to "shake hands with religion." Unlike Donne, who produces neologisms frequently, King's Latinate words are used chiefly for satire—the Pope's "timpanous and excrescent titles," or the "triturations" of the learned—though he occasionally anglicises Latin or Greek theological or philosophical terms when expounding scholastic theories in *The Lord's Prayer*. Sometimes, he uses colloquial phrases to lighten a long and difficult theological explanation, as in the many delightful, brief images in the ninth book of *The Lord's Prayer*—for example, "Can the Judge of all the World play booty with his clients?" His style is at its most natural in such openings as "I need not tell you the occasion of our meeting" (Duppa's funeral), or "You will easily judge *Thunder* and *Earthquakes* improper Prologues to usher in such a Triumph as the *Inauguration* of a King" *(1661)*. Reading aloud reveals many passages with the inevitability of which one is conscious in all good prose: the onomatopoeia of "like a flash of lightening, leapes out and dies at once" in the first Lent sermon, or (in the beginning of *The Lord's Prayer*) the rhythmical strength of "even as Aaron stood in the doore of the Tabernacle, betwixt a displeased God, and a wretched people."

King's style is less vivid than Joseph Hall's, with his pictures of London life, and his familiar address: "Dear Christians, I must be sharp, are we children or fools, that we should be better pleased with the glittering tinsel of a painted baby from a pedlar's shop, than with the secretly rich and invaluable jewel of Divine Truth?"[103] Nevertheless, King as well as Hall moves at dramatic moments into the present tense, as in his vigorous description of the trial of Charles I: "But this brought not their design to effect. . . . Now they have invented a *Law*, They cannot find a Judge to Execute it. The Office is tendered to all the Robe here left behind."

King's use of rhetorical devices is less heavy than that of either Donne or Andrewes; there is less wordplay, and it is usually subtle, even at his most metaphysical in the Act and Spital sermons. In Duppa's funeral sermon, the chasing of the word "division" to show that Death, his theme, is the true divider, is an isolated example of persistent play. For the most part he uses only brief phrases like "indefinite, nay infinite," or "Mercy presupposes misery," very different from Andrewes's famous "Gabri-el . . . Micha-el" passage, or hauntingly beautiful cumulations in Donne such as "I shall rise, from the dead, from the darke station, from the prostration, from the prosternation of death."[104] Nor is King's alliteration and assonance of the "bloody blameful blade" variety but unobtrusive, to make a sentence more effective: "The stile of his survay runs universally" *(The Lord's Prayer XI)*, or the complex interlocking alliteration in the first Lent sermon of "For my part, I thinke Plato spake no paradox but plaine truth; since amongst all the curious Caskets of Nature wherin the secrets of Art and Knowledge are lockt up there is not any so loose, so false a Cabinet as the *Heart*." His puns are subtle too, intellectual and not unattractive even to modern sensibilities: "These organs of our Bodies are His, and the Musicke they make is by Him" *(The Lord's Prayer XI)*; or (a pun in *1621* that depends on knowing that the seventeenth-century word for plough is "to ear") "I pity that pastor who is put to plough the rocks when the ear is too hard for his advice to enter"; or finally, one depending on "ala," the Latin for "wing," which introduces an extended image drawn from hawking, "the alacrity of our Faith beating in our Prayers."

His favourite devices, like those of the Fathers he so loves, are rhetorical question, antithesis, and parallelism. Sometimes (particularly in his earlier work) there are whole paragraphs of questions, like the passage in *The Lord's Prayer XI* beginning "What monuments of Shame then doe these erect to them and at how easie a rate doe they purchase confusion?" At best, however, King uses such questions to capture his hearers' attention by a direct appeal, particularly in the midst of theological exposition. Often they bring out the metaphysical quality of his wit: for example (in the ninth sermon of *The Lord's Prayer*), "Would you not judge him mad, who, being come to an Anchor in a safe Road, would, like the Dolphin, hunt the storme, and chuse to ride it out at the Maine Sea?"

King's careful antithesis and parallelism result as much from his close familiarity with the Bible as from conscious rhetorical style; like Hooker's, his words merge with the biblical phrases, imparting to his prose (which only reveals its full beauty read aloud) the sonorous rhythms of the Authorised Version. "Things past and future are eternally present with him, whose Title and Motto is *I am that I am,*" (from *The Lord's Prayer II*) or, "Though we began our Calculation with the stars, and layed the dust of the Earth for Cyphers, yet shall wee want number to compute how many ages are behinde to come of this Kingdome's date which here we pray for" (*The Lord's Prayer IV*). Balance in the Lent sermons is more obviously euphuistic and old-fashioned "Senecan" (as it can be in both Hooker and Shakespeare): "that may be true but this more Safe. I will hope wel of the one, yet beleeve better of the other"; or "A certain death is better than a doubtful Reprive: and a Sociable Woe sweeter than a solitary Content. Mirth and a Wilderness is a strange Anticke: but Misery sequestred from reliefe or advice, a very Monster." In *The Lord's Prayer X*, a polemical passage is made more pithy by antithesis: "To beleeve this is more dangerous than his Pity was foolish"; the three following clauses are strongly balanced: "All . . . All . . . All." Paradox is another device frequently and naturally used, as in Duppa's funeral sermon: "I begin there where all must end, with Death."

Undoubtedly, King's school and university training would have led him to copy passages from his reading into a commonplace book; his use of the same quotations on the preeminence of monarchy before and after the wars suggests this, together with the similar passages on memory that appear in both the 1621 and first Lent sermons, and the passage on present time found almost verbatim in both the first Lent sermon and at the end of *The Lord's Prayer VI*. His set pieces on youth and age, on the dove, on the transience of human life, probably also stem from such a book; passages like these relieve even the workaday style of the Restoration sermons. A commonplace book may also lie behind "characters" on the popular pattern (for instance the picture of Death in *Duppa*), though he uses these rarely compared with Hall, who was also a verse satirist. Equally popular sources of moral wisdom in the sermons are the frequent proverbs, both Latin and English, and the emblems in words, such as Persecution in the 1621 sermon, with her pavilion hung round with trophies of death, and Sin in *The Lord's Prayer X* with a whip at her back.

In 1662, at the age of seventy, King stated in his Visitation sermon his views on style in preaching, the fruits of a lifetime's meditation on the subject. Principal among them was his regard for decorum, which he calls "decency." In this, like his general abhorrence of extremes in thought and behaviour, he anticipates (as we have said) the eighteenth century. He agrees with Bacon and the Senecans in rating meaning higher than the elaborate presentation favoured by those preachers he calls "Hunters of Words," who "assail the Auditory . . . with tinkling words" irrelevant to their text; they should remember that "A Vessel at Sea, which bears more Sail than Ballast, is ever apt to over-set." On the other hand, King stresses that "to apparel our Discourse in more Ceremony than becomes the subject, or to use none at all are Extremes alike culpable": "Many have been . . . more ridiculous in an affected Plainness, than others in their studied Curiosity." Every dress is not suitable to religious truth: "That Language which commends the Stage would misbecome the Pulpit: Light conceits or flashes of unseason'd wit prophane that holy ground. And again, that bitter Style which in a Declamation were an ingenious Satyre, translated into a sermon might prove a Libel." This long, quotable section on the right choice of words and style may be compared with passages on the subject from later and better known sermon writers like Joseph Glanvill.

King's earlier comments on translations of the Bible (particularly the Latinate Douai version) and his praise for the elegant classical style of Apuleius or Seneca indicate that he was always aware of words. The Visitation sermon shows that this derives not only from his naturally poetic ear, but also because of his high view of the role of preaching: "In our Alchimy, wherein we labour to make Gold out of Clay, and by perswasions to prepare that Earth which we bear about us for final glory, The subject we undertake must fix our words, else we do but *Beat the air.*" He has a very modern awareness of the power of the media.

IMAGERY

Berman rightly observes that the movement of King's thought "depends on logical expansion rather than upon progression. Ideas are restated and redefined by an almost endless series of metaphors and images."[105] As a result, the thought is less dense than Donne's: King takes the words of his text and savours them, meditating upon them by means of his shifting images, which are in themselves a kind of progression of thought. Though his prose shows flashes of metaphysical wit to bring home a point, King has a sensitivity that prevents him from producing tasteless or incongruous images to make them more memorable through shock (as even Donne and Andrewes notoriously did on occasion). There is indeed the delight of surprise, but in a gentler mode: man sending away unwelcome better thoughts in the first Lent sermon "as Felix sent away Paul, *I will heare Thee some other Time*," or the childless monarch in *1661* despatched "to his last Bed like a despised Lamp, inglorious, and in the Dark." Extended conceits are more frequent and more self-conscious in the early sermons, for instance the violently metaphysical image in the Spital sermon of Christ's "hands and feet, forcibly entered by hammer and nailes, which possessed themselves of his whole stocke of life, and almost all the treasure of his bloud"; or the elaborate comparison developed at the beginning and end of *The Lord's Prayer*, between the clauses of the prayer and the writing of a letter.

Like Donne's, King's imagery makes much use of light and water. King's many sea travel illustrations, however, must be drawn from books like *Purchas his Pilgrims* (dedicated to his father by the author, who had been the Bishop's chaplain), for as late as 1636 he told Henry Blount, in a commendatory poem for his *A Voyage into the Levant*, that "from my Countrye's smoak I never mov'd."[106] Images of war and siege in the prewar sermons, though vivid (like that at the beginning of the tenth section of *The Lord's Prayer*) are also likely to be secondhand, for King, unlike Donne, was never a soldier. Both authors, however, had on their shelves the Roman military writer Vegetius. King's medical and horticultural images also have a literary ring; the garden or ship of the commonwealth, and images from a river and its banks, doors, windows, and locks are conventional. Nevertheless, when he takes such well-worn ideas as the mediaeval concept of the Book of Creatures, from which we can read of the existence of God, he adds some independent metaphysical twist: in the first Lent sermon, for instance, the book becomes a ledger book, and God its index. Others of King's images are drawn from heraldry,[107] from maps, alchemy, building and pargeting, and country matters like a dog worrying a flock, or a red sky presaging a fair day. Frequent images from hunting and, in particular, hawking, suggest it was his, as well as the Court's, favourite sport—his library possessed a mediaeval treatise on hawking attributed to the thirteenth-century philosopher, Albert the Great.

One misses the short dramatic scenes from daily life that delight in the sermons of Joseph Hall and Donne, but there are pleasant, brief allusions to familiar everyday topics such as the spectacles in the first Lent sermon, useless because cased up at the girdle; or such as the type in *The Lord's Prayer X*, broken up by the printer after each book and replaced in the fount; or the children's arrows in *The Lord's Prayer IV* "which fall backe as fast as they shoot them up." King may perhaps have been shy: he talks less about how people behave than Hall or Donne, and unlike Donne in particular, he rarely uses "I" or "you." On the other hand, he uses "we" more often, placing himself alongside the sinners in his audience, focusing their attention on God and Heaven's glory. Donne spends more time dramatically presenting his own sinful reactions so well that his audience can readily identify with him.

King's two most frequent sources of imagery are portrait painting and the worlds of law and accountancy. Apart from conventional comparisons between art and nature, his painter is often a copier, producing dead colours and a blurred impression, in one instance compared unfavourably with the work of "Tintorit and Holben"—perhaps there had been difficulties over family portraits.[108] His law references (doubtless much more to the taste of that litigious age than to ours) are from all aspects of the law courts: pleas, leases and lawsuits, wills and legacies; there is even what sounds like a contemporary legal joke: "If thine adversary take thy coat, give him thy cloak, for if he have it not, thy Atturney will." This is the world of Henry's uncle Philip King the Auditor, from whom, perhaps (as well as from the erstwhile lawyer Donne), came the legal books once in King's library, so useful to an archdeacon.

KING AND DONNE

There is no doubt that John Donne was on intimate terms with Bishop John King and his family.[109] The two men were both part of Sir Thomas Egerton's household from 1598 to 1600 (when Henry King was eight years old and already at Westminster, Donne's old school) and they were linked constantly thereafter. John King, as Vice-Chancellor of the University of Oxford, was probably instrumental in Donne's being made an honorary Master of Arts in 1610, by which time Henry King was himself at Christ Church, of which his father was then Dean. As Bishop of London, probably exactly a year before Henry King's ordination John King ordained Donne, who then became rector of Sevenoaks in Kent, the parish church of Knole, home of Richard, third Earl of Dorset, to whom (probably during the same period) Henry King was chaplain. It is therefore hardly surprising to find, when from 1621 to Donne's death in 1631 the two men were neighbours in St. Paul's Churchyard, and both were on the Cathedral's administrative chapter, that they had a working relationship such as that I suggest below.

Inevitably, after Fraser Mitchell's allegation that King plagiarises Donne, it is necessary to consider whether this is true of the two occasions in which a whole sermon of King's closely echoes one of Donne's. The first is King's Act sermon on Psalm 32:5 and Donne's on Psalm 32:4, 5 (tentatively dated by Evelyn Simpson to Lent 1624 or 1625—King's sermon may confirm that dating).[110] The second is King's first Lent sermon (1626), which echoes Donne's Valediction sermon (1619).[111] There are also resemblances between both the first Lent sermon and the third section of *The Lord's Prayer* to Donne's *Essayes in Divinity*, first printed by his son in 1651.

King could only have known these works of Donne in manuscript. The Valediction sermon, which survives in more manuscript copies than any other, was pirated in *Sapientia Clamans* in 1638, but not finally printed as Donne's, in *XXVI Sermons*, until 1660. Some of the manuscript's variants, like the use of the word "momentane" (used twice by King and only found in this manuscript sermon of Donne's) bring it closer to King's sermon. Many of the images and examples of the two sermons are the same: memory's position in the hindermost part of the brain, the Creation account in Genesis, the man who hoarded in barns and was called to reckoning, the firstfruits due to God, the analogy of God's courts. King uses these images to reach different conclusions from Donne's, however. Memory, for instance, is like the last day in an almanack— neither is unimportant because it exists at the back. Donne follows through the course of the seven days of Creation, developing their mystical meaning in human life (in the manuscript versions, he also relates each day's work to contemporary controversies). King uses them briefly, to demonstrate the speed of man's fall from grace, created in the morning of the sixth day and yet surrendering to the Devil "before the evening of that same day." Donne treats firstfruits at length; King only alludes to them to contrast what is left for God if we wait to turn to him at the end of life, "when for a fragrant flower, wee present him with a dry stalke and withered leafe."

On the other hand, where Donne drew brief sketches of youth and age, King develops fully their respective strengths and weaknesses. From the fate of the fool in St. Luke who heaped goods into barns, Donne launches into a characteristically terrifying speculation about Hell and its devils; King uses the story to warn his hearers that they can be certain only of the present as a time for repenting sin. He particularises what Donne refers to as the "Court of Heaven" as a "Court of

Audience," and though he uses similar analogies—waking dreams, lightning, Paul's words about Apollos, and many others—again, they are developed to different purpose. King also uses different quotations from the same Fathers that Donne uses. Moreover, his sermon considers, as Donne's does not, the second half of their text from Ecclesiastes, *"while the evil days come not, nor the years draw nigh, when thou shalt say, I have no pleasure in them."*

This is, to say the least, an unusual form of plagiarism, an act King seems unlikely to have committed, if one remembers his scrupulous honesty, for instance, over acknowledging secondhand references in his margins: Augustine quoted by Biel, for example. In fact, at some points, King deliberately takes issue with Donne's conclusions in the Valediction sermon. It becomes clear he is actually developing a dialogue with it. Memory he claims is not, as Donne states, a quicker, surer way to God than Will or Reason, but is weak and unreliable. By creating terrifying pictures of the torments of Hell and the endless fire the soul will endure because it can never be destroyed, Donne attempts to persuade his hearers not to leave repentance to the end of life. King, though he agrees that "a repentance protracted and delayed to the last hours of life, borders upon Destruction," shows in contrast that, as Christ's forgiveness of the penitent thief dying on the cross indicates, we should not "lay such a stumbling block before the feet of those that are now falling into earth" as to suggest their last-minute penitence is not acceptable. He ends, "all I enforce from hence is not to terrifie, but to hasten them . . . That they may employ this short allowance of Time to the best Advantage."

The tone of the two sermons differs as one imagines the characters of the two men must have differed. King's is more restrained and gentle, more concerned with increasing the hearers' personal devotion, less subjective. He grieves at humanity's ingratitude for God's mercies and our obsession, instead, with the injuries done to us; he speaks of grace and redemption. Donne, as always, disturbs his audience by his farsighted understanding of the human motivation for sin; he stretches his hearers' minds and imaginations further. Nevertheless, King's sentences flow more musically, with a calm beauty that probably in its own way was equally effective.

King's educated Court audience would certainly have been delighted by such a dialectic in-joke as answering Donne's sermon, so well known that King could hardly have hoped to get away with plagiarism (particularly using the same text). It is a form of metaphysical wit akin to the allusions to other contemporary verse found both in manuscript verse commonplace books and in contemporary drama.[112] It seems pertinent to ask whether such a close relationship between sermons was an isolated occurrence, or whether a survey of contemporary material, at least of Court sermons, would show similar examples. Sermons, frequently taken down by their hearers in shorthand, must have circulated quite as often in manuscript as verse did. Fewer collections survive, presumably because their manuscripts received more usage, as a source of devotion, but the many bound volumes of individual sermons that survive from the middle and end of the century witness to their great popularity.

Comparisons between the second related pair of sermons, using Psalm 38:5 as their text, will be found in the introduction, and the notes to the Act sermon. The two preachers agree here more closely in their interpretation, and both may owe something to Hooker's sixth book *Of Ecclesiastical Polity* (which complicates the relationship). At points, however, King again may address Donne's points (his self-denunciation, his acceptance of "lesser" sins), and he uses the same biblical illustrations—the ten lepers, Adam and Eve—to serve entirely different ends. In one instance only, at the end, King's wording on calamities is so close to Donne's as to suggest that one of them referred to what the other had written. There is no evidence that Donne's sermon preceded King's and it survives in no known manuscript, being first printed by his son in 1660—if it came first, King most probably was shown the text by Donne; he could alternatively have heard it preached. King's sermon was printed at Oxford, shortly after its delivery. Until a more conclusive date can be offered for Donne's sermon, the direction of influence may be an open question.

The other instances of close relationship, though not so extensive, are more striking, since there is no way King could have known Donne's *Essayes in Divinity* other than by borrowing it in manuscript, presumably from Donne himself. The allusions (and it is unthinkable that King wrote the passage identified in the notes to the seventh sermon of *The Lord's Prayer* without Donne's work in front of him) follow the same pattern of divergence and answer as in the other sermons.

King indeed seems not so much to be imitating or plagiarising Donne, as writing his own sermons in the context of, or with an awareness of Donne's; one last example illustrates this clearly. King in the Lent sermon has "Wee write the benefits we receive in water, they leave no tracke behind them," which assumes, but never explicitly refers to, the Armada in Donne's parallel image: "If thy memory have not held that picture of our general deliverance from the Navy (if that mercy be written in the water and in the sands, where it was perform'd, and not in thy heart)" (*Sermons* 2.238). It is as if Donne's words echo in King's ears and inspire him with a new creative way of using them. It is in this same way (see the notes on King's reading and to individual sermons) that King seems to be aware of poems by Donne and George Herbert, as well as the plays of Shakespeare and Ben Jonson.

Indeed, the relationship between Donne, the ex-lawyer, and the younger Henry King, trained in theology at Oxford and son of a clerical family, ordained only one year later than Donne, is by no means so obviously that of Donne the skilled practitioner and King the deferential follower, which those few who have written about them both seem to suggest. Henry King has much of his own to offer in his quite individual and attractive prose rhythms. (He is, moreover, a valuable source of contemporary information as well as a seventeenth-century literary figure to be reckoned with.) Nevertheless, the bad press that his sermons have received, in the first instance from Fraser Mitchell and more recently from Horton Davies, influenced by Mitchell, inevitably has prejudiced modern readers against him. The aim of this edition is to allow King to speak for himself.

HENRY KING'S READING

King belonged to a small group of seventeenth-century preachers who, like secular writers such as Robert Burton and Thomas Browne, used in their prose secular classical and humanist writers alongside theological authors and the generally acceptable ancient historians. Moreover, Henry King, like a comparatively small number of other sermon writers (who included John Donne, Bishop John King, and their friend Bishop Thomas Morton) carefully indicated all, not merely biblical, references. Donne's and King's margins are particularly interesting, since they can be linked to some extent with the books known to have been in their libraries, providing a valuable picture of contemporary reading habits.[113] King is sometimes meticulous enough to give the date and page reference of the edition he is using. As a result, for instance, the sole reference to Archbishop de Dominis in his work (in the 1640 sermon) can be matched by the sole graphite marking in the corresponding edition at Chichester, just as the various quotations in the same sermon and in *1661* from King's 1593 copy of George Buchanan's *De Iure Regni apud Scotos* are all marked. On the other hand, some of his classical and humanist allusions, which he evidently regarded as so well known as to need no reference, remain unidentified. Who is Philip's boy in *Duppa*, for instance, who held out "to youth a skull, to age a coffin"?

As with most contemporary preachers, however, at least half King's quotations and references are from the Bible, from which, in turn, half are from the Psalms; after these, the greatest number come from Isaiah, the Book of Revelation, and the gospels of St. Matthew and St. John, in that order; comparatively few are from that favourite Calvinist source, the historical books of the Old Testament. King's pre–Civil War sermons usually quote the Geneva translation of his childhood and occasionally its Calvinist gloss. The Authorised Version was not printed until he reached Oxford—he calls it "new" or "new-fangled" for many years, though by the Restoration he invariably uses it. Sometimes his earlier sermons present instead his own translation from Latin or

Greek sources, in preference to Geneva. One unsolved puzzle is the Latin version other than the Vulgate he sometimes quotes; it is *not* his own retranslation, because it is also used by his father, by John Donne, and Joseph Hall. In it, Philippians 1:23 reads "Cupio dissolvi" and 2 Timothy 2:12 reads "Si compatimur, regnabimur." It is not the reading of the earlier commentators King mentions, like Lyra, Hugo Cardinalis, Thomas de Vio, or of the polyglot bibles (all of which use the Vulgate text). It is not from the Protestant Reformers Erasmus, Calvin, Junius, Tremellius, or Beza. (Perhaps this is a case in which a specialist from another field may produce the answer!)

The Psalms in English are a different case, however; King generally uses Coverdale's translation as preserved in the Book of Common Prayer, which would be familiar to him from the daily offices of Matins and Evensong, both at school and in the cathedrals to which he was later attached. (At St. Paul's, indeed, the Psalter was divided between the thirty prebendaries, who were expected to recite their section daily—King's psalms, as Prebendary of St. Pancras, were numbers seventy-seven to eighty-one)[114] When his psalm quotations vary from the Prayer-Book version, therefore, this may be through relying on faulty memory. His "misnumbering" of them, however, is often due to the variance in the Prayer Book and the Vulgate and Septuagint numbering between Psalms 10 and 147.

Donne, who was brought up as a Catholic, frequently used the Vulgate, but it may surprise that King used it as well and that his untranslated short phrases from "the vulgar" (as he calls it) imply an expectation that it would be familiar to his hearers. International scholarship was, of course, still conducted in Latin, and the Vulgate was the standard Latin version. King clearly was completely at home in Latin: the autograph notes in his books at Chichester use that language. In the sermons, even the English chroniclers Stow and Holinshed are cited from Latin versions of their work, and the Chichester catalogue shows that King once owned Latin versions of foreign writers such as Machiavelli, Castiglione, and Guiccardini, who were already translated into English by this time.

The Septuagint, the early Greek translation of the Old Testament, from which King quotes the Psalms in particular (see, for instance, the *The Lord's Prayer VI*) and to which he refers by name in the Spital and 1640 sermons, was probably also familiar from schooldays, since Westminster was one of the schools that pioneered the teaching of Greek and Hebrew. The great sixteenth-century polyglot Bible edited by Arias Montanus (still at Chichester, in the 1609 edition) provided him not only with the Greek and its Latin translation but the Hebrew and the "Chaldee" or "Syriac" (Aramaic) Paraphrase, to which both he and Donne refer. Unlike Donne, however, who seldom uses Greek authorities and then only in Latin translation, King seems to have known Greek fairly well.[115] On the other hand, again unlike Donne and his own brother John, King rarely refers to Hebrew, and then it is either transliterated or cited in general terms as in the sermon commemorating the execution of Charles I: "the *Hebrew* reads the *Singing Men and Singing Women*."

King refers to two other versions of the whole Scriptures: the Latin translation of Junius and Tremellius, of which his 1593 copy is still at Chichester, and the clumsy, official Catholic "Rhemist" translation, "blinding the English with so much Latine that they disguise it from vulgar apprehensions" *(The Lord's Prayer VI)*. He also criticises its gloss for distorting the meaning to promote Catholic doctrines repugnant to the Reformed churches—a criticism the Catholics levelled in the opposite direction at the Geneva gloss.

Donne's sermons show his fascination with etymology and the byways of language; King only rarely examines parallel texts in detail, but when he does (in the Spital sermon, for example), like Donne, he uses the commentaries of the Jesuit Lorinus for his incursions into the Syriac and Ethiopian. After the Fathers, his textual explanations come chiefly from the glosses of Hugo Cardinalis and Vincent of Lyra; among the Schoolmen he most frequently uses Aquinas, but also Alexander of Hales, whom he dubs "acute," and Gabriel Biel; he does not, however, use Duns Scotus, a frequent source for Donne. Donne's indebtedness to mediaeval thinkers is again understandable from his Catholic upbringing; Henry King's may seem less so, but it must be remembered that the Oxford curriculum remained virtually mediaeval until after the Restoration.[116] He quotes

Aquinas more frequently than Basil or Tertullian and as often as St. Bernard (Donne's favourite Father after Augustine, and also Joseph Hall's). Unlike Donne, however, he rarely entertains the Schoolmen's more fantastic metaphysical speculations, on the soul, angels, and the like: he criticises them for dealing "altogether upon distinction," claiming they "would if possible divide Christ's seamlesse coat."[123]

Sixteenth- and early seventeenth-century Anglican theologians drew on the early Fathers because they lived in the period when the infant Church seemed closest to its Founder's intentions. To Henry King, they are more than an authority "our adversaries the Papists" could not challenge; they are valued elder colleagues, "the Doctors of our Church," and as alive to him as admired lecturers of his Oxford days, or founding fathers of the Elizabethan Church like Richard Hooker.[124] It is possible to draw tables, like those in the Potter and Simpson edition of Donne's sermons (indeed, Horton Davies has done just that for *The Lord's Prayer*) to show King's total number of references to the Fathers in his mere twenty-one sermons: some 118 to St. Augustine, 39 to Jerome, 30 to Ambrose, 18 to Chrysostom, with scattered quotations from Basil, Leo, Gregory Nazianzen, Tertullian, and obscure Greek Fathers like Nilus Martyr, Isidore the Pelusiot, and Mark the Hermit. Apart from demonstrating his great love of St. Augustine (indicated by the markings in his fine seven-volume Paris 1555 edition at Chichester), these numbers distort the picture, however. The Chrysostom references in *The Lord's Prayer* and the sixteen to Alexander of Hales exist because King needed their commentaries on Matthew 6, the chapter in which that prayer occurs. Moreover, despite his serried references on occasion (scrupulously acknowledged where secondhand), he maintains an independent judgement. He is not deferential to the Fathers merely because of their antiquity and will disagree even with Augustine. Justin Martyr, he considers, "grossly errs" in his view of the will of God *(The Lord's Prayer V)*, and Origen was "a man of rare Parts and great Wit, but subject (as great Wits are) to the extravagancie of conceit" *(The Lord's Prayer X)*.

King frequently acknowledges his debt to the Protestant Reformed theologians, Calvin, Luther, and Zanchius among them (their books, with others by Peter Martyr, Oecolompadius, Musculus, and the rest are still at Chichester), but it may be significant of a move away from Protestantism as a result of the Civil War, that he does not quote them, any more than the Geneva Bible, in the printed Restoration sermons. King seems less interested than Donne or Hooker in the course of church history, though he uses the ecclesiastical historians, from Eusebius to Baronius, as a fruitful source of anecdote. His references to contemporary Catholic theologians, to mediaeval councils of the Church, and even to the reforming Council of Trent, partly show his wish to refute the Papists from their own texts, but also show a far-from-Puritan openness of mind. He shares some less common Spanish and Jesuit sources, apparently uniquely with Donne and Bishop Thomas Morton, for whom Donne acted as a research assistant during the Oath of Allegiance controversy from 1605–1610. It may be that all three were using the library of books Morton's biographers say he began collecting at Frankfurt in 1602, which in the time of his friend John Overall was housed in St. Paul's Deanery—an arrangement that possibly may have continued into the period when King was writing, when Donne had succeeded as Dean.[119]

Henry King's attitude to the classical writers he uses more than most contemporary preachers is ambivalent. Apt or witty quotations from beloved school texts, Virgil, Ovid, Horace and the other satirists, especially Juvenal, are useful, but their presence in sermons (frowned on particularly by Puritans) needs care—they are, after all, pagans. So though they may provide sound moral teaching, Homer, King says, speaks "fainingly," Tacitus, pronouncing on the divine right of princes, sounds "more like a Christian than a Heathen," and Seneca, whom he quotes even more frequently than he quotes Aquinas or St. Bernard, he still refers to as "the Pagan philosopher." When classical writers' style is under consideration, however, King speaks as a humanist, prefacing his quotations with remarks such as "Apuleius elegantly writes."[120]

King's English reading is unrepresented in the books that survive from his library, all in Latin, but clearly he knew well the work of the Elizabethan travel writers and chroniclers and of at least two contemporary dramatists, Shakespeare and Ben Jonson.[121] There are echoes of *Hamlet, Lear,* or *Macbeth* over whole areas of sermons. For instance, one is aware of *Macbeth,* act 1, scene 3, behind a long section of the second Lent sermon (which is particularly full of Shakespearean echoes) beginning: "How hopelesse is my Redresse, when amazement seizes the Organs of reason, and every faculty that should assist me is confounded, when only feare is predominant, and the perplexed Phantasie, like a false glasse, multiples the danger, and makes each mischiefe looke far bigger than it is?" And, "Those who in the Dialect of the Ryalto are the Best, those whom the Exchange cals Good men" (*The Lord's Prayer VIII*) was surely suggested by *The Merchant of Venice,* act 1, sc. 3, just as the first scene of *Volpone* lies behind passages in the Spital sermon on avarice, on riches ("the golden body of that Saint"), and on gluttony—the notes suggest other reminiscences, not only of *Volpone* but also of *The Alchemist.* Similar echoes suggest King must have known John Donne's poems (in manuscript of course because not then published) and possibly, through their mutual connection with John Donne, those of King's contemporary at Westminster, George Herbert, which did not circulate generally in verse miscellany manuscripts. Even without the evidence of the sermons, it is clear, from the fact that King wrote verses to accompany gifts of Burton's *Anatomy of Melancholy* and Overbury's *Wife,*[122] that he knew well English seventeenth-century prose and "character" writers. Besides, he had read Montaigne's *Essais,* perhaps between the first edition of *The Lord's Prayer* and the second, which contains a reference to it.

King does not seem to have shared Donne's interest in modern science, as his derogatory remarks in the Spital sermon on science and medicine in relation to the ending of the plague make abundantly clear. On matters medical, he cites the ancient Greek physician Hippocrates, and on astrology, Aristotle's *De Caelo* (quoted not in Greek but in Latin, from the Coimbra edition), rather than Kepler or Galileo. His world is therefore still geocentric, as he states explicitly at the beginning of *The Lord's Prayer VII;* but of course, for the purposes of poetry, so were Donne's "imagined" corners of the earth, and Milton's cosmography of Heaven and Hell. Alchemy clearly fascinated King, from the many images it provides (though he cites no texts). He rejects "wilde astrologie," however, agreeing with Cassius that our faults lie in ourselves and not in "loose stars" or "angry planets" (for example, in *The Lord's Prayer V*). Though he would have studied mathematics and sometimes draws images from it, again it does not interest him as it did Donne: he speaks slightingly of its "great many idle lines" *(1621).* Nevertheless, the sermons reveal the well-stocked mind of a scholar just as much as does the prose of a Robert Burton or Thomas Browne.

Details of less well-known authors to whom King refers, with the sermons in which they are cited, will be found in Appendix 1.

NOTES

1. Lawrence Mason, "Life and Works" 227–89; Percy Simpson, "The Bodleian Manuscripts of Henry King," 324–40, and "John and Henry King: A Correction" 208–9.
2. Bod. Rawlinson MS D. 1361, fols. 389–97. King's cousin, George Duncombe, may well have been Oughtred's brother-in-law: he married Judith Carrell of Surrey, and Aubrey relates that Oughtred also married "a Mrs Caryl (an ancient family in those parts)" [*Brief Lives,* 290].
3. Baildon, *Records of Lincoln's Inn,* 2:182.
4. E.g. BL MSS. Additional 25303 and its copy Additional 21433; Harleian 3910 and Lansdowne 777, see M. Hobbs, "Early Seventeenth-Century Verse Miscellanies," 182–210.
5. See introduction, *King and Donne,* and Hobbs, "Pale Imitation."
6. Maclure, *Paul's Cross,* 11; and Crum, *Poems,* 8–9.
7. Hannah, *Poems and Psalms,* xvi–xix; and King, *1621.*
8. See Crum, *Poems,* 236 for the Bishop's elegy.
9. Donne, *Sermons* 9.38 and 296–315. See also "Style" in introduction.
10. Donne, *Sermons* 7.30.

11. Ibid. 9.302.
12. Cf. Thomas Browne, "I love to lose myself in an *O altitudo,*" in *Religio Medici,* c. 1636 (*Works,* 1.9). In 1624, Browne was in his third year at Broadgates Hall, Oxford, and could have been present in the University Church when King preached; Donne also uses the exclamation, three years later than King, in his fourth Prebendal sermon, 28 January 1627: "*O altitudo!* The wayes of the Lord are past finding out" (*Sermons,* 7.305). All three men, of course, could have taken it independently from the Vulgate translation of St. Paul.
13. Fuller, *Worthies,* 133.
14. Donne, preaching in 1622, must have spoken for over two and a half hours (*Sermons* 4, no. 3) and Pepys's editors cite one by Isaac Barrow that lasted three and a half hours (Pepys, *Diary* 3.58, note 2).
15. Donne, *Sermons* 6.212-34; Hall, *Works* 5.212-24.
16. Donne, *Sermons* 4.1-2.
17. Crum, *Poems,* 10. As recently as December, 1989, a source for the relationship between Spelman and King has emerged from Sotheby's catalogue of the Trumbull Papers (now in the British Library). Lot 18, a letter signed on 30 March 1628 by the shareholders of the Guiana Company, includes the names of Henry King (the first intimation of his involvement), Henry Spelman, and also Roger North. This is a striking instance of the truth of my suggestion in the introduction, at the beginning of "Civil Wars and Interregnum", that at this period, new evidence from other fields may yet give a different slant to the known facts. Spelman's book was written in 1626—the 1628 letter provides a reason for his gift to King in that year, when they were associated through the Guiana Company. Moreover, copies of two of King's poems by his amanuensis Thomas Manne occur, for a so-far unexplained reason, among the North papers in the British Library (Additional MSS 27407-8). It seems the connection may have been found.
18. See Hobbs, "'To a most dear Friend'."
19. See Hobbs, "More Books" and The Refounding."
20. Gardner, *Elegies,* lxxxvii-viii. See also the preface of this volume, note 6.
21. Joseph Hall preaching at court on Whitsunday 1640 (*Works* 5.419-20) underlines the length of time he had been absent: "in my last sermon at the Court, I gave you the Character of Man"—that had been in 1634.
22. Letter to Edward Bysshe in 1656, in connection with Dugdale's *St Paul's,* quoted by Hamper, *Dugdale,* 318.
23. Berman, *Henry King,* chap. 3.
24. Text in Cardwell, *Synodalia* 1.380-15. Part of the anger against the canons arose from Convocation's continuing to sit when Parliament, with which it was usually co-terminous, was dissolved, in what Claire Cross called "a final Laudian act of provocation" *Church and People* 197.
25. Quoted Berman, *Henry King,* 58.
26. There have been few attempts to synthesise such material from theses, transactions of county record societies, and biographies of individuals, though recent collections of specialist essays move toward this, e.g. *Origins of the English Civil War* ed. Conrad Russell (1973); *Reactions to the English Civil War,* ed. John Morrill (1982); *The Interregnum* ed. G. E. Aylmer (1972). Robert Bosher's pioneering work *The Making of the Restoration Settlement* (2nd ed., 1957) is still the most useful ecclesiastical guide to the period, though it took a hard knocking from I. M. Green (himself invaluable for the next stage) in *The Re-establishment of the Church of England* (1978); the relevant chapters in Ronald Hutton's *The Restoration* (1983) provide the best single synthesis, though his conclusions are made less accessible by the inadequate index.
27. See Peter King's article "The Episcopate during the Civil Wars" in *English Historical Review* 83 (1968); and Victor Sutch, *Gilbert Sheldon* (1973); though Sutch, also, believed (p. 36) that after the initial sequestrations, most of the bishops "were so demoralised that they were content to sit quietly, doing nothing."
28. Bosher, *Restoration Settlement,* 26-27. Green, apart from including Chichester among those bishops who continued to make appointments during the Civil Wars (p. 115n), says of King only that "he had been sheltered by yet another of Duppa's numerous nieces during the Commonwealth period" (p. 120).
29. Crum, *Poems,* 18 and note. (She was apparently unaware that from the time of Richard Montague, all bishops of Chichester had been granted the rectory of Petworth, to supplement their very meagre income from the see.) The paten and flagon she mentions are now in the cathedral treasury.
30. Arundel Castle Archives, MS A. 91 (an account book). The entries run from 1642 to 17 August 1648. I owe this discovery to Mrs Ruby Reid Thomson.
31. King's will is *PRO:* Prerogative Court of Canterbury wills, 136 Coke. The Restoration petition is reproduced in Hobbs, "Restoration Correspondence," 142.
32. Crum, *Poems,* 20-21 and Bod. MS Rawlinson D. 1361, fols. 389-97.
33. Crum, *Poems,* 21, n. 3. Richings is about five miles from Eton and nearer Langley, the home of Dorothy Hubert, King's sister. The duration of the "college" seems uncertain, since Hales apparently stayed until 1655, yet King addresses a letter from Langley in 1651. This accords with Wood, source of all subsequent

accounts: "he mostly lived in the House of Sir *Richard Hobart*" (*Ath. Oxon.* 2.432, quoted by John Walker [*Sufferings* 11] who adds "and, if I am not mis-informed, was in a manner Sustained by his Charity"). There are particular expressions of gratitude to the Huberts in King's will, which reinforces the picture in the correspondence of Gilbert Sheldon, Henry Hammond, and Brian Duppa of the real hardships undergone by the sequestered clergy in England, a necessary corrective to the recent somewhat unsympathetic picture drawn by such writers as Claire Cross ("The Church in England 1646–60," in Aylmer, *The Interregnum*), in their attempt to redress contemporary exaggerations of such sufferings.

34. Crum, *Poems*, 117–32. I am not convinced of King's authorship of the first elegy for Charles I in Crum (110–17), which was not printed by him in the Restoration edition of his poems in 1664; phrases in the second, on the other hand, recur, like others from his "Elegy upon Sir Charls Lucas, and Sir George Lisle" (Crum, *Poems*, 101–10), in *Commemoration*, see notes to that sermon.

35. Harold Smith, *Ecclesiastical History of Essex*, 239.

36. For the history of the books, see Hobbs, "The Refounding of Chichester Cathedral Library."

37. Quoted by Crum, *Poems*, 55.

38. Bosher, *Restoration Settlement*, 42.

39. The same reason Sutch thought accounted for the prominence accorded, both then and now, to Hammond over Sheldon, who wrote little, yet is (I think convincingly) shown by Sutch to have been the real "Architect of Anglican Survival" during the Interregnum.

40. Parr, *James Usher*, 567. King's verse translation of the Psalms (1651) brings out their relevance to contemporary Royalist sufferings under the Commonwealth.

41. *Letters and Journals of Robert Baillie*, 3 vols. (Edinburgh, 1842), 3.400, quoted in Bosher, *Restoration Settlement*, 122.

42. On the false rumour of his death, Duppa significantly describes him as "a freind whom I could have ill have lost in these times" (Duppa, *Correspondence*, 162). "I do not love my letters should be fly-blown before they come to you," he grumbled audaciously about censorship in 1651 (Duppa, *Correspondence*, 45). There are also constant mysterious references to "an other business," "another employment," or journeys that temporarily prevent his writing to Isham. The search of his house at Richmond and the removal of his papers in September 1659, show his caution was justified. For Dillingham's reference see BL Harleian MS 3783, fol. 178.

43. *Ath. Oxon* 3.841: King's Visitation sermon and his correspondence show Wood's information was inaccurate. Joseph Hall had laid himself open to similar accusation before the wars when he tried to keep the peace in his new diocese of Exeter, see "Some Specialities in his Life," in Hall, *Works* 1.xxv–vi.

44. Burton's letter was transcribed in 1859, from the correspondence of Sir William Wilson of Sheffield House, to whom it was addressed, by R. W. Blencowe, "Paxhill and its neighbourhood," *SAC* 11.33, since when the whole correspondence has disappeared. The circumstances make the authenticity of the letter indisputable, however. One of the chaplains invited to accompany King was probably Lancelot Addison, father of the essayist Joseph (see *Ath. Oxon.* 2.970); the other was possibly that Thomas Wilkinson for whose preferment King contended with Sheldon (see Hobbs, "Restoration Correspondence," 148–50).

45. Green, *Re-establishment*, 82–83. (His case that Charles intended to balance the churchmanship of episcopal appointments, regardless of earlier promises, would have been strengthened by a knowledge of Burton's letter.) Of the nine bishops still alive by then, only three were translated; Norwich, which in Nicholas's lists was intended for Warner of Rochester, was given instead for reasons of policy to the Presbyterian Edward Reynolds. For King's reorganisation of the diocese, see Hobbs, "Restoration Correspondence," 143–44. In anticipation of the Restoration, he had already ordained on 25 and 26 May 1660 and instituted to the parish of Newick, where his brother-in-law Sir John Millington, Elizabeth King's second husband, lived. Most of Chichester's ecclesiastical records are resumed only after Bishop King's death, however, in 1670 (perhaps because of the legal and administrative inexperience of his Restoration vicar general, Lambrook Thomas [Green, *Re-establishment*, 119]). The scattered evidence for the years 1660–70 in the diocese of Chichester urgently needs correlating.

46. Pepys, *Diary* 1.195, and Lent preachers 1660/1 in White Kennett, *Register*, 368.

47. Green, *Re-establishment*, 22–4.

48. Hammond actually preached for Accepted Frewen, who was ill, at Whitehall in 1633. Green says Frewen was appointed "Despite (or perhaps because of) his moderation and inexperience" (p. 92). In comparison with King, the other candidate, this parenthesis rings true.

49. How they came into his possession is an unsolved mystery. A possible link is Charles II's emissary from the Continent, Eleazor Duncon, a canon of York. Apart from their connection over the projected episcopal consecrations, his name, spelt variously as Duncan and Duncombe, suggests that he may have been related to King through his cousin, George Duncombe (see my introduction: "Interregnum").

50. The House of Lords journals show King present and, in the first three years, active on committees

whenever the House sat, from the time the bishops were re-admitted to Parliament in November 1661 until his death, with the exception of winter 1662–63, when, like many other peers, he was ill.

51. The sermon was printed by Henry Herringman, who with Richard Marriott had brought out King's poems in 1657, supposedly without his consent. The fact that King always used Herringman thereafter as his printer further strengthens the argument that this was merely polite fiction.

52. There are additional passages in *1661* from George Buchanan, for instance, and the inaccurate marginal reference "15.18" for the quotation from Proverbs 15.8 was also inaccurate in *1640*, where it reads "5.8."

53. It seems unfortunate that King should subject Charles II to a biblical disquisition about a man with two wives and the need to acknowledge the firstborn as heir, even if he is not the son of the best loved. He could scarcely have been so tactless as to suggest that James Crofts, Charles's bastard by Lucy Walter, as a Protestant should inherit the throne, regardless of what offspring might be born of the recently projected lawful union with the Roman Catholic Catherine of Braganza. (In fact, King at the end expressly welcomes the possibility now present of an heir to the kingdom, and Charles, after all, commended the sermon for publication.) King may perhaps allude to Charles I's warning on the night before his execution (printed in *Reliquiae Sacrae Carolinae* [1650]) to the young Duke of Gloucester that the government would try to make him ruler in his elder brother's place.

54. It is not so surprising that King claims this is his first funeral sermon. As a diocesan officer, he had not, like Donne at St. Dunstan's, combined the duties of a parish priest with those of the cathedral. It does make less likely his authorship of the manuscript funeral sermon for Lady Katherine Cholmondley (d. 1657), which follows King's elegy for her in Bod. MS English poetry 30, however (Crum, *Poems*, 27, 49).

55. SRS 68 (1971), 228. Chichester's *Articles of Visitation* published in London before 25 March 1663 by Henry Herringman (Keynes, *Bibliography* 78) were virtually identical with those used in the dioceses of Bath and Wells, Exeter, Hereford, Lincoln, and Winchester; see Green, *Re-establishment*, 135–38.

56. White Kennett, *Register*, 286, under the date Michaelmas 1660; Bod. MS Addit. C.308, fol. 163v.

57. Hobbs, "Restoration Correspondence," 146–47.

58. Pepys, *Diary* 4.69, 6.54 and note 3. King was possibly the first (despite Margaret Crum's opinion) and certainly not later than the second, to preach this commemoration sermon at Whitehall, see Crum, *Poems*, 26.

59. John Bernard, *The Life and Death of . . . Dr. James Usher*, 1656. (His text, he continues quaintly, is "Like the Æthiopians, striving for preheminency by their blackness.") The sermon would be known equally to Nonconformists and Anglicans, since Ussher was universally respected for his striving to find an acceptable liturgical compromise, and Cromwell had given him a state funeral. Atterbury's sermon was preached at St. Andrew's, Holborn (see Francis Atterbury, *Sermons* p. 3).

60. Milton had escaped execution for treason (partly through the good offices of Andrew Marvell) but in 1665 was still living in retirement. King may have believed the rumour of Milton's death put about by his friends for his safety (see A. N. Wilson, *Life of John Milton*, 203).

61. The book was printed illegally, ostensibly at the Hague though actually in England, on the day of the King's funeral, 8 February 1648/9. It reached thirty editions within the year and was translated into Latin by John Earle (see F. Madan, *A Bibliography of Eikon Basilike*, Oxford: Clarendon Press, 1949). F. J. Shirley, who considered Gauden might have falsified book VII of Hooker's *Ecclesiastical Polity*, thought like myself that the matter of authorship still might be in doubt (*Richard Hooker*, 47–50).

62. Bod. MS Additional. C.308, fol. 55v.

63. SRS 68:231, 232.

64. Evelyn, *Diary* 3:524.

65. It was a stone from Bishop John King's memorial, with the single word "Resurgam" (I shall rise again), which the workmen brought to Christopher Wren after the Great Fire, and which he took as his motto in the rebuilding of St. Paul's.

66. Fuller, *Church-History* 11.194.

67. More and Cross, *Anglicanism*, lxxv.

68. Parr, *Life of Usher*, 567.

69. *Golden Remains*, (London, 1688), 18; cited McAdoo (*Spirit of Anglicanism*, 15), to whom, with Collinson, Kendall, and Tyacke, I owe much of the background of this section. (Hales nevertheless became King's chaplain during the Interregnum.)

70. Morrill, *The Church in England 1642–9*, 98, in *Reactions to the English Civil War*.

71. King is echoing the seventeenth of the Thirty-nine Articles of Religion: "Predestination to Life is the everlasting purpose of God, whereby (before the foundations of the world were laid) he hath constantly decreed. . . ."

72. *Ath. Oxon.* 2.432.

73. More and Cross, *Anglicanism*, 69; for the Calvinist view of Rome, see Tyacke, *Anti-Calvinist*, 153.

Notes to the Introduction

74. Others, Donne and Hall, for instance, use a similar comparison: one must be wary at this period of claiming orginality—Horton Davies (*Angels from a Cloud*, 117) praises Theophilus Field's original image of the five senses as the Cinque Ports in a 1628 sermon: Henry King had already printed it in 1627.

75. Cosin, quoted More and Cross, *Anglicanism*, 516, and see also p. 530; Francis White used similar arguments against "Jesuit Fisher" in 1624 (quoted More and Cross, *Anglicanism*, 514–15.

76. Donne, *Sermons* 9.152; Bald, *John Donne*, 404–5, describes how Donne in 1630 took Smith's yeoman, Christopher Ruddy, before the Court of Aldermen for his unseemly conduct in church.

77. Hall, *Works* 5.81.

78. In his edition of Brownrigg's *Fourty Sermons* (London, 1661), William Martyn speaks of Brownrigg's similar high esteem "of our English Liturgie . . . that it could not be expected to see Religion prosper & flourish again amongst us, till that excellent Book . . . were re-established" (sig. G2).

79. For Hooker, see McAdoo, *Spirit of Anglicanism*, 1–11.

80. Noel Malcolm, *Marco Antonio De Dominis*, 64.

81. Donne, *Sermons* 8.119; he died in 1631, before the monarchy was seriously threatened by Parliament, but King was already preaching on the subject in the 1620s.

82. In fact, as Archdeacon of Colchester, he apparently did not: T. A. Mason (*Serving God and Mammon*) regarded the failure of three archdeacons, of whom King was one (see Laud, *Works*, 5, part 2, 332 and note), to return annual reports for the diocese of London to Bishop Juxon that year as a sign of increasing resistance to Arminianism; though it may have been due to no more than administrative inefficiency or pressure of other work. To Nicholas Tyacke ("Puritanism, Arminianism and Counter-Revolution," 140, in Russell, *Origins*), the Laudian view of episcopacy is "the idea of a holy priesthood with consecrated property rights," the complement to a "theoretical advancement of royal absolutism in the secular sphere." He makes an interesting correlation between the Arminian bishops' seeking to bolster their status by divine right, and the need (of Laud and Juxon, at any rate) "to compensate for a sense of social inferiority" because of their backgrounds. Henry King, born into a clerical elite, did not think the point worth making.

83. Mason, *Serving God and Mammon*, 61–62; Crum, *Poems*, 136–39.

84. White Kennett, *Register*, 650; Crum, *Poems*, 17.

85. Pepys, *Diary* 10.222–23.

86. Mitchell, *English Pulpit Oratory*, 176.

87. Like Jeremy Taylor, however, Frank, a later writer, was undoubtedly influenced not only by distinguished earlier preachers, in particular Andrewes, but also secular writings, including those of Donne and Thomas Browne.

88. Mitchell, *English Pulpit Oratory*, 168.

89. John Sparrow ed., *Poems* xvii–xviii.

90. See introduction, "King and Donne" and Hobbs, "Pale Imitation."

91. Mitchell, *English Pulpit Oratory*, 169.

92. Ibid., 170.

93. Mitchell's desire (Ibid., 136–37) to allot seventeenth-century preachers to "schools" led him to set up the moderate Calvinist Henry King as an "Anglo-Catholic" (an anachronistic term for that age anyway) and then censure him for not conforming!

94. Mitchell, Ibid., 176.

95. Davies, *Like Angels*, 51–52, 161–64.

96. The chief authority is still George Williamson, *The Senecan Amble*; see also J. W. Blench, *Preaching in England in the late 15th and 16th Centuries*, and (with caution) Mitchell, *English Pulpit Oratory*.

97. *A Priest to the Temple* (Herbert, *Poems*, 235).

98. Donne, *Sermons* 8.191.

99. John Sparrow ("John Donne and Contemporary Preachers," *Essays and Studies* 16 [1930]) notes that at least by Laud's time as Bishop of London (i.e., from 1628), preachers had to bring with them a written copy of any Paul's Cross sermon they were about to preach, and in Bod. MS Rawlinson D.399, fol. 115, is a note from Laud to that effect (dated only "29 November"—probably to Henry's brother John, but it may have been to Henry) warning that the sermon was "not to exceed an houre and a halfe in both Sermon and Praier."

100. Crum, *Poems*, 50.

101. For instance, "centinell," "stolne," "wils," "aboord," "bloud," "retrait," "goodnes," "cal'd."

102. Evelyn Simpson, *Prose Works of John Donne*, 258, and John Sparrow, "John Donne"; Hall, "Some Specialities in his Life," in *Works* 1.xxvi.

103. Hall, *Works*, 5.134.

104. Donne, *Sermons* 1.86.

105. Berman, *Henry King*, 72.

106. Crum, *Poems*, 83.

107. The family were very conscious of their heraldic bearings: most of their memorials carry the family coat of arms and a reference to their (probably mythical) descent from the ancient kings of Devonshire. At the Restoration in November 1661, Henry was made member of a House of Lords committee to regulate the granting and use of coats of arms.

108. A fine 1620 portrait of Bishop John is at Montacute House, on loan from the National Portrait Gallery, and portraits of Henry and his brother John are at Christ Church, Oxford; Chichester City Council owns one of Henry King as Bishop. The respective painters are unknown, but Bishop John's portrait has been attributed to Nicholas Lockey on stylistic grounds; see John Ingamells, *The English Episcopal Portrait* (Paul Mellon Centre for Studies in British Art, 1981), 256–57.

109. See Bald, *John Donne,* 282–83.

110. Donne, *Sermons* 9.38, 296–315.

111. See Hobbs, "Pale Imitation."

112. Ibid., 79 n.7.

113. For Donne's books, see G. Keynes, *Bibliography of Dr John Donne,* 263–79, and Hobbs, "More Books," 590–92; for King's books: Hobbs, "Refounding," 189–205.

114. See Donne, *Sermons* 6.29. Donne preached a course of sermons on his own psalms; none of King's extant sermons draws texts from his.

115. "Donne's knowledge of Greek was very small, almost negligible. He knew just enough of the Greek New Testament to be able to quote an occasional word" (Donne, *Sermons* 10.317).

116. In the 1650s, Henry Hammond was still recommending in a book list for Mr. Staninough, tutor to Sir Robert Pye's sons, "Aquinas Secunda Secundae" (the part most frequently quoted by King), together with "the Moralists, Greek (if the disciple be capable of them, or els Latine," Cicero, Seneca, and "some parts of Petrarch," along with contemporary writers (J. W. Packer, *Transformation of Anglicanism,* 87). McAdoo instances Cosimo de Medici being welcomed at Oxford as late as 1670 by a dissertation against Copernican astronomy (*Spirit of Anglicanism,* 3).

117. *An Exposition upon the Lord's Prayer IV.* See, however, King's incursions into numerology in *The Lord's Prayer II, VI,* and *VII.*

118. Of Hooker, King wrote to Izaak Walton (*Lives,* 4) "though I dare not say I knew [him]; yet, as our Ecclesiastical History reports to the honour of S. *Ignatius,* that he lived in the time of S. *John,* and had seen him in his Childhood; so, I also joy that in my Minority, I have often seen Mr. Hooker with my Father."

119. Bald (*John Donne,* 202–10) gives a useful brief account of Morton.

120. His claim that Seneca speaks divinely may be more than a stylistic comment, however: the Greek Fathers held that (like Virgil for his Messianic Eclogue) Seneca, though pagan, would be admitted to Heaven, because according to tradition he had corresponded with St. Paul.

121. King elsewhere uses a phrase from *Henry VIII* (act 4, sc. 2, lines 121–22), in his poem "The Retreit" (Crum, *Poems,* 235, line 12). The publication of the First Folio in 1623 had made Shakespeare's texts readily available; Ben Jonson had published his *Works* in 1616.

122. Crum, *Poems,* 154–55.

2
Editorial Principles

The original spelling and capitalisation have been retained, except that *i/j, u/v,* the long *s* and the double *u* have been made to conform with modern usage. Contractions representing *m* and *n* have been expanded, as have contracted endings of Latin and Greek words.

In order to direct the modern reader's attention away from distracting inessentials to the more important matters of meaning and style, I have edited the texts a little. This has been in three main areas:

1. The original *punctuation* is sometimes so heavy that it impedes the flow of a sentence and thereby obscures the meaning, particularly in more theological discourses, such as the Act sermon. King almost certainly must have overseen the printing of the sermons. To a great extent, they reflect his practice in the extant poetry manuscripts, where his intention was clearly rhetorical, as a guide to reading aloud—we are apt to forget that all reading was done aloud, even in libraries, until the eighteenth century. It seemed acceptable, therefore, to make the punctuation of the sermons exercise some similar helpful function for the eye of today's faster silent reader, by removing some heavier commas, semicolons, and colons (which would have been allied to timed pauses). At the same time, I have where necessary added commas to elucidate the phrasing, full stops to divide long involved sentences, semicolons to divide ideas, or a dash or parenthesis where King is in danger of losing his construction. Overlong paragraphs have been divided and some single-sentence ones joined together for easier comprehension.

2. All proper names, all references to words in the sermons' texts, all Latin and biblical quotations, and many metaphors and allusions are italicised in the originals, a much heavier use of the device than in Donne's printed sermons. *Italicisation* has been retained where used for emphasis, or to point to an antithesis or comparison, but omitted where merely conventional: i.e. for proper names, which are in any case capitalised, or for reiterated reference to a key word. Italicisation occasionally has been added, on the other hand, to indicate King's translation of a Latin or Greek quotation, usually where I have omitted this from the transcript.

3. Because the first aim of this edition is to make King accessible to a modern reader, longer Greek and Latin *quotations,* usually from the Fathers, have also been omitted where (as usually happens) King supplies either a translation or a paraphrase with them. In the three or four cases where he does not, their removal has been indicated in the notes. On the other hand, most of the short biblical phrases, tags, and classical quotations integral to the rhythm of King's prose style have been retained, with translations at the foot of the page where the meaning is not apparent from the text. (Single-word or very short Latin or Greek phrases have been translated in square brackets within the body of the text.) I have to some extent used by ear here: if a passage has few quotations, I have left proportionally more than if it is heavily weighted with classical words. The *Greek* (see preface) has been transliterated into roman type and italicised, and all but essential accents removed. As I pointed out, few scholars today are familiar with Greek, and since sound is one of the criteria of King's choice of word, transliteration makes it possible for a reader to reproduce this without knowledge of the Greek alphabet. Moreover, so many modern words derive from Greek that in some cases, the meaning will become apparent from the transcription.

In the *margins* King's own abbreviations are reproduced for the most part but have been standardised in the following respects:

1. *Biblical quotations* are given uniform roman type and modern pointing where the originals were sometimes italic (for instance, throughout *ELP*). Where the editor has corrected references, the correction is italicised; where complete references are supplied, they are italicised and also bracketed and use the standard abbreviations of the Revised Standard Version of the Bible (the list of abbreviations also includes unfamiliar Latin marginal abbreviations used by King).

2. *Other sources* have been similarly standardised: authors' names are in roman type, their works in italic; additions or corrections are again in italic and bracketed.

3. Where Latin or Greek *marginal quotations* have been omitted, the omission of a Latin quotation is indicated by a square bracketed [*a*] and of a Greek one by a square bracketed [*b*].

4. King's *original pagination* will be found in the margins, in square brackets.

Where there is more than one edition, significant textual variants are shown in the notes. The text used for *1621* is the third edition, for *An Exposition upon the Lord's Prayer*, that of the 1634 edition, the second impression. Material added in this addition is enclosed in double brackets (⟦,⟧). The glossary includes not only unfamiliar words, but those changed in meaning since the seventeenth century, such as "humerous novelist" (*Lent 1*).

THE SERMONS: ABBREVIATIONS

1. SERMON TITLES

1621	November 1621	Paul's Cross: "supposed Apostasie" of Bishop John King.
Act	July 1625	Oxford: *David's Enlargement*. First sermon on the Act Sunday.
Lent 1	Lent 1625/6	Whitehall: *Two Sermons*.
Spital	Easter 1626	Spital: *A Sermon of Deliverance*.
Lent 2	Lent 1627	Whitehall: *Two Sermons*
ELP	1623–1628	
(also as *The Lord's Prayer*)		*An Exposition upon the Lord's Prayer*.
1640	March 1640	Paul's Cross: Anniversary of the Inauguration of Charles I and the death of James I.
1661	May 1661	Whitehall: Inauguration and Birth of Charles II.
Duppa	April 1662	Westminster Abbey: Funeral of Brian Duppa.
Visitation	October 1663	Lewes: Visitation.
Commemoration	January 1665	Whitehall: Commemoration of Charles I, King and Martyr.

SERMON TEXTS

1621	John 15:20: Remember the word that I have said unto you, the servant is not greater than the Lord: If they have persecuted me, they will also persecute you.
Act	Psalm 32:5: I said I will confesse my sinnes unto the Lord. And thou forgavest the iniquities of my sinne.
Lent 1	Eccles. 12:1: Remember now thy Creator in the dayes of thy youth.
Spital	Psalm 91:3: For he shall deliver thee from the snare of the Hunters, and from the noysome Pestilence.

The Sermons: Abbreviations

Lent 2	Psalm 55:6: And I said, O that I had wings like a Dove, for then I would flee away, and be at rest.
ELP	Matthew 6:9–13: Our Father (etc.)
1640	Jeremiah 1:10: Behold, I have this day set thee over the nations, and over the Kingdoms; to Root out, and to pull down, to destroy and throw down, to build and to plant.
1661	Ezekiel 21:27: I will Overturn, Overturn, Overturn it, and it shall be no more, until he come whose Right it is, and I will give it him.
Duppa	Psalm 116:15: Pretious in the Sight of the Lord is the Death of his Saints.
Visitation	Titus 2:1: But speak Thou the things which become Sound Doctrine.
Commemoration	2 Chron. 35:24–25: And all Judah and Jerusalem mourned for Josiah. And Jeremiah lamented for Josiah, and all the Singing-men and the Singing-women spake of Josiah in their Lamentations to this Day, and made them an Ordinance in Israel; and behold they are written in the Lamentations.

2. BIBLICAL ABBREVIATIONS

(According to the Standard Revised Version, together with King's Latin abbreviations)

Old Testament

Gen.	Genesis	Hos.	Hosea [Hosee]
Ex.	Exodus	Obad.	Obadiah
Lev.	Leviticus	Jon.	Jonah
Num.	Numbers	Mic.	Micah
Deut.	Deuteronomy	Hab.	Habbakkuk
Josh.	Joshua	(Abbac.)	
Eccles.	Ecclesiastes	Zeph.	Zephaniah
Song	Song of Solomon	Hag.	Haggai [Aggee]
(Cant.)	Canticum Canticorum)	Zech.	Zechariah
Is.	Isaiah	Mal.	Malachi
(Esay)		*Apocrypha*	
Jer.	Jeremiah	Wis.	Wisdom
Judg.	Judges	(Sap.)	Sapientia [Wisdom])
(Judic[es])		Ecclus.	Ecclesiasticus
1 Sam.	1 Samuel	Ezdras	Ezdras
2 Sam.	2 Samuel	*New Testament*	
1 Kings	1 Kings	Mt.	Matthew
2 Kings	2 Kings	Mk	Mark [Marcus]
(1 & 2 Reges)		Lk	Luke [Lucus]
1 Chron.	1 Chronicles	Jn	John [Johannes]
2 Chron.	2 Chronicles	Act[s]	Acts of the Apostles
Ezra	Ezra	Rom.	Romans
Neh.	Nehemiah	1 & 2 Cor.	1 & 2 Corinthians
Esther	Esther	Gal.	Galatians
Job	Job	1 & 2 Tim.	1 & 2 Timothy
Ps[al].	Psalms	Tit.	Titus
Pro[v].		Heb.	Hebrews
Lam.	Lamentations	Jas.	James
Ezek.	Ezekiel	(Jac.)	Jacobus)
Dan.	Daniel	1 & 2 Pet.	1 & 2 Peter

1, 2 & 3 Jn	1, 2 & 3 John	Col.	Colossians
Jude	Jude	1 & 2 Thess.	1 & 2 Thessalonians
Ephes.	Ephesians	Rev.	Revelation
Phil.	Philippians	(Apoc.	Apocalyse [Revelation])

3. OTHER MARGINAL ABBREVIATIONS

art.	articulum [article]	l[ib].	liber [book]
c[ap].	capitulum [chapter]	pars	part
fin.	in fine [end]	ser[m].	sermon
hom.	homilia [sermon]	tom.	tomus [volume]
lect.	lectiones [readings]	ult.	ultimum [last]

AV	King James's Authorised Version of the Bible (1611)
BCP	Book of Common Prayer
Gk.	Greek
L.	Latin

3

The Sermons to 1627

1621

TO THE MOST EXCELLENT AND ILLUSTRIOUS PRINCE, CHARLES, PRINCE OF WALES.

Your Highnesse may please to remember how great an interest your Princely Mother, our late Gracious Queene, vouchsafed to challenge in my deceased Father: accounting Him as one of Hers, as most truly (next the professed band of dutie to his dread Soveraigne, whose first-sworne Chaplaine he was after his Majestie's happie arrivall in these parts) by all the tyes a Royall Mistris might engage a Servant, he was. Since that Starre was taken from our sight, I know not whether else ought Shee could call Hers might so immediately refer as to your selfe. I am sure it was His study, while he lived, to consecrate his best endeavours to the Branches of that Royall stocke, and by that line of duty drawn from Her merits, to measure out His bounden services to Her Line, chiefly to your Highnesse; Who, I have cause to thinke, doe yet beleeve you had a faithfull Orator and Servant of Him. Since, then, by double right he was devoted to your Highnesse, by his owne acknowledgement and by the purchase of your especiall favours towards Him, I durst not entitle any other Patrone to the remainder of what he was, his Memory, without leave from your Highnesse. But as it was my filiall duety to vindicate a wronged Father, so I held it the tribute of my civill duty to tender it first to your Hands, that it might take sanctuary under your Princely wing. Thus borne up, the Truth I write shall boldly flie into the bosome of those climes where it was first discoloured, and if their foreheads be not meretriciously steeled with impudence or growne flint, fetch backe its owne proper hiew, or their shame.

It is not a forward presumption in me, but the cause, which makes your Highnesse' patronage my chiefe scope; upon which tearmes it will not be inglorious for you to undertake it. For whilest you shall protect abused Innocence, your Goodnesse will stand pitched at the just height your Greatnesse now doth, one degree from a *Defender of the Faith*. Long may you flourish, to make all good men happy in your protection, and may that heart want the prayers of good men to releive it, which doth not as faithfully sue to Almighty God for all addition to your Happinesse as he who is

Your Highnesse' most
humbly devoted
Servant,

HENRY KING.

JOHN 15. vers.20:
Remember the word that I said unto you, The servant is not greater then the Lord. If they have persecuted me, they will also persecute you.

I Will not strive to attire my Text in any other fashion; the plaine naturall dresse it now weares will best sute it and my intendment.

A SERMON PREACHED AT PAVLS CROSSE, THE 25. OF NOVEMBER. 1621.

Upon occasion of that false and scandalous Report (lately Printed) touching the supposed Apostasie of the right Reuerend Father *in God*, IOHN KING, *late Lord Bishop of* London.

By HENRY KING, his eldest *Sonne*.

Whereunto is annexed the Examination, and *Answere of* Thomas Preston, P. *taken before my* Lords Grace of Canterbury, touching *this Scandall.*

Published by Authority.

AT LONDON,
Imprinted by FELIX KYNGSTON, for *William Barret.* 1621.

The parts shall be, as the Propositions, Three: Division:
I. Is monitory, and as it were an *eisagōgê*, Introduction or Preface to the rest: *Remember the word I*   I.
said unto you.
II. Is a Principle, a ground of infallible truth, both in Ethick and Œconomick rules, in Humanitie   [2] 2.
and Divinitie: *The servant is not greater then the Lord.*
III. Is an Inference upon an Hypothesis: *If they have persecuted me, they will also persecute you.*   3.
  I begin in order.

  Remember. I know not what better exordium a Preacher can make, or from what foundation the   First Part:
frame of his speech can more happily arise then from this, which is the first stone in this pile,   *Remember*
Remember. It is the best charge the Priest can give, and the first lesson the People should learne;
else, like children that read only by rote, they shall spend much time and understand nothing. It is a
taske can never be urged too often—*Manda remanda*—nor can it ever be learned too perfectly. An
age is not enough for this precept, but when seven yeeres are run out, they may begin again and
finish an apprentiship long as life, yet misse that freedome and perfection they seeke: *Ars longa,*
*vita brevis.**

  Since therefore much is to be learned, and either we want time or capacity or memory to   [3]
comprehend it, the right way to profit an Auditory & not cloy, is to let them digest what they have
bin taught, and not heare new lessons before the old are remembred. For as eating much meate and
not keeping it argues a better appetite then concoction, so hearing much and retaining none shewes
a quick eare, but a dull devotion.

  There are many now adaies who never thinke they have preaching enough, but as exquisite
gluttons lay all markets for fare, so doe they lay all Churches where there is any suspicion of a   Gregor. Nazian.
Sermon, and all is *estiazein tōn akoēn,* to glut their eares; nay, the same Father speaks them more   *Epitaph. Caesar*
fully: *they goe not so much to feed, as delight their eares,* and to satisfie that wanton itch of   Ibid.
hearing, which like a Tetter, the more it is rubbed, the more it spreads. I wish there were more
practising, on condition there were less preaching. A man may heare so much that he may ston the   [4]
sense and be like the Catadupes, whom the continuall fall of Nile makes deafe. Cisternes that have
more powred into them then they can hold must needs run to wast; and men that affect to learne
more then they have brains to comprehend, waste their Pastor's labour and their owne patience. It is
good counsell for one to eate no more then his stomacke can beare, for too full feeding engenders
nothing but surfets; and I thinke as good counsell will it be, to heare no more then hee can carry
away. For were the retention good, the nourishment would be more solid, and Christianitie acquire
that full growth, for want of which wee are but Impes and Zanies in respect of those that lived in the
Primitive Church.

  No wonder, then, if Preaching may breed surfets, that so many Crudities lie in the stomacke of
this Citty; that so many Fumes and giddy vapours flie up into the head, to the no small disturbance
of the Churche's quiet; that so many hot spirits, like Canons overcharged, recoyle against all   [5]
Discipline, breake into diverse factions, and with the splints of those crackt opinions doe more
mischiefe then deliberation or Justice can suddenly salve. I speake no new unheard language. This
communitie of Preaching hath brought it into such cheape contempt with many, that as if the gift of
tongues were prostitute to Idiots and Trades, you shall have a sort of Lay Mechanicke Presbiters of
both sexes—*Prædicatores* and *Prædicantissae*—presume so far upon their acquaintance with the
Pulpit, that they will venter upon an Exposition, or undertake to manage a long unweildy prayer,
conceived on the sudden though not so suddenly uttered. Nay, they are so desperate, they will
torment a Text, and in their resty Conventicles teach as boldly as if they were as well able to
become Journeymen to the Pulpit as to their owne Trades. I cannot but think of the story of the
poore Asse that carryed the goddesse Isis so long to and from the Temple, that at last, hee began to   [6]
take state upon him, and would needs play the goddesse. So these creatures have so long travelled

---

*Art is long, life short.

betwixt the Temple *portantes mysteria,* and conversed with the sacred *mysteries* of Religion, that they begin to flatter themselves in an opinion of worth which none would suspect, and forgetting their former condition, will needs turne Teachers. If this be the fruit of so much preaching, it is high time that command bee now reversed, Son of man, *Lift up thy voyce like a Trumpet:* rather, *Son of man, sound a retreit and be dumb,* in admiration to see Coblers & Artizans usurpe that holy Office:

> *Frange leves calamos, & scinde Thalia libellos,*
> *Si dare sutori calceus ista potest.**

Let none thinke my meaning is to finde fault with the multitude of Preachers who (without envie) were never more nor better; neither to taxe the devotion of such who frequent those exercises. Far be it from me. I onely strike at the abuse. I pitty that Pastor who is put to plough the rocks when the eare is too hard for his advice to enter; and is tasked, like Belus his daughters, to fill *pithous tetrêmenous,* Sives and Pitchers without bottome, for such are our hollow Formalists. And I blame that people who, like thirsty lands, still gape for raine yet no signe of softening; or as men sicke of an Atrophy, eat much but thrive not. When *Manna* shall grow stale and common, and stinke in their nostrils, it is time to diet such mis-governed feeders and stint them to their measure, as Israel was to an Omer. I wish they would heare no more then their memory could master. A little lesse preaching, and some more praying would doe well: For so they might gaine more time and obtain a better faculty for the *remembring* of what they learne.

The roome is now prepared, wants onely the Ghest to fill it, who followes in the next place: *The word that I told you.*

Wisedome is its own Herald, and the words of worthy persons need no waymakers to prepare attention save themselves. But when both these concurre, and the name of the Authour presents it selfe in the front to credit the errand, it must needs take strong hold in the hearer.

In both these respects doth Christ plead for regard. First, in respect of his own person: *I said.* That *Ego sum* uttered by him in the Garden strucke such awe & terror into his enemies, that they did homage to the sound of his voyce by falling flat to the ground. It is to bee hoped, then, that when his discourse knockt at the eares of his Disciples (like the Spouse in the Canticles: *Open unto me, it is I*) his owne would both know and obey his voice: especially since that now, like one preparing to leave the world, he began to give his latest charge, and to bequeath such lessons to them as might both warne them of what should befal, and comfort them in their sufferings.

The words of dying men are precious even to strangers; but when the voyce of one we love cals to us from the death-bed, O what a conflict doe his words raise! How strongly doth griefe and affection strive to inclose them, knowing that in a short space that tongue, the organs whereof yet speake, was to be eternally tyed up in silence; nor should the sound of his words salute our eares any more!

Secondly, in respect of the words themselves: *Remember the word that I told you.* If rarenesse and opinion make Jewels precious, what value shall we put upon our Saviour's words, *who spake as never man spake,* within whose lips the mines of knowledge were included? *The words of the Lord are pure as silver seven times tryed, better then Rubies;* nay, *huper chrusion kai topazion: more precious then gold or Jewels.*

Now if they be of such high esteeme, where should Jewels els bee put but in a Cabinet; or where should gold be disposed but in a Treasurie? Both these is *Memory.* First, it is a Cabinet, placed in the closet and bedchamber of the soule, the Braine, the safest Keepe in man's Cittadell; one Key it hath, *Reminiscentia,* which opens it, and without that it still remaines locked. Secondly, it is *Ærarium animæ,* the soule's Exchequer, like that *Gazophulakion,* the *Treasurie* in the Temple, into

---

*Break your soft pipes, O Muse, and tear up your books, if shoe-making gives such skills to the cobbler.

which the mites of knowledge and learning are cast. Unto this doe all the Arts and Sciences, humane and divine, offer; the precepts of the Law, the golden rules of the Gospell are in this coffered up. And as the Temple in Jerusalem was maintained in repair by the Treasurie, so are the decayes of the temple of Man's body repaired at the cost of the Memory. When tentation hath shaken the building, when sorrowes and despairs, like tempestuous drifts of raine, have beaten thorow us, lo, from this Store-house do we fetch props to upbeare our declining faith, by calling to minde the gracious promises of Christ. Here finde we comforts collected from the Gospell, to cast off the stormes which beate upon us. [11]

If then such riches lie here in banke, no marvell if our Saviour wish his Disciples to locke it up sure: *Remember the word I told you;* knowing that the place is not built of brasse but fraile and brittle; and that there is a thiefe still lurking about the doore, even that great Thiefe who at first robbed man of his Innocency, and upon the least advantage would spoyle us of those comforts and carry the words away, as in the Parable. Besides, it hath many Pick-lockes which oft times wrench it open. First, *wine,* whose subtile fumes unrivet each joint of it, and loosen the cement which held it fast; for you shall note that deepe drinkers have but shallow memories. Secondly, *women:* I seeke no further instance then Samson, into whose besotted affection Dalila crept so farre, she made him forget his safety. Weake though shee was, she forced a secret from him which all the Philistims could not wring out: which lost, he lost himselfe, eyes, liberty, life and all. Thirdly, *ingratitude:* this is a witch indeed, a sorceresse, whose drowzie inchantments make us even forget God. Matth. 13:19 Judg. 16 [12]

If then we be apt to forget him, how shall wee bee able to retaine his *words?* or how *remember what he hath said,* when we cannot remember the good hee hath done for us? It is a crime none can acquite us of. What is become of all his wonders? Whither is the memory of his great deliverances fled? May I not aske of them as of things worne out, or as he did of the Kings of the Nations: *Where is the King of Emath, and the King of Arphad?* Surely they are gone, all lye extinct and lost. And as the grave of Pompey had not so much as an inscription, to distinguish the dust that covered his victorious body from ignoble slaves, and cowards or to shew, *Here lyes Pompey,* no more have those once glorious dayes now any difference in our memory or esteeme. They lie promiscuously raked up in the dust of time, without any monument set over them to tell they once were, no Rubrick or capitall letter inserted to distinguish them from the common heape of dayes piled up in the Almanacke. 2 King. 19:13 [13]

I know your City-feasts keepe their annuall circuit. The inauguration of Officers and choice of Wardens to each Company want no ceremonious forme to set them forth: for the better solemnizing whereof, Samson is brought unto the feast, and the first dish must be a *Sermon.* An Italian Atheist scoffingly said he was wont to goe to Church that hee might returne with better devotion to his dinner. Be the thought of my applying it to you far from me, as I know the intent is from you. The piety of many grave and good men in those societies fully resolves me that it is devotion, not forme, which makes them desirous of that act. Yet none can deny but some there be, and those not a few, who suppose Sermons at such times are rather for convenience then otherwise; that as *Moses' silver Trumpets* served to call the people together, so they to assemble the ghests; as if there were no difference betwixt a Sermon and a Wake, or preaching were become as necessary a complement to a Feast as wine or musicke. But those times whose memory should be precious passe by without Sermon, or so much as the courtesie of the day; no Annals or yeerely feasts to keepe them up, but in stead of a mention there is a blanke, and solemne silence in stead of an Anniverse. [14] (Num. 10:1–3)

Pardon my plaine language. I professe ingeniously I speake not against the practise, but comparatively. Let their Elections and meetings want no grace the Pulpit can afford them. Let them (in the name of God) performe those lesser rites, but so that they omit not greater duties: for to bee diligent in things indifferent or needlesse, and neglect necessary services, is at best but a precise kind of Poperie—to value Tradition above Scripture, and set more by man's institution then God's. When we shall see shallow customes out-face Religion and the shadow have more honour then the substance, blame none for speaking: [15]

Nam quis iniquæ
Tam patiens urbis, tam ferreus, ut teneat se?*

When the two Sunnes appeared in the firmament before the great famine and plague in the time of Richard the first, that apparition eternized the day to all posteritie, nor is the fame of it yet dead. Our times have seene as great a wonder, yet so short-liv'd, that it hath not worne out the age of a man before it selfe is almost worne out; as if the Chronicle thereof had been writ in the same element the deliverance was wrought on, Water, where no tracke of the storie nor character of the hand that wrote it could abide—That time, I meane, when two Moones appeared in our Hemisphære at once, the one in the skie, the other in the Sea: a fatall prodigious Crescent, the hornes whereof, like the *Hornes of the Ram which stood before the river, were high, pushing Westward and Northward and Southward, so that none might stand before him.* Yet by the furie of the *Goate that encountered him upon the floods* were those Hornes broken, and that threatning Crescent, like a Meteor, wain'd and went out. A Meteor indeed, for it had just the fate of a Meteor, the matter of which it was compacted being blowne asunder, and by the windes scattered upon each adjoyning shore. Heere was enough to give life to a story so long as the world should last; but we are drowned in Lethargie, whom neither mercies can allure nor prodigies awake. I will not seeke an instance beyond this, though I could many: and I would to God our unthankfulnesse were bounded here, that though we are unmindfull of deliverances which are without us and concerne our bodie's peace, yet we might be more apprehensive of such as by neerer relation concerne our soule's good.

But not the greatest blessings that ever befell mankinde are free from this canker of oblivion: the Death and Passion of our Saviour, and the Redemption which by that act was purchased. For how is it possible, if wee remember that Christ already dyed for us, we should still crucifie him afresh, and by our sinnes (each whereof is a new crosse and burthen to him) adde afflictions to his former sorrowes? That wee should wound him daily with our blasphemies; and with serpentine tongues, sharpened with othes and swearings, fetch new streames of blood from him? Or can it be beleeved we retaine the memory of our Redemption and the deare ransome Christ paid for our soules, when we set so low a rate on life as to lay it to stake for each brawle begot of wine and choler, apt to hazard our owne and others' soules for revenge of the lye given, and *Facili redimunt qui sanguine famam*—to spend our too cheap blood in fetching back that thing which wise men never lost, *Reputation?*

O yee sonnes of men, when will ye be wise, or when desist from being authors of your owne wretchednesse? You have bin long put in mind of these faults; it is now time you should remember to amend them. Be but you willing, and you need not to despaire of remedy: the cure is easie and the balme familiar if applyed--*Tantum recordare: onely Remember.* Remember what Christ hath said, and you will the better remember what he hath done for you. This is the right method, the probation which Christ requires from his: *If ye love me, keepe my sayings;* and if you will perfectly remember me, first *remember what I told you.*

But is this all that Christ requires, only to *remember his Word?* No, there is a farther scope: *Thinke not the duty of a Christian is discharged by hearing onely, unlesse thou doe what thou art taught.* For to keepe the Commandements in memory and to breake them in thy course of life, to remember Christ in thy words and forget him in thy deeds, is to mocke God, and foole away thy salvation.

Briefly thus: Let the people know it is no speculative, but a practick memory Christ lookes for; and to remember his words is to practise them. What shall it availe if thou have memory beyond Cyrus, who could call every souldier in his armie by name? What good, though the evidence of Time were recorded in thy braine, though thou keepe a Chronicle of all occurences since Adam, and couldest remember more history then Baronius wrote? Surely if thou retaine all, yet practise

---

*For who is so long-suffering, so unfeeling towards this vicious city, that he can hold himself back?

none, if it be for theory and not use, thou art but like a Granary locked up in the time of dearth, or a sword sleeping in the scabbard when it should bee drawne. Such knowledge doth but *Animam prægravare:* comber the soule, as Saul's armour did David; and is only like the Persians' glittering munition, which Alexander said was for Spoile, not Fight. So this knowledge doth spoyle the owners and make their condemnation the greater, when they shall know the right way yet hold the wrong, heare so much yet doe so little. Let no man thinke it enough to spend the day in hearing, or by frequenting a multitude of Sermons to advantage himselfe; for though he count his Lectures as the Papists their Pater-nosters, by the beads, yet if he be *An hearer of the Law, and not a doer of it,* hee prosecutes against his owne soule. Each Pulpit is to him a Tribunall, and every Preacher a Judge to pronounce sentence against him. Such as these are lyable to the woe which Christ denounced: *Woe unto you, Scribes and Pharises, hypocrites, that impose such heavie loads* upon your Preachers, *but touch them not with the least* of your actions. Nay, they are guilty of the blood of their Preachers, as Jerusalem of her Prophets: *O Jerusalem, Jerusalem, that slayest the Prophets which were sent unto thee!* For with tasking them to too much paines, they weare them out, and make Martyrs of them when there is no time of persecution.

 Againe, let the Preachers know here is a *Memento* for them too. They must not onely tell the people what they should doe, but by their examples shew them the way—*Oves ipsum sequuntur:* the sheepe follow him; therefore it is presumed the Shepheards must goe before. *Who shall heare him, who heares not himselfe?* Or *Domine, quis credet auditui?* Who shall beleeve his report, who by a life unsutable to his words discredits his own errand? It is Isidore Pelusiota his counsell, *that life and doctrine may consent:* for he preaches best *Qui dicit non Lingua sed Vita*—who lives as well as he speakes. Therefore *Let not their hearts & tongues jarre,* but let their actions bee interpreters and comments to their words, and their lives the counterparts of their doctrine. For if their faces stand to Jerusalem and their hearts to Ashdod—teach others well but follow not their owne lessons—they doe but (as Nazianzen speakes) build up with one hand and plucke downe with the other. What shall I say of them? They are as Guardians that have other men's soules in wardship but neglect their owne; or *like whetstones, they set an edge on others'* devotion *yet themselves* are dull and *cut not at all—*

> *Funguntur vice cotis, acutum*
> *Reddere quæ ferrum valet, exsors ipsa secandi.*

Or lastly, they are like Conveyances of land, instruments to seate others in the Kingdome of heaven, yet themselves have no part in the state they convey. They stand in the Pulpit like Moses on the Mount Abarim, and onely shew the people a Land of promise, which themselves must never set foot in.

 I have bin long in the passage to my Text; the copious matter would not dismisse me sooner. One note and I passe it.

 Of all faculties in man, *Memory* is the weakest, first waxeth olde, and decayes sooner then Strength or Beautie. Of all powers in man it is least at commaund (the will not so little). A man may be master of his invention and of his tongue, but who could ever boast himselfe the master of his memorie, or promise to himselfe that would not fayle? Which makes God and his Prophets, Christ and his Apostles, strengthen it with so many admonitions: *Remember and forget not. Remember thy Creator in the dayes of thy youth;* and many the like both in the old and new Testament. Now as generally in all things we are forgetfull, so in nothing more then in things belonging to our woes: Either we dare not, or cannot, remember miseries which must befall us. The Mariner loves not to heere of stormes; nor states rockt in securitie, of warres; nor can wanton youth endure the tidings of sicknesse or age that must surprize it.

 Naturally all hate reproofe, nor have we patience to heere of judgements that must follow: *for all these God shall bring thee to judgement.* To such remembrances wee are deafe and averse:

Monitoribus asperi,* and their preachings wee banish from our eares, as Amaziah did the words of Amos, when he foretold Jeroboam's death and Israel's captivitie: *Gradere, fuge in terram Judah:* O thou Seer, goe flie away into the land of Judah, *and prophecy there, but prophecy no more at Bethel.* They that will please these times must steepe their words in oyle, sooth and flatter; *though they see, they must say nothing,* or if they doe, they must *speake plausibly.* We love to heare of faire dayes which no misfortune clouds, and crie with Hezekiah that *Nothing but peace may sound in our eares:* for sorrowes and persecutions wee abhorre to thinke on and, like those in the Prophet, *Put farre away the evill day. Hunc voluit nescire diem:* such blacke crosse dayes as these we curse out of the Ephemerides, and excommunicate them from all societie with the yere, as Job did his birth-day: *Let the day perish to all memory, let darknesse and the shadow of death staine it, and let forgetfulnesse like a cloud dwell upon it.*

Just cause then had our Saviour, being to warne his Disciples of calamities and persecutions that should ensue, to stirre them up to *Remember,* that, as the wise man advised, their end might be in their sight. *Remember the word I said unto you, The Servant is not greater then his Lord.*

Second part: The servant is not greater then his Lord

There is nothing so much sets out the Universe as *Order,* to see how subordinate causes depend of their Superiours, and this sublunary globe of the Celestiall. Were not this method, what could hinder a second *Chaos?* For in the World's beginning, all lay in one common wombe of darkenes. It was onely order, and that Method God's *fiat* brought a long, which gave distinction and visibility to things: a heaven above the earth, and light to separate day from night; Man as Lord to rule the Creatures; and God himselfe Lord over all. Should all have been equall, what had man beene better then the beasts, save only his shape? Or what the Serpent worse then other Creatures, save onely for his malice? What active predominance should *Fire* have had above the other Elements? Or what priviledge could that Sire of generation, *Heate,* challenge above unactive *Drought* or *Moysture?* Grant equall force to the Elements, that the qualities of the one should not bee more operative then another; like a *Mare mortuum,* [Dead Sea] stupid to all motion, would the World be, and *Nature* so be calm'd that the seasons of the yeere would be lost. *Heate* should not name the Summer nor *Cold* the Winter: instead of *Winter* and *Summer,* a blended mixture of the qualities, a lazy luke-warm season, would last all the yeere.

Unisons yeeld no Musicke, for Harmony consists of variety in stops higher and lower; and equality amongst men would breed nought but confusion. Looke up to heaven and reade over that bright booke, you shall see an inequality of light in those celestiall bodies. *Astêr asteros diapherei en doxê: One starre differeth from another in glory:* so was it allowed by God, who at the review of his worke found all to be *valde bona,* very good. And one man differeth from another in glory, in honour, in riches, in abilities of the minde; *which disparity in worth makes the world more beautifull.* All were not borne to be rich, nor all to be wise, nor all to teach, nor all to rule, but some for *Disciples,* some for *Masters;* some for the *Throne,* some for the *Mill;* some for *Servants,* some for *Lords*—Which distinction we owe unto these two *Relata disquiparantiæ*† (as Logicians terms them), *Dominus* and *Servus.* These were the two differences which in the Heraldry of Nature were first put to blazon the coates of all mortality, and make a distinction betwixt the elder and younger house, the Inferiour and Superior: for (saith Saint Augustine) *As men, all are alike; but the respects of* Lord *and* Servant *make a difference amongst them.*

To make it more plaine, looke once more backe, and see the host of heaven governed by these rules of subjection and superiority: *fecit Deus duo luminaria magna*—God made two great lights, unto which the lesser are servants and tributaries, borrowing their lustre from them. And as in heaven, so in earth hath he ordained *Luminaria magna,* greater lights and higher powers, to goe before his people. Though I am not of opinion with that insolent Spaniard Juan Puente that God's

---

*Harsh to advisers,
†Things related by opposition.

Margin notes:
(Horace Ars Poet. 163)
Amos. 7:12
Esa.30:10
(Is. 39:8)
(Amos 6:3)
Lucan (7.411)
[25]
Job 3:3,5
[26]
[27]
1.Cor.15:41
[28]
Gen.1
Tomo primero de la conveniencia de las dos

meaning on the Text is to be restrained to those two *Catholique Lights* set up by him in the front of his booke, in which hee hath taken upon him to adde new devices and Mottoes to the Shields and Scutchions of them both: under one, the word *Luminare maius ut praesit urbi, et dominetur Orbi;* under the other. *Luminare minus, ut subdatur urbi, & dominetur Orbi.** But let him passe for a profound Sycophant. I hope the Kings of the earth shall never come to that nonage, to make them Guardians of their Crownes. Those lights are well where they are, and best shine in their owne Orbes. I feare they will bee too dim to give light to al the nations of the world—I am sure too hot and scorching for our Climate. Thankes be to God wee need no addition. We have our *Luminaria magna* of Religion and State, shining like Lampes in the great assembly of Parliament; and a *Julium sydus,* an imperiall Starre, whose peacefull influence hath many yeeres blest our Land. May it bee long ere this Sunne goe downe, or by his set leave us in darknesse and mourning! Nor may there want a succeeding Ray, a Beame of that light, to shine in the circle of this Throne, so long as those *Duo luminaria magna* in Heaven, the Sunne and the Moone, shall runne their course!

Since, then, it is established *per leges universitatis,* by the law of God and Nations, that the Lord must rule and the servant obey, it were preposterous, nay monstrous, that the *servant should bee greater then his Lord.* Let no man whom Fortune hath subjected and made a servant be grieved at his lot, or thinke too meanely of that vocation. To serve is no base office, nor is slavery the badge of servants, but obedience: *Servants, obey your Masters.* It is no neglected title of drudgery, that alters man from his creation, but a title of dependance that still referres to a superiour, and as man should doe, lookes upwards. *Men* and *servants* are names neere a kin. There was but one Authour that made Man, and the same made Servants: even God himselfe, whose decree was *That every soule should bee subject to the higher power.* He then that is stubborn resists not man's, but God's ordinance.

Servi are not slaves, but *humiles amici,* inferiour friends. *Ye are my friends* saith Christ to his Disciples; *they are* Fellowes; nay *they are* Brethren.

There are no slaves but such as serve either their owne or other men's crimes. *Sinne brought in the first thraldom;* but since the glad tidings of liberty & release was brought by Christ, who cancelled the *Chirographum lethale,* the deadly Indenture, that none may thinke it an abject duty to serve, he the Lord hath dignified the calling by taking upon himselfe *morphên doulou—the forme of a Servant.*

Againe, let not the Lords of the earth, whom soveraignty hath lifted above the common ranke of men, thinke so highly of themselves that they contemne all below them, since that *Lord* or *Master* are not onely stiles of preeminence but of care. For this cause, a Master is called the Father of his family, and the King is *Pater Patriæ,* the father of his Countrey. In the Prophet you shall finde *Dominus* and *Pater* joyned: *If I be a father where is my honour, if a Master where is my feare?* Let them remember that as they have many below them, so they have one that is farre above them, a Master and Lord Paramount, even *Dominus dominantium;* that though they be gods on earth (*dixi quod dii estis*), yet still but men, and breathe one common aire; that though fashioned *ex meliore luto,* of better clay, yet *lutum,* still but *clay:* and are *eiusdem farinæ*—of the selfe same *grane,* though sifted by birth and fortune from the branne of vulgar men. For when all the sheafes in the field did homage *to Joseph's sheafe,* all were but sheafes, linkt in one band of brotherhood from earth and from the wombe.

But whither doe I presse this poynt? My Text is no plea of Jurisdiction, no Charter to prove only the Master's prerogative above the servant: which though it naturally arise from hence, yet is not this all. That is a granted Maxime: our Saviour's meaning is larger, and implies that his Disciples, being but servants, *must not expect better measure at the hands of men then their Lord had found* (so the Glosse); and therefore, as they might not scorne or thinke much to runne those courses of

---

*The great light to be over the city and to rule the world . . . The lesser light to be subject to the city and to rule the world.

[Marginalia: Monarquias Catolicas la de la Iglesia Romana y la del Imperio Espanol. En Madrid en la Imprenta Real. 1612; [29]; [30]; I Pet. 2:18; Rom. 13:1,2; [31]; Sen.Ep.47 Joh.15:14; Sen.ibid. Aug. Hom.42 in orat. Dominic.; Aug.; Phil.3:7; [32]; Mal.1:6; Colos.4:1; Psal.82:6; Gen.37:7; [33]]

hazard and reproch which hee himselfe had past, so neither take upon them, out of pride, to do more then he. Thus doth he express himselfe: *If I, your Lord and Master, have washed your feet, ye ought to wash one another's feet.* There hee gives them an example of *Humility*, heere of *Patience: If they have persecuted me, they will also persecute you.* To strengthen which perswasion, he argues from this Axiome: *The servant is not greater then the Lord.*

[Joh.13:16]

[34] A just truth and not to be contradicted; but Rome denies it, and that great Heteroclite in Religion, the Pope, thinkes it too scant for him to be circumscribed by presidents, either of the Apostles (though he calls himselfe *Peter's successor*) or of Christ himselfe, whose *Vicar* hee is proclaimed.

Hee will ducke and complement as low as may be, stile himselfe *Minimus Apostolorum* and *servus*, yea, lower yet, *servus servorum*, a servant of servants. Yea, and yet the Fox wants attributes deepe enough to earth his pride in. You know what in another case Saint Augustine sayes—it is true in this: *Those that will build high, lay deepest foundations.* Nor ever was insolence so high flowne, but before it tooke wing, it raised it selfe from the ground. *Brutus* will kisse the earth, though his thoughts aime at the government of Rome; so will the Pope lessen himselfe, and contract his greatnesse into short titles (as the Snake hides her length by folding her selfe up into many gyres and doubles), kisse the ground, even when he meanes *to build his nest in the Starres;* when he aimes, not at Rome's alone, but the world's supremacy.

[Aug.Ser.10: de Verb.Dom.]

[35]
[Obad.1:4]

Thus, like a Falcon, he stoopes lowest when he meanes to soare highest, and his ambition, like a bullet spit from the mouth of a Cannon, first grazes and then mounts. For behold, from these low foundations, from this flat and bottome of dissembled humility, he hath built a Tower loftier then Babel, on the highest pinnacle whereof, as on a Pharos, the Banner and Flag of his Supremacy is hung out; hath cast up a Mount equall to Olympus, on the top whereof himself stands, like the *Tempter* upon that *'Oros hupsêlon lian—exceeding high hill,* from whence he shewed Christ all the Kingdomes of the earth. Loe, from hence doth he overlooke the world and the Kingdomes of it, and to maintaine the Idoll of his supremacie, with an *Omnia dabo,* sets them all to sale, proclaiming unto the Kings of the Nations, *All these will I give, if ye will fall downe and worship me.* But amongst them, if there bee any that refuse to adore this *Golden Calfe* or question his usurped supremacie, *Res fisci est:** straight hee seazeth their Crownes and, as due to him by forfeit, bestowes them most bountifully upon any who by force of Armes can get them.

[Mat.4:8]

[36]
[Vers.9]

[Juvenal (4.55)]

It is not long since he gave away our Land upon the same quarrell (that I may name no Germane examples, not of yesterday but to day), yet (thankes bee to God) the Title proved so difficult, and the possession so hard to get, that he who thought it already his was faine to disclaime the suit, and with losse of fame and costs returne home. Thus doth hee sit *in Templo Dei,* opposing himselfe against, and exalting himselfe above *all that is called God,* that is, all Kings of the earth (who are stiled Gods: *Dixi quod Dii,* and *Christi Dei:* Christs, the Lord's Anoynted) which will not acknowledge him their Head, as being impatient to heare of any Deity equall or greater then himselfe. Nor against these onely doth he advance himselfe, but he doth *theomachein:* fight against the God of Heaven and his Christ.

[2 Thes: 2]

[Psal.82:6]

[37]

Take a short survey of his practice, and you will find no greater opposition betwixt the sides of the *Diameter,* nor larger distance betwixt the two poynts of heaven, *North and South,* nor more enmity betwixt the words *Christ* and *Antichrist,* then their persons. Our Saviour Christ when he entred Jerusalem came riding meekly upon an Asse, no attendants but his Disciples and a few poore Villagers; but Kings have walkt afoote whilest the Pope hath rode, and Emperors, like Querries, waited on the stirrop. Christ *washed his Disciples' feet* and *wiped them;* but the Pope hath caused Emperours to kisse his feet. Christ taught us to give unto Caesar: *Reddite Caesari;* the Pope bids take from *Caesar the things which are Caesar's,* not the Tribute, but Crowne and life too. Christ refused to be called *good,* as holding it a stile fit for God alone; but the Pope is patient of a stile so

[Math.21:5.]
Frederick 1 waited on Pope Adrian's stirrop.
[Joh. 13:14]
[Math.22:21]

[38] [Math.19:17]

---

*The thing is forfeited [to the State]

farre above it as superlatives can stretch him, *Optimus Maximus,* and *Dominus Deus noster Papa, our Lord God the Pope.*

 Christ instituted a *cheirotonian, Imposition of hands;* but the Pope hath practised *podotonian,* an *imposition of feet.* For Cælestine the fourth crowned the Emperour Henrie the Sixth with his foot, and spurned it off againe with his foot, dismissing him with a curse of Excommunication. So, as *Christ laid his hands upon them and blessed them,* the Pope laid his feet upon the Emperour and cursed him. Now judge their contrariety, and see if this *servus servorum,* servant of servants, the Pope, take not more upon him then ever Christ, the *Lord of Lords,* did. Finally, the Popes (that I may omit the impiety of their owne persons, some whereof have been Arians, as Liberius; some Nestorians, as Anastasius II; some Heretickes, as Syricius, Cælestinus, &c.; some Sorcerers, as Alexander VI, Sergius IV and 17 besides; some Atheists, as Leo X, who called the Gospell *a fable of Christ*)—the Popes (I say) for these many Centuries of yeeres have beene such profest enemies to Christ that there have beene no persecutions, Massacres, Invasions, Powder-plots, but they have come out in a sort *cum Privilegio*—with their allowance, their encouragement, their privity. At their feet have the garments of all those Jesuiticall Assassinates beene layd down, as *Stephen's executioners* layd theirs at Saul's. Nor doe we yet finde better measure (looke but to the other side of the sea, and then judge). Nor can we hope better, but the voyce of the Ancient Churches by them persecuted cries unto us, in the words of my Text, as Christ to his Apostles: *If they have persecuted me, they will also persecute you.*

 I am arrived at my last point, which needs no long discourse. *It is a matter fit rather for meditation then proofe,* and is a story acted, and no supposition; so that our Saviour's *Si persecuti,* If *they have persecuted me,* is now turned to an assertion: *They have persecuted me.* Since the quarrell in the garden betwixt the *Woman* and the *Serpent,* the devill never wanted Seconds to take up his weapons against the promised Seed. God told her, *Ponam inimicitias, I wil put enmitie betwixt you,* and did hee not keepe tutch?

 Marke the whole passage of our Saviour's life, & tell me what day was not to him a Persecution. So soone as he saluted the light, to avoyd Herod's bloody Inquisition which pursued him, hee was constrained to flie the land, and like a banished sojourner make Egypt his abiding place. When Herod deceased, and he *vocatus ex Egypto*—*revok't*—was he yet secure? No, but in the house of his friends (as Zacharias) so used, that Barbarians would have dealt more mercifully. Amongst his own countreymen the Jewes, unacknowledged and unregarded, scorned, reviled, belyed: *Hee hath a Devill, He is mad, He blasphemes.* Sometimes conspiracy to throw him headlong from a Cliffe, sometimes to stone him. Thus was hee shuffled up and downe from coast to coast, from the City to the field, from the Gadarenes to Samaria, from dry land to sea, yet no sayles able to make speed from his Persecutions, but *Mare nos repellit ad Barbaros**—each shore hee tutch't at was an enemie, nor found his wearines the benefit of a resting place whereon to lay his head. As a Partridge from the fowlers, so fled he from the cruell Priests and Scribes, who were *They* in my Text, the Actors in this persecution; and like a *Roe in the wildernesse* was he pursued. Many darts throwne after him; many toyles pitched for him, for they *sought how to take him in the snare.* All which, though hee long avoyded, yet never did they give over the furious chase, till faint and wearie, on the top of Calvary their cruelty overtooke him, where with nailes and speare they goard his harmlesse body, and bereaved that Just one of the life they long had hunted after.

 When the Principall is slaine, partakers must looke to bleed: nor can the Armie hope for mercy when the Generall is put to the sword. One life sacrificed cannot appease an incensed enemy, nor could the life of Christ, though the best among the sonnes of men, quench the bloody thirst of the Jewes; but being flesht upon the Leader, they are eager after the *Heard,* and having rent this *Lambe*

---

*The sea drives us back to the Barbarians.

Bzovius *Annal. Tom. 13. Extra.in Verbo Significasti: Tit. 14.cap.4*

(Mk.10:16)

[39]

Act.7:58

[40] Third part: *If they have persecuted me, they will also persecute you*
Calvin *Harmon.*
John 15:20
Gen. 3
Verse 15

Matth.2:13

[41] Zach.13:6

1 Sam.26:20

Cant.2:17

[42]

from the fold, they seeke to worry the whole *Flocke*. For the divel's commission was not like the command of the King of Syria: *Fight neither with small nor great, save onely against the King of Israel;* but as that in Zachary, *Arise, O sword, and smite the shepheard;* and not him alone, but *let the sheepe be scattered*. Spare none, neither Lord nor Servant, Master or Disciple, but extirpate all. Downe with the glorious Temple of Christ's body, *Downe with it even to the ground,* and let not *one stone of that building,* one Disciple, survive to re-edifie the demolished Church. You see the sad Patrimony of the Apostles, and that (as Hugo Cardinalis hath it) *the warre descended to them by inheritance,* and persecution was their lot and portion. For so was the will of the Testator: *If they have persecuted me, they will also persecute you.*

Sinne is a fruitfull parent, and never yet wanted issue, but as poyson runnes successively thorow the veines, so have her agents drained thorow al successions of time. The tyrannies of God's enemies towards his Church never ended where they began, and though the persons changed, the malice did not. As in a Campe the word goes from Centinell to Centinell, so in this, *Abyssus abyssum invocat*—one misery called up another: and as the Carthaginians' hate to Rome was by the Fathers assigned over and intailed to the sonnes, so was the cruell tradition of shedding the blood of Saints delivered over by predecessors to their following generations. *Finis unius mali gradus futuri:* one persecution hath trod upon the heele of another, and where the old went off, new Scenes of mischiefe have taken their Cues.

The Monarchies of the world have not shifted oftener their Seates then the Empires of death and Persecution. The first persecution began in Egypt in the time of Pharaoh; from thence it was derived to the Jewes; when they failed, the Arians and Easterne Heretickes went forward with the Chase; & *Ubi desinit philosophus, incipit medicus** where these wrangling Sophisters of the divell left, the Jesuites began. Those onely, the great *Paracelsians* of the world, whose practice is Phlebotomy, to let States' blood in *the Heart-veine,* and deale altogether in metals and minerals, Steele and Gunpowder—Creatures so prodigiously dexterous in their art, that they are now become the onely Inventories of mischiefe: All the shallow elementary examples of trechery formerly practised serving to them but as a garden of simples, from whose composition they have extracted a Quintessence of such speeding operation, that it is able to make an Earthquake greater then Nature ever durst owne, and in a moment purge a whole Kingdome into nothing. Thus hath the divell his Infantry belonging to his Campe, and where the old Garrisons were worne out, new supplies to make good their places: *They shall also persecute you.*

Persecution heere is no single appellation of misery, but a compound of all cruelty. I cannot give a fitter Embleme to express it then that possest man (Mark 5) who *dwelt among the Tombes, bound with fetters and chains,* so mad and raging doth it runne about the world, keeps its court amidst the graves, and her pavillion hung about with the trophees of death: fetters, and whips, rackes and strappadoes, halters and swords, stakes, and fire. Besides, this hath a name as numerous as his: *My name is Legion* (saith the possest) *for we are many;* so is Persecution *Nomen multitudinis,* a collective name of Multitude. In it, many *Legions* of ills, the Burse of Tyranny, and (which speakes all) a full Inquisition is included: Persecution of the body and affliction of the mind, persecution at home, persecution abroad, and not only *Persecutio manus*--violence offered to the body—but to the Good Name, by slanders and calumnies. *For it is not the sword alone, nor the fire which makes a Martyr*. There is *Martyrium famae,* Martyrdome of fame, as well as *vitae,* of life. A man may bee a Martyr without blood-shed, and *sicca morte*—by a dry death—attaine the Crown of a Confessor, even by suffering persecution in his fame and honour, which is (as Anselme calls it) *persecutio oris,* the persecution of the mouth. Neither is this less grievous then the former: it rather exceeds it as farre as the price of fame is above life. *Feare not those which kill the body* (saith Christ). This is more exquisite and kils, if not the soule, that which is next in value, the Good name.

One of these two mischiefes, *Os gladii* or *gladius oris*--either the materiall sword of the

---

*Where the philosopher leaves off, the doctor begins.

executioner or (if not so) the sword of a two-edged lying tongue—hath runne thorow all the ancient Apostles, and most of those *Hæreditarios Discipulos,* later Apostles, who in their severall ages have succeeded in the Church. Christ himselfe was not free from it—was not hee branded with the name of an Impostour after his death? And the Disciples were *made Theaters of misery* in their lives, of scorne and infamy in their deathes. Tertullian
Math. 27:63 Heb.10:33

Thus did the Arrians scandalize the great Athanasius; And as executors unto them, the Romish Priests & Jesuits, with their frontlesse imputations, have strived to darken the glorious truth of our Church and Religion by traducing the Professors, and on their ruined credits sought to build up their owne rotten cause. [48]

Luther was defamed *for lewd life, and conversing with the divell,* and that he had *hanged himselfe;* Bucer, for denying Christ at his death; Œcolampadius, for dying suddenly, when hee was sixteen days sicke in his bed; Calvin, for dying distracted and desperate—an aspersion which, my Author saith, Bolsecke himselfe recanted in the Synod with teares; Beza given out for a Convert, and a revolter from the Protestant Church to theirs—All which so grosse and false, that some with their owne pens confused the calumniations cast upon them; and amongst the rest, Beza, after the report of his death and conversion, published his owne defence and their perjurious falsehood in a tract called *Beza redivivus, Beza revived.*

Bozius *De signis Ecclesiae* L.23 c.3
Lindan *Dialog.* Cochleus Hieron. Bolsec. *in eius vita.*

[49]

I have yet one instance of the selfesame quality, as false as that though not so well confuted. One, indeed, too many by that, and so deare, that I could have wished He had not so soone been added to this catalogue of wronged Worthies. But that wish is vaine, and like Him lost, and by that losse am I furnished with what most willingly I would have wanted, a sad example. Your conceit already lookes thorow me, and my meaning is articulated in your apprehensions before uttered in words.

One he was, knowne to all enough, to me more neerly, as being tyed to him in double bonds, of *Canon* and of *Nature;* Sometimes the Bishop of this See, or to use the phrase of Saint John, the *Angell of this Church,* though now taken up into a better Hierarchy, the society of Angels in heaven. I had cause to thinke hee now was out of the reach of detraction, and too high fixed to be traduced, but I see flouds of reproche throwne after him by the Papists, as after the *woman in the Wildernesse.*

Apoc. 2

[50]

For my owne part, I thought once not to have meddled at all in this subject, knowing that *Rerum irrecuperabilium felicissima est oblivio:* unhappy losses are happily forgot; much lesse with the slander raised after him, supposing it too light upon the Ballance to poyze or sway any wise man's beliefe.

Againe, I could not judge it but as very ridiculous or malicious. If ridiculous, I hoped, like a fume it would have vanished (for *mendacia diu non fallunt*),* and having arrived at nine dayes, the age of a wonder, died in laughter. If malicious, I held best not to take notice of it; For injury is no injury if not apprehended. *Omnis iniuria in sensu patientis* (saith one): to own a scandall crownes the revenge of the Authour, whereas neglected, it quickly findes its owne grave.

Cyprian

But I see this spurious Brat hath found too many Nurses since it was exposed, and like a Snowball, by rolling is growne greater, and *as it hath acquired more age, so also* (with those that wish it so) *more credit*. Therefore, because impudent avouchings make wise men somtimes doubt and the ignorant stumble, and for that I would not with a guilty silence seeme to betray a Truth, or confirme their errour who take all for granted which is not contradicted, I have at last adventured to speake: Not that I hold my selfe fit or able for this taske at any time, much lesse now, but onely for that I hoped what I should say might win more beliefe, as having been an eare-witnesse, and which is more, *oculatus testis,* an eye-witnes, of all his last passages, and could beare record against his Accuser's falshood, as Saint John did of the truth, *Quod vidimus, quod audivimus,* &c.

[51]
Minut. Felix

1 Joh.1

Yet alas, what can I say! What proportion will words hold against peremptory assertions? I have

---

*Lies do not deceive for long.

nothing to convince them but a plaine unglost deniall: *Petilianus dicit, Ego nego*—They *say it is so, I know it is not;* and in a just case, it is Rhetoricke enough. Let bad causes shrowd themselves in suspected apologies: Trueth needs no clothing, but as a principle, scornes proofe or demonstration. Besides, it were difficult to proove a Negative, much harder to refute an untruth by the tracke. You may as well descrie the Eagle's path, or define that which is a twinne of the same litter, *non ens.** Neither finde I any such President from that Incarnate Truth, Christ Jesus, who being accused by clouds of false witnesses, answered either nothing at all or very little, according to his owne prescript: *Let your communications bee yea and nay.* And yet, if I would seeke evidence to cast them, I would looke no further then their owne Jurors, but *ore ipsorum*—from themselves—fetch circumstance to confute them. For I never yet knew any Lye so close built, but there was some **loope-light for the Truth to discover it.** This is *mendacium fenestratum,*† hath many wide windowes for you to behold it.

First (you know) Hee whose conversion they now urge had been long an eye-sore to them, railed on by many of their Pamphleters, Parsons especially, and that other unchristened Jesuite (for he hath no name, or else shames to put it to his booke) who thought it would be credit to his worke if he could bring in the name of Doctor King, thogh but in the Rere and Post-script. Judge, then, how can this Report cohere, to detest him living, to defame him sicke, yet claime him dead? Were it true, there is little policy to trust a reconciled enemy, but being so false, it is most impious and diabolicall to belie the dead. For *insidiari calcaneo,* which Gregory expounds to be *Finem vitæ,*‡ is the divel's proper passion.

Secondly, for the Authour of his conversion they alleage such a one who sure uttered words which no man ever heard, and acted feats which none could see. For had he been a Substantive visible or to be understood, and no Jugler nor dreame nor aire, nor meere metaphysicall Notion, we, who were scarce ever absent, should at one time or other have descryed him. But peradventure it was a night-piece, and not fit to bee perused by every light. Well then, apply their owne *Ignis fatuus* to it, and grant them as much as they can suppose, and marke if it appeare not farre worse.

You must presume first Mutes onely for the *Actors* in this *Scene,* thoughts or wishes to have been *Embassadours* in this parley; for what Mercury flew on this errand? What servant or friend imployed, to disclose the purpose of his Conversion to the Confessor? Did he by inspiration know his minde, or venter to him unsent for? That were strange, unlesse some walking *Frier* or *Fairy* from Saint Omer's or Doway gave him intelligence; or else some whirle-wind rapt him and bare him to the house, as the Angell tooke up Habakkuk by the haire of the head and set him in Babylon.

Next, a prison doore opened at all houres of the night, either by corruption of the keeper, or by miracle, as it opened to Saint Peter; Free passage thorow each ward, accesse without impediment into the house, nay, bed-chamber of this sicke Patient; attendants either none (which were unlikely) or sleeping—belike such as garded the Sepulcher whilest our Saviour's body was stolne away by his Disciples! Whether the servants slept or no, I will not dispute: sure I am, the *Tares* are sowne by *Seeds-men* envious and dangerous, *Seminaries* and Priests.

Thus you see, like *Mathematicians,* they draw a great many idle lines, have many concessions to bring their conclusion about, and when all comes to issue, their maine Agent proves *Corpus Mathematicum,* a meere imagination next to, yea just, nothing.

Nothing indeed, for bearing any part in this designe. A man first (by their confession) so unfit to reconcile any to their Church, that hee is by them *disavowed for a Sonne or Member of the Catholike Church.* Besides, they make him no lesse then *a Persecutor, worse then Luther or Calvin, or then a Reprobate.* And secondly, such a one who for his owne particular had professed to many, and often, that *He had never set foot within the gates:* yea, and disclaimed it utterly, with a *Non*

---

*not-being.
†a lie with windows in it,
‡to lie in wait for [bruise, AV] the heel. . . . The end of life

novi hominem: he did not know the face of his suggested Convert. The foulest mouth of them al cannot disprove this.

But they thinke, belike, all gaine-sayings are fruitlesse, since it is already entertained at Doway for Orthodox and by them licensed to the Presse. So that what before was onely *Fama volans,* a flying report, is now *liber volans,* a flying booke. I confess it, and withall know the disadvantage, that there now stands a whole *Impression* against mee: yet let them know, a Truth, though but breathed into the aire, carries more power then a printed Lye. If ever any, this is one, and of the grossest *edition.* I now perceive their intelligence is as false as their quotations, and both as equivocall as themselves. The best is, this is not the first Libell which hath flowne from their presse, witnesse the *Three Conversions,* the *Life of Saint Francis,* the story of Garnet's strawe, and of our Lady of Loretto, *Calvino-Turcismus,* and that which outstrides the largest fable in Ovid, the *Golden Legend.*

Yet I would be glad to do the Author al right: one thing I must commend him for, that in setting down the Conversion of this our Bishop, he is so briefe, following that rule of the Poet, *Breve sit quod turpiter audes:* short stiles best suite opprobrious and unjustifiable subjects. For like *the Dogge at Nile,* he laps but fearefully & straight flies off. Neither do I so much blame him. He did but there, as in all other parts of his booke besides, shew his skill in Poetrie, and that he was a Graduate in that eighth science which they beyond Seas have added to the seven others, *Arte calumniandi,* the art of slander; that hee had studied Saunders, Parsons, Cochlaeus, and Bolseca better, perhaps, then Saint Augustine or the Scriptures.

Besides, being now invested a Priest (and I know not whether Arch-priest), it is not unlikely but, as Philosophers are bound to study *Aristotle,* so he to reade over and study *Caiphas the high Priest,* and by custome to let loose some Barrabas, some pestilent Pamphlet, to humour the Synagogue of Rome and advantage their cause, all which considerations doe somewhat extenuate his fault. But for the *Surveyour* of his booke, Matthew Kellison, that would faine have the world take him for a politicke wise man and a solid Criticke, as having measured out Religion by the Acre and taken a Geometricall *Survey* of it, I know not how to excuse him. Certainly, if hee had been halfe so carefull to search the truth as he was busie to survey Religions, he would never have suffered himselfe to be so grosly guld with every fabulous Gazette and idle Corante that posts betwixt England and Doway.

I desire not to bee mistaken; I come not hither to pleade against them, nor to pleade for Him whom they have so palpably injured. Let obscure names hire a *Panegyricke* to varnish them over: faire and perspicuous Texts need no dictionary or glosse to construe them: such I take Him to be. That He suffers under their mis-report hurts not him; it rather gives foyle and lustre to him. It was the honour of dead *Patroclus* that two armies fought for his Corps; and it was the glory of *Moses* that an Arch-angell strove with the divell for his body: and if two Religions strive for him, as the Councell did for Paul, or that *Urbs septicollis*—seven-headed city—contends for the new birth of his faith as the seven Cities did for Homer's birth, can it lesse be then an honour, and such a one which Christ vouchsafes not to all? Many have died, but *frustra peritura cadavera,* as subjects not worth a contending for, past in silence. Therefore the Apostles, when they were convented and imprisoned, *Ibant gaudéntes:* they went in triumph, greatly rejoycing that they were held worthy to suffer reproch for the name of Christ and for his Gospell.

So that it is not his hurt—the hurt is, as Rome meant it, yours if you beleeve it, *for by beleeving it, you make your selves Authors of it.* If any should labour to perswade that Snow were black, his foule report could not sully it; and though you might thinke him shamelesse that would averre it, you would take him to bee mad that should beleeve it. Thus is his case more miserable that is rashly credulous to depravations of other men, then hee that first forged them. The deviser of them knowes they are false, nor can he by telling make them true; but hee who beleeves them alters the property, and dogmatizes them for truth. And as the Artizan who casts or carves the Image is not the Idolator, but he that worships it when it is made—*Qui colit, ille facit*—so neither is hee so much the lyer that tells the lye as he that beleeves it, being told. It is Saint Hierom's advice: *Doe not thou authorize slanders by giving credit to them, lest thou make the crime thine.* It shall bee my advice to all that heare me, and to such as heare mee not, for *not to receive or credit opprobrious calumniations cast out against our brethren* is one of the degrees of innocence and happinesse recited by the Psalmist. Do but remember, that if God hath denounced a wo against those that speake evill of Good *and rob the righteous of their good names,* he hath also a woe for them who consent unto the theft.

But my perswasion is misplaced: you are not such before whom I need to cleare him of this defamation. I hope with modesty I may use Saint Hierom's words: *he had deserved better ranke in your estimations then so.* For did he so long runne his course thorow this Churche's Zodiack and as a true Diocesan visit each Pulpit within your City (some of them oftner), & not onely taught within it, but *kath' holes tês perichōron: in all the adjoyning villages* where hee lived, never allowing his numerous affaires so much as a Sabbath or Sundaye's rest, whilest he was able—so, by his unwearied industry, telling the world that they which for gaine, or ease, or for ambition aimed at Bishopricks, mistooke that weighty calling, since that (as Theophylact speakes) when Christ made his Apostles Bishops and Superintendents of his Church, he appoynted them *not so much to Lord the flocke, as to feed it*—Did he all this, and with that zealous care, that as a Torch, hee consumed himselfe to light others, and when Himselfe should faile, provided, so farre as in him lay, for a succession in his Blood to *set* hand to the same *plough:* having dedicated in his desire all his Sonnes (in act Two) to the Ministery of this Church, and by no meanes willing to heare of any other course (though otherwise invited by Gracious offers for some of them in particular) to be undertaken by them, save that function alone? And can it be conceived he should, after all this, turne a shifter of his Religion?

Let me aske, with better right then did Zedekia, *When went that Spirit of God,* which had accompanied him thorow all the passages of life, from him? Great buildings, before they fall, give warning of their ruine by inclining some way or other; what argument did hee ever give of his Revolt? Or that, like Ephraim, having bin so long harnessed, so long militant in God's battels, so long a Captaine in the Armie, he should in the last day of battell turne backe, when hee had now but one enemie to incounter, *Death?* That he should forsake his Colours, or like a *ripsaspis* and Renegado, recant that faith which much contention and with losse of Spirits he so long had maintained? Had his resolution wavered this way, how could he have disguized so apparant a relapse from those reverend Bishops who were his familiar and frequent visitants; and especially his most honoured friend the Lord Archbishop of Canterbury, who was with him on the Wednesday before his decease? The end of life ever answers the beginning, is the old rule. If so, who can imagine that One who began in opposition to the Church of Rome should end in Apostasie and reconcilement to it? Nay, that good Father is confident: *It is incredible he that lived so well should make so inglorious an end.*

Nor was this confidence in him any way abused, neither his end disproportionate to his beginning. Hee that had so long taught others how to live was by his owne infirmities tutord in the art of dying. It is not strange he should bee perfit in this lesson, since for a long time (to use the Apostle's word) *He dyed daily,* his sharpe agonies having made his life but *bion abion:* no better then a living death. Unto this wholly doth hee address his thoughts, and admonished by his increasing paines, as from the tongue of the Prophet sent from God to summon Ezekiah, *he sets his house in order.* Where first he resolves himself into his *principia naturalia,* bequeathing his Soule to God that gave it, his Body to the dust from whence it was taken; and not onely so, but *In principia fortunæ:* hee resolves his fortunes into their beginnings, acknowledging, with all thankfull duty, that under God, our gracious Soveraigne had been the maker of them.

I will not conceale his owne words, dictated in his last Testament:

"First, I bequeath my soule into the hands of Almighty God, beseeching him for Christ Jesus' sake, my most blessed Saviour, that as it hath pleased him even from my mother's wombe to take mee into his speciall favour and protection, and to continue the same unto me thorowout all the passages of my life, especially under my most gracious Master and Soveraigne, the Instrument of his goodnesse and bounty to me and mine for these eighteene yeeres; and hath vouchsafed me, though the unworthiest of many, to bee a Minister of his holy Word and Sacraments; so it would please him in this my time of sicknesse and grievous infirmity to hold mee up by his right hand, and to vouchsafe mee the comfort of his holy Spirit, that I may patiently indure this crosse and affliction which he hath laid upon me."

A Petition as soone granted as desired. Nay, I may say as it is in the Prophet, *Antequam clament, ego exaudiam*—God heard his prayer long before it was framed in this place. For from the first beginning of his sicknesse, hee was indued with such a *Spartana patientia,* well knit patience, that some of his Reverend brethren, comming purposely to comfort him, professed they found more comfort from him then they could bring; and though hee might truly say with David, *I am weary of my groning,* and *Every night wash I my bed with teares,* yet never did any impatient murmure (it was a religious boast in the Lord uttred by himselfe) breake from his lips against that high hand which had so long humbled him: neither did that *Petra, rocke-stony,* disease grow so fast within him, but his Christian resolution hardened as fast, and his faith, built as firmly on the true Rocke of his Salvation, Christ Jesus, with the Invocation of which Name hee began and ended the day, using most frequently those words of Saint Paul, *Cupio dissolvi, & esse cum Christo*: I desire to bee dissolved.

[Esa.65:24] [67] [Psal.6:6] [Phil.1:23]

But before he loosed from this shore, considering hee was bound for a long voyage, he was not unmindful first to take in *Viaticum animæ,** the holy Sacrament; which hee professed in the presence of some especiall friends, his wife, children, and family, appoynted by his owne invitation to accompany him to that feast, as Christ to his Disciples: *his soule had greatly longed to eate that last Supper,* and to performe that supreme Christian duty before he left them. Yea, hee so hungred and thirsted after that Bread of life and that Cup of salvation, that though all solid sustenance was become odious to his palate, now quite disabled from taking it downe, yet he professed duty and Religion should prevaile above his weaknesse, and he would force himselfe to eate that sacred Bread, which as it was the first he had in many dayes before tasted, so was it the last. His Chaplaine ministred to him, who (let me not omit) having read the Confession for that purpose, was by him commanded to reade it over againe. Having happily accomplished this service in all our hearings, he *gave thanks to God, that hee had lived to finish that blessed worke* (it was his owne speech) and after a short prayer, conceived by himselfe, hee dismissed the company.

Sir Henry Martin his [68] *Chancelor, M.Matthias Caldicot, M. Philip King his Brother, John King his second Sonne, and my self,&c.* Luk. 22:15

Doctor Cluet, Archdeacon of Middlesex

[69]

Such was his devout preparation, and so long did he observe the tedious Vigils before the festivall of his dismission. His day of Rest was now come, which, as if reserved by God's favour, was that very day his Saviour dyde on, Good Friday; & that time of the day when our whole Church was exercised in prayer, according to the custome of that Day (neere eleven of the clocke in the forenoone); as if he had stayed to take the helpe and advantage of good men's devotion to set him forward—a day which might incite Prophets and Patriarkes to desire to end on, being truly *Dies meus* (as Christ said), *My Day*: a good and blessed day, and of all others most proper to crown and dignifie the end of good men.

John 8:56

Drawing now fast to his end, and ready to hoyse saile for another World, he requests the valediction of our prayers at the parting. Our obedience forthwith actuated his wil: straight was his bed incompassed with mournful Clients, ready to offer up a religious Violence to heaven for his sake. First, he expresly causeth his Chaplaine, now his ghostly Father, to reade the Confession and Absolution, according to the ordinary forme of Common prayer in our Liturgie. Which ended, and our prayers having taken a short truce, as awaiting somewhat now from him, he bids the curtains to be quite throwne open, and whilest we kneeled (not unmindfull of his Episcopall office), to shew

[70]

---

*Food for the soul's voyage,

80 THE SERMONS TO 1627

<small>Deut.11:29</small> hee was not so exhausted but hee had yet One Blessing in store, hee distributes a benediction round about, to every one of us there present; so that his Bed was now like the Mount Garrizim, from each corner whereof a Blessing resounded.

His speech here felt a stop, but neither our Prayers, nor His understanding; for testimony whereof, desired by his Chaplaine to make some signe his heart went along with us and tooke the <small>(2 Kings 2:11) [71]</small> same course our Prayers poynted out, with a most speedy hasted elevation of Hands he expressed that his Heart, like Elias before the Charriot, yet kept pace with us, though his tongue could not; and though he wanted Organs to ejaculate his Prayers, the ejaculation of his eyes, darted up to <small>Acts 7:55</small> Heaven, now supplied that want. There they yet fixt, as if eyther he had with Stephen *beheld the Heavens opening* for his admittance, or meant to marke that place whither his Soule now bended, or else that his Body was emulous to have gone along with it. For we might perceive that (like the <small>Joh.20:4</small> *two Disciples* that *ranne to the Sepulcher:* they both ranne to seeke Christ, but that *Other Disciple outranne Peter*) the Soule, too swift for the Bodie, left it behind.

<small>Joh.19:40</small> And yet that followed with the best speed it could make and *ligatum linteis,* wound up in a bare winding sheete (as far from superstitious Pompe after it wanted breath as himselfe ever was, whilest <small>[72]</small> he had breath to reproove it in others or to forbid it in himselfe),* *Introivit monumentum,* came unto its Sepulchre, his corps being borne thither by men of eminent degree and worth in our <small>Act.8:2 [b]</small> Church—like those who carried Stephen to his grave (Act. 8:2)—the very even before that blessed morning wherein those two Disciples came to Christ's. This difference betwixt their Epitaphs: on Christ's Grave, *Resurrexit:* hee is risen; on this Servant of Christ's: *Resurgam,* I shall rise; and in the meane, rest in assured hope to bee partaker of the Resurrection of the just.

There now, committed to the Earth by that Reverend and most Orthodox Prelate, in Religion and <small>Where also was present the Lord Bishop of Ely.</small> learning equally absolute, my Lord Bishop of Coventrie and Lichfield (who concluded the last Act of the intire affection mutually borne betwixt them living by honouring his dead Corpes with rites of Buriall), doth it peaceably rest: and let me heere rest. For in my owne particular, it must ever be a <small>[73]</small> part of my Prayer (and it is a wish I would not be so unthriftie to venter but upon good assurance nor settle it elsewhere): *Sic mihi contingat vivere, sicque mori:* May my course of life be such, and <small>2 King.2</small> may my end be like his. Or if it be too much ambition for me to crave *Eliah's spirit,* that is, to live like Him, an humbler Boone shall content me, to possesse his Mantle: that is, to Dye in the profession of that Protestant Faith in which he did.

I have touched upon a sad string, a subject to which affection and sense is quick; I could not <small>Homer *Odyss.*</small> lesse in pietie then *epikterea ktereisthai,* as Telemachus to his Father, or as the Latines: *Parentalia perficere*—perform my last Parentall Dutie and act these *Justa,* Rites (though not *Exequias,* Funeralls) to His memorie, which will longer survive in the brests of good men. Nor could I more then in this sort *Parentare iniuriis*—out of so just a provocation as *wrong done to a Father,* take that temperate Revenge of a Slanderer as to disproove him. My Speech here findes a *Deliquium* and <small>[74] (Phil.1:23)</small> *Cupit dissolvi*—labours in the period. Suffer it to gaspe a few minutes, and it suddainely expires.

Let no man doubt or waver, or think the worse of *Religion,* for that so noted a Professor is traduced. These are stale tricks with our Adversaries, since it hath been long their practice, like the *Lunaticke* in Athenaeus, ever wont to stand upon the Key of the Cittie if any fayre Shippe of rich <small>Acts 9:15</small> burthen (any noted *Ekenos ekloges*—vessell fraught with knowledge and true profession of the Gospell) had made to the Haven, to crie, *It is theirs, it is theirs!* Againe, let no man be confirmed that this Scandall is true, because they so peremptorily beleeve it. Such is their impious Credulitie, that it is grown a Maxime among them to beleeve any thing, were it never so false, were it Contradiction, so it made any way for them. For those very tongues which out of malice gave out,

---

*He commanded in his Will, his body to be buried in the Cathedrall Church of S. Paul, without any Pompe or solemnities, onely with a Tombestone with this Inscription, *Resurgam.*

in time of his sicknesse, That through impatience he had offred violence to himselfe, those very same, after his death, out of the abundance of their Romish charitie, would perswade the world he died Reconciled unto their Synagogue—for I may not call it *Church,* unlesse it be *Ecclesia malignantium, Ecclesia maledicentium.* Nor let this Lye proove more authenticke because *Printed;* that rather discredits and weakens it, and you have now more cause to suspect it then before. It is a ground in their Religion that *Unwritten traditions have more authority then written Scriptures.* And if so, why should not we take them at their word and make as slight and scornefull reckoning of their writings as they of God's? [75]

Canus *Loc.lib.3 cap. 3[a]*

Lastly, that none may wonder or be perplexed, or through a nice misprision suspect there could not but bee some ground for this farre-blowne *Calumnie,* let him but *Remember the word that Christ sayd* and what He Suffered, and then all wonder will end in satisfaction. For who can thinke it strange that Christ's servants are slandered when Hee, their Lord and Master, could not avoyd the poysoned breath of *Slander*? If His Innocence had no protection but that He on no ground at all was belyed by malicious tongues, surely on as little ground will they belie any Disciple of His: *For the Servant is not greater then his Lord.* And (saith Christ) *If they have persecuted me, they will also persecute you.* [76]

Why then, Let it satisfie all the world and his owne fame that this (now dead) *Disciple hath had but the same fate and usage his Master had.*

Matth.10:25

It is the glory of Imitation to counterfeit the life, and *Art* is most proper, when it most resembles *Nature.* The Apostles were but Copies drawne from Christ; their perfection, therefore, must needs be greatest who come neerest to the Originall. And that *Disciple* is a true Disciple who learnes not the Lesson but the *Master,* not only suffers for Him but in degree and qualitie as like as may be to Him. This is truly *Discere Christum*: to learne Christ; this is *Induere Dominum Jesum*: to put on the Lord Jesus; this is to *Partake the sufferings of Christ.* They who durst partake his sorrowes shall share with Him in joyes; they that are *sicut in terra,* shall be also *sicut in cœli,* For so hath the Spirit assured us. *Si compatimur, conregnabimus: If wee suffer with him in earth, we shall raigne with him in Heaven.* Behold, a voyce hath bid me write, *Blessed are ye, when men revile and persecute you, and say all manner of evill for my Name's sake falsely: Rejoyce and be glad, great is your reward in Heaven.*

[77] *(Rom.13:14)*

(2 Tim 2:12)
It was the Motto of his Episcopall Seale

Matth.5:11,12

TO THE READER

[L3v]

How little I affect to be in Print needs no Apologie to any who either know already it was the desire of some my most Honourable friends, whose intreaties were commands to me, or but consider the subject which first set me a worke, a Slandered and traduced Father: unto whom duty and necessity urged me to doe this right. And I cleerly professe, if a true relation of his end may doe him right, I have faithfully performed it, and have given the world so just an account of Him, as if I should have made my conscience' last shrift to God. Whether I have uprightly stewarded his honour and my owne faith, I leave to the strict judgement of any who are able to distinguish colours and discerne Truth from Imposture; being confident as innocence can make a man that none are able to disallow the reckoning. *Si vera dicam, Deus testis; si mentiar, Deus vindex.**

As therefore the acquitting of His integrity was the prime motive which entred me into this Quarrell, so now the clearing of my owne fidelity was a secondary motive for the publication of it. First, that they might not thinke, by false alarms and the confused outcries of Report, to beare downe a good cause, or so easily to triumph in their supposed victory as if none durst affront them, I thought good in the meane time thus on the sudden to checke the rumour, till haply some more deliberate pen (which they shall not long or vainely expect) may quite race it out. And though this

---

*If I shall tell the truth, God will be my witness; if I lie, my avenger.

byrth of mine were more hastily formed, I hope it will not be untimely, for *Truth never knew abortion,* but like a starre newly risen to discovery, hath its being of old, though the observation was but late and moderne.

[L4] Secondly, to let those calumnious tongues who gave out my Revolt also, as well as my Father's (both true alike), know I have not yet so doted on their part, or dis-affected my owne, as to leave my *Countrey* or *Religion;* nor, I thinke, ever shall, except my understanding, wits, and above all, the Grace of God leave me, or their persuasions have the same power over me as Mercurie's had over Sosias, that they can make me beleeve *Ego non sum Ego:* I am not the Son of such a Father. And what in this case, on my owne behalfe, I write, is likewise avowed on behalfe of my second brother, JOHN KING, entred into the same orders as my selfe; who also had his share in this lewd imputation as well as my selfe; for we are not more brothers in nature then (by God's mercy) in this resolution.

Thirdly, to take the liberty of adding and explicating some remarkeable circumstances which better become a Margin then a speech.

Lastly, that though the slander hath hitherto got the start, the Detection might at last be set in a course to overtake it. Which taske *Sermo transiens,* a Sermon pronounced, could not so throwly effect, except it were also *Sermo inscriptis,* written. A course no way improper, for *A Writer is in some sort a Preacher: though* his *tongue* be silent, his *Pen* preaches, and a Sermon preached from the *Presse* sometimes edifies so much the more then from the *Pulpit,* by how much the Report is carried further. So that the audience, which before was but *Parochiall,* or at most Provinciall, may be this meanes grow more Generall and (as it were) *Œcumenicall.*

Gerson *De laude script. consider. 1.*

And now, having committed it to the view of all men, I will not prejudicate or doubtfully forestall the beliefe of any. I make no question but all will rest satisfied, except those wayward dispositions who are *resolved afore-hand not to be satisfied at all,* having banished all reason from them without hope of repeale. Such, though unwillingly, I must leave to their owne hardened obstinacy—*Stultos iubeo esse libenter:* and suffer fooles gladly, that will be so against my consent.

[L4v]

If they can yet flatter themselves with any advantage this fiction may affoord them, I shall not envie them that Paradise into which their fond imagination hath put them. I rather pitty the poore shifts they are driven to, for the keeping of their weather-beaten Cause a-float. All the harme I wish them is, that they would leave off this thredbare trade of Calumny, especially towards the Dead, grow better acquainted with speaking and writing the Truth, and not conversing with her at such a distance as now they doe. Or if they will needs be *Architecti mendaciorum,* still hammering untruths, I would advize them to lay probable foundations, and chuse such *Materials* as are more malleable and (in the world's esteeme) not so impossible for them to worke upon as He they have heere selected. For every wood will not make a Mercury, nor is every good man a fit mould to cast Them a Convert in.

Farewell.
H.K.

ACT

DAVID'S ENLARGEMENT

PSAL. 32. VERS. 5

I said I will confess my sinnes (or transgressions) unto the Lord. And thou forgavest the iniquitie of my sinne.

Act 83

This Text hath two generall parts: The first records *David's Repentance*. The second, *God's mercy* to him.

The former part contains these severall circumstances:
1. *A resolution: I said.*
2. *The Act resolv'd upon:* Confession—*I will confesse.*
3. The *Subject* of that confession: *Sinnes or transgressions.*
4. Their *pluralitie* or the *Extent of his confession:* not *sinne,* but *sinnes*—A terme implying both their generality and number. For although the *Septuagint* read *anomian,* the Hebrew is *sinnes.* [2]
5. Their *propriety,* which he assumes to himselfe: *Mea, my sinnes.*
6. He specifies the *Confessor: unto the Lord.*

In the latter part, I onely observe two circumstances.
1. the *Readinesse, and Propension, and speed* of God's mercy. *He sayes he will confesse,* &c. and presently, *Tu remisisti: Thou forgavest.*
2. *his Bounty,* set downe in such terms as may convey unto him the most liberall pardon: *Iniquitatem peccati,* the very formality of the *Sin*—not *my sinne,* but the *Iniquity of my sinne too,* both the Act, and the Obliquity; both the Guilt of the sinne, and the Punishment due unto it.

The contemplation of a religious worke doth much affect a good man, and howsoever the Act onely crownes him, yet the purpose delights him. *I was glad* (said David) *when men said unto me, we will go into the house of the Lord.* See with what pious Alacrity he utters his intentions to an Act of Religion: it doth him good but to speake of it. And here you may discerne as much Alacrity in his intended repentance, when he records the very determination, that which at first was either barely design'd by his thoughts or at most but said: *I said.*

1.
I said
(Ps. 122:1)

Words in God's Method are the Introduction to Deeds: His *Fiat* was the Seminary of all being, for *he said onely, and it was done.* That man who sayes well is engaged to equall his words; else like a Bankrupt, he forfaits that good opinion his pretences and speeches had wonne. St. Augustine sayes *Verba sunt folia: Words are as leaves;* and in good trees, leaves are the pledges of fruit that ensues. He that onely speakes, and does not, is not a fruitfull Christian; rather he is like a Sycomor, whose issue is nothing but a leafe. This is not enough. *Fructus quæritur* (saith the same Father): God expects from us what David here exhibites—*fruit, not leafe,* or not leafe without fruit. He sayes devoutly, and from those seeds, a repentance to a new life springs: *I said, I will confess,* &c. It is a *Deliberation,* or it signifies as much as *Decernere, Constituere: to purpose* or *to resolve.*

(Ps. 33:9)
[3]
Aug. *Serm.5 de verb Dom.*

Marlorat
Lorinus

Resolutions are the Moulds wherein Actions are cast; and no man can define a Deed better then to call it the effect of what our purpose had contrived. And every purpose is a silent Dialogue betwixt the Soule and her Faculties, by whose consent that which we resolve is established. For man is a *Theater,* wherein are many subtile spectators, waiting upon every action. He is a short Modell of a *Common-wealth:* Each Sense is an Agent, each Faculty an Officer. Hee hath his Common-Pleas in his Common Sense; his Chancery in the Conscience; he hath his Projectors, and those as busie as the State hath any—Thought and Phantasie, and the quicke Imagination. The Memory is his Recorder; and lastly, the Tongue is the Speaker in this Assembly, who reports those Acts which are designed: *I said.*

[4]

But our Intents doe not always come to publication, nay, they do not always need it; and then the office of the tongue is not required. A resolution may sometimes speake without the Organs of utterance; it may be intelligible, it may be audible, and yet not vocall, as Saint Ambrose speakes of Susanna: *Conscientia loquebatur ubi vox non audiebatur.**

Ambros. *Offic. lib. 1. cap. 3*

In religious purposes that determine in God, and in which there is no parties interested but God and the soule, there is no necessity to use words. Words are but the Interpreters of our mindes one to another, but as Midwives that deliver our thoughts; and however betwixt Man and Man this verball trafficke be necessary, yet betwixt us and God, that sees our thoughts before the tongue

---

*Conscience spoke where no voice was heard.

TWO
SERMONS.

VPON THE ACT SVNDAY, BEING the 10th of Iuly. 1625.

Deliuered at S.t Maries in Oxford.

PSAL. 133. 1.
Behold how good, and how pleasant it is, for brethren to dwell together in vnitie.

OXFORD,
Printed by I. L. and W. T. for WILLIAM TVRNER.
Anno Dom. 1625.

DAVID'S ENLARGEMENT.

THE MORNING SERMON ON THE ACT SVNDAY.

Preached by HENRY KING, Inceptor in Diuinity, one of his MAIESTIES Chaplaines in Ordinary.

PSAL. 18.36.
Thou haſt enlarged my ſteps vnder mee, that my feet did not ſlip.

hath formed them into syllables or set the stampe of language upon them, it is not so. He reades us in the power of speech, and not onely in the Organs which actuate that power: Hee is the *cardiognōstês, so well acquainted with the heart* that he dictates to it, as it doth to the tongue. And therefore, hee that understands our words whilest they are *in Principiis*, in their conception and parentage, whilest they are yet *Intra causas*, lodged and couched *within their causes*—(as Saint Augustine expresseth it: *Vox mea nondum in ore erat, & auris Dei iam in Corde erat*)*—He, I say, that knowes our thoughts, not onely before we utter them in words, but before wee our selves know what we shall next thinke, cannot need a *Dixi, I said,* to informe him of our purposes. Since his intelligence precedes our thoughts, hee cannot but take his information from them, better then from our words; and so the sense of the Text will hold as well in a *Cogitavi* (as one Translation of ours reades it: *I thought* I will confesse) as in a *Dixi, I said.* For in God's apprehension they are all one, and no way distinguisht, save in a little Priority of time; for *thoughts* are words' elder Brothers, and the Dialect they speake is our Mother tongue, the originall language of Mankinde which never yet suffered confusion.

[5]

When the tongues were dispersed at Babel, the thoughts were not; and howsoever each Nation be distinguished in his peculiar speech, we all thinke alike; even as anger and laughter have the same wayes of expression in all parts of the world. So that this *Dixi* was not so much the language of David's Tongue, as of his Heart, *Corde pronunciare erat: He spake* unto God *in his Thoughts*, which are the most constant, most unalterable dialect, and therefore most proper to expresse the certainty of that Act which followes upon this Resolution in the next part, His confession: *I said I will confesse, &c.*

(Gen.11:9)

Aug. *In Psal.32*

Sinne is the weightest of all sorrowes. The Apostle calls it *kat' exochên, The thing that presseth downe*. 'Tis the heaviest calamity man can suffer under: *Iniquitates meæ gravatæ sunt super me,* cryes the Psalmist: *Mine iniquities over-burden me.* Our blessed Saviour was so sensible of this weight, that in his fearefull conflict in the garden he profest *His soule was heavy unto death.* They were our sinnes which so deprest his invincible patience that he sweats, and that unnaturally, in the bearing of them. And in his complaint, where he puts the sorrowes of the whole world in ballance against his owne—*See all ye that passe by, if ever sorrow were like my sorrow*—the reason of that *Non sicut* [not like], which turned the ballance on his side, was because the sinne of Mankinde lay in his scale, which like a Mine of Lead (or as Zachary stiles it, *Talentum plumbi*)† out-weighed all the rest. Now as sometimes a sad story lightens the heart of him that told it, and sorrowes finde ease by the relation; so doe sinnes: *Est aliquid fatale malum per verba levare.*‡

2. *I will confesse*
Heb.12:1
Psal.32:4
[6]

Lament.1:12

Zach.5:7

(Ovid Tristia 5.1.59)

He that hath opportunity to unfold his griefe hath made the first approach to comfort, and he that hath the Grace to acknowledge his fault is in a ready way to pardon. There is no affliction so great as his that wants a tongue to utter it, and there is no sinne of such a desperate malignity as the silent sinne, when the Offender is dumbe and speechlesse. *A misery lodg'd in the heart* is like an Exhalation inclosed within the Earth, which shakes the foundation of Reason and Patience; or like a dampe, it *overlayes the Spirits: Strangulat inclusus dolor.* But when it hath found an issue by the Eye to weepe out at, or a vent by the tongue, streight it growes tamer. When once a window is opened to give it Aire, that fume which would have stifled us breathes out, & cleares the roome.

(Ovid Tristia 5.1.63)

[7]

Such a Meteore, such a boysterous Exhalation is sinne. What strange convulsions doth it cause within the soule? How doth it contract our hopes of Mercy, and like an East-winde dry up and wither our comforts? What stormes, what guilty conflicts, what blacke cloudes of despaire doth it raise in the Conscience? But so soone as a sinner recollects himselfe, is brought to a remorse, how calmely is the storme allayed by a religious contrition! how sweetly doth this cloud discharge it

---

*My voice was not yet in my mouth, yet the ear of the Lord was already in my heart.
†A weight [Greek measure] of lead.
‡It is something to relieve a deadly evil by words.

selfe when it relents into a showre of penitent teares! For 'tis the most naturall way for *sinne to evaporate by the eye* (as Elias Cretensis sayes). Lastly, how gently doth this dangerous vapour breathe out by a devout confession—*I said, I will confesse*!

Our Lawes so farre prejudicate silence in a malefactour that waves the ordinary and open way of tryall that they account him a Fellon against himselfe, a conspiratour against his own life, and guilty of his owne bloud; holding him worthy of no death but such an one as, like a monument of shame, serves to object his silent contumacy: As if it meant to crush out and, by weighty expressions, force the confession of that fact from the dead body, which no perswasion could winne from the conscience whilst the party yet lived.

David himselfe professes, that whilst he remained speechlesse, he found a great abatement in his comforts, a generall consumption wasting both his body and minde too: *When I held my tongue my bones consumed—Quoniam non protuli ore confessionem ad salutem, omnis firmitas mea in infirmitate consenuit** (so Saint Augustine paraphrases him). Thus you see his silence corrodes and macerates him even to the bone; but so soone as he opens his mouth and disguises not his sinne, straight he findes a spatious enlargement, in the forgivenesse of all his sinnes. One sayes rightly that sinne is the *disease of the soule, an Epedemicall sickenesse whereof the whole world labours.* There is nothing so pernicious to this Malady (saith another Father) as silence: *Silence foments and cherishes the infirmitie.* Therefore, by the rules of cure, nothing can be more medicinable than Confession, Which (in Origen's phrase) is *vomitus sordium,* a clearing the Conscience of those vitious obstructions which nourish the soule's diseases, distempering the Complexion of our Faith so as we grow cold in Religion; and either want appetite to serve God, or capacity to learne his Law, or heate of zeale to concoct what we have learned, or palate to taste the comforts which wee should find in applying God's mercy unto us. [8] *(Ps. 32:)* Verse 3

Aug. *In Psal.32:3*

Ambrosius

So that there is not such a speedy redresse of Sinne as a penitent confession. Yet not such a Confession as the Church of Rome would submit us to, which is (to use Cassander's words) a racking or *torturing the Conscience,* which no wise man would endure, *no reasonable man approve.* Indeed those on that side have made this, which Christ intended the happy instrument of our peace with God, as the *Master-key* to open into all the secrets of Christendome: as a *Picklock* to possesse them of these mysteries of State whose knowledge hath troubled, nay endangered, all parts of the World where the Romish colours have bin advanced—A tyrannicall way of knowledge, to make the Practitioners feared and hated at once. 'Tis justly theirs: *Scire volunt secreta domus, atque inde timeri*†—A curious *Engine* wherewith they wring out any small designe that may make against them, under paine of Damnation if it be not declared; but take a libertie to seale up in secrecy any Deed, though never so horrid (be it Murther or Treason), so advantagious to their cause. And this though the Confessor knowes, being put to his Oathe, he may lawfully sweare he doth not, since *he knowes it only as a secret, but not to reveale:* they are the very words of Franciscus à Victoria. Cassand. *Consult., art.11*
[9]

Juvenal
(3.113)

Artic *184,pag.96b[a]*

I doe not here derogate from the use of Confession, for by the Churche's appointment, we practice a forme of publique Confession in our Liturgie. Nay, in this place we finde a Private Confession, made by David unto the Lord, which is no lesse necessary for us then him. 'Tis against that Auricular Confession of Rome I here speake, which so clogges our Christian Liberty that it layes a *necessity* upon us to confesse unto the Preist, or else denies us our salvation. And besides the necessity layed upon us, it tyes us to an *impossibility,* exacting the particular enumeration of all the Sinnes & several sorts of Offences whereof we are guiltie—a taske which the Prophet David utterlie declines, appealing from this unjust imposition in the words of the Psalme, *Who knowes how oft he offends? Lord cleanse me from my secret sinnes.* [10]

Psal. 19:12

---

*Since I have not brought forth of my mouth a confession, for salvation, all my strength has grown weak with infirmity.
†They wish to learn the secrets of the house, and thence to be feared.

Let the other side, then, for the countenance of their way of Confession, urge that Embassie addrest to Charles the Fift from the Governours of Norimberg, touching the reviving and re-establishing of Auricular Confession amongst them, upon a pretence that since that custome was left off, their Common-wealth swarm'd with sinne much more then formerly. Which proposition of theirs the Emperour in effect did but scoffe at and deride (even by the Confession of Lorinus the Jesuite, who reports it), Intimating unto them that they would never have sought so much at his hands, but that it seem'd they wanted a sufficient engine to examine Malefactors: supposing that the Ecclesiasticall Rack, when the Preist should undertake them in an Auricular Confession, would make them discover more then the politicke Rack, or all the tortures the publicke Executioner could give them.

<small>Lorinus *Com. in Psal.32*</small>

Let them object to us, as Eugenius the Fourth, in the Councell at Florence, did to the Greekes: *Why doe not your Preists exact this Confession?* As we refuse not private Confession made to God, nay sometimes a *private Confession* to our ghostly Father the Minister, who hath authoritie to divest us of any scruples which may arise in our Consciences, and to pronounce an *Absolution* upon our hearty *Repentance:* Yet we will not loose or betray our Freedome so much as to do that Act by *constraint* which ought to be as *free and voluntary* as David's resolution in this place: *I said, I will confesse.* We have no reason to stand to the courtesie of Rome for that Pardon which Christ hath freely given us; nor yet to suffer her *Merchants* to erect a new Staple, or put an Impost upon our salvation, which is exempt from all Custome, from any acknowledgement, save onely to Christ, whose worke it was. We have no cause but to be very well assured that we may be saved without *Auricular Confession;* since in that sacred Booke which, we beleeve, contains all that may conduce to our salvation, we finde no tracke or mention of it.

[11]

Bonaventure grants that however the Formall part of Confession, the power of Absolution, were instituted by Christ, yet the Materiall part, which is the Detection of the sinne and the necessity of disclosing it, was not so. For at the most, it was onely insinuated by Christ, but promulgated by St. James: *Confesse your sinnes one to another.* In which place (as Bullinger well inferres), they that understand aright will finde a reciprocall obligation layed upon the Preist to confesse to the People, as well as the People to the Preist. And for any better Evidence then this to confirme their opinion out of the Gospell, I am confident they have none. We finde when our Saviour cleansed the Leper, hee had him *goe and shew himselfe to the Priest,* and *offer the gift which Moses commanded,* but he bad him not *confesse to the Priest.* And to the adulterous woman, he gives a *Vade: Goe,* but not to any Confessor. Nay, we finde no Confession taken from her by himselfe: the whole Condition of her Absolution in that place is *Vade, & noli amplius peccare—Goe, and sinne no more.*

<small>*Ad Sentent.lib.4, quæst.17.distinct.3*
Ja.5:16
Bullinger *Decad. 4,ser.2 de poenitent.*
[12]
Mat.8:4
(Levit. 14:2)
(Jn. 8:11)</small>

But Eckius and others answere that the power of Absolution was not as yet assign'd over by Christ unto his Church, and therefore our Saviour neither practised it himselfe, nor sent them unto any Priest: which, had it been, 'tis likely he would have done. Well then, graunt him as much as he alleadgeth, that the Commission to Absolve was not as yet given to the Apostles; and it shall appeare that in those very words wherein Christ conveyes this Authority to them, Auricular Confession receives its deathe's wound.

In the Gospell of St. John, when he tels them *As my Father sent me, so send I you,* Hee there gives them authority to *remit or to retaine sinnes,* but not to exact any Auricular Confession. Hee doth not there erect any Tribunall for the Priests, where they should sit as Judges over men's Consciences, to acquite or condemne at their pleasure. This is not the meaning of *to Remit* and *to Retaine.* They do not import a *Judiciary power* (as the Church of Rome unwarrantably assumes), but a *Ministeriall power,* to publish the mercies of God to repentant Sinners, and to denounce his vengeance against the obstinate and impenitent. This is St. Jerome's Interpretation upon those words *Quicquid ligaveris in terris, &c.—whatsover thou shalt bind on earth shall be bound in Heaven, and whatsoever thou shalt loose,&c.—*where he says that, as the Leviticall Priest is said to make the Leper cleane or uncleane because he pronounced him so, even thus the Evangelicall

<small>John 20:21
[13]
Hieron.*In Mat. 16:19*</small>

Priests in the Gospell Remit or Retaine sinnes because in their preachings they declare which sinnes are remitted, and which retained by God. Even thus Peter Lombard, distinguishing God's way of Binding and Loosing from the Churche's, sayes that God by himselfe remits sinnes, who cleanseth the Soule from all spots, and looseth it from the Debt of eternall Damnation; but he hath not granted this to his Priests: to whom notwithstanding, hee hath given power of *Binding and Loosing,* that is, of *shewing men to be bound or loosed.* Pet.Lombard *Lib.4.Dist.18*

Thus you may see by how unjust a Title the Church of Rome would usurpe a Dominion over men's Consciences (as she pretends a Soveraignty over the world), ayming at Supremacy in all; Either wilfully, or ignorantly, mistaking our Saviour's Commission for Binding and Loosing (as Hierome complaines): *Istum locum Episcopi & Presbyteri non intelligentes, aliquid sibi de Pharisæorum assumunt supercilio,* &c.* Loco citato [14]

Let me but mention to you likewise upon what slight pretences they ground their *necessity of Auricular Confession,* cosening the ignorant people with that smooth and plausible imposture wherein they say the Priest cannot remit sinnes unlesse he know them, and he cannot know them unlesse men will confesse them unto him. Then which Proposition nothing can be more false. For the Priest may Preach and Publish Remission or Retention of sinnes to those whose faults he knowes not: And those men, by a faithfull application of what they heare, may receive the Remission of their sinnes, who never revealed them to the Minister, but confessed them unto God alone. Which way of Confession *is truely and onely necessary unto Salvation—I said, I will confesse my sinnes unto the Lord.* Richardus à Sancto Victore *De Clavibus*

But I urge this point no farther: Cassander's temperate conclusion shall bring me off; I am of opinion (saith he) There had beene no Controversie about this point of Confession, had not some ignorant and importunate Physitians corrupted this wholesome Medicine with their drugges of Tradition: *By which meanes they have made it onely a snare to entangle and involve the simple; and an Engine to torment, not to ease, the Conscience of those that seeke unto them.* We, for our parts, hold *Confession necessary,* though we lay *no necessity* upon men *to confesse to the Priest;* nor doe we prohibit that in some cases. Nay, we account it an happy discharge of a troubled soule to impart it selfe to the Minister of Christ, from whose lippes he may receive such spirituall Comforts as his Office can minister and the Scripture allowes. Ever provided that this be left indifferent to the penitent, to doe or not to doe as he thinkes good; that it be not a constrained, but a voluntary Act, as David's here, freely arising from his owne inclination: *I said I will confesse.* Cassander *Consult.Art.11* [15]

The Greeke is, '*exagoreusō kat'emou, I will declare or confesse against myselfe:* So that this Act is an Accusation rather then a Confession. 'Tis true that every confession of a sinne is an Inditement of the Sinner; and yet is this such a kinde of tryall as serves to acquite, not to condemne: *In Confessione, sui accusatio, Dei laudatio est.*† In the course of our Law, the Malefactor's Confession is the strongest evidence, and casts him without any other Verdict: but in God's Courts, to pleade guilty is the way to procure an Absolution. He that at the Barre of his owne Conscience arraignes himselfe in this World, shall never be arraigned at the Tribunall of the Great Judge in the next: *If wee would Judge ourselves, wee should not be judged.* Dorotheus writes of a devout man, that being askt which was the best course to come unto God, replyed, *ever to accuse one's selfe.* Let me therefore use the Prophet Esaye's words: *Do thou first declare thine iniquities, that thou mayst be justified.* He bids thee be so early in the acknowledgement of thy faults (saith Origen) *that thou maist prevent the Devill, who is ever ready to accuse thee.* In doing thus, wee disarme our old Enemy, and take away the sting of his malitious accusations, which have no power to hurt us, since by condemning ourselves, we have saved our selves. I end in Saint Augustine's words: *Confesse* Aug.*Ser.8.de Verb.Dom.*

1 Cor.11:31
[16] Dorotheus *Doctrin.7*
Esay 43:26
Origen *Homil.3 in Levit.*

Aug. *In Psal.29*

---

*Not understanding that position of priest and bishop, they take to themselves something of the superciliousness of the Pharisees.
†In confession, accusation of self is praise of God.

what thou hast done against God, and then thou shalt, to thy comfort, confesse what God hath done for thee. Thou shalt have cause with David thankefullie to commemorate God's favour in a *Tu remisisti,* in the forgivenesse of thy sinnes: *I said, I will confesse my sinnes.*

<small>3.
Sinnes

Juvenal [9.*103*]
Ecclesiast.10:20 [17]
Gen.4:10 Job 20:27

Habac.2:*11*</small>

Sinne is a loud argument, which if it want other tongues, will relate it selfe. Should a man bee silent, it would by guilty confessions betray it selfe. Sinne is the worst secret that can be. I know no bosome where it is safe. There is no creature, no element, no privation, night nor silence, but is able to pursue and detect a sinner: *Servi ut taceant, iumenta loquentur.** Beasts have a verdict to passe upon wicked men: *A bird of the aire shall carry the voice, and tell the matter.* Earth will cry Cain guiltie, or if earth doe not, *Heaven will reveale the iniquity.* If both be silent, yet *the very stones out of the wall* (within which the sin was acted) *shall cry against him, and the beame out of the Tymber* (like a double witnes) *shall answere it.*

<small>Nilus Martyr
Parænes.99</small>

Doe not therefore flatter thy selfe in the closenes of thy transgressions. What ever disguises night, complying with thy darke purposes, may put upon thee, there is nothing can disguise thee from thy Maker. Canst thou be so stupified, so besotted in thy sinne, as to suppose when other eyes behold thee not, God doth not? Thinkest thou, by drawing a Curtaine about thy Bed, or by putting out a candle in thy Chamber, to hide thine incontinencie from God, or darken his knowledge? Foole, thou canst not! Thou bearest a Lampe in thine owne brest, thy conscience; that is *luchnos* (saith Nilus), *a watching Candle,* that burnes at midnight, and will light the Judge to descry thee. Or if that taper burne dimmely, if it have wasted into a snuffe, so that thou hast no Conscience, or but a seared one, which lies smothering in the socket, and can onely glimmer, not shine; why yet, God is (as Basil saith) *holophthalamos, all eye,* to survey thee. Or if thy transgressions have made thee so loath'd an Object that he will not looke upon thee, should he examine thy cabinet friends upon whose secrecy thou relyest, the silence and the darkenes of the night, they would turne Traytors to thee and discover thee to him: *Night would convert it selfe into a Noone, and Silence prove a speaking evidence against thee.* Since therefore thou canst lurke under no concealment, why doest thou not confesse that which it is impossible for thee to hide? Why deferrest thou to resolve with David, *I will confesse my sinnes?* If thou confesse not thy sinnes, they will confesse thee the greater sinner: And if thou wilt not owne them here, in a religious acknowledgment, they will owne thee hereafter, in a finall Condemnation.

<small>[18]
Leo Ser. 5 de Quadrages</small>

<small>4.
Their plurality: Sinnes

Act.5:3</small>

This plurall, *sinnes* or *transgressions,* as it implies our many alliances to sinne, and the multiplicitie of our sinnes, Actuall and Intentionall, so it admonisheth us to confesse them all. God, as he is a franck pardoner, so he loves a liberall confession, wherein nothing should be kept back. Yet (not to perplex any man with the strict enumeration of every crime, as the Papists require) I confesse the wilfull keeping back of sinnes may be as dangerous as Ananias his deteining part of the price. But for all that, thy condition is not damnable (as Rome perswades) though thou hast forgot some sinnes which thou hast done, if so be thou slightest none of those which thou remembrest.

<small>[19]

Senec.
Dorotheus Doctrin.7
Vers.5
Psal.62:8</small>

It is the Doctrine of the Church of Rome that some sinnes are such diminutives, such Peccadillo's, so small, so veniall, they are not worth a mention, nor doe they need a pardon; But doe not thou beleeve so. This negligent extenuation of faults is as pernicious a sinne as any—A presumption unheard of amongst the Fathers of the Primitive Church: Who (if we will credit Dorotheus) were wont to *keep a reckoning, & to aske God pardon for the very least and slightest offences* of which they were at any time conscious. David in this Psalme, in the preceding words, frees himselfe of all suspition of concealment or palliation of his faults: *Mine iniquity I have not hid.* And Psalme the 61: he summons all, in a generall exhortation, *to powre out* and empty *their soules before God.* And because he would be sure not to be understood here short of his meaning, he puts *sinnes* in the plurall, which enwraps all, greater and lesser. For so Marlorat, in his *Ecclesiasticall Exposition,* renders the word *Prævaricationes,* Prævarications: which are not onely facts of

---

*Should the slaves be silent, the beasts will speak.

malice, but collusions too; and may containe our intended sinnes, as well as committed. For so he explicates himselfe, *David coram Deo se sistens, sensus omnes suos effudit.** Marlorat

Wilt not thou confesse thy riots as well as thy Murthers? the pollution of thy thoughts as well as of thy Actions? Christ thy Saviour suffered for both; he bled for both. Though thy *great sinnes* opened the wide River in his side, and the currents in his hands and feete: thy *smallest sinnes* scracht him in the thornes which he wore upon his head, or at least opened a Pore in his sacred Bodie. For how knowest thou but that, as he bled for thy *crimson sinnes* (as Esay calls them) through those larger wounds, so he sweat bloud for the sinnes of thy thoughts; that, as he suffered for thy great offences upon the Crosse, so he suffered for thy lesser crimes in the Garden: that, as he did undergoe a publique passion for the one, so he had an antepassion for the other, in his Agony: that, as for thy foulest transgressions he became a *red Sea*, a true Jordan, a sanguine River, the head of which streame began at Mount Calvary; So, before his Ascent thither, in a lower place, not farre from the Brooke Cedron, he suffered his body to become a *Marish*, when for thy sake the bloud wept out at every Pore.

[20] Esa.1:18

(Mt. 26:36)

Joh.18:1

Take heed, therefore, how thou underratest any sinne, since in the Inventory of thy Saviour's passion, they were all rated: He dyed for all. And do not neglect those faults which are the smallest in thy Catalogue: For even that sinne which *whispers* now, and is only *peccatum susurrans*—carried about in a still report, and in the common fame, wounds and traduces thee but closelie—will in a litle time become *Peccatum clamans*, a shrill and *crying sinne*. That which is now a Grane in weight, may prove a Pound; and that which was but a single fault at first, by an unblest fæcundity may multiply into Sinnes. For *Culpa culpam excutit;* one sinne is strooke out of another; like sparkes, they convey fire one to the other. Doe not suffer, therefore, the *Embers* of sinne, any loose thoughts or vitious Imaginations, to lurke within thy bosome, least at length those subterraneous fires breake out like Ætna and burne thee in their hot *Flames. Minutæ guttæ pluviæ, nonne flumina implent & domos deiiciunt?*† Thou seest, the raine which causes the land floud at first onely distills in small drops; take heed then how thou lettest any vice drop in upon thy senses. If a temptation insinuate into thine eares, or onely beat in at the casements of thy eyes, those litle flawes, those cranies, if not stopt betimes, will make way for the ruine of the whole Fabrike. Marcus Eremita excellently saies that Sinne is *Diktuon poluplokon*, like *a subtile net,* consisting of *many foulds*: which, if not warily avoided, will entangle the whole body. Whensoever therefore that *Fowler,* whose taske hath bin *to ensnare soules,* offers his Net at thee, seekes to fasten a small sinne upon thee: quit thy selfe betimes, by a Repentance, and in a true confession discharge thy selfe of all thou knowest, even to thy smallest trespasse; Remembering that wise saying in Ecclesiasticus: *Qui spernit modica, paulatim decidet*—He that contemnes small faults shall fall insensiblie. And to make this confession of thine more perfect, as thou acknowledgest the Offence, so acknowledge the Offender. *Qui rem non tacuerit, non tacebit authorem:* If thou confesse the Fact, and yet deny the Author—say thou hast sinned, but blame some others as an Occasion or Accessory to thy sinne—thou do'st not then accuse thy selfe, but endite another; thou do'st not make a just confession. but by a Recrimination seeke to excuse thy selfe. David, here, makes no such coy or faint confession; He doth not say onely *what was done,* but *who did it,* confesses a Propriety & makes title to those sins: *My sins.*

[21]

Aug.citat.a Biel, Lect.72.de Missa

Biblioth. Patrum Grae.Lat. To.1

Ecclesiastic. 19:1

Senec.

[22]

We are all naturally prone to transfer our sins upon others. Adam cries, *The woman which thou gavest me:* And Gabriel Biel mentions some that used to blame the Planets which raigned at their Nativities for the sinnes unto which they were enclined. If they had ill dispositions, Saturne was in fault; if they were Theeves, Mercurie made them so; if incontinent, an amorous Venus was to be

5.
My sinnes Gen.3:12

Lect.72 de Missa

---

*David, standing in God's presence, poured forth all that was in his soul.
†Small drops of rain, do they not fill up the rivers and bring down houses?

blam'd, not they. A folly worthy of no refutation but laughter, did I not see it possessed some in that high nature that they do not onely accuse the Influences of Heaven, but pronounce God himselfe, who gave motion to those starres, as the Author of their sinne. Most strange and fearefull illusion! that any should imagine God a Plotter for Damnation; that he should combine with the Devill to supplant soules; that he should make a Prison, and then make Offenders for that prison; that he should build a Hell and cause men to sin, that they might be condemned unto that place of Torment.

O farre be the thought of this from our hearts! Let God be glorified, and all men reputed blasphemous Lyars that speake or imagine thus. Let us say with the Psalmist: *I have sinned, and I alone;* and in these words acknowledge, *I will confesse against my selfe* those sinnes which I have committed against thee; resting upon that excellent conclusion of Fulgentius, *Non potest esse illius Author, cuius est ultor:* It is impossible that God should be an *Agent* in sinne, whose office is to *avenge* sinne, and to punish the sinner. For if thou say or thinke otherwise, thou wilt prove a devill to thy God, slander and accuse him to his face of sinne, who is the Confessor to receive the acknowledgement of thy sinne, *The Lord: I said, I will confesse my sinnes unto the Lord.*

Psal. 51:4.

[23]

6. *Unto the Lord*

(Book of Common Prayer: General Absolution)

We take a liberty to tell God those things which for shame we dare not communicate unto men: *Multi quod scire hominem nolunt, Deo narrant* (saith Seneca). He spake in the worst sense; 'tis true in the best. We need not be ashamed to discover our selves, our Actions, our Thoughts, to God; who, *as he delights not in the death of a sinner,* so neither glories he in the shame of a sinner. When we shrift our selves to men, we adventure our credits upon their secrecy; and confesse to our owne disadvantage, since it is in their power to betray us.

If the Conclave of Cardinals would have suffered S. Chrysostome's Caveat to have bin entered amongst them, they never would in the Laterane Councill have decreed a necessity of Auricular Confession, nor in the Trent Councill have established that former Decree. *Take heed how thou tellest thy defects to a man* (saith Chrysostom), *least he cast thee in the teeth with them:* and in the very next words, he flatly prohibits the necessity of such private confession, leaving our meditations upon the scope of this text: *Thou art not to confesse to thy fellow servant least he may divulge it, but to him that is thy Lord, that careth for thy soule; to him, that is most mild and curteous; to him, that is thy Physitian: I said, I will confesse my sinnes unto the Lord.*

Concil.Trident. Sess.4.can.5. Homil.4 de Lazaro

[24]

But doth God need an informer? Did he not know David's sinne before his confession? or cannot he know mine, unlesse I tell him? Yes surely, he knew them before. But he knew them as my Judge, not as my Confessor. He knew them, but not that way which most delighteth him and is best for me, in a repentance. In a word, he knew them before, but he knew them to my Condemnation: He knew them not to my Comfort, so as to forgive them, till he received them from mine owne mouth: *I said, I will confesse my sinnes, and thou forgavest.*

2 Part.
1.
Thou forgavest
(Song 2:12)

(Lk. 24:47)

[25] Marc.2:7

Like the tidings of *release* unto a *Captive,* or a reprive unto a condemned man: so is the sound of this word *Tu remisisti,* thou forgavest. It is the *savour of life* unto life; a reviving or recovery from the death of the soule, Sinne; and an earnest of a new life, both in the Body and the Soule, in the new Jerusalem. 'Tis the *voice of the Turtle,* the true language of the Gospell, derived from his lippes that left the blessing of his peace upon all that love the Peace of his Church; that *legend of mercy* which Christ commanded his Apostles to divulge in all parts of the world, *for the remission of sinnes.* This was the end of Christ's comming into the world, *to save sinners,* his owne peculiar worke; who alone, as he hath *the property to have mercy,* so hath he the sole *power to forgive.*

(Book of Common Prayer: General Absolution)

That the Church hath a power to remit sinnes also is true in a subordinate sense, that is a *Ministeriall,* a *Declaratory* power, as our Liturgie fully expresses it: *and hath given power and commandement to his Ministers to Declare and Pronounce to his people, being penitent, the Absolution and remission of their sinnes,* &c. But he hath given them no *Judiciary* or *Authoritative* power, to pardon absolutely of themselves. This is God's prerogative, he alone doth that act; the Church but reports it. He signes the deed; the Church as a witnes testifies it; he hath the originall power to absolve, the Church hath power, not to dispence, but to pronounce his absolution; he grantes and seales the pardon, the Church conveyes and publishes it; he hath the possession, the true inheritance, as of the Throne, so of the keyes of David. The Church hath but the use and custody of those keyes: by which she opens and shuts, yet not at her owne pleasure, as if she could hang new locks where she listed, or make new dores for sinners to goe out at, but with a limitation: Shee must not presume to goe farther then those Keyes lead her. So many roomes as Christ hath opened by those keyes, she may open or she may shut. The Ministers, who are his Dorekeepers, should take too much upon them if they should presume beyond this.

Mistake me not, I doe not in any sense of diminution call the Ministers *Dorekeepers,* as if I would inferre their office determined at the Church-doore. No, their keyes open farther then so; and by vertue of them, they may goe as high as God's *Presence Chamber,* the Church there: to receive and to deliver his messages to his people; to signifie his pleasure to them, either for the Remission or Reteining of their sinnes. But beyond this, their keyes will not lead them. They cannot open God's *Privy Chamber,* where all his secret Counsells, his Acts of mercy or of judgement, of Pardon or Condemnation are concluded: this is accessible to none but God himselfe. They are not able with any key in their bunche to open that doore. And if by violence they shall attempt to breake it open, as the Successors of Peter have done for many years, sitting there as Counsailours joyn'd in Commission with God, nay *sitting as God* (saith S. Paul), to condemne or to absolve like him; let them know, in this they have committed a Riot not lesse then Lucifer's; and their aspiring insolence must expect a Præcipitation as violent and deepe as his. [26]

2 Thess.2:4

I have almost lost my selfe in this Labyrinth of Papall usurpation; I retrait to my text in S. Ambrose his words, who hath briefly stated and limited the Power of Preists' Absolution. In the forgivenesse of sinnes (saith he) men use their *Ministery,* but exercise no right of any *Authoritie:* men aske, and men pronounce, but the Deity graunts: *Tu remisisti, Thou forgavest.*

Which speech doth not onely intimate his *Power,* but his *readines* to forgive. See in what a forward terme David expresses God's alacrity and propension to mercy, setting it downe in the Preterperfect tense—*aphêkas,* thou hast forgiven—as a thing past in graunt before the suit was commenced. Seneca spake it of the Court: *They were prone and speedy to doe injuries, but their benefits came slowlie from them,* and with difficulty. 'Tis otherwise with God: he is of no slacke Power, nor doth he foreslow his favours to mankind, seeking to put a price upon them by delay. *God is not slow or slacke concerning his promise,* saith S. Peter: Or if he be slow he is *slow to nothing but to wrath* only. [27]

2 Pet.3:9
Psal.86:15

In that Act which was the swiftest execution of his vengeance, the Floud, howsoever then that suddaine Inundation surprised the World, came upon it unawares *whilst they were eating and drinking* (as our Saviour saith), yet when it was done, *He is sorrie.* Though he *repented he had made man,* and from that repentance put on a resolution to destroy him; Yet after his destruction, he relents into mercy, he is sorry he had demolished and annihilated his creature by water, though most deservedly; and then makes a Promise and Covenant never to *destroy him so againe.* Did he not give Abraham leave to dispute and argue Sodom's reprieve, to plead a Pardon for it, after his sentence was past and the Executioner ready to give fire? Yet for all that, he heard him out, till he had said all he could say; till he had made all his Abatements, from Fiftie even to the last Ten. And when he sate downe before Niniveh, and had beleaguered it with his Judgements, yet you see he gives them faire Quarter: Fourty Dayes to parley and to make their Composition with Him. Nay, he allowed Rebellious Israel Fourty yeares: *Fourty yeares long was I grieved with this generation*—so slow is he to wrath, so loath to execute his vengeance.

Mat.24:38

Gen.9:15
Gen.18

[28]

Jon.3:4
Psal.95:10

And yet He is not so slow to punish, but he is by many degrees swifter to shew mercy and to forgive: *He that knows all things,* (saith S. Ambrose) *is ignorant only of wayes to delay his Mercies;* which are as instant as his worke was in the first Creation, *Said* and *Done* at once. How doe his winged blessings out-flie our suites? chiding our sluggishnes, in that no diligence we can use is able to keepe pace with him, nor our earliest importunity speedy enough to overtake his bounty: who gives oftner then we can aske, and more then we have capacity to apprehend. 'Tis not enough that he tarry till we come unto him, unlesse he prevent us by comming unto us ere we set out; that he suspends his blessings till we seeke him, unlesse he first seeke and call upon us, as he did upon Eliah: *What doest thou here, Eliah?* that he stay till our petitions wooe him, unles his favours first sollicite us, and give us cause to thanke him, not to aske. He thinkes his goodnes hath no advantage, no victory over our necessities, if he should onely *heare us when we call*, unles, as he prophesses by his Prophet Esay, *Antequam clametis, ego exaudio*—he begin to us and *make our answeare before we speake*. He thinkes his mercy would prove tardy if it expected our suit, unles he granted it before our motion.

Therefore in the 2 Sam.12. when Nathan admonishes David of two great sinnes, he no sooner in a religious humiliation dejects himselfe, crying *He had offended;* but the Prophet speedily raises him with the comfortable tidings of his Absolution; and in such a Phrase as if God had antedated the pardon before the sinne was committed. For he tells him *the Lord hath also put away thy sinne*. Not he *will*, or *does*, but already he *hath* put away thy sinne. You may perceive a gratious hast too in the remission of his sinne in this place: he but *confesses,* and God *forgives* him. Nay (saith S. Austin), he makes no confession, but a promise onely: *He sayes he will confesse, and upon that promise, God immediately grants him a large pardon: Tu remisisti, Thou forgavest the iniquity of my sinne.*

2.
The iniquity of my sin

The extent of his *grace* is as large, as unlimited, as his *mercy* is sudden. God, as he is no slow, dilatory God: so neither is he a sparing close-handed God. As he doth not suspend his favours, or hang long in the deliberation of his pardon to sinners: so neither doth he give them in a lame, imperfect fashion, but large, and full, and ample as is himselfe, *In quo omnia plenitudo:* who is the spring of all bounty.

He doth not *veniam dimidiare*, distribute his mercy by halfes, keepe men betwixt life and death, panting betwixt hopes and feares, as if he should send a pardon when the prisoner is halfe hanged. No, *Non de dimidia, sed perfecta remissione hic disserit Propheta.**

God doth not lease his pardons for life onely, adjourning the short punishment in this world with a purpose to inflict it æternally in the next. His hand is not so scant—*non arctatur, non clauditur fine, nullas habet metas Divina clementia*† (saith Bernard). And Hierome in his translation dates this remission with a *semper* [always], to signifie the duration, the continuance of it, which is as long and lasting as his goodnes, that hath none end.

Nor yet doth he remit the *Eternall* punishment and retaine a *Temporall*, to be paid in this world in an imposed pilgrimage, or a purgatory hereafter (boldly saith a writer). Therefore one of our English Translations reads, *Thou forgavest the punishment of my sinne.*

Let those then that list to be abused, commute or fine for their release at Rome, suffer the Pope to pare their salvation, and take fees out of God's Pardons, which he bestowes freely. We will receive our Absolution neerer hand, and lesse wasted in the carriage: *Let our Israel trust in the Lord, for with the Lord there is mercie, and with him is plenteous Redemption—Copiosa Redemptio:* a bounteous remission; for he shall wipe out all our sins, neither take vengeance on us in this life, nor in the life to come.

If he do lay a crosse, a calamity upon us in this life, as he did upon David for the scandall he brought upon Israel by Uriah's death and the adulterating of his wife; afflict us, as he did him, in the losse of a child; or send a Pestilence to scoure the land, as he did his—In which sense Euthymius sayes of him, *Mors remissa est, sed noxa vel damnum exigebatur per subsecutas calamitates*‡— Yet for all this, God doth not inflict this *Sub ratione pœnæ*, as a vengeance, but a chastisement; not as a punishment, but a fatherly Correction; not as a Minister of his wrath, but an evidence of his love. *For he chasteneth the Children whom he best loves.* And so you see, he corrects the bitternes of his Judgements with intermingling mercy amongst them; *Pellit pestem a peste* (saith one): he

---

*The prophet is not talking about half measures but complete forgiveness.
†The Divine mercy is not restrained, not enclosed by a boundary, has no limits.
‡Death is remitted, but affliction or loss is required through subsequent calamities.

takes out all malignity from his judgements— as S. Paul saith, he pluckt out the sting of death: *O mors, ubi aculeus tuus?* [I Cor.15:55]

Last of all, he doth not onely remit the punishment of the sinne and reteine the Guilt, treasuring up that *in diem iræ*—to presse against us *in the last day*—but he forgives that too. He doth not quench the flame and leave a sparke behind, to kindle his wrath or to incense him hereafter. No, *Tu remisisti iniquitatem peccati mei, Thou forgavest the very iniquity of my sinne,* the enormity, the *Obliquity* (as Aquinas calls it) so that *that distinction of the punishment and of the guilt is frivolous and out of season here.* God forgives the sinne at the very roote. And as Elisha, when he cured the waters, *cast salt into the springs:* so God, to make a perfect cure by his Absolution, heales us at the heart, because that is the roote of sinne. *Aphêkas aseboian tês kardias,* saith the Septuagint: *thou forgavest the iniquity, the impurity of my heart.* [32] [2 King.2:21]

Thus you may perceive there are no Arrerages left in God's Audit; he forgives both the *Guilt* of the sin & the *punishment,* both the suit & the damages, for he requires nothing but a true confession: *If we confesse, he is faithfull and just to forgive us.* This makes a full expiation and attonement for all our sinnes. Therefore he that confesses and repents, as it were Levies a fine with God to cut off all punishment, in the present or in the world to come. For this *Remisisti* is *remisisti in æternum,* our everlasting *quietus est;* a generall acquittance, for the breadth and extent of it like his mercy, which is exceeding broad, exceeding large, and againe like unto his mercie for the duration and date of it, which endureth for ever. [1 Joh.1:9] [*Chaldaean Paraphras.*]

I am at my farthest, even lost and confounded in the vast subject of God's mercy; which like *a deepe sea* through which I cannot wade, stops my passage; so that here I can onely stand upon the banck, and cry with S. Paul, *O altitudo, O the depth of his mercy.* [(Rom. 11:33)]

In which devout extasie I will end; onely borrowing a short *Gloria Patri,* and some sounds like those which environ the mercy Seat, from the Prophet David's song of thanksgiving: *My soule, praise thou the Lord, and forget not all his benefits; which forgiveth all thy sinnes, and healeth all thine infirm[i]ties; which redeemeth thy life from the grave, and crowneth thee with mercie and compassion.* To this glorious God, full of compassion, who crowneth us here with *mercy* & will crowne us hereafter with *glory,* be ascribed all *honour* and *thanksgiving* for ever. Amen. [33] [Psal. 103:2,3,4] [v.8]

SPITAL

A SERMON OF DELIVERANCE

Psal.91.3.
For he shall deliver thee from the snare of the Hunters, and from the noysome Pestilence.

I stay not upon unneedfull Preface, to shew with what accord the Text suits this Time. The Israelites' *Passeover,* and the Christians' *Easter,* wherein Christ our Passeover was slaine, beare record that this Festivall was founded on two most memorable Deliverances, the first from *Ægypt,* the last from *Sinne.* To which General Deliverance what Title you make, common Religion and Faith must teach. But the particular Interest you have in the latter part of my Text, Your Citie's happy recovery from her late mortall Sicknesse, and your Gratitude instruct you. [2]

The Argument of the Text is *Deliverance. Liberabit: Shall deliver.* [Division:]
The *Author: He shall deliver.*
The *Subject* on whom it is wrought: *Thee.*
The *Danger* from which He delivers, which is twofold:
1. From the *Snare of the Hunters.*

A SERMON OF DELIVERANCE.

Preached at the Spittle on Easter Monday, 1626.

Vpon Entreatie of the Lord Maior *and Aldermen.*

Published by Authoritie.

And
Dedicated to the Citie of *London.*

By HENRY KING *D. D.*
One of his Maiesties Chaplaines
in Ordinarie.

LONDON,
Printed by IOHN HAVILAND, for *Iohn Marriot.* 1626.

2. From the *Noysome Pestilence*.
I take the Text in the Method it lies.

    It is no flat or low expression to discipher God by a *Pronoune* rather than a *Name,* but the most eminent forme of speech that may be. He that can take the just dimensions of this *autos: He,* shall finde it a word of an exalted sense, capable of none but the worthiest constructions: A word fit to blazon Honour without diminution of the least title, and able to reach the highest superlative, *Him that sits above the Heavens.* I finde no higher glory at which Pythagoras sometimes aimed but to possesse himselfe of this poore Pronoune, nor could his Schollers who so much admired him speake his worth in a fuller stile, or make a nobler mention of him in any Attribute then *autos, He:* That Pythagorean *autos epha—He said it*—being of as indubitable truth as the Pythian Oracle, not to be doubted or disputed but beleeved. What ever claime He or his Schollers for him could lay to this word, I am sure was only usurpation, since the right belongs properly to God, who is *He, exochio* [the Mightiest], that prime Active power who made Heaven and Earth; whose *Ipse dixit* was of such Authority, that it proclaimed Him not only the God of *Truth,* but *Power* too. For you see the whole Creation waited on his word: *Dixit & facta sunt, He said the word, and all which he said was done.*   I. *He*   [3]   (*Ps. 33:9*)

    We need not then search for other Attributes to speake Him. In this one sillable, *He,* all that we can thinke of Him is spoken. If the whole World be a *Booke* penn'd and composed by God: If all the severall sorts of Creatures be the *Pages* of that Booke, this *autos, He,* is the *Index* that points and directs us unto every *Leafe.* 'Twas He that made this firme Masse on which we tread, laying the foundations so sure *it cannot be moved:* 'Twas He that lighted those great Tapers in the firmament, whose successive government distinguishes our Times, our Dayes, and our Nights. 'Twas He that levied those bright Powers in Heaven, which like a ranged Battell march and move in their order. 'Tis He that regulates the Influence of the Starres, *restraining the Pleiades* or enlarging them, as he thinks good. 'Tis *He that brings the winds out of his treasures—Arise, O North, and come, O South, and blow upon this garden* of the Earth. 'Tis He who keeps the Snow and Haile as it were in Banke, and hath a *Magazin* in the Clouds, where his Munition, his Artillery, the *Thunder* and the *Lightning* which he darts against his Enemies, are laid up. 'Tis *He that shuts up the Sea with doores,* bounding the Wave with a Banke: *Hitherto shalt thou come, but no further; Here shall it stay thy proud wave.* It was Hee that epitomiz'd this large Volume of his Creation, abridging the greater World in the lesser world, which is *Man,* his Masterpiece, drawne from no meaner Copie than the Originall, *God* himselfe, whose Image he beares. And last, It was He that, when the workmanship of the Devill, upon a perswasion to make him better, had blurred the Image of God which was pourtrayed in Man, renewed this defaced Picture, and by a gratious Deliverance freed him from that hand unto which his owne Disobedience had surrendred him.   [4]   (*Ps. 93:1*)   Job 38:31   Cant.4:16   [5]   Job 38:8,11

    See how just a Report this *autos* makes of him, how it trackes and followes him through the whole catalogue of his works, even to my text. All which though it be perfectly able to name, yet it is not able to name *Him.* In Job 38. where God acquaints that servant of his with his greatest Workes, yet when He comes to discover himselfe that did all those, He speaks out of the Whirlewind that which Job no more understands than he sees the speaker, that which rather poseth then resolves him, *Quis est?—Who is He* that hath done all this? And certainly, when the busiest search hath beene made after Him, the best information is taken from this *autos.* 'Tis He, that *Almighty, most high,* that Cause of Causes, Primitive Essence, from whence all Being is derived— That *He* whom we can express in no English but *God,* nor can we define that sacred Stile by any thing but Himselfe: He that is Himselfe, according to his owne Message, *I am that I am*—He who, from our inability to utter Him, raises this Trophee to Himselfe, that He is too great for our expression, an Argument fitter for our *Faith* than our *Words,* with more ease beleeved then spoken.   [6]   Verse 1   (*Exod.3:14*)

    Thrice happy we, if we had still looked on Him at that holy Distance, if prophanation had not trenched upon his Honour so far as to dare invoke that Sacred Power, whom all Attributes are too narrow to containe, in an Imprecation or an Oath, who never should be mentioned but in our   [7] prayers; And in stead of offering a devout violence to Heaven in those prayers, offred a literal violence, setting our mouths against Heaven, like Cannons planted for Battery, to discharge nothing but Blasphemies against the Lord of Heaven and Earth, from whence we purchase a lucklesse victory: whilst we thus besiege Heaven, we winne Hell.

The Jewes bare that reverence to their *Tetragrammaton,* the Name of God, that they never named it but in the Temple: But how many are there amongst us, who are more familiar with *God* in a Taverne than a Temple, where the intemperate heat of Wine inflames those Tongues to violate Him, which ought to be inflamed with holy zeale to confesse and praise Him? How many be there whose sinnes are their best Catechismes, that apprehend no knowledge of God but to sweare by; that never Take that *Name* into their mouthes, but to breake a Law by taking it in vaine; Inverting their Creed—instead of *Credo in Deum,* I believe in God, into *Iuro per Deum,* I sweare by God.

O wretched familiarity of man with his Maker, where God is growne so cheape to be despised! Such acquaintance, as it begins in an ungratious boldnesse, so must end in forgetting. For as Christ told those that intruded upon his knowledge with a *Domine in nomine—Lord in thy name* wee have cast out Devils—so shall hee dismisse those who by their Diabolical Blasphemies have cast out God: *Depart from me, I know you not.* Never must they be acquainted with any other kinde of Deliverance than that in the Gospell, to be delivered over to Judgement. Festus tould Paul He should goe that way his Appeale lay. They have Appealed unto Judgement, in calling God as a Witnesse to their Oaths, and therefore cannot without a speedy repentance make title to his *Mercy,* or lay claime to that *Deliverance* which speakes him a loving Father as well as a powerfull God: *Liberabit, He shall deliver &c.*

2. *Shall Deliver*

There needs no Comment, nor doth this Dialect require an Interpreter beyond it selfe. At this word *Deliverance,* as at a Labell, the Seales of God's love to Mankind are affixed: Seales so authenticke that they need no hand to signe the Instrument. This word like a loud Herauld proclaimes the Author. *Mercy* speakes God in a shriller, more audible accent than *Power.* For His mercy is above all his workes or attributes. The pennons of the Cherubins that stretched their wings over the Propitiatory and were a covering to the Mercy-seat, would want Extension to shadow the unconfined Mercy of their Maker, which covers them, and like a coole comfortable shadow, shelters us from the scorches of the last Judgement, which will breake out in fire and brimstone. The Creation of Man was a large Evidence of his Power, but the Deliverance hee wrought, in repairing the Decayes of Nature, a worke beyond the Spheare of Power. *It was a harder taske to save a sinner, than to make a Man.*

He that before might doubt what person this *autos* denoted, in the next word, *Liberabit, He shall deliver,* takes his full resolution. God's Titles are his Workes, and the best of those Titles is his best Worke, *Deliverance.* Tis God's fashion (saith Saint Ambrose) *Non respondere nomen sed negotium,* rather to declare himselfe by the business he Acts, than a Name, which is of little use when the Description is Radicall, and so essentiall as this *Liberabit, He shall deliver.* I finde several Readings of the word: *He hath delivered*—so the Arabique and Æthiopick, which Lorinus professes to follow. Others reade it in the Present: *He doth deliver;* but the Septuagint is *rhusetai, He shall,* or *he will deliver.* From which I only note unto you, that God's favours are not circumscribed within the limits of any Time. Salvation belongs to our God in all Places, at all Times, and in every Tense wherein the Grammar can forme or Religion invoke it.

Wee must not so interpret the word as if his Deliverance lay yet under Promise, not wrought nor performed amongst us; as if it were only future, expected, but not come: *He shall deliver;* nor yet *Liberavit, He hath delivered:* take it as a past act now out of Date, which he hath once done, but wil no more. Though his Judgements stand as single Presidents, recorded to have bin once done but disavowed for ever being done againe (as doth the Deluge, after which God is said to repent Him, and then contracts with Man never to destroy him againe by water), yet his Mercies are Leading cases, which God is well content we should still urge. They are Patternes, by which Hee is often

Spital

pleased to worke. Like fruitfull Copies that multiply by Imitation, they disperse themselves through all successive generations of Time.

And though men allow it not, God gives us leave to draw his favours into Example, emboldning us to prescribe upon his goodnesse; bidding us bee assured that if He did formerly bestow his blessings on us, He is still able to paire and fellow those blessings againe; That He is the God of Succession, as well as of our Forefathers (unto whom if his hand of bountie were liberally extended, it is not closed to us). His mercy is not shortned, nor the Arme of his Deliverance reservedly shut up within his Bosome. That Arme is stretched out still, ready to embrace *Filios e longinquo, The Children from farre,* that is, the last remotest Generations of the world as well as the first. What in the Method of his Goodnes He hath Once Done, He did it to act over againe. *Sicut erat in Principio semper erit:* There is no change in his Mercy, no more than in Himselfe, who *is Yesterday and to day, and the same for evermore.* He hath, He doth still, He will deliver. [12]

Esay 43:6

Hebr. 13:8

It was a speech of Seneca, being to treat of an Argument, though unlike this, *It was an easie taske to report God's Story*; We have heard with our Eares, and our Fathers have declared the Mercies he hath wrought for his people. Knowledge, Experience report, Tradition and Histories are full fraighted with the Annals of his Deliverance—Deliverance of all kindes, by an Invasive Armie or single combat, as in the Duell betwixt David and Goliah. Deliverance in all Sexes, wrought by the hands of women as well as men—Jael's hammer was no lesse victorious than Gedeon's sword; and the Naile she drave into the Temples of Sisera as deadly as the speare of Jonathan. Judith, the widow of Bethulia, stands in the triumphant list of Conquerors as well as Judas Maccabeus, who like a Lion, never turn'd his backe to the pursuit of any Enemy; And the head of Holofernes, by her strucke off, proved as terrible to the Assirian Host as the head of the Gorgon worne in the shield of Perseus, which turn'd all that look't upon it into amazement and stone. [13]

(1 Sam.17:38–51)

(Judg.4:17–22) (Judg.7:9–14)

(1 Sam 14:1–14)

(Judith 13)

And since I am in the Catalogue of female Wonders, let it not seem a Digression, but a glory both to our Nation and our God, whose Instrument shee was, to say that our Elizabeth, that unpatterned Mirrour of her Sex, that onely Example of masculine heroick Vertue which the latter, or indeed any times produc'd, hath as many Pennons, as many Streamers hung about her Hearse, as many Trophees of Conquest to adorne her pretious memorie, as any of those names who whilst they lived were wedded to victorie, the Edwards or the Henries—They that ran the hazard of so many dreadfull Battels, they that stood the shocke of Warre against so many enemies, forraine and domesticke, making from every place their Retreits with Honour to themselves and advantage to their Kingdome. [14]

But I lose my selfe in this vast subject of God's mercy, acted in so many shapes and by such various wayes, that they require a Chronicle to give you information, rather than a short discourse. Let me carry you once more backe, and leave you upon the holy Story of the Scriptures, and from thence you will soone conclude that *Deliverance* is God's Title, confirm'd to Him not only by the confession of those records, but by the Obedience of every Element. [15]

Which to serve his purposes have changed and altered their properties. The fire hath laid by his heat, and the churlish element of water growne tame, that it might be a preservative to such as God was pleased to save. His three servants walked in that Vault of flames as in an Arbour, the fire having no more power to hurt them than the gentlest breath of Aire that nourishes, not kills, those that take it in. When He led his people out of Egypt He was not only their *Leader* but their *Hoast* too, both their *Captaine* and their *Army.* He was their *Vaunt* & He was their *Reregard.* Whil'st they were under March He went before them in the *Pillar of Smoake and Fire,* both to discover and cleare their passage. But when Ægypt had them in Chase He came behind them, interposing Himselfe betwixt the Armies as a trench or stronger Bulwarke to keepe them asunder. And when He brought them to the Red Sea, the obedient Floud recoiled against its own streame, flowed backe against it selfe to give them way, making the waves a solid Wall whilst they recovered the other Shore.

Dan.3:25

Exod.13:21

[16]

Which Deliverance referr'd to an higher. For Egypt was figuratively the Captivitie of Sinne, and Christ our Saviour was typed by the Paschall Lambe. So that the whole storie of that deliverance was not consummate till Christ's passion, whose *Consummatum est* [It is finished] concluded all the preceding types, fulfilled the Law and the Prophets, and put a Period to the great worke by Him undertooke for Mankind.

To warrant which Digression of mine from the first Person of the Trinity to the Second: it is the Opinion of some that this whole Psalme pointed at the Incarnation of the Sonne of God, taking that *Habitabit in umbra* &c. to signifie the wombe of the blessed Virgin, where the Divinitie lay veyled and shadowed in flesh; And *Sadai* in the Hebrew (mentioned vers. I) to be one of the Names of the Messias, denoting Him, as the sense of the word carries it, *who was the only sufficient sacrifice for the sin of Mankind.*

But my purpose is not to dispute his Title to this Psalme; I only plead his right to my Text, so far as the Title of *Deliverance* enforces it, Which was His by the full allowance of Faith and Scripture. It is a Rule in Divinitie that *Opera Trinitatis ad extra sunt Indivisa:* in an externall consideration, The works of the whole Trinitie which looke outward are undistinguished and common. What one Person does, all doe, because all are but *one* and *the same God.* Our Creed attributes the Creation properly to God the Father, and yet you see (Gen. 1) the whole Trinitie exercised both in the Act and in the Consultation when Man was created: *Faciamus, Let us make man.* By the same latitude of speech we communicate Salvation to the *whole Trinitie,* though the peculiar right and strict proprietie of the Idiome belong to the *Second Person,* at whose comming Salvation arrived upon the Earth. *His Chariot brought Deliverance into the World* (saith the Prophet), Himselfe being not only *Sōtêr,* a Saviour, but Salvation in the Abstract: *Who of God is made unto us wisdome and righteousnesse and sanctification and redemption.*

He that was a Deliverer by an early promise, so soone as the first Man's ruine made him capable of Redemption, being *that Seed of the woman which should bruise the Serpent's head:* He that was the Soule of every Sacrifice, all which were but Hostages of that greatest Propitiation by his bloud: The Prophet Esay gave him *Liverie* and *Seizin* in this Title, *Ecce Salvator tuus venit—Behold, thy Saviour commeth.* And (Luc.1) the Angell which proclaimed Him puts Him in the full possession: *To you a Saviour is borne.*

A Title unto which He was justly fitted, in every Action of his Life declaring that He was not only the Saviour of the *Soule* in forgiving sins, but of the *Bodie* too, in curing the diseased, in cleansing the Leprous, in dispossessing such as were possest of Devils, In opening the doores of every sense—Eares barr'd up with deafenes, and Eyes that had never bin acquainted with any thing but Night and Darknes. He was a Saviour Actively and Passively; a Deliverer by way of *Purchase* and *Redemption;* a Deliverer by way of *Rescue,* and a Deliverer by way of *Conquest* too. He purchased us from the wrath of God, and rescued us from the jawes of Death and Hell in his Passion; and He triumphed over those Enemies in the victorious Act of his Resurrection.

When the first Man had sold himselfe to sin, & in that luckles bargaine concluded us, his wretched posteritie—passed us away into the power of the Devill, who bought him from all Obedience—He then stood forfaited to the wrath and justice of God, as having violated the conditions unto which God at first bound him: For so runs the Indenture; *Quo die comederis,* &c.—*In that day thou eatest of it, thou shalt die the Death.*

Upon which trespasse his Charter was cancelled, and the priviledge of his birth reversed, God now seizing backe into his hands the possession of that happines wherein at first he was instated. The Earth was cursed out of her plenty into weeds and barrennes, his wife doomed unto the sorrowes of travell, and himselfe bound to preserve life by a perpetuitie of sweat and labour. So that since his happines and whole being was now confiscate, he had no possibilitie to discharge the debt, but like a miserable Debtor, must have languished in his imprisonment, had not the Son of God become his *Surety,* had not he undertaken to satisfie the offended *Creditor.*

Which He did, and with no meaner Sum then the unvalued drops of his bloud, tendered at six severall payments. The first at his *Circumcision,* which was the opening of that Exchequer which never shut up till the full ransome was paid. The second in the *Garden,* where in his painfull Agony He sweat more bloud for us than we ever wept teares for our selves. The third at his *Scourging,* when his backe was *plowed up in furrowes,* and his whole flesh, which was now *Caro discontinua [broken up]* indeed (as Cajetan calls it), had not so much skin to fence it as would distinguish one wound from another, *the heavy chastisement of our peace now upon him* having made his whole body but one wound. The fourth was at his sad *Coronation,* which proclaimed Him not only *virum dolorum,* a man of sorrowes, but a King of sorrowes; when the sharpe thorny Crowne, not fitted but beaten to his head, opened so many weeping issues in his Temples that He was now *unctus sanguine vulnatorum* (as David spake of Saul)—anointed with his owne bloud in stead of Oile. The fift was on the *Crosse,* where upon a most unjust Statute enacted by the clamour and importunity of the Jewes, who still cried *Crucifie him, Crucifie him,* his whole body was extended for the Debt, his hands and feet forcibly entered by hammers and nailes, which possessed themselves of his whole stocke of life, and almost all the treasure of his bloud, saving only so much as was reserved for the Sixt and last payment, w[hi]ch his *side pierced with the Speare* powred out when he was dead. Wherein, to shew that he had fully perfected his bloudy Audit without collusion or reservation, that he had paid *exaton kōdrantên, the utmost farthing,* even to the last drop; That he was not onely *Exinanitus, emptied* and devested of his Divine Attributes, but *Evacuatus,* in a literall, corporeal sense *Evacuated* and Powred out, He sent forth that thin watrish moisture which lodgeth with the bloud, in so much that his witnes saw at one Wound a double current of *water* and *bloud* flowing out.

[21]
Psal.129:3.

Esay 53:5.

Esay 53:3.

(2 Sam 1:21)

[22]

Joh.19:34

This was the fearefull Method of his Redemption; at this *bloudy Rate* did he repurchase God's favour which wee had lost: *Pacificans per sanguine suum, making our peace* with God, and *redeeming us to God by his bloud*—that is, as well re-enstating God in us, as us in His Favour. Which was a true Redemption, a payment so full, that the Apostle avowes the bargaine as purchased for a valuable Consideration: *Pretio empti estis magna*—Yee are bought at an high rate.

Col.1:20
Rev.5:9

[23] I Cor.6:20

But yet, though by this payment the justice of God was satisfied, the malice of the Devill, more unsatiate then Hell or Death, under whose arrests Man now lay, would not bee satisfied, nor would he give consent that the Prisoner should be released, though the Ransome were paid. Therefore our blessed Saviour, by way of *Rescue* as well as *Purchase,* was faine to deliver him from his unjust Jaylor.

Pharaoh held out an obstinat siege against God's Commands, and in that Rebellion stood the danger of Nine Plagues. He did not thinke the Destruction of his Cattell, or Famine of his Land valuable Plagues to ransome such a Nation as Israel from his bondage, and therefore would not be induced to *let them goe* till the immediate Arme of God *rescued* them, and then, forced to it by his sword, that had the whole Land upon an Execution *(for there was no house wherein there was not one dead),* He did not only dismisse, but urge them to a departure.

(Exod.7–13)

Exod.12:30
[24]

Of such Rescue as this did man stand need of: Treatie or Composition would not prevaile with the deafe Grave, which uses not to let out any that lie under his silent ward, but still calls for more. And therefore, see how our Saviour prepares himselfe for this Combat, encountring the Enemie upon the evenest termes that might be, for he engaged only his *Humanity* in this quarrell, not bringing his *Divinitie* in sight till the Battell was wonne: To let them see (saith Leo) Hee did not contest with them upon apparent disadvantage, He would not fight against them with the Power of his Godhead, which must needs over-match them, and keepe himselfe unhurt, but entered the lists for Man as Man, not Impassible, not Invulnerable, but with a body subject to all that man is, Sinne and Corruption onely excepted. *This holy one could not taste corruption* (saith David), though *He was wounded* and *killed for us,* as Esay and Daniel prophesied of Him. And that they might not complaine of the disadvantage of ground, Hee invaded Death in his owne Quarters. In Golgotha was his Battell pitched, which is the Field of death. In which Field the most eminent but indifferent peece of ground was chosen out, Mount Calvary; w[hi]ch by the opinion of some Fathers, Justin

Leo *Serm.5 de Pass.*

Psal.16:10
[25] Esay 53:5
Matth.27:33

Martyr & others, was the very grave where Adam's body was interred. *Ubi cadaver, ibi Aquilæ*—where should Eagles congregate but where the Carkase lies? Where could Christ better combat for Adam's Libertie than at the Prison doore, upon the Tombe where Adam's Body was shut up? There did our Saviour meet Death, and in a Passive Defensive Warre suffered him to prevaile upon his Bodie, seeming to give ground at first, that so he might foile him by a greater Stratagem.

He knew that *Calvary* was but the Outworkes of Death, from which slight Fort, raised only with dead men's bones, if He should have beaten Him, He well understood there were other lower workes, stronger Redoubts unto which Death might have retired; and therefore, that He might be sure to get within him, to be admitted into the strongest of Death's fortifications, like Souldiers that sometimes surprize an Adverse Towne by putting themselves into the Enemie's Colours, Hee disguised Himselfe in the wan pale Colours of Death. He died, that so getting his Accesse into the Grave, he might beat Death in his owne Trenches.

Which hee performed, and having by this defeat rescued the Prisoners from their bondage, the third day proclaimed his Victory and Resurrection. Three daies he lay in Earth, like sleeping Samson in the lap of Delilah, *linteis involutus:* manicled and *bound with linnen cloathes,* as you reade in the Gospell. He might truly say, *Cinxerant mee funes Mortis:* The snares or cords of Death compassed me; but *it was impossible for him to be holden with those cords* (saith another Scripture). And therefore, *loosing the sorrowes or Bands of Death* (so the Syriack reades it), he came out. His incorruptible body lay indeed like a dangerous surfet in the Stomacke of Earth, which was unable to digest it or by assimilation to turne it into its own substance, as by that common chyle of putrefaction ordinary courses convert into Earth; and therefore it must needs cast Him up againe, or perish by that distemper.

And cast Him up it did, as Ægypt ejected Israel, laden with their owne spoiles. In that Triumph He disarm'd Death, broke off the sharpe point of his dart, tooke out his sting: *O mors, ubi aculeus?* He led captivitie captive, and by this Ascent, *gave gifts*—liberty and enfranchisement—to Men.

His glorious *resurrection,* which most properly we now commemorate, stiled his *Deliverance* in the loftiest key that glory or conquest could be strain'd up to; A Deliverance wrought by a high hand to manifest his Godhead & cleare our Faith; which though it were sorely shaken by his Death—Before that *we trusted* (saith Cleopas) *that it had bin He who should have delivered Israel*—yet it recovered againe and was established by his resurrection. A Deliverance by which he quitted Himselfe as well as us, *Salvator corporis sui* (that I may use S. Paul's phrase, though in another sense), by repossessing the power he put off, as well as by releeving us. His *Passion* spake him Man, His *Resurrection* God: Every circumstance of his Arising raising us by so many steps and staires to the confession of his Divinitie.

How well did He interpret that Text of S. John, *Habeo potestatem ponendi animam & reassumendi,* when in a most powerfull manner He *reassumed* that life which was not ravish't from Him by the Jewes' Tyrannie, but *laid downe by Himselfe:* The strong guard that was set to make good his Monument, nor the Monument which was sealed up to make Him safe, being unable to resist his passage. In a God-like disdaine of the vigilant Malice of the Jewes, He made a dead sleepe, like that which fell upon the first Man when his Rib was taken forth, lock up the senses of his drowzie watchmen, that thought to have lockt Him up and kept his Body like a Relike, cased up in Marble. And though the jawes of his Tombe were close shut upon Him, without any externall helpe to wrench them open or to remove that weighty stone which lay at the mouth of the Grave, *He issued out,* making his Escape as subtile, as unconceiveable.

For Aire to breath out at the least cranny and vent it selfe when it is imprisoned, is Naturall; but for one bodie to passe through an other (I say not by Penetration of the Dimensions, but a Miraculous Cession) is above the Power of Nature. For flesh and bones thus *to make way through the solid Rock* is even more then Miracle, and not lesse than Divinitie; to which Nature, though to her own prejudice, gives way. It was very much, I confes, *Propria virtute,* by his owne Power, to raise His Body from Death; but to raise it in this fashion, by such a proud unpractised experiment, for a close Prisoner to Baile Himselfe, to quit the Jayle, yet be beholding to no Key to let Him out save his owne Power, which is the True Key of David, must needs advance the Dignity of the Deliverance, and of Him that wrought it. [30]

Thus did our blessed Saviour arise from his Grave: *He came forth of Himselfe, when the Vault was shut.* For though we reade that the *stone was rolled away from the mouth of the Grave* by the Angell, Yet (saith Hierome) *We must not thinke the Angell came to open the Sepulchre and helpe Christ out.* That stone was not removed by the Angell till he was gone (saith Justin Martyr), and the cause why it was removed this only, *to declare the truth of his Resurrection.* An action worthy of Him, and most sutable to his Birth (as Athanasius infers): *He that through the Virgin doores of his Mother's wombe came into the world without impeachment to her Virginitie; He at his second Birth came from the Wombe of the Earth without any violation of the Seales that closed Him in.* Gregor. Nazianzem Mat.28:2 [31]

This glorious though scornefull Triumph did He make over His Enemies, to let them see that it was His owne sentence, not their Power, which made them His Executioners; and that when He was pleased to revoke their Commission, no Fetters could bind or Prisons immure Him, being, as the Psalmist speaks, *Solus inter mortuos liber:** And also to confirme us that He who, being bound, was without other help able to unloose Himselfe, is much more able to enlarge us when He is free. Psal. *88:4*

This Act of His Resurrection was but as a Tutor to indoctrinate our Faith, *an Exemplary Act to assure our Arising.* And not only to be the *Example* of our Rising, but the *Cause* too. For His owne dignity was He *Primitiæ Mortuorum,* the *first-fruits of the Dead,* the first that rose. 'Twas fit His sacred Body should have the Precedence from Death to Life: and it was necessarie for us that He should be first, *that so He might be the cause of our Resurrection:* according to that rule given us by Aristotle, *Illud quod est primum in quolibet genere est causa omnium quæsunt post.†* Tertullian [32] I Cor. 15:20 Tho.Aquin. *part. 3: quaest.53, art.1* Arist. *Metaph.2*

As therefore the fruit of this Deliverance by his Resurrection was wholly ours, so should the acknowledgement too; as it was the greatest victory, so it should have the largest Panegyrick. I read that the Grecian Churches, in memory of our Saviour's Resurrection, were continually wont, from Easter to Whitsontide, to use no complement when they met but only this, *ho Christos aneste ek necrōn: Christ is risen from the dead.* It was the salutation which past betwixt them, in stead of a God save or giving the good time of the day: *Christ is risen.* And the others were wont to make no Reply, to thanke them in no other Phrase then this, *alethōs aneste ho Christos*: 'tis true, to his Glory and our Comfort, *Christ is risen.* O that this happy Meditation might so incorporate with our thoughts, that our sleeps and our wakings, our dayes & our nights, our studies and whole discourse might be nothing else but Resurrection. [33]

We cannot in any lower gratitude discharge the obligation we owe Him, then to remember and mention this his Deliverance hourely, which was performed for his Glory, but our Good. God said he would get him honour upon *Pharaoh,* but *Israel* had the spoile, the fruit, the Deliverance: so Christ's was the War, but ours the Peace setled by that War. Peace with God & Peace within our selves, to calme all those distractions which from the apprehension of Death might arise to trouble us. *Quare tumultuaris anima?* Wherefore, then, shouldst thou be disquieted, O my soule? trust in God, for He is thy Defender, thy Salvation. Why shouldst thou be afraid to meet with that death which thy Saviour hath so tamed and corrected for thy sake, that it is not now so much a punishment, as an Entrance to a better Life. *(Ps.43:5)* [34] Aug.*Tom.10 [a]*

Thou canst now no sooner cry with Saint Paul, *Quis liberabit?* Wretched man that I am, *who shall deliver me* from the Body of this Death? but thy Faith will make a sweet reply from this Text, *Ipse liberabit,* He shall deliver thee. Rom.7:24

Mercy presupposes *Misery,* for *Mala est causa quae misericordiam requirit;* and a *Deliverance* presumes a *danger.* Both which misfortunes met in this one subject, to make Man's condition wretched and hazardous at once. I stand not to repeat the priviledges which Man lost. Since the 3. Thee Augustin.

---
*(Alone) free among the dead *(Book of Common Prayer* translation)
†That which comes first in any species is the cause of all things which come after.

ruine of our first Father, we have no Story that is memorable but our Woes, wherein as we have much to grieve, so we have somewhat to boast of even from them. For they qualified us, they gave us a capacitie to exercise the mercy of our Saviour. They were our miseries, our sins which drew downe Christ from Heaven to Earth. O happy Day, when such a blessing as the Son of God arrived! and (I had almost said) Happy misfortune, which occasioned that Arrivall! It had bin a kind of pity (pardon the speech, which not envy to our well-being, but Honour to my Redeemer urges) for Man not to have bin miserable, for then the rich mines of Christ's love never had bin discovered, but like his treasures, lyen buried in ignorance, whereas now their discovery hath enriched *Man's* Fall with that Priviledge which the *Angels* that fell were denied. Those collapsed Spirits, like dying Stars, vanish't into sulphur and darkness. Their ruin'd condition had no help from Christ to raise them up againe; Whether it were because their sin was more unexcusable then Man's, who was Passive in his Mischance, being seduced by the Serpent, whereas they had no Seducers but Ambitions and Themselves: Or whether (as Pet. Lombard out of S. Augustine gives the reason) *because the whole Angelicall Nature fell not*—though many fell in that Apostasie, yet many stood: whereas the whole Nature of Man was lost in Adam's depravation—I will not dispute. Certaine I am Christ suffered not for the Angels that fell, but only *for us Men and for our Salvation*. The Angels that stood *had this benefit by Christ's Passion, that they were confirm'd in their blessed State, so that they could not fall* (as some hold): But those that fell away received none at all. The Psalmist says, God in his Creation made *Man a little inferiour to the Angels;* but Christ by his Redemption advanced Him above many that once were Angels. He suffered those that fell to convert into Devils, choosing out of Man's ruines to repaire and make up their Number againe. *As he tooke not Angels, but the seed of Abraham;* so he delivered not Them but Man. For *unto which of the Angels did he at any time say* (that which he daily speakes to the meanest soule that sues to Him) *He shall deliver thee from the snare of the Hunters?*

4. From *Snares* and from *Hunters*? *Ergo-ne nos Bestiae?* Tis Saint Bernard's *Quære; Are we turned Beasts? Yea,* (saith he) *undoubtedly Beasts,* both by the confession of the Psalmist, who compares *Man to the Beasts which Perish;* and by the evidence of our owne Nature. The Verdict of our own Sinnes finds and concludes us Beasts. Our wild untamed Appetite, which never yet could be empaled within the bounds of Reason or Religion, by any Lawes of God or Man; Our brutish Affections and headstrong Passions have transformed us into all the Savage shapes which the world ever produced: Rebellious as the unyoaked Oxe, and like the Horse (in Jeremy) *neighing* after forbidden Beds; like the Lion in Fury, the Ape in Affection, the Wolfe in Rapacitie, the Beare in Gluttony, and the Swine in Drunkennes. Certainly, when man hath thus metamorphosed himselfe, when He is become a wildernes stored with such strange beasts, it is not strange, when his Vices have made him such store of game, if Toyles be pitched to take or Hunters pursue him.

Tis Hierom's Observation that this word *Hunter* is ever taken in the worst sense thorow the Scripture: They were the worst Men who were reputed the best Hunters—Nemrod, whose stile is a Great Hunter, and Lamech, and Ishmael, and Esau. The Prophet could not find a fitter Appellation for *Tyrants* then to call them *Hunters,* and in Jeremy, God threatens his disobeying people that he would submit them *to many Hunters:* The Ring-leader of which Band is the Devill. He is the chiefe Ranger, and his circuit or walke the whole World, which he compasses, *seeking whom he may devoure.* The Prey he hunts for is the very *best and choisest* the world yeelds: *Cibus eius electus,* the soules of Men, whose destruction is his Sport. A Murtherous sport, worthy of him who was a *Murtherer from the beginning.* To which purpose his Bowes are bent and his Arrows ready upon the string, to *shoot at such as are upright in heart.* The Dogges accustomed to this Chase are the same that worryed Actæon, our owne violent passions and Sins. Saint Ambrose names the whole Packe: *Ambition, Ryot, Pride, Lasciviousnes and Avarice;* These are the Dogs of Chase that never suffer us to rest. To make good which Metaphor, he brings the Apostle's Text, *Flee Fornication.* Saint Paul would never bid thee Flee, did not these make hot pursuit after thee, being still maintained and encouraged by the Devill as their *Huntsman.*

It was this same Hunter who, upon the old quarrel betwixt the Serpent and the Seed of the Woman, followed our blessed Saviour from the day of his birth, first casting off Herod's Bloudhounds, that drew all Judæa for Him; to avoid whose cruell Inquisition, He was faine to flie to Ægypt, and take cover there. By which avoidance, when that Crie was at fault, when that Persecution ended with Herod, upon whose death Hee returned from Ægypt into his owne Countrey, the Devill singled him out againe in the Wildernes, where *Three dayes he tempted him,* seeking to surprise or winne Him by promises. Which failing, he attempted to circumvent Him by the wit and fallacie of the Rabbins, Sophisters of his own instruction. But when both these, and all else he could doe, was defeated, He finally unkennelled the whole multitude of the Jewes: *Circumdederunt me canes multi*—Many Dogs then came about Him, whose mad, unsensible malice, being set on by the Priests and Scribes, never gave Him over, but like Hounds in full cry, whose mouths had learn't no note but *Crucifige—Crucifie him, Crucifie him*—they ran Him from the Common Hall to Calvary, where they killed Him in view; Hanging Him upon the accursed Tree as a sad Spectacle to God and Angels and Men.

[40] (Mt.2:14)

Matth.4:1.

Matth.22:15.

Psal.22:16.

The very same Hunter who in this maner Butchered Him, seeks hourely to make his Prey of us, arming the hand of every Persecution, and suborning all the Temptations Wit or Invention can presse to make us, who are the *members* of Christ, tast the same Cup of bitternes which He our *Head* then did. Only here is our comfort, that as the Devill in pursuing Him foiled himselfe, was taken in his owne malitious snare, so the Protection of God will arme us so that all his fiery Darts, like harmeles drops of dew, shall fall from us; that He, who hath *sealed his servants in their foreheads,* hath imprinted also that victorious Motto on their soules, *Non prevalebunt: The gates of Hell shall not prevaile against you.*

[41]

Rev.7:3

Matth.16:18

Doe but observe how in every Action performed upon our Saviour, the Devil wounds himselfe. In admitting His body into the Earth, he contriv'd and let in his owne ruine: As the *Trojanes* made themselves guilty of their Citie's Sacke, by receiving the Horse within their Walls which powred out so many armed Bands into their streets. In wounding Him he healed us: *For by his stripes are we healed.* In that bargaine and sale which Judas made, hee signed the Acquittance for Receit of our Ransome. In the *Crowne of Thornes* and *Robe of Purple* He declared our Triumph. In giving him the *Vineger* tempered with Gall, He fulfilled the Prophecie; And with the *Speare* piercing his side, let out two Sacraments, *Baptisme* and the *Sacrament of his Bloud,* as sure Seales to confirme unto our soules the Truth of our Deliverance.

[42]

Esay 53:5

Psal.69:21

O wonderful power ('Tis Saint Ambrose his holy Extasie) but more wonderfull mercy of our Redeemer, who thus retorts the Devil's malice, making him in his owne Assaults destroy himselfe! Well may he persist to invade our frailty by his Temptations, which wee cannot decline, our whole life being nothing but *a long temptation* (as Saint Chrysostome calls it) but yet he shall not captivate or conquer us by them, God's grace having instill'd this fortitude into us, that wee may say *Disrumpamus vincula eorum: We will breake the bands in sunder* where-with he would entangle us—*He shall deliver Thee from the Snare of the Hunters.*

Ambros. *Lib.1 de Poenit.cap.15*

[43]
Psal.2:3

This *Snare* is our sinnes, and those sins weav'd and made up by the practise of the Devill, who by suggesting the delight and opportunities of sinne takes us in our owne Net. One cals it *diktuon poluplokon,* a Net wrought with many subtile threads, made of as many cords as there are Vices. *These are Cords* (saith Salomon), Cords to bind us hand and foot, and make us sacrifices for the pit of Darknes. It is the misery of Man that in no place is he secure from these Snares. Destruction like a warder lies at his doores, and rather then Hee will want danger, hee lyes in ambush for Himselfe, for *Corpus ipsum laqueus—His owne body* is like *a Net* cast over the soule, which intangles her, & restraines the freedome of her faculties. When Man sins, and by excuse strives to diminish or defend the sinne, like a Flie caught in the Spider's web, the more he struggles to get out, the more he implicates himselfe. He that hopes to make good one sin by another, does ill and seekes to mend it by a lye, drawes Esaye's woe upon himselfe, *Iniquitie with Cords,* and ties the knot so fast, that nothing but Judgement and the Sword can cut it asunder.

1.
Snare
Marc.Eremita
Prov.5:22

Bern.*In Psal.90*

[44]

Esay 5:18.

A beleaguered Citie is not so streitly hem'd in as Man is environed at every Port of his Five Senses, which are attempted by severall Assaults of the Divell. *He seeks to involve us,* not only by habituall sins, whose long custome hath made us familiar with them, but upon all emergent Occasions brings us acquainted with new Crimes. Hee bribes the Eye to wound the Heart, and by those windowes of our bodies, He throwes in Lust like wild-fire; For the cure of which Fever in the bloud, he sends us to such a strange Physitian, whose remedy is worse then the Disease. You may find her Character taken by the Wise-man: *A woman whose Heart is a snare, and her Armes like chaines* to captivate the sinner. Thus the bed is a snare, and the boord too—*Mensa laqueis,* Our *Table* is become a *snare,* to betray us to riot and excesse. Our Ambition intangles us in those affaires which oft-times ruine us. And our Abundance, our Wealth, is but a vitious Steward to take up sin at any rate. Riches ill employed are but like Bauds, to procure those costly Vices which meaner fortunes cannot purchase.

It was not therefore without just cause that Salomon termed Riches *a Snare*. The Apostle calls them a *Temptation,* and a *Snare* too. The desire of them bewitches and ensnares the soule in the cares of the world; and the indirect waies by which they are oft-times compassed are as Gives and Fetters to clog the Conscience.

How many be there, that to compasse an inheritance on Earth to bequeath to their Posteritie, sell away their interest in Heaven? How many be there that live by Cosenage, and thrive by Oppression, that like *Plagiaries* make it their trade to hunt and catch men, building their owne fortune, like a Citie founded in Bloud, upon the ruine of others? yet are so far from recognition of their sin, that with those in the Prophet, *They sacrifice* unto *their Net*. They glory in their Art of Circumvention, taking all wayes that lead to profit for safe and Legal.

I pray God that within *this Citie* there be not too many of this sort, that there be not amongst her severall Mysteries too many Nets of this making. 'Tis Saint Ambrose his rule, *Wheresoever Extortion or Deceit harbour, there are Snares.* (A learned Spaniard interprets the Snare here to be nothing else but Cosenage, *Enganno*.) And the Prophet David makes his Report, *I have seene these Snares of Iniquitie and Deceit in the Citie*. I would faine beleeve (as I wish) this Citie were no part of his Survey. For I come not to upbraid, much lesse to accuse you; no, not so much as upon the common fame. Though some may be guilty, God forbid I should prejudicate all; I dare say many are not. The utmost of my scope is onely Admonition, that they which practise such Arts, desist, and by a Repentance *untwist those Nets* which the ancient Deceiver of Mankind hath wrought to deceive them with.

I am *glad for your sakes* (as Christ told the Disciples upon the death of Lazarus) that I may truly use that language to your Citie which the Spirit did to the Church of Thiatira: Though I could say some things against Thee, Yet I can say some things for Thee too. *Novi opera: I know thy workes and thy love and thy service, and thy deeds of piety, that they are more at the last then at the first.* Your good workes, daily amplified by the addition of Benefactors, stand to your Honour, not only upon Record but publique view, all eyes being able to beare you witnes that you have not beene only carefull to see the bountie of your Predecessors employed the right way, according to the pious meaning of the Doners, but as Heires to their goodnes as well as to their fortunes, you have adorned their Monuments, and provoked by their happy Examples, upon their foundations you have raised more stories of Charity, enlarging your owne fame no lesse then you have enlarged your Munificence.

Your *Bridewels* for the employment of idle persons.

Your *Hospitals* for the entertainment of the Aged and Nurserie of Orphans.

Your *Spittles* for cure of the diseased.

Your *Bethelem* for the distracted.

Your *Pesthouse* for the separation of the sicke: as necessarie a servant to your Citie as any—though the narrowest peece of all your Beneficence, considering the number which in an infected time throng thither.

All these, as they have ennobled you to the whole Christian world, so, I trust, they have endeared you and your Citie to the care and preservation of God, who no doubt will largely repay upon your succeeding Generations the charity in these kinds expended for his sake. [49]

Since, therefore, your goodnes is imprinted in so faire a letter that men not only may see and read, but have cause to glorifie Him who is the Author of all goodnes for you, his Instruments (since your good deeds are growne into such a storie), 'twere much pity, but more shame, that any foule notorious sin should deface or blot so faire a Catalogue; That any loud clamorous sin of Oppression, or the cries of Men undone by Extortion, should drowne the prayers of those many Orphans and distressed people unto whom your liberall Alimony gives just cause to sollicite Heaven for all blessings upon you.

Let me then beseech you for your owne sakes, as you regard your owne peace and the prosperitie of this Citie, that if any where amongst your treasures you finde *Pretium sanguinis* [the price of blood], any unjust unconscionable gaine, wrung from the throats or extorted from the calamities of others; If you there find the Orphan's Patrimony or the Widowe's Dower; throw it out, as the Priests did the wages of Judas, for these are also *the price of bloud*. The living of the poore is his life. *Take heed, therefore, how you make your chests Cemeteries to burie men quick, lest they become Gulfes to swallow you too,* and like true Tombes, cause the golden body of that Saint, which lies there enshrined, to crumble into Dust and become nothing, before the next Generation comes to possesse it. Upon such Tombes as these, S. James hath wrote the Epitaph; *Divitiae vestrae corruptae—Howle and lament, yee rich, for your riches are corrupt, your gold is cankerd.* There is a secret Judgement which, like an East wind, blasts the Owners and dissipates ill gotten gaines; like a worme at the Root, it smites both the Tree and the Branch, causing the fruit to become like the Apples of Gomorrah, which posteritie shall no sooner touch, but it shall fall into ashes. For to speake truth, how can that Father thinke the inheritance he leaves should be long liv'd, when together with the estate, the sin by which he got it is entailed upon his Heire?

(Mt.27:6)
[50]
Mat.27:5,6.

Ambrose *Lib.2 Offic.Cap.16*

Jac.5:2,3

[51]

And againe, Not as a Party but merely an Adviser, let me beseech you, upon no lesse obligations then God & your Soules, as you tender the favour of God and peace of your Soules: If, when with Peter, *you let slip your Nets* upon those waters where you may freely trade for profit, you chance to enwrap amongst the common Shoale of gaine *Quæ Dei sunt* (as Christ calls them): *any thing that belongs to God,* and part of his or his Churche's due, let not any such gaine land at your houses, enter it not into your Audit, nor account that amongst your *Supers* which is your *Onus,* and will prove a burthen to your Conscience. If by mishap any such light into your Net, throw it out againe, it is *Merces operarii, The hire of the Labourer,* the wages of your Minister: restore it backe to its owne naturall current. As Fishers when they have taken any Royall game present it to the King, so *Reddite Deo,* redeliver it to God, for *Res fisci est ubicunque natat.**

(Jn 21:6)
(Mt 22:21)

[52] Jac. 5:43
Luc.20:25
Juvenal.(Sat.4.55)

The deteining of it may prove dangerous, and in the end confiscate you. Certainly, the advantage by it is not sufficient to counterballance the damage. A little of this *leaven* may *sowre* your whole lumpe; and but one foot of Churchland taken into your estate, like the King's Waste, may alter your Tenure in God's blessings, and bring your whole fortune into Wardship. Those that be peccants in this kind, let them not ever trust to their smooth sailing. Though their advanced Prow beat off all suits that dash against them like water, yet let them know the least defraudation of God is *Sacriledge,* and Sacriledge is a lading which in the end will sinke the best and ablest Bottome. Undoubtedly, as God for the just payment of his Tithes promises a plentifull Harvest and full blessings—*Bring yee all the Tithes and prove me &c.*—so the wilful deteining may exasperate Him, in stead of freeing you from Snares, *to raine Snares upon you,* and *to plead against you with Pestilence and bloud* (as he threatens by Ezekiel), bringing that danger upon you which else he will surely *deliver* you from, *the Snare* and the *Noysome Pestilence*.

[53] Malac.3:10
Psal.*11*:6
Ezec.38:22

2.
And from the Noysome Pestilence

The Greeke is *apo logou tarachōdous*—literally, from the terrible Word. Symmachus reads,

---

*Whatever swims is forfeit [to the State]

Calumniarum sermonem, the *speech of Calumnie;* and Euthymius, *verbum perturbationum,* for there is no greater perturbation to the mind then slander. Death attired in his ugliest shape appears lovely to Detraction. How many be there that with more equall temper could endure the sword of the Executioner, then the *Sword of the Tongue,* to wound and traduce their Fame? How many be there unto whom a burning Fever is not so torrid, as *glōssa phlogizomenē,* the *scalding tongue* of a Rayler? The sting of the Scorpion is mercy to the blacke tooth of a Backbiter, whose fangs are like envenomed Arrowes, and under *whose lips the poyson of Asps.* No disease is so incurable as this, no Plague more dangerous. S. Augustine plainly calls a *Detractor* the *Pestilence.* The burnt unwholsome Aire which corrupts the bloud whilst the *Dogstar* raignes is not so pernicious as the rotten breath of slander, which casts a leprous skurfe upon the whitest reputation, and bespeckles even Innocence it selfe.

This sharpe killing word didst Thou, blessed Saviour, sustaine for our sakes ('Tis S. Bernard's sweet Meditation). By falshood wast thou betrayed, and by perjurious witnesses belied to the most shamefull Death, that Thou mightest deliver soules from that which is *verbum asperrimum,* the *most killing word,* the voice of Judgement pronounced upon impenitent sinners: *Goe yee cursed into everlasting fire.*

I fixe not upon this Interpretation, though very warrantable, but follow our English Translation, which justly agrees with the Hebrew: *From the noysome pestilence,* which literally imports that contagion a Schooleman defines to be *a sicknes which usually is to all,* and hath lately bin to us, *so mortall.* Thus Lorinus also, out of Authentique Copies, reads it *A peste pessima seu qualibet pestilenti,* or *de peste ærumniosissima.* The Chaldee paraphrase is *de Morte atque Tumultu,* from *Death* and *Tumult,* which I take to be a just Periphrasis of the Plague, that being of all others the most tumultuous kind of Death: Since, like a furious Torrent that beares downe trees and houses, it sweeps whole Families, whole streets, nay, whole Cities, insomuch that the living have not bin sufficient to burie the dead. Such a Mortalitie as this was there in the ninth yeere of Edward the second. Nor is it only tumultuous in regard of the Numbers that die, but in regard of their Buriall too: When every Churchyard is made *vallis Mortis,* the valley of Death, and the bodies piled and built one upon another make (in Job's phrase) a *rick* rather then a *Grave,* where, for want of earth, one coarse is covered with another.

Which must needs beget this Epithet *Noysome,* putrifie the Aire so much, that (as Solinus reports of the Lake Avernus and the dead Sea, whose steame kills all that draw it in) birds flying over those Cemeteries have dropt downe, and Men that suckt it up, like children overlayed by their Nurses, have bin impoysoned by that Aire which nourished them.

Kingdoms and States are called Bodies, because *Metaphorically* they are so: The King is the Heart, the Counsell the Braine, the Magistrate the Hand. And there is this true Accord betwixt those *Politicall* and *Naturall* Bodies, that they have distempers like us, their Agues that shake them, their sicknesses and their Deaths too. As there is an appointed Time for Man upon Earth, so for all Man is Lord of. Empires have their Periods, and those Periods to them as Graves to us. Babylon and Persia, and Greece, and Rome, which successively buried one another, the last Surviver (as Executor to the rest) inheriting all that the Three first had, shew that Monarchies sicken, & like Men die, sometimes of Age, oftner of Wounds. It hath bin observed that one whole part of the Earth hath bin sick at once. For in the yeres 1349 and 1579, an Epidemicall sicknes ran thorow all Europe: But Evagrius writes of a Plague that overspread the whole World. To speake more directly, some diligent Observers have delivered it as Dogmaticall that particular Cities have their *Criticall* Dayes, their *Climactericall* Yeares, and that most constantly.

Every third yeare (saith Boterus) is a climacterick, dangerous and fatall to the Grand Cairo in Ægypt, in which three hundred thousand commonly die of the Plague; And the fift or seventh to Constantinople, the Mortalitie costing her scarcely fewer then two hundred thousand. Our Land, and in it our Metropolis, London, our Mother Citie, hath, like Jerusalem, mourned in the Dust for the calamitie of her Children and death of her Inhabitants. We have had our *Climactericall* yeares, as well as other places. Some have noted the Twentieth or thereabouts to have bin mortall to us, which though it hath held currant for these two last Visitations, I draw not into conclusion that it should still hold. I thinke rather the whole Land sensible of the losse of her DEBORAH, and our late most gratious SALOMON of ever blessed Memorie, whose Exequies deserv'd a lamentation not lesse then that which was made for *Josiah* in the *valley of Hadadremmon*, to performe rites worthy such Funerals, mourned in Death, shedding *Lives* in stead of *Teares*. Zach.12:11

For any other cause, certainly I am perswaded it is not in the discretion of Nature to dyet her selfe, to set out her sicke dayes no more then to appoint her well, but meerly in the direction of God, who uses her but as his handmaid, to effect his purposes when and how He pleaseth.

It was one of Manes his Phanaticall dreames amongst many others, that a certaine Spirit in the aire, called *Messor*, diffuses that contagion which breeds the Pestilence. His drift was only to establish that Diabolicall conclusion of his concerning his *Two beginnings*, one whereof produces good, the other bad, and so to joyne an other Power in commission with God. And surely they that impute God's judgements to Nature, and because they are able to trace an Infection to the first Body that died, or can distinguish betwixt a contagion received *Per contactum* from other bodies or occasioned by an infected Aire, conclude a *Pestilence* to be nothing else but a Malignitie of course, proceeding from an ill conjunction of Planets or the concurrence of some other disaffected causes in Nature, derogate from God, and are in a faire way to Atheisme. [59] Epiphan. Aug.

I can by the helpe of Philosophie and observation assigne some probable reason of the *Earthquake* or *Thunder*, defining the one to be a vapour included in the bodie of Earth, which with strugling to get out shakes it; and the other to be but the collision of two Clouds, and in them the contestation of two repugnant qualities whose strife begets that fearefull Blow. But yet, if I looke not beyond *Nature,* if I apprehend no Power beyond these that directs and formes those fearefull Judgements, I might justly feare to be the next marke at which those Judgements should aime, to be swallowed up, or to be Thunderstrooke. Let not *Sophistrie* or *Philosophie* deceive you, let them not lull you into a securitie to make you fearles of God's anger, by fathering his Judgements upon *Chance* and *Nature*. There is no Judgement, as there is no Mercy, wherein you may not discerne *Digitum Dei,* the hand of God, directing it, be it Wind, or Storme, or Haile, or Lightning, or Infection—all are but his ministers, to *fulfill his will.* [60]

Psal.103:21
Vers.6

The Pestilence is *his Arrow*—'Tis called *Sagitta noctu volans;* directed against his People either for *disobedience* and breach of his Lawes (as Deuteron. 28:21) or for *Pride*—For David's presumption to number the people, God abated Seventy Thousand of his number by the Pestilence—Or for unjust *Avarice*, for *Extortion* or *Simony;* Or for *Lasciviousnes*, by the example of Sodom drown'd in *Mari pestilentico,* and turn'd into a Lake; Or for *Gluttonie* and *Excesse,* as Numb.11:33—*Whilst the flesh was yet betweene their teeth, the wrath of the Lord kindled, and smote the people with an exceeding great Plague.* [61] 2 Sam.24:15
Ezek.7:15 *(Gen.19:24)*

Nay, it hath yet a neerer dependance upon His will, insomuch that it is called *Manus Dei,* the hand of God—so Exod. 9:3,15 and Jeremy the 21:5,6. And David, making choise of the Pestilence then of any of the two other punishments there proposed unto him by the Prophet Gad, accepts it in this Phrase, *Let us fall into the hand of the Lord.* Now as none but *his bow* can shoot this Arrow, none but *his hand* manage this heavy Judgement, so no hand but His can cure the Wound which it makes: He *woundeth, and he bindeth up againe: Ipse liberabit,* He shall deliver Thee *from the Noysome Pestilence.* 2 Sam.24:14

Job 5:18.

Pliny writes that Locris and Crotone were never infected with any Plague; other Historians and Travellers, that as the Plague in Ægypt and Barbary rage their fixt Time, so also they decrease at their day. It commony slakes in Ægypt when Nilus overflowes; at Aleppo, when the Sunne is entering into Leo. Alexander ab Alexandro reports, That a great Mortality was stayed in Rome by the Investing of a Dictator. And Thucidides saies the greatest Contagion which ever brake out in Greece was cured by the advice of Hippocrates the Physitian, who caused them to cut downe all their woods and burne them, by which Action the Aire was purified, and upon that successe they [62]
Mr.G.Sands *Relation,lib.2. pag.97*
Dier.Genial.lib.1. cap.6
Thucid.*lib.2. Bel.Pelopones.*

110 THE SERMONS TO 1627

<small>Lactant. *Lib.2 De Orig.Erroris cap.8*</small>

would have made Hippocrates a God. Lactantius mentions a like Cure performed by Æsculapius the Physitian upon Rome, sicke of this Mortality.

[63] I know *Physicke* and *Industry* have wrought admirable effects amongst the Heathen, and amongst us. But I shall never Deifie the Physitian for the Medecine's sake. 'Tis God's permission to the one, God's Blessing upon the other which enables all meanes of recovery. Salubrity of Aire is His Gift; shift of Places, smells to prepossesse the Senses, but for Him had been unbeneficiall. Our best Cordialls and Antidotes, should His Mercy contribute nothing to their working, would invert their Nature, and become *Poisons*. Helpe I am sure they could not, nor, had they helped us, wee had still languished under the tyranny of this Noysome Disease, had not He made Man's industry prosperous for recovering of some, and for the generall safety of all said unto his Angell, *It is enough, stay now thy Hand.* Just cause then have we all to praise Him in this Panegyrick, *Ipse liberavit:* He hath delivered us *from the snare of the Hunters, and from the Noysome Pestilence.*

<small>2.Sam.24:16</small>

Conclusion
<small>(Ps.130:7)</small>

That I may now looke towards my Conclusion.

[64] You see how *copious the Redemption of the Lord is,* how his Deliverance extends itselfe over all dangers: there is no Buckler either to beare off the Darts of Satan or fury of an Enemie but this; there is no Amulet to resist or cure infection but this. So that *Deliverance* is a title of which God hath just cause to be jealous. No Rivall must share in this glory; He is the prime Actor, other Men or Meanes but meerely his Instruments, his subordinate Ministers. *Mihi vindicta* is God's Motto: *Vengeance is mine, I will recompence;* and He speakes it in as loud a phrase, *Mihi misericordia—* Mercie is mine, *I will have mercy on whom I will have mercy.*

<small>Heb. 10:30</small>

<small>Rom.9:15</small>

I can never then sufficiently wonder at that Church who hath not only Mangled His Titles to distribute them amongst the Saints, but have done that which the barbarous Souldiers would not, Divided the *seamles Coat of his Passion,* and with Saints' Merits Patch't the entire Garment of our Salvation: Imparting the highest Deliverance that ever was wrought—that Deliverance, to effect which Hee was delivered into the hands of sinners; That Deliverance which with many stripes and wounds He purchased; That Deliverance which He earned, as Adam did his bread, by the sweat of his brow and the labour of his hands: Hee sweat for it in the Garden, and Hee bled for it upon the Crosse—This Act of Deliverance have they maimed, some amongst them daring to affirme that *Christ hath not so satisfied for all,* but that each man must suffer and satisfie for himselfe in particular (so the Rhemists): which must either conclude Invaliditie and Insufficiencie in Christ's sufferings, or unjustice in God, who for one Offence will be paid twice, first by the Surety which is Christ, & then by us who are the Principall Debtors. Others broching it for truth that Christ died not for both Sexes, was not the *Saviour of Women, but Men only*—An assertion of Postellus the Jesuit, who in Paris put forth a booke entitled the *Victory of Women,* wherein he writes that one Jane was sent from God to be the *Saviour of Women:* Contrary to the purpose of Christ, who Died for All, gave himselfe for All; and directly opposite to the meaning of God, who at the cleansing of the Leaper commanded them to offer Lambes of both kinds, *Male and Female:* To shew (as Isychius excellently inferres) that Christ died for both Sexes, Women no lesse then Men.

<small>(Jn. 19:23)</small>

[65]
<small>(Lk.22:44)</small>

<small>Rhem.Test.Annot. in Rom.8:17</small>

<small>Jesuit Catechis. lib. l. cap. 10</small>

[66]
<small>Levit.14 Isych.lib.4 in Lev.cap.14</small>

But a third sort, to justifie their praying unto Saints, by a learned trick Divide the Office of Christ's Mediation amongst them, and by this Distinction of *Mediator Intercessionis* and *Redemptionis,* defeat Him of halfe his right. They confesse that Christ only died for us, and so became our *Redeemer,* but every Saint is an *Intercessor,* to sollicite God on our behalfe—A Position which the Apostle plainly contradicts: Our Redeemer and Intercessor are both one. *We have* but one Intercessor (saith he) *one Advocate with the Father, Jesus Christ the Righteous, and he is* our Redeemer, *the Propitiation for our Sinnes.*

<small>1 Joh.2:2.</small>

If they have parted this great Streame of Deliverance, which concernes the salvation of our *Soules,* you cannot wonder if with more confidence they multiplie Deliverers for the *Body,* if they cut that River by which Health and Temporall safetie are conveyed unto us into as many lesser Currents as the Thornes opened Rivelets of bloud in our Saviour's head—certainly, I think they have exceeded the comparison. *Old Rome* had Tutelar Gods for every Province, and Houshold

[67]

Gods for every Family: Gods for every Office, for the Farme and for the Field, for Warre and Peace, for Sea and Land, for Disease and Health. And *New Rome* hath created as many Saints to fill those Offices as formerly they had Gods. They have a Guardian Saint for every place: for their Sellar and the oversight of their Ale, Lewis a Minorite; for every Season, for every Trade, for Fullers and Coblers; For every Creature, even for their Hogges; For every Disease, even to the Toothache (for that cure, Apollonia); for the Falling-sicknes, S. Valentine. And as if there were no Balme in Gilead, they fly to S. Roche and Sebastian for remedy from the Pestilence. Rivius *L.I de Supersti:[a]*
Rivius loc.cit.
Henr.Steph. *Apolog.Herodot.cap.38*
Sohn *De Cultu Dei.Thes.90*

Blessed be God that neither their Saviours nor Saviouresses, nor the efficacie of strange Mediation is any part of our Creed. We *digge no new Cisternes* (like those in Jeremiah) but fill our Pitchers at the Well of Life, Christ Jesus, Imputing our Mediation and Redemption, our Deliverances Temporall and Eternall, to Him alone. [68]
(*Jer.2:13*)

Though by many seducements Rome, like the *Bramble* in Jotham's parable, hath invited us to repose under Her Shadow, yet by the mercy of God we have not yet betaken our selves to any other shelter but of Him and His Christ. We yet dwell (and I beseech God we still may) *sub umbra Altissimi, under the shadow of the most High.* Blessed is that People that abide under it. *Thou shalt not be afraid for any Terror by Night, nor for the Arrow that flyeth by Day; for the Pestilence that walketh in Darknes—Quoniam Ipse Liberabit &c: For He Shall Deliver Thee.* Judic.9:15.
Psal.91,vers.1
Vers.5
Vers.6

Should we forsake this Shelter, of all other Nations we were the most unthankfull. Never did any People since his Elect Israel receive such liberall Testimonies of his Love, or taste so many Deliverances as we have. Whether I understand by the Snare *Clancularias inimicorum machinas* (as Marlorat interprets it)—Privie Conspiracies plotted by Domesticke Traytours to supplant us—or publique Invasions by forren Enemies; the Literall Plague of Disease and Noysome Pestilence, or the Metaphoricall Plague of Sinne; Dangers of the Body or of the Soule—*Sive clam occultis arbitus insidietur nobis Sathan, sive aperto Marte nos oppugnet paratum fore Dei auxilium**— Amidst all these difficulties, we have found that *his Faithfulnes and Truth hath beene our Shield and Buckler.* [69]
Calvin
Vers.4

We may justly engrave upon the Pillars of our State the Prophet's Inscription: *When thou passest thorow the waters I will be with Thee, that they doe not over-flow Thee, and when thou walkest thorow the very fire, Thou shalt not be burnt, nor shall the flame kindle upon thee.* Esay 43:2

When Spaine *rose up like a Floud* (as Jeremy speaks of Ægypt), and like a *Dragon in the Sea* (it is Ezekiel's comparison) *troubled the waters with his Fleet;* when every ship was ballasted with destruction, and the pregnant sailes swelled with fury more then wind—*Thus saith the Lord your Redeemer,* the *holy One of Israel; for your sakes have I brought downe* (that Sea-built) *Babel. They were all fugitives, and the Chaldæans cried in their Ships*—He smote that Multitude, whose pride was higher wrought then the Seas that bare them, and by the Breath of his rebuke made them fly *like dust before the Whirle-wind:* Every Billow chasing them, and as it were, having them upon the Execution, till at last the Rockes became their Monument, and the fierce Northerne Sea their Grave. Jerem.46:8
[70] Ezek.32:2
Esay 43:14
Esay 17:13

Againe, when the malice of some English Jesuited Pioners soughts to undermine the Kingdome, to blow up both Prince and People with Gunpowder, He snatch'd us like Brands from the mouth of the Furnace, and by discovering the bloudy Trap, Delivered us from the snare of those Fowlers: *The Net is broken, and we are escaped.* Psal.124:7

And now lastly, when a contagious Sicknes, like a vultur, fed on many parts of the Land, but chiefly on your Citie—a Disease which I cannot better describe then in Cyril's words: *A Disease greedy and cruell, that devour'd all ages and Sexes without pitie or distinction;* making a promiscuous Prey upon the *Shepherd* as well as the *Flocke;* and in contempt of Cure, with the same wound striking the *Physitian* into the grave with the *Patient*—In this late dreadfull Time, when Death held [71]
Cyrill.Alexandra *Glaphyr. lib.3 de Lepra.*

---

*Whether Satan will lie in ambush for us secretly with hidden arts, or whether he may attack us in open battle, the help of God will be at hand.

his solemne Triumphs amongst you and the Grave, even glutted with the dead, like a bad stomack sent up unwholesome smels to annoy the Aire, finding her selfe unable to overcome the bodies shee had swallowed, so narrow was the stomack (I meane the burying Places) and so great the Multitude that daily cloyed it: When every house was endorsed with Death or Desolation, the Inhabitants either extinguisht or fled; and the Sanguine Crosse set upon the doore—Not like the sprinckling of the *Paschall Lambe's bloud* upon the *Israelites' gates* in Ægypt, for that was a Convenant of life, but like a fatall Kalender, bare witnes of the sad dayes which the miserable dwellers were forced to compute, shut up from the comforts and society of Men, and Lying at the Mercy of such an Enemie as would allow no Quarter, but oft-times emptied the whole house—Who was it that Delivered you from this Enemie? Was it an *Arme of Flesh,* or was it any other then that *Power* in my Text? No. *Ipse liberavit, He was the Deliverer.*

He delivered you from that Danger, and that beyond Hope: A very few weekes saw Death's Computation abated from Five Thousand Two hundred and five to One. Though the storme were very violent, yet it lasted not long. Though it tooke away Great Numbers, yet compared with what it had done formerly, and (unlesse thus happily prevented by God) might have done now, it will appeare a gentle Visitation. Our Chronicles mention a Plague, Anno 21.Ed.3, so violent that it made the Country quite void of Inhabitants, there being scarcely any left alive:

> *Funestos reddidit agros*
> *Vastavitque vias, exhausit civibus urbem.**

Neither did He accompany this Visitation with those Calamities which have wasted other parts. Eusebius relates a Plague in Greece, in the Time of Maximinus, which bred such Desolation, that the empoverish't Countrey endured a Famine more grievous then the Plague, such a Famine as constrained the Noble Matrons to goe a begging for reliefe, and so enfeebled the wofull Inhabitants, that they lay gasping in every Angle of the Streets, *Having no strength, nor voice, nor spirits left, but only to professe their Hunger.* Tho. Walsingham mentions such a Famine that accompanied the Plague in this Land.

But God was more mercifull then to scourge You with Whips strung with these Two Scorpions at once, Plague and Famine. Neither did he prolong your punishment, making you Lye long under his fearfull strokes, as other Places have done. Philostratus reports a Plague in his Time which lasted Fifteene yeares; but Evagrius trebles the Time. He writes of one that continued Two and fifty years. I may aske with the Prophet, *Numquid melior est Alexandria?* Is *London* better then *Alexandria?* or *England* lesse sinful then *Greece?* No, but God's Mercy was more abundant, more speedie to us, Dating his heavie Judgements to as few weekes as the least of those Contagions lasted yeares. *He hath Delivered you,* And *He hath Delivered you* so soone.

Not to weary you (yet how should you grow weary at the Repetition of God's Deliverance towards you?) He Delivered many of you that staied at home. And whereas Volateran, treating of the Cures of Pestilence out of Titus Livius, delivers this Maxime, *That nothing could keepe off the Plague but shift of Place,* He controlled that Position, making your owne infected houses safer to you then others' Country houses, or the clearest Aire to which they could retire.

And yet He Delivered you that fled too, by staying the hot pursuit of your Enemy. For though you went from the infected place, you could not have outgone his Judgement that could have overtaken you. I told you the Pestilence was called *the hand of God,* and God's hand could have reach't you at any distance, had not He sanctified your flight. It was observed that in the great Plague at Greece, if any to avoid the Infection had removed into some Citie of safety and better Aire, they only died that thought by flight to shun it. But God dealt not so with you; He blest your Flight, your Secession, your Removes.

---

*He filled the fields with graves and laid waste the roads, and snatched away the city from the citizens.

Neither hath He in them only blest you, but in your returne also, bringing your Tribes backe againe into your Citie, uniting all her scattered Lines unto their proper Center; and assembling them in the very place from whence the growing sicknes this last yeare frighted you, making you translate the solemnitie to another Place.

And He doth still deliver you by continuing this *His Deliverance,* whose fruits are Health and Safetie unto us all. For though the Mortality be now happily stayed, yet let me tell you, it is rather as yet Slumbred then Extinguished—*Non desunt venena sed torpent.* There are bad relicks enough to awake it againe. In bedding or garments infected there is *Contagio residua,* a lurking, a residuous contagion, able to cause a Relapse no lesse fearefull then the late Disease. Though it be raked up in Ashes, yet amongst these Ashes there be some sparkes which now and then discover themselves, that may raise the Flame as high as ever. God grant that either our owne Securitie, in adventuring too soone upon Things or Places that yet may retaine Infection, or especially our foule sins, which shew we have forgot God so soone as his Rod is taken off us, doe not kindle His Anger freshly against us, lest we be utterly consumed. [76] Seneca

Last of all, that I may trace God's mercifull Deliverance even as low as the Grave, He hath delivered those that died by this contagion: some of them from their pressing *wants and exigencies,* more grievous then Death—*A peste ærumnarum* (as Junius and Tremelius read it); Others from Toile and Servitude; but all of them from a wretched sinfull life, so putting a Period to many calamities, many sorrowes, many discontentments, by one Death. [77]

And He hath yet *a future Deliverance* for us, later then that which was their last; not only from Disease, which is the Bayliffe of the *first Death,* but from Sin which exposes us to the danger of the *second Death*—That greatest Deliverance in whose purchase He bled, and for whose Assurance He rose againe. The Deliverance, first, of our Soules from our sinfull Bodies, when Death by giving Nature a Bill of Divorce, shall sever them from each other, and they must take severall Sanctuaries, one above in the Bosome of Abraham, the other in the Bosome of Earth. And then the finall Deliverance of those Bodies from the Earth againe, unto whose custodie they were committed, when by a new indissoluble union, they shall be remarried one to another, and both together united to their Head, Christ Jesus, by which union they shall be married to the Joyes of His Kingdome, unto which in their Election they were contracted. [Lk.17:22) [78]

On this Assurance, as on a Rock, rest all our comforts. We shall not need to feare what can become of this Earthy stuffe we beare about us in our Bodies, since our Soules like *Gedeon's lamps* shall burne bright when these *earthen Pitchers* are broken. And what ever Fate shall break these Pitchers, these Bodies of ours, whether the violent hand of an Enemy or a fiercer Disease, an Higher hand will recollect the scattered Relicks of our Frailtie, and by infusing nobler qualities of Glory and Incorruption (for this corruptible must be invested with incorruption), make them in stead of Clay, vessels of Honour, fit for this Kingdome. (Judg. 7:16)

I Cor.15:53

So long as by our Faith we are allowed a recourse unto this pretious Balsam, Death can looke grim in no dresse, nor Death's most fearefull Executioners affright us. The very name of *Resurrection* so sweetens the bitternes of Death that, enamoured on the Joyes it leads to, we have rather cause to court then feare it. Whether we perish by the *sword,* Peace softer then Rest shall close our Wounds; Or whether by the *Pestilence,* this thought shall abate the horrour of that Noysome Disease: *It may appeare a Comfort, rather than a Calamity, to fall with a Multitude.* That company, that *communion in Death* shew's us, through a sad Perspective, the joyfull *communion of Saints,* unto which we in the next life shall be admitted. And although, like a tempestuous *Autumne,* it shakes us by heaps into our Graves, our Extraction will be more orderly, in better Method then was our Buriall. For *unusquisque suo ordine:* we shall *Arise in Order.* That confused tumultuous kind of Death shall not disguise us from the knowledge of our Maker, who will distinguish each Bone, and give it to the right Owner. Nor can the deepest dungeon of Earth, the lowest Grave, deteine us, since our Deliverer will be our Baile. He that hath the *Keyes of David* keeps also the *Key* of our Prison. By that *Master-Key,* He will unlocke our Graves, those *doores of Mortalitie,* and with it will [79]

Petrarch *De Remed. utriusque fortun.lib.2. Dialog.92*

I Cor.15:23. [80]

TWO SERMONS
PREACHED AT WHITE-HALL IN
Lent, March 3. 1625.
And
Februarie 20. 1626.

By
Henry King, D. D. one of his Maiesties
Chaplaines in Ordinarie.

LONDON,
Printed by IOHN HAVILAND,
1627.

He open the *everlasting doores*, giving us our entrance into Heaven. After which happy Resurrection, we shall live, not *sub umbra altissimi*, under the shadow, but in the bright Sunshine of God's presence, and the comforts of his Spirit, and the fruition of our Redeemer, who is both our *Resurrection* and our *Life*. Amen.

LENT 1

TO THE SACRED MAJESTIE OF MY SOVERAIGNE LORD AND MASTER, KING CHARLES.

Most Gratious Sir:
To invite you to this cold service is to bid you to losse, and to practise part of that trouble upon your Eye, which hath already exercised your Eare. If it appeare an importunitie, I dare not excuse my selfe, but humbly sue for Pardon. Which my owne cleare purpose and your Bounteous Inclination assures me you will not denie, When your Majestie pleases to consider, I doe but restore what in the intention and Course of my service was Yours before. Nor might I presume to communicate it, unlesse I obtained Leave from you, and it had first passed your Princely Hand. Then, as you have ever beene my Gratious Master, vouchsafe to dignifie by your acceptance the meane endevours of him who, though he erre in point of discretion, will never erre in the Zeale and Dutie which becomes

Your Majestie's most loyall
and humbly devoted Servant
HEN. KING.

A Sermon preached at White-Hall in Lent.
1625.

Ecclesiastes 12.1. *Remember now thy Creatour in the dayes of thy youth.*

My Division is plainly thus:
1. A *Monition* to quicken the Memory, *Remember*.
2. The *Object* presented to it, the *Creatour*.
3. The *Application* of that Object, *Thy Creatour*.
4. The *Distance* at which wee must take him, *Youth*.
5. The Light by which we best may view this Object, *In the daies of thy youth*.
6. The *Time* which hastes to bring us home and set us neere unto God, *Now*.

I wonder why Tertullian was so stiffe and peremptory in that assertion of his, *Animam oblivionis capacem non cedam—That the soule could not forget;* holding Plato paradoxicall for affirming it could and did. For my part, I thinke Plato spake no paradox but plaine truth; since amongst all the curious Caskets of Nature wherein the secrets of Art and Knowledge are lockt up, there is not any so loose, so false a Cabinet as the *Heart;* nor in the whole masse of Creation is there so thanklesse, so forgetting a Creature as *Man;* Who began early to practize his ingratitude, and that hee might justifie the Prophet's complaint which charges him *with rebellion from the wombe,* made himselfe perfect in the lessons of forgetfulnesse from the first day he could remember he was made Man.

It hath beene knowne that some old Persons have lived so long that they have outgon their reckoning, outlived the computation of their time, not being capable of so much Arithmeticke as to say how old they were. Which faile of memory is pardonable in such relikes and ruines of Nature, whose pregnant imperfections have dispensed with their understandings and given them now a priviledge to dote. But how shall we excuse, or indeed how thinke charitably of Man? who in his best state, in the freshnesse of his youth and vigour of his intellectual faculties, revolted from his creation.

For whereas a little before, God in the reasonable Soule had advanced his owne *Colours,* imprinted his owne *Image,* and for a richer testimony of his love, *Creavit quandam Trinitatem ad imaginem suam* (as Bernard hath it): gave him leave to weare the sacred mystery of the Trinity, as an Ensigne & badge of that high Order unto w[hi]ch his Maker intended him, in his Soule's three faculties, consisting of Understanding, Will and Memory; yet for all this, he willingly defaced and blurred the glorious Image of his Maker, and recoiling from his obedience, *exchanged those three purer faculties wherein the blessed Trinity was at first pourtraied for a confused masse of imperfections.* His Memory became, like himselfe, perfidious and impotent, his Knowledge darke and besotted, his Will perverse and most corrupt.

<small>Bern *Ser.Parv.1*</small>

<small>Bern.ib.</small>

Who then is able to wonder enough at his disloyalty, or speake his falshood in so high an Accent as it deserves? who forfeited all his titles to Happinesse in lesse time than the readiest tongue can relate it. That when he was new from the Mint and hand of his Composer, the Articles betwixt God & him for his Allegeance not yet fully dry, himselfe scarce warme in the possession of the World then given him, flew off from his Allegeance, and with such speedy precipitate violence, that he left but very few houres betwixt his creation and his fall.

<small>Gen. 1:31</small>
<small>[5] (*Irenaeus Advers. Hæres.* 5.23)</small>
<small>Gen.3:6</small>
<small>Vers.8</small>
<small>Vers.23</small>

In the morning of the sixt day was Man made, and before the evening of that same day had he, upon the Devil's short parley, surrendred up his innocence & libertie, quite sold away his Patent, the priviledges of his birth, and at that scornefull rate wherewith we purchase the love of children, *for an Apple.* For this is evident out of the Text: *In the coole of the day God walked in the Garden,* and having received the confession of his guilt, *cast him from thence,* making the same light a witness of his admission into Paradise and his expulsion.

So that his happinesse was but like a waking dreame, which vanished before his bed-time; or like a shadow, in the morning with him, at evening behinde him, past and forgotten.

How much more happie are other creatures in their deformities, than Man in all his perfections! It is a kinde of comfort which deformitie hath, that it cannot impaire, but may enjoy that being without the envy of any, or danger of growing worse; so cannot wee, who are not yet at the bottome of our miserie, but still in danger of falling lower. How well were it for Man-kinde, if we might glorie in that infirmitie which beasts may doe: they cannot be sayd to have lost what they never had, nor to forget what they never had organs to remember. We had a great deale lesse sin to answer for, could we say so too. Man once had what he now hath lost, and for default of a little memorie at the first, hath taught us to forget wee might have beene happie. And therefore (saith the Psalmist) *Man being in honour had no understanding, but was compared to the beasts that perish:* Nay, it had beene well if he had not sunke below that meane comparison. In the Prophet Esay God justifies the gratitude and knowledge of the verie beasts above man's: *The oxe knoweth his owner, but my people would not know, nor owne, nor remember me that made them.*

<small>[6]</small>

<small>Psal.49:12</small>

<small>Esay 1:3</small>

Certainly, were our memories as strong as are our sins, were we as retentive of God's great favours as we are of the slightest injuries which affront us, there were no need of precepts to quicken our Remembrance, but rather of drowzie Opiats or Mandragora's, to dull and stupifie the braine, that workes too strongly upon the apprehension of a wrong. There would be no use of Tutors to instruct us in the Art of Memorie, but we should cry, as Themistocles sometimes did to that famous Artist who undertooke to teach him that Art, *Mallem oblivisci doceres:* I had rather thou wouldest reade some Lectures of Oblivion to mee, that thou couldest teach me to forget, for there be many things that I remember too well.

<small>[7]</small>

<small>(Cicero *De Oratore* 2.74)</small>

Man's nature is a wondrous master-peece of perversenesse, a mettall not to bee wrought upon by soft and easie wayes. He that thinkes by laying the obligation of a good turne upon us to make us remember him, takes the wrong course. We are not so soone apt to forget any, as those who have done best for us, nor is there any so certaine meanes to make us *Remember,* as by doing us some unkindnesse or hurt. Wee write the benefits we receive in water, they leave no tracke behinde them longer than the verie doing; but for our injuries, wee print them in capitall letters, *that hee that runs may reade them*—*Scribunt in marmore læsi:* We write them in Marble with points of Daggers for Pens, and in such Inke as Dracoe's lawes were writ in, Bloud. By such fearfull Charters as these doe too many contentious spirits amongst us hold their wrongs.

[8] *(Hab. 2:2)*

Pardon the speech, I thinke if God had not done so much good for our soules as he hath, we should better have remembred, beene more mindfull of him. Our Saviour askt the Jewes, *for which of his good workes they ston'd him?* Certainly we expell God from our thoughts and memories for no other quarrell but this, his good deeds. Any crosse by him throwne upon us awakes the slumbring faculties of our soules, *Vexatio dat intellectum:* like a warning-peece discharged at Sea, it makes us stoope and come in. *En hêmera thlipseōs ekekraxa: In the day of my trouble I sought unto thee.*

Joh.10:32

Psal.86:7

Our hearts are tough and stubborne as the Adamant: and as nothing but the dust of the Diamond can cut or shape it, so nothing but our owne Dust, Miserie, and Affliction can cut our hard hearts into any forme of duty or obedience to our Maker.

[9]

With what strange eyes doth man looke, that sees cleerest in an Eclipse, when God frownes upon him? and unto whom the puddled troubled waters of adversitie are the best perspectives to shew him God? How frowardly doe wee combine against our selves? We shut up our apprehensions, yet wee understand; wee winke, yet thus blind-fold, we see God against our wils. We know not well how to remember him, and yet wee know worse how to forget him; for everie thing wee meet discovers him, and everie creature without our enquirie doth not onely give us cause to *Remember,* but in visible demonstrations makes us see the Creatour.

Indeed *Mundus nil nisi Deum revelatus:* The whole universe is nothing else but an Evidence, a Revelation of God; everie creature *Paideutêeion tês theomoisias,* a master in his Science, to instruct us in the knowledge of our Maker. Those numberlesse Atomes of dust on which wee tread bid our feet, as wee walke, informe our heads of his infinitie: That hee, whose power did compact this great bodie of the earth, and from the aggregation of those small Atomes made it grow into such a magnitude, is no more to bee contained in finite numbers than is that dust.

2.
Creatour
[10] Basil [Adv. Eunom. 5)

We cannot open our eyes to looke up to *Heaven,* but at those casements we let in the confession of *His Immensitie.* When wee consider how many starres there fixt are bigger farre than the Earth, and then againe lose our selves in the capacious extent of that Greater Bodie which contains those starres, we finde this *Maximé* to collect our scattered, confounded apprehensions: that He who made those orbes is farre more immense than is his worke.

Nay, even whilest we thinke all this, yet are not able to weild our owne imaginations, to graspe, or circumscribe, or confine in any limit of Sea or Land, of Earth or Heaven, our quicke thoughts, or give a reason why they in an instant comprehend all these: From this our owne incapacitie and inabilitie to understand or know our selves, wee may learne how much more incomprehensible our Maker is. So that everie thing is so full and pregnant in the proofe of its Creatour, that I may cry with David, *Quo aufugiam a spiritu tuo? Whither shall I flie from Thee?* In what darke corner of the world shall I hide my understanding from taking notice of Thee? Not all the curtaines of night drawne about the Soule, not all the thicke vailes of ignorance, darker and blacker than the night, not all the blinde retreats w[hi]ch a guiltie conscience hath sought, or w[hi]ch is more, wisht for, to shrowd it selfe from the justice of the Creatour, is able to conceale our apprehensions so low that the confession of God shall not reach us. *Abyssus abyssum vocat*—this is a theame which hath pierced as low as the region of darknesse, which *one Abysse hath related to another.*

[11]

Bernard *Meditat.1*

Psal.139:7

(Ps.42:7)
[12]

The power of the Creatour is a perpetuall Tradition which day and night successively deliver. *One day telleth another,* and where the light failes, the night goes on and repeats those discoveries which day hath made: Just as the Memorie wraps up the speculations of the Phantasie, to deliver

Psal.19:2

118 THE SERMONS TO 1627

them backe againe to us, so oft as our use requires them. The beames of the Sunne, which illuminate each part of the *Horizon,* stile Him the Father of light, and the moist collection of the clouds which *drop downe fatnesse* upon our Land speake Him the God of plentie.

<small>Psal.65:12</small>

And if there be any so stiffe in their misbeleefe that will not bee informed by these still Messengers that daily deliver Him to our thoughts, He hath louder Heraulds to proclaime Him, creatures that in a more exalted note voice the greatnes of their Creator. There is no Meteor, but in this argument is able to be our Interpreter; the tempestuous winds that *breake the Cedars of Lebanon,* the quicke ejaculations of the lightning, which have sometime made the palaces of Tyrants the tombes and funerall piles of their Owners, have evinced deafe Atheisme, and made it acknowledge the Creatour. By such boisterous messengers as these did He once treat with the Jewes, for wee finde in the Gospell, that when all the miracles our Saviour had wrought amongst them, nor his preaching, uttered in such a Dialect *as never man spake in,* could induce that stony-hearted people to beleeve his Deitie: the Elements, in disdaine to see their Maker made the subject of their scorne and tyrannie, undertooke the cause, and like victorious Advocates, vanquished their incredulous malice. The violent earth-quakes, that not onely affrighted the upper world, but shooke the territories of death, leaving the graves without their Tenants, and dislodging the bodies of many Saints which had long slept in the earth; the unnaturall darknesse at Noone-day; the *Rending of the vaile of the Temple;* and above all, the Rhetoricke of thunder perswaded, nay, extorted this confession from them, *Of a truth, this was the Sonne of GOD.*

<small>(Ps.29:5)
[13]

(Jn.1:46)

[14] Matth.27:54</small>

Thus you see, that as God out of stones can create sonnes to Abraham, so from everie peece of his creation can he raise proofes of the Creatour. For all creatures are but his tongue to speake him, and the mutest of them all is articulate, hath a peculiar language to utter Him: *Cœli ennarrant*—Heaven declares—and Earth reports, and all that move in the one or on the other convay the praise of Him that made them. Therefore the Psalmist summons all things, animate and inanimate, all seasons, all conditions, Angels and Men, Light and Darknesse, Dragons and Deepes, Wormes and Vegetables, to praise the Lord. Indeed, the whole universe is but God's *Lieger-Booke,* wherein his Acts are written; everie Species is a line in that booke, everie peculiar work a character for Man to read his Maker. And sure, with much delight are the most of us willing to read this booke: the curiositie of the stile and varietie of the storie invite all eyes to run it over.

<small>(Mt. 3:9)

Psal.19:1

Psal.145:10</small>

It is a most pleasing kinde of Geographie, in this large Map of the created world, in the Celestiall and Terrestriall Globe, to contemplate the *Creatour:* But when wee come to apply this studie, to bring it neerer to our selves, considering God not in his exteriour creation but as he is *our Creatour,* in this application of the Object most faile:

<small>[15]</small>

Remember thy Creatour.

It is the generall vice of Man, *he loves not to bee acquainted with himselfe.* Like an humerous Novelist, he travels other Countries, but is not able to give any account of his own: so censorious & criticall in surveying others that he is still finding or making faults in them, but so indulgent to himselfe, hee will not peruse his owne brest. The Elephant doth not more abhorre the represent-ment of himselfe in the cleare streame, than Man declines all those occasions which might present himselfe unto himselfe: Choosing rather to live disguised in those phantastick dresses wherein flattery or selfe-love attires him then to set his lookes by the true glasse of reason, which might make him understand himself—Like those old Impostors the Soothsaiers, *better read in the fate of others than their owne.* Wee love alwaies to be studying other men, when wee should first begin at home, and make our owne bosomes our chiefe Libraries.

<small>3.
Thy Creatour
Bernard
(Meditat.I)

[16]

Seneca</small>

Which is the maine cause that we are so raw, so ill studied in the knowledge of God, for (as S. Bernard): *so much as I profit in the science of my selfe, so neere come I to the apprehension of my Maker.*

<small>(Bernard
Meditat.I)</small>

And yet it is not sufficient onely to know him, unlesse thou knowest him the right, the best way.

Lent 1

When the Philosopher would interpret himselfe what he meant by knowing, he does it thus: *Scire est per causam scire.** The knowledge he meant reacht as farre as the discerning of the first cause; so the knowledge of God here understood is not shallow or superficiall, only as he is in a generall consideration the cause of things, a *Creatour* at large, but in a neerer dependance, *Thy* Cause, *thy* Creatour. Aristotle [17]

True speculation doth not alwaies hunt objects at the view, nor must it stop at the numerous effects wrought by the Creatour—This is rather to make thy selfe acquainted with the History of the Creation, than the knowledge of thy Creatour—but it must threed the whole Herd of the visible Creatures, and with a most intent undiverted eie trace & follow him home unto the place elected for his aboad, *thy Soule,* w[hi]ch is his *Temple.* And as Mary, when she went in quest of her Saviour, stopt not at the empty Monument, but searches and followes him so farre that she discovered him under the disguise of the Gardner, and then casting her selfe at his feet takes possession of him, with this acclamation, *Rabboni,* which is in effect as much as Thomas his gratulation, *My Lord and my God:* So, when thou hast trackt him to his retiring Chamber within thy selfe, in the humblest postures of obedience falling downe before Him, Apply Him to Thee, and derive thy selfe from Him as the Author of thy being, *Thy Lord, Thy Creatour.* John 20:*11*
Verse 28
[18]

To remember or to know God Historically is a wilde unusefull theory. If thou canst make no neerer approches than such, the devils have profited as farre in Faith as Thou: for *Diaboli credunt*—They beleeve the History of Christ—but such a beleefe doth no good at all. An Historicall faith which gazes on Christ, and takes Religion at a large distance, can never save any. (Jas.2:19)

There must be a neerer scale to bring thee to heaven, *Fides iustificans,* a justifying, a saving faith, which consists in the laying hold on Christ, and applying his merits to thee.

Was ever any fed by the report of a Feast? or had any consultation of Physitians such good successe that it could talke the Patient into health? The sight of meat nourisheth not me, nor can my wounds heale at the relation of other cures. Poisons and Antidotes have all one effect upon me, if not ministred; and a soveraigne Plaister is as unbeneficiall as a corsive, if not applyed. Christ is both my *Feeder* and my *Meat,* my *Physitian* and my *Remedy.* If my Faith concoct him not in the Sacrament, if it apply him not in my Penitence, my wretched soule lies under two dangers, of a Famine, and of Death. [19]

Woe unto me if I know God onely by Report: my salvation will then prove as barren as my knowledge. Nor shall I enjoy any thing of it beyond the name. I may heare of Heaven, but never must set foot within the gates. Religion and Faith are but aiery emptie sounds, if we possesse nothing of them beyond the words. The fruit of either consists in their Application. 'Tis true that Christ is the Saviour of the World, but that an uselesse truth to me unlesse my Faith entitle me to Him, and by appropriating his worke, be able to call him *my Redeemer.*

Therefore Luther saies well that *Meum [Mine]* and *Nostrum, [Ours]* these two words, are the summe of all Christianity. In that Master-peece of prayer, the first thing our blessed Saviour taught his Disciples was to possesse themselves of God under the stile of *Pater Noster, Our Father.* Luther *In Galat.*
1 & 3
[20]

In these stiles of *Mine* and *Thine* is not onely the whole world owned and divided, but the possession of all God's promises are delivered and taken by those termes. And surely, if we were as apt to pleade our Titles to Heaven as we are forward, though we wrestle with many troubles of suit, to maintaine our right in Earth, we would not then so easily forfait the remembrance of God as we doe, but with Jacob's resolution hold him even by force, making Him ours by all the ties which might confirme a just possession. (Gen.32:26)

But we are better Stewards for the world then for God: with more thrift doe we husband our Estates then our Time alotted for our Repentance; with fuller intention doe wee pursue the businesse of Earth, than the great businesse of our Salvation. Either our thoughts are so taken up in

---

*To know is to understand the cause [of what we know].

Temporall affaires that there is no roome for God: Wee *Remember* not *our Creatour* at all; or not so much, or not so oft, or not so early as wee ought—*In Iuventute,* In the daies of our Youth: *Remember thy Creatour in thy Youth.*

4. *Youth* is a headstrong unruly thing, rash in his apprehensions, violent in the execution of his designes, that acts first, and considers after. It is an easie combustible matter, apt to take fire at every Traine. It is like Wax, chafed and tempered by the excesse of heat raigning in the bloud to receive the seales of damnation, and the impression of any sinne. It is like a beleagured Citie assailed on all sides, the Cinque Ports of his Senses so blockt up with severall Temptations, that it is not safe for him to looke out at any of them. Oft-times even with the Aire his Nostrils sucke up the savour of Death, and an harmonious witchcraft ever deludes his Eare, whispering to the abused Sense that those Actions Ambition or Delight prompts him to, become his yeares.

In so much that the many Invasions unto which hee lies open and unguarded, might justly require this Admonition to fortifie him.

But yet it was not onely the contemplation of Youth's pronenesse to doe ill which occasioned it, but as well the consideration of his abilities to serve his Maker, which moved the Wiseman thus farre before hand to be-speake Man's younger yeares for God. Trees that are newly planted beare the fairest and best relisht fruit, whereas longer growth impaires them both in beauty and taste.

Salomon himselfe, whose Sunne-rise was so glorious, & in the morning of his reigne exprest so much maturity of judgement in deciding Controversies, so much devotion to God, and received so much approbation from him againe, that whereas God did in a manner but sojourne with his Fathers in a Tent, he had the honour to make him his guest, and to raise a standing house, a Temple, for him to dwell in—Yet for all this, in the declining of his yeares hee set as in a blacke cloud, darkly and ingloriously. For he fell by the practise of his strange Wives, who alienated his heart not onely from the remembrance of what himselfe once was, but from his Creatour, who had advanced his Throne above his Predecessours.

It doth not therefore ever follow, that the discerning of age is better than youth's. It may be sometimes more stayd, but never so cleere: a dimme sight lookes longer and with more intention upon its object, and wee know the reason—because it can take but a slow survay of what it sees. Yet who will denie, but that he who weares his eyes in his head sees better than one that weares them cased up at his girdle. A spectacle may present things bigger than they are, yet not so truely; for any addition unto truth is Imposture, as well as to detract from it. I may walke well enough by a candle enclosed in a Lanthorne, though I cannot read by it so well as by a taper, whose free light is not immur'd or shadowed at all.

Undoubtedly Adam's youth, I meane his morning and first part of his birth-day, was his best: and so I doe not say is, but should be ours. Man should be then most Man when the Ministers of Reason are most active, all which flag in his evening; and therefore as they decrease and lessen, so must hee. Hee that remembers God but a little in his youth, by the rule of Nature should quite forget him when hee is old; and then wee know the doome that followes: *Hee that hath no remembrance of God in his life time, shall be forgotten by him in death.* Hee that hath expended his young dayes in ryot, shall grow old in want. He that hath beene unfruitfull in the former part of his life, must needs be barren at his death. Nay (saith S. Cyprian) *He that never blossom'd in youth, whose goodnesse never put forth into a flower, can never beare fruit when he is old.*

It is a great adventure for a man to let himselfe loose at One and Twentie, and thinke to reclaime or take himselfe up againe at Threescore: when decay hath prevailed upon him, and age cast as many wrinckles upon his minde as hee weares upon his fore-head. To have lived till Fiftie or Threescore is a faire kalendar of time, but vertue doth not go by that kalendar. To be old is not to be wise, nor doth antiquitie leave off the vices which it nourisht from youth, but oft change[s] them into worse. Men use not to be superannuated in sinne: rather, their impotence so deeply seduces their judgement in their latter times, that they give their evils leave to prescribe upon them, and plead custome.

I speake not this to credit youth or diminish age, or by any rude comparison to take from riper yeeres that reverence which their goodnesse or experience may challenge. I confesse, and must deliver it from a more authenticke mouth, that *Amongst the ancient is wisdome*. I do not here set youth as an emulous opposite to age, contesting for prioritie, nor put the person of the younge in balance with the old. I onely conferre Man's younger time with his elder, his past dayes with his present: which is no more, in effect, but to compare man with himselfe, and such a comparison can disparage none. [Job 12:1] [26]

The scope of all I can say discharges it selfe briefly upon these two issues, to *prepare youth*, and to *hasten age*, as a *Monitor* to the one and a *Remembrancer* to the other.

Since ill customes grow strong upon us when we are weakest, I should advise those that are the Guardians of youth, and whom the care of a family employes, to enter them betimes in the Schoole of Vertue, and season these new vessels with Religion, knowing that caskes long retaine the taste of their first liquors which were infused into them. [I.]

Youth is a fertile garden, and though the heat and ranknesse of the soile bee apt to send up many weeds, yet if well drest in the fore-hand of the yeere, it is capable of faire plantations. Manure it therefore betimes whilst it is Spring, and it can looke upon the drooping Autumne at a great distance. Such a plot to worke on as is Man in his prime, such a *planter* as Paul, and such a *waterer* as Apollos, would make it in short time *theou geōrgion*,* fit to be reaped by *Angels,* and inn'd by *God*. [27] [1 Cor.3:9]

Aristotle was so precise in admitting schollers to his Morall Lectures, that he would have them past their wardship first, thinking their greene capacities could not bee mellow enough for his *Ethicks* till Thirtie at least. But Christ our Master was of another minde; his *Sinite parvulos*, &c—*Suffer little ones to come unto me*—encouraged parents and supervisors of children to enroll them in his Bands, his Church, before they were Masters of so much tongue as to name Christ. What though their narrow apprehensions cannot reach the high principles of faith? In a few yeeres, their understandings, elevated with their statures, will grow up to them, and the accession of a little time digest those precepts which their infancie drew in into the constant habit of a good life; not bowing themselves into any crooked postures of errour, nor forgetting that straight forme into which their first education wrought them. Therefore it was the counsell of the wise King, *Traine up a childe in the way he should goe in* at the doore & entrance of his life, *and when he is old he shall not depart from it*. Such happie blossomes in youth are the prognostications of a rich Autumne. And the wise Heathen, upon the same ground, undertakes for the felicitie of that state and those subjects who enjoy the blessing to have a religious Prince, train'd up in goodnesse from his infancie, set over them: *Nulla erit processu temporis, etc.* [(Ethics 1:1)] [Mar.10:14] [28] [Prov.22:6] [Seneca]

I need not (though without flatterie I might) give it English, nor would I speake it in any lower vulgar language, but onely the language of thanksgiving to Almightie God, who hath placed upon this Throne such a King; whose religion sprang up with him from his minoritie, and whose riper yeeres exhibit this fruit, which each day fals plentifully into the observation of all that are about Him, That He is not only the Defender of Religion, but morning and evening a Personall Actour in that service; Not only carefull to enact lawes for the the continuance of the Gospell, but making Himselfe a Law and a glorious Example to his whole Court. [29]

Lord, thou that knowest this truth, and bearest mee record: I doe not mingle this as an officious Parenthesis in my Errand, rather to adde glory to my present Master than to Thee—Never, O Never be unmindfull of Him who so early and so oft *Remembers Thee*.

I have performed my first intent, in doing the office of a Remembrancer to the Elder, touching the

---

*God's field (Gk).

2. Education of youth; This last concernes themselves. And it were a shame for those that undertake the manage of others' time to be unthrifty in their owne; to teach such as are submitted to their care to set out towards Heaven in the Morning, and yet themselves not follow till the Evening. I doe not prejudicate a gray-headed Penitence, though I must needs preferre the younger; that may be True, but this more Safe. I will hope wel of the one, yet beleeve better of the other.

[30] Winter voyages are very dangerous and uncertaine, by reason of the North-winde which is then let loose upon the Earth; and sure, hee were not wise that might take his journey in the Summer, yet by delaying his Opportunity would expose himselfe to the inclemency of the weather or fury of the Sea. Old Age is Man's Winter, witnesse that Snow which covers his head, more cold and lasting than the Russian Frosts, which scarcely the raging Dog-starre can thaw. Youth is his Summer, wherein the better temper of the Aire, the cleerenesse of his skie (wherein are fewer clouds, lesse stormes to hinder his prospect to Heaven) promise a more successfull voyage. Therfore whilst wee can see our way, whilst those Pilots which direct the body are able to discover that Shoare Eccles.12:3 whereunto wee bend our course, whilst our Lights are not damm'd up, *nor they wax darke which looke out at our windowes,* Let us fix our Eyes, our Faith and Memory constantly both upon the Journey, and Him who is able to reward our travell.

[31] God did not place the Memory in the hinder part of the head that wee should Remember Him last; Nor did he place our last Day below all other Daies in our Almanacke that wee should make it the farthest part of our Reckoning. By Christ's rule, our Last must be First, and as the end of every Action is first in the intent of the Author, so should God be freshest in our Memory and our End alwaies in our sight.

How can He that preceded all Time take it well at our hands to be put backe unto the last minute of Time? How can He that requires the first-fruits of our Lands be content with the Latter harvest of our Lives? How can He that expects a sacrifice of a sweet smell but distaste our unsavory zeale, when for a fragrant flower, wee present him with a dry stalke and withered leafe, the lees of our Age for the Vintage of our youth.

Prov.8:17 *They that seeke mee early, shall finde mee* (saith He), so if He bid us come at morning, our owne inexcusable neglect forfaits the appointment if wee go not till the Evening. Let us therefore [32] (Ps.130:6.) *Prevent the morning watch*—not deferre our journey till the dusty Evening or Twilight of our Daies, but set forward whilst we are yet a few houres from the dawning of Time, and (as the Apostle Hebr.3:13 speakes) *Whilst wee can say to day.*

In the dayes of thy Youth.

5. How every attribute lessens and shortens life, to make us understand what shadowes and dreames
In the of happinesse take up our Time! Our whole Age, our Delights, and their Fruition as short as is the
dayes day—yea, much shorter, since oft-times our Pleasures, our beloved sinnes and their Repentance lodge but three Minutes asunder.

The Schoolemen distinguish the day into Temporall or Morall. By the Temporall day, they understand that common Measure of Time whose compasse is 24 houres.

Eccl.12:2 By the Morall day, they meane our Prosperity, whilst our *Sunne is not darkned,* in which cleare [33] unclouded Time wee are most apt to forget God: As it is said of Rehoboam, who when hee had 2 Chron.12:10 established the kingdome and strengthened himselfe, *forsooke the law of the Lord*. And then the sense of the Text is, that we not only then thinke upon God when want of his helpe & our owne Misery prompts us—like Mariners at Sea, whose religion oft-times rises or falls with the wave; who with Jonah's Shipmates, pray devoutly in a storme, but in a calme lay their devotion to sleepe till the next Tempest wake it—But in our happiest condition, in our abundance, before adversitie like a (Eccles.12:) blacke cloud overshadowes us, *Whilst the evill dayes come not, nor the yeares wherein thou shalt* Verse 1 *say, I have no pleasure in them.* Upon which Interpretation, though proper to our Authour's purpose, and warranted by the best Expositors, I dare not at the end of my journey embarque my selfe, but insist upon the literall meaning and Temporall acception of *Dayes,* taking the *Dayes of our youth* for that short portion of Time set out for Man's being.

Which is best computed by Daies, & that *Stylo veteri,* the stile being drawne downe from our Fore-Fathers. Jacob, demanded by Pharoah how old he was, calculates himself by *Dayes,* and those summ'd up in sorrowes in stead of houres: *Few and Evill have beene the Dayes of my Yeares.* If hee, whose Age doubled ours at the largest extent, numbred his Time by Dayes, wee, that are bedwarfed both in our Stature and our Yeares so many spans below him, by what short measure shall wee take our life? Dayes are too large a size; For when wee thinke that halfe our Time is Night, which wee sleepe out; and of the other part which wee call Day, much is laid out upon Ceremony & the circumstance of Life, our Dressings, our Meales, our Visits, our recreations—I say, when wee consider this, wee shall confesse that *Minimum est quod vivitur,* nay, lower yet, *Punctum est quod vivitur, & adhuc puncto minus:* Life hath the *least* share in our Dayes, the Dimensions of it appearing no bigger than *one sand* in the Houre-glasse to the whole houre, or lesse than a *small point* to a Line.

Wherefore, then, doth improvident Man sooth himselfe with the imagination of many yeares to come, when his whole Time is comprehended in a few Dayes? nay, begun and finisht in one Day: *As at first the Evening and Morning made the Naturall Day, so Youth's morning, and Age's evening make but one Day of Life.*

What haste, then, ought wee to make in our Conversion? when our whole terme is bounded by such narrow Confines, and the flying Minutes in their sly Motion beguile us so fast, that wee are not sensible of time's stealth, or our owne declining to the Evening. Why doe wee so adjorne religious duties (sending away those better thoughts which bring God neere unto us, as Fœlix did Paul: *I will heare Thee some other Time*) when wee are not Owners of so poore an Election as to promise another peece of Time which may bring those thoughts and us together again? *He that hath promised thee a Pardon this Day for thy Sin, hath not promised thee a Reprieve for thy Life one day longer.* And therefore, if thou dismisse Christ when he knocks for entrance at thy heart with a *Vade & cras revertere, Goe and come againe to mee to morrow,* thou forgettest Christ's summons in the Gospell, *Stulte hac nocte:* Foole, thou hast no assurance of thy soule this night, nay, past this minute; and therefore *Now* collect thy selfe, delay not beyond this instant: *Ecce nunc tempus acceptabile, Now is the accepted time.*

[34]

Gen.47:9

Seneca

[35]
Biel *Lect.70 de Missa*
Genes. 1:5

Acts 24:22

August.*Serm. 16 de verb. Dom.*
[36]

Prov.3:28
Luc.12:20
2 Cor.6:2

Remember Now Thy Creatour.

Of all the severall distributions of Time, there is none that we can lay claime to but the Present. *The past time is not now, the future is not yet, onely the present may be called a time, and that, only, called ours.* Therefore Aristotle delivered it in a blunt, but true phrase, *Wee have no interest in time beyond this present Now:* And that so short, that like a flash of lightning, it leapes out and dies at once. That which I call *Now* lasts no longer than the verie syllable which delivers it to your eare, but changes in the mid-way, past and gone in that breath which named it.

Thus doth Time incessantly feed on us: it eats upon our dayes, digesting them so fast and greedily, that our *Future,* which was a minute since before us, not yet arrived, is in the twinckling of an eye behind us, lost and swallowed up in the wide gulph of time *Past.* O wretched condition of Man-kinde, that stands accountant unto God for everie sand that moves & passes thorow Time's Houre-glasse, yet scarse is allowed so much of time as to number his receipts and to compute his charge, which powres and empties it selfe so fast upon him, that his Present is suddenly mingled with the Past, and all the severall pensions and contributions which out of Time's Exchequer are payed to life no sooner grow due, but they become Arrerage.

In which fickle momentany flights, what securitie have wee in life? How shall wee make up our Audit with God for these summes so hastily throwne upon us, but by laying hold upon this instant, *Now?* Nay, how shall wee possesse our selves of that *Now* of time, which vanishes as it appeares,

6.
Now
Aug. *Confess.*11
Artist. *Phys.lib.*4
[37]

[38]

but by preventing it, by anticipating the day before it climbe too farre out of our reach, and our Sunne in a precipitate descent haste towards the West?

'Tis hard for a routed Armie to re-enforce it selfe in the end of the day, or but to make an orderly retreit; and it is as hard for man in his old age, when an Armie of infirmities mustered against him make the ministers of Reason disband, and everie disease hath him upon the execution; when the approches of death affright his dayes by looking in at his windowes, and by knocking at his doore disturbe his rest, making his nights sleepelesse, to deliver up a cleere undisturbed account to God, or to retire without confusion and disorder unto the dust from whence he was taken.

[39] It is not a perfect will when the Testator is not in perfect memorie. I would bee loth to make my last Audit with God in worse state of minde than my Audit with the world: the not disposing of my goods being but a trifle to the not disposing of my soule. My goods, if I have any, will find an owner (though I appoint none) when I am gone: a brother, or a friend, or a childe; but if on such loose unsettled termes I part with my soule, who shall owne it? He that by the right of creation hath best title to it, and made it mine, will not receive it backe from me, unlesse by my assignement, unlesse my prayers and my penitence make it a Legacie fit for Him.

It doth concerne me therefore to bequeath it to Him betimes, whilst I am in my right minde and perfect understanding—as S. Augustine advises, *Age pœnitentiam dum sanus es*—before my weake age confine mee to my chamber, or sicknesse lay mee on my death-bed. But then to leave off sinning when I am readie to leave life, argues I would yet sinne longer if I might live; That it is necessitie, not my owne will, divorces me and my vices. Such a bed-rid recantation as this is scarce worth the name of a Repentance. For I cannot so properly be said to repent mee of my sinnes, rather my sinnes repent themselves of mee; nor doe I discharge them, but more truely they discharge me, casting me off as an unusefull minister, unable and unfit now to serve them any longer.

S. Ambrose pronounces a woe upon them who put a period to their licentious courses and life together. S. Augustine goes neerer: *A repentance protracted and delayed to the last houre of life, borders upon destruction.* But yet, though it be so dangerous, so neere the brinke, it is not desperate. God forbid that I or any should miscensure the late conversion of a dying sinner. Christ's pardon to that condemned, nay, executed man upon the Crosse shewes that his mercie is not limited by any circumstance of time. Farre therefore be it from us to lay such a stumbling block before the feet of those that are now falling into earth, as to Imagine the penitence of Him that *hath waxed old in his iniquities* (as the Prophet's phrase is) should not be acceptable to God. Though young-begun devotion be more durable, an elder is not unwelcome. God accepts a late conversion better than none; for *Omnis ætas habilis Deo.**

Whilest wee have any interest in life, we need not despaire: wee are not past the acceptable time, or the day of our salvation. *Any part or moment of life is capable of God's mercie in the remission of sinnes.* 'Tis true that after death, God's Court of Audience is shut up, all prayers returne emptie, and repentance is ineffectuall: but the last part of age, though it be the picture of death, 'tis not the originall. Though it bee the *Vigill* and *Eve* of our last Festivall, *wherein wee shall finally rest from all our labours,* yet it is not death. There is yet a *Nunc,* a *Now;* there is a sparke of Life, rak't up in the embers of Age, able to kindle hopes as high as our Salvation. Therefore the Psalmist invites the Children of the Winter, *Snow* and *Haile* as well as *Fire, old Men* as well as *Children, to praise God.*

There are none that can so *Adæquaté,* so truly, so punctually be said to possesse this *Now* as old Men: For they have but barely this present Minute, so much of Time, and no more. 'Tis true that Youth hath no Assurance of Life past this very Instant, but Age hath no Hope beyond it—

Vitæ summa brevis,
Spem vetat inchoare longam.†

---

*Every age is fit for God.
†Life's brief span forbids thy entering on far-reaching hopes.

Yet all I enforce from hence is not to terrifie, but to hasten them, as devout Ananias did Paul to his Conversion, *Nun ti melleis? Now why tarriest thou? arise, and wash away thy sinne:* That they may employ this short allowance of Time to the best Advantage; that since they *Now* have so little Day to travell by, they gird up their Loines, and hold that pace which Eliah did before the Chariot of his Enemy Ahab, *Runne,* not creepe, being as swift and instant in their preparation as death is on them. Lest the consideration of themselves, that they are now, like trees loosened at the root, falling into earth, and *as they Now fall, so must they for ever lie, whether to* the right hand or to the left, to Mercie, or to Judgement; or else the consideration of that great journey which they are now going, from Earth to Heaven, and their fear of being benighted ere they get thither, having so small a time to journey in, perplex and dissettle their thoughts, making them amazedly cry out, as they did in the Prophet, *Woe unto us, for the day declineth, and the shadowes of the evening are stretched out.* {Acts 22:16; (1Kings 18:46); [43]; (Eccles.11:3); Jerem.6:4.}

The Conclusion and Summe of all is, that wee beseech Almightie God to feather us with the wings of the morning, that wee may begin our flight to him betimes; that wee may *Remember him in the dayes of our youth.* But if like sluggards wee have outslept our Morning, yet that He will vouchsafe us his grace, to bring us to Him in the After-noone or Evening of our life; That He will entertaine us into his Vineyard in his owne time, whether it bee at the *Sixth,* or *Ninth,* or *Eleventh Houre.* I know the morning is the best to enter upon this taske; And to hide our selves out of the way, or out of a presumption to deferre it to the latter part of the day, is Sinne and Danger. {*Conclusion*; [44]}

But yet if wee can stand in Christ's way, to bee called by Him at any of his houres, wee need not feare that wee are tardy, or doubt our recompence. They that were hired at the Eleventh and last houre had their penny as well as the earliest *that had borne the heat of the day.* And *Nicodemus had his access to Christ by night.* {Matth.20:9; John 3:2}

What, then, though our Life's short Taper be wasted to a snuffe, and almost burnt out: if that snuffe of our dying candle will but last so long, that wee may see to *Praise God before our death;* if it will but serve to light us fairely towards our graves, wee shall not then feare to goe unto our last beds in the darke. Our Bodies will sleepe in their dust without a candle, and for our Soules, they will need none, being translated into that region of light where there is *no need of a candle,* but the brightnesse of God's face holds on the day everlastingly, not suffering the night to rivall it any longer. Where their spring never droopes, nor their *Youth* declines; where the presence of their *Creatour,* whom they *Now* contemplate, perpetuates that *Now* unto them, fixing it to an Eternall Consistence of Time, which cannot alter or get beyond them, and makes their Fruition as Immortall as their Joyes. AMEN. {Ecclus.17:27; [45] Revel.22:5}

LENT 2

A SERMON PREACHED
at White-Hall in Lent.
1626.

Psal. 55:6.
And I said, O that I had wings like a Dove for then would I flee away, and be at rest.

I know that some Writers interpret this Psalme in a Mysticall sense of the Passion of Christ, and the Persecution of his Church; And apply this Text to our Saviour's Resurrection, desiring to Ascend up into Heaven, and to assume his proper place at the right hand of his Father. {Gloss; Hilarius; Hieronymus; [2] Cassiodor.}

But my discourse runs not by that Compasse; I take it Literally, as it is the complaint of David, and the History of his distresse, flying from Saul's fury into the Wildernesse of Ziph: Or as others will have it, from the conspiracy of Absolon and Achitophel. {Lorinus; I Sam.23; Vatablus; Arias}

Under whose Person I shall consider the Misery and disquiet of Man's life, Bewailing his wretched condition, and desirous to Go out of the world:

A SERMON PREACHED AT WHITE-HALL IN
Lent 1626. February 20.

By
Henry King, D.D. one of his Maiesties *Chaplains in Ordinary.*

LONDON,
Printed by IOHN HAVILAND,
1627.

O that I had wings like a Dove, for then would I fly away, and be at rest.

1. To give you a cleerer view of the troubles which distemper Man's life: Behold him first with David in a sad solitary *Consultation*, debating with Himselfe how hee might compasse his Flight, *And I said*.

2. The *conclusion* unto which hee growes, as comfortlesse as the other: wherein his Escape is only form'd in his Imagination and Wish, *Quis dabit? O that I had*, &c.

3. The *meanes* of his conveyance or subject of his Wish is *Wings*. [3]

4. The *Quality:* wings *like a Dove*.

5. The *use* he would make of them: his flight, *For then I would flie away*.

6. The *End* of his Flight, and Scope of his Wish: *Rest—I would flie away, and be at rest.*

My Meditations are now on wing, and I shall make but a short and speedy flight thorow each circumstance.

There is no greater torment to the Minde than suspense, when Men are unresolv'd in their courses, and uncertaine what to doe. But when amidst this anxiety they are exposed to solitude, when they are left to themselves with all their Sorrowes and Feares about them, I know not unto what higher pitch Calamity can be wrought.   I. *And I said*

A certaine Death is better than a doubtfull Reprive; and a Sociable Woe sweeter than a solitary Content. Mirth in a Wildernesse is a strange Anticke; but Misery sequestred from reliefe or advice, a very Monster. The Oratour said, hee would not live alone in Heaven without a Companion to communicate his Joyes unto.   [4]

I dare not say so. But sure, the Society of Angels & Saints contributes very much to those unutterable Joyes: And then, if the *Communion of Saints* be an Article in my Creed, to cheere my languishing Faith, I have good cause to put the *Desertion*, the being forsaken of Men, into my Letany, and pray against it. The *Dereliction* of the Father was so exquisite a Torment, that it caused the Sonne of God to confesse the weight of it by his loud cry upon the Crosse, *Why hast thou forsaken me?* The apprehension of it did some way daunt that invincible Patience, which all the preceding Agonies could not shake. For amidst them He was *Ut Ovis coram tondente*, Dumbe and silent *as the sheepe before the Shearer;* Onely this affliction broke open the sacred doores of speech, which before, Silence had lockt and seal'd up, forcing Him in the highest accent of sorrow to expostulate his forlorne Condition. The curse of Men or vengeance of God can finish in no more fearefull issue than Desolation. Nor could the mournfull Prophet, whom griefe had made eloquent, bewaile Hierusalem in a more learned Dirge, or write a sadder Epitaph upon her ruines, than *Desolata est*—she is left alone, desolate, and forsaken, and there were none to comfort her.   Matth. 27:46   (Is. 53:7)   [5]   Esa.64:10

If this Desolation in misery crack't the very Axle-tree of Heaven, and made the Sonne of God, *who upholds all things*, shrinke under the weight of it, what Sonne of Man, though strong as Atlas, can stand below this burthen, and not perish underneath it? Affliction lookes cheerefully when it may repaire to such as will afford it Pitie or Comfort; But when it is straightned, and lies under a solitary Confinement, it is the very picture of Despaire. If mishap single mee out and I fall in Company, a Friend may raise me up againe; but *Væsoli*—if I fall *alone*, when I am left and given over to my selfe, *Woe is mee:* What hand shall then lift me up, or who shall raise my soule from that dejection whereinto Calamity hath throwne her? How hopelesse is my Redresse when amazement seizes the Organs of reason, and every faculty that should assist me is confounded; when only feare is predominant, and the perplexed Phantasie, like a false glasse, multiplies the danger, and makes each mischiefe looke far bigger than it is?   Hebr.1:3   Eccles.4:10   [6]

Concluded under this Misery shall you finde David. He lies here under the pursute of swift Enemies: and which is worst, naked, and ungarded; left to Himselfe, to consult with his owne troubled bosome what course of safety to take. Which Deliberation of his is attired in the same Livery his Fortune now weares, Pale and Distracted: He calls for helpe, and the best relief his Judgement can furnish him with is but the name of a Rescue; and rather a desire of his Escape, than the meanes how to effect it, 'Tis but a *Dixi, I said*—He doth but talke of it. To promote which Purpose, he would become a Debtor to a creature of the Aire for wings, to helpe him from the Earth; and to procure this Courtesie, he is constrained to use the fruitlesse mediation of an Agent more emptie than the Aire, a Wish: *Quis dabit: O that I had* this Opportunitie of Flight!

Though David be the Historie, Man is the Morall: whose condition at best is as full of anxietie as David's. If David had enemies, he hath more. And if he had cause to wish his departure, hee hath so too. 'Tis unsafe for him to stay here, and yet uncertaine when he can get off. Onely Desire is his Pilot, which lookes at a great distance upon his deliverie; and his wishes bespeake that happinesse which yet hee is not neere unto:

O that I had, &c.

'Tis a miserable releefe when we can onely heare the sound of comfort, but feele none. Wishes that are laden with the richest blessings reach not farther than the Eare, but die there: as sparkes, leaping from the fire, lose their noise and light together. Did ever the Historie of a Medicine cure a sick man? or the smell of a feast feed one that was hungrie? or the contemplation of Libertie baile a Prisoner? If so, then haply I may be induc'd to thinke that wishes have somewhat in them besides the sound, and are more than meere shadowes.

Shadowes indeed, dilated or contracted according to the Phantasie, from whose uncertaine Light they are cast. They are but as meat set upon the Herse of the Dead, for shew, not use; or like Dreames, whose successe is as emptie as their Birth. The day will not rise a minute the sooner for my wishing; nor shall a man have a whit the more because hee desires an Addition to that he hath. Those desires may bring him lesse quiet, lesse contentment, not more wealth. Let me apply the words of Esay: our wishes at best are but *as a Night vision, as an hungrie man dreameth that he eats, but he awakes and his soule is emptie.*

As their releefe, so their Parentage is miserable. Our words have a fuller Pedegree than our wishes, for those spring from plentie, *Out of the abundance of the heart the mouth speakes.* But wishes spring from Penurie, they are the Dictates of our necessitie, and the onely Grammar by which they are taught to speak is Want, which prompts us to wish what we have not.

There is not in the World any thing so lawlesse as our desires, which like Freebooters, *rifle others to enrich us.* There is not any thing so wilde as our wishes. Reason cannot bound, nor Religion reclaime them, but like *Haggards,* that goe out at everie cheake, they flie at all game that crosses them. We rove and bangle after everie Fortune, most eagerly pursuing that which wee are prohibited, and affecting least that estate which wee enjoy.

Qui fit Mæcænas, ut nemo, quam sibi sortem
Seu ratio dederit, seu fors obiecerit, illa
Contentus vivat?*—

'Twas a question long agoe proposed, but never to be resolved, so long as Fortune or Nature have any interest in Man. Our mindes lie in our bodies, just as sicke men in their beds, who by tumbling and tossing from one place to another thinke to gaine ease, yet by their unquiet Motion heighten their Distemper.

We varie our desires, shift our Imaginations from one Object to another, in which wildernesse of thoughts we lose our selves; and by this confused way, the more wee seeke after Rest, the more we tire our selves. Either we grow wearie of the State of the Times, or of our owne; wearie of others, or of our selves. We thinke our good daies (if wee have any) fly too fast; but our Ill ones, as if govern'd by that *Sunne* which stood still in *Gibeon,* hang too long over our heads: which makes us oftimes,

---

*How comes it Maecenas that no man lives content with the lot which either his own choice has given him, or chance has thrown in his way?

Lent 2

ere it be Noone with us, ere wee have arrived at halfe our age, to wish it Night. Thus, to helpe the lazie Motion of Time, to get the start both of it and our owne miseries, wee plume our selves for flight, and our Wishes are *Wings*:

> *O that I had Wings!* [11]

As sparkes flie up, so should Man's thoughts. The flame without Instruction can finde out its owne Center; but all the Lessons or Instructions Divinitie can reade will hardly raise Man, who is a sparke lighted from the Deitie, or make him beare up unto his proper Sphere. As other winged Creatures, so the Soule hath her flights too, and the period of those flights is Heaven. Her proper Motion, then, is to goe to Mount, to worke up: Should shee forget that Motion, the verie forme of the Bodie would quicken her Memorie; which is therefore built in that streight upright figure, to make us understand that as our future aboad, so our present Contemplation must be Heaven.

3. *Wings.*

Ambros. *De Virg. Lib.3*

When other Creatures, in signe of Homage to the earth that bare them, decline downewards, and with dejected postures confesse their whole Parentage to bee nothing else but Dust, into which ignoble Element they shall be taken backe againe, and so digested into their confused Principles, as if they never had beene—When all their Memorie is shut up in earth, and determines in that corruptible Masse out of which they were at first extracted: Man, like a Monument of Honour, like a Pillar or Pyramid erected for the glorie of his Creatour, points upwards at Him. And though his Base or Pedestall bee grounded in Earth, his head is in the Clouds, like that great Tree in Nebuchadnezzar's vision, whose plantation was earth, but his *Height* reach't *Heaven*. How much, then, doe those Men degenerate from their Creation, whose groveling Meditations are ever bedded in Earth; and like Moles, buried below the cares of this world, worke under ground, more zealous to finde out the Veines and Mines of Treasure lockt up within the Wombe of the Earth, than to make themselves capable of those richer blessings, which are treasur'd up in Heaven. [12]

Dan.4:10, 11

I doe not justifie one sinne by another, nor by any diminution of the one contend to make the other plausible; but by way of Comparison I dare be bold to say, the Ambitious Man hath more of Man in Him than the Covetous, and bates lesse of his pitch. A Hawke that keepes her wings, though shee bee otherwise ill-conditioned, and flie not true, does lesse degenerate from the Aierie than one that, being throwne off, uses to take stand upon the ground. [13]

The proper Motion of my soule is to ascend, and though an aspiring Man makes his ascent by the wrong staire, hee more preserves the dignity of his being, gives more testimony that He hath a soule, than a wretched drudge of the World. And (though it be farre from me to commend either, both being execrable) I should rather Pitie a Phaëton falling in a brave Misfortune, than a low Slave of the Earth, that never would looke up to the skie, nor care's for any Sun-shine, save onely that which his bright Sunne of Metals, Gold, casts.

To take up this loose Excursion, and to fix you where I left—Earth is no competent Object for Man's thoughts. If the Soule's Active Faculties lye still emprisoned within that Body of Clay which she informes, the Dull sense would be as faire a difference of Man as Reason and the discursive part. Anatomists would have the soule learne to contemne the World from the very figure of the *heart,* which is dilated upward, but pointing and narrow below, to shew wee should touch the earth only *In Puncto*. Our Meditations must rather glance, than fix upon the businesse of the World. And therefore the Soule (in Böetius), sensible of her owne Elevation, confesses shee hath wings to lift her farre above the contemptible earth: [14]

> *Sunt pennæ volucres mihi,*
> *Quas sibi cum velox mens induit,*
> *Terras perosa despicit.**

Boetius *De Consol. lib. 4. metr.1*

---

*I have the wings of a bird, which my swift mind puts on and despises the earth she hates.

S. Ambrose makes the Application: *Since, O Man, like a Bird thou hast the Liberty of Wings, why doest thou clog thy flight with the cares of this world? Why doest thou set up thy Rest on Earth, that shouldest build thy Tabernacle in Heaven, and Nest above the Starres?*

<small>Ambros. *Ser.14 in Psal.118*
[15]</small>

But every Plume makes not a like speed, nor flies at the same pitch. As in the feathered Creatures there are diversities of wings: so there are degrees of Knowledge in men's soules, and diversities of flights. Some have quicker and more lofty apprehensions than others, some have Eagle's wings, some but the wings of the Sparrow. The Woman in the *Revelation* had the wings of an Eagle given her to accelerate her flight, and carry her into the Wildernesse. But David in the *Psalme* had onely the wings of the Sparrow to convey him from danger which pursued him: *Anima ut Passer erepta*—*My Soule is escaped as a Sparrow from the Net.*

<small>Revel.12:14

Psal.124:7</small>

Here for this Escape, He desires a wing of larger stroak, stronger to maintain a flight, and more able to goe at stretch from that mischiefe which threatened him—*the wings of a Dove:* For she is held to have the speediest wing for the time she flies of any other Fowle. Therefore Euripides, when he would commend swiftnesse, does it in this Phrase: Not inferiour to the Dove, whose nimble pinnions even cut the Aire with their quicke Motion.

<small>[16]</small>

Radit iter liquidum celeris neque commovet alas:

<small>Virg. *Aeneid*.5.(217)</small>

O that I had wings like a Dove.

'Tis a judicious regular Phantasie that workes by an authenticke Coppie. Did all our wishes, all our desires determine like this, we should not then at any time blush to owne them: nor need wee feare though they were printed on our foreheads.

<small>4.
Like a Dove</small>

'Tis S. Paul's Rule, *That wee covet the best Gifts.* I thinke the Prophet here was Example to the Apostle's Rule, who shapes his Wish by the very best of all flying Creatures, The *Dove,* Embleme of unspotted Chastity, of white Innocence and harmelesse Simplicity.

<small>I Cor.12:31</small>

The Dove hath ever been lucky to Mankinde. It was the Dove that had the dignity to be dispatched, as the first Embassadour that ever went betwixt God & Man, after the Deluge, discharging the trust of him that sent her out of the Arke so well, that she gave him ocular proofe of the falling of the Waters: Returning home with a Banner of Truce displayed in her Mouth, and bearing the Articles of God's convenant and Man's Peace sealed to him in the Olive Branch, which she presented to Noah. And when the Spirit of Comfort came from Heaven to rest upon the head of Christ, he borrowed onely this shape to descend in, making his first visible apparance in the forme of the Dove. Which dignity our Saviour preserves to her in an high measure when He courts his Beloved the Church under this Stile, *My Dove.* And againe in the Gospell, where he vouchsafes to make the Dove his owne Text and our Coppy, proposing her in his Sermon as a Patterne worthy the imitation of all Christians, *Estote Simplices ut Columbæ: Be ye wise as Serpents, simple as Doves.*

<small>[17]

Gen.8:11

Matth.3:16

Cant.2:10, 14

Matth.10:16</small>

If the world had quite lost the Character of all Morall goodnesse, wee might profitably search for it and recover it in the Dove. Milde and soft, and calme as the stillest Aire, having no Malice to sowre, *no gall to dis-sweeten her Temper* (I may truly apply that of Wisdome): So loving to her Mate, and so True, that shee hath given life to a Proverbe by her properties—*True as the Turtle* is the highest language conjugall loyalty can speake in. *Never stain'd by adulterous Couplings,* but of so reserv'd and cold a Chastity which the hot flames of Lust cannot thaw.

<small>[18]

Wisd.8:16.</small>

Not Loose, and yet most Free in her conversation, for shee loves Company, and therein shewes Chastity is not onely confin'd to Nunneries. A sociable woman may be as honest as a Recluse, and though free, more chast and vertuous in her Mirth, than many a Cloystred frailty is in her devotions.

She is no light gadder like Dinah, no stragler from her house like the factious Separatist, that flies off from the Congregation. 'Tis one of the Dove's notes that *Gregatim volat:* she will assemble with the Flocke. Not tainted with excesse in her feed—She eats for hunger, not wantonnesse. Her

<small>[19] (Gen. 34:1–2)</small>

---

*She skims her way in the clear light, nor do her swift wings move at all.

habitation, though not Curious, yet Cleane, and White like her own Thoughts. In the Choice whereof she imitates the wise Builder in the Gospell, laying *the foundation of her House in the rocke.* Matth 7:24
Cant.2:14

And for her lodging, 'tis not like the proud Daughters of Tyre, soft and lascivious. Her Nest is hard, and this hardnesse (saith a Writer) signifies Repentance and strict life; to represse & choake the growth of those weeds which People of dissolute addictions, pamper'd in ease and Ryot, like ranke soiles send forth. (Ps.45:12)
Hugo Cardinal

It was Job's speech, *Moriar in nidulo meo, I shall die in my Nest.* I doe not wonder, then, if David here going in quest of a Peace not to be found on Earth, & of that final Rest, which onely can compose the troubles that distemper life, wish to be furnished both with Instruction and Meanes for his flight by the Dove: First desiring her Vertues to Qualifie him, to make him capable of that last Quiet, and then the speed of her wings to haste unto it, *O that I had wings like a Dove, For then would I flee away.* Job 29:18

[20]

I Blame not any for being wearie of his stay here, or desirous to leave the World. Sure, the World, now froward and peevish in her old Age, growes wearie of her Guests, and makes more speed to bee gone from us then wee can to *fly away* from it. For let us set out never so soone, all that we can call happinesse here on Earth hath already taken Wings, and Flies before us. *Riches have Eagle's Wings* (said Salomon) *to flie away from the Owner:* so suddenly is the World's wealth annihilated and shrunke to nothing. And for those Graces which Honor or Favour contribute unto us, the *Giddie Wheele* of Fortune turnes about so fast, that none can take sure footing there. 5.
For then would I flee away

Prov.23:5

The Apostle sayes, some Men's ills doe *proagein eis krisin: leade the way,* anticipate Judgement. I am sure all our good meets with its Criticall day before wee our selves doe, who generally outlive our best Times, and survive all wee could have wisht ours, save onely our Miseries: So fleeting is the plentie or glorie of the World, so short a stay doe those blessings make with us. [21] I Tim.5:24

Should they stay longer, wee could not stay with them. Infirmitie and Decay thrust on our Earthy Bodies with such violence to their Center, which is the Grave, that as in a Scene, our Entrance and our Exit are but a verie little distant from one another. Therefore the Philosopher, when hee was askt what life was, gave a briefe but significant resolution in his dumbe shew, when he but Turn'd and so went out. The Motion of our Time is so precipitate, that as if the dayes of our life were measured by that *winged Sunne* in Malachy, the Minutes flie away so fast, even our Thoughts cannot lackey, nor our Desires keepe pace with them. Malach.4:2

The *Shadow,* or the *Dream of a shadow: skias oneiros,* which was Pindarus his Expression of Life, or *the Weaver's shuttle, or the Winde,* are too slow Comparisons for Life. When wee have named all, wee must conclude with Job: *Dies mei velociores—Our dayes are swifter than all these.* [22]
Job.7:6, 7

So that wee cannot stay here, nor, if we could, doe I finde any thing to make us enamoured of staying. When I consider that each day addes to my sorrowes, or which is worse, my sinnes, making their guiltie account rise still higher in the Doomesday Booke, how can I better make my abatements, than by going hence? Since *living here I cannot but continually sin,* how shall I flie the dangerous occasions of sinne, but by *quitting Life,* and *flying away? O, therefore, that I had wings to fly away.* Aug.in Psal. 54.11

Againe, when I consider with Job *The tedious monethes of vanitie which I am made to possesse, and the wearisome nights which are appointed for me;* and that (as Salomon saith) *All is labour and sorrow and vexation of Spirit:* Can any man blame me to take Saint Paul's *Cupio dissolvi* into my mouth? *I desire to bee dissolved.* 'Tis but Justice, being thus toiled out with Labour, and overwatcht with Care, at length to bid the world Good Night, and wish my selfe that rest which is the End of David's wish, *O that I had wings like a Dove: for then would I flie away, and be at Rest.* Job 7:3
Eccles.1.*14*
Phil.1:23
[23]

As the shadow to the servant who hath wrought in the heat of the day, or Reward to the Hireling, or sleepe to the Traveller; so sweet, so desirable is Death to one wearie of Life. *Man goeth forth to* 6.
And be at Rest his labour till the Evening, saith the Psalmist. All life is but a laborious Day; wherein, as Inheritours of Adam's curse, wee eat our bread in sorrow and sweat. Onely Death is our Evening, in whose succeeding Night, wee burie all the troubles of our Day, taking possession of a quiet which wee might wish for before, not taste till then. Compar'd to this, all else wee call Rest is counterfeit; it beares the Name, but not the true stampe, and rather resembles than is Rest. Sleepe, which is the best, most cunning Picture of Rest which the curious hand of Nature ever drew upon us, is but a Picture, and by the Rules of Art, a Coppy must lose much of the Originall. If ever Rest were drawn to the life, 'tis in that most exact Night-peece, Death; wherein all memory of preceding trouble is so slumbred, that no relick awakes to disturbe the quiet which it affords. But 'tis much otherwise with us that Live here, whose busie Cares, not content with the Latitude of Time which Day allowes them, encroach upon our Nights; when, though the Doores of sense are lockt up in sleepe, with false Keyes they enter at the Phantasie, which they affright with visions and distemper with Dreames: making the same cares which bring us to bed keepe Company with us there, and become our Alarums to raise us in the Morning. *Thus the very Rest which we take is a toyle!*

O miserable condition of Mortality, when the relaxation of our Bodies is our Minde's exercise, when our recreations are a Businesse; when our Vacation is a Terme; when our broken sleepes, and our Rest interrupted with thoughts, like the Intermissions of a Fever, cannot properly bee termed an ease, but a lesse paine. But thus hee *gives his Beloved sleepe:* This is the rest which even the Darlings of the World and Lords of the Earth take here. I would it were not too true, That they often sleepe worse, never better than thus. Nor will the numerous Cares, which like a wreath of thornes, empale their heads, and swarme within the circle of a Crowne, give them leave to expect more quiet, till they shall exchange their Ivorie Beds for a Grave, their Canopie of State for a Coffin, their Sheets for a Shrowd, their rich Mantles for a Coverlet of Dust. They then shall finde a *Chamber in Death* will be a more quiet Dormitorie than a Palace; and (as Job sayes) *Glebæ* (so the Chaldee Paraphrase renders it)—*The clods of the valley, shall bee sweet unto them.* They shall rest softer upon that cold pillow of earth than on a Bed of downe.

Therefore, *Fæliciores mortui vivis,* happier are those that Sleep in Death than any that Live. For *they* (saith the Spirit) *rest from all their labours.* Their perfect Peace is sign'd, when wee here in our War-fare cannot obtaine a *truce for the Night,* nor will our Disturbances allow us quarter in our Beds; Nay, scarcely in our last and lowest Beds, our Graves.

Wherein (let me truely say) though wee enjoy a quiet Rest compar'd to that wee had here, yet even that, compar'd to the Rest wee shall hereafter enjoy, when that *Dies Refrigerii, Great day of refreshing* is come—I say, that Rest which Death allowes is imperfect; and the Grave will appeare rather a *Resting place* than a *Rest:* As a Traveller sits downe to ease himselfe a little on the way, that he may be fresher to hold out the latter part of his journey. Certainely, as (in the language of the Schooles) there is *Beatitudo viæ,* a Beatitude on the way, before wee reach our Countrey: so there is *Requies viæ, A rest by the way.* And in that high Road of Nature, Death, is this seat, this Resting place erected, where though wee sit downe, we cannot stay; Though wee dispose our selves to sleepe there for a Time, that sleepe is not our Everlasting Rest.

Though wee there *Rest from our labours,* wee doe not Rest from our Hopes: *Caro mea requiescit in spe*—We still *Rest in Hope.* And Hope is a watchfull, sleepelesse qualitie, that will keepe us waking, and knocks at the Doores of our Graves, using the Call of Micah to raise us thence, *Arise and depart, for this is not your rest.* That Hope sollicites God for the re-union of the Soule and the Body. And the Soule, though after her separation admitted into the Presence of God, loth to partake that happinesse without her Bodie, hastens God's comming, that shee may the sooner meet with her Companion againe, *Veni cito* [come quickly]. And the Bodie, though peacefully compos'd in the Dust, wearie of the darke lodging and tedious Night which over-shadowes it, wishes for the Morning of the Resurrection as earnestly as Job did for the Dawning of the Day: *When shall I arise, and the Night bee gone?*

'Tis not enough then for us, *Quiescere in pace:* to rest in our graves in Peace. Our Peace is not compleat till wee shall Rest in Glorie; nor will our Faith bee satisfied, till it determine in Fruition, and wee are made partakers of that Beatitude which yet we apprehend only in Beleefe. Then our Rest shall bee perfect, when this *Quies* shall become *Acquiescentia,* an Acquiescence which is the highest Degree of Rest—the Delight and Content which arises from the Contemplation and the possession of this Rest; when Christ shall say unto us, as the Prophet David does unto Him in the Psalme, *Arise and come into thy rest.* Psal. 132:8

To finish all. The Rest which David in this Wish aimes at, lies higher than the Grave: Heaven is the Resting place hee meanes; and that Celestiall Rest in Glorie, which will succeed the Resurrection of the Just, is the Period of Christian Faith. The attaining of this Rest shall be the End of my Flight and your Application. Conclusion

I shall perswade well, and you apply profitably, if wee rightly prepare our selves for this Rest. As the Body hath Preparatives to procure Rest, so hath the Soule too; but the Ingredients are quite different. Physitians of the Body use to prescribe *Mandragora* and drowzy *Opium* to call on sleepe. But the *Great Physitian* of our soules hath in his Gospell tempered our preparative to Rest with Active stirring Simples. The cup hee gives us is not a *Cup of slumber,* but of watchfulnesse, and the full Receipt, *Vigilate & orate: To watch, and to pray here,* that wee may Rest hereafter. A sleeping heavy Christian, like the drowzy Bridemaids in the Gospell, may enjoy that mischiefe which David prayes against, *Sleepe in Death,* but never Rest in Life. To prevent which Lethargie, and to lighten the soule of all impediments and dull obstructions which may retard her Motion, 'tis fit before wee take *our Flight hence and be no more seene,* wee take an exact survay of the Conscience, *which close Cabinet admits no scrutiny, no spectator but God & our selves:* where, if we finde any weighty Crime that oppresses, or Secure sin that besots and stupifies the Soule, that we endevor to expell that cold venome by the pretious Antidote of Repentance; that wee disburthen our selves by Confession, and by a devout Sorrow throw out the dangerous lading. [29]
Calix soporis
Esa.51:22
Matth.26:4
(Mt.25:1–12)
Psal.13:3
Psal.39:13
[30] August. *In Psal.54*

It was an Heathen's advice: *Nemo cum sarcinis enatat*—an Encombred Man cannot swim. If we adventure thorow the waters of Death, Nature's Dead Sea, with such a Mill-stone hanging at our Neckes as a Mortall sinne, wee must not hope to recover the safe shoare, but drowne everlastingly, and perish in that bottomlesse Gulfe. If wee hope to flie up to our finall Rest with such Manacles about us as the violence of hands, or such shackles as the transgressions of our feet, swift to pursue all occasions of sinne, how presumptuously doe wee tempt God, and delude our selves? When such a weight as Guilt, or (in Zacharie's phrase) *such a Talent of Lead* as sinne depresses and holds us downe, the powerfull Wings of the Cherubines shall never be able to lift us up from the Earth. Wee must therefore first shake off these Fetters, these Chaines, devest our selves of this weight, and by applying the mercies of Christ to us, *Cast* the heavy *burthen* of our sinnes upon him, who is willing to take them off us. Seneca

Zach.5:7
[31]

Psal.55:22

And then, being alleviated, lightned of our burthen, and capable of Flight, the Prophet DAVID will fit us with Wings, *The Wings of the Dove.* These Wings saith Ambrose, are *good Conditions, habituall Vertues.* For this goodnesse must not be slight and superficiall, and Temporarie, but Constant and lasting to the end. They onely that continue to the end shall bee crowned with this Rest. Or else these Wings are our *Prayers,* that like the Angels in Jacob's vision, Ascending and Descending, maintain our traffique with Heaven: or (saith Saint Augustine) they are *Charitie* to those that want, and forgivenesse of such as have offended us; these (saith hee) are a paire of Wings to convey us to Heaven. Or they are Repentance, which is the seale of our peace with GOD. Ambr.*Serm.26*

Id.*Lib.3.de Virg.p. 32*
[32] Genes.28:12

Hieron.*Lib.2. Ep.10.ad Rustic.*

In one word, these Wings are the qualities of the Dove: Mildnesse, and Simplicity, and Innocence, and Cleannesse, Properties that divide the rich blessings both of Earth and Heaven; for *the Meeke shall possesse the Earth, and the Cleane in heart shall see GOD.* A mildnesse which furie cannot exasperate, nor heighten to a Revenge; but rather is content to suffer wrong, or to remit it, or by a secession desires to shunne both the Person that did the Injury, and all provocation of returning it together. (Which Saint Ambrose and other Writers collect to have beene the intent of Matth.5:5, 8

Ambr.*Lib.1.Offic.cap.21.*
Lorin. *In Psal.54*

[33] David in this avoidance of his unjust Enemies.) A Simplicity never adulterate or discolour'd with Hypocrisie; A pure white Innocence, never sullied with Levitie, nor bespotted with foule action. Rare and certaine capacities to wing our soules, and to promote our flight into the Tabernacle of Rest. When the Psalmist askes the question, *Who shall abide in thy Tabernacle, or who shall dwell in thy holy Hill?* The demand is answered punctually: *Hee that hath cleane Hands, and a pure Heart.*

Psal.15:1

Psal.24:4

When wee are fethered with this happie Plume, when our Prayers have obtained these graces from God to qualifie our last Flight which shall end in *Glorie,* and then with their advanced *Wings* beat at the Gates of Heaven for Entrance, those *everlasting Doores* shall *open* themselves wide to our Admission, and the *King of Glorie,* Christ himselfe, vouchsafe to receive us, sealing unto us our Eternall *Quietus est,* as hee did to that poore Accountant in the Gospell,

(verse 7)

[34]

Matt. 25:21

Well done good and faithfull servant,
Enter thou into the Joy of
thy Lord. AMEN.

An Exposition upon the Lord's Prayer

TO
THE SACRED
MAJESTIE OF MY
SOVERAIGNE LORD
AND MASTER,
King CHARLES.

Most Gracious Sir;
   Though I have had two Masters, I never had but one Patron. When by the direction of your Majestie's Blessed Father, my first Royall Master, somewhat was done to disprove that (since confessed) scandall touching my Father's Revolt from his Religion, I then addressed my selfe to Your Princely protection, which You so liberally afforded, that my emboldned Duty afterwards instructed me to presume upon Your goodnesse in the like kinde. I confesse, this weake testimony of my service in God's Church tooke life from the Example of Your Glorious Father's worke (I meane that excellent Meditation of his upon this Prayer) and my purpose was to have dedicated it unto Him, as an humble acknowledgement of the many gracious encouragements which I received from his owne mouth in the times of my Attendance on Him. But though my Purpose died with Him, my Obligation did not. That lives in You, whose vouchsafed favour both derived and increased it, by assuming me to your Service, when the consideration of mine owne inability and the losse of my Master made me content to lose my relation to the Court. Then, Gracious Sir, since it naturally descends on You by Two Titles, both as His Executor and my Master, be pleased once more to enlarge the bounty of your acceptation, and to receive this Tribute from his hand who is ambitious of nothing but leave to weare Your Cognisance, and to write Your Name in the Front of his labours. This afforded Goodnesse and my gratitude will successively prompt Devotion, by making it my daily practice to pray for the addition of all Blessings upon your Royall selfe, with that Religion and Loyalty which fits

Your Majestie's most humbly
devoted Servant,

HENRY KING

I. AN EXPOSITION UPON THE LORD'S PRAYER

MAT. 6:9
After this manner, or thus, pray ye.

This Text is but a preface and no more, or like a Curtaine hung before some rare peece. Behind it is delineated the curious Archetype and Master-peece of all Prayer, whose Author is Christ. From

AN EXPOSITION VPON The Lords Prayer.

Deliuered in certaine Sermons, in the Cathedrall Church of S. *Paul.*

By *Henry King* Archdeacon of *Colchester,* and Residentiary of the same Church.

Orationi lectio, lectioni succedat oratio: breue videbitur tempus quod tantis operum varietatibus occupatur. Hieron. Epist. ad Lætam.

The Second Impression.

LONDON,
Printed by *Anne Griffin.* 1634.

I. An Exposition upon the Lord's Prayer

which originall copy, all our prayers, so farre as imitation and our weake Art can counterfeit, are derived and drawne.

The parts are three:
First, an Injunction: *Pray;*
Secondly, a Pattern: *Thus,;*
Thirdly, the Persons: *Yee.*
From the Injunction I will observe three Circumstances:
First, the *charge* it selfe, that Prayer is *ex Præcepto*.
Secondly, the *Necessity* of it.
Thirdly, the *Excellence*.

I first shew prayer is *ex Præcepto*. To prove which needs no other argument than the forme or modification of the word:

Pray; or as the Vulgar, *Orabitis:* ye shall pray—both Mandatory. However, then, Halensis stiles it only *Documentum,* a lesson, Saint Augustine confessed it to be a *Jussion,* or command; And Aquinas plainly shewes it is a *Precept*.

Christ never decreed any thing in vaine, and therefore whersoever his command is laid, it calls for obedience; and the oftner he repeats his command, the greater tie doth it leave on our duty. The Injunction in this place hath divers conformations and ligaments, all which, like so many cords and fastenings, binde it to our memory and observation. *Clama ad me & exaudiam:* Call on me. Pray for the peace of Jerusalem. *Subditus esto Domino & ora illum. Orate ne intretis in tentationem:* Watch and pray. *Petite & accipietis:* Aske, and ye shall have. So here, *proseuchesthe,* Pray.

Nor was this barely given in charge, but exemplified by the Author, Christ himselfe. Hee that in his Gospell taught us to make *Prayers* and *Supplications* did himselfe pray also; and that not a few times, nor in few places. For what place was there wherein this High Priest found not an Oratory to pray?—The Mount, the Garden, the Crosse: so that I may truely say of Him, *His whole life was nothing else but a long Prayer.*

My second circumstance, concerning the Necessity of Prayer, naturally flowes from this. For if Christ, the Lord and Master, found Prayer an act worthy to exercise him, how great a necessity is implyed from us, whose whole composition is nothing else but *Wants and Necessities?* All which are onely supplyed by our Prayer. There is our Harvest, and from that seed doth the increase of God's blessings multiply upon us. Those two maine props of life, our *Raiment* and the *staffe of bread,* are the donatives of Prayer, witnesse that Petition under which they and all else wee need are comprised, *Give us this day our daily bread.*

For which and other benefits, wee have no other commodity to trafficke or exchange with God but Prayer; the onely rate at which his mercy is purchased, and the currant Coine in his Exchequer. Therefore *Pray.*

A most beneficiall yet easie taske, enjoyned only for man's good, Almighty God herein dealing with us, as those Benefactors whose bounty sets the poore a worke for charity, not profit; not for any advantage they meane to make of their labour, but what meerely reflects on themselves, that they may give them an occasion to earne a living. So from the solicitation of our praiers doth God take occasion to extend his mercies unto us. Not that our prayers have any worth or merit, or *that they advantage Him, but our selves.* When he bids us *Pray,* he doth but fit us with a capacity to receive what he desires to give.

Hee might indeed bestow upon us his Favours without the suit of our Prayers, but that were a double derogation, first from his Gift, and next from his owne Soveraignty.

He that can make himselfe so cheape to give unask't, certainly gives that which is not worth taking, else hee would never make such haste to bee rid of it. Thus to fore-stall a suit instructs him that receives to neglect, not to thanke the Doner. Suit puts value upon a gift; nor is that ware held marketable which proffers it selfe unto the buyer. There is a modesty to be used even in doing favours; for it is an unmannerly kindnesse that intrudes on the accepter, and an impudent good turne which like a prostitute wooes him that should receive it. Such is the curious disposition of man to undervalew and grow weary of whatsoever he comes easily by: *Cito data vilescunt*. There is no bread so sweet as what is earned with sweat, and *no gift so prized* as that which is obtained with greatest difficulty: *Quicquid quæritur optimum videtur*. Therefore, before God gives, it is fit he understood in a few words the desire of his clyent, lest he should offer a blessing to *one that had no will to take it*.

Aug. ser.5 de verb.Dom.
Petronius Arbit.
August.

[7] Againe, if God should give without petition, it were an impeachment to his royalty. We see ordinarily men are content to enter covenant not to receive their due unlesse upon demand, nor will the Tenant offer his rent, if not first required and called to make a tender: and shall wee thinke to receive from God's hand mercies which are not due unto us *ex debito*, but *ex mera gratia*—not of right, but of grace—without entreaty and request? The most bountifull master that lives, though he lease out his profit, wil not lease out his right, & though hee expect no money payment, yet will he reserve some slight acknowledgement, though but a pepper corne. Kings themselves, when they have rewarded such as well deserved by the gift of Manours or Lands, yet will have those on whom they confer such favours hold them by some service, which service they will have acknowledged by some kind of homage, by some sleight penny-fine or the like.

[8] 'Tis true, such paiments as a Pepper-corn or a Peny adde nothing to the revenew of the Temporall Lord, more than the confession of his right and Royalty, yet are they of such high consequence to those that hold their estates by them, that to contemne one of those little ones makes their whole fortune escheat into the power of the Lord. Just so is it with us Christians: wee have a Lord by whose goodnesse life and our being are demised unto us, a bountifull Master, who hath endowed us with all our temporall blessings in this life, and by his promises given our hopes a title to eternall blessings in the life to come. For all which unprized mercies, he hath reserved nothing to returne unto himselfe, save onely the thankfull sacrifice of our prayers. A light and easie payment to God, yet of more weighty consequence on our behalfe than *Ingens auri vis*, a Mine of treasure. For *Prayers* are our Quit-rents, our Homage, our suit-fine, *Census nostræ subjectionis*—by this service doe wee *hold our estates* in his blessings. So long as we pay unto him these rents of devotion, so long is our tenure safe and our title to his goodnes unquestionable. *Open thy mouth (in prayers) and I will fill thee with good things*. But when once we shut our mouthes, when we neglect this dutie and service, wee then forfeit his favour in the present and hazard it in the future.

Gerard Aphorism.
Psal.81:10

[9] Such and so great is the necessitie of *Prayer*. And yet so great is the impudence of the Pelagian, or rather the Devill, whose fee'd advocate he was, to cry downe the use and exercise of Prayer, which had so often repell'd his assault and foil'd him, that from the proud insolent Sophistry of Free-will, he would argue it needlesse to trouble God by asking either perseverance in faith, or conversion from sinne; whereas it is (saith he) in each man's free election and choice either to stand or fall. An assertion to bee hissed at, not answered, being quite contrary to Christ's rule, who layes so much weaknesse to our charge that wee have not power to thinke well, much lesse to will that which is good, without his assisting grace, nor to avoid one danger hanging over us without the same grace preventing. By this Grace are wee elected from the wombe, and by it also are we *holden up ever since we were borne*. 'Tis his grace that we Pray, and againe, 'tis his grace which answers our Prayers: like a cloud doth this Grace still hang over our heads, but the dew thereof drops not downe upon us unlesse first resolved by the breath of our *Praiers*. Let therefore our Prayers ascend up unto him, that so his Grace may descend on us.

[10] Psal.71:6

Enough to disprove Pelagius, but not to stop the mouth of other Heretikes, who out of the infallibility of God's prescience would conclude the act of Prayer needlesse. Whatsoever (say they) God hath foreseene must come to passe, whether wee pray or not, because his knowledge cannot erre. True, but let them know, the same God who fore-saw what should bee, fore-saw also that we should pray unto him, *the act of Prayer being necessary to obtaine and impetrate those things at God's hands which he in his mercie forsaw hee should bestow upon us:* This is Saint Augustine's opinion.

Aug.De Civit. Dei, lib.5.ca.10

I. An Exposition upon the Lord's Prayer

Since then God hath fore-seene a Necessite of our Prayers, let each one fore-see his owne good so much as to petition him continually: This act of invocating him being so necessary to salvation, that *without it no meanes to salvation.* Almighty God is easie to bee found, but hee will first be sought; and his hand ever open to give, if devoutly ask't and intreated. For so is his owne rule, *Petite & dabitur vobis:* Aske first, and then have.

I am now come to consider the *Excellence* of this act of Prayer, which from hence is cleare, Since that, instead of all the abolished sacrifices of the old Law, this only remains unto us. This is our morning and Evening sacrifice, our cleansing sacrifice and our sinne offering. This cures the maladies of the diseased soule. It is our Incense offering, *Spirituale thymiama.* And for the greater glory of it, Carthusian observes that the stile of Incense is attributed *to no other Theologicall vertue so truly as to Prayer.* Like incense doth it fume up, making a sweet smell in the nostrills of God. Therefore the Psalmist prayes, *Dirigatur oratio mea tanquam incensum:* * Which (saith the Glosse) was but a figure of Prayer. A Censer full of this Incense religiously offered diverts the wrath of God, and enterposes it selfe betwixt his anger and those whom it threatens: even as Aaron stood in the doore of the Tabernacle, betwixt a displeased God and a wretched people.

Such a strong prerogative hath Prayer, which God seemes to acknowledge, when with a familiar anger he chides Moses for that his prayers hindered the execution of his vengeance upon Israel: *Let me alone, that my wrath may wax hot upon them.*

Lastly, in stead of the *Elevatum,* the Heave-offering, *Elevatio manuum,* the Elevation of our hands in Prayer, now serves. Blessed are they that can lift up cleane hands in this sacrifice, for they shall surely get the victory. When Moses his hands were held up, Israel (you know) prevailed, but when they were let downe, Amaleck got ground. The morall is thus: When wee pray, our sinnes retire, but when we let that act fall, they charge us with double force.

But our prayers are unweildy and heavie, witnesse the Disciples singled out to accompany Christ when he prayed in the Garden, who at that time found so heavie a weight of slumber hanging over their eye-lids, that they were not able to watch, no, not one houre. 'Tis requisite then they should have props to beare them up. As Aaron and Hur were Moses his supporters, so must Faith and Perseverance be the supports of Prayer. Held up by these, they ascend boldly and without let unto the Throne of God; but if these faile, like dull and lazie mists drawn from the earth they rise not to any height, but fall backe upon those places from whence they are exhaled, or vanish with that breath which sent them up.

Not to insist long on this Encomium of Prayer: It is our scaling Ladder—*Oratio iusti penetrat nubes;*† our Engine of Battery, by which Heaven is beseeged and *suffers violence* (as Christ said). 'Tis our weapon with which we wound our enemies, nay, with it even God himselfe is wounded, as the Spouse in the Canticles cries: *Charitate vulneror.*‡

It is a thing so strong and potent, that it prevailes with (though not against) the Almighty. *Oratio hominis res est omnipotentissima*§ ('tis Luther's devout Hyperbole). This wrestles with God as Jacob with the Angell, and will not part without a blessing won from him. Therefore Saint Hierome saith, *God, that cannot by any forces leavied be overcome, yet confesses himselfe vanquished by the publican's prayers.*

'Tis the Rudder which keeps our soules steady *in aquis multis,*‖ when crosse winds and the billowes of persecution beat upon us. 'Tis the Compasse by which we saile: when all is clouded, no Starre of comfort shining out unto us, this holds us in the right course till we againe discover mercy—*Out of the Deepe have I called unto thee and thou heardest me.*

Lastly, 'tis our Key which opens the gates of Heaven, bee they lockt never so fast: *Oratio iusti*

---
*Let my prayer be counted as incense before thee.
†The prayer of the just penetrates the clouds.
‡I am wounded with love.
§The prayer of man is a thing most omnipotent.
‖In many waters.

clavis Cœli. With this Key did Elias open the windowes of Heaven shut up for some yeares in drought; and with this doe we let downe the former and the latter raine on us.

But a Key, you know, hath many wards, and requires Art to make it, which Art we can no where else learne but from Him who hath *Potestatem clavium,* the Keyes of David, to shut and open at his pleasure. Here then let us borrow our skill and fashion our Prayers in his Mould, by that excellent patterne here in his Gospell left unto us,

Pray thus.

Out of the forme and fashion of which Prayer I observe two things. First, it was a set forme of Prayer, not made upon the sudden but composed with premeditation. Secondly, it was *Short* and compendious. Both which circumstances are here commended to our imitation and use:

Pray thus.

First, it was a *set* forme. The Art of Prayer is not a lesson obvious to all, but full of difficulty: Saint Paul tels us, *Yee pray not as yee ought,* and the Disciples confest their unskillfulnesse in this act when they desired their Master to tell them how to pray, as John taught his Disciples. To answer which request of theirs, he dictates unto them this manner of praying. Prescription is a good warrant, and therefore hee prayes best that prayes by Precedent. Yet it is a disease raigning in many now a daies to affect sudden conceptions of Religion better than mature births. I doe not know what should induce them, unlesse out of a jealousie lest any should finde out a Newer or Narrower path to Heaven than themselves, they thus forsake the Churche's beaten road. For my part, I must needs suspect that these sudden unsetled fits of praying, that take men like quames, cannot but argue some kinde of crazinesse and distemper, if not in point of Religion, at least in Opinion and Ceremony.

Sure I am God likes not raw Sacrifices, no more than rash vowes. *Bee not rash with thy mouth, and let not thy heart bee hasty to utter any thing before God. Before thou prayest prepare thy selfe.* And David refuseth to offer unto God a gift which *cost him nothing.* Why then any should presume to tender him a raw unseasoned meditation that cost no paines nor studie in the shaping of it but, like an Abortive, is conceived and borne at the same instant, I cannot see.

Our blessed Saviour, it should seeme, chose rather to be at a certainty with us for his service, than either to put us upon sudden shifts, or stand to the curtesie of any voluntary Motions or Revelations or Enthusiasmes of ours for his allowance. To which end, hee prescribed a constant Method of Prayer, *Pray thus.* In honour and imitation whereof our Church hath also fixt and rested upon a setled course for her Liturgie in the Booke of *Common Prayer.*

In contempt of both which, however, some giddy separated men preferre their owne phantasies, not onely rejecting our Common Prayer, but even Christ's Prayer also; leaving it out, as a thing not worthy to joyne with their inventions, either privately in their meetings, or publikely in the Pulpit at the end of their Prayers (a contempt you know contrary to the Canon or good manners). Yet, for all this, I hope there are none here sowred with that Leaven, or that need to be perswaded whether a stolne and ignorant Conventicle should sway more in this point, than a learned and reverend Convocation.

Hugo Cardinal deprives, in his judgement, such factious men as these of either understanding or reference to Christ. But the Councill of Toledo deprives those Spanish Priests of their function who held this Prayer was not to bee used dayly, but onely on the Sunday.

Mistake me not, I doe not say no Prayer should be used but onely the *Lord's Prayer.* The Geneva note renders it rightly—Christ binds not to the words, but to the sense and forme of the Prayer. Nor doe I disallow extemporall Prayers, when need or occasion shall require. Seasonably used, they are the fruits of a ripe well-tun'd Devotion: *My tongue is the pen of a ready Writer;* but affected out of nice desire to bee singular, or opposition to the allowed formes of Prayer, they are the Symptomes of a dangerous folly.

I doe not deny him a good Artizan that workes by the strength of his owne phantasie, yet all will grant hee workes truest that workes from a Copie. And though a voluntary exprest upon an

I. An Exposition upon the Lord's Prayer

Instrument shew the sufficiencie of the Musician, yet I should thinke that Musician who undervalues all set Lessons in comparison of his voluntaries hath more of Arrogance than Skill. Just so is it in Prayer.

I prejudice no man's gift, and let me advise no man so much to prejudice this excellent gift of Christ's Prayer as to exalt his own Meditations above it. All I will say to such men is this only, *Iudicium fidei sequere & non Experimentum tuum** is a safe Rule, & I wish they would follow Christ's Rule, which is *Regula fidei*—the Rule of *Prayer* as well as *Faith,* and the discipline of the Church—a little better, and not, like Empericks, presume to practize without booke. [20]

My second observation was the shortness of Christ's Prayer, who having found fault with the multitude of the words used by the Heathen (Vers. 7), takes order to mend it in his patterne. A garrulous talkative zeale is unpleasant and unnecessary. It consists not with the modesty of Faith. Nay, in the judgement of Saint Chrysostome, such a tumultuous suit to God is *rather an act of Impudence than Devotion.* To what end doest thou use a *multitude of words* in thy Prayers? God that form'd thee reads the unwritten Language of thy thoughts; thy hidden desires and imaginations are plaine and legible Characters in his eye. Why then shouldest thou assault his eare with superfluity of speech? Unlesse thou doubtest he heares thee so seldome, that when thou art speaking thou wilt be sure to say enough to him. Or *thinkest thou God is a sleepe,* and must bee waked with loud clamour? Or doest thou distrust his apprehension, that he understands thee not at first sight, or cannot construe the meaning of thy petition without a long paraphrase? Like him Saint Chrysostome reprehends, who prayed in such a forme of language as if he meant to tell God somewhat which he knew not before.

2. *A short forme of Prayer.* (Mt. 6) Tertul. *lib.de Orat.*[a] Chrys. *in Mat* [b]

[21]

Chrisostom, citat a Gabr.Biel, *Lect.64 in Missam*[a]

Be so modest as still to remember God is a Judge, that needs take no informations of thy cause from thee; *When wee lay open our wants, we doe not tell it to incline God a thing he knew not before,* but by that declaration incline his Mercy to us: *Your Father knoweth whereof ye have need before ye aske him.* Misery is a subject that requires the briefest History that can bee to set it foorth. 'Tis best, therefore, in opening the complaint, to use but few words in Prayer, considering (as Saint Hierome speakes) *wee come not to present God with a Narration, but a Petition,* and not to discourse with him, but to pray to him.

Augustin. Chris.*in Mat.6*[b] Matth.6 : 8

[22] *Epist.ad Probam*

I must hereagaine prevent the misconstruction of any that can bee jealous my meaning is bent against much praying—God forbid. I say with my Author, *I speak not against much praying, but much speaking* in our prayers; for, saith Saint Augustine, *He that talkes much in his prayer, is a bad performer of a good action;* he overdoes a dutie, and so by double diligence growes troublesome; especially being that this duty is not acted by the tongue, so much as the inward affection: *Plus fletu quam affatu.* Nay, a man may be silent, and yet pray loudly: *Deus non vocis, sed cordis auditor;*† as Saint Ambrose spake of Moses, *Qui cum taceret, clamabat.*‡

August.ibid. Cyprian Ambros.*Offic. lib.1,cap.4*

I exhort all to frequent prayer *Mane, Meredie, Vesperi,* for so often David Prayed: at *Morning, Midday,* and *Night;* and our Saviour Christ, we reade, *Tertio abivit:* prayed *thrise* in the Garden within a very short space; but pray in few words, for so did Christ.

[23]

I know many there be who deride our short prayers, and Cartwright scoffingly termes our Collects, *Shreds;* but if they be shreds, they are such as have more worth in them than a whole peece of their uneven, ill-spunne meditations that follow his Tenets.

August. *Epist.121.* (ad Probam)(a)

Confutatio in Rhemist. Testament, in Matth.16:21.

Saint Augustine writes that *the religious men in Ægypt were wont to make very frequent, but very short prayers:* which practice he commends to us, this being most consonant to the Wiseman's speech, *God is in heaven above, and thou upon earth, therefore let thy words be few.*

Eccles.5:2

Pray yee.

This part is my application; I shall not need any labour to make it fit, since the words, barely

[24] Part 3. *Vos*

---
*To follow the decision of faith and not your own experience.
†God is a hearer, not of the voice, but of the heart.
‡Who while he was silent, cried out.

repeated, apply themselves. They were Christ's Disciples unto whom he gave this exemplified injunction: I trust so are we. Nor doth this speech with lesse propriety or necessity belong to you then it did to them.

So that you see the Disciples themselves were taught. If they, who had such a *large proportion of grace,* and *gifts of the Spirit infused,* thought it no disparagement to be directed and tyed to a patterne, I doe not see why any of meaner endowments should think themselves too wise to learn of Christ, or to *Pray after his manner.*

Againe, though Disciples, and in that neere relation to Christ, then corporally present with them, yet for all that they must pray.

[25] The best that lives upon the earth, though he can boast never so neere an alliance to Christ, hath need of praier, else all his goodnesse can be no *Supersedeas* for temptations. A wall'd Towne is no protection from the enemy without a garrison to beat him from the walls, nor doth the place secure it, but the watch. So the strength of man's owne righteousnesse is no fortresse to secure him, unlesse religion guard him and that his prayers stand centinell—*Watch and pray*—solliciting the Watchman of Israel to defend him in all assaults. There is no faith so well built or freed from decay that needs not bee repaired hourely by the invocation of God's assistance. The just man falls *Septies in die*—seven times a day. How oft then falls he that hath no claime to righteousnesse, nor any title but what is derived from his sinnes? He therefore that is fallen must pray that he may rise, and *Qui stat videat ne cadat:* Hee that yet stands must pray to prevent his fall. For (as Saint Augustine) *Prayer is the base, the pedestall of faith.*

August.*Serm. de verb.Dom.*
[26]

There be many that never serve God but when they need him—*Quando bella, quando fames &c. tunc putatur invocandus Deus**—and then indeed they will pray earnestly, as Jonas his Mariners call'd upon their Gods in the Storme; but in the calmes of prosperity they are tongue-tide, as if then there were no use of God.

1 Thess.5:17

'Tis a dangerous opinion for any to thinke hee hath no need of God. And 'tis high time God should grow weary of doing good to that man who growes weary of serving him. An intermittent pulse is one of the fore-runners of death, and a cessation from Prayer, which is the Soule's pulse, shewing all her sicke distempers, wants and grievances, is the argument of a desperate forlorne condition. Therfore the Apostle exhorts us to pray *sine intermissione,* continually, without any stop or intermission. In what state soever thou art, sicke or in health, 'tis fit thou pray: do'st thou want? Why, pray that thou mayst be supplyed. Do'st thou abound? Yet doe not like the Horsleach, being full straight fall off, but pray still. Consult thy owne brest, and thou wilt find thou hast as great cause to pray in the daies of thy prosperity as of thy misery, if not to implore God for any thing thou hast not, yet to praise and blesse his bounty, who gave thee all thou hast. For to give thanks is to pray, and *Thanksgiving* as well as *Petition* is a Species of Prayer. So Aquinas.

[27]
Aquinas 2a:2æ q.83, art.17

Therefore I say as was said to Israel, *When thou shalt passe the River, and God shall bring thee into a Land that flowes with milke and hony,* give thee an exalted full fortune, still empty thy bosome in thanksgiving unto him, and with Jacob remember with what staffe thou passed'st over the Jordan of thy meane poore estate.

Minut.Fœlix. (*Octavius*)[a]

Gloss.in 1 Thess:3: Sine intermis sione orate.

Lastly, in what condition soever thou art, whether in abundance or in want, be sure to offer up unto God the fruits of a cleare conversation and of a good life, for a good life is a practicke forme of Prayer, as pleasing to God as any thou canst offer—*Semper orat qui semper bene agit:* Hee that lives well prayes still.

[28]
Seneca

To close all, Pray, and I say againe, Pray. Let thy uprising and thy down-lying, thy going in and thy comming out, bee hallowed by Prayer. It was a divine meditation of a Philosopher: *When thou awakest thou canst not tell whether ever thou shalt sleepe againe, nor lying downe to sleepe, whether ever thou shalt wake:* therefore pray at thy uprising, and pray at thy downe-lying, *Ut te in*

---

*When there are wars, when there is famine, etc., then they think to call upon God.

ipso quietis exordio divina meditantem somnus inveniat.* Nor, when thou goest out, whither thou shalt returne; take therefore Saint Hierome's advice: *When thou goest out, fortifie thy selfe with prayer; and when thou returnest,* like the strong man in the Gospell, *Stand in the doore of thy house with thy prayers.* Ambros.*Lib.3.de virg.(ca.1.)* (Mt.12.29)

Finally, because thou knowest not how soone thy borrowed life will be required backe and thy soule taken from thee, whether in the mid-day of thy age, or in the evening, therefore let thy morning meditation be spent in beseeching God that thou maist not be taken from thy selfe in that horrour and distraction when thou art unsetled and unprovided; and againe, *because the Day of the Lord comes stealing on like a theefe in the night* (who can tell whether *hac nocte,* this approaching night) let us all conclude this our Evening Sacrifice with humble and hearty Prayer unto Almighty God, that at the comming of the Bridegroome (which cannot now be farre off) we may not bee surprised sleeping, but being furnisht with Oyle in our Lamps, our eye-lids waking, wee may enter in with him; that when the last everlasting night of this world shall come, we may in the morning of the next world rise to life that shall know no end. *Amen.* [29] Gerard *Aphorism. Sacr.* (Matth.25:10)

II. OUR FATHER WHICH ART IN HEAVEN

[30] Mat.6.9

I have drawne the Curtaine; and now the Master-peece of Prayer, wrought and conceived by Christ, begins to discover it selfe. Of which, before I take a stricter view, like men arrived at some curious building, who first examine the situation and modell, give mee leave a little to fix my contemplation on the outward parts of this Fabricke, to consider the Forme of the Prayer before I open the Matter.

This is the Psalmist's method, who being to discourse of Sion and make a spirituall corography and description of the beauty thereof, directs the eye of the beholder first to the walls and battlements, to walke round about the out-works, and to *number the turrets* thereof. Psal.*48* Vers.*12*

A faire and spacious front promises a faire inside; and if our pitty or wishes could prevaile, there should bee no faire well-proportioned body but should have as faire a soule to inhabit it, and a disposition suting the exteriour lineaments: *Orandum est ut sit mens sana in corpore sano,*† for 'twere a foule solecisme that the Cabinet should bee better than the Jewell which is contained within it. [31] (Juvenal, *10.356*)

If Salomon should have built only a faire Porch or a beautifull Gate, and a Temple disproportionate to his Porch, he had then drawne men's Religion into their eies, and made them more zealous to gaze without then to pray within. But his Fabricke was better cast. So much ornament, so much cost beautified the inside of his Temple, that the outward Pile served as a bait to attract the people's devotion, and prepare them by the exteriour Modell sufficiently to prize and admire what was contained within. Happily, by describing the Courts and Gates and Porch of this rare Building, erected by a greater then Salomon, my discourse may attaine that good effect, to prepare your piety for the entrance into it.

The outside of it comprehends enough to exercise your attention, as the Landskip of Jerusalem contained matter to hold the eyes of those that most curiously looked upon it. That had *many Turrets,* This hath *Seven,* raised from those seven *Petitions* in *Christ's Prayer.* View it in the natural mold whereinto it is now cast, and you will finde it like Minerva's Sheild composed by Phydias, which consisted of many excellent parts, all which made but one intire Shield; yet taken asunder, each part that belonged to it was a compleat worke. So consider this Prayer as it now lies all together. The plates and joints and severall matters make but one Christian Buckler, to ward and [32]

---

*So that sleep may find you at the very beginning of your rest, meditating on things divine.
†Your prayer should be to have a healthy mind in a healthy body.

avert all necessities that may befall us; yet resolved into parcels, every Limbe and Member and Gradation is a perfect Buckler to beare off our particular wants.

It is like that famous Target of Ajax that was *Clypeus Septemplex:* consisted of seven folds; this is *Oratio Septemplex,* a prayer consisting of seven requests. That Buckler was Dart-proofe, impenetrable, and this prayer an impenetrable Shield, to *resist the fierie darts of Satan.* If I would insist upon the allusion to the number of these Petitions, I might compare this whole Prayer to the constellation of the Pleiades or seven starres in Heaven; Or to the *seven starres* in the right hand of the Sonne of Man, being fit Lights and Tapers for the *seven golden Candlesticks* there mentioned, to bee set up in those *seven Churches;* and not in them alone, but in all the Churches of the world where Christ's name is known and adored.

Or I may liken the parts of this Prayer to the seven Planets, eminent above all the other starres of the Firmament. For as some of those Planets move neerer to the earth, others higher and farther off, so is the motion of these seven Petitions: some of them move and solicite God for *Earthly* things, as the foure last of them; others for *Heavenly and Eternall,* as the three first, *Hallowed bee thy Name, and thy Kingdome come,* &c.—Saint Augustine hath taken their just Height and motion.

I purpose not to inlarge my Discourse by commending the perfection and dignitie of the seventh number, which some gather out of Naaman's command to wash *seven times* in Jordan; or as Lyra upon that place when Elias bade his servant *goe seven times* and looke towards the Sea, after which he discovers a cloude of raine. So, saith Lyra, *after the seven misteries of our Saviour* (viz. His Conception, Birth, Baptisme, Preaching, Passion, Resurrection, Ascension), *abundant showres of grace* fell upon the earth.

I know every *seventh* yeare is reputed a Climactericke; and *seven yeares* the rate of a man's life; and *seven dayes* the account of our week—and *seven Petitions* the number of Christ's Prayer.

But 'tis not my taske to consider this Prayer by Number but by Weight. God regards not how many prayers men string with their Beads, but with what devotion they send them up; nor doth hee keepe a Score or Tally of our Petitions, though he bottle up and number each religious Teare shed in the vehement imploring of his Grace. The Excellence, not the Arithmetike of this Prayer, is my object, which Hugo Cardinalis commends unto us in three observations, the *Dignitie, Brevity,* and *Fulnesse.*

For the Dignity, Christ was the Authour of it—*Qui fecit vivere, docuit orare.** And if he were the Author, of whom God said, *This is my beloved Sonne in whom I am well pleased: heare him,* it must needs follow that for his sake this Prayer is more audible in the eares of God, and more acceptable, than any we can make.

For the Briefnesse of it, Saint Cyprian saith this is that *verbum brevians,* short compendious Oration, promised in Esay to the world. The reason why it was comprised in so few words are severally alleaged by the Fathers. One is, *that it might be more portable in our memories,* that so it might bee sooner learn't and oftner repeated; that hee who dayly uses it might not thinke it tedious, and hee who knowes it not might want all excuse for his ignorance of it. Therefore Saint Augustine gives a strict charge that young children should first of all learne this Prayer, being no burden at all to their memory or capacity. The last reason for its shortnesse is to shew us the most wordy voluminous Prayers are not ever the best, or soonest heard by God. (Alexander Hales summes up all the commodities of it thus shortned together: *Ob illius brevitatem facilius scitur,†* etc.)

The last Argument of this Prayer's excellency is the fulnesse and weight of it. In few words it involves most copious matter, and though very briefe, yet it is of an ample sense: *The sense of it is as large as the Body is little—It is the summe of all we can request at God's hands,* that is, of all which wee can justly and piously request. Sometimes we desire of God what is unfit for him to grant, or us to receive: therefore, saith Saint Augustine, *Si recte & congruenter oramus, nihil aliud*

---

*He who made us live, taught us to pray.
†On account of its brevity it is more easily known.

II. Our Father which art in Heaven

petere possumus quam quod in oratione Dominica positum est.* It consists of seven Petitions (saith Biel) and *Seven is a number that includes the universe of goodnesse.* And this is the Exception which the Brownists take against it, because 'tis so ample. Saint Augustine makes a particular demonstration of it. If you run thorow all the Prayers of good men and Prophets set downe in the Scripture, all the severall Petitions in the Psalmes, You shall find (saith he) none of them but may be reduced to these seven Petitions, as the common places of all Prayer. When Christ sayes, *Pater clarifica nomen tuum,* what is it else but *Hallowed be thy name?* When the Psalmist cries, *Ostende nobis faciem: Shew us the light of thy countenance,* What is it but *Thy kingdome come?* When he sayes againe, *Direct my steps in thy paths, that my feet doe not slide,* what is this but *Fiat voluntas, Thy will bee done?* Againe, when Salomon prayes unto God, *Give mee not poverty nor riches,* what is it but *Give us our daily bread?* When the Psalmist sayes, *If I have repayed evill for evill unto any,* what is this but *Forgive us our trespasses, as we forgive others?* When it is said, *Take from mee concupiscence,* is it not as much as *Lead us not into temptation?* Lastly, when the Psalmist cries, *Erue me ab inimicis: Deliver mee from mine enimies,* is it not as much, in effect, as *Libera nos a malo: Deliver us from evill?*

You see the large capacity of this Prayer, how that it comprehends the subject of all other prayers; and not them only, but even all Christian discipline, as Tertullian writes: for which cause he stiles it *Breviarium totius Evangelii,* the Abridgement of the whole Gospell, Such plentifull Rivers streame from this Seven-headed Fountaine. So that as the seven Armes of Nilus watered and made fertill all Ægypt, so doth this Prayer, springing from seven Petitions, which are *Deprecativæ* or *Optativæ,* water the whole Christian world, preventing and deprecating all mishaps and supplying our wants.

So that in this short Prayer, as in a little Orbe, the Sonne of righteousnesse moves. From hence doth every Starre, every faithfull servant and Confessor of Christ (for they are Incarnate Starres), borrow a ray of light, to illuminate and sanctifie the body of his meditations—The Church in her Liturgie, and the Preacher both enjoyn'd to use it. A small quantity of this Leven seasons a great lumpe of Devotion, and a few spirits give taste & quicknesse to much liquor. This Prayer is a *Quintessence* extracted by the greatest Chymist that ever was, from Him that brought Nature out of Chaos, Separated Light from Darknesse, and extracted the foure Elements out of Nothing. All parts of it are spirits: *Quæ enim spiritualior oratio?*† And the mixture of a few graines therof with our prayers proves the strongest and best Christian Antidote. Let us gladly *use that forme of Prayer which Christ our Lord hath taught us* ('tis Cyprian's inference), and give unto God what the Sonne of God gave unto us. *It is a familiar and friendly tribute to present God with his owne.* A petition cloth'd in Christ's words will finde the ready way to heaven, and *a speedy access into the eares of God.*

And when the Father acknowledges his Sonne's words in our Prayers, hee will acknowledge and ratifie that promise, which through him he made unto us, that *whatsoever we should aske him in his sonne's name should not be denied.*

Thus have I at full surveyed the Forme or Outside of Christ's Prayer. I am now come to the Matter, to enter the inward roomes, into which my Text is the doore that leads me; serving as a Prologue or a Frontispeice to the whole Prayer, which is divided into three generall Parts: Into an *Exordium—Our Father which art in heaven,* &c; *Tractatum,* a Tract, which is the seven Petitions; *Conclusionem,* a Conclusion—a Ratification of the Prayer, *Amen.*

Or if you please, I will call this whole Prayer of our Saviour's a Letter, consisting of foure parts or complements:

An *Endorsement* or *Superscription* directing it to the party, viz. God, *Our Father,* and to the place, Heaven—*which art in Heaven.*

---
*If we pray rightly and fittingly, we can seek no other than what is set out in the Lord's Prayer.
†For what prayer is more spiritual?

146 AN EXPOSITION UPON THE LORD'S PRAYER

2. The *Contents*, following in the severall Petitions, from *Hallowed be thy name*, &c., to *Deliver us from evill*.

3. A *Subscription* or *Under-writing*, found in the latter part of the thirteenth verse and immediately following the last Petition whereunto it is joyned, *For thine is the kingdome, the power and the glory for ever*. [42]

4. The *Seale* that closes up all, *Amen*.

Division of The Text

My text is the *Endorsement*, the Superscription; or it is the the *Exordium* of the Prayer, wherein, as Rhetoricians use first of all to implore the Attention and Benevolence of their Auditors, so doe we from hence begge God's attention and inclination to our requests by a double Insinuation:

1. First of his *Goodnesse*, in that we stile him *Father*.
2. Secondly of his *Power*, in that wee acknowledge him the *Lord of Heaven, Qui es in Cœlis*.

Both which circumstances conduce to his Praise and Honour (saith S. Ambrose).

Lect.64 in Miss.

Gabr. Biel divides this *Exordium* more punctually into foure parts, for so many wayes herein do we win upon God's favour:

1.
2. From the greatness of his love to us when we call him Father. [43]
3. From the liberall communication of his goodnesse to us, in that we say *Our Father*.
4. From the immutability of his Essence, intimated in these words, *Qui es, Which art*.

From the high domination and power he hath over us when we say *In Cœlis, Which art in Heaven*.

'Tis most requisite when we speake to God, we should use a decent Method, an orderly proceeding, since he is the *God of Order*. 'Twere a rude presumption for any to sue unto him in that fashion which they would not use unto men, if their superiors. When wee make any request unto them, we hold it manners to prefix some modest introduction before the suit, wee doe not bluntly discover it at first. If thou begin a Petition with this homely phrase, and in this peremptory manner, *Give mee what I require*, can it avoid the censure of rudenesse?—As if thou cam'st to command, not intreat, and to challenge or lay a claime to a favour, not to sue for it. And canst thou hold it fit to petition Almighty God without some preface, as well to confesse his power as to declare thine owne modesty? [44]

Sen.Lib.2 de Benef:cap.2

Humblenesse becomes the person of a suitour. *To beseech* is a terme that confounds an ingenious man, dejects and casts downe his looks, as asham'd that his eye should follow the suit which his tongue preferres. Which bashfull recognition of his wants finds an easie way to pitty: whereas he that begs in arrogant termes or impudent behaviour shuts up the hand of bounty, and destroyes the good intention of the giver. The dejected *Publican* in the Gospell stood fairer and better justified in our Saviour's estimation than the *Pharisee*, insolently bragging of his worth.

Luke 18:14

You shall finde in the Scripture that Prophets and holy men, whensoever they spake or prayed unto God, used some Preface, to prepare his eare and to make way for their words. When Abraham besought God concerning Sodome, he begins, *Let not my Lord bee angry if I speake that am but dust and ashes*. And Moses, pleading for the people, begins, *If I have found favour in thy sight*. And when David prayes unto God to forget *the sinnes of his youth*, he makes a commemoration of the goodnes and mercy of God, *Remember, O Lord, thy tender mercies*, &c. *even for thy goodnesse' sake*. It gives life and hope to our Petitions when before wee aske, we urge God with the precedents of his owne goodnesse. This kinde of acknowledgement is *Ad plus dandum invitatio*, a fit preparing of his favour; and wee invite him to grant againe when we revive what already he hath done. Good cause then had our Saviour to lay the ground of our Petitions on God's *fatherly* care and love to us, by bidding us cry *Our Father*: That as Orators, before they plead, use some *Exordium* or *Preface* to make the Judge favourable to their causes, so wee, being to speake unto the Judge of Heaven and Earth, might by this beginning make him propitious to our Prayers. [45]

Gen.18:27
Exodus 34:9
Psal.25:7
Vers.6
Vers.7

[46]

Calvin

Wherby let mee note unto you, formes of Oratory and Rhetoricke are allowed in our Devotions: *Eloquentiam non pugnare cum simplicitate religionis.** Nor doth Christ dislike an elegant Prayer.

---

*Eloquence does not war with simplicity in religion.

II. Our Father which art in Heaven

And let mee tell those men who have such an unlearned conceit of God's service, that they thinke it a trespasse of high nature to staine their Discourses with a Latine sentence, or authority of Fathers quoted in their owne dialect; or that make it a nice case of Conscience to present God with a set studied Prayer, or any other forme of speech than *Quod in buccam venerit:* what comes into their heads whilest they are speaking, when the tongue strives with the Invention for precedence or at least both goe together—that if they please they may bee more elaborate, take more paines and time for what they speake then an extemporary minute or an instant, unlesse they finde it more for their ease to keepe unto that naturall vaine of theirs, unstudied or unlaboured; and hold it a better protection and excuse, for those that know little, to condemne Learning and all that know more then themselves. [47]

I confesse that *Pia rusticitas*, Devotion clothed in the rudest phrase that can be, is to bee preferred before eloquent hypocrisie, and an holy Ignorance is better than learned irreligion. I would advice all men to use more Religion than Rhetoricke in their Prayers; yet none can deny but that an eloquent Meditation, so it be not affected, and so it doe not *Exercendæ linguæ magis operam dare quam menti mundandæ,** is acceptable both to God and Men. [Hieron. *Ep. ad Tranquillin.*] [Gloss]

View the Scripture, the Dictate and worke of the Holy Ghost: you shall finde that for the elegance of the phrase and weight of the words, it passes all the weake shallow Oratory of Man's tongue. Therefore Saint Augustine calls it *the venerable stile of the Holy Ghost.* And in the Gospell, the Jewes acknowledged our Saviour for the best Rhetorician that ever was: *He spake as never man spake.* The practick perfection of which Eloquence he hath declar'd in nothing more then in this Prayer, which in a narrow compasse comprehends the summe of all Oratory, Brevity, and Elegance and Perspicuity. [48] *Confess.L.7:c.21* Joh.7:46

Pater Noster. It may be askt who is here meant by *Pater*, whether the word be taken *Notionaliter* and *Personaliter,* for God the Father, the first Person in the Trinity; or *Essentialiter,* essentially, as it is refer'd unto the creature made and conserved by God, in which sense it appertaines to the whole Trinity, *for the whole Trinity is one Father, as one God.* It is resolved by all that when we say *Our Father,* we meane and pray unto the *Trinity,* and that by good right. [I. Our Father Biel *Lect.64.in Miss.* Biel *Lect.Cit.*]

In the beginning, it was the Trinity which fathered all mankinde: *Faciamus hominem,* which originall title of Son to that Father Man might still have preserv'd, had he not by his wilfull disobedience made a forfeiture of it. For though God had setled an estate upon Adam, it was not so firmly intailed but that it might bee, and was, quickly cut off. His sinne did dis-inherit him, and us in him, dispossest him of the Garden, his first Mansion and Patrimony, and devested him of the title of a Sonne: For hee was then no more *filius Dei,* the Sonne of God, but *servus peccati,* sinne's bond-slave. Nay (saith Saint Augustine), *before Christ's mercy, the Devill only had title to him,* and in that bondage was he concluded till that time; by whose mediation God was reconcil'd to Man, and the lost Sonne acknowledged by the right Father: *Iam non servus est sed filius; quod si filius & hæres.* So that Christ, having now by grace restor'd to Man what originally hee lost, purchased the title of Sonne by Adoption. Since that we tooke from Creation was extinct, he held it meetest that, as God now tooke us for his children, wee should also in our Prayers claime him for *Our Father.* Since we had received *Spiritum Adoptionis filiorum Dei,* the spirit of Adoption should crie *Abba, Father:* So beginning where Adam left, and directing our supplications to that Father which first made us, the *Blessed Trinity.* [49] Gen.I [Serm.151 de Tempore] Gal.4:7 [50] Rom.8:15

Which though it be here meant, yet is not the Essentiall name, as *Deus* or *Dominus,* God or Lord, used, but a Personall *Father—Voca me patrem* (as 'tis in the Prophet): *Call me not Lord, but Father.* Jerem.3:19

Saint Chrysostome gives the reason. God (saith he) would be called *Father,* and not *Lord,* that hee might give us more confidence of obtaining what wee sue for. Servants doe not always finde an easinesse in their Lords to grant what they aske, but Sonnes presume it. Therefore *A Prayer that is sweetned with the Name of Father,* how much comfort doth it beget in the heart of him that [51] Bernard

---

*Serve rather to exercise the tongue than adorn the mind.

pronounces it? *Can a woman forget her childe?* Yea, though she forget to be kinde, to bee naturall, yet will not *I forget to bee mercifull,* saith our heavenly Father.

Hence Saint Augustine fitly notes the priviledge which the Christian hath above the Jew: *You never finde that the old Israelites were allowed to call God "Our Father";* no, as Servants still, they stile him *Lord.* But unto us Christians hee hath afforded this grace through his beloved Sonne, to say unto him, *Our Father: Dedit potestatem filios Dei fieri his qui credunt.**

This Prayer then is the Prayer of Sons, fit onely for their mouthes who acknowledge God for their Father; it is the *Bread of Children, non catulis proiiciendus:* not lawfull to bee taken into the mouthes of any that are not his Children. But yet say it be; admit that men of prophane lips and perverse life, *that hate to be reformed, take these words into their mouths.* Say Esau, the Father of the Reprobate, spake in the language of Jaacob and cry *Our Father,* how is this Sacrifice accepted by God when it is offered up from such unhallowed Altars? Doth hee answer to that call of *Father?* Or stands it with his honour to account them Sons? Either it must follow that they say false in saying *Our Father,* and saying false, sinne in saying the *Lord's Prayer* (for *verbum mendax iustus detestabitur*)† or that God must father children which are none of his, but such to whom he sayes, *Vos ex Patre Diabolo estis.*‡ The doubt seems subtile, but easily answered by acute Alexander Hales: A wicked man may say this Prayer and not sinne or lye, so he say it not *Indicativè* but *Optativè,* not Implying but Wishing that God would be so gracious as to be his Father, which wish is lawfull. Againe, this Prayer is *Oratio communis,* a common universall Prayer, *said in the behalfe of the whole Church of Christ, which hath many sons;* therefore though Atheists or Reprobates cry *Our Father,* they include not themselves, but only speak the language of the Church, which reapes what they sow; for their owne lips must not taste the fruit and effect of this sweet vintage, as having no part in God nor in the Church. So that unto such men, this Prayer is like weapons which cowards or unskilfull men weare, to arme others, not to defend themselves. Though they use the words & syllables of Christ, they want the Spirit that animates the words, and though they have the Sword of Prayer, they want the Arme of Faith to wield it. Like as the Epyrots told the Turks (when they vaunted they had won the sword of that victorious Prince of Epyre, George Castriot): *Though you have the sword of Scanderbeg, yet you have not his arme.*

2. *Noster: Our Father*

I need not set any marke or difference to distinguish those false spurious children from the true. The next word *Noster (Our)* shuts out them from the Church, and seperates them from the number of God's elect children who can, only, and may justly, call him *Our Father.*

Meum and *Tuum,* these words *Mine* and *Thine,* have beene the seeds of Envie and Contention ever since the world was habitable. From these little graines hath the Lawe's large Harvest growne up. These were they which at first invented, and ever since exercised our Termes. The common Barritors, causes of all rents and schisms in the Common-wealth's body, These have blowne the coals of strife, occasioned brothers to goe to law with brothers, nay, brothers to destroy one another. If Abel should have ask't Cain upon what quarrell he kild him, he could have stated his controversie in no other terms but *Meum* and *Tuum: Thy Sacrifice is better accepted than Mine.* These have been the accur'st removers of neighbour's bounds and land-marks, have entitled the vigilant Oppressor to another's patrimony. These were the bloudy Depositions that cost Naboth his life: Had he relinquished his right to the Vineyard and not call'd it *Mine—I will not give thee my vineyard*—he had preserv'd a friend of Jesabel, and a life too. These two little Monosyllables, *Mine* and *Thine,* they are the great Monopolists that spanne the wide world, that, like Abraham and Lot, divide the land betwixt them yet cannot agree, but are ever wrangling and quarrelling about their shares: like those two factious brethren Eteocles and Polynises, who never could be reconcil'd, living nor dead; for when they had slaine one the other, and were put on one Herse, one funerall

---

*To them that believed he gave the power to become children of God.
†The just man detests a lying word.
‡You are of your father the Devil.

II. Our Father which art in Heaven

pile, their ashes fought, & the flames that burnt the bodies, as sensible of the mortall fewd which was betwixt them living, divided themselves. How many actions and suits begun upon these termes *Mine* and *Thine* have survived those that commenced them first, and descended from the great Grandfather to the Heire in the fourth generation?

Since, then, these two had occasioned so much strife, so much mischiefe in the Politicke Body, Christ would not have them admitted to make any faction or rent in the Mysticall Body of the Church. But as he was the Reconciler of God & Man by his bloud, so would he shew himselfe the Reconciler of Man and Man, shutting up all opposition of *Mine* and *Thine* in this one word, as the common Peacemaker: *Noster, Our Father*. [56]

'Tis Atheisme for any to say *Pater Tuus*, God is *Thy Father* and not *Mine*. 'Tis presumption for any to say *Pater Meus*, to call God *My Father*. 'Tis Saint Ambrose his Caveat: *Christ alone can call God "My Father."* for God is his Father by nature, ours onely by Grace. Unto Christ he is *Pater specialis*, to us *Pater communis*, not in speciall but common. *Have we not all one Father?* 'Tis meetest then we should say in one voyce, *Pater noster, Our Father*. [Gloss / Idem, Vid.Biel / Malach.2:10.]

In teaching us to say thus, Christ taught us also a two-fold Lesson.

First of brotherly charity: we must not only (as Saint John saith) *Love one another*, but Pray one for another, brother for brother, neighbour for neighbour, the Priest for the Congregation, and the Congregation againe for the Priest. Thus doth the practise of our Church instruct us in the Liturgie: *Dominus vobiscum, The Lord bee with you*. There the Priest prayes for the people; and the people againe pray for the Priest when they answer, *And with thy spirit. When brethren thus unite their forces and prayers*, they are so fortified that the power of Hell cannot make them disband. If we are commanded to doe good unto all men, it followes, *a maiori ad minus*,* that at least wee must pray for all men. A good wish is better cheape than a good worke, nor will they afford a reall benefit to their brethren that will not pray for them. Hee that thinkes himselfe borne only for himselfe contracts and straightens the freedome of his being. The most noble and Christian resolution, therefore, is for a man to study his brother's good as well as his owne; *Nec sibi sed toti natum se credere mundo*.† [1 John 4:7 I. / [57] Chrysostom [b] / Prov.18:19 / (Lucan 2. 383)]

Secondly, a lesson of humility. When he hath thus combin'd the race of men together in one fraternity, given the lowest and meanest as good right to call him *Father* as the highest and best amongst us, Hee would not have any to prize themselves so much as to scorne and dis-value all below them. God is a God of the valleyes as well as the hils, nor is he a Father of the rich and noble, but of the poore too. Be their qualities and degrees never so different in the account of the world, summ'd up in the account of this Prayer they are all even. As but one sacrifice was appointed for the rich and poore, so Christ hath appointed but one Prayer, but one appellation for them all, *Pater noster*, Our Father—*The King and the Begger, the Lord and the Slave, all concurre and say "Our Father."* [2. [58] / Chrysostom [b] / Exod.30:10 / August.Hom.2]

God is no partiall Father, nor is his eare partiall; hee heares and accepts the one as soone as the other. For our Prayers doe not ascend in their ranks, nor doth the poore man's Petition stay to let the great one's goe before; but when we pray, God comprehends us all under one common Notion of sonnes and suitors. *From hence let them learne this equall lesson, not to disdaine any*, though the meanest, *for their brethren, who have God for their Father* as well as themselves. [[59] / August.ib. / Chrysost.[b]]

I have held you too long upon these first words, *Our Father*—indeed, beyond a *Pater noster* while. But I shall quickly dismisse you, for my speech is now arrived at the end and period of our Prayer's journey, Heaven: *Which art in Heaven*.

Thither it now bends; but being in the ascent and rising up to it, give me leave a little to breath by the way, to rest a minute upon the contemplation of God's Essence, intimated in these words, *Qui es*. To *be* is predicated of none so properly as of God (Exod. 3:14). He takes an attribute, [*Which art*]

---
*from the greater to the less.
†to believe himself born not for himself but for the whole world.

denominates himselfe from his Being: *ho ōn—Thou shalt say unto the children of Israel*, I am *hath sent me unto you*. Againe, our Saviour sayes, *Before Abraham was, I am.*

Lastly, Saint John characterises him by his Essence: *ho ōn, ho ên, ho erchomenos*—Grace be unto you from him *that Is, that Was, and that Is to come*. He is indeed *Ens Entium, Ens primum*, and *Ens simplicissimum*—The first, purest, most independant Essence. The world and the creatures in it, and we ourselves, are but Derivations from that Primitive Being: *In him we live, and move, and have our Being*.

As he is the most absolute, so the most immutable Essence. (*Qui es* signifies *Immutabilem subsistentiam*.) The circumstances of Time measure not nor alter Him, as neither feeling the accessions multiplied, not the waining and decrease of Times.

Things past and future, are eternally present with him, say the Schooles, whose Title and Motto is *I am that I am*, or as the Chaldee Paraphrast renders it, *I will be what I will be: Yesterday and to day the same for evermore*.

In a word, he is that Immense Being in whom these three vast transcendents, *unum, verum* & *bonum*—unitie, veritie and goodnesse—knit and meet together and make their aboad. He is *Maximè unus,* because most invariable; *Most True,* because most absolute and independant; *Most Good,* because the Author of all Good, nay, Goodnesse it selfe in the Abstract.

So long, therefore, as wee conforme our selves to his Will, retaining our goodnesse, so long we preserve our *Being,* it may bee said *we are;* but when wee once leave off that, we leave to *Be: we are only privations,* or what is worse, Beasts and no men. There is no true existence but Vertue. A good man is a Copy & Image of God; God is ever neere unto him, he ever neere unto God, neere to Beatitude, neere to Heaven, nay he is Heaven: *Wheresoever sinne is not, there is Heaven*. If a sinner be called Earth (as in *Genesis* 3, God tels Adam after he had sinned, *Thou art Earth*), certainly, a just man by as good right may be tearmed Heaven. His Conscience is a Firmament, *Simplicissima, solida, pelucida* (as Aristotle defines Heaven)—cleare and serene, and solid, not to be shaken or daunted. This is it which, whilst he lives here, makes him shine cleere in report and the esteeme of the world, and hereafter will cause him to shine more brightly in the Kingdome of Glory: *Iusti fulgebunt sicut Sol.**

Thus you may perceive this short stay hath not hindered or disadvantaged our proceeding a whit, but rather set us forward and brought us a neerer, though a lower way to Heaven, since we have here discovered an Heaven upon Earth.

For Heaven is not always taken materially for the place where the Saints abide, but spiritually, for Angels and Saints, or for good Men. So Saint Augustine interprets this place.

But why *Cœlis* in the plurall number? Is it onely an Hebraisme? Or to give us an occasion to dispute whether there bee more Heavens than one? Whether Heaven bee divided into severall Classes and roomes and stories and degrees, because the Psalmist mentions the *Heaven of Heavens,* and in the Gospell we read, *Glory in the highest Heavens?* Whether there be three Heavens onely, because Saint Paul was rap't to the Third, or whether so many as Philosophy supposes, Ten?

Or is it said *Qui es in Cœlis* to limit God and tie him to a place, as if he were onely in Heaven, not in Earth, as Aristotle thought?—As if hee did not *fill both Heaven and Earth* with his presence; or as if he were not in all places, and at all times, in this place, at this present, in this assembly: in us, as one hath it.

For none of these reasons was this circumstance *In Heaven* put here; neither to egge our curiosity to dispute of Heaven, nor to restraine or confine God, who is All in all and above all, as Saint Gregorie excellently: *Deus est inter omnia, non tamen inclusus; Extra omnia non exclusus, infra omnia, non depressus; super omnia, non elatus.†* The true reason why hee is sayd to be *In*

---

*The righteous will shine like the sun.
†God is among all things and not shut in by them, outside all things yet not remote, above all things yet not set over them.

Heaven, is to lift up our hearts, and our hands, and our eyes, and our contemplations unto the Lord. When Christ bid us say, *Our Father which art in Heaven,* he did it that hee might remove our thoughts from the Earth, and fix them on Heaven and the things above.

Whither, since I have at last conducted your Meditations, there will I leave them. Now they are placed at that pitch, there let them rest; I will not by any further discourse call them downe or settle them lower. I have discharged the full scope and purpose of my Text, Which was onely to direct your Prayers to the right Place, Heaven, and to the right Object, God our Father.

I know our adversaries the Papists set their Disciples a lower course, directing their Devotions to Compostella or Loretto or the Shrines of Saints, or the Sepulchre at Jerusalem; but these are no objects for our Religion or piety. Heaven must be the receptacle of our Prayers. Shall we seeke to Christ amongst the Graves or Tombes of the dead? The Angell long since answered them, *Resurrexit, non est hic: Hee is not here, he is risen.* And if we ever hope to finde him, our prayers must rise after him, Goe up unto that place whither he is ascended, *Heaven.*

Againe, though their Prayers goe to the right Place, yet they are not delivered according to Christ's direction, unto the right Owner, *Our Father,* but unto Saints and Angels—they calling them Father that are but brethren and fellow-servants: as the Angell told Saint John, being about to worship him, *See thou doe it not, I am thy fellow-servant, and one of thy brethren which have the testimony of Jesus: worship God.* Nay, I would to God it were not true that they prayed unto stocks and images, saying unto the worke of the Carver and the Crucifix, *Thou art my Father.*

But howsoever they thus grosly will mistake their way and mis-place their prayers, and if not disclaime the true Father, yet joyne other Step-fathers unto him, let us goe unto the right Father, and to him alone, sending our Prayers as Christ hath directed them, not leaving them by the way, or delivering them to the hand of any officious busie Saint that would intercept them: that we give not him cause to complaine of us as he did of Israel, *I have children that will not acknowledge me.*

Happy is that people whose God is the Lord (saith David), but much happier that people whose Father is the Lord; and ('tis the step unto which Tertullian advances the Emphasis) *happy are they that acknowledge God for their Father,* that at the last day hee may owne & acknowledge them for his sonnes: *Come ye blessed Children, &c.*

Cajetan *in Mat.6*
Chrysostom[b]

[65]

Mat.28:6

Revel.19:10

[66]

Esay 1:2
(Ps. 144:15)

Tertul. *De Orat.*

III. HALLOWED BE THY NAME

[67]

Our meditations have now rais'd themselves unto the first step of this seven-fold scale of Prayer; From whence wee have the advantage to take a fuller view of the whole body thereof, and to consider the order of the Petitions, as well as their severall matters. So that the more wee contemplate this Theme, the more must we admire the perfection of the Lesson, and the singular method of the Teacher. 'Twas not enough that hee instructed us what to pray, prescribing universall remedies for our Necessities out of this precious Salvatory, but hee must shew us also where to beginne the cure. 'Twas not enough for him to levy this Masse of Devotion, to have mustered and drawne together the object of all Petitions into these seven Battalions, but as hee is our Captaine and Leader, so *he will goe out with our Armies. He will teach our hands to warre, and our fingers to fight.* He will direct us in this spirituall warfare, wherein we assaile our heavenly Father and offer a devout violence to his Kingdome—How these Christian forces, these Troopes of Prayer must be ranged; which Battalion must advance first and begin the fight.

This Petition stands in the head of the Troope, being brought up before the others to acknowledge the power of that Name which could give successe to all we sought for in the rest of them. Constantine wore that victorious Motto in his Banner, *In hoc vinces.* Well may I write upon the front of this Petition, *Hoc nomine vinces: by this Name* shalt thou obtaine the victory. It was the Motto of the most succesfull Warriour that ever led the host of Israel, *In nomine tuo conculcabo: In thy Name I will tread them downe that rise up against mee.* Since then our aime is to tread downe our necessities, which would else depresse and keepe us downe; since wee are to fight against our

Psal.60:10
Psal.144:1
[68]

Euseb.*De vita Constant.L.1: cap.22*

Psal.44:5

152 AN EXPOSITION UPON THE LORD'S PRAYER

spirituall enemies, temptations, and the evills which this life exposes us to, it was most fit wee should beginne with that *Sacred Name* which is the beginning of all good to us, and puts an end to all our miseries:

Hallowed be thy Name.

This way of proceeding is just and naturall; for whereas Aquinas saith: *Prayer is the Interpreter of our desire;* Biel in that observes the order of these Petitions holds the same course our desires doe. Now our intent and *desire first begins with the end:* God and his glory is the end of all Christian service. *All motion, all operation takes beginning from Him,* and by returne terminates in Him. For this cause then doe our Petitions, which containe *the blessings of earth and the blessings of Heaven,* blessings Temporall and blessings Eternall, first exercise themselves upon what conduceth to God's glory before what concernes our owne profit, beginning with Heaven and things concerning our future life in the Three formost requests of this Prayer, and then descending to Earth and what appertaines to the present life in the Foure last.

Biel tearmes this Petition *Actum Charitatis,* an act of love: *This is a well-regulated love, that empties and powres out itselfe into God's honour,* who is the Fount of love (as Saint John sayes), *For God is love.* Wherein you may see the difference betwixt the love of the world and the love of God: By the World's Maxime, our love should beginne at home with our selves, but by Christ's more authenticke rule, it must beginne with God: first serve Him before our owne turnes. God requires the first-lings of our Love as well as of our Fruits; and as Saint John tels us, *He loved us first,* so must wee love him before and above our selves. Our Saviour, jealous of this precedence in our affection, askes Peter, *Lovest thou me more than these?* Intimating, by the manner of the question, how high a trespasse it was to preferre any temporall respect before Him. But in the Gospell of Saint Matthew, hee makes a more open declaration of himselfe in this point: *Hee that loveth Father or Mother, Sonne or Daughter, or any thing more then me, is not worthy of me.*

From whence let us collect thus much, that all private respects must wait on God and his service; we must not intend our owne honour above God's. He that strives to consecrate his own name before God's takes a course to raze himselfe & his name out of all memorie, but *Him that honours me, I will honour,* saith God. Wee must not study our owne profit more than God's glory; or, like those that Christ said followed him not for his Doctrine, but for the bread he gave them, place that Petition *Panem nostrum &c: Give us our dayly bread,* before *Hallowed be thy Name* and the two that follow it.

For he that is the *Bread of Life,* Christ Jesus, hath in the Method of this Prayer controled such disorder in our desires, hath taught us that *Non in solo pane*—wee must not live onely by Bread, but by Faith in his Name, and hope of his Kingdome; and that *Fiat voluntas tua—To doe the Will of God*—should bee our meat and drinke, as Christ sayes it was his.

'Tis not abundance of worldly blessings which should take up our meditations or desires, but the advancement of his glorious Name, who hath created those Mines and Veines of treasure in the Earth. Salomon ask't not at God's hand Wealth but Wisdome, nor did he covenant with him for gold and silver when he dedicated the Temple, but that whensoever hee or his people should worship and invocate his Name in that Place, he would be gracious and propitious to them. And *He that was a greater than Salomon* taught us in his Gospell first to seek God, *to seeke the Kingdome of Heaven and the righteousnesse thereof,* and then all other temporall things should be abundantly conferred on us.

Therefore here, wee doe not pray in the first place for our owne advantage, but God's, not studious of our profit, but zealous for his glory. *Non nobis Domine, non nobis, sed Nomini tuo da Gloriam;* Not *give unto us,* but *to thy Name* give the Glory. *Sanctificetur nomen tuum:* Hallowed bee *thy Name.*

The parts I propose exceed not the number of the Words.

1. First, I shall speake of *Nomen,* Names in generall, Men's Names.
2. Secondly, *Nomen Tuum,* The Name of God.

III. Hallowed be thy Name

Thirdly *Sanctificetur,* How his Name is *Hallowed;* which to expresse and set off more perfectly, I shall shadow my discourse with some darke and contrary colours, shewing also *In quibus non sanctificatur:* By what this sacred Name is prophaned.

The use of *Names* from the beginning was distinction, to separate creature from creature by their severall appellations. The names of the creatures are speciall stiles to distinguish their species, which they beare since Adam's time, who had that favour permitted him by God to be the God-father to his workes; for *Hee brought the Beasts and the Fowles unto him, and hee gave Names to them;* which yet (for ought wee know) continue unaltered.

Yet are those Names the badges of our ignorance, not imposed from a knowledge of their internall being or to discerne their Natures, but like other common marks, shape & colour, to discerne them from one another. [[Should we travell over the History of Creatures, wee must confesse with S. Hierome that the most of them we know onely by their names, we never saw them, unlesse perhaps in some Map of Affricke, or in Gesner. And of those which are obvious to our eye, wee know little besides the Name, saving those uses which wee put them to. As for their Constitutive Formes and Intrinsecall proprieties, those have been secrets and mysteries, hid from the most subtile indagation of Philosophy.]]* For not the Tree of Porphyry, nor Logick, nor Philosophy, nor Aristotle himselfe, nor he that pretended to have travel'd further into the Story of all creatures than men of common faith dare beleeve, Plinie, could ever assigne the Essentiall difference of any creature. So that we must content our selves with a wide speculation, and since we can discover no better Evidences by which to know them, hold it sufficient to distinguish a Horse from a Cow by *Hinnibilis,*† and a Asse from a Lion by his Braying.

The Names which men beare are individuall, for though there was no use of particular Names to every beast, to Man, who was a creature form'd for society and commerce, for rule and the survey of all the world—nay, was to be sub-divided into a multitude of Nations—there was a necessity of particular Names for all the successions of his race. That common title of Humanity, *Man,* might serve to give him sufficient distinction from creatures of a different kinde; yet amongst his owne rankes was no way competent to signifie either Number or Sex. Nor could the disparity of conditions or degrees amongst Men bee enough to separate one from another, without Names: *One Starre differeth from another in glory* (saith the Apostle), and yet every Star hath its severall Name, *For God cals them by their Names.*

The names of men therefore have beene like partitions, to divide the Families of the world, like fences to keepe one tribe from encroaching upon another. And when there was no other Heraldry found out, Names only were the difference of the elder and younger House, of the Noble and the Base, of the Bond and of the Free, of Isaac and of Ismael, of Israel & of Edom. [[Which practise is retained in all parts of the world (for ought I could ever finde) save only in China, where the daughters have no Name besides the Sirname, but are called after their age and order. And amongst the Atlantes, who have no Name at all. And lastly, amongst the Troglodytes, who give their children the Names of Beasts and Birds, calling one Ramme, another Oxe, &c.]]

Primitively, all or most names were significant, pointing out not only the Person, but his Quality and Beginning, As God entitled *Adam* from the Mould wherein he was cast, and the principles whereof hee was made, *Earth.*

Others in Scripture have beene denominated from their Professions (a practise continued unto our times), or some remarkable accident, as *Israel* from *Jacob,* and *Paul* from *Saul.* [[*Moyses* was named by Pharaoh's daughter *Mosche,* which in the Ægyptian tongue imports his being drawne out of the waters, of *Mascha, Extrahere.* And *Esther* was stiled so from her singular Beauty, of *Seter,* which in the Persian language signifies a *Starre.*]]

The Grecians held that Names were prognostications, and imported that Fate which the Owners

---
*Double brackets indicate material added in 1634 edition.
†The sound of neighing.

Margin notes:
3.

I. Nomen: Of Names in generall, and their first institution [74]
Gen.2:19, 20

Hieron. *Lib.2:* *Epist.* 22, *Epitaph.Nepotiani*

[75]

[76]
I Cor.*15*:41.
Psal.147:4.

Purchas. *Pilgr. Asia.lib.4.c.18. §.4.*
Aretius *Problem 83*[a]
Aretius loc.cit.,*p.* 285[a]
All Names at first significant.
[77]

Rabbi Abenezra citat. a Joh. Weemse *Christian. Synagog Lib.1:cap.1.p.21.* Id.*pag.* 22.

154 AN EXPOSITION UPON THE LORD'S PRAYER

were to run thorow, as *Hippolitus* had his death written in his Name, *Torne with horses;* and *Priamus* (of *Priamos*) forshewed that his starres had sold him to captivity, which he must buy out by ransome. Whether this rule held as just, and bare that fatall truth in others, as it did in those Two, I meane not here to discourse. Sure I am, in the intent of Scripture, most Names there were propheticall, for *Abraham* had God's Covenant of multiplying his Seed sealed in his Name, and the sacred Name of *Jesus* was a lowd proclamation of of the Deliverance which was brought into the world by that Name. S. Augustine tels us the crown of *Stephen's* martyrdome was platted in his Name, for *Stephanos* signifies a Crowne.

[margin: [78]]
[margin: Aug. Serm.2.de Steph.[a]]

And as there were prophecies of Good desciphered by them, so also of Evill: For *Achitophel* was a title of Ruine, *Jeroboam* of Rebellion, *Jezabell* of Woe.

I know there are many amongst us who are curious observers of Names, and will conclude some to have beene more ominous, more unluckie or unfortunate, more lasting and short-lived than others, which by no meanes they will endure to bee put upon their children. ⟦As Montaigne observes, some Names were ominous and Fatall to some Princes in their particular Kingdomes, as *Ptolomy* in Ægypt, *Henry* in England, *Charles* in France, *Baldwine* in Flanders, *William* in Aquitaine.⟧ Saint Chrisostome makes mention of some in his time that would have their children called only after the names of those that lived longest, out of a perswasion that the Name might conduce to the addition of their Yeares. ⟦Surely, for my part, I can commend no Rules to be observed concerning Names but only that of Socrates, who advised Fathers to take care their children had Good and Easie Names, that so their Persons might not be reproached by their Names: As Martial tels one, *Sed tu Nomen habes aversum.**⟧ I hold the choise and imposition of names, so they be not scurrile or scandalous, indifferent and free to all; though I cannot allow that conceit which misleads many so farre as to beleeve our fortunes or our ages are contrived in our Names. Should a man bid Methuselah for one Gossip and Salomon for another, I doe not see, for all that, why hee should have a longer terme of life or a larger portion of wit than others, that have names neither so durable nor so discreet.

[margin: Montagn.*Essay. Lib.I:cap.*46]
[margin: [79] Chrysost.*Hom.*22 in 1 Cor. 4]
[margin: Martial *Epigr.* (4.19.2)]

Some by glorious actions have ennobled meane Names, and others, by degenerating from their titles, have forfeited them to infamie. Judas, by the signification of his Name, should have beene a *Confessour,* not a Traytour; and Lucifer an *Angell of light,* not the *Prince of darkenesse.* ⟦I could give you later instances even in some Popes, whose prodigious lives have shamed all their Names. Who would suspect by the Title that Benedict 8, whose Name signifies *Blessed,* had beene a Conjurer and a Cursed Inchanter? or that John 23, whose name imports *The Grace of God,* should have deserved so ill of the world as by the voice of a Councill to bee stiled *Diabolus Incarnatus,* an Incarnate Devill? Nay, Polidor Virgill tels you it was the practise of the Popes ever since the time of Sergius 2, Who changed his disgracefull Name *Bocca di Porco,* Swine's mouth, into *Sergius,* ordinarily to assume Names quite contrary to their Natures. If hee were a rusticke, ill-bred man, he was called *Urbanus,* that is Civill; if a Coward, *Leo,* a Lyon; if a Tyrant, *Clemens,* Gentle or Merciful; if an Atheist, *Pius,* Devout and Godly. I speake not of this to prejudice any, much lesse to put them out of conceit with themselves by reason of their Names.⟧

[margin: [80]]
[margin: Concil. Constant. Sess.2]
[margin: Polidor Virgil, vid.Helin.Geograph. pag.183]
[margin: [81]]

I am perswaded 'tis in man's owne election to over-rule the misfortunes which wilde Astrologie guesses at, or his Name threatens:

Sapiens dominabitur astris.†

The miseries of our lives are rooted in our Nature, not in our Names. There is no man throughly miserable, but hee that makes himselfe so, and no Name fatall but unto him that beleeves it.

So my life be good, what disadvantage is it if I be Christned with a By-word instead of a Name? I am sure when I goe downe into my grave, I shall leave it there, nor shall it at the last day rise up with me: for he that *will change our vile Bodies,* will also change our vile Names; at our admittance into

[margin: Philip.3:21]

---

*But you have an unlucky name.
†The wise man will have dominion over the stars.

III. Hallowed be thy Name

his New City, hee will impose upon us his *New Name,* His better Name, that *everlasting Name* which shall not bee put out. <small>Apoc.3:12 / Esay 56:5</small>

To finish this Nominall discourse: For the Time when Names were given, I finde no set day till the covenant of Circumcision was established, and then they used to Name and Circumcise their children at once. So we reade in the Gospell, *When the eight dayes were accomplished that they should circumcise the Childe,* his *Name was then called Jesus.* By which custome we are yet governd, forbearing to Name any till their Baptisme, which succeeded the Circumcision in the old Law. <small>Luk.2:21</small>

In former Ages of the world, Men had onely one Name, but as the world multiplied, so did Names also. The first Sirname we reade of in the old Testament, I take it, is 2 Sam 20:1, *Sheba filius Bichri cognomine* (so the Vulgar reads it), but the New Testament mentions divers.

Yet the Romans, not content with one name (as Varro sayes their Founder Romulus had no more) or with Two, as most of their succeeding Kings, swelled into no lesse than foure, bearing as many Names as a Pinnace hath sailes—their Maine, and Fore, and Top, &c.—for they had their *Prænomina,* their *Nomina,* their *Cognomina,* their *Agnomina.* I never lately heard of so many, but onely in *Eudæmon Johannes,* who sure had more witnesses than ordinary, else I wonder how he came by so many Names.

Wee in our practise are satisfied with Two, the *Sir-name,* which is *Nomen gentilium,* the name of the Tribe or Family from whence wee issue, and the *Christen Name* received at our Baptisme. In the giving whereof, though (as I said before) an undenied Liberty bee left for the chusing of any, either Hebrew or Ethnick, yet most commonly wee beare such Names as wee finde mentioned in the Scripture, either of Prophets, or Patriarkes, or Christ's Saints and Apostles, which wee chuse, not for that reason Stapleton alleages on behalfe of the Pontificians—*that we thinke they become our Guardians,* or that we are enrolled into their companies, capable of their intercession and custody, *because wee beare their Names*—but to put us in minde to imitate the vertues of those holy Men whose Names we have. <small>Stapleton *In Fest. Johan.Baptistæ*</small>

A practise of a pious meaning; how ever, wee know many amongst us that swerve from it, chusing, out of a nice singularity or a suspition of circumstantiall Idolatry, to impose any Names but the Names of Saints. To decline which, they christen their Children with Propositions and wholsome Sentences: yea, they impose plaine challenges upon them in stead of Names, as *Sin defy, Fight the good fight of faith,* and the like.

But I should neither much blame nor censure them did they not doe it out of grosse affectation, and insolent opposition to the customes used by us.

No more of Humane Names. I have held you too long in this Argument. If you now expect I should give an account of that time I have spent in this discourse, or shew what it conduces to *Nomen Tuum,* to the *Name of God,* I must confesse I followed that generall Liberty which the word *Nomen* afforded, which Quae being so fitly given by the Text, I held it not impertinent to premise somewhat concerning Men's Names, that you might more plainly discerne the difference betwixt *Nomen,* and *Nomen Tuum:* God's Name and Ours.

Well may we distinguish Man and Man by their severall Appellations, but God, whose simplicity is ineffable, whose Essence most indivisible, wee cannot. *When there are many, there is need of Names;* where but one, the paucity and singularity is distinction enough. *There being then but one God,* (saith Trismegistus) *he needs no Name.* Besides, as wee want strength of Sight to discerne and capacity to estimate Him, so we want Titles whereby to circumscribe his infinite, *Immense,* Being. Shall the tongue of Man graspe and fathome Him in one narrow Appellation, whom the world's continent, nor Heaven more spacious than it, no, nor the heart of man, vaster and more capacious than them both, is not able to comprehend? There is therefore no use of Name with God; the disproportion is so great betwixt him and our Finite Attributes, that wee disparage and detract from his greatnesse when we strive to expresse him by any Names. The imposition of Names emplies a priority of Worth, of Time, and of Knowledge, so that as the *Lesser is blest,* so is hee <small>2. *Nomen Tuum: Thy Name* Minut.Fœlix Lactant.*Lib.I: cap.6* Minut.Fœlix Xixtus *Sentent.*</small>

Named by the Greater. But who hath preceded God in Time, as that hee was acquainted with his pedigree, or in knowledge, *that hee knew his being,* or in dignity, that he could denominate him?

Amongst Men, *Names illustrate and reveale the knowledge of the thing Named,* as Damascen defines them; but with God they shut it up, they darken and diminish that knowledge of Him which is imprinted in our apprehensions. Doe we stile him *Father,* or *King,* or *Lord?* Why, by these same Titles doe wee call mortall Men; so that wee both contract his Essence and dimme our owne capacity whilst we fix on those Appellations. *Remove those weake helpes*—a Spectacle argues an infirme eye. Thy understanding will be more sharpe and cleere to discerne Him without a Name. Better is it onely to conceive than to Name God, for our conceit is more ample than our language; and 'tis more Glory to God when in a silent Contemplation wee confesse Him farre greater than we can utter. Let us bee religious to sanctifie, not curious to search his Name. 'Tis good for us *to bee busied in his Statutes* (as the Psalmist's phrase is), not in his Attributes. The one will guide us in the way of Peace, the other will confound us. *Let passe then all busie searches, they doe hurt.* For thy service and adoration, thou needest know no other Name but God. That Title is enough to give aime to thy Petitions; that Object powerfull to grant them.

Looke not therefore after any other Name, *Quia nec invenies,* (one answers roundly): if thou dost, 'tis but lost labour, *thou shalt never finde it.* God hath no Name distinguished from his being—*Deus est Nomen suum:* Hee is his owne Name. Lactantius quotes out of Mercurius Trismegistus, that to prevent all study which men might make for finding out his Name, He is *without Name.* Dionysius says, Hee is *Innominabilis,* impossible to be Named—Which if it be true, then is this Petition nullified. If God have no Name, why doe we cry, *Sanctificetur Nomen Tuum*—Hallowed be thy Name?

The Schooles wipe away this scruple with a distinction: As the Name imports the composition of *Substance* and *Quality,* so *it cannot suit* with the simplicity of God's Essence, for God hath no composition, either Naturall or Metaphysicall; but as it only signifies *Notitiam,* anything by which Hee is notified and by which wee strive to expresse Him, so He may be said to have a Name.

Yea, He hath many Names, *Vel potius Cognomina** (saith Arias). Petrus Galatinus reckons out of the Rabbines Threescore and Twelve Names, which they multiplyed into Ten sorts, so that, according to their calculation, they amounted to *Seven Hundred and Twenty* in all.

But contract them according to our Numbers, and you shall finde very many, yet all those too few to give us a sufficient declaration of Him. The cause of which multiplicity of Attributes springs from our owne imbecillity (saith Zanchius), for they were not assign'd to intimate that really there were many distinct severall vertues in God, but that by means of them, Hee might the better descend to our capacity; and we make shift to signifie Him by Many, since One Attribute was too narrow to comprehend his Incomprehensible Greatness.

Some Names there be (saith Saint Ambrose) expressing his *Divinity,* others his *Majesty.* The Schoolemen distribute them into Three rankes. First, *Essentialia,* as Verity, Eternity, &c. Secondly, *Notionalia,* applyed to each Person, as Paternity, Filiation, &c. Thirdly, *Appropriationis,* which though they agree to the whole Trinity together, yet are they attributed severally to every Person; as Election to the Father, Redemption to the Sonne, Sanctification to the Holy Ghost. Some Names God hath from everlasting, as his Attributes of Power, of Goodnesse, of Truth, &c. Some are relative, which beganne in Time, as Creator, Lord, &c., for he was no Lord before hee had servants, nor Creator before the world was made. Lastly, hee hath some which bee rather signes and effects then Names; as his Workes, his Word, his Sacraments; whereby neverthelesse Hee is knowne to his Church as perfectly and distinctly as men by their Names. And 'tis agreed by all Authority of Fathers that the Profanation and abuse of his Word and Sacraments are apparant breaches of the third Commandement, *Thou shalt not take the Name of the Lord thy God in vaine.*

Such and so many are the Names of God, and yet *this large variety no way empaires the*

---

*Or rather cognomens.

III. Hallowed be thy Name

simplicity of his Essence. Rather, I should think it a good Morall way of expressing God's infinity by an infinite number of Attributes. What hurt or blemish is it to the Diamond, though you put severall rates upon it? the quantity and the lustre is still one and the same: so is God.

Neither doe those Attributes of his which began in Time cause any alteration or change in his Eternity. For (saith Saint Augustine) One and the same peece of money is sucessively called a Price, a Debt, a Pawne, a Tribute; yet those appellations change neither the metall, nor the weight, nor the Impression. How much easier, then, may we apprehend the Immutability of God's substance amidst these his Attributes, *In whom there is no shadow of Change*. [92] James 1:17

There being then so great a Number of Names belonging to God, Biel proposes the doubt which of them the Text means when wee say, *Hallowed be thy Name*. To which I answer briefly, that whereas Saint Augustine says *Nomen est quasi Notamen,** that which Alexander Hales infers is most certaine: *Whatsoever denotes or expresses God unto us is his Name*. And therefore, we must sanctifie every one of those notifications, sanctifie Him in every Attribute, in everie Circumstance by which his knowledge is conveyed unto us. Which how it is done and how omitted, how God's Name is Hallowed and how profaned, in briefe instances I shall declare, being the last part of my discourse due to this word *Sanctificetur: Hallowed bee Thy Name*. [93]

First, *Just* and *Mercifull* are God's Names. Now, we sanctifie the Attribute of his Justice when wee leave unto Him the righting and avenging of our wrongs, for *Vindicta mihi* is his prerogative: *Vengeance is mine;* and we offer violence to this blessed Name when, urged with a distempered haste and fury, we wreake our selves by offering violence unto our Brethren. When we rely wholly on his Mercy, confessing that there is no Name under Heaven which can save but only that of his Sonne Christ, we sanctifie that Attribute, whereas when we flie to Saints' intercession, and from rotten Shrines look for Deliverance, we abuse and vilifie his Name. 3. *Sanctificetur* Deut.32:35

Secondly, the *Sacraments* and *God's word* are his Names. When we reverently receive those sacred Representations of his Bodie and Blood, bringing along with us neither obstinate hearts, nor stiffe rebellious knees that will not doe their duty to Him, for fear of Idolatry to the Bread, we then sanctifie his Name; whereas comming thither irreverently, or unprepared, we scandalize those holy mysteries, and *condemne our selves*. When we live according to the *rule of Faith,* his holy Word, when we doe not disguise our selves with the Mantle of Religion, making it a cloake of of maliciousness, and using religious pretexts but as a way to compasse sacrilegious designes; when wee doe not, as Sixtus complained of some, *Magis gentilizare quam christianizare,†* committing nothing that may be prejudiciall to the Faith we professe, or unworthy the Christian Name borne from our Baptisme, we *Hallow God's Name;* but when wee invert the order of those words, doe the contrary, we then take *his Name in vain*. For *Nomen inane crimen inane:* There is no greater crime than Hypocrisie, when men cover a rotten heart under a religious Title, and have no part of goodnesse but the Name. [94] Rom.8:1 I Pet.2:16 Ambros. *De Virgin.* [95]

Of this Hypocrisie none are more guilty than the Jesuites, none more frequently take the name of Jesus in vaine than they; In whose tumultuous breasts the Lion and the Lamb cohabitate, yet not in that sense the Prophet meanes, but as Christ interprets those in the Gospel, *wolves in sheepe's cloathing:* cruelty coloured over and hatched on the outside with holinesse, Meere pit-falls strewed with Religion, as Coffins with flowers, to cover the ruine of many a State swallowed up by their policy. Aug.*Ser.18 de verb.Dom.*[a] (Mt. 7:15)

Lastly, we sanctifie the Name of God when wee never speake or thinke of Him but with a religious reverence: We must not talke of Him as of a common Argument, fit for all times or all places. How did the Hebrewes tremble to take the *Tetragrammaton* into their mouthes? Nay, it is recorded that only the High-Priest, and that in the Temple and on the Day of Expiation, was held fit to pronounce the Name of God. Ludovicus Vives [96]

---

*A name is as it were a distinction.
†Make Gentiles rather than Christians.

158 AN EXPOSITION UPON THE LORD'S PRAYER

How is it then that Men presume to play with His Name? with scurrile wit, vented in every idle pamphlet, deriding both Him and His service. How is it that, without acknowledging any distance with Him, they make their tongues every where, in all places, so familiar with Him, that out of an ill nurtur'd familiarity, they will not in his owne peculiar, his proper place, the Church, where his Tabernacle and Habitation is fixt, scarce honour Him with a bended knee or an uncovered head—cheap low-rated complements, which they passe upon all other occasions and are content to cast away upon every one that hath but leasure to entertaine them—as if either God were not there present, or his presence not worthy of that regard?

[97] Is the Temple of God so much disesteemed since the Veile was rent, since the Traverse was taken away and the *Wall of Partition* (that deni'd the people accesse into the Holy Place) broken downe, in comparison of what it was before? When it was free only for the Priest to enter, Men made a Religion even to looke towards it; but now, when the *Sanctum Sanctorum,* wherein the Propitiation betwixt God and his People is made, wherin the sacrifice of Prayer is daily offered up and the Sacraments administered, is free and open to every commer, so little reverence doth the place finde from them, that even the Service, more awfull than the place, cannot win that reverence they owe it—as if the outward worship of God had past away with the old abolished ceremonies, and with them were now extinct.

Exod.3:5 — God's Name must be sanctified, as by our Inward, so also by our Outward worship, by the Gesture, as well as the Heart. Why else did hee command Moses in the old Law to *put off his shooes when he stood on holy ground?* Why doth the Apostle in the New Law tell us that *Hee who*
I Cor.11:4 — *prayes with his head covered dishonoureth his Head,* God and his Christ? Or why doth hee publish
[98] Philip.2:10 — that Decree enacted by divine Authority, that *At the name of Jesus every knee should bow?* That many take a perverse liberty, some out of a wilfull neglect, others out of a precise superstition, to trespasse upon either of these precepts, is true; but how any way they can discharge themselves of those duties, or excuse the neglect, I cannot see, if they but thinke it is no order in the *Mosaicall Law,* but a Decree in the *Gospell* which bindes them to it.

In a word, if the old Israelites were so timorous and sparing to use the Name of God, unlesse in
Psal.78:56 — weighty occasions, Let me aske with David, *Why doe wicked men tempt and provoke God?* By daily prophanations of his Name, by an habituated Blasphemie, by a trade of swearing, rending open the wounds of Christ their Saviour, and making new issues for his Bloud to flow out at their Mouths? accounting it a grace, not a sin, to enterline their discourse with Oathes; not thinking their words have either their just Ballast or true cadence, unlesse poised and bound up with Oathes
[99] instead of Periods. How happy were our assemblies, did not this loud sinne reigne in them! How happy were wee all, if wee could reserve this sacred Name, not for our talke, but for our Prayers, doing that which the language of my Text invites us to, *Sanctificetur Nomen Tuum: Hallowing the Name of God.*

Conclusion. — To end all: how we abuse the Name of God wee plainely see, but let me aske this once for all—
Luke I:49 — How can wee sanctifie it? Is not Holinesse his Attribute: *Holy is his Name?* Nay, not onely the Act, but the *power to hallow* all things (for so saith Arius Montanus, the Hebrew word imports *Sacrare*), and as John Baptist said to Christ when He came to bee baptized of him, *Commeth hee to be*
(Mt.3:14) — *Hallowed by us, who are men of profane lips and polluted lives?* Doth God want that Sanctity which wee can lend him? Doth he need the helpe and advantage of our Prayers? Or hath Christ taught us here to pray for Him as well as our selves? Saint Augustine makes my reply: *Intellige, &*
[100] *pro te rogas.* Marke well the sense of the words, and thou shalt finde 'tis for thy selfe, for thy owne
Idem — benefit, for thy owne sanctification—thou prayest not for God, Thou prayest that the Name of God, which is holy in itselfe, may also be sanctified by Thee; Thou prayest that His Word, His Sacraments, which are His Names, may bee vindicated from all abuse. Thou prayest that his
Cajetan *In.Mat.6*[a] — glorious Name may be sanctified here *on Earth, as it is in Heaven,* where the Angels cry aloud *Holy, Holy, Holy, Lord God of Hosts.*

Lastly, thou prayest (saith Saint Chrysostome) that His Holy Name which sanctifies all things

IV. Thy Kingdome come 159

may also sanctifie Thee. For without His Grace thou canst not Name Him as thou oughtest in thy Prayers, and unlesse first anointed with his Holy Oyle, thou canst not Hallow that Name whereof the Scripture testifies: *Thy Name is like a precious Ointment poured out.* That therefore the odour of this Name may prove unto us the *Sweet savour of Life and not of Death,* let us daily beseech that God who ownes that Name. *Si tu quæris Nomen Dei, quærit & ipse Nomen Tuum:** If thou shalt forget his service, and take no notice of his Name in this life, He will not know thee in the next— *Verily I know you not.* But if thou seeke the honour of His Name here, thou shalt see his Glory and his reward hereafter. If thou call on the Name of the Lord in these thy dayes, He will in His Great Day call on thy Name, *Veni Benedicte: Come thou blessed.*

Cant.1:3
[101] 2 Cor.2:16
August.
(Mt.25:11)
Mat.25:34

Now the God of all Mercies grant us his gracious assistance, that we may so sanctifie his Name on Earth, that our Names may bee writ in his Booke of Life in Heaven. *Amen.*

IV. THY KINGDOME COME

[102]

A Kingdome is no common Notion, no popular Theme, but very nice and dangerous to bee discussed. It was the Admonition of Pindarus to speak temperately and cautelously of the Gods: the advice holds as well for those that are the Gods of the Earth, Kings and their Kingdomes.

'Tis growne a fashion amongst some that would pretend a deeper reach than men of ordinary compasse to speak no language but State, and with that mis-becomming freedome, that their usuall discourse is no better than a Libell. Such contemplations as these, when they move out of their owne sphere, and are versed by persons not qualified with the liberty or capacity to handle them, are full of hazard.

From the pulpit they sound worst of all, that being a place not priviledged for censure, but erected as an Oratory wherein to pray for Kings and Kingdomes.

[103]

'Twas never well with Christendome since the Romish Clergy left Divinity and studied Politicks. Had the consideration of States never entred the Conclave of Cardinals, and had the Jesuites not entred into the secrets of Kingdomes, but like Regular men lived within their Cloister, many Princes had gone downe to their Graves *Sicca morte,*† with white winding sheets, not stained or discoloured with their owne bloud.

Juvenal
(10.113)

If at any time we will mention the King or Kingdome, let it be in our Prayers: our Commission reaches no further. For our blessed Saviour did as straitly charge us, by the mouth of his Apostle, to pray for Kings and the present prosperity of those Kingdomes he hath established on Earth, as by his owne Mouth he hath taught us to pray for the comming of his Heavenly Kingdome, *Adveniat Regnum tuum; Thy Kingdome come.*

The parts are two:

First, the *Object* of our Prayer, *Regnum Tuum: Thy Kingdome.*

[104] Divis.

Secondly, the *Petition,* by which wee desire to bring it neere to us: *Adveniat, Thy Kingdome come.*

But did hee teach us onely to Pray for Kingdomes and Princes, and not also to give thankes for them? Certainly, if the Apostle's rule hold, that we must *give Thanks for all men,* much more for those that are the best of Men, Princes; and if for Princes, how much more for the Best of that ranke—improved to that Superlative, not by the partiall rate of our affections (which might be allowed to value him in that degree, because ours) but weighed in the unpartiall balance of Merit, which cannot lie, nor needs the least graine of flattery or favour to make Him more currant in the World's opinion?

---

*If you seek the Name of God, he himself will seek your name.
†By a dry death.

160 AN EXPOSITION UPON THE LORD'S PRAYER

Prince Charles his returne from Spaine. Octob.6.1623

[105]

Methinkes I should not goe on in this subject and not allow Him a roome in it; nor can we effectually pray for the comming of Christ's Kingdome, and not first give Him thanks for the comming home of our owne.

Indeed our Kingdome shifted place, our Iland swam from us and made an Inroad upon the Continent, where awhile it stucke. Yea, our Hearts travelled from us, bound on a voyage in which all our Hopes were adventured.

They are now return'd, and wee fixt in our owne Center againe. And shall we be tongue-tied? Shall wee not blesse *the God of Jacob,* who hath brought backe the *staffe of our Jacob,* wherewith he past over that *Jordan* which divides these Kingdomes, crossed the River to come to us, and hath restored safe from the floud the *staffe of these Kingdomes,* which went out from us and crossed a Sea greater than Jordan? Shall we not praise his goodnesse, who, when our hopes were imbarqued and put to Sea in so rich a Bottome as the Prince, brought both Him and them back unto us without wracke or miscarriage in the Adventure?

[106]

I Thes.5:18

Luk.18:11

Yet some may say, this Ceremony is ended, and therefore suppose the repetition of it sounds out of date. I thinke not so. Hee that imagines thankes can bee at any time unseasonable is not of Saint Paul's minde, who bids us *Give thanks alwayes*. And hee that thinkes, when God hath given him a share in any blessing, that he can pay him at one breath, and after a short *Lord I thanke thee,* may sue out his *Quietus* as if hee owed Him no more; or that thinkes his gratitude for this particular Blessing, which was kindled and lighted with his Bonfire, should burne out and end in it, is not of my minde.

The mercies which God affords us require many dayes of payment: we cannot discharge them at one entire solution. Some blessings God hath bestowed on us for which we have taken above five thousand yeares to satisfie him—so long have we beene thanking Him for our *Election,* which was more ancient than the world; and his Church hath these sixteene hundred yeares beene levying Thanks to pay him for the *Salvation* he sent into the world by his onely Sonne—and yet the summe is imperfect, the greatest part behinde, unpayed.

[107]

In Caligula

I am not so mad to compare these ancient mercies of God with any later—New benefits hold no proportion, nor deserve to be named with them—yet this I know: God, that did allow so many Hundred yeares of thanksgiving for Spirituall blessings, doth allow a few dayes for Temporall. And if so, I come within my time to pay my thankes, nor can I forfeit any thing to his discretion that will censure this mention unfit or unseasonable. Not to trouble you with a receit of many words, Sueton writes: when the newes of Germanicus his welfare came to Rome, the people welcomed it with Lights and Fires, and this shout, *Salva Roma, Salva Patria, Salvus Germanicus*. Turne it to *Britanicus,* and the Acclamation upon this happy returne may be ours; *Salva Patria, Salvus Britanicus*—our Country is safe, our Prince is safe; God grant that both He and It may long continue so, He secure in It, It secur'd by Him. And as He is the Branch of a most Royall Stocke, may He spread like Him, that our Hopes may rest and build in his Boughes, and under them the Church and Common wealth be sheltered.

[108]

Nor let it seeme uncharitable or unchristian to anathematize them who doe not beare a part in this Joy, and in this Prayer for the good of our Kingdome, from having any part in the Kingdome of Christ which here we sue for, *Adveniat Regnum tuum*.

Kingdome

John 18:36

There is no eye so dull, but that discernes the *Kingdome* here specified not to lie so low as Earth; nor is that Temporall Kingdome of Christ, which the Jewes vainly expect, here meant. Our Saviour himselfe hath told us, The Kingdome which he promises, and we pray for, *is not of this world*. Yet are the Kingdomes of the Earth Christ's, by the surest Titles that can be, Inheritance and Purchase. He that is the Lord of the Cittadel commands the Towne; and hee that is possest of the Hils, is Lord of the inferiour Valleyes. By an higher prerogative of Domination, than, must it follow, that He who is the King of Heaven is King of the Earth too: For Heaven is the originall Copy of all Kingdomes, as Christ of all Kings.

[109]

IV. Thy Kingdome come

Let me not seeme to lead your Meditations out of the way or meaning of my Text, if I stay them a little upon the Temporall consideration of *Regnum Tuum,* touch upon the Kingdome of the Earth. My Method thus strengthened will run but the same course wee ourselves hold. From earth we travell upwards towards Heaven; and from the generall consideration of *Regnum Tuum* will I conduct your attention to the Kingdome of Christ.

The Romish Pilgrims are content to beleeve their neerest way to Heaven lies thorow Arabia and Palestina, the Holy Land; but I hope our Climate is not a whit out of the way. Saint Hierome assures us *Et de Hierosolymis & de Brittannia, æqualiter patet aula celestis:* Brittaine is as neere Heaven as any other Kingdome of the World, and I dare undertake to carry your Meditations as soone thither from hence, as if they travelled by Jerusalem or the Sepulchre. Hieron. *Ep.ad Paulin.de Institut. Monar.*

In fetching of which compasse, I pretend only to prove (what none can contradict) that Hee that made Heaven and Earth is King of Earth as well as Heaven. However, then, the Devill was so franke to offer Him all those Kingdomes which hee shewed in that large Map of his mentioned in the fourth of Matthew, he sought to bribe Christ but with his owne, for hee needed not the Devil's usurped claime to strengthen his title, since all was his before. The Earth is the Lord's, and all the Kingdomes of the Earth are but Copyholds belonging to *Regnum Tuum,* His Kingdome, as the Capitall Mannor, and hold from him. [110]

Heare by what Evidence.

'Tis true, the first Adam was heire of the world, and invested with a kingly Power *To Rule over all the Earth,* but those conditions and Covenants which God made with him being not observed, his title, forfaited by disobedience, became void, and reverted into His hand againe that first gave it. In the third of Genesis, vers. 17, God Re-enters, and in vers. 24, Adam is ejected. Neverthelesse, God at that time did not otherwise make seisure of it, but that it might bee redeemed againe whensoever the debt of Adam, and the weighty arrerage which his seed had runne into, was satisfied. Gen.1:26

[111]

By Christ, the *second Adam,* was this debt discharged, and by His Bloud was *Death's Bond,* that *Chyrographum Lethale* mentioned by the Apostle, cancell'd and washt out. So that the World, forfeited to Justice and lying as a desperate Mortgage, not possible to be redeemed but onely by the Sonne of God, now became His purchase. God surrenders and yeelds up both Title and Possession to Him: *I will give thee the Heathen for thine inheritance, and the ends of the Earth for thy possession.* In the verse following, hee puts the Scepter into His hand, and in the sixth verse proclaimes the Coronation, *I have set my King upon Sion.* (Col. 2:14)

Psal.2:8

Vers.6

Thus Christ, being enthronized in the World's Kingdome, hath ever since set His owne stampe and figure upon every kingdome thereof, Feare and Majestie. A Roman Historian writes that when Vespasian was saluted Emperour, the transfiguration of his State shone in his face, which appeared much brighter than before. Indeed every King is, as it were, a rich Medall cast in Christ's owne Mould, and beares that awfull Motto of safety written about his sacred Person, *Nolite tangere Christos meos: Touch not mine anointed.* A spell of most approved vertue, for we have often knowne that the Majesty which a King beares about him hath beene a charme to fright treason from him, by disarming and casting downe the hands of such who came provided and furnished for his Death. The lookes of Marius, though his high fortunes were now levelled with the ground on which he lay, so appaled his Executioner, that instead of wounding him, hee drops his sword from his hand and cries for mercy, *Parce, o Imperator.** Yea, the very sound of Christ's voice in the Garden, when the darknesse of Night concealed his face and begat an uncertainty of Him whom they sought, made his surprisers retire, and doe an homage to his Person *by falling to the ground.* [112]

Psal.105:15

[113] (Jn 18:6)

Besides, hee hath declared how close this *Tuum* hath bound the Kingdome to Him, by undertaking the substitution of Deputies here on Earth. 'Tis his condition, *Thou shalt make no King but whom the Lord shall choose;* and in Aggee, He exercises that power: *I have chosen Thee.* And Deut.17:15
Agge.2:23

---

*Spare me, O Emperor.

162 AN EXPOSITION UPON THE LORD'S PRAYER

<small>Prov.8:15</small> again, by the confession of the wisest and greatest King that ever was: *Per me Reges regnant—By me Kings reigne*—that is, by my permission, my appointment. The Psalmist gives the reason: <small>Psal.22:28</small> *Quoniam Domini est Regnum—Because the Kingdome is the Lord's.*

<small>*The Pope no disposer of Kingdomes.*</small>   If it be cleere, then, that *Regnum tuum* is Christ's peculiar, if he be the Disposer of Scepters and Soveraignty, by what right doth the Pope undertake to bestow both them and the Allegeance of Subjects as he pleases? Or what wrong can he complaine of, if those persons it concernes deny him to be their Judge and Visitor?

<small>Psal.2:9</small>
<small>[114]</small>   I never read that the *Iron Scepter* which bruises the Nations was put into his hands; and though he will needs keepe the *Keyes,* surely the *Chaines and Fetters to binde Princes and Nobles* were no part of his charge. The Psalmist left them with Christ, where they yet remaine, unlesse hee hath since purloined them. Yet I know the Canonists have lifted him up to as high a pitch as that was <small>Baldus</small> from whence the Devill overlookt the Kingdomes of the world, *Princeps omnium, Rex Regum: King of Kings. Pater dignitatum, sicut sol pater planetarum* (so cries another): the Father of Principalities, from whom Emperours receive their power as the Moone borrowes light from the Sunne. And againe, in that blasphemous acclamation of the Conclave to Pope Julius, *Tu es omnia, supra omnia, omnis potestas tibi data est in Cælo & in Terra:* Thou art all, above all, all Power in Earth and Heaven is entrusted to thee. Yea, had those flatterers beene silent, he hath beene forward enough to be his own trumpet: *Ego sum Papa & Cæsar, Cælestis & terrestris Imperii Dominium habeo,** so Boniface proclaimed himselfe.

<small>[115]</small>   But for all this, these Sycophants onely speake what his Ambition strives to bee, not what of right he is or should be. These lying Texts are more authenticall to prove him Antichrist, then King of Kings or a disposer of the Nations. For what lesse can he be, that would devest Christ of that glorious Attribute, to put it on himselfe?

Since that time he layed by the keyes and presumed to unsheath the Emperour's sword, Christendom hath felt, to her smart, that sword could never yet finde the way into its scabberd againe. 'Twere a great deale better for Christ's Vicar to meddle with his owne Church-Booke, to bee content with his wax vailes, his Commutations and Tributes, his Impost upon the Bordelli—those Candle-rents, as being Petty Tithes, wee confesse due to his Vicaridge—but for Scepters and Kingdomes, they are great Tithes, and only proper to Christ, whose Vicar he cals himselfe.

<small>[116]   Revel.19:16</small>
<small>1 Tim.6:15   Psal.103:19</small>   Again, if it be *Regnum Tuum,* Christ be the supreme transcendent Monarch—*King of Kings, and Lord of Lords,* and *Solus potens Rex Regum,*† and (as the Psalmist) *His kingdome ruleth over all*—how can any other appropriate the Earth's Kingdomes to himselfe, or lay claime to an universall Monarchy?

<small>*No universall Monarchy*</small>   'Tis an hatefull inclosure to hedge in the World at once; and a License which none but a Geographer can justifie, to quarter Sea and Land in one Globe. Did God appoint to each Body a Peculiar Angell, and did he lesse to those Greater Bodies, Kingdomes and common wealths? The <small>Ephes.4:5, 6</small> Apostle tels us there is but *one Faith, one Baptisme, one God, Father of all, which is above all,* yet we have no Text that there should be but one King. When God tooke asunder the world, and scattered it into severall people and severall languages, certainly he never meant any man should peece them together againe, or make them understand one Tongue, but Christ alone, whose Trumpet in the end of the World shall speake to them in such a language that shal be heard and <small>[117]</small> understood alike of all. Then indeed the curse which scattered them shall be repealed, but not till <small>(Jn 10:16)</small> then, and all shall be reduced unto one Head, that there may be *One Shepherd and one fold.*

The Poet saies Alexander was almost stifled with a conceit that the World was so narrow for him, hee wanted Aire and elbow-roome in it—:

<small>Juvenal *Sat.*
(*10:169*)</small>   *Æstuat infœlix angusto limite mundi.*

And Plutarch writes, He wisht for more worlds than one, fearing that which was discovered was too

---

*I am Pope and Emperor, I hold the right of dominion over the heavenly and earthly empire.
†Alone the powerful King of Kings.

IV. Thy Kingdome come

small a prize for him to conquer, and would be too quickly won. I confesse this became him well in an Apothegme or a Verse, but in plaine-meaning Prose, for any man to be so vast in his desires as to effect no lesse than the whole World's soveraignty is a prodigious avarice, too great for our Wonder. He indeeres himselfe too far into God's favour that thinkes the Earth was made onely for him, as the Flouds for Leviathan. Sure, Almighty God, that cals himselfe *King of Kings*, intended more Kings than one. [Revel.17:14]

In the Psalme we finde a Plurality, *God standeth in the congregation of Princes*—there, God is President of that Royall Assembly. And in another Psalme he speakes to them: *Be wise O ye Kings of the Earth,* wise to preserve and understand their number, as well as their obedience unto Him. For should there bee one onely supreme Power on Earth to whom all the rest should bee subordinate, they were not then Kings but Viceroyes, nor could their States be called Kingdomes but Corporations, rather held at the Devotion of Him that gives the Charter. [[118] Psal.82:1] [Psal.2:10]

To come off from this Argument: wee finde in the Revelat. *The Crownes of all the Kings cast at the feet of the Lambe.* The reason is there given, *Quoniam dignus: Hee alone was worthy to be the Lord of them all.* If there bee any more worthy of them then Christ, let him stand up and claime them. Till then, we shall acknowledge no singular Power, no Lord Paramount nor universall Monarch but Christ alone; And untill that Interrogation of Job bee solved, *Quem constituit alium super terram, aut quem posuit super orbem?** we will turne his *Quaere* into a *Thesis,* and say, *Hee hath appointed no one to Lord the whole Earth besides himselfe.* [Revel.4:10] [[119] Job 34:13]

I have done with the Temporall consideration of *Regnum Tuum.* I come now to the stricter acception of it, which is Spirituall, in which sense *Regnum Tuum* imports a Kingdome different much from the other. For those other Kingdomes are *Occidentall,* wee looke on them as on the Sunne setting and declining to Night; but this Kingdome is in the East, and the aspect of it is like the morning Sunne, which fairely rises to our Prayers. Those Scepters are delivered over from hand to hand, but this is *Sceptrum æternum,* not successive, but Eternall—as the Psalmist saies, *Thy Throne, O God, is for ever, the Scepter of thy Kingdome is a right Scepter.* Lastly, Earth's Kingdomes beare the difference of the younger house, they are *Regna transeuntia,* Moveable Kingdomes, which goe and come, change and decline; but this is *Regnum Adveniens,* not yet Come, but Comming. Yea, when it is Come, it will be *Adveniens* still; when it hath growne as old as the World, seene as many yeeres as we reckon from Adam, there shall come after them a terme longer liv'd than the first, and still the succeeding date shall bee double, till at the last the Account outgrow all Arithmetick. Though we began our Calculation with the stars, and layed the dust of the Earth for Cyphers, yet shall wee want number to compute how many ages are behinde to come of this Kingdome's date which here we pray for, *Adveniat.* [*Tuum: Thy Kingdome*] [Psal.45:6] [[120]]

The Schoolemen, that deale altogether upon distinction, and would, if it were possible, divide Christ's seamelesse Coat, have variously divided this Kingdome of His, made it an Heptarchy. For they doe not only understand by *Regnum Tuum* that Generall Administration whereby he governes all things, or the Kingdome of Grace, or that of Glory, but they make *Regnum Scripturæ* and *Regnum Ecclesiæ Militantis*—The Scripture and the Church—Kingdomes. They make *Locum Beatitudinis,* the place where the blessed Saints contemplate God, a Kingdome: Nay, by a bold figure they erect a Throne in the King's owne Person, take Christ himselfe for a Kingdome. [[121]]

For all which, I deny not but they may have colourable warrant from the Scripture; yet I shall not hold their course, or stay to view so many Kingdomes as their Discoveries have travelled thorow.

I rest upon that proper construction of *Regnum Tuum,* which imports Christ's Administration as He is head of the Church, and by his sacred Word (which is the Law whereby his Kingdome is governed) subjects the Faith and obedience of his servants to himselfe.

Which acception will fully determine in two others contained under it, *The Kingdome of Grace,* and the *Kingdome of Glory.* And however the last of these is the finall Object of our Prayers, yet is

---
*Who gave him charge over the earth, and who laid on him the whole world?

the first a disposition and necessary meanes to attain the other. He that prayes for the Kingdome of Glory and hath not a sufficient stocke of Grace to maintaine and beare up that Petition, builds without his foundation. He is like one that attempts to flye without wings, or like a Projector that, in going neerer waies to profit or preferment than by the beaten path, beguiles himselfe at last; he sends up his Prayers as vainely as children doe their Arrowes into the aire, which fall backe as fast as they shoot them up.

The Kingdome of Glory presumes that of Grace; As the Peace which God gives us in this world is a pledge of our future peace in the other, so is Grace the earnest of our Glory. None can be admitted into the Triumphant Church but who hath first served in the Militant, and none can be made free of the Kingdome of Glory, but hee who hath served his time in the Kingdome of Grace. Therefore by good right doe we here pray for the Kingdome of Grace, as well as for the Kingdome of Glory.

Yet our *Adueniat,* when it referres to the Kingdome of Grace, doth not looke on it as on a thing altogether absent, but as not yet fully come. The Kingdome of God indeed hath beene come amongst us ever since Christ's time, and wee have lived under the raigne of Grace ever since the Law was abolished and the Gospell establisht, but this Kingdome is yet straitened, beares not its full bredth, nor is it arrived at its perfect growth. Wee therefore yet Pray *Adueniat,* for the dilation, the increase, the perfection of this Empire.

So long as the *Holy Scripture,* that rich Cabbanet wherein the Graces and Mercies of God are lockt up, is opened with the right Key, understood in the true upright meaning of it, and preserved in that height of dignity which Christ appointed to it, not wrested to make Heresie authenticall, nor abased so low as to make Tradition Judge of it; so long (I say) as the lustre of it is not dim'd, but the dignity preserved religiously amongst us, so long have we the earnest of Salvation and pledge of Grace deposited with us; but where it is quite lockt up from God's people, and the Keyes kept in the Pope's Chamber, that the Laity cannot open it at all, nor, when it is opened, must understand it any way but how hee pleases, how it serves best for his advantage; Where tales and Fables beare more authority than Divine Stories; Where the Legend is instead of Bibles, and man's stupid Traditions valued above God's Scripture, I feare the Kingdome of Grace hath lost much ground there, that there it is, since the first comming of it, almost gone, almost extinct, and that the curse which was throwne upon the hard-harted Jewes that would *not see what they saw, nor understand what they read,* hath trenched very deepe upon it. *Auferetur Regnum Dei a vobis:* The Kingdome of God shall bee taken away from you—That is, *the true understanding and estimation of the Scripture* shall be removed from you.

Our *Adveniat* therefore must stand in the Gates of our lips to disperse this Canker, that it never eat upon our Church, that the dangerous teeth of this curse never fasten upon us, but that the Word of God may still be as open to our Understanding as it is free and open for us to Heare in all Churches of this Land.

Againe, so long as the Gospell of Christ, which is the Evidence of his Grace, is minced or dam'd up in any Circumstances, so that the Current is hindred and cannot flow with a free liberall streame, it shewes the Kingdome of Grace is not fully come. Wee must therefore open the course with our *Adveniat,* pray that the Obstacles may be removed, and those Sluces that either stop or divert the naturall Current of it may bee taken up, that so it may finde no let or opposition through the Christian World. Let me adde Saint Chrysostome's exposition: So long as our earthly affections are predominant, and a perverse will over-rules the understanding, so long as the flesh is in rebellion against the Spirit and prevailes, the Kingdome of Grace is not yet come. But when the Spirit hath subdued the Earthly Man, 'tis an Infallible token of the Kingdome of Grace. Our *Adveniat* therefore prayes for the setting up of this Kingdome in man's selfe (which the schooles call *Regnum animæ*) as well as for Christ's Kingdome. Hee that by Religion and reason hath subjected that earth which lies in his Temper, he (saith Chrystostome) is Lord of himselfe. And Gerson, out of that old Maxime, *Si vis tibi omnia subiicere, subiice te rationi,* inferres: Hee is not fit to reigne with Christ in his Kingdome *who hath not first overcome all worldly passions, and beene King over himselfe.*

IV. Thy Kingdome come

Lastly, whilst *the sound of the Gospell hath not gone out into all Nations,* whilst there is a World layed open to our discovery which hath not discovered Christ, not heard of Him (like those in the Acts, who had not heard whether there were a Resurrection or no) the Kingdome of Grace is not yet come so amply as it should bee. Wee must therefore daily propagate it in our Prayers, beseeching God that all Nations may entertane his Truth, that so Christ may be Lord from *Dan to Beersheba,* from Sea to Sea, from one side of the continent to the other. And then, where there is this Extent of Grace, where there is this Unity of Faith and Harmony of Religion through the world, 'tis the immediate fore-runner of Christ's last glorious Advent. The Kingdome of Grace is then at a Period, and gives way to the last Monarchy which ever shall be, *The Kingdome of Glory,* which is the full scope of our *Adveniat: Thy Kingdome come.* (Acts 17:32)

[127]

Thus wee can make shift to delineate, though in a rude imperfect Modell, the Kingdome of Grace, but the Kingdome of Glory we cannot. On that we are permitted to looke at the distance whereat Seamen discover Land, and our hopes are as remote from us as they from Harbour, which they onely beginne to ken, and no more. Or as Moses from the top of Abarim survaied the Land of Promise, and tooke possession of the Soile with his eye, so from this Mount of Grace are wee permitted to descry that higher Mount of Glory, whose top reaches the highest Heavens; To taste it in the promise of the Gospell, and take possession of it *Oculo fidei,* with the Eye of our Faith, till ourselves being seated in it, the Eyes of our Body shall hereafter see all that we now beleeve.

Numb.27:12

[128]

Wee are suffered to discerne that to bee our Gole, may descry the Host of Heaven, Angels and Saints there assembled, and have a glympse of *that Crowne of Righteousnesse* which Saint Paul speakes of, and read that promise writ in the Circle of it, *Si compatimur conregnabimus*—that we shall after that great day of Coronation reigne for ever with Christ. But here our eye dazles, dimme and unable to behold any more; the Consequence of that blisse is unutterable, the Measure of it not to bee taken by so weake a Perspective as the Eye. *The Eye hath not seene, nor the eare heard, nor can the heart of man conceive the joyes which are comprehended in that Kingdome of Glory.*

2 Tim.4:8.
2 Tim.2:12.

1 Cor.2:9.

So then the Kingdome of Grace is not our Petition's full scope, it only is the Harbinger to fit us for the life of Glory, as John Baptist was to prepare the way for Christ. And as John Baptist could no otherwise describe the Excellencie of Him that was to come after him, but onely by accusing his owne unworthinesse: *Non sum dignus, I am not worthy to untie his shooe-latchet;* so can wee no way discipher the Kingdome of Glory and the joyes there treasured up, but by professing our selves unworthy to utter, and unable to figure it in any other Mould but in our wishes and Petitions, praying to God *That it may come.*

[129]

Luk.3:16.

But what language doth this *Adveniat* naturally speake? What is our meaning in this Petition? Doe we accuse God of slacknesse, that He tarries too long? or doe wee dare His comming? Or doe we doubt it, like those in the Prophet *Qui dicunt festinet,* which call for his comming: *Let him make haste.*

Adveniat: Thy Kingdome come
Esa.5:19

Or doe we thinke our request can prevaile with Him to alter the prefixt day of his arrivall, to change the Jesses of that great Journey, and come sooner than in his eternall purpose he hath decreed? Certainly none of these. This Petition doth not argue or complaine of God's slownesse, no more than the Saints in the Revelation, that cry from under the Altar, *Usque quo, Domine? How long, Lord, holy and true?* &c. Nor is it so ill bred as to presse or quicken Him, but it shewes the alacrity of our Faith beating in our Prayers, by which we doe *Festinare ad spei nostræ complexum:* a little *anticipate our Hopes,* and labour to get a little ground, a little advantage of that Time, which upon even termes will out-flie us. For if we lie still, and bee not before hand with it but suffer it to overtake us, we are lost. 'Tis so speedy and we so dull, we cannot keepe wing with it, but shall bee cast behinde so farre as the foolish Virgins were, nor can wee ever bee able to recover that ground which our slow improvidence hath lost. Againe, in this *Adveniat* we doe not sue to God to change his purpose of comming, but rather beseech him to change our vile bodies, that so we may goe the

[130]

Revel.6:10

Tertul. *Lib.de Orat.*

(Mt 25:1–12)

---

*If we endure with him, we shall also reign with him.

166 AN EXPOSITION UPON THE LORD'S PRAYER

sooner to Him, uncloathing ourselves of the burthen of our flesh, and crying with Saint Paul, *Cupio dissolvi, I desire to be dissolved and to be with Christ:* and winging ourselves with the Prophet David's wish, *O that I had wings like a Dove, that I might flie away and be at rest.*

Lastly, 'tis no impatient voice of a man weary of God's stay, or not content to tarry his leisure, but rather like the shout of men harnessed & prepared for the Battell, which declares our readinesse to encounter Him, not silently awaiting his comming, but whilst he is yet on his way, making out to meet Him, and standing ready to welcome his arrivall, his Journey toward us, with the loud acclamation of an *Adveniat Regnum tuum: Thy Kingdome come.*

I have spoke all, and in this short Paraphrase upon the *Adveniat* in my Text, delivered the full use we all must make of this Petition: which is, to make our selves as ready for the Kingdome of Glory as that is ready for us, to set our selves as neere to God as the approaching day of his Kingdome is neere to us. John Baptist long since proclaimed this Kingdome to be at hand, and in the Revelat. that *Ecce venio* [Behold I come] tels us the King of Glory is not farre off. O then (as it is in the Psalme) *Lift up your selves, yee everlasting Gates, that the King of Glory may enter in.* The Heart is the gate at which Christ must enter, 'tis the Fort, the Cittadell which hee would have yeelded into his possession: *My sonne give me thy heart.* Let us therefore prepare our Hearts for the entertainment of so great a Guest, that so our soules may hold the same course hereafter, which our Prayers here doe. If wee cry unto Him *Adveniat,* pray for his comming, yet are unready and unsettled against that Day, we doe not love but feare his arrivall. And then, if this *Adveniat* breath from a soule distracted with feare, our Petitions runne counter; the point of them is turn'd against our owne breast, we pray against our selves. *Doest thou wish for Him whom thou fearest?* How shall God beleeve thee, when thou thus jugglest and playest the Hypocrite with Him, when thou makest a request to Him which thou art afraid lest He should grant unto thee?

Thinke how miserable were thy case if Hee should take thee at thy word, and when thou sayest *Thy Kingdome come,* should suddenly at the instant come upon thee, before thou had'st time to recollect thy selfe, and to repent this Hypocrisie of thy Prayers.

Thou hast no way to rectifie and set straight thy Prayers but by rectifying thy selfe: *correct thy perverse wayes,* and amend thy life, lest if God take thee unprovided, thou finde by late and wofull experience that thou hast *prayed against thy selfe.*

'Tis most true, *Repentance* is the best preparative for the Kingdome of Glory commended to us by the Great Physitian of our soules: *Repent, for the Kingdome of Heaven is at hand.* He that against that time shall bee enabled with Grace to lay up so good a stocke for himselfe as a *New life,* is furnished for a glorious voyage into the *New Jerusalem.* Nor needs hee bee afraid how soone Christ's second *Advent* will bee. This onely preparation doth Hee require of us, and if He yet deferre His comming a while longer, 'tis onely for our good, to give us time thus to provide for his entertainment, as He himselfe warnes us: *Et vos estote parati.* We doe not stay for Him, no, He stayes for us.

Behold, his preparations are all made; O that ours were made also. Heare from his owne mouth: *Omnia parata,* All things are in a readinesse; *Paratæ sunt nuptiæ,* the Marriage is at hand: *Parata est Cœna,* My Supper is ready; and *Paratum est Regnum,* My Kingdome is long since prepared. Blessed is that man who can truly answer him, *Paratum est Cor meum:* Lord, my heart is ready, my heart is ready. He shall be sure to be one of those to heare that joyfull Reply from Christ againe, *Possidete paratum vobis Regnum:* Enter into that glorious Kingdome prepared from the beginning of the world.

V. THY WILL BEE DONE IN EARTH AS IT IS IN HEAVEN

Hitherto our Petitions have beene in the ascent, raising and working themselves upon the wings of this Prayer. They are now climbed to the highest pitch, the *Culmen & fastigium:* Top of this Mount of God. For the contemplation of God's will is next in height to his owne Presence, nay, 'tis

V. Thy will bee done in Earth, etc.

Himselfe. We can put no difference betwixt his *Essence* and his *Will*. Now because this is otherwise in Man, whose Will is a faculty of the soule, and not his Essence:

My first part shall be to shew the difference betwixt *voluntas tua* and *voluntas Hominis*, God's *Will* and *Man's*.

Secondly, I shall declare what this Will of God is, and the severall Acceptions of it; which is the contemplative part, Involving *Totum theologiæ*, the whole body of divinity.

Thirdly, how this Will of His is to bee fulfilled; which is the Practicke part of the Petition, and indeed *Totum Religionis*, the Maine Scope of Religion, In the performing whereof the whole Law and the Prophets are fulfilled: *Fiat, Thy Will be done*.

Lastly, I shall present unto you the Patterne proposed unto us, according to which, Religion and our Endevours must worke: *Sicut in Cælo, In Earth as it is in Heaven;* and this is the perfection of this Petition, which is the Exemplary part.

First, of the consideration of *voluntas Tua* and *Hominis, God's Will* and *Man's:* Like the distance betwixt Heaven and Earth, such is the disproportion betwixt God and Man. God sees not as Man sees, nor doth He Will like him. The Will of Man is moved by occasion, altered by chance, but the Will of God, like the Persian Lawes, stands irrevocable, neither to be resisted nor reversed.

When Adam's privilege was called in, the Will was abridged too, and allowed lesse freedome than before. If it now have any Liberty, 'tis Negative. It is in a Man's owne Will and choice whether he will do any foule fact, perpetrate an Ill, for *Homo est libere malus*,* nothing compels or laies an inevitable necessity of sinning upon him; 'tis free for him to avoid it. No loose Starre bawdes him in his inordinate desires, no angry Planet guides his hand to Murther, no watry Influence urges him to that familiar sinne now growne a fashionable complement, Drunkennesse. Hee may avoid the Actions of sinne, though not the Offers. Those *Primi motus*—motions and seeds of sinne which are scattered upon his whole being—will bud and put forth a blade. Though the Heart of Man be never so well manured by Grace, and sowne with graine of better value, for all that, Originall sinne will send up those ranke weedes, those wild tares, to grow amongst our best Harvests, as the remembrances and Characters of that taint wee beare about us.

Now although Man be *Libere malus,* he is not *Libere bonus:* Though it be in his Election to act no mischiefe, 'tis more than he can undertake to doe any Good; yea, or to thinke well, without the assistance of God.

The liberty of Will consists not *In indifferentia ad utrumque contrariorum* (which is the state of the question, and the termes of quarrell betwixt us & the Papists touching Free-will)—in *an Indifferency* to Will that which is Good or that is Evill—but only *In immunitate a Coactione,* in *an immunity* from any Coaction. A man is not good against his Will, nor is there any Necessity of sinning layed upon him.

So that this Liberty is clogged with Restraint:

Cum fugit a collo trahitur pars longa catenæ†

It is a negative freedome, like that which is indulged to Prisoners, who are allowed the liberty of the Prison to goe freely about the house, but may not exceed that circuit (if you can call it a liberty not to weare shackles), or else have leave to walke abroad with their Keepers, or be confin'd to one roome: this is such. Man is not left indifferent to himselfe, but still waited on by an Abridgement.

To speake more properly, Man hath such a freedome over his Will as Keepers have over Lions in their grates, who permit them a kinde of liberty: they doe not tye them up, but let them walke about in their Cels, and can choose, keeping them within those bounds, whether they shall doe any hurt; but it were a dangerous presumption to inlarge them further. As dangerous is their boldnesse who dare impute to Man the liberty of doing well, or give the latitude and scope to Will which, if it [is] not bridled, and with a strait hand held in, is wilder then the wildest of creatures.

Man may rudely Cast and Project good things, Intend and Meane towards Well, yet all this is but

---

*Man is freely evil.
†When he flees, a long piece of chain is dragging from his neck.

168 AN EXPOSITION UPON THE LORD'S PRAYER

Purpose, but Pretense, 'tis not Action. He must wait on God for the finishing his good intents. For though hee may cast the Modell, lay the Plat-forme of Vertue, he cannot raise the worke without higher assistance. *Except the Lord build the house,* in vaine is all other endevour. Upon which foundation Damascen builds his conclusion: *We have in our eye and contemplation what to doe, but cannot determine upon it, or effect it without God co-operate with us.*

But howsoever Man be thus confin'd in his Will, God is not in His. He is *Liberrimum agens,* such an Agent as attends not the concurrence of Causes or Times for accomplishing what hee would have effected. All times are seasonable to Him, all causes give way to his prerogative, who precedes all causes that wee can call First; and with such a prompt passive obedience, that He *no sooner Wils anything, but that Will is moulded and made up into a Work.*

His Will speakes in no other tongue but his Workes, and what wee in our language and translation call Workes, is in the Originall nothing else but his Will. Hee doth not *Velle* first and then *Facere:* first Intend and then Act, but these runne even together. If there bee any prevention in either, 'tis in the Action, forward to obey his Will.

You never read a *Voluit,* but you see a *Fecit* goes along with it. *Quicquid voluit fecit: Hee hath done whatsoever hee pleased.* Whereupon justly doth Saint Augustine inferre, *God's Will is the highest and the Primary Cause of all motion and action.* Damascen inlarges it farther: *His will both makes and conserves all things,*

Besides, the Will of Man is but a Quality, an adherent Companion to the soule, rather *Consequens essentiam animæ* then *Essentia ipsa,* a Consequence, not an Essence. Hee that writes most boldly of it stiles it but *Pars animæ,* part of the soule. But the Will of God is not *Pars Dei,* a part of the Deity, but entirely It selfe, *not an affection, or a quality, or an elicit act, but the very Essence.* 'Tis not a distinct thing in God to Will and to Be, but the same. And as it is all one in Him to bee Good and to bee God, so *it is all one in Him to Will and to bee God,* Such an Identity is betwixt the Essence of God and his Will; in which Justin Martyr grosly erred, holding that God's Essence differed from his Will.

They are both Convertible, and yet the Master of the Sentences well notes that the Conversion holds not round: *Howsoever it be true to say, 'tis all one in God to Will as to Be,* we must not for all that say God Is whatsoever He Wils.

The distance then appeares so large betwixt these two Wills, of God, and Man, that 'tis fit I set the tearmes of my comparison wider than at first I did. For Heaven and Earth are lesse distant from each, than God's Will and Man's. As remote as they seeme to our apprehensions, yet they meet in Logicke: one Predicament contains both Heaven and Earth, but *Voluntas Hominis* and *Voluntas Tua toto genere differunt*—differ in the *Genus:*—God's Will and Man's will not to be reconciled in one Predicament, the Will of God being a Substance and the Essence of God, Man's but a Faculty and Accident.

Lastly, the Will of God and of Man differ sometimes as contraries. Man's will is carried to those Objects which the Will of God is not to grant him. Oft times we wish abundance and a smooth life, not made rugged or sowred with Crosses, when God in his wisdome knoweth want is better for us, and that calamity best makes us understand both Him and ourselves, according to that *Vexatio dat intellectum.**

We covet long tearmes of life, addition of daies, both to our selves and those wee love: when we see God withstands our wishes, dealing more mercifully with us than wee are able to apprehend or chuse for our selves. What the Poet spake of the false gods, with better right may I of the True God, *Charior est illis homo quam sibi.†* Out of this provident care of us he cuts us off early, before age hath reacht his mid-way, and by this diminution of yeeres as well prevents the growth of sinne in us as takes us from the sense and sight of those woes which hang over the last times. He deprives us of

---

*Trouble brings discernment.
†Man is dearer to them than to himself.

V. Thy will bee done in Earth, etc.

our dearest comforts, takes from us the chiefest blessings which the World yeelds, for whose sakes wee are content to grow enamoured of the World, not being desirous to forgoe it for Heaven till that tedious age seize us, wherein we are not fit or able to live any longer. By which sad lesson Hee lets us know that 'tis in vaine to dreame of any Heaven upon Earth, of any perpetuity of worldly blessings; and admonisheth us that wee should weane and desettle our affections from them betimes, fixing our eyes upon better objects. For by the path of losse and Affliction, Hee leads our eyes and drawes up our Meditations to that Tabernacle of rest, that place of everlasting comfort, whither he hath taken our friends before us.

I have easily discharged my first Part, touching the difference of God's and Man's Will. My second is an harder taske, to shew what this *Voluntas tua,* Will of God, is: indeed an impossibility, if we understand by it his Hidden and Secret Will. For who hath beene the Lord's Counsellor? Who hath knowne his minde so farre as to bee acquainted with the mysterie of His Will? What finite tongue is able to define such an infinity as it? As no Name hath signification enough, no Attribute breadth or capacity competent to import his Essence, so neither is any definition capable of *His Will,* which is Himselfe. If any could be assigned certainly, the *Genus* of that definition must be Mercy. Resting upon that, we shall be sure the *Definition* will not bee much wider, and not a whit narrower than the definition, but holds the best and most equall proportion; for you shall finde that His Will is ever apparel'd in Mercy: *As I live I would not have the death of a sinner.* Mercy was the Foundation of all his workes, which are but the issues and fruits of his Will. In Mercy did hee found this vast Globe of the World, and *The whole earth is full of his Mercies.*

Yea, and when his Will was to contract the greater World, to cast it in a lesser Mould, comprising the whole Universe in Man, that Decree, that Act of his Will was accompanied with a Mercie greater and more ancient than the other, whereby he did Pre-elect Mankind to Salvation *Ante iacta mundi fundamenta:* long before the foundations of the greater World were layed.

Which superlative Mercy was rooted in his Will. Such a Mercy unto which Hee was not perswaded upon Conditions, either *Ex præuisa Fide* (as the Arminian holds)—a prevision or foresight of Faith; or *Ex præuisis operibus,* any forestalled Merit; or for Good workes which Hee foresaw at our Election (as some of the Papists flatter themselves); but *Ex mera Gratia & Beneplacito,* moved and led to it by his owne gracious inclination. There was no preceding cause that induced Him, no contract that tied Him to this great worke of Mercy save onely his Will. *Desponsavi te mihi in æternum: I* have contracted *thee,* not thou thy selfe. *Even so, Lord, was it thy good Will and Pleasure.*

I dare not give way to a further inquiry, or let our curiosity, though steered by Dutie and Religion, trace this secret Will of God any higher. 'Tis dangerous to hunt such abstruse mysteries at the view, or looke too neere, lest a perpetuall blindenesse punish our presumption, as Uzzah for daring to touch the Arke was strucke dead.

Wee will here call downe our Contemplation, and as they that looke on the Sunne reflected in the water see him more perfectly & more safely than if they should gaze on him in his owne Sphere wherein he moves, so will we behold the glorious Will of God by reflex in his Word. Thus looking on it, we shall bee able to satisfie our selves in so much as becomes Christians, not over-curious to understand.

Moses cast a Mantle over his head, and would not suffer his eye to meet God comming towards Him, or open it selfe at the face of God, but onely to looke after Him being past; so may wee. Though it be full of hazard to looke on his Will *a priori,* in the face of it, in the Motives or occasions which first induced the operation thereof, we are allowed to survey it *a posteriori,* in the Backe-parts, the effects and consequences, for they are visible and unvailed, being the markes and discoveries of his Revealed Will.

To this end, and to let in our apprehensions more cleerely to the knowledge thereof, the Schooles distinguish variously of the Will of God. There is *The Absolute Will of God,* that ordaines a Being

[145] 2 Part: *Thy Will*

Ezek.33:11

[146]
Psal.33:5

Mat.25:34.

[147]

2 Sam.6:7

[148]

I
Biel *Lect.69
In Miss.*

unto all things, *Sibi in aliquo complacens, ut sit vel fiat** (so he illustrates it), which is againe divided into two Other, *Voluntas Antecedens*, taken to signifie his Eternall Ordinance, wherein He forecast what He would doe; or *Consequens*, which imports his Providence, whereby Hee sustaines those creatures which he hath produced.

(2) Secondly, there is a *Manifestation of his Will*, whether it be in his Workes, which are the fruits of his Will, or his Word, which is the Evidence of his Will, directing us to the knowledge what Hee would have us doe (A sense Tropicall and Figurative, yet most proper to informe us); and this is scattered into five divisions or species. First, *Permissio*, his Permission in Allowance or Privilege to things, without which they cannot be. Secondly, *Impletio*, the Perfecting or Fulfilling of them. Thirdly, *Consilium*, his Revealed Decree. Fourthly, *Præceptum*, his Positive Law, his Precepts, wherein he teaches and commands us to doe what is acceptable in his sight. Fifthly and lastly, *Prohibitio*, the Restraint Hee layes upon us, His command for the eschewing those Actions which are contrary to his Will.

[marginal: Aug. Enchirid.]

Peter Lombard is of opinion that the Will of God, which in this Petition wee desire may be done, is taken *Pro Præcepto aut Consilio Dei.†* So that the meaning and Paraphrase of it is this: We desire God to enable us for the performance of that which his will instructs and bids us doe.

You see into how many severall acceptions *Voluntas tua* is scattered, which notwithstanding doe not vary or diversifie God's Will, but our Apprehensions of it: *God hath not many, but one Will: however, wee treat of that one Will many wayes.* And yet this Treaty ends not our taske, which is not so much to Dispute of his Will as to Doe it. I therefore leave this contemplative part, and goe on to the Practicke, which offers it selfe in the next Circumstance, *Fiat voluntas: Thy Will bee done*.

[marginal: 3. *Fiat: Thy Will be done.* Esay 46:10]

Here some may object and aske, Doth God need our *Fiat*? Doth He not perfect whatsoever He Wills without leave from us? I read it as one of God's Mottoes, *Omnis voluntas mea fiet*: Every jot of my Will shall be fulfilled. And if so, why doe wee give him our *Fiat*?

If any subordinate Magistrate should under-write the King's Letters Patents, or a Constable signe a Proclamation (which is the immediate Herald and Messenger of his Will), as if those acts were so feeble and bashfull that they could want countenancing or approbation from him, would you not thinke him lunaticke? What then can we thinke of ourselves, if we in our Petitions annex a *Fiat* to *voluntas tua*, Thy Will be done?

[marginal: Esa. 46:10 Jac. 1:17. Bradwardin *De causa Dei, Lib.1: cap.23, Corollar.*]

Againe, is not the Will of God inflexible?—*Voluntas mea stabit*, My Will, like a peremptory Decree, must stand. Is it not immutable, unalterable, like Himselfe, *Apud quem non est transmutatio*, with whom there is no shadow of change? If then his Sentences of Vengeance and of Mercy stand fixt, concluded and determined, *Not by any Alterable, Revocable Will, but Absolute and not to be repeal'd;* If we prejudicate our Petitions, knowing the fruitlesse successe before we make them; If a despaire to prevaile with God, and an impossibility either to promote or hinder his purposes, hang upon our lips and clog our words as they goe up, why doe wee trouble God with an importunate service, or put our selves to an unfruitfull taske, praying for that which without Heresie, and the concession of Mutability in God, we cannot obtaine?

[marginal: Lib.1:cap.28 *in fine*]

Bradwardin tels us, *It was an Error which lay on the Ægyptians, that they thought Sacrifices might divert God's purposes,* alter his resolutions. May it not be imputed for as great an error unto us, if wee imagine that our Prayers (which are our Sacrifices and Holocausts) can alter God's Will, or disturbe his Method, which must goe on whether we pray or be silent?

But to take away these busie scruples, and to wipe them out, *Una Litura,‡* from any weake imagination to which they shall object themselves: I grant it a truth that the Pelagians (of whom we may reade in Saint Augustine, *Lib. de Hæres.*) anciently, and since them Petrus Abailardus (as Alphonsus à Castro), and many more, I doubt not, besides him (though I am sure not those religious

[marginal: Alphons.à Castro *Lib.11*]

---

*Greatly pleasing himself that in each, it should be or be created.
†As the command or counsel of God
‡With one blot.

V. Thy will bee done in Earth, etc.

men whom Alphonsus in that Chapter injuriously, and without any ground to bee taken out of their workes, couples with him: Wickliffe, Hus, and Luther, whose precious Memory I will not wrong so much as to seeke to vindicate them from such blasphemy against the use of Prayer, never but highly extolled and devoutly practised by them)—I say, the Pelagians, and some other Heretikes, out of a malicious practise of theirs to discountenance the use of Prayer and to make it uneffectuall, objected God was Inexorable, a hard peremptory Master, whose Will would not bee altered, concluding with those in Malachy, *Vanus est qui servit Domino:* 'Tis to no end to serve or pray unto God. Mal.3:14

But yet I see not why this Conceit should so transport them, or stagger any others. If any sparke of that Heresie to this day lurke amongst us, or lie raked up in any schismaticall bosome, let them know that the hinderance of God's Will is not the scope of our Prayer, but the execution of it; for we literally beseech Him that His *Will may be accomplished*. [154]

What his secret Will is, we looke not into; but we are sure Prayer is a condition of His Revealed Will. The Law bids us pray, *Ora pro iis sicut præcepit Dominus;** and the Prophets bid us pray, *Orabit me,* &c., and the Gospell bids us pray, *Orate ne intretis in tentationem.*† Yea, so necessary is this act of Praying, that without it, God will not send downe his blessings to us. 'Tis the *Medium* to convay unto us those mercies which in his secret Will he hath decreed to bestow upon us. God will not save a man against his owne mind, or without his own desire. Though he made thee without thy advice or knowledge, and did not call thee to counsell when hee elected thee to life, yet for all this he hath left some part of thine election to bee made up by thy selfe. Thou must *worke out thy Salvation* by thine owne importunity. Though thou hast His *Word,* and the Warrant for thy deliverance from death be signed and enrolled and registred in his Booke, though it hath past his Mouth and his Hand, yet He leaves thee to bee thy owne Solicitour for procuring the Seale to bee put to it. Though He hath graciously promised thee a pardon, 'tis in his Court of Heaven as in our common Fores: that Pardon profits not thee, is indeed no Pardon, unlesse thou sue it out. God will not save thee if thou implore Him not, nor shalt thou beleeve He can, if by thy Prayers thou doe not begge an unwavering Faith, a constant beleefe in his Mercy, built and grounded upon the promises of his Word. Levit.16:34
Jer.29:12 Luk.22:40

[155]
Phil.2:12

In briefe thus: we doe not here pray that God would Change His Will, but alter Ours, and give us grace to conforme our crooked inclinations according to that Rubricke, that strait Rule of our Faith. We doe not take upon us by a kind of concession to authorize God's Will or desire Him to do what we cannot hinder, but we petition Him to authorize us, and to enable our weaknesse to performe his Will. Wee first desire an aptitude to Will those things that are acceptable in his sight, and then to Doe them: *Fiat Voluntas Tua,* Thy Will be done. [156]
Cyprianus

The Commandements are His Will. We doe not presume so much on our owne strength or perswade our selves wee can fulfill them, as the Rhemists doe, but retire to God from whom they came for his assistance—such is the humble voyce of our Letany: *Incline thou, O Lord, our hearts to keepe these Lawes.* Rhem.Test.Mat.
11

Againe, 'tis his Command and Will that *Wee beleeve in the Name of Jesus Christ* (Joh. 3:23). Therefore wee cry to him in the Gospel, *Domine adauge fidem:* That Hee would helpe our unbeleefe, and confirme his faith in us. Luk.17:5

Againe, it is the Will of God we should be sanctified both in Soule and Body, that we abstaine from fornication, from oppression, and fraud. And here the Precept is most seasonable, justly set for the Meridian of this City, of which I may speake, as Gregory Nazianzen did of Alexandria: *Civitas quam vix multa virtutis exempla salvare possunt*‡—It is such a City as hath need of Prayers, within whose wals sinne hath too long kept his quarter; where fraud is ever predominant, [157]

---

*Pray for them as the Lord commanded.
†Pray lest you enter into temptation.
‡A city which many virtuous examples can scarce save.

172 AN EXPOSITION UPON THE LORD'S PRAYER

and Cozenage reputed a thriving Trade, not a Crime; where Oppression lurks in the bosome of Authority, being sometimes clad in the Colour and Robe of Justice; where uncleannesse is growne so impudent it seekes no darke Retreats, no suburbes or blinde paths, but broadly lookes day in the face, and takes a pride to out-stare honesty, now a dayes so dis-esteem'd and out of fashion that 'tis held only the Birth-right of Fooles.

[158] Now as this *Fiat* is *Vox infirmitatis,* the voyce of weaknesse, invocating God for strength and supply, so it is *Vox Obedientiæ,* the voyce of Obedience. Where this *Fiat Voluntas Tua,* Thy Will be done is truly said and meant, it is the pledge of our submission, yeelding obedience and assent to God's Will. Of which Obedience I seeke no example but Christ's. He who was obedient in the highest Degree (for that Obedience exalted Him to the Crosse) can best instruct our Wills in the passive Lessons of this vertue. He that in this place taught us to say, *Thy Will be done,* in the 26. Chapter of Matthew, there demonstrates to us by example what Hee taught here by Precept. For on the Eve and fearefull Vigils preceding that great Festivall of Tyranny, His Passion, after three severall Charges made upon Him in the Garden by different Agonies, when our faint infirmity and the guilt of our sinnes made him seeme to shrinke a little and give backe, having Thrice besought his Father that *Cup might passe,* yet for all this Hee comes on againe faster, and more resolvedly than Hee seem'd to retire, making this *Fiat voluntas tua* three times the Period of His Prayer: If it may not passe from me but I must drinke it, *Thy Will bee done, not mine. Not as I will, but as Thou wilt.* Upon which words Tertullian excellently glosses: *though Hee was both the Power and Will of His Father, yet to tutour our Obedience by His owne Example, Hee submitted Himselfe to the Will of His Father.*

[159] Mat.26:39
Tertul. *Lib.de Orat.*

Phil.4:11 Lastly, it is *Vox Patientiæ,* the voice of Patience, and sounds like that *Ecce paratus sum,* I am ready to undergoe thy Will, O Lord. Hee that hath perfectly learnt Saint Paul's Lesson, *To be content in what condition soever he is,* that Man is a confirm'd Christian. Happy is hee that with a cheerefull countenance can looke upon all the changes of life:

Horat. *L2:Sat.7.* (84–85)

> *Sapiens sibique imperiosus,*
> *Quem neque pauperies, neque mors, neque vincula terrent;**

[160] that with an even unmoved Temper can wellcome all fortune, not tempted by his Felicity to forget God, nor urged by his afflictions to murmur at Him, that when hee hath lost his venture by Sea, or his comforts by Land, suffers no tempest or rebellious perturbations within his owne brest, but parts with his wealth as Bias did with his at the sacke of Priene: *Ille hæc ludibria fortunæ ne sua quidem putavit*—considering his riches as hirelings, destin'd to change their Masters—and parts with his friends as the noble Roman did with his Sonne, of whose death, when he had received the notice, he entertain'd it with this manly reply, *Ego cum genui tum moriturum scivi:* I knew hee was not immortall, and *when hee first became mine, I received him upon such conditions as that I reckoned Death might make him not mine*—He, I say that can thus unaltered looke upon his Crosse, speaking Saint Augustine's language and with his devout heart: *Let the world stand or sinke to its first foundations, let my fortune fall under those ruines, yet my Faith and Patience shall not sinke, I will still blesse that God that made the world,* and made me; Hee that thus meets the affronts of Death and Fortune, giving them Job's thankfull, though sad, farewell, *Dominus dedit, Dominus abstulit: The Lord gives, and the Lord takes away, blessed be the Name of the Lord—* such a man hath well *Learn't Christ,* and made a just application of the Apostle's Doctrine, *In all things give thankes for this is the Will of God.* 'Tis most certaine God owns them for his dearest *children* (divinely speaks Seneca) *who obediently bow to His Justice;* who, though Thunder-Strooke, his Arrowes sticking fast in them, yet blesse Him that afflicts them, and adore the hand that hurt them.

Tul. *Paradox.*

Sen.*Consol. ad Polyb.*

Aug. *Serm.29 de verb.Dom.*
[161]

Job 1:21.
Ephes.4:20
1 Thes.5:*18*
Senec.*Consolat.*

---

*The wise man, whom neither poverty nor death nor chains can frighten, has control over himself.

V. Thy will bee done in Earth, etc.

How unkinde, how curst soever thy fortune be, how violent thy afflictions, let not thy Patience prove a Ruffian. Lay thy hand upon thy mouth, and let that which was once thy Master's be thy Motto, *Sicut Ovis coram tondente:* Like a Sheepe dumbe before the Shearer; for thy taske is to suffer, not to reply or complaine. How grievous soever thy losses be, either of goods, or health, or (that which of all others trencheth deepest upon our affections) of friends; amidst those losses bee sure thou doe not lose thy selfe, and then be as sure thou shalt one day finde againe those whom thou here missest. [Act.8:32] [162]

Methinks the very connexion of these two Petitions, *Thy Kingdome come, Thy Will be done,* are like strong grapples and ties to hold a Christian and his patience together. How can a man but gladly suffer the deprivation of his friends, when hee thinks they are landed and arrived at that Kingdome which we dayly pray to come unto? When hee remembers they are gone before to that happy place whither wee, with all the Sailes Devotion can beare, with all the speed Prayers can make, follow after? Surely, not to bee thankfull to God, but repine at his Will for lifting them up to that height of Beatitude, were an ingratitude next Atheisme, and to lament them whom we beleeve to have gained an everlasting state of happinesse were madnesse, not sorrow, and rather envie than affection.

Thus are wee arrived at our furthest point of this voyage. These mixt meditations, compounded of contrary ingredients, Bitter and Sweet, Affliction and Patience, Sorrow and Joy, Mortality and Heaven, have brought us to the last part of this Petition, which is the Exemplary part, *Sicut in Cœlo, sic in Terra: In Earth as it is in Heaven.* [163]

Man was a creature made up in imitation of his Maker:—*Imago Dei,* the Image of God—*to put him in remembrance that he should continually work after that Originall Copy which God gave him from Heaven:* Thus Saint Basil. God commanded Moses to doe according to that hee had received from Himselfe in the Mount; and our blessed Saviour, who knew well to worke his Elect by the best Copy, prayes that his Disciples might not *onely be where Himselfe was,* but *Sicut* too: *as the Father and He was.* Wee expect to bee Changed, and that our *vile bodies shall one day bee made like Christ's glorious Bodie.* That Faith, that beleefe for the alteration of our Bodies, should therefore in the meane time daily preach unto us the change of our crooked corrupt Minds, to make both Them and our perverse Wills *Sicut eius,* obedient and conformable to his. [4 Part: *In Earth as it is in Heaven* Basil *Institut.Ad vitam perfectam,cap.2* Joh.17:11, 24 [164] Phil.3:21]

To live *Sicut in Terra,* according to the times and fashions of the World, is quite out of the rode of Heaven. Christ's Method was contrary to the world's: in his last Legacy he bequeathed *Pacem non sicut Mundus,* a Peace to his Disciples not like the peace of the World; and hee expects a like proportion from us, that we should not *vitam Mundi agere,* not live to the World, but to God; not passe our dayes as Worldlings, and Sonnes of the Earth, but as *Filii Lucis,* Children of the Light. [Joh.14:27 Ephes.5:9]

Wee must leade our lives *in,* but not *by* the World: *Sicut in Cœlis, non sicut in Terra.* Earth is a bad copy, lame and imperfect. Let Beasts make that their object, the levell of their thoughts. Man's exalted strait forme bids him looke up, invites his Contemplation to the things above, not the things below. That man degenerates from Nature much, from Grace more, that proposes unto himselfe low ignoble patternes. [165]

Imitation in its proper Motion ever ascends, for the Sphere of Vertue is mounted high, and all *Good is derived from above. Sufficit Discipulo ut sit sicut Magister:* Christ hath said there is no competent congruous samplar for the Disciple but his Master; nor must any Christian know any other *sicut,* but *sicut in Cœlis:* He must only patterne himselfe by Heaven. [Hieron, *Epist.21*[a] Jac.1:17 Mat.10:25]

I stand not to amplifie this point. Only to repeat the several Interpretations which learned Men give of *Cœlum* and *Terra* in this place is a sufficient morall and Application.

First, Saint Augustine understands by Heaven the Angels, and by Earth, Men; upon which hee grounds this exposition: When we pray *Thy Will be done,* &c., we *desire that as the Will of God is performed by the Angels in Heaven, so it may also be fulfilled by men on Earth; that Men may be as obedient to God's Will as are those blessed Ministers of Heaven,* who readily fulfill all his Commands. [I. [166] Biel loc.cit Id.pag.143]

174 AN EXPOSITION UPON THE LORD'S PRAYER

'Tis not enough to know the Bible, or bee able to repeat the severall volumes of his Will, unlesse a practise be joyned to this speculative science of Christianity. Knowledge what to doe and forbearance to doe what we know, hastens our Condemnation, and addes weight to it; *That servant* Luk.12:47 *who knowes the Will of his Master, but does it not, shall bee beaten with many stripes.* Isidor Pelusiot says, it is a *most impudent Hypocrisie* to call God Father, yet doe nothing worthy his sonne; to cry *Thy Will be done,* and yet doe nothing agreeable to that Will.

Isidor.Pelus. Epist.24:L.4

[167] 2. The Glosse in Matth. 6. interprets these words *De carne & spiritu,** understanding by *Heaven* the Intellectuall Faculties in Man, which exercise their acts in the head and upper Region of the Body; by *Earth* the sensitive, which keepe their quarter in *Inferioribus,* below. *We pray that the flesh may not resist the good motions of the Spirit;* that the dissolute appetite rebell not against Reason; that Anger or Passion breed no tumult, no intestine warres within man's selfe, nor distract his thoughts from the service of God; but that Will may bee governed by Reason, Sense subordinate to the Intellect, the Flesh to the Spirit, and all these obedient to the Will of God; *that no worldly* Cyprian *respects may hold downe our Meditations from Heaven,* but that the love of God and his service may bee predominant above all earthly pleasures or profits.

3. Other of the Fathers out of these words *Sicut in Cœlo,* &c., extract this charitable use: *to pray for* [168] *our enemies,* understanding by *Cœlum, Ecclesiam iustorum;* by *Terra, Congregationem peccatorum:* by *Heaven,* the Church; by *Earth,* the Congregation of sinners, and such as either know August. not Christ aright, or not at all. For their conversion to the true Faith doe we pray in this place. And the same Father recites out of S. Cyprian: *The Church prayes not onely for the constancy and* Id. *Lib.de bono* *perfection of Faith in the Elect, but for the Inchoation of it in those that are yet Unbeleevers,* that *perseverantiæ* they also might be enlightned, and have a stocke of Faith whereon to build their Salvation.

An excellent Christian-peece of Charity, which I wish were more in request with some Roman Catholikes than the practise of their Church shewes. See the difference betwixt a Protestant and a [169] Popish Charity—They solemnly Banne and Curse all Heretikes foure times a yeare, and on Maundy-Thursday the Protestants; but we in our Church, the day after, Good-Friday, in memory and imitation of our blessed Saviour, who prayed on his Crosse for those that crucified Him, devoutly pray for them, that God would give them cleerer Eyes and softer Hearts, that He would reduce them and all others who either out of wilfull malice or out of ignorance wander from the Joh.10:16 Truth, to his Fold, that *there might bee but one Shepherd and one Flocke.*

(4.) Some take *Cœlum* and *Terra* literally, and interpret *Terra* to signifie Men that dwell on Earth, Heaven the Materiall Body of the Celestials, consisting of divers Orbes, of Planets and Starres—all which, as they are carried about in a Regular motion, no way Exhorbitant or Eccentricall, but according to God's Ordinance; so we desire God that here in the Sphere of his Church we may [170] move in a like Regularity, not transgressing his commands and our appointed bounds; that as the Sunne runnes his race about the Heaven, so may we discharge our progresse on Earth, going forward in all goodnesse, passing from one Vertue to another, till having runne thorow the whole Zodiacke of the Vertues, and all the Degrees of Goodnesse, wee may reach our highest Degree, the Josh.10:13 felicity of Saints in Heaven. And as that Sunne stood still in Gibeon whilest Josuah pursued the adversaries of God, so must our Faith have its Solstice, and our hearts stand undaunted and unmoved in defence of Truth and the Gospell against all those that oppugne or labour to supplant it. Esa.38:8 And lastly, as the Sunne went backe and made his retreit from the Diall in Ezekiah's time, so must we sometimes be Retrograde—that is, retire from the habit of our sinnes, and by unfeined Repentance turne backe unto the God of our Salvation, from whom, as lost Sheepe, we went astray.

5. Finally, Saint Chrysostome doth as it were binde up these various expositions of *Cœlum* and [171] *Terra,* and applies them all briefly according to that excellent Rule of the Apostle, *Ut conversatio* Phil.3:20 *nostra sit in Cœlis,* making the full meaning of our Petition this, *That our Conversation may bee in*

---

*Of the flesh and of the spirit.

Heaven, and wee our selves may so live out our Pilgrimage on Earth, that wee be not excluded from the joyes and fruition of Christ's glorious Kingdome in Heaven.

This is the Period, the resting place of all our Hopes, and of our Faith; it is the end of our Prayers, it shall also bee mine. I conclude in the words of the Psalmist, *Beati qui custodiunt:* Blessed are they that know the Will of God and observe it; That yeeld Him such a setled Obedience which affliction cannot shake; That have learn't to beare their Crosse without murmur; and though wounded, give thankes with holy Job, *Though hee kill me, yet will I trust in him.* That, if at any time rebellious passions dare turne head to reason, or dispute with God, Why goe I thus heavily and oppressed? Why doth thy vengeance single me out? Why dost thou lay this burthen of sorrow upon me? are able to refute and choake it with *Voluntas Domini:* Be not disquieted or troubled, O my Soule, *it is the Will of God.*

Lastly, whose Patience is so well vaulted, that no weight crushes, but strenthens it, making it more close and firme; whose resolution is so bold, that like Atlas, they stand, not lie under their burthen; and though Fortune or the Hand of God have cast them never so low, yet on that dust, those ruines that cover and bury them, write this for an Epitaph: *Voluntas Domini facta est*—The Will of God is done, and *Blessed bee his Holy Will.* They that can thus court their sorrowes, thus entertaine and give them such a welcome, that can so Christian-like endure the *Will of God* in this kinde here on Earth, let them not feare nor doubt, nor bee confounded, but know, in the confidence of Christ's promise, that *It is the Will of God,* after those trials on Earth, *to give them a Kingdome in Heaven.* Where it shall be no more with them *Sicut in Terra,* as it was on Earth; for there shall bee no more sorrow, nor teares, nor affliction, nor night, but an everlasting Day of happinesse, and a fruition of Joyes, which shall there beginne but never end. *Amen.*

Conclusion

Job 13:15
[172]
Psal.42:11

Luk.12:32
[173]

VI. GIVE US THIS DAY OUR DAILY BREAD

[174]

The life of a Christian is not therefore tearm'd Spirituall, that wee should live like Spirits without food; Neither did our Saviour, when hee said *The love of the world is enmity with God,* intend to put that mortall Opposition betwixt us and the world, that wee should cast off all worldly respects conducing to a supply of our wants. Hee whose goodnesse gave us Being, gave us then also meanes to preserve that Being, *Meats for the belly* (saith S. Paul) and *Herbs for the use of man* (so the Psalme). I confesse there are many Texts to hold the Body in subjection, but none to destroy it; For hee that bids us fast, bids us not starve, and he that bids us in the Psalme, *Not to set our hearts upon riches,* bids us not begge.

Nay, there is no Text that doth, by advancing the price and estimation of the soule, devest us of a just regard of the Body. S. Ambrose says the Body is *Tunica animæ,* the Coat, the Vesture of the Soule. He therefore that casts off all care of it, uncloathes Nature and discovers the shame of his understanding. Though the Soule must have the highest regard, the Body must have a share and a degree in our regard. For how can wee justifie the neglect of that Body for the present, which God hath decree to Glorifie hereafter? Of which future Glory he hath given this earnest, that hee hath alotted a roome in this Prayer meerly for things conducing to the Bodie's provision.

1 Cor.6:13
Psal.104:14
Psal.62:10
Aug.Ser.33 de verb.Dom.[a]
[175]

It is not strange that God, who hath taken so strict an Inventory of Man that the very *least haire of his head* is entred in his Registry, should be so tender of the whole Body. He that so precisely rates each Ligament, each small Threed that ties the parts of the Body together, could not lesse than provide for sustenance to hold the maine Essentiall parts, Soule and Body, together.

Mat.10:30

Against all, therefore, that professe the Science of Want and Willing Poverty, against all those that tyrannize over Nature, and execute a justice upon themselves beyond God's Commission by starving the Body, let mee oppose this Petition, as an inducement to them not to bee cruell to their owne Flesh, and as an argument of God's impartiall care of the Body as of the Soule. And you may

[176]

observe how farre hee carries this care, even thorow all his Actions and our courses. There is not so great a disproportion betwixt the Soule and the Body as betwixt God and Man; yet in those acts which concerne our profit and his Glory, Hee so farre condescends to us, that Hee allowes us more time for our advantage than He takes to Himselfe. Of the Seven dayes in the weeke, Six He allowes to Man's industry, to doe his worke in, to buy and sell, to plant Vineyards, and to reape the fruits of the Earth, reserving only one Sabbath, the Seventh day, for the adoration of his Name.

And of the Seven Petitions in this Diarie, this *Ephemerides* of Prayer, Christ hath ordained a more liberall share to Man than to Himselfe; for onely Three of them directly and immediately concerne his Kingdome and the Honour of his Name—the Foure last were intended for helpes to accommodate Man whilst hee lives here in the World.

This Petition is our first step to Earth. In the three former wee made our ascents and approaches towards Heaven; here our Devotion flies at a lower pitch, and stoops at the World. *Naturaliter, quod procedere non potest, recedit:* By Nature's Rule, *when things are at the highest, they must descend.* When the Sun hath clomb up to the remotest part of our Tropick, and is placed at greatest distance from our *Hemisphære,* hee traverses his course, and by another Tropick falls neerer to us againe. In the three first Petitions wee were neerer the Sun, neerer that place where the Throne of God is fixt and the *Sun of righteousnesse* moves, Heaven. Here, wee as it were cut the Line, are in a new Climate. The Two Globes of Earth and Heaven here divide themselves, this being the first side of the Terrestriall. On which I shall describe unto you six Provinces that offer themselves to our view.

1. First, the Necessity of asking, implied in this postulation, *Give.*
2. Secondly, *Ordo Petendi,* the order in which our Petitions must be ranked, which is exemplified in the Method of this Praier, which requires Heavenly Blessings before Earthly, and teaches us to intend God's Honour, and the performance of his Will, before our owne Necessities.
3. Thirdly, *Qualitas petendorum,* the Quality of what we aske, *Bread.*
4. Fourthly, *Modus petendi,* the Measure or Bounds of our Petition, *Quotidianus: Daily* Bread.
5. Fifthly, the Petitioners for whom wee aske, *Nobis:* Give *us.*
6. Sixthly, the Date of the Petition, *Hodie: This day.*

I. It is the blessing of Clients to meet with easie Patrons, such as will bee mollified with Petitions. Wee are not sure there bee many of this soft temper in the world: but we are most certaine God is one. A mercifull Lord that yet never closed his eare to shut out the Praier of such as invok't Him, nor contracted his bounty for bestowing mercy where it was implor'd. So gracious, that He ever gives where Hee is faithfully askt, yea, and sometimes antedates his favours, by *hearing us before wee call,* and granting our requests before we give them language to utter themselves in.

*Multa Dii dedere neglecti:**

The Poet gave that free testimony of his false gods; how fully is it verified in the True God? He confers his Grace on many that seeke it not. Indeed, if God should give us no more than we aske, we should receive very little, but if no more than we deserve, nothing at all.

Of such a profuse benignity is Hee, that for feare lest our owne Necessities should not bee imperious enough, urge us fast enough to seeke his helpe, Hee with them laies his command on us and indents with us, makes a perpetuall Covenant that wee shall require his assistance when wee need it: *Call upon mee in the day of trouble, so I will heare thee, and thou shalt praise mee.* O the riches of his Mercy, that prevents the dull suiter, and bespeakes subjects to conferre his blessings on! That descends so low as to solicite us to sue to him; That contracts for our Prayers to be sent up for our good, as He doth for his owne sacrifice; and is afraid of nothing more than that wee will not aske so much and so often as He is willing to bestow!

How different is the World's custome from his! There is a wretched kinde of tenacity predominant in the disposition of Man, who is generally in nothing more close than in giving, nor more

---

*The Gods though neglected give many things.

VI. Give us this day our daily Bread

reserv'd than in doing good to his brethren. There is scarce one amongst many that with a serene contented looke receives a suit. *Who is there almost that comes within the view of a Petition, but turnes away his head?* as if there were no spectacle so odious as a poore man's supplication; or else reviles, or non-suits him with a frowne; or *faines occasions to shake off the importunate Client* and excuse his owne benevolence; or, if he bee surprised so that hee cannot avoid the giving of somewhat, either hee gives so slowly, or unwillingly, or disdainfully, that hee destroyes the nature of his good turne. *Sen. De Benef. Lib.1:cap.I.* [181]

When I consider with how much delay commonly the charity of Men is stupified and besotted, with how much insolence oft times their benefits are seasoned, I cannot but conclude them most happy, whose free independent condition exempts them from committing a servile Idolatry to Men, so that they know no *Fore* but the Temple, and understand no use of Petitions but in their Prayers. A suit commenced in God's Court will finde a swifter decision, and cheaper Issue, than in ours. There is sometimes that unconscionable impost set upon the favours of Men, that Clients must sue long and yet pay too. But God's come at an easier rate, *Sine pretio,* without money, though *Non sine petitione,* not without Prayer. Esay 55:1
Mat.7:7

Wee must pray then for the supply of our wants; but not only pray—*Hoc genus dæmoniorum non eiicitur sola prece:* Necessity is a bad Spirit, that will not be exorcised or cast out unlesse wee joyne our owne endevours to our Prayers. When Adam forfeited his obedience and shut God out of his heart, the eare of God and the bounty of Nature were at once barr'd against him; for at first the Earth wore her commodities in her forehead, visible and eminent, but after Man's fall, she by Gods command call'd in her blessings, conceal'd her fruits, and in stead of that plenty wherein once she was apparrelled, now only weares that barren attire which God's curse cast upon her, *Thornes and Thistles.* From which Curse nothing can rescue or redeeme her, but Prayer and Labour: Prayer to open the eare of God, and Labour to open the Earth and search for those riches which lie hid within her bosome. So that, both these being requisite to supply Man's wants, it were a lazie presumption for any to suppose that the saying of *Lord, Lord,* should win God to give them bread for which they would take no paines at all. [182]
Matt.17:21

Gen.3:18

[183] Matt.25:11

Now as wee must not onely Pray, and not Labour, so neither must our Labour goe single, without Prayer: for though it be our industry that opens the Earth with the Plough or the Mattocke, 'tis Prayer that must *open the windowes of Heaven* for the *former and latter raine,* to blesse the labour of the Husbandman. Whosoever digges, or ploughes, or sowes, or plants, it is *God alone who gives the increase.* A Fortune collected meerely by man's industry, without God, shall melt away at the second generation, nor shall it have the blessing of continuance, unlesse it be evicted by suit at His hand who is able to prosper the worke of our hands. The Apostle tells us, *Ye fight and warre but get nothing, because yee aske not.* A man may struggle with necessitie, and wage a continuall warre with his wants, but never get the upper hand of them, never obtaine that victorie hee hath sweat for, Abundance and Plenty, unlesse Devotion bee mingled with his Labours, unlesse he hath prayed, as well as sweat for it. 'Tis therefore best wee all take the advice which the Spirit gave the Church of Laodicea, *I counsell thee to buy of mee gold that thou mayest be made rich,* to purchase a Patrimony by thy Prayers from God, and to lay the foundation of thy Fortune in Religion and a good conscience. 2 King.7:2 Jerem.5:24

I Cor.3:6

Jac.4:2

[184]

Revel.3:18

I passe from the *Necessity* of our Asking, to the *Order.* Wee must place Spirituall blessings before Temporall, and begin at God, from whom all things assum'd their beginnings. For as Hee hath the Priority of Essence and Power, being the *Prima Causa* and *Primus Motor:* first Cause and first Mover, so must hee have the prioritie in our observance and duty. Else what a solœcisme were it, that He, who preceded the World in his owne Being, should bee cast backe and come behinde the World in our account? This were (so farre as in us lies) to degrade our Maker, and to make God, who is *Antiquus Dierum,* the Ancient of Dayes, Puny to his owne workes. 2.
Ordo petendi

Dan.7:9

God hath stampt a method in the Grave, and made the parent of Confusion, Death, sensible of order; for the Apostle tels us, *Wee shall not rise but in our order;* and shall wee live so pre- [185]
I Cor.15:23

posterously to disorder Him who is the *God of Order,* by denying that place and dignity wherein hee ought to stand in our affections?

Rivers that take their beginning from the Sea flow backe againe, and pay a thankfull Tribute to the Ocean by powring themselves into the lap of their first Parent. 'Tis a just and equall gratitude that the Soule, who was infused by God, and tooke her first birth from Him, should, so soone as shee is able to apprehend her owne Parentage, so soone as her Intellectuall Faculties bee full summ'd, and the wings of Meditation and Prayer can carry her upward, take her first flight to Heaven, her Native Soile, there to confesse the Power and Goodnesse of Him that made Her.

Hee were a most perverse Scholler, and learnt counter, that should begin at the wrong end of the Alphabet, and so trace it upward. God is the first Letter in the Christian Alphabet, for He is *alpha,* and therefore to be first studied, to have the first roome in our thoughts. And againe, hee is *ōmega,* the last, and for that hath another capacitie, another right to be first with us. The end, though last in execution, is ever first in the intention. God is the end, to whose Glory we and the world were made. Hee is the Terminus whither wee all tend. Let Him then and his Kingdome possesse the chiefe roome in our desires, and then we shall bring home the Wise man's counsell to our selves, *Let thy end be alwayes in thy sight.*

God cannot endure to come in the Rere of our meditations, or bee rankt lowest in our regard. He that commanded the *First Fruits* of the Earth as his due, will expect *Primitias Labiorum,* the Firstlings of our Love and Devotions too. For this cause, He bids us Remember him in our beginning, *in the Dayes of our Youth.* And the Psalmist dedicates the first part of the Day to his service, *Early will I call upon thee.*

Wee see in the common practise that till the Custome bee paid, the Trade is not free or open: so whilst the First-fruits, which are God's Custome, rest unpaid, wee cannot expect a profitable Trafficke with Him, or successe in our owne affaires.

The Story tells us, that when Jaacob, pressed by the famine which reigned in his Land, sent to Egypt for victuals, hee considered the dignity of the Governour before his owne necessity, and honoured him with a present, the best hee could provide, before hee askt for Corne. Wee were not true Israelites, if wee more regarded meats and drinks than *to doe the Will of God,* or preferred *Panem quotidianum,* our Daily Bread, before *the Hallowing of his Name.*

Certainly, to begin with God is a faire Introduction to all other blessings. *They that feare God can lacke nothing* (saith the Psalmist). Hee hath given them meat that feare him; and *though Lions suffer hunger, they shall be fed.*

It was David's conclusion, and demonstrated in his Son Salomon, whose election God so well approv'd in that hee sought Wisdome before Glory and Religion above Riches, that hee told him because he had asked those things, He had not only granted what he requested, but what hee asked not, Riches and Honours in greater measure than any of his Predecessors ever had. Christ, who was figured in Salomon, by the Method and Order of this Prayer teacheth us that all Petitions are best coucht for our advantage when they begin with God and his Kingdome. For so hee comments upon his owne Method: *First seeke the Kingdome of God and the righteousnesse thereof, and all these things shall be added unto you.*

This being premised touching the Order of these Petitions, my third point followes seasonably, which is *Qualitas petendorum,* the Quality of what we aske, *Bread.*

S. Augustine, as loth to eat before hee had reconciled Christ's two Texts that seeme to thwart one another, moves the doubt; Why our Saviour teaches us here to pray for what wee eat, and yet elsewhere precisely forbids us to be solicitous what wee should eat. But the Father doth not sooner move the scruple than solve it. Alexander Hales hath made up his answer in a short distinction: There is (saith he) *Solicitudo curiositatis,* a curious care to please the palate with variety of diet, and there is *Solicitudo diligentiæ,* an honest diligence that aimes but at a competent allowance to resist hunger. 'Tis onely the first solicitude Christ forbids, not the last.

Certainly, if wee measure this Petition Literally according to its Object, wee shall finde the Word

VI. *Give us this day our daily Bread* 179

pretends no curiosity. 'Tis but Bread wee aske: The smallest, most temperate request which Poverty can put up, and the lowest rate Bounty or Charity can be seized at. You see how small a breadth the word carries in our acception, yet Saint Augustine in his construction enlarges it very farre, and will have it signifie all kinds of meat; *Panis pro omni cibo.* But the Hebrew stretches the sense so wide, that under this word *Bread* it hath involved all things that tend to the sustentation or support of our life, as Health, Plenty, Peace. And as *Manna,* the Bread from Heaven, humoured the palate so farre that it counterfeited all meats, and relisht to him that ate it like that his Appetite most longed for; so doth this Bread apply it selfe to all necessities, importing whatsoever conduces to our preservation. [190] Wisd.16:20, 21

Insomuch that S. Ambrose justly inferres, *No Petition within this Prayer is of so large demensions as this.* For Literally in it wee pray for Meats and Drinks. And because Meats without a Stomacke are a torment, not a blessing, wee pray for health of Body, that wee may enjoy the Earth's fruits, and *eat the labour of our hands.* And because a Land which is made the Stage of Warre, whereon her bloudy Scenes are acted, banishes all Husbandry (for where the Sword is busie, the Plough stands idle), wee pray for peace, that wee eat our owne Bread; that every man may sit *under his owne Vine, and under his owne Figge-tree;* that Warre fright not plenty from us, or make us slaves to want and famine, but (as it is in the Prophet) *Our Speares may be turned into Sithes, and Swords into Mattocks.* I finde also that victory is figured under the title of *Bread:* for Joshua tels Israel God would give the people of the Land of Canaan for *Bread* to them. Psal.128:2

2 King.18:31
[191] Micah.4:3
Numb.14:9

By these severall steps doth the signification of this word *Bread* dilate it selfe; thus wide doth it stretch in the naturall meaning, and the Mysticall sense is as ample as the other. For as it signifies *Panem corporalem,* that Bread which nourisheth the Body, so doth it also *Panem vitæ & justitiæ,* that Bread of Life which is the Word of God, wherewith the Pastors feed Christ's flocke. And, wee may imagine, hereupon it is that S. Augustine interprets those Five Loaves wherewith our Saviour fed the Multitude to bee the *Pentateuch,* the Five Bookes of Moses. Besides, it signifies the Sacrament, which the Psalmist calls *Panem Angelorum,* and the Author of the Booke of Wisdome *Panem de Cœlo,* Angels' food and Bread from Heaven. Ecclesiast.11:1

Matt.14:17
Psal.78:25
Sap.16:(21)
[192]

Lastly, Righteousnesse may bee called *Bread,* for our Saviour's Sermon in the Mount implies as much when hee termes them *Blessed that hunger and thirst after righteousnesse.* Matt.5:6

This is the summe of all that the Schooles say concerning the word *Bread.* Which is broken by them into Five parts: First, *Corporalis,* our common Bread. Secondly, *Spiritualis,* Bread in a spirituall sense, which is *Panis Justitiæ,* Righteousnesse. Thirdly, *Doctrinalis,* the Doctrinall Bread distributed by God's Dispensers, the Preachers. Fourthly, *Sacramentalis,* that hallowed Bread which wee receive in the Communion. Fifthly, *Æternalis,* that eternall Bread of Life which we hope to bee partakers of in the World to come, of which our Saviour sayes, *Ego sum panis vivus.* I may adde one other Species of Bread, which the Psalmist cals *arton dakruōn,* Bread kneaded with our teares, which is the Bread of Repentance and sorrow for sinne past. Joh.6:35
Psal.80:5

I shall not erect any large discourse on these foundations. Only thus: Wee must remember, *Man lives not by Bread only, but by the Word of God.* And that even the Soule, our best part, hath her decayes as well as the Body, and requires a repaire as speedy. She is sensible of wants and pinings, hath her part of Hunger and Thirst, and that in a degree so farre exalted above the corporall hunger as her subtile essence is sublimated and refined above the Body: In which kind of sense the Psalmist sayes, *Hee sent leanenesse into their Soules.* Matt.4:4
[193]

Psal.106:15

Therefore, because the Word of God is our Soule's food, and Hee in the Prophet hath threatned a famine more dangerous than that of Bread, *a Famine of hearing his Word,* Let us daily beseech Him that Hee will be pleased to continue both this Bread unto us, and the number of such as are to distribute it; That so the plenty which blest his People may dwell amongst us, and we may speake the Psalmist's language: *God gave the Word; great was the multitude of the Preachers.* Amos 8:11

Psal.68:11

Againe, because the Bread which wee eat in the Sacrament is *viaticum animæ* (as S. Augustine stiles it), the bait or provision to strengthen the Soule in her journey; because it is both the Antidote [194] to resist the venome of sinne, and the Physicke to purge it away when it is collected (for so S. Bernard says, 'tis *Medicina animæ*); let us beseech the great Physitian that hee would revive our sicke Soules with that *Bread,* and give us often leave to wash our wounded consciences in that *Cup;* and that the administration of his Sacraments, which are the Evidences, the visible Seales of his grace and favour, may never bee cancelled or suppresst till that time come when we shall eat and drinke with him in Heaven.

4.
Daily Bread

Modus petendi, The measure of the petition, is included in this word *Quotidianus: Daily Bread.*

I finde the two Evangelists S. Matthew and S. Luke somewhat differently translated in the Vulgar. S. Matthew hath *Panem supersubstantialem;* S. Luke, *Quotidianum.* I meane not to dispute the cause of this difference, or the truth of the translation. I am content to take the Schoolemen's reason, that S. Mathew spake to the capacity of the learned, but S. Luke spake to the understanding of the rude and unlettered as well as the other. *Supersubstantialis* (saith Alexander Hales) is a word that few understand, but *Quotidianus* is the more easie and familiar. Therefore because this Prayer was to be commonly used by all sorts of Men, the Church determined to use this word *Quotidianus, Dayly Bread,* as most proper to informe all understandings.

[195]
Alex. Hales *Part 4:quæst.10, pag.175*

But upon this ground and concession, let mee aske unto whose capacity did the Rhemists fit their translation, when they read, *Give us our supersubstantiall Bread?* Did they intend it for the use of Scholers, or generally for the People? If for them, why would they offer with strange dresses to disfigure our Mother Tongue, to attire it in the Roman garbe, blinding the English with so much Latine, that they utterly disguise it from vulgar apprehensions? I cannot conceive what darke designe they had in obscuring the Text with so much unknowne compound sophisticate Language, using not only here, but thorowout their whole Translation, such words as but Schollers none can understand, unlesse (besides that plot in which their whole faction hath long laboured, to benight the Church of Christ, and cast a generall mist of ignorance to blinde the World that it should not discerne his Truth) they have a plot upon God himselfe, and would, if it were possible, make Him speak in as unknowne a tongue to the Congregation, as they themselves speake to the People and teach the People to pray unto Him.

[196]

Wee that studie perspicuity embrace the common, and by best judgements most approved, word; *Quotidianus,* both because by it *Generalius exprimuntur petenda*—'tis of more spacious signification than *Supersubstantialis,* carrying both the Materiall and Spirituall sense—Yet how ever it bee in it selfe of so significative an extent, 'tis set up to us as a Boundary, to limit our vast desires, and empale the wilde appetite. If we may compare this petition to a Terrestriall Globe, this must be the Meridian to girdle it about, by it must wee take the length and bredth of our requests; 'tis the seize, the measure of our markets, as the *Omer* was Israel's daily stint for the collecting of their *Manna,* which was their *Bread.* We here are tied to our allowance and proportion like them: *our Daily Bread,* that is, so much as is sufficient for our daily sustenance. The Syriacke Translation expresses it fully: *Panis indigentiæ,* Bread to resist Hunger, and repaire Nature.

Biel *Lect.70 in Miss.*

[197]

Exod.16:16

Neither did Christ put this Epithet into our mouthes onely to bridle the appetite, but the Will too, and all the covetous motions springing from thence.

What meanes then our wastefull excesse in Meats and Drinks? Our learned witty Gluttony, which exercises all the Elements, Earth, and Aire, and Fire, and Water; which tortures the backs of beasts to carry, and braines of men to devise new Sacrifices to offer daily to their devouring Idoll, the Belly, which many serve more than God? The Roman Poet loudly exclaimes against it:

[198]

*O Quæsitorum terra pelagoque ciborum
Ambitiosa fames!**

Lucan *(4.375–6)*

Certainely if we but considered how little expence Nature puts us to for her support:

---

*O the ambitious hunger for food sought by land and by sea.

VI. Give us this day our daily Bread

*—Quam paucis liceat traducere vitam,
Et quantum Natura petat;* (Lucan 4.378)

how that the staffe of Bread is sufficient to waft and carry us thorow Life's whole journey, wee should see that God's hot indignation glowes against us as much for the prodigious abuse of his Creatures this way, as for any other sinne. How can wee excuse our selves to Him, when wee lay out on one meale a yeare's allowance, and waste as much provision in a few houres, as were sufficient to releeve the famine of an Army? *When thou devourest at one Feast what would suffice thee for an hundred dayes, thou eatest not* in God's name, for 'tis not *Panis Quotidianus,* thy *Dayly Bread,* but the *Bread of many dayes.* [Aug.*Ser.in Monte* [199]]

Againe, what meanes the *Joyning of house to house,* the carefull collecting of an estate purchased with losse of Time, and perhaps of Conscience? Which if Fortune deprive us not of whilest we live, we must part with when we die. If we considered how little of that earth wee buy must one day hold us, in how narrow a grave our corps shall lie, this meditation well apprehended were enough to entombe all avarice. Wee should account it madnesse, not providence, and not thrift but profusion, to lay out so much care in compassing that which wee must enjoy so short a time. Apuleius elegantly speakes: *Ad vivendum sicut ad natandum is melior, qui onere liberior*—Hee swims best that hath the least weight to encomber him; and hee lives happiest who least troubles himselfe about the world's pelfe. Minutius Fœlix interprets him: *A large provision for so short a voyage as Life, is a perplexity, not an helpe;* and a burthen not a supply. I end this point with S. Augustine's paraphrase upon this Petition: *Aske* not superfluity of things, but *so much as is necessary for thy use.* Cloath thy request in Salomon's words, *Give mee not riches nor poverty,* and thou thereby doest not crosse but vary these of Christ. [Esa.5:8] [[200] Ser.105 de Tempore Prov.30:8]

Nature is not unreasonable in her desires, nor chargeable in her fare: See the whole Bill of fare, and Catalogue of her utensils set downe, *The chiefe things of life is Water and Bread, and cloathing and lodging to cover thy nakednesse.* They who have all these things have enough, they want nothing but the Apostle's contented minde, *Habentes victum & vestitum, his contenti simus:* When wee have food and raiment, let us therewith be content, and give God thanks. [Ecclus.39:26] [I Tim.6:8]

Concerning our Spirituall Bread, that doth not so much require a Limitation, as a Caution. Receive the holy Sacrament so often as thou canst prepare thy selfe: S. Bernard allowes it thee every day, if thou darest allow it thy selfe. [[201]]

Heare the Word of God preached in abundance, take in at thy eare *Quantum sufficit,* so much as is sufficient—or if that bee too little, as much as thou listest—but take heed the frequent reception of the one doe not make thee loath and undervalue thy Lord's Supper, nor the plentifull hearing of God's Word make thy devotion surfet.

Omnis saturatio mala, panis vero pessima: A surfet of Bread (in the opinion of the Physitian) is of all surfets the worst; but in the sentence of the Divine, a surfet of that Bread which is the *Word of God* is of all Bread-surfets the most desperate. [Hyppocrates]

There is one condition concerning this *our Bread* which I cannot passe: It must be *Panis datus,* Bread given to us from God, not *Panis arreptus,* extorted and wrung from the throats of others. For God will not blesse that kinde of men which vultur-like lives by rapine and preying on their brethren. Such as these doe neither eat *Panem nostrum,* their owne, nor *Panem Quotidianum,* their *Daily Bread,* but (as it is in the Psalme) *ton laon en brōsei artou: They eat up the people in stead of Bread.* And howsoever it digests with them in this World, I feare they must looke to bee fed in the next with that diet which Ahab threatned to Michaiah, *The Bread of sorrow and affliction.* [[202] Psal.53:4 2 Chron.18:26.]

The Petitioners are intimated in this word *us: Give us.* That wee aske not for our selves in particular, *Give mee,* but *us,* is a Lecture of Charity. The Apostle professes if hee had all the World, all Gifts, all Faith, and had not Charity, whatsoever hee had or could doe was as nothing. [5. *Nobis* I Cor.13:(1, 2)]

I may in allusion to his speech boldly say, if God have bestowed his gifts upon us in the greatest abundance, if hee have fill'd our Granaries with Corne, and multiplied our flocks in the fold, yet hath

182 AN EXPOSITION UPON THE LORD'S PRAYER

<small>Ephes.4:2</small>
<small>[203]</small>
not enriched us with that *Brotherly love* wherewith we should *support one another;* If hee hath not given us a bountifull heart, and a charitable hand to give some of our goods to the releefe, and some of our bread to the nourishment of the poore, Hee hath given us but halfe a blessing. Wealth is but a confused lumpe, till bounty shape and put it into forme; but a dead uselesse peece of earth, till Charity inanimate and quicken, and by sending it abroad make it currant and by distributing it to severall hands give it heat and motion.

<small>Gal.6:10</small>
The Apostle bids us, as to *Love all,* so to *Doe good to all.* A man that doth good to none but to himselfe is a hatefull incloser; hee empales Gods bounty, by usurping a strict propriety in those blessings which he intended for the common releefe of mankinde.

<small>[204]</small>
As no part of the body was made only for it selfe, so no man. Wee are all one body whereof Christ is head, and therefore one another's members. As wee are all parts of that mysticall body, so are we also of a Politicall. Of which body, as the King is the Head, and the Counsellors the brain, so the Rich man is the stomacke that receives the good of the Land. Now as the stomacke receives the meat not to retaine it still there, but to disperse it into all the parts of the body, which must bee fed by that nourishment; so have Rich men their wealth, not to hoord up, but to disperse amongst the needy: for *Dispersit, Dedit pauperibus,** is the Rich man's office and commendation too.

<small>Psal.112:9</small>
Doe but observe how God waters the Earth by severall Veines and Channels. Shall the Channell say to the dry ground, I will retaine my waters, and shut up my banks from releeving your barrennesse, when the Channell is but the conveyance of that blessing to the World? God oft times reaches unto us his benefits by others' hands. Hee hath made the Rich his Almoner, his hand, to contribute unto the necessities of his brethren; for *Per eum qui habet iuvat egentem; per eum qui non habet probat habentem:†* If then hee bee of such a cruell retention to close and shut up himselfe against the poore, hee resists the ordinance of God, by with-holding that good which He intended to convey to others by him. Christ teaches us to say *Our Bread,* and *Give us:* wee heare not of any in the whole Booke of God that sayes *My Bread,* but onely Nabal, who is therefore both *Churle* and *Foole* upon record. Let him that hath Bread, *scatter it freely upon the waters,* for so God shall make it *Panem Quotidianum* in a lasting sense, by feeding him and his posterity Daily; and, as Elisha told the widow, *Neither the meale in his barrell, nor the oyle in his cruse shall ever suffer a diminution.*

<small>Aug. Ser.205 de Temp.</small>
<small>Leo Ser.5 de Quadrages.[a] [205]</small>

<small>I Sam.25:11, 25</small>
<small>Eccles.11:1</small>
<small>I King.17:14</small>

<small>6, Hodie</small>
This Day. As 'tis the date of the Petition, so must it also be the date of our solicitude. From whence I shall onely raise these short Lessons, and so end.

<small>I.</small>
First, wee must know that our care of Temporall blessings ought not to be prolonged so farre as either to impedite devotion, or make life tedious. Care is an uselesse companion to Christians. For let the apprehension of it worke never so strongly on thee, It can neither *Adde to thy stature,* nor yet diminish the growth of thy sorrowes. And though it may change thee from thy selfe, by making thee old and gray-headed in youth, it cannot change thy Fate. 'Tis an unnecessary affliction of the minde, since Man hath no cause to doubt his providence or love, who both *feeds the Fowles* and *cloathes the Lillies.* Let us therefore take our Saviour's counsell, *Cast our care upon the Lord,* and bid the morrow care for it selfe.

<small>Matt.6:27</small>
<small>[206]</small>

<small>Chrysost.</small>
<small>V.26 & 28</small>
<small>Matt.6:34</small>

<small>2.</small>
Secondly, 'tis put as a Motive to quicken our Pietie, and invite us to a continuall exercise of Prayer. Therefore though thou beest full, though God hath given thee, as he gave Israel, *Bread enough,* though thou art liberally replenisht with the blessings of earth, and He hath fill'd up the measure of thy desires, let not thy abundance perswade thee to shake hands with Religion, as Lot did with Abraham when hee grew too great—As if Prayer were but a needy service for beggers, not the rich. Doe not thou, like a Fort Towne, because thou art victualled for many monethes, presume upon thy strength, or stand upon thy owne guard, as if thou couldest hold out a siege against all necessities: Like the rich man in the Gospell, who having fill'd his barnes and store-houses, bid his

<small>Gen.13:11</small>
<small>[207]</small>

<small>Luk.12:19</small>

---

*He has distributed freely, he has given to the poor.
†Through him that has, he helps the needy; through him that has not, he tests him that has.

VI. Give us this day our daily Bread

soule rest securely in the confidence of his wealth. Know, God with one fit of an ague can shake thy strongest Fortification; That Hee can cut off thy supplies, and breake *thy staffe of Bread* as he did Israel's; and by the battery of one hot disease, even in a night's skirmish, beat thy soule out of her fraile Cittadell: *Stulte, hac nocte.** Psal.105:16
Luk.12:20

If thou beest full, therefore, praise God in the daily practise of thy Religion, *Give thankes to him alwayes,* and pray unto him continually, that his hand may not bee shortned towards thee to plucke backe his favours from thy possession—I say, *continually pray.* Thinke it not enough to come to Church upon Sundayes, or serve God once a weeke, and forget Him till the next Sabbath's All-in awake thee. As it was a constant daily sacrifice which the Priest offered in the old Law, so must thou offer up to God *Diurnum, Hodiernum sacrificium:* a sacrifice of Prayer for the sanctification of this Day, and each present Day unto thee. For Almighty God no more likes an intermittent, unequall, broken Devotion, than a Physitian doth the Pulse which falters in its pace, and beats at uneven time. 2 Thess.1:3
[208]

Now as thou must not discontinue God's service, so neither must thou anticipate, putting two dayes' Devotions into one; or thinke to serve God so long at once, as will serve for thrice. Thou must not deale for God's blessings as thou doest for Reversions, whose purchase precedes the possession. God doth not use to make any such estate in his favours, nor allow such early payments. Hee is not so needy of thy service, as that he should take it before hand. Pay thy Vowes when He requires, and thy Prayers when they are due, *Hodie,* This Day: *To day* in the present, *that is, every day, for the present comprehends all time.* Yesterday was the Present, This Day is, To Morrow will bee. Pray unto Him this day, and if He give thee leave to stay till the morrow become a *Hodie*—that to morrow this time, thou maist say *To Day*—Pray unto Him then also; and so let thy unwearied zeale still proceed, still keepe pace with Time, not ceasing to travell over the whole Kalendar of Dayes, untill it hath found that *Acceptable Day* wherein God will seale the full pardon of thy sinnes. For be sure He hath laid up *That Thy Day* amongst the rest, yet conceal'd it from thee, that Hee might engage thee in a perpetuall, assiduous, indefatigable search of it. Aug. *Epist.ad Probam*
[209]
(2 Cor. 6:2)

If we marke it, God's Conveyances and Patents of Grace runne in the Present, and are signed with a *Hodie: This Day have I set thee up over Kingdomes and Nations*—so he tels the Prophet Jeremy. Againe, *The Lord hath avouched thee this Day to bee his peculiar people.* And thus also doe his Pardons run. He tels the Theefe on the Crosse, *Hodie mecum eris in Paradiso: This Day thou shalt be with mee in Paradise.* If therefore we in our Counterpart shall vary this Date, or performe that duty, which on our party wee owe unto Him, in another stile, wee nullifie this Grant, and forfeit the whole Indenture of his favour. Jer.1:10
Deut.26:18
Luk.23:43
[210]

Let us therefore *Heare his voice to Day* (as it is in the Psalme): *Hodie si vocem eius audieritis—* that is, all the Dayes of our Life; and *Hodie,* Let us to Day, and in a continued course of Prayer all the Dayes of our life, beseech Him to heare ours: That He would vouchsafe to speake unto every one of us in that gracious language wherein he bespake his Deare Sonne, *Hodie genui te*—This day have I begotten you anew, this Day have I accepted of you for my children, and setled on you the Inheritance of my Kingdome, which shall never be revoked or reversed, *That ye may eat and drinke at my table in my Kingdome.* Psal.95:8.
Biel. *Lect.70.de Miss.146*
Psal.2:7

Luk.22:30

Lastly, it objects our frailty, and puts us in minde of the shortnesse of Life, In which wee have no Terme but the present, no State but a *Hodie, To Day,* For we are here to day, and gone to morrow. Of all the numerous distributions of Time, which multiply from Minutes to Daies, and from thence grow into Yeares, wee can claime no share, no portion but so much as is measured out in a *Hodie,* one Day. For as the Evening and the Morning in the World's beginning were the first Day, so *Mane Iuventutis* and *Vespere Senectutis*—our Morning of Youth and Evening of Age—in the computation of Life make but one Day. Of all the species of Time which Philosophy hath fathered upon it, we can pretend to none but onely the Present. For what is past we have not, and what is to come wee know 3.
[211]
Gen.I

---

*Fool, this night. . . .

184 AN EXPOSITION UPON THE LORD'S PRAYER

<small>Senec.</small> not whether ever wee shall. *Wee are sure of nothing but the Present,* and not sure of that neither. For *who knows the compasse of his Dayes?* Nay, of one Day, of this *Hodie*? Who knowes whether this very Minute may not be the Period of the Dayes of his Life?

Since therefore wee have so small an Interest in the World, let not our soules fix there, or make <small>[212] Psal.120:5</small> their habitation amongst the *Tents of Kedar*. Let us not still looke downward, lingring after the <small>Exod.16:3</small> Bread, or the Temporall Benefits of this Life, as Israel did after the *Fleshpots of Egypt,* but addresse our selves for a new Voyage: Remembring that when our strength and stomacke shall faile, when age shall cast a generall numnesse over us, when this our Bread shall grow insipid and our palate tastelesse, there is a new Table, and another kind of Bread, provided for us in the Kingdome of Christ. In stead of this *Panis Quotidianus*—Our Dayly Bread—*Panis Crastinus* (for so Saint <small>Hieron.Comment. in Mat.6</small> Hierome writes that some Hebrewes translated this place), a *Future Bread,* which wee shall eat the Morrow after this World's Day concludes. Such Bread which, when we have once tasted, will leave *no more hunger* to succeed it; and such a Morrow which shall have no new Day apparant to inherit that Light which died the Evening before. For this Life's *Hodie,* which wee call *To Day,* shall bee <small>[213]</small> turn'd into a *Quotidie, Every Day,* in the next; but without difference, or vicissitude, or alteration. That Every Day shall be but One entire Day, produced and lengthned into a *Semper,* a blest Eternity, whose duration shall bee like our Joyes, both as unutterable, as endlesse. Amen.

[214] VII. AND FORGIVE US OUR DEBTS, AS WEE FORGIVE OUR DEBTORS

Christianity is an active Profession, full of Religious importunity, that will not suffer her Disciples to fix their minds or meditations too long on Earth, but elevates their thoughts to that Meridian whose highest degree is Heaven. Indeed it were unreasonable that the Servants should slumber <small>Mat.8:20</small> upon that pillow whereon our Great Master, the *Son of Man had no roome to lay his head*.

Earth is but as the Center in the midst of a Circle, and how ever our apprehensions thinke it a great Body (as in it selfe it is) yet compared to Heaven 'tis but as a little Ball. If those 1022. Starres <small>Conimbricens. Lib.2.de Cœlo: oap.12 [215]</small> whose bignesse the Astronomer concludes to exceed the dimensions of our whole Terrestriall Globe appeare to our view not like Leaves or Lines, or Characters writ in that great Volume of Heaven, but onely like small Points and Periods: Imagine, then, to one that should from that exalted part of the Firmament survey the Lower World, how like an Atome or little Mote would this huge heape of Dust appeare whereon we tread? If to man's subtill and most sublime thoughts Earth be so smal a thing, what an unequall distribution should that man make of his thoughts, that could content them with such a Trifle? What an Emptiness and Vacuitie would inhabit that soule, which when it hath Capacity and Receit fit to comprehend the Foure points of Heaven—nay, Him whose Essence is larger than them, God—should contract and lessen it selfe, and let out all his roome to entertaine so small a Guest, so scant a Tenant as the World?

'Tis a just proportion to allow the cares of this life as much roome in our thoughts as the quantity and breadth of that Stage whereon wee move is, compar'd to Heaven. 'Tis, in respect of that, onely *Punctum,* and therefore wee are taught wee should only*Tangere in puncto,** touch it but lightly, give <small>[216]</small> it onely a short entertainment in our meditations. See how short a stay our Blessed Saviour makes upon the World, who onely glances upon it *in Transitu,* in his way and passage thorow this Prayer, not touching it directly but in one of the Seven Petitions, which is the very Center of the whole Prayer, as Earth is in respect of Heaven: *Give us this Day our daily Bread. This is the only Petition* <small>Cajetan In Matt.6</small> *which includes Temporall blessings:* For (as Cajetan sayes further), The three former Petitions *aske those things which conduce to the Glory of God, and the three last remove and deprecate those evils,* those transgressions which make us uncapable of his Kingdome, and unfit to doe his Will.

---

*A point . . . Touch at a point.

VII. And forgive us our Debts

Now therefore, as to a Man that stands upon this Center of Earth Heaven is his Object, whether he lookes Diametrically from one side to another, or whether hee view the large Circumference that environs him, *'Tis Heaven that on al sides terminates & confines his eye:* so, if we consider the middle Petition, *Give us this day,* &c., whether wee looke backe, Heaven is behinde us in the Three preceding Petitions; or looke we forward, 'tis before us againe in those Three which follow it.

Thus you see, like men set on shore for refreshment and provision of some necessaries for their voyage, we are cal'd aboord againe. Christ did only Land us upon the World's shore, in that middle Petition, to refresh us in the midst of our Travels, but Hee purposed not to affoord us any long stay, for you may see Man's meditations here imbarqued for the furthest point of Life's Voyage. For the clearing of which passage to his last Home, hee uses all diligence in these three last Petitions, which are as it were his Harbingers, to remove all impediments which might retard him in the course of his future Beatitude.

See, in this, Man making his peace with God and the World, compounding with his Creditor, God, and with his Debtors, Men, at one and the same rate: *Forgive us,* &c. *As we forgive them,* &c. See him in the next, preventing all future arrerages that might lie upon him, or make his *Onus* [debit] swell up and become great againe, when he prayes for grace to avoid the occasions of sinne, *Lead us not into Temptation.* And behold him in the last, suing out his everlasting *Quietus est* [quittance], not to bee encombred with after-reckonings or troubled with the fearfull punishment in another World for sins acted in this—*Deliver us from evill:* Which is the scope of what most of the Schoolemen write concerning the latter part of this Prayer.

This of my Text is a suit, limited by a Condition. The former part is the Suit, wherein we solicite the mercy of God for remission, *Forgive us.* Secondly, we specifie the danger wee would be delivered from, in this word *Debts.* Thirdly we acknowledge the proprietie of the Debt, that it is *Ours,* run into by our owne defaults, *Forgive us our Debts.*

The latter is the Covenant upon which the validity of God's Grant to us and the confirmation of the suit depends, a Reciprocall Mercy which we promise to shew unto our Brethren that have injur'd or offended us, comprehended under the stile of *Our Debtors*—*As we forgive our Debtors.*

The first part is a Discharge wee seeke from God, a privilege from former arrests, a Freehold wee labour to purchase from Him, *Forgive us.*

The latter contains our Bargaine, and the consideration wee tender Him in lieu of his goodnesse to us, Forgivenesse to our Brethren.

I remember Hieron. in his Epistle *ad Paulinum* speakes of the Booke of Job, *Singula in eo verba plena sunt sensibus:* Every word in it is of import. And Gerson makes this conclusion of the whole Scripture, *Nihil in iis otiosum reponi putandum est:* there is nothing in them contained but is materiall and of use. Nay, *Singuli verborum apices* (saith another): *Every point and tittle is of consequence,* according to that our Saviour said. Now if every word in Scripture hath its weight, much more every word in this Prayer, which is the Epitome of all Scripture, and as the Spirit extracted out of the whole Booke of God.

I must not then passe by this Copulative *Et dimitte: And forgive us,* which Christ hath prefixt to this Petition, without a Note, at least without mentioning the Schoolemen's reason why this Petition is coupled with a Conjunction, and so the next after this, whereas the Three first are not tied together by any such band. The cause is, saith Hales (and Biel, who recites him), for that the three former imply such a necessary connexion one to the other, that they cannot be severed; For the *Name* of the Father cannot so heartily be blest and *hallowed* by the Children, unlesse they expected an Inheritance in the *Kingdome* of their Father, which should devolve on them; Nor were they capable of that Inheritance, were there not a conformitie betweene their Father's *Will* and Theirs.

So though there be three Petitions, they have but one scope, one and the same Increated object, the Fruition of God's Presence; Unto whose Kingdome, as in a journey, all the steps Wee take are but one continued Motion tending to the place we go to, how ever that motion be diversified in our

margin notes:
[217]
Thom.Aquin. 2a, 2æ q.83:Art. 9.in conclus. Id.Salmeron To.5.Tract.51 [218]
Division: First part.
Second part. [219]
Gerson Part.2: ser.de 4 domibus
Mat.5:18 [220]
Hales part.4: q.37
Biel Lect.72 de Missa
[221]

186 AN EXPOSITION UPON THE LORD'S PRAYER

Gate. So those three first Petitions are but our steps, they are but one spiritual Progresse in which wee make our approaches unto *our Father which is in Heaven*. Those then, being inseparable, could admit no tie to hold them together, their necessary dependance one upon the other being their Cement, which combines them so close they appear but one peece: but 'tis not so with the rest of the Petitions, which though they conduce to the same end as the former, yet they goe by severall waies. They are severall subjects, and therefore needed a Conjunction, which as it unites them, so it *argues the diversity of the thing united* (as Biel). The Three first could not be dis-joyn'd in God's grant, These may; for God may give abundance of Temporall blessings, and yet give no Remission for sinne. He may give Riches *In Pœnam* [as a punishment] to men that employ them, so as they onely by them purchase their finall condemnation. He may bestow the fat of the Land upon a Miser that cares not what extortion hee practises upon his brethren. He may bestow his Bread upon a Prodigall, that abuses it in Riot and Surfets, from the fulnesse growing into a wanton disorder which pampers vice, and encourages those Temptations of sinne wee here pray against. Thus have I shewed you the reason of this Conjunction; From whence I proceed to the first part of this Text, the Suit: *Forgive*.

[margin: Biel loc.citat. [222]]

Wherein I purpose not to dispute the propriety of the terme *Dimitte*, whether it had not beene better exprest by *Remitte*, since as Salmeron well notes, *The Church by "Dimitte" understands Forgivenesse or Remission of sinne:* An Act which though God hath imparted to his Church by a direct Commission given to the Ministers—*Whose sinnes ye remit they are remitted, and whose sinnes yee retaine they are retained*—yet is the power originally in Himselfe:

[margin: I. *Forgive* Salmeron *Tom.* 5:*Tract.51* [223] Joh.20:23 Mark.2:7]

Who can forgive sinne but God alone? Forgive us.

Never did Man speake in so naturall a Dialect as this. Other Petitions displayed the condition and temper of his Faith, this only shewes the condition of his Nature. Those implied the happinesse he hopes for hereafter, this the weighty miserie he lies under in this World, Sinne. What better method can the convicted hold than to submit? or what more proper favour can the condemned sue for, than their pardon? There is no such acceptable forme wherein wee can present our selves to God as in Repentance, nor is the accent of any word uttered by the tongue of man so sweet in his eare as the confession of a fault.

For how should the acknowledgement of a sinne but delight God, when the conversion of a sinner affects the whole hoast of glorified Spirits in Heaven?—*Est enim gaudium coram Angelis, &c.** Such a confession as this is the first step to a Convert: *To aske forgiveness, and to confesse the fault, are in effect all one*.

[margin: [224] Luk.15:10 Tertull. *De orat: cap.7*]

In the practise of our Law, wee finde it is not safe for a delinquent to put himselfe upon his purgation, if his guilt lie in pregnant proofe: Peremptory attempts of justification rather exasperate Justice, which is in nothing more softned, than by one who (strooke with remorse) pleads guiltie to his Inditement. 'Tis just thus in God's Courts, who deemes it a contumacie in Man to diminish an offence committed against Him by vaine apologie or excuse; when wee are sure that many by anticipating his Justice, and by an unurged Confession of their Crime, have appeased the Judge, and acquitted themselves. The Publican's bashfull contrition, that was afraid to make his approaches too neere the Altar, and ashamed to looke that way his sinne had ascended, won pity from his lips who had the power to absolve him, whereas the proud garbe of the Pharisee, who (saith S. Augustine) *Superbe gratias egit*†—thankt God for a favour he never had—was condemned.

[margin: [225]]

He that thinkes to beare up himselfe by his owne merit, hangs a golden weight about his necke, that will choake him at last. A man must not thinke to turne the scale of God's Justice by justifying himselfe. That which hee thinks Righteousnesse in himself is not so indeed; and that which is so, is not his but God's, Lent and Imputed by Him. 'Tis a proud ingratitude therefore for a Man, enricht

---

*For there is joy before the angels. . . .
†Proudly gave thanks.

VII. And forgive us our Debts

onely by Devotion and Loane, to lift up himselfe against that hand from whence he borrowed it: As if he should take up money, and then goe to Law with his Creditor that lent it.

Even thus, a man that glorifies himselfe in the conceit of that Righteousnesse which he received, not from Nature but from Grace, not by Acquisition but Infusion, affronts God with his owne favours, and receives a *Brest-plate* (for so the Apostle calls it, *Loricam Iustitiæ*) out of his Armorie, to stand out and wage a presumptuous warre against Him. *Hee that defends himselfe, dishonours God,* and wrongs his owne soule; *therefore accuse and discommend thy selfe, for so thou canst in nothing* lesse wrong God, or *more right thy selfe.* Say with David, *Forgive Lord, bee mercifull to my sinnes,* and thy conscience shall finde that voice of pitty suggested to it which he reports, *Thou forgavest my sinne.* [226] Ephes.6:14

August In *Serm. de verb.Dom.*

Psal.*(51:1)*

This word *Forgive* is the Key which opens the wounds of Christ, and gives a ready passage to the Mercy-seat. Hee that can use this Key dexterously with that Christian skill wherewith the Artist who first formed it instructed the Disciples, cannot doubt of the successe. *He that taught us to aske forgivenesse, promised to grant what we sued for:* And that upon an everlasting record kept by Ezechiel, where wee may finde a Pardon Dormant for all sinnes whensoever we should sue it out— *At what time soever a sinner shall repent, I will blot out all his offences.* [227] Cyprian *De orat. Dom.*

Ezech.18:22, 27

If wee consider the condition of the Suitors, *Us* Men, wee shall then finde it necessary to be sued for at all times. Man and an infirmity which makes him prone to sinne are inseparable companions; His faults with their unblest societie will accompany him whilest he lives. And if he always sinne, he hath no remedy but always to pray for his redresse in the forgivenesse of sinnes. *Us*

Aug. *In Psal.29*

To presume *that Man should be Impeccable,* when none that ever was apparelled in our flesh but only the Sonne of God was so, *is a dangerous and false presumption.* Can it be beleeved (saith Leo) that Man should flatter himselfe with an opinion of integritie? Man, that hath more alliances to sinne than to Adam, from whom the Pedigree of his Guilt is derived, *whose first offence left a perpetuall obligation of sinne upon us*—A sinne which anticipates his birth, and when hee is borne growes up and waxeth like him; who is an Ancient in transgression before his birth, nay, before his conception, guilty in both, as being *Borne in iniquity, and conceived in sinne?* [228] Leon.*Ser.5 de Quadrages.*

Aug.*Ser.15 de verb.Dom.*

Psal.51:5

Since therefore Man cannot but offend, the Schoolemen's cautelous doubt, which they put if in case a man that sins not sayes this Prayer, is defeated: whereas it is a sinne to suppose a separation of sin from Man's Nature. If we say we have no sinne, wee give God the Lie, who sayes wee have. The very deniall convicts us, and into the number of our hidden faults casts one that is evident, an untruth. So that wee have so much the more sinne, in that wee shew so little truth.

S. Augustine sayes the Pharisee's insolent gratitude was reproved, not because hee gave God thankes, but because he thought himselfe above God's pardon. And the same Father deduces his odious arrogance to this issue, that he *needed not say "Forgive us our trespasses"* (For so he enforces). But admit the impossible supposition that there could bee found a man devoid of sinne, what inconvenience could the saying of this Petition bring? Nay, it would prove a large advantage. *Say thy branch be yet greene,* not blasted by the breath of sin. *Why for all that, thy root is dead,* and thou hast no meanes to keepe that mortifying Gangrene from invading thy selfe but by imploring God's prevenient grace, lest that rottennesse bee transfused into the limmes of thy Tree. [229]

Aug. *Ser.36 de verb.Dom.*

Id.

Aug.ib.

Say thou art fallen into no actuall sin, why, this Petition is a warning to tell thee that thou maist; For thus S. Cyprian: *it puts thee in minde thy actions may be foule, and that thy intentions are so.* [230]

To goe a little further. If thou hast hitherto committed no foule transgression, this Prayer like an Antidote strengthens the complexion of thy Faith, and helpes thee to resist the contagion of sinne. Nay, it forespeakes God thus farre to antedate thy pardon, in that it brings Him to an easinesse to *forgive* thee, when thou doest sin. And when he hath forgiven thee, when by his gratious pardon thou hast got thy absolution from sinne, the continuall repetition of this Prayer addes new seales and confirmations to that Pardon which Hee hath already granted. So that I may conclude of the use of this Petition, as Leo doth of the Sacraments, that they are profitable for all, Good and Bad:

Leo *Ser.5 de Quadrages.*

188 AN EXPOSITION UPON THE LORD'S PRAYER

so is this Petition advantageous unto all—unto those that have sinned, *ut quod nondum habent accipiant:* that they may *receive what yet they have not,* Remission of sinnes; Unto those that are absolved of their sinnes, *ut accepta custodiant:* that they may *preserve the integrity* which God's Pardon hath renewed in them. Thus it raises up those that are fallen, and it confirmes those that yet stand, lest they should fall.

To end this point: S. Bernard, out of the consideration that wee sinne often, concludes a necessitie of our frequent suing unto God to *Forgive us.* But S. Augustine will have not only those that have sinned, but the justest and most upright to use it as oft. And you shall finde that Lyra and the Glosse, by the authoritie of S. Augustine (whom they recite), interpret those two months (which by S. Augustine's computation are threescore dayes) desired by the daughter of Jephthah to bewaile her Virginitie, to bee the Six Ages of the Church: That is, from Adam to Noah, from him to Abraham, so to David, so to the Captivity, from thence to Christ, and from his time to the End of the World. In al which Ages, *The pure Virgin Church in all her Congregations laments the sins of her People, daily crying unto God* in the voice of my Text, *Forgive us our trespasses.*

Justly, therefore, because Man is a creature apt to sooth himselfe in the conceit of Merit and Inherent Righteousnesse (as doth the Church of Rome too much), and because this opinion had prevailed so farre on some that they presumed to leave out a branch of this Prayer (for so did those Precise Hereticks the Cathari), exempting themselves from the communitie of sinning like other men—Justly (I say) did a Councill decree, that *He that was most righteous might truely* use this Prayer, *and necessarily ought* to say, *Forgive us our debts.* Nay, it further decreed, that if any man presumed to say that Saints or holy men, when they used this forme of Prayer, spake not on behalfe of themselves (as being endowed with that measure of sanctity they needed it not) but on behalfe of such as were sinners, that man should be anathematized & concluded under a curse.

Forgive us our Debts. There bee some debts of which 'tis impossible wee should be discharged, as that Generall Debt wee owe to Nature by Death, A payment which without difference all must equally make, as well the Prince as the Vassaile, the richest as the meanest: *Debemur morti nos nostraque.** To die is as true, as good a Debt as any the world knowes. For the levying of which Debt, there is an Extent upon all Mankind, and a Statute recorded by S. Paul, *Statutum est omnibus semel mori:* It is decreed that all must die once. This is a Decree not to be reversed, a Debt which is not possible to be declined.

There bee other Debts from which it were a sin in us to sue for a release, as our Obedience to God and his Law, our Love to Him, our thankefulnesse for all the favours and mercies He hath conferred upon us. Wee doe not here sue to be freed from these payments (saith Salmeron). No, they are heavier Debts, and of a different condition, Debts which we borrow of as many Creditors as wee have sinnes, The worst sort of Debts that can be; and yet not Doubtfull or desperate Debts (Twere well they were so), for no secret conveyance or deed of trust made underhand can delude that Creditor, who will require an account for them.

How happy were a great many, if after the beggering of other men by their oppressions, if after the fraudulent purchases of much wealth, and the erecting of an high fortune of their owne upon the ruine of their poore Brethren—first chewed & ground by those fearfull Milstones, the Upper and the Lower (for there are both), *Use* and *Use upon Use,* and then swallowed downe and digested in a Mortgage—they could bequeath those sinnes from themselves, as they doe their estates, or by an absolute Deed of Gift make over their Guilt, assigning the punishment for their ill-gotten wealth to their Executors. But 'twill not be. God is a cleere-sighted Creditor, who cannot bee mockt out of his Justice; and the Vengeance due unto sinne is such a Debt which neither can be entailed upon the Heire, nor by any forfeiture escheat into other hands save the hand of God; nor be sold off, as men sometimes make bargaines for others' *Debentur,* nor any way be alienated. They are *Debita nostra,* such Debts whose propertie cannot be altered, *our Debts,* assur'd by such a Title as Gehazie's Leprosie was unto him, that it should *cleave fast.* The father cannot transferre them to his sonne,

---

*We and what is ours are owed to death.

VII. *And forgive us our Debts*

but they wil revert to their first Owner: For thus God hath said, *Every man shall beare his owne burthen;* And in the Prophet hee protests plainly, *The Sonne shall not beare the iniquitie of the Father, nor the Father of the Sonne.*   Ezek.18:20

That by *Debts* are meant *Sinnes* is apparant by the interpretation of another Evangelist, who was well able to comment upon the text of his Master, I mean S. Luke. For that which S. Matthew here cals *Debts,* he reads *Sinnes: Forgive us our Sinnes.* And in the fourteenth verse of this Chapter, S. Matthew thus expresses himselfe, that *Debts* are *Trespasses.* 'Tis usuall in Scripture to express *Sinne by the name of Debts:* For so in the Parable we find this debt diversly rated and comprehended, under the name of *Talents* and *Pence.* And justly. For as pecuniary Debts differ in their summes, and Coynes vary in their valuation, so doe Sinnes. The reason why Sinne is stiled Debt, Tertullian renders: *because it binds a man over to a future account;* and *in the day of Judgement every offence wil be required and charged upon the delinquent* (So Fortunatus amplifies it).

Debts are Sins or Trespasses
[236] Luke 11:4
Matt.6:14

Tertul. *De orat:cap.7.*
Mat.18:24, 28

Id.
Pamelius *Annotat. in Lib. Tertullian De orat., ex Fortunato*
[237]

As there is a difference in Debts, some being greater and others Lesse, so is there in Sinnes too: Some are more hainous, and shal have a severer punishment than sins of a lower degree. And yet all Debts, from the greatest to the least, are payable, and all sins, from the foulest to the cheapest, from the wilful Offence to the sin of Ignorance, are punishable. The quantity of the Debt doth not make it more a Debt, though it make it greater. He that lends a penny is a Creditor in as true a sense as he that lends a pound; and one that is indebted but in a small sum, hath as much right to answer it backe from whence it was borrowed, as he that is ingaged in a Million.

It being then granted that there is the same reason in Sinnes as in Debts, it followes by necessary consequence That by the rule of Justice, the least sinnes are as liable to punishment as are the least Debts to payment. From which conclusion I ground a direct Antithesis against the Church of Rome, which allowes the conceit of venial sins—For so their writers distinguish sin, *in Mortale & Veniale:* into Mortall and Veniall; whereas there is no sin, [[saith Hieron, committed against God's command]]* which is not mortall. The debt of sin is Judgement, and the Valuation Death. Therefore as the smallest Coine which beares the King's Impresse is currant as well as the greatest, so the sleightest offence hath its proportionable rate and value in the account of God's Justice as any of an Higher Nature.

No sinnes Venial

Hieron.*Lib.*2:*Epist.* 20 ad *Celantiam*[a]   [238]

Who will deny that Pilferings are Thefts, or that our Lawes punish Theft as well as Murther? or who knowes not but that hee Robs a Cottage, though hee take little, nay though he take nothing, is in as much danger of an Arrainement as hee that robs a Palace? There is no sinne wee can commit which is lesse in quantity than the point of any of those Thornes which were platted in Christ's Coronet, & yet the least of those Thornes prickt Him, the least drew Blood from Him. Shall wee then so farre undervalue any sinne, as to call that Veniall which was rated in any degree of Christ's sufferings or proportion of his Bloud—That pretious unvaluable Blood, whose least drop had beene enough to pay the ransome of the whole World, and make a full expiation for all sinne?

[239]

There is nothing more dangerous to a Christian than to sleight or diminish an offence—To say to thy selfe, I have done no murther, I have committed no Sacrilege, I have violated no man's Bed, nor defiled my owne Temple, which is my Body, but the holy Ghost's Chappell: These are sinnes which might bring mee in danger of damnation, but I have done no such. If I have thought ill, that Thought was never brought to an Act; though it sprang from my infirmity, yet that infirmity never had strength to bring it forth, but like an Abortive, it perisht againe in that womb wherein it was conceived. Therefore I hope God will be more mercifull than punish my purposes with death, to condemn mee for that I never did, for that which was onely form'd and cast in my imagination, not full shaped.

Surely I hope so too. And our hope in Christ's Mercy is a *Rocke* whose foundation will never faile. But yet for all that, like wise builders, wee must build the right way, or else our building will prove in vaine. And certainely, he that trusts upon the diminutions of a sinne builds upon the falsest foundation that may be. For to let small sinnes run on, out of a hope that they are not worthy God's

[240]

---

*Material in double brackets added in 1634 edition.

taking notice, or, if Hee doe take notice, that they are not worthy of his anger, is not Hope, but Presumption, and so our Hope is turned into a sinne.

Alas, we flatter our selves in our securitie if we thinke there be any Veniall sinne, or if we thinke that our Thoughts or lascivious lookes are onely the Abortions of sinne, and not sinne. Hee that imagineth evill is the Author (saith Salomon), For *The wicked thought is sinne.* And Christ hath pronounced that incontinent wishes are adulteries: *He that seeth a woman to lust after her, hath committed adultery.*

<small>Prov.24:8, 9</small>

<small>Matt.5:28</small>

So then, Thoughts are sins, and Lookes are sins, which (not repented) will, if not absolutely condemne (which though I am not peremptory to pronounce, I dare not be so coole in God's cause as to deny), yet prove as sluces to let in damnation, and worke wholly unto that unhappy end; as the smallest Leake which is sprung at Sea may, if neglected, let in water to drowne the tallest Ship. Therefore if the Tide of sinne have washt, though never so lightly, over thy Banke, if a Temptation have floated in upon thy Soule by any of thy Five Ports, thy Senses, make up the Breach betimes, lest a tide or two more overwhelme and lay thee quite under water. Had thy Mother Evah done so, had she not lookt upon the beauty of the Fruit, shee had not tasted it, nor for it had shee tasted the sorrowes of Child-bearing which that curiositie derived upon her. Had she then closed her eye, Death had never closed the eye of any childe of hers.

[241]

Stop then thy eare against those Romish charmers that would besot thee with the confidence of *Veniall Sinnes*—I meane, that some sinnes are so little thou needest not aske pardon for them. Exorcise that plausible mischiefe with S. Augustine's Spell, *Ne minima contemnat, qui in maxima labi nolit:* Despise not the smallest sinne, for even that is a step to a greater. Remember, thou maist multiply Pence till they come to a Talent; so thou maist linke sinne to sinne, till they make a Chaine long enough to dragge thee into perpetuall bondage with the Prince of Darkenesse, long enough to reach from Earth to Hell, till the multiplication of those Acts grow into a Habit, become great and strong, and heavie enough to sinke thee into the Bottomlesse Pit. Remember too, that as the least Coines, even to the Farthing, have their value, so also the least Sins shall have their Punishment. For the Justice of God hath put a price upon every Sinne: Christ mentions the Farthing, and will not abate even that in His Audit, when he says, *Thou shalt not goe out till thou hast paid the utmost farthing.* Upon which the Glosse excellently comments, and to the shame of many Doctors in the Romish Church: *By the Farthing he understands the least offences, because none of all them shall passe unpunished.*

[242]

<small>Matth.5:26</small>

And when, remembring this, thou shalt deliver it over unto thy meditations and digest it into thy beleefe, so oft as thou shalt apply this pretious balme tempered by Christ to heale thy wounded conscience and to wipe out thy sinnes, whensoever thou shalt cry unto him, *Forgive our sinnes,* thou wilt include sinne in the Latitude: *All thy sinnes;* and sinne in the Number, the very least of all thy sinnes; Not closing thy eyes at Night, nor opening them at Morning upon any affaire, till thou hast sued for thy release from all, And running over the History of thy Dayes and Nights, left none unrepented, whose omission might endanger thy salvation.

[243]

Forgive us our Debts. There is not so naked, so penurious a thing as Man. *Naked was he borne, and naked shall hee returne,* devested of all but his sinnes. Wee have no peculiar but this, nothing that we can call *Ours,* but only our Faults. Except that luckelesse patrimony, I know not what we can lay claime to, either that is without us, or in us. *Bona Fortunæ*—Wealth—acknowledgeth no Soveraigne but Fortune, wee are not Masters of it. And though it abide with us as an Hireling, perhaps till the end of our daies, then it surely takes leave—often before that, becomming any one's save his whose it last was. Nothing of all wee had goes along with us but our Winding sheet; for other things wee have gathered, the Psalme says *wee know not who shall enjoy them*—sure wee are, wee shall not. And for that forme which makes so many enamoured of themselves, can any call it Theirs?—When all the Pargets Art hath invented are not able to Coat it against the violence of Time and Weather, nor by all their fillings to repair those decayes and breaches which sicknesse hath wrought upon it? The Breath we draw, is that ours? Is it not suckt & borrowed from the next

<small>Nostra</small>
<small>Job 1:21</small>

[244]

<small>Psal.39:6</small>

Aire? Our best part, the Soule, is it any more than a Loane, deposited for some yeares with the Body, after whose expiration it reverts to *him that gave it*? And lastly for our Body, is it any thing else but a Lumpe of walking clay, a little Earth inanimated; the certaine restitution whereof wee owe unto the *Dust* from whence it was taken?

What is there then of our whole selves which we can call *Ours*, unlesse our Sinnes? These are effects springing from our owne depraved Nature, the fruits of a Vicious Crooked Will, our true Legitimate Issue, though borne against all Law both Humane and Divine. They are *Nostra*—Ours—by many assurances, *Ours* by all Titles both of right and possession. Therefore Hugo Cardinalis, upon the words of the fifteenth verse (*But if ye forgive not men their trespasses, neither will the Father forgive yours*), makes this inference: *Rightly doth Christ call them* Your *Sinnes, because they are the only Acts wherein Man is the Prime Agent*. These are the only revenues of Nature, and the possession of Mankinde. Such an undoubted Inheritance and Possession, of which wee can no way devest our selves but by conferring our Title upon Christ, who was content to accept it, and by *casting our sinnes upon Him* who became *Sinne for us:* that He might free us from the penalty of sinne, making the Crosse a Bloudy Evidence of that right hee claim'd in our Punishment, and a Trophee both of his Love to us, and of his victories over Death and Hell and Sinne.

The Intercession of whose Bloud daily solicites our pardon, and seales unto our Conscience the Forgiveness of these Sinnes we here sue for, *Forgive us our sinnes*.

VIII. AS WE FORGIVE OUR DEBTORS

I am upon an argument of Debts, and may assume S. Augustine's beginning to some Auditors of his. I must confesse my selfe indebted for the handling of this Text, betwixt the first part whereof & this last hath passed so large a time that it is now become a stale Arrerage. And though the Contagion which lately dispersed us hath diminished many of those hearers unto whom I was a Debtor, I am ready to discharge it to you, being desirous to pursue my first intent (though sometimes by other service interrupted) of going thorow the severall Petitions of this Prayer.

This Petition, I told you, was a *Suit* limited by a Condition. The former part was the Suit, this the Condition on our behalfe: wherein wee covenant with God, whom wee daily offend, for his Mercy and Forgivenesse to us, *As we forgive* and shew mercy unto such as have offended us.

So that this whereon I am now to insist is the *Counterpart*. From whence I shall shew you in generality how we are mutuall Debtors to one another;

That wee are Debtors for some things which wee borrow not, yet wee owe and must make payment;

That there bee some Debts due unto us from others, yet wee must not require them, which are Trespasses committed against us; And these we condition with God that we will remit: *We forgive our Debtors*.

The last circumstance enforces the Petition upon our selves, precluding us, and making us incapable of God's Pardon, if wee forgive not our Brethren *Sicut:* Forgive us, &c. *As we forgive,* &c.

We are Debtors, contracted to this title ever since the bargaine of our Forefather, which left us indebted to the Justice of God and Penalty of sinne: Since the severall discharges whereof by Christ, wee yet hold a firme interest in the name. The Reciprocall Offices which passe betwixt man and man are Debts: Relations—whether *Æquiperantiæ*, or *Disquiperantiæ*, as Logicians distinguish—of Distance or neerer ties, the References of Command or of Affection, of Duty or of Service, derive this stile of Debtors upon us. Friends that are linkt in a Paritie of minde, Husbands and Wives who by a nearer union are conjoyned, Masters and Servants that in a more unequall manner referre to each, and lastly Parents and Children, that by two sure knots of Bloud and of Obedience are fastned together, are Debtors, by mutuall respects owing themselves to each. These Offices of Service, or Affection, or Duty, are so good Debt, that not onely wilfull neglect of them, but omission, forfaits us to the censure of God and Man.

Joh.13:34 Our blessed Saviour bound us by a Precept to *Love one another—Diligite invicem*—and therefore whatsoever wee pay not upon that common Bond, wee stand indebted for, both to our
[250] Brethren and to Him.

Ephes.5:22; 6:1 Subjection is the Debt of the Wife to the husband, Obedience of the Children to their Parents,
Vers.5 Loyalty of Servants to their Masters; And the not payment of every such Debt where it growes due makes the Arrerage Sinne.

To strengthen which Obligation, you shall finde that they are al enterchangeably signed. The
Ephes.5:29 same Spirit who enjoyned Submission to the Wife hath levied also upon the Husband a tender
Vers.28 Affection, like unto that wherewith God loves his Church: Literally, *they owe it to their wives,* saith S. Paul.

Coloss.3:21 So Parents owe somewhat to their Children in lieu of their Obedience: They must not grieve nor
Ephes.6:4 provoke their Children, no more than they must dishonour them. Nor must the Master prove a Tyrant to his Servant, since besides the wages hee contracts for, there is a favourable respect to
[251] Ephes.6:9 descend upon him, like that which the great Lord of Heaven shewes unto us.

And yet, how ever these Precepts run enterchangeably, obliging both parties—as well the *Relatum* as the *Correlatum*—I must tell you, the violating of the Conditions on one part doth not make the other void. An ill Master, or an hard father, or a worse Husband, do not disoblige Servant, or Childe, or Wife, from those respects which God's Commands hath cast upon them as Debts. When equality of desert or correspondence in those parties failes, our Obedience unto God, under whose sentence wee must stand or fall, should supply their defect.

Unnaturall harshnesse or rigour in Parents doth not slacke the Tie of Filiall Duty: Though they forget to be Parents, Children are bound to remember them, by their Obedience, that they are so:
(Exod.20:12) Since, though Nature's Deed be cancelled, God's Statute, which conveyes an *Honour* upon the *Parents,* is still in force.

[252] Ephes.5:29 Though the Husband hate or prove cruell to his owne flesh, if hee forget *the Wife of his Bosome,*
(Gen.2.21) to whose building the first Husband that ever was contributed a Rib from his owne side, the wife must not make his unkindenesse a Bill to divorce her regard from him. If upon every distemper or frenzie of our Head the Body should take advantage to revolt; if the Heart, growne hot with indignation or unkindnesse, should by any sudden Allarme which passion strikes her into, cause the Bloud to boile above the usuall height, or make her Pulse beat a running precipitate March; if by awaking the Humors shee should cause the stomacke to cast up ill fumes, or the side to send splenative Damps into the Head, this were not the way to cure, but quite to discompose and disorder the frame of Wedlocke so much, as that it could never be peeced together againe.

Lastly, if any Superiours, Lords or Master, by the ill manage of their authoritie, should prove grievous or Tyrannicall to such as are subject to their Commands, this default of theirs must not
[253] arme an inferiour hand against them, nor doth it acquite Inferiours from their subjection.

Rom.13:1 We owe unto the *Higher Powers,* in what ranke or title of domination soever set over us, a service as tribute, assured by two Seales, of love and conscience. So that if any that are above us send not downe those graces which inferiours may look for, they must not think to pay themselves by stoppage, or to right themselves by with-holding the Duty which they are bound to performe, but
Rom.13.5 must still proceed in their observance, if not so much for Love, yet for *Conscience' sake*. These are Currant Debts, which we Owe and Require, Pay and Receive.

There be other Debts which wee borrow not, and yet wee Owe them: such are Deeds of Charitie.
(2.) Of which Debt, how ever Manes, that notorious Heretike, discharges himselfe (who it should seeme studied the Art to save his Purse more then to save his Soule, it being his thriftie Heresie that *Deeds of Charitie* are unlawfull); And though the *Anabaptists* and *Family of Love* by their
[254] uncharitable practise would have no Mercy move but in their owne Sphere, towards their owne

VIII. *As wee forgive our Debtors* 193

Fraternity and Sect, accounting all releefe extended to others extravagant, and as Bread throwne to Dogs; Yet had He or They beene but halfe so precise in husbanding their Conscience as their Estates, they would have been of another minde. Better Men, I am sure, were and are. *Thy Bounty* (saith S. Ambrose) *is the poore man's Revenew, nor is Thy Rent more due to Thee, than thy Almes to Him. God made the rich and the poore for one another* (saith August[ine]). Poverty is a subject allowed by Him to exercise the Piety of such as doe abound, and abundance is but a surplusage to support the poore; So that a rich man whose abilities make him capable of doing good, if he do it not, forfeits the maine cause for which God enriched him. Ambros. *Offic.* *Lib.1:cap.11*[a] Aug.*Ser.25* *de Verb.Dom.*

The Gospell carries these sins of Omission higher, making them not lesse than perpetrated facts. By that Rule and in that Language, all Defect in Charity is Cruelty; Not to give is as much as to take away; Not to succour the distressed is in effect all one as to spoyle them. If I feed not the hungry, I starve them; if I releeve not, I destroy. [255]

Nay, our Saviour carries it yet higher, making, according to his rate, trespasses of this Nature not Morall Vices but Capitall Crimes, whereby through our unkindnesse to our Brethren *He is wounded: I was sicke in prison and yee visited not mee; I was hungry and yee releeved me neither with your Bread nor your Drinke; I was naked, and yee cloathed mee not.* Nor can we plead Ignorance, or excuse our selves with *Lord, when saw wee thee hungry, or sicke, or naked?* since our Saviour professes, *In not doing it to them, wee have omitted it towards Him.* Give mee leave in Saint Augustine's phrase to raise this Debt yet one step higher, and I then fall off: *If hee endanger his owne safety that cloathes not the naked, what shall become of Him that devests the poore,* and by Extortion makes pillage of his Brethren? Matt.25:42 Vers.45 Aug.*Ser.20* *de verb.Dom.* [256]

I passe from these debts which we owe and must pay, to other Debts which are owing to us, and yet wee must not exact them: 3.

We forgive our Debtors.

If this Gospell should have the same construction that the Law hath, taken to the Letter; *Forgive our Debtors*, it would scarce prove *evangelion, Good Tidings*, or wellcome newes to many a Creditor. Those who in the Dialect of the Ryalto are the Best, those whom the Exchange cals Good men, would pray worst. Christ's Prayer to them would become as terrible as his Scourge, and doe as much as that did, *Drive the Money-changers out of the Temple.* I feare most Bankers would then turne Recusants, and not onely forbeare to use the Lord's Prayer in the Congregation, lest before witnesse they should release their lendings, but even in their chambers would bee afraid to use it, unlesse they might expugne the latter part of this Petition, as the Cathari did the former. It would then grow a profitable part of Religion, a Motive to Devotion, to bee in Debt, and none would be so zealous to pay their vowes to God, as they that would not pay their Debts to men. Joh.2.15 [257]

I read that upon the intreaty of Nehemiah the Hundredth part of the Debt was remitted by the Creditors, and all Mortgages restored to the owners; but the Greeke History tells us that Licurgus and Solon, seeing how much the People of Lacedemonia suffered by being overcharged with Debt, burnt all the Bonds and obligations of the Creditors in the Market Place. Such a Bond-fire as this in our City would smell sweeter than the Arabian Triumphs, wherein Spices are their Fewell, and create a greater Jubilee amongst us than ever was held in Rome. I am sure men would get more by the remission of their Debts than the Pope can give them by the remission of their Sinnes, since those who repaire thither pay more for his Acquittance than the Pardon or whole Lease of their Sinnes is worth. Nehem.5:10 [258]

But not to send any Creditors away discontented by preaching *Forgivenesse of Debts* (as the Gospell saies the young man went from Christ sorrowfull when he bid him *Sell his Possessions and give them to the poore*); not terrifie the Rich with any imagination or sound of Losse, as if their love to God could make them Losers, or that they must suffer in their Fortune for Religion's sake: Let mee tell them this Text beares another sence. These *Debts* are *Sinnes*, and the *Debtors* are such as have offended or wronged us: so S. Luke reads it. And therefore, if there bee any Debtor who, to detaine his Debt and have a colour not to pay, should appeale to the Letter, hee may remember Mat.19:22 August. *Lib.2 de ser.Dom. in Monte, cap.13: Tom.4* [a] Luk.11.4

there is a Text which disables him to borrow—*Nemini quicquam debeatis sed ut invicem diligatis:* Owe no man any thing but to love one another. If it were established as a Law that none should lend or borrow but from this stocke, there could bee no currant true payment of this Debt but to owe it still. Obligations of Courtesie and Affection are not like common Bonds, Dated and Cancelled at a Yeare—the older they are, the firmer, since Time not superannuates but improves them, and still, the more wee owe, the more wee pay.

I know some Councils and other Popish Writers are Literally for not payment to some. A Romish Debtor is actually released of all Debt or Contract with an Heretike, saith their Canon. Which makes mee remember that in the Psalme, *The Righteous lendeth, but the wicked borroweth and payeth not.* What large Indulgences doth Rome afford to her Children, which Cancels their Debts and Pardons their Sinnes at the same rate! What better Religion can dissolute men chuse than Popery, which privileges them to owe without payment, and to sinne without punishment?

But not to persist in this Diversion: The Text intercedes not for a release of *Debts,* but *Sinnes.* Our Commission is to preach Forgivenesse of Sinnes. And yet, though we have no warrant to preach Remission, wee have warrant to preach Forbearance of Debts. *'Tis a kinde of robbery for one that is able to restore what hee borrowes, to keepe it from the Owner;* nor is it violence, but justice to force him to a restitution. But to presse an unable Debtor is Tyranny, and makes the Creditor accountant for such a sinne which his whole Debt cannot buy out. Such as these, Christ's Parable instructs us to forbeare; and where he mediates for longer day, 'tis irreligion not to grant it. It is lawfull for any man to call for his owne, but he must doe it in a temperate, Christian way. I may deliver a truth in that phrase and those circumstances that it may sound like a Libell; and I may require my owne in that harsh fashion, that it shall appeare Extortion rather than Equity.

There bee some men so punctuall and peremptory upon their Debtors that, impatient of reason or delay, they punish their breaking of Day for payment with imprisonment. With ill Debtors, that would delude them, they have some colour to deale thus; But with such from whom they can receive no present satisfaction but their Body, nor expect any possibility of satisfaction but by a patient forbearance, and giving them a longer respit, to deale thus is neither discretion nor conscience. Is the carcase of a poore Debtor languishing in a Jayle better security than what they have already? Or doth that wretched pawne of his Body satisfie the Debt? If not, what madnesse is it in them when a Debt is doubtfull, to take a course to make it quite desperate? What barbarousnesse is it in them, because a man is already disabled for satisfaction, by a cruell restraint upon his liberty to disable him for ever? I am afraid to thinke what will become of such flinty hearted men, who sacrifice their brethren to ruine, and starve poore Debtors, onely to feed the wolfe of their revenge. *If hee bee in danger to bee chain'd up in eternall darkenesse who visits not the Prisons, what chaines are preparing for him whose cruelty fills them?*

For such men as these, *Father forgive them,* or at the least reduce their cauteriz'd dead consciences to this sense of their owne misery: that without a speedy repentance shall reprive them, they are lost, and that they never must taste droppe of thy mercy, unlesse they shew that mercy unto others which they expect from thee. For wee covenant for thy forgivenesse *Sicut dimittimus:* As wee forgive our Debtors.

In Matthew 7, it was a Maxime which our Saviour Christ gave to his Disciples, *Whatsoever yee would that men should doe unto you, even so doe yee unto them*—A Maxime so just and equall, that even Heathen men adored it. Severus the Emperour was so much affected with it, that he caused it to bee engraven in his Pallace and upon the publike Buildings; And besides, out of a reverence to the Author, determined to have built a Temple for Him. But how ever hee was crost in that purpose, we finde this very sentence gave occasion to Ulpian, chiefe Counsellour to Severus, to frame that Conclusion which is amongst the Pandects: *That every one should expect that right upon himself which hee gave others.* Camerarius writes that upon an old Monument under which Apollonia Geria was buried at Rome, they found this inscribed: *Quod quisque vestrum optaverit mihi, illi semper eveniat vivo & mortuo*—Let that befall you alive and dead which you wish to mee.

VIII. As wee forgive our Debtors

But to leave these Stories, Our Saviour in his Gospell, to put a greater dignity upon this Rule of his, professes it is not only a Law to governe the Actions that passe betweene Man and Man, but is also a Covenant established betwixt God and us, who will doe unto us as wee doe unto our Brethren, exercising the same measure, the same degree of rigour or mercy on us as wee expresse towards them: *With what measure ye mete, it shall bee measured to you againe,* and with what judgement yee judge, yee shall bee judged. Which is the perfect scope of this Petition, wherein hee doth not promise to heare us, or allow our Prayer for Remission of our Sinnes, but upon condition that wee forgive those that trespasse against us—Forgive us *Sicut: So,* and no otherwise, but *As we forgive.*

[264]
Mat.7:2

Therefore Cajetan well saies, wee as it were judge our selves, and *define* how farre the mercies of God shall extend to us, when wee either contract or dilate them according to the limits of our owne Charity to others. Nay, wee as it were *enter Bond with God that we will expect no mercy from Him, if wee shew none.*

Leo *Ser.5 de Quadrages.*

To what a strange equality doth the goodnesse of God levell it selfe for our sakes! At first God was man's patterne by which hee was wrought and made up, *Factus ad imaginem*—according to his Image. Now man is God's, who formes his Actions by a Samplar within us, the complexion of our Conscience. So Theophylact saies, *God takes patterne by my actions, and whatsoever I doe to others, the same will hee doe to mee.* You see what a necessary dependance there is betwixt the Mercy of God and Ours, when God implies Ours as a Condition not to be dispensed with, or rather as a Previous Disposition which must precede His: *If thou have ought against thy brother, goe and first be reconciled, and then come and tender thy Gift.* In vaine doest thou make thy approaches to the Altar, and thinke to bee accepted before God, when thou leavest behinde thee that fume which sweetens the sacrifice of thy Prayers: thy Charity with Men. Therefore S. Luke delivers it absolute, *Forgive &c., For wee forgive those that are indebted to us.*

[265]

Matt.5:23

Luk.11:4

So you see there is a necessity laid on us: Woe unto us if wee forgive not, for then the handwriting of Death which stands against us must never bee reversed. Wee shut out God's mercy from us, if wee first shew it not to our Brethren. But yet the necessity holds onely on our part. It doth not necessarily follow, if we forgive others, God must therefore forgive us. Our Remission I confesse may bee a Motive to incline God, not a Cause to necessitate or compell his Mercy to us. *God saies hee will not parly with us,* unlesse wee first be reconcil'd; and yet hee tells us not, when we are reconciled, that our Act of Reconcilement must conclude Him. It doth not follow, it I commit Adultery and remit a Grudge, that upon my Act of Forgivenesse God should quit Scores, and pardon my Incontinence. Such bargaines as these would open a large way to Atheisme and all licentiousnesse.

[266]
Mat.18:35

Aug.*De civit. Dei,L.21:ca.27*

God's mercy is not subordinate to ours, but most free and independant; no merit of ours can buy it, nor any action wee can doe produce it as a consequent. Our mercy shewed to others is not the cause of God's, but a Motive to incline His, and to qualifie us with a capacity to receive His. *Neither did Christ in these words absolutely promise His Remission, but by an exhortation excite ours*—Calvin states it rightly. For which speech, Stapleton in his Antidote bitterly inveighs against him, as being willing to quarrell with the Truth if Calvin spake it. Yet I will not wreake the injury upon Stapleton—wee are upon a Theme of Forgivenesse, and Stapleton himselfe, but five lines after this hot accusation, cries Calvin mercy, urging his words to refute himselfe: *God will not upon any other tearmes take us to favour, but as wee take those into our mercy who have offended us*—Hee will not forgive our Debts, but *as wee forgive our Debtors.*

[267]

Stapleton *Antidot. Evangel.in Matt.6:15*

[268]

Let the devout ejaculation therefore of Hugo Cardinalis be the Preface to my close: Good Lord, grant us that gift of Charity, *that we may remit unto others the wrongs which they have done unto us,* and bee thou gratious *to remit our trespasses committed against Thee.*

The Light of Nature, Reason, and the True light, Christ Jesus, tells us it is better to forgive, than to retaine an injury.

Is it a Calumny cast upon thee? The noblest revenge is silence or neglect. S. Basil as highly commends that Philosopher Pericles who to a tedious Railer made no reply, as we doe Conquerours. Indeed, 'tis nothing but our apprehension which quickens slander and gives it life, which if despised, would returne upon the Author, and like a weed, perish in that ranke soile which bare it.

Is it a law-strife, in which many a man wrangles out his time? S. Paul tells thee tis more wisdome to sit downe: *Is there not one wise man amongst you, but Brother goeth to law with Brother; why doe ye not rather take wrong?* And our Saviour tells us 'tis better husbandry *to agree with an adversary* at any rate than stand out, for there is nothing got by it: If any man sue thee at the Law to take thy coat, *let him have thy cloake also;* for thou shalt spend more to recover one, then both are worth. Therefore if thine adversary take thy coat, give him thy cloake: for if he have it not, thy Atturney will. And since thou art sure to lose it both wayes, 'tis better to yeeld it upon quiet termes, than after much vexation lose it in the costs of thy warre.

Or lastly, is it a quarrell, whose decision ends in bloud? *Quæ utilitas in sanguine meo?*—Give mee leave to use the words: *What satisfaction can my bloud give thee* for an injury? Or what can my death adde to thee but a new sinne, whose clamour can never be appeased untill it have awak't justice, and let loose that vengeance which thy remission might still have kept muzzel'd and tied up? What strange prodigious Spirit of wrath is it, that like an *Incubus* overlayes thy judgement, and makes thee value the satisfaction of a wrong above the favour of God, and sooner forfeit Heaven than thy Revenge?

O what a rebellious thing is Man, whose passions and perturbations that power which calmes the angry Sea cannot allay! *Sub iussione Christi mare audit, & tu surdus es?*—Shall the Wind or the Flouds bee more obedient to Him than thou? In every such storme of fury call up thy Religion and *wake Christ* (who *sleepes* in thee when thy Passions are awake), as the Disciples in that tempest did, with their loud cry, *Master helpe us, or wee perish.* For if He sleepe still, thou art utterly lost, and wrackt upon thy owne Coast. Nay, if thou suffer these vindicative gusts to prevaile upon thee, the storme will grow so loud, that thou shalt Want voice to cry and to wake him. Whilest fury or malice is in thy heart, the tongue of thy Prayer is either quite tyed up, or if it doe speake, it speakes Death unto thy soule. If thou cry unto God to *forgive thee, as thou forgivest,* in that cruell hypocrisie of thine thou signest the warrant for thine owne death. Thy not forgiving thy brother turnes thy Prayer into a Curse, and like a Comet makes it shoot vengeance into thine owne bosome.

Mercy was the last Legacy which thy Saviour bequeathed, whilest that Sunne of Righteousnes hung upon the Crosse and was neare his Sun-set. He would not goe downe in wrath, but in forgivenesse: *Father forgive them.* O let not Him see the *Sunne go downe upon thy wrath.* It is not with thy Conscience as with the Skie. A Red Evening prognosticates a faire day: But if the Evening of thy Life be Red, if it bee died or discoloured with bloud, the Morning of the next World will rise foule and lowre upon thee, nor shall any sound but of Judgement and Horrour salute thy eare— Awake to Judgement, thou that wouldest not sleepe in Mercy. Whereas if here thou *liest downe in peace* (as David speakes), reconciled to men and to thy selfe, thou shalt finde (no doubt) the fruit of this reconcilement on Earth sealed in Heaven, in the *Forgivenesse of all thy sins. AMEN.*

IX. AND LEADE US NOT INTO TEMPTATION

This part of the Praier is rather a Deprecation than a Petition, fitly ensuing that which precedes it: Wherein, as wee sued for the discharge of sinnes committed, so here wee deprecate all new occasions which may revive those sinnes. *Leade us not into Temptation* (So Biel glosses it), *Lest relapsing into our foule habit of sinne after we have been cleansed, our latter condition proves more dangerous than the first.*

Alexander Hales makes the object of this part Concupiscence: which is Vice's Seminary, the mould wherein sinne is cast, the beginning of all Temptations. It is Christ's Method to stop the

IX. And leade us not into Temptation

Primos motus peccati: Conceptions of sinne—prevent ills in their cradle, kill them in the Bud, before they acquire strength or opportunitie to ripen.

Lest any should misconceive the words, and (because wee pray unto God *Not to leade us into Temptation*) make an affirmative inference, that *He* might be the Author and *leade us into Temptation,* I shall first shew

God is no cause of Evill
Nor an occasion of it by Tempting any
Yet He permits Temptation.
What, and from whence, and how Various this Temptation is, who the *Authour* of it,
Who the *Deliverer* from it, my ensuing Treaty will disclose.

My first taske is to shew *God is no cause of sinne.* For is there any so farre gone in errour, as to suppose the cleere Fountaine of all goodnesse can be the foule Sewer of Sinne? Can Good and Evill flow from the same head? Or can the Judge of all the World play booty with his Clients, receive a Praier with one hand, and deale a Curse with the other? 'Tis true, the tongue can *blesse* and *curse* with the same breath; but God, who gave it motion, making it the Organ of Speech and interpreter of the Heart, made not the perverse language which the tongue utters. Cursings were never stampt in his mint, but cast by him who is the Author of Lies and Forgeries. Contraries never rose from one spring, nor doe the brackish and sweet waters flow from the same Rocke.

What a Monster, then, should that man breed in his imagination, that should pronounce God the Authour of Sinne? If nature abhorre to teeme with Opposites in one and the same wombe; If the Grape and the Thorne, the Figge and the Thistle, be births which one stocke beares not; If bitter and sweet bee qualities which necessarily derive themselves from a different parentage; then much more are *Good & Evill* Births which the God of Nature never yet reconciled in his Acts. And sooner shall Nature runne counter to her selfe, inverting her even course, sooner shall the congealed frost lodge with the fire and Winter become the preposterous Mother of the Harvest, than the true *Father of Light* bee brought to father the spurious issue of Night, Sinne and Errour.

As there is none good but God alone, so nothing but goodnesse can proceed from Him. And if wee devest him of that proprietie, we act a robbery upon Him which his Vegetable Creatures are not capable of. Christ sayes, *A good tree bringeth forth good fruit;* And if wee say lesse of the Author of all good fruits than of the Tree, doe wee not conclude his goodnesse to be of lesse growth than it?

Such a deniall as this is, at the easiest construction, a folly of as large extent as his that denied God. *Dixit insipiens:* There is one foole in the Psalme, that sayes there is no God; And there is another foole (saith S. Basil) who imagines God the Author of evill.

Such is the madnesse of many, that *out of a desire to extenuate or disguise their faults, they impute them to God,* by false criminations traducing even the God of Truth.

Strange presumption of the Creature, that dares make Him guilty of his deformities who in the originall Copy of his workes never knew any lamenenesse or imperfection! For upon the first review, his Penman records that he approv'd them all for good.

Therefore S. Augustine saies right, *God made Man, but Man made himselfe a Sinner.* And it is S. Bernard's free confession, *Si peccavi, ego peccavi.** He is so farre from blaming God, that he will not blame *Destiny* or *Fortune:* nay, he accounts it a slander to accuse *the Devill* as the Author of his Sin. 'Tis true that the deceit of the Devill was the Prologue to sinne; his perswasions laid the first traine by which Man's will was inflamed, he kindled his desire with curiositie to know; but the Cause was in Man's selfe, a Perversenesse & Disobedience in his *Will.* Aske the Prophet, and he will tell you, that there lies the head of sinne: *As the fountaine casteth her waters, so shee her malice.* If man's Will had beene suitable to his first abilities, hee might have stood unshaken by any assault of the Serpent: *It was in his Power, at his owne election, not to have fallen*—he might stood

---

*If I have sinned, it is I who have sinned.

if he would—but his Will *declined and forfaited* that power. *Therefore, because hee rather chose to fulfill his owne vicious purpose than God's command,* God left him to the fearefull consequence and punishment of the sinne by him committed. If then Man's Will were the cause of his fall, what an addition should that man make to his sinne that would make God accessary to that fault, whereto onely himselfe consented?

As God is not the Author of sinne, so neither of Temptation: which in the definition of the Schooles is *A motive or provocation to ill;* and *The end of a Tempter is to seduce and make ill.* How then can it stand with his goodnesse to be a Factor for reprobation, or a Confederate in that Act which he abhorres?

I know, *Temptation* is the concurrence of Time and Place, and subjects appliable to both; And however in it selfe it be lesse than the Fact, yet considered in the Author that invites sinne by these opportunities, it shall farre outgoe it. The infirmitie of a Sinner may sometimes find excuse or pity, but what shadow of excuse can shelter his malice that drew him to the Act?

'Tis more hatefull to bee sinne's Bawd, than to be the subject of it. The first is the Active part of Vice, the last is Passive. The first Nurses it, the last receives it; And if the milke be empoisoned, you will rather blame the Nurse that gave it, than the Childe that drew it in. 'Tis not the Wax, but the Impression of the Seale that fortifies a Conveyance, and makes the Deed. Man is a thing easily perswaded to errour—*Cereus in vitium flecti:* like wax wrought to a softnesse, that will receive the Figure of any Vice. And yet we blame not his softnesse, but lament him whose credulitie and easie temper betrayes him to every Temptation.

If wee lay the occasion of Man's fault aright, wee must lay it on the Tempter. At his allurements did Adam's obedience relent, his perswasions heated him with the inordinate desire of knowledge. Hee chafte this wax, mollifying it with such art that it received his Authenticke Seale of damnation, by which Sin was made currant in the World. Had there beene no Tempter, happily Men had never beene acquainted with Sinne. And we may justly thinke it was the Serpent made him familiar with that mischiefe, which his innocent disposition then knew not.

Temptation, then, is but an instruction How and When to sinne, a subtile engine serving to encourage and give aime to those faults which our frailtie is perfect in without a Prompter. *'Tis but a deceitfull Glosse set upon Vice to make it look amiable,* As the Physitian wraps his bitter Pills in Gold, only to beguile the Phantasie of his Patient. And if so, for Religion's sake let us impose a better office on God than to bee the Devil's Factor in procuring sins. *Farre be it from us* (saith Tertullian) *to thinke God contrives or consents to Man's ruine* or, like a Broker for Hell, underwrites our Bill of Sale.

If I would stretch my thoughts to the very center and lowest degree of basenes, they could not thinke a vilenesse below a Seducer, an office which posed that great Master of language, S. Hierome, whose sharpe pen knew to display the darkest Vice and dissect the foulest Body of sinne; but to deale with this hee had not words nor art enough, is faine to cry for helpe to expresse himselfe: *What shall I say of thee, thou childe of the Serpent, minister of Satan, who by thy seducements hast couched many sins in one?*

'Tis more Religion to deny God, than to make so inglorious a confession of Him as to repute Him sinne's Agent. The *King of Glory* is an usurped Title if hee trade in deeds of shame; nor is Hee a competent Judge of sinne, if his practice makes Him confederate in the sinne which Hee condemnes. *Let no man therefore say when hee is tempted, "I am tempted of God", for God cannot be tempted to evill, neither tempteth he any man.*

But doth God not Tempt? How then shall wee reconcile Scripture to Scripture, Moses to S. James? who tells the people, in Deut. 13, *Tentat vos Dominus Deus vester; The Lord your God tempts you.* S. Augustine reconciles both by a Distinction. There is *Tentatio Deceptionis,* and *Probationis;* or (as he expresses himselfe elsewhere) *There is one kinde of temptation wherein God proves and makes triall of the faith of his servants, and this himselfe sometimes vouchsafes to owne; and there is another temptation of deceit, which allures men to sinne, whereof He is by no*

IX. And leade us not into Temptation

meanes the Author. Notwithstanding, though He be not the *cause* of it, He *Permits* even this—so Alexander Hales. God may be said to Lead us into Temptation, *not that He effects it, but that he gives way to it, which is by a Desertion, and the withdrawing of his helpe* (as S. Augustine exemplifies it). Alex.Hales *part.4:pag.177* Aug.*De ser.Dom. in Monte,1:2, c.14:Tom.4*

In which I have unveiled the sense of this Petition, which is not to imply God a party in Temptation, but a Deliverer to rescue us from it, or to avert and hinder and breake the force of it. *Ne inferas* or *Ne inducas,* that is, *Ne patiaris induci*—so S. Augustine explaines. And S. Cyprian reads it, *Suffer us not* to be lead into Temptation. Cyprian *De Orat. Dom.* [284]

But *Permission implies Consent:* nay, it is a kinde of Will, one of the five branches into which the Will is subdivided; and so neere allied unto the Fact, that the Tragedian delivered it for truth, *Peccatum qui non vetat cum potest, iubet:* Toleration of a fault makes an Accessory, and *not to hinder a mischiefe when 'tis in his power, is to command it.* How then shall wee acquite God for being Accessory to the Temptation, since He who by his least word might hinder, suffers it? Or how is Hee unguilty of Adam's fall, *when He permitted* the Serpent *to Tempt him, whom Hee knew would fall?* Tis Lombard's question. The Reply is easily form'd, nor can he that weighs it aright impute any the least part of Adam's trespasse either to God's Foreknowledge or Permission. Senec.*Traged.* Petr.Lombard *Lib.2:dist.23*

First, for his Prescience. 'Tis true, God foresaw man would fall, yet did not his foresight cause it. *Hee foresaw that lucklesse event, but not established it, not compeld it, not conjoyn'd it.* For as He Foresaw it, so He forewarned Adam, dealing plainly with him, that if he eat of the forbidden fruit, he should die the death. Were it not strange proceeding, to endite mee of Conspiracie for telling another of a danger which hee might have shunn'd but would not? If it be injustice to Man, 'tis irreligion to God. Therefore we cannot lay the fault of Adam any where but on himselfe, who would not apprehend the danger by taking that warning which God gave him. *God no way the Cause of Adam's Fall,* [285] *either in regard of his Prescience or permission*

Now in his Permission of the Tempter, God was lesse culpable than in the other. Neither doe I see what God could have done more to prevent man's ruine than what He did, unlesse He should have lockt him up against all attempts by making him impregnable, and deafe to the tongue of the Charmer, and so incapable of temptation. Which had God done, he had some way degraded the dignitie of his Workemanship, by forming him so that he could not be corrupted, but must be good whether he would or no. 2.

[286]

It was more Glory to leave him to the libertie of his Election, and more Honour for Man to have the *Power to resist Temptation,* than to have beene guarded with such a privilege as that he *Could not bee tempted at all.* Petr.Lombard *L.2:dist.23.*[a]

This Power had Man, by vertue whereof he might have stood the shocke of any Temptation; had he not willingly disabled himselfe. So that he cannot complaine that he was vanquished, since he never stood out at all; *he yeelded upon parley, not conquest; nor was he overcome, but by a base composition surrendred himselfe.* Nor can he complaine that God preordain'd him to destruction by giving him a Crazy Temper, putting so much Earth and frailtie in his constitution which must needes depresse him. *We cannot thinke that an ill complexion which was so made up that man might not have sinn'd if he would;* Nor can wee lay any blot upon God's justice *for punishing him who wilfully and without constraint yeelded himselfe to sinne.* Augustin.

[287]

Petr.Lombard *L.2.dist.24*

You may observe how carefull God was in preventing Man's ruine, who did not only warne him of the Danger when hee was yet out of the Distance of it, but in the very conflict it selfe suggested a meanes to evade it. *He did* (as St. Paul sayes) *with the Temptation make a way to escape.* For though he suffered, that is, not Inhibited the Tempter, yet He Inhibited him to appeare in any other shape but of the Serpent. The Devill, to effect his ends and to beguile us, can transforme himself into an *Angell of Light.* But here he was restrained for [from] assuming that or any other shape but the worst, That so our first Parents might take warning from his outside, and suspect the danger of his Offer and Treaty from the forme of the Tempter. 1 Cor. 10:13

[288]

Which great mercy, began to our first Parents, He continues to us. As He restrained then the Manner of the Temptation, so doth He still limit the Power of it towards us. When He brought Job to the test, suffering the Devill to be the Minerall to separate that pure Gold from the drosse which embased all the rest of his linage, his bad Friends and worse Wife, He bound his hands, suffered him to doe nothing but by His speciall Warrant. When Hee submitted his substance to his malice, Hee excepted his Body: *Upon himselfe shalt thou not stretch out thine hand.* And when Hee enlarged his Commission upon his Body, hee charged him to attempt nothing against his Life, by every step and proceeding directing his malice to a fortunate end, that after this probation, hee might enrich Job's latter daies with blessings more ample than the first.

Let not then a misgovern'd curiositie thrust thee into any impertinent searches or suspicious thoughts of God, as if Hee conspir'd to make thee sinne by scattering temptations in thy way for thee to stoope at; neither be so irreligiously acute to see more in God's permission than He meant.

If thou wilt needs know why God suffered Temptations, Let this pious resolution silence all other questions of this nature, with this answer rest modestly satisfied: *He suffers Temptation for our good,* not to occasion our Fall, but *from thence to take occasion to crowne us.* From those Temptations, which wee are assisted by his Grace to withstand, He takes occasion to reward us. And let mee say with one who (I hope) devoutly meant it: for those Temptations which vanquish us, *Hee suffers them, that from thence wee may borrow some colour to excuse our faults:* For those Delinquents finde an easier way to pardon that can say, though they did the fact, they were drawne and tempted to it.

If, then, Temptations have so blest an Issue, why doe wee shun them in our Praiers? Why doe wee not rather cherish and desire them? The Schoolemen, as peremptory in the stating of a doubt as they are bold in their *Quæres* [Questions], doe halfe affirme That they are to be desired. *The weakest sort of Christians* (say they) *must pray for patience and victory if Temptation assaile them. But Christians of better growth, that dare presume on their owne abilities and God's assistance, may profitably desire it.* To strengthen which assertion they urge S. Gregorie's speech, *A Saint, next vertue, covets nothing more than Temptation.* For my part, I should easily subscribe to them, could they produce any of so confirm'd a beleefe which Temptation could not shake; but since I finde none of that proofe—no, not amongst the Disciples, whome Christ upbraids with the title of *holigopistoi,* men of little faith—I shall rest in that modest determination of S. Chrysostome and Theophylact: *Wee are all at best unprofitable Servants, and at strongest too weake to wrastle with a Temptation.*

Therefore wee must not wilfully thrust our selves into the mouth of danger, or draw temptations upon us. Such forwardnesse is not Resolution but Rashnesse, nor is it the fruit of a well-ordered Faith, but an over-daring Presumption. There is no Ship so tall built or strongly ribb'd, which can be confident shee will not founder in the next storme: nor is there any man of such a confidence who, if a Tempest or Temptation rise up against him, can bee assured that at the instant he can call up so much Reason and Religion as to withstand it.

Would you not judge him mad who, being come to an Anchor in a safe Road, would, like the Dolphin, hunt the storme, and chuse to ride it out at the Maine Sea? Is it not enough thou hast an Antidote to expell poison, but thou must turne Emperick upon thy selfe, hazard the empoisoning of thine owne Body, to try the power of thy Medicine? 'Tis no discreet Religion which seekes out dangers and glories in Temptations; nor is hee *wise to salvation,* who presents himself to that hazard which Christ taught him to pray against. *To hazard a set battell in hope of a doubtfull victory, is to out-dare a man's judgment,* saith S. Hierome. 'Tis possible that he who exposes himselfe to the danger of a fight may overcome, but 'tis probable he may fall: The perill is certaine, the victory doubtfull. In un-needfull Temptations, I had rather distrust my selfe, than make trial of my strength in apparent disadvantage.

Certainly I will pray against Temptation: 'tis my Saviours rule, *Orate ne intretis in Tentationem: Pray lest yee enter into Temptation*—but if it surprise mee, I will pray to Him *Not to lead mee into it,* that is, not to deliver mee into the power of it, but to give me grace *to beare it manfully.* Which is the full scope of this Petition, so Isidor. Pelusiot expresses it: *Not to be swallowed up in Tempta-*

IX. And leade us not into Temptation

tion. And Thomas Aquinas is bold to say that herein *wee doe not pray that wee be not Tempted, but that wee be not Overcome by Temptation: Non petimus ut non tentemur, sed ut non a Tentatione vincamur.* Th.Aquin.*2a.2æ quæst.83;art.9 in conclus.*

The Glosse sayes, He is *Lead into temptation* who is overthrowne by it. So that *'tis not ill to bee Tempted* (Christ you know was, and yet without sinne)—*the mischiefe growes by yeelding to it.* In this sense doe I understand S. Augustine's words, where he distinguisheth betwixt *Tentari, & In Tentationem induci.* The First implies the Trials God layes on his Servants, the Last those Occasions of danger into which, by withdrawing his helpe, He suffers us, by the various Ministers of sinne both Externall and Internall, to be lead. Gloss in Mat.6

[294]

Which are so many, that if wee will compute our danger, wee need not send out our wishes to meet Temptations or bring them home to us—they come too swiftly, and unbidden, like rough winds that blow from every corner of the skie; and in that number as if each minute were computed by them, So plentifull is the spawne of sinne in our waters. Therefore S. Bernard cries out, *Woe is mee! I am environed with warre,* and *hemm'd in on all sides with Temptations.* 4. *Temptations*

Biel fitly compares them to the creeping things of the earth, which are numberlesse. S. Bernard likens them to the little Foxes in the Canticles, which with cunning insinuation lurke in every branch of our Vine, in every angle of the Body, nourished at our owne boord and by the same diet which feeds our Passions. *The cause of perturbations and passions arises from the humours,* and these perturbations are the Tinder at which the Devill lights his Temptations. Gabriel Biel *Lect. 77 de Miss.*
[295] Bernard *In Cantic: Ser.64*
Bern.*Ser.4.in fest.omn.Sanct.*

To make which more plausible, 'tis ever his cunning practise to attire them in that dresse and Livery which best suits each man's Humour and Complexion. To the phantasie of the Melancholy he whispers nothing but horrour, plying him with all Objects that may bring him to madnesse or despaire. To the Sanguine Complexion he presents those wanton delights whereunto naturally it leanes. The Phlegmatick, like Marishes which every Tide overflows, he seekes to lay quite under water by the habit of that moist vice which, like a Deluge, covers the greater part of the Earth, Drunkennesse. Lastly, the Furious and Cholericke hee prompts to quarrels, cherishing that unruly flame so long, till he have made them beleeve that Murder is the triumph of Reputation; so causing them to purchase the opinion of an unhappy valour by Bloudshed. At which lucklesse period he leaves them, to the torture of a Guilty Conscience in this Life and the fearefull expectation of vengeance in the next. Thus doth the Devill, like a politique Enginer, besiege us in our owne works, turning our Passions, like Daggers, upon our owne brests. [296]

'Twas this busie Tempter who made a suit to Christ to sift and winnow his Apostles: *Satan hath desired to winnow you as wheat.* Is it not time then to put in our Crosse plea? To make it our suit to Christ to keepe us from his sleights, that wee be not entrapt by him whose trade and businesse is to deceive—Suffer us not to be seduced by him whose proper office it is to Tempt, *Lest we be tempted by him that tempts.* Luk.22:31
Aug. *De Civit. Dei,lib.6*
1 Thes.3:5

But though the Devill be the chiefe Instigator of sinne, the Flesh is the Instrument. Nay, saith Origen, *Were there no other Devill, wee have one at home,* an invisible Devill that lodgeth in the Bloud, *the seditious Appetite,* which urges us to perpetuall mutiny against the good motions of God's Spirit. This Devill of Concupiscence, which *daily entises and drawes us away* (as S. James hath it), must wee exorcise too; beseeching God that He will not, by forsaking us, deliver us over to our selves, nor suffer our owne lusts, which maintaine the hot Trafficke with Hell, to betray us to Shame and Perdition. [297]

Jac.1:14

Againe, because every new Opinion or strange doctrine (wherewith our Times, like over-ranke soiles, abound) is, as Vincent Lyrinensis calls it, a *Temptation,* drawing a Traine of new Sectaries after it; because our Religion is planted betwixt two extremes, both which have but one End, leading us by different pathes to destruction. Wee beseech God so to confirme us, that wee bee not delivered into the power of their perswasions who, upon the false foundation of *Merit,* raise up a Babel of Presumption, from whose steepe and elevated top they precipitate their giddy followers (as the Tempter, when he had carried Christ to the highest pinnacle, would have cast Him downe). Nor [298]

Matt.4:6

yet suffer us to bee dejected or depressed by the heavy Doctrine of those Teachers whose tongues are heavier than the hands of Moses, when he was supported by Aaron and Hur. Indeed they preach Moses, not Christ—a pound of the Law for a dramme of the Gospell; never well but when they are busied in arguments of Judgement and Reprobation; with which Killing Letter they wound those Consciences which they should bind up, their Doctrine being *Non tam Ædificatio quam Tentatio*—not to edifie but to demolish, to plucke downe the *Living stones* of Christ's Church by despaire.

Suffer us not to be seduced by either of those Spirits—the one is a Spirit of Aire, the other of Fire—But let thy calme, peacefull Spirit so compose our Faith, so settle our Religion, that thus established it may rest sure upon its owne Base and Center, the *Word of Truth*, not to be shaken by these, or disordered by any the like Temptations. For *To depart from Faith* by Apostasie, nay to bee brought into any degree of Revolt, either by recoiling against the Truth, or by any unsteadinesse, any hesitation to stagger in it, *is to be Lead into Temptation.*

Lastly, because the whole World feeds us with vanity, and foments us daily with delights, wee here beseech God to uphold us that wee fall not on these rockes of Temptation, or bee induced, for the short-liv'd happinesse of this world, to forfait the everlasting joyes of the World to come.

For as *Hee* only can lead us into those joyes, so *Hee* alone can *Lead* us out of the Labyrinth of *Temptation,* wherein without His guidance wee are apt to lose our selves.

However, then, those Arch-hereticks Pelagius and Cælestius will not be beholding to this clew to bring them out, nor will have this Petition so understood as if men implored God's helpe to hold them up from falling by Temptation, presuming it in their owne power to resist sinne and not to accept of a Temptation (which Opinion is sharpely sentenced by severall Councils), yet *We have not so learned Christ;* Nor beare wee so sleight regard to that Prayer which his lips authorized as to thinke any part of it superfluous, or that Hee would instruct us to make a suit of that unto his Father, which was in our owne power to grant or to deny. Wee are assured, though there be many Windowes, and Ports and Doores for Temptation to enter at, there is but one Key, to let us out or to locke us up against it, God's Assistant or Prevenient Grace. *By thee shall I be delivered from an Hoast* of Temptations, cryes the Psalmist; And it is God's voluntary promise, *Liberabo te ab hora Tentationis*—I will guard thee so sure in all thy wayes, that no Temptations shall prevaile against thee.

Which promise He performes either by giving us ability to decline them when they offer themselves at us, Or by allaying them in such fashion that they become healthfull Medicines to cure, not poysons to corrupt us; and happy Probations, not to waste but to refine us—As Gold runs purest from the Furnace, finding no abatement of the substance, but the drosse only; Or by apportioning them to our strength, that they doe not over-match us; so though Hee gives us not Peace, yet Hee gives us meanes, by a faire defensive warre, to hold out the siege against them.

Be this then our comfort, that as Temptation hath some ill in it, so it hath much good. It was said of the Conspiracy against Julius Cæsar: If in that action there were any thing of glory, it belonged to Brutus, but all the malice and cruelty of the designe was imputed to Cassius. I make a juster application: Whatsoever good is occasioned by Temptation, we must ascribe it to God, but the malignity which accompanies it belongs to the Devill. S. Augustine saies, God's purpose in imposing trials is not to hurt; And S. Ambrose says, though *the Devill tempts to destroy us, yet God,* when either Hee tryes us or suffers us to be tempted by him, *doth it to crowne us (Diabolus tentat ut subvertat, Deus tentat ut coronet).*

Blessed be the Spirit of Comfort, that disposes his malice to our happinesse, and so fortifies us that, though He suffer us to be tempted, *He will not suffer us to bee tempted above our strength;* Who though He may some way Permissively be said to *Lead us into Temptation,* doth not put us upon any Forlorne Hope where wee are sure to perish, but in the noblest sense of Leading, *Leads* us as a Generall doth his Souldiers, encouraging them to give on upon the enemy in the assurance of a victory; or as Hee lead our Generall Christ Jesus to be tempted of the Devill. Blessed bee our

Leader Christ Jesus, who in his Gospell hath left a rich Legacy to comfort us in all our conflicts: *Be of good comfort, I have overcome the world.* Wee are to bee assured in the Apostle's confidence: *In that he himselfe was tempted, hee is able to succour us when wee are tempted.* And blessed be the God of Hoasts who, through the Intercession of his Sonne, will give us the *Victory* not onely over *Temptation,* but over our Last Enemies, *Hell* and *Death.* Amen.

John 16:33
Heb.2:18
[303]

X. BUT DELIVER US FROM EVILL

[304]

Christianitie is but a Spirituall Warfare, and the chiefe weapon is our Prayer—*Arma nostra preces & lachrymae:** You know who was the Generall of the Field and Leader of this Battell, who ordered the Files, ranked the severall Petitions of this Prayer, and cast it into this Sevenfould Forme.

It is not only the propertie of an expert Generall to give on upon the Enemy, but to goe off as well. Hee must not only provoke his Souldiers to make bold Charges upon the Adversaries, but when the day is ended, provide for a safe and honourable Retrait. Our blessed Saviour, that Hee might shew himselfe a perfect Leader, not only able to instruct us in the fight but carefull to bring us off againe, see how he hath ordered the manner of our Retirement; Guarding our returne with safetie and fortifying the last part of his Prayer with the full Power and fruit of his Mediation, *Deliverance:* As He once placed the Pillar of Fire behind the Israelites, to secure them from the danger of the Egyptians, who then had them in chase.

[305]

I know, if wee only looke with carnall eies, no Prospect offers it selfe to our view but feare and terrour on all sides: *Temptation* (like Egypt) at our heeles, in the preceding Petition; and *Evill* (like the Canaanite)—nay, the extremity of all Evills, beyond the Temporall Scourage of Ashur, the Punishment of Sinne—before us in This. So that we might for ever languish in that distracted amazement which seized the Servant of Elisha, when hee beheld the whole Country of Samaria begirt with Souldiers and no meanes of Escape. But when Faith hath cleared, and devout Prayer obtained that favour at God's hand for us which the Prophet there did for his Servant, the Opening of our eyes, we shall then perceive that our Trenches are stronger then all the workes raisd by the Enemy; that there are many Powers levied in this name of *Deliverance;* that Chariots of Fire are our Convoy, and as he there confessed, they that are with us are stronger than any that oppose us. Indeed, *If God be on our side, who can be against us?* Who can doubt of successe in his Prayer or safety from all danger, when Salvation beares him off and Deliverance marches in his Rere-gard?

(Ezek.32:22)

2 King 6:15, 16, 17

Vers.17 [306]
Rom.8:31

Deliver us from Evill.

The scope then of this last Petition is Deliverance: *Libera nos,* Deliver us.
The Danger wee desire to bee secured from: *A malo,* from evill. That is,
Evill Present, and Evill to come: *A malo Culpæ, & a Malo Pœnæ*—From the *Evill of Sinne* in this World, And from the *Evill of Punishment* in the World to come.

Division
1.
2.
1.
2.
1.
Deliver us

God did not onely intend his owne Glory when Hee raised up so excellent a peece of Building as Man, but had a Purpose also afterwards to Glorifie that Creature whom Hee then made. How that Building was defaced, or who was the accursed instrument to demolish it, I mention not here: The meanes of his Reparation, not the Manner of his Decay, is now my Argument.

[307]

To this repaire of ruin'd Man, and the re-setling of him in that way of Glory unto which the Ordinance of his Maker first disposed him, nothing contributes more than Prayer, which is the very Picture of our Mediator, daily soliciting the accomplishment of that happy worke which Hee undertooke for us, *Deliverance,* and whose maine intention is to prop us up from falling into the Habit of Sinne, and from that Habit to the lowest degree of Woe, Hell fire—*Deliver us.*

'Tis sometimes seene that Griefe makes us eloquent: I am sure danger often makes us devout.

---

*Our arms are prayers and tears.

Necessity prompts men to seeke releese, and the apprehension of an ill, ready to fall upon us, sends us to God for shelter.

Doubtlesse Religion owes much to feare. Petronius, an understanding Heathen, affirmed that the Heathens his Brethren did owe the Invention of their Gods to it:

Primus in Orbe, Deos fecit timor.

[308] 'Twas feare at first opened the eye of Nature, & made her, even blindfold, to groape after some Deity that ruled the World, and kept all the Elements in awe.

In the Prophesie of Jonas, wee finde that the fearefull Tempest gave motion to those men's zeale which perhaps before was wholly becalmed, and the working of the Sea wrought them into a Religion. When the Wind and the Billow chide loudest, the shrill accent of their feare was heard above it; The tumultuous exhortation of each one to pray unto his God spake in as much noise as the storme. Nor did the terrour of their Shipwracke, which then threatned them, employ the industry of their owne prayers, but reacht so farre, that it awaked the sleepy Devotion of Jonah: *What meanest thou, O sleeper? Arise and call upon thy God, if so be that God will thinke upon us, that wee perish not.* I doe not wonder if a furious Sea frighted those Sailors into Devotion, since the Disciples themselves, having put to Sea, and running the like hazard by a storme which had neere buried the Ship, forgetting the confidence wherewith faith should have armed them, and remitting al trust either in the goodnes or power of their Pilot, (then aboord with them though a sleepe), being now almost growne desperate by their feares, raised Him with this loud cry: *Master save us, we perish.*

Jonah 1:6

[309]

(Mt.8.25)

[a] There is nothing so naturall to Man as to call for helpe, because there is not in the World a creature exposed to so much want and danger as hee. And how ever the Cathari, out of the proud conceit of their owne Purity, omitted this Petition, wee know the very Condition of his Being is a Misery, and his Conversation full of Sinne. Well may our tongues then bee perfect in the language of this Petition, *Deliver us from evill,* When Nature and Conscience, our owne Infirmitie and the expectation of an heavier sentence prompt us to it. Danger even now grapples with us, and Judgement waits so close upon us, that both in Veiw and at Distance, Neere hand and Farre off, for the Present and for the Future, in Possession and in Reversion, our miseries are intaild upon us. Where there are so many Quues given us, we cannot but be expert in the repetition; and when woe is the constant Scene, *Libera nos* should bee our Mother Tongue: Deliver us from Evil; *A Malo Præsenti & Futuro:* From ills Present and to Come.

[310]

2. From Evill

This is the Dialect of Nature and of Conscience; By the Rules of this unhappy *Syntaxis* doe they both most congruously speake. Life is a Misery, and Sinne a Sting, and Death a terrour. Life exposes us to the assault and opportunity of Sin, and Sin binds us over to the sentence of Death at the last Sessions, when the World shall bee arraigned in flames. *Deliver us* therefore *A Malo Vitæ:* from an *Evill Life,* and from a *Worse Death.*

I. A Malo vitæ

Wee first grow familiar with our Evills when wee take acquaintance with Life, Whose whole Voyage is so clogg'd with variety of encombrance, that 'tis an affliction but to carry our Contemplations thorow, or travell it with our thoughts.

[311] I know, in the sense of many a wretch, Death is an happinesse, and there can be no such exquisite torment as to prolong an unwilling life. I doe not onely include in this speech those whom Misery hath tired out, and so made weary of living: Wee must allow them to be partiall, and justly to prejudicate Life. My speech reaches to all, and in this Generall Appeale I make Common Understanding the Judge, and on that ground pronounce that there is none who indifferently weighs the troubles of Life when it is calmest, and our quiet in Death, but will rest upon S. Ambrose his Conclusion: *So abundant are Life's Crosses, so scarce the Comforts, that compared to it Death is an Ease, not a Punishment,* and a Curing Medicine, not a Corrosive.

When we shall thinke that these bodies of ours are made up only to be dissolv'd againe, As Printing-Characters are put together only to serve the short purpose of the Author—which done, and the Impression finished, they are taken asunder againe, and throwne into their Cells; When we shall thinke that discord lodges in our Temper, that the contention of the Elements rules the Bloud, and that the victory of every predominant Humour and Qualitie in the Body turnes to a mortall Disease to strike us into Dust; When wee shall thinke Youth is a hot Fever, and Age a cold Palsey; That one-and-twenty is a Temptation, and Threescore an Affliction; That the Entrance of Life is with Labour, and the Catastrophe, the utmost extent of it, a meere inveterate Sorrow; we shall finde good cause to approve their Custome for the best, that used to mourne upon the Birth-day, and laugh at the Funeralls of their Friends, welcomming the Nativity of their Children with teares, but celebrating their Deaths with Feasts.

It was the speech of Gregory: *If wee judiciously apprehend the whole cast of life, or our owne Actions, wee shall perceive* a perpetuall Sentence, a Doome hanging over us, *That our Dayes are evill,* and all the Circumstances of Life or Time, but as *so many Titles to misery.* Which may not onely warrant us with S. Paul to desire a dissolution, *Cupiens dissolvi;* but with Elias, fainting under the consideration of his sorrowes, to make a voluntary resignation of his weary life, *It is enough, O Lord, take my soule.* Deliver us therefore *a Malo vitæ,* from those Evils and Crosses which make Life distastefull or dangerous to us.

It were happy if all Man's Misery were lockt up in himselfe, if the summe of his unhappinesse consisted in his owne sorrowes; for then Death would Cure, at least Finish them. But the Steme arising up from his corruption flies up to Heaven, and breeds ill odour in the nostrils of God: God is exasperated and troubled, nay, grieved by his Sinnes. *Præbuisti mihi laborem in iniquitatibus tuis*—'Tis his Complaint in Esay—*Thou hast wearied mee with thy sinnes.* Because therefore this Dilassation, this tiring of God, this abuse of his Patience may kindle Him into a flame of displeasure, we pray to be delivered *a Malo Culpæ,* from those sinnes which endanger his wrath: *Deliver us from this Evill.*

I know, each Sinne beares a Whip at the Backe, and like the Scorpion carries a Venome which few Antidotes can expell.

Vice is its owne Mulct, and every bad Thought is but a new capacity of Vengeance. Our Affections are our Penalties: The Master of the Sentences calls them *Pœnales Affectus.* Our owne Passions, like Plummets tied at the feet of men throwne into the Sea, weigh us downe. Anger, like a Calenture, burnes us up; and Drunkennesse, like a Dropsie, melts us into water; Gluttony choakes us with surfet, and Incontinence rewards us with disease. Job saies the sentence is now absolutely past and gone out upon the wicked, *His bones are full of the sinnes of his Youth;* And so filld, that hee cannot lave them out of his Conscience, or empty them into the Grave. That earth which annihilates all other things cannot concoct such a crudity as sinne. The faults of Life survive in Death, *Et cum eo in pulvere dormient:* and as men sleepe upon their owne condemnation with the Axe under their Pillowes, so wee on them. *They sleepe with us in the Dust,* and when the last Earthquake shall shake off those hills of Dust that cover us, those sinnes will rise up with us, and produce an Evidence whose bloudy Character Time or Rottennesse could not blot out; by which they will deliver us unto a Torture more Immortall than the malice of our Inditement.

If our Prayers, then, rest onely here, and sue for no further Deliverance then *A Malo Culpæ,* from Temporall Miseries and Diseases, or from those Mischiefes which actually our sins cast upon us in this Life, they travell but halfe way, leaving the greatest part of the Journey, of best advantage or of most dangerous Consequence, behinde them.

We therefore enlarge our Petition, and pray to bee delivered *A Malo Pœnæ,* from *the Evill of the last Punishment;* for this is the full scope and meaning of the words.

And yet wee doe not exclude the avoidance of those Punishments which are laid upon us whilest wee live here. The Attachment of a Principall involves al that are Partakers. Sinne is a Party in Death, and Temporall Punishments are as Decrees binding us over to an heavier Sentence, unlesse a Timely Penitence reverse that Sentence and sue out our Pardon. The Fever in my bloud is a Figure

206 AN EXPOSITION UPON THE LORD'S PRAYER

of the last Fire which will burne both Body and Soule, if the Teares of Contrition quench it not in the meane space.

As, therefore, in the latitude of this word *Evill* wee pray against all kindes of Evill, whether they be *Mala Naturæ* or *Culpæ* or *Pœnæ: Naturall Evills,* as Deformitie of the Body, Blinde, or Lame; Misse-shapen Births such as Monsters are made up in; Or *Morall Evills,* Sinnes that deforme the Soule and make the Minde of Man a Monster or Prodigie to affright even himselfe; Or lastly, *Evills of Punishment* ordained for the vindication of those sinnes; So, under the title of *Punishment,* we are allowed to pray against all kinds thereof, whether they bee (as the Schooles distribute them) Temporall, or Eternall.

And yet Bonaventure apparells some of these Temporall Punishments laid upon us in such a Phrase as makes them rather to be embraced than shunn'd: *There be some Punishments ordained for the overthrow of God's Enemies; There bee others appointed for the Reclamation of his Servants*—of which sort are those Fatherly Corrections and gentle Visitations whereby God humbles us, to raise us up to a higher degree in his favour and set us a step neerer Heaven. These are the Christians' Presse-money, whereby God bindes them to his service. *Castigat omnem filium &c:* He chastens every sonne hee loves. Wee doe not pray against these Castigations, that conduce to the bettering or improving of our Soules; These are not angry Curses darted against us, but Blessings: *Beatus quem tu corripis.*

They are the other, Vindicative, Punishments wee seeke to decline: Those that speake in Mortall Diseases, in Famine and Bloudshed.

Nor doe we only pray against these. All Earth's Punishments, compared to those that are treasured up against the day of wrath, are Mercies.

This Petition is but an Armour to beare off the heat of the last fearefull Day. Famine, or Warre, or Disease, can onely kill the Body, but the finall Punishment is an eternall Warre, waged with my Soule and Body too, that never admits a Truce; A Famine which time cannot determine nor Comfort releeve. As our Saviour bids us rather feare those can kill both Body and Soule, than those who onely have power to destroy the Body: So hath Hee instructed us rather to pray against the everlasting Torture of the Soule, than the Momentany Discrutiations of the Body. The principall aime of this Petition is leveld against the principall Misery, the Eternall Punishment of the Life to come—*Deliver us from Evill.*

By which *Malum Pœnæ,* Future Misery, what is meant, what *Species* of Punishment it is, I shall first shew by a Negative, and then Define.

First, this Evill is not *Purgatory*: For that which hath no being cannot be the subject of this Petition. Purgatory (I confesse) is a fine Tale for a Romanza, but a ridiculous History to bee brought into a Church; It being capable of no colour of Truth. And therefore it was one of the wisest Acts the Council of Trent ever did, at that time when it decreed *That the Doctrine of Purgatory should be beleeved by the people, taught by the Bishops and Priests,* even in the Body of the Decree to prohibit any Disputation or curious search after it. They suspected, and justly, it would lie open to too much infirmity, and shame the Abettors by the folly of its Pedigree. For what ever they vaunt in the Præludium to the Ninth Session, bringing the Holy Ghost, the Scripture, and the Fathers to authorize their Invention, Undoubtedly the Father was an Amorite, the Mother an Hittite. It owes the true Parentage, the Naturall extraction, to Philosophy and Poetry.

It was first phansied by Plato, foure hundred yeeres before Christ, Who in his booke *De Anima* reports the severall successe of deceased Men. Those (saith hee) who have lived very well, are convayed to the purest Regions and Islands of the blessed; Those that have lived but indifferently are wafted over Acheron unto a Fiery Marish, where they suffer for a time, and then *kathairomenoi apoluontai*—being Purged and Purified in that Fire, they are released; But Mortall, Capitall Offenders, *aniatōs echontes,* they are cast into Tartarus, from whence there is no release. Virgil confirmes this:

X. But deliver us from Evill

*Aliis sub gurgite vasto
Infectum eluitur scelus aut exuritur igni.**

So Homer, *Odyss. (alpha* and *gamma.)*
So Ovid, 2. *Fast.*
And so the Alchoran, *Artic. 10.*

Here, then, without all controversie it began, and from thence obtained some credit amongst men addicted to the reading of Philosophers and Poets.

Origen, a Man of rare Parts and great Wit, but subject (as great Wits are) to the extravagancie of conceit, was the first learned Convertite that named it in his Writings. Who, notwithstanding though he held a Purgatory, held not that any Prayers were availeable to deliver Soules from thence. And besides, his Purgatory differs very much from that of the Church of Rome. The Romish Purgatory takes place immediatly after the end of this life, Origen's not till after the day of Judgement. The Church of Rome holds their Purgatory is ordained for men of a middle condition or state of goodnesse, Origen extends his to all, even the very best. (It is the fift Article for which hee was condemned.) His Authority gaind amongst his many Schollers some private Adherents, but yet found such cold entertainement in the Greeke Church, wherein he lived, that in the Councill held at Basil (Ann.Dom.550), upon an Apologie then delivered by the Easterne Pastors, it was scornefully exploded and by full consent cast out, as a new groundlesse imagination—So the Apologie runs: Wee never heard from the Doctors of our Church there was any such thing as Purgatory. So, then, howsoever the Councill of Trent give it out for a thing generally currant in the Catholike Church, you see it was not so, since the Easterne Church opposed it from the first. And so Roffensis (whom they have reason to beleeve) confesses: *The Greekes to this day doe not beleeve there is a Purgatory* (&c.) It was then rejected by the Greeke Church, yet not extinguisht so, but that it began to breake out againe in the Latine—I meane Nam'd, but not Defin'd as a thing *De Fide*.

S. Augustine, though hee mentions it, concludes nothing for it; nay, hee is so farre from that, hee confesses ingenuously it began from the Platonicks and Heathen Authors. And in his booke *De Hæres.* hee registers Origen's opinion of Purgatory for an Heresie—which had hee beleeved, sure, hee never would have done.

In this uncertaine manner, for a long time, like a sparke raked up in Embers, it lay, sometimes glowing, but with no confident apparance at all, untill the Councill of Florence, held Anno 1439. There it was set a foot and decreed for. In which Session, though they allotted it a being, they could not assigne it an *Ubi*: They would have it somewhere, but neither they nor any Writers since them could ever yet resolve *where*. Some will have it to bee in Hell; from whence a new question springs, *An Gehenna & Purgatorium sint in eodem loco?*† Others, in the Center of the Earth. Eckius placeth it in the bottome of the Sea. But Lorichius, in a distempered Conscience and troubled Minde. Olaus Magnus translates it to Heckelburge, in Norway. Bellarmine, out of Gregory *(Moral. lib. 15: cap. 30)*, contends that Purgatory is in Mount Ætna or Lipara, or Hiera and the rest of the Vulcanean Islands. But because the matter which nourished the Fire in those places hath (as Fazellus reports) long since failed, Surius layes the Scæne at Hekla in Iseland, *Quod ibi erumpant Flammæ.*‡ It was ill lucke that Tierra del Fuego, in the South of America, was not discovered in his time. It had been the best use that Region could ever have beene put to; And I am perswaded that in the whole world a fitter place, either in regard of compasse of Land, or plenty of Fire, could not have beene thought of to receive this plantation of Purgatory.

---

*Others have the wickedness with which they are stained washed away beneath a huge whirlpool, or burnt away by flames.
†Whether Hell and Purgatory may be in the same place?
‡Because flames burst out from there.

Æneid.6:(741–42)

Vid.Chemnitium
*In Exam.
Concil.Trident.
Sess.9:Decret. de Purgator.*
[321]

[322]

*Apolog.Græc.
pag.119*

Roffens.*Art.18:*
pag.86.b.

[323] Aug.*De Civit. Dei
lib.21:c.13*
Haeres.43

Eckius *In Enchirid.*
Lorich.*Instit.Cathol:
De 12 Fidei
Artic.*
[324]

Fazellus.Id. *De
Ætna, ad Annum
1554*[a]
Surius *Hist.
ad Annum1537* [a]
Vid. Ortelium.

Of the eruption of these fires, see Purchase *Pilgrim.part.3:
pag.939*

As they could never agree about the *Place,* so neither about the *Tormentors* in Purgatory, whether they were Angels, as some thought, or Devils. Neither about the *Torments,* whether they consist of Fire onely, and then whether that Fire be Corporeall or Incorporeall; or whether of Water and Fire; or of Frost and Cold; or of none of these, but of disturbed affections, perplexed with faint Hopes and certaine Feares: So Lorichius.

Neither about the *Duration* of those Torments, whether all the Soules condemned to that Fire languish there untill the day of Judgement, as Dionys. Carthusian; Or some onely, and not all, as Beda; Or whether they lie there onely for the space of Ten yeares and no more, as Dominicus à Soto; or untill the Pope pleases to enlarge them, as others. Or whether they have intermission from their paines upon Sundaies and Holy-dayes, as Durandus and Prudentius (cited by Bellarmine); Or whether those paines by little and little are remitted and diminished, as Bellarmine.

Neither about the *Causes* or Occasions of Those Torments—Whether Veniall sinnes are onely punished there, as Gregor., or Veniall and Mortall sinnes too, as Eckius. Nor, lastly, about the *Condition* and State of Soules in Purgatory. For some hold that the Soules punished in that Fire endure a Torment which surpasseth all the most exquisite Torments in this life. But the Rhemists thinke the Soules in Purgatory to bee in a more happy and blessed Condition than any men that live in this World. And Tho. Aquinas, with Bellarmine, thinke it probable *Animas Igne Purgatorio tortas, pro nobis orare & impetrare** (Both which are cited by Emanuel Sà, *Aphorism. Confessar. in Purgatorium.*).

Yet notwithstanding, the Councill of Trent makes nothing to swallow downe all these incongruous, phantasticall conceits of Purgatory, and to digest them into a Canon with Decrees for that Spurious, Lunaticke Monster—which is onely full-shaped and made Legitimate there. Yet not out of any foundation, either in Reason, or Scripture. For whereas that Councill boasts of Scripture's Authoritie to shoare up this rotten building, it is so false that their owne Writers who had the reputation of Learned, by name Petrus à Soto and Petionius, acknowledge there is no Text of Scripture which Proves or Names *Purgatory.* There is but one place to make it colourable, and that in the Apocrypha (which they are faine for that and the like Purposes to make Canonicall), where Judas Machabæus made a Collection of two Thousand Drachmes, which he sent to Hierusalem to offer a Sinne-offering—And that, for ought they know, was for the Living rather then the Dead, That the whole army might not perish for their sinne, who under their Coats, contrary to their Law, had hidden the Jewels consecrated to Idols. Even as Achan did the Wedge, for which so many were slaine flying before the men of Ai.

And although (verse 44) Praying for the Dead bee mentioned, wee finde Judas did it in contemplation of the Resurrection—not a word of bringing Soules out of Purgatory. For other texts of Scripture alleaged by their side, they are but forc'd impostures, and meere distorsions.

Thus have I delivered the full History of Purgatory, which all learned men of their owne side know to bee true. And I will bee bold to doe them that right, as to say: However they are well content, for the great commodity which thence ariseth to their Church, that common ignorant people beleeve it for Truth, I cannot bee perswaded they themselves beleeve it at all.

'Tis a Politicke Case of Profit, not of Conscience, which makes them willing to hold it. Just like Demetrius in the Acts, who not for the zeale to Dianae's Temple at Ephesus, but in respect of the advantage to his owne Trade, exasperated the tumultuous people against Paul. His Exordium is, *Sirs, you know by this Art wee have got our goods.* Upon which Principle (I suppose) the Pontificials are willing to maintaine their conclusion for Purgatory.

'Tis certaine, their most gainefull Copyholds and Tenements hold of Purgatory as their chiefe Mannor—Their masses for the Dead, their Pilgrimages, their Bathes for the Soule, Vigils, Anniversaries, Indulgences, Workes of Supererogation, Holy Water, Exequies, their Oblations at the

---

*That the souls tortured in purgatorial fire pray and beseech for us.

X. But deliver us from Evill

Shrines of Saints: All which Candlerents would fall to ground, were this conceit of Purgatory removed, which, onely, keepes them in repaire and Tenentable. Wee for our part neither feare nor credit it, and therefore not include it in the scope of this Prayer.

The Evill wee pray against is the *Sentence of the Evill Day, the Day of Wrath, of Blackenesse and Tempest, of Vengeance and Fire;* Whose sequele is, to them that have done ill, incessant Torment in the Lake of Fire and Brimstone. 'Tis consonant to our Creed to acknowledge no Third place betwixt Heaven and Hell: The one for the Righteous, the other for the Reprobate. *They that have done good shall goe into Life Everlasting, and they that have done Evill into everlasting Fire.* [A Malo Gerhennæ] [330] Athenas.Creed

A Father defines a Sinner to be the substance of all Misery, both in this world and in the next. Whilest he lives here, his Conscience, like a sad Perspective, shewes him Hell; and when hee dies, hee feeles what hee but feared before. To make up which, the Extremity of all Ill concurres, *Pœna Damni* and *Pœna Sensus:* The Paine of Losse and the Paine of Sense, One to torment the Soule, the other the Body; Whilest hee shall both languish in a perpetuall Exilement from the sight of God, wanting the comforts of his gracious Presence, and in a most exquisite sense endure all shapes of Torment multiplied upon the Body. This is the *Worme* that gnawes, but *never dies;* this the *unquenchable Fire* that continually feeds on them who are cast into it, but never consumes it selfe or them. (Mk. 9:48)

When I have said this, no man's curiosity (I presume) will expect a more punctuall Description of this *Summum Malum*—Highest Degree of Evill; Or desire to be resolved what kinde of Fire it is, whether Materiall or Immateriall; What Place it hath, whether in the Body of the Earth, or in the Aire; What Intermissions, what Duration. [331]

I am not so well skilld in the Chorography and Mappe of Hell, as those that undertake both to dispute and Define these things. 'Tis a Theme rather to exercise our Feares and Devotion, then our Enquiry. If any scrupulous Atheist there bee that denies Hell, as Almaricus did; or doubts it, as Dyonisius; or beleeves it only in an Allegoricall sense, as the Family of Love and those ancient Hereticks mentioned by S. Augustine did, I pray God they doe not fetch their resolution there too soone—Like that unreasonable Philosopher who, denying the Fire to burne, was by his enraged Antagonist thrust into the Fire, that he who would not be instructed by reason, might be confuted by sense and demonstration in the Flame. [Aug.DeHæres.]

What this Gehenna is, Tertullian will sufficiently resolve: *It is a Treasure of Fire which will breake out at the last Day.* That this fire *differs from that culinary Fire which serves our use,* there is no controversie. That there shall bee a difference in the Torment, wee may boldly pronounce for Truth: For as all shall not bee rewarded with equall degree of Beatitude, so neither shall all Sinners bee punished alike. Adultery, and Theft, and Murther, meet in one and the same Center Hell, but the Theefe and the Murtherer shall not burne alike. Undoubtedly Bloodshed shall have more Heat, a greater intension of Flames. But for the Intermission or Cessation of each Offender's Punishment, that must bee hopelesse. However it bee imputed to Origen that (in this more mercifull than God) hee hath shortned the date of that fearefull Judgement, assigning certaine Paroxismes to conclude that exalted Fever of Fire, and putting a Period not onely to the Paines of the Damned, but of the Devils themselves: To beleeve this is more dangerous than his Pity was foolish. [332] Tertull. Apologet.cap.47 Cap.48 August. De Civit.Dei Lib. 21:cap.17 [333]

All *Epithets* are too narrow to comprehend, all language too light to expresse the weight of those Torments, all Arithmeticke too little to calculate the duration of them. It is *Mors sine Morte, Finis sine Fine, Defectus sine Defectu:* An Immortall Death, a dying yet never determining Life, an Endlesse End, a Plenty of all Misery, but Dearth of all Comfort. The Punishment of Hell is a torture that kills not, A Judgement that executes eternally, but never finishes the execution. 'Tis an everlasting Calenture, a Disease under which the Body ever languishes, but never impaires, Where, though the Body bee the fuell, yet the un-devouring Fire feeds it; Like the Salamander, which is nourished in the Flame; or the Liver of Prometheus, which grew as fast as the Vulture gnawed it. [Tertull.Apologet:cap.48]

The least sparke of this Fire may serve to kindle our Devotion, and the contemplation of so great [334]

a danger give Religion a tongue to call loudly to the God of Mercy to *Deliver us from this Judgement*—May teach us to make this *Libera nos a Malo* the Antiphone of our Letany: *Deliver us from this Evill.*

Nothing but the breath of Prayer can coole, nothing but the Teares of contrition and Penitence quench this fire.

Let it then bee our care betimes to strive to allay this Combustion, which, if neglected, growes too violent to bee appeased; and whilest we live here, to lave from our eyes those religious shoures which may extinguish it. Whilest our Oyle is yet in our lampes, and these Candles of Nature, our Eyes, not sunke downe within their Sockets, the Doores of Heaven lie open to our Prayers; but when wee are once benighted with dimnesse, clos'd within the *Chambers of Death,* the Gates of Heaven are shut. Either wee cannot pray, or if wee doe, our Prayers knocke at Heaven as at a Gate of Brasse, for it is now become so, and like a Mine of Adamant, Deafe and Impenetrable, beats backe the voice.

[335]

(Lk. 16:24)
Lactant.*Lib.1: cap.15.*

The successelesse Petition of *Dives* will shew that the *Soules condemned* to the Pit of Sulphur are so *farre from release,* that they cannot make their approaches to the first degree of comfort. The Ocean of God's Mercy, then dry as the Pumish, hath not one drop that can be purchased or wrung out by any importunity: The Fountaine of Living Water is onely free to Life. Nor will the Balme of Gilead cure the second Death. When the Fever is upon us, preventing Physicke comes too late. Prayer and Penitence are unable to remove the fits of the last Criticall fire when they are upon us; but if they be seasonably and timely applyed, they doe not only Bale us from Judgement by *Delivering* and Guarding *us from Evill,* but like Starres, fix us in that glorious Firmament where is the fruition of All Deliverance, Salvation, and Peace, and Joy for evermore. Amen.

[336]

[337] XI. FOR THINE IS THE KINGDOME, AND THE POWER, AND THE GLORY, FOR EVER. AMEN.

When I first entred upon this Prayer, I compar'd it to a *Letter,* which is a Justifiable Metaphor; For all *Prayer is the Interpreter of our Minde and Desire* (so Aquinas defines it). Nay, tis both the Letter and the *Bearer* too: *Per nuncium orationis*—so S. Augustine. To a Letter or Epistle doth this Prayer agree in each circumstance. First, for the Endorsement or Superscription, whereby it is directed *to God, Our Father,* &c. Secondly, for the Contents, which are branched out into seven Petitions. Thirdly, for the *Coronis* [Crown], the forme of Conclusion, or Subscription, which is the matter of this Text: *For thine is the Kingdome* &c. I might for a need finde a date for it, though a large one, in these words, *For ever.* And lastly here is a Seale put to it, *Amen.*

2a.2ae:q.83

[338]

The Direction and Explication of the Matters severally contained in the Petitions hath beene my former Subject. That which remaines here, to make up my last treatise, is like that Civill and Mannerly Ceremony which wee usually referre to the latter part of our Letters, wherein wee mention our acknowledgement and Farewell together.

I doe not call it a Ceremony any way to diminish or lessen the dignity of the words. They have their weight and Authority confirmed by Him who dictated the rest. Nor are they unnecessary or uselesse, though onely annexed, not incorporated into the Prayer. Though our essentiall Parts, as Soule and Body, be the maine Foundations of our Being, none will deny but that the Integrals, as Hands and Feet, are necessary assistants both to serve and adorn our Being.

[339]

Of the nature of Integrall Parts are these words; which as they have their Decencie, so they are Necessary too.

Ambrose *De Sacrament.L6.c.5*
(Ps. 92:1)
(Jas. 1:5)

They are the gratefull acknowledgement of God's goodnes, *with whose mention, as wee begin our Prayers, so 'tis fit wee end them. It is a comely thing to sing praises unto God* (saith the Psalme). And the Apostle will tell us, *They that aske must be confident that hee of whom they aske hath power to give, for else they doe not aske in faith.*

XI. For thine is the Kingdome, etc.

You see in what a qualified sense I call this Doxologie a Ceremony. I wish some others had not in a proper sense used it as a Ceremony, fit onely to bee annulled and abrogated. The Latine Copies are deficient in setting it downe: Whether they were loath one Evangelist should speake more than another, for Luke hath it not at all; or whether they suspected that these words were additions to the Prayer, wanting the privilege of our Saviour, who was the Author, to make them Authenticall. Erasmus, it should seeme, was transported with this conceit, and hath not so much forfeited his Temper or Judgement upon any thing of like consequence, as this. For in his Notes upon Matthew, he peremptorily delivers it that they which annexed this Conclusion to the Lord's Prayer did patch up the Prayer with their owne idle invention—leaving a greater scorne upon these words, which in good manners he might have left disputable whether they were Christ's or no, than upon any Apocryphall writings, which without controversie he knew to be but man's. Maldonat the Jesuite deales more calmly. He does not vilifie the words like Erasmus, but onely seeks to excuse the Latines for leaving them out: Supposing, as Erasmus doth, that their use began from the Greeke Church; who, he thinks, were like enough to make the addition here, as they added the *Gloria Patri* [Glory be to the Father] to the end of each Psalme, and likewise to the Angel's Salutation of the blessed Virgin these words: *hoti su etekes ton sōtêra hêmera.** Or as they used to close their Sermons with this Doxologie, *hoti soi estin doxa, kai kratos, kai basileia,* ascribing, as wee doe, *all Honour, and Power, and Dominion unto God.*

I will not looke so farre into the meaning of the Holy Ghost as to dispute whether these words were not borrowed from the speach of David (I Chron. 29:11): *Thine (O Lord) is Greatnesse, and Power, and victory, and Praise; for all that is in Heaven and in Earth is thine. Thine is the Kingdome, O Lord, and thou excellest, as Head over all.* 'Tis not unlikely that the same Spirit might speake the same thing here againe, though in a shorter phrase.

This I am sure is granted on all parts and confessed by Maldonat, that not onely the Septuagint, or the Fathers of the Greeke Church, Chrisostome, Theophylact and Euthymius, recite the words, but the Hebrew and the Syriacke, which were the Originall Copies. And 'tis not unfitly noted by Chemnicius that S. Paul, mentioning the sense of the last Petition, addes this clause too: *And the Lord shall deliver mee from every evill worke, and will preserve mee unto his heavenly Kingdome, to whom be glory for ever and ever. Amen.*

Let then this truth be granted, that the Testaments Originally had this clause, and reason (if not authority, which outweighs Erasmus) will confirme us that this is no unsuited Argument, patcht in to stuffe out the Prayer, but added as a most apposite and devout Close, not only to informe our desires that their maine scope must terminate in the Glory of God, but to teach us that the severall Dictates and Petitions in Christ's Prayer are radicated and founded in God alone: To weaken thereby the pride of such who vaingloriously impute the successe of their Prayers rather to their owne merit than the mercy of God. So Calvin inferres.

But if his credit be too light to counterballance him, I thinke in any indifferent judgement, S. Chrysostome will turne the scale. For he makes these words to have a necessary relation to the two last Petitions, being annexed by our Saviour *tharriōein, to embolden and fortifie* the faith of his servants. He was loth to leave their Meditations upon two such dangerous Rocks as *Temptation* and *Evill,* without a Tide or a flash of Mercy to fetch them off; And therefore adjoyned these words, to establish them in a confident beleef that Hee, who taught them to pray against the Kingdome of Satan or Power of Sinne, was able to destroy them both, and in the meane time willing to confine them so that they should not prevaile against them. For all the Principalities and Powers, whether of the Aire or of the Fire, of Light or of Darknesse, must stoope and bow under His Scepter, who hath Dominion over Sinne and death, Heaven and Hell: *For thine is the Kingdome, the Power, and the Glory,* &c.

---

*Because you bore our Saviour.

The Summe of the words is but an Investing God with his owne Title, which are three, set out

[344]
I. By an eminent Declaration:
  1. *The Kingdome*
  2. *And the Power*
  3. *And the Glory.*
2. Their Duration, *For ever,* or as our Liturgie hath it, *For ever and ever.*
3. The forme under which they are conveyed upon God, *Tuum est,* &c: *For Thine is,* &c.
Lastly, the Seale of the whole Prayer, *Amen.*

I.
The Kingdome

God, who at first imparted his Image to Man, in that act derived some of his Authority upon him too, To rule the World as his Vicegerent upon Earth; By which He lifted up Man to the Contemplation of his Divine Majestie and Kingdome. When man but thinkes over his owne and the World's History, hee must needs in the end of his travell land upon the consideration of that Majestie whose Prerogative put him into the possession of the World. Philosophers beginning but

[345]
at the Foot of Motion could trace it up to the Head, and by that speculative study arrive at the first Mover. So when Man judiciously survayes his owne being—how all Creatures are subordinate unto him, to serve either his Necessities or his Delight; how himselfe hath Dominion over them, Reason over Him, Faith over Reason, and God over Faith—must confesse that the top of all Dominion and Supremacie is in God alone.

S. Basil sayes a King is *horatos theos,* a visible God, but God *basileis ahoratos,* an invisible King. So the King is the Glasse thorow which we may behold God: Hee is his Picture, and yet resembles Him no neerer than dead Colours doe the Life. For Death doth not only rule in his Complexion and the Temper of his Body; but even all those faire Colours of State and Shew, of outward Pompe and Command, of Glory and Authority, which set him off shall in a little Time

I Cor.7:31[b]
starve and fade, like those which the hand of the Painter hath laid upon his Picture. As the Fashion

[346]
and Symmetry and Beauty of this World passes away, so also the fashion of those that rule the

Gregor.Tholos.
*Syntagm.Juris
lib.18:cap.1*
Num.14

World: *Principalities grow old and infirme, they sicken and die;* An *Empire* hath its funerall pile, as the Emperour his Hearse; *Kingdomes* expire like the Kings, and they like us. For though they have the title of *Gods,* they are but mortall, miserable Gods, like their gorgious Statues, which the stroke of an hammer breakes into dust. Every sleight distemper is able to depose and thrust them into earth, imprisoning all their Glories in a little Coffin, from which low Captivity their whole

Psal.82:7
Exchequer cannot buy them. *They shall Dye like common men;* And not onely their Bodies, but

Psal.146:4
their *Thoughts perish.*

Hee then that takes the Altitude of God by the King goes a regular way; but hee that rises to no higher an estimate of God's Power then the King's, degrades that high Authority which gave Kings theirs, and makes Him lesse by whom they were made so Great. All the severall Lines of Regality

[347]
are united in God, as the whole masse of Light in the Body of the Sunne, but in an higher exaltation of Majestie, in a more eminent degree. The phrase here specified sounds no lesse; *The Kingdome.* Which small Particle speakes Him in his fullest stile, importing the difference of his State and the Advancement of his Prerogative above all the Kingdomes of the Earth. *A King,* or *A Kingdome,* is currant Language thorow most parts of the inhabited World, Pagan or Christian. But since the Truth of God was revealed in his Word, or That Word translated into other Tongues, never was it knowne that *The Kingdome* was translated in any Tongue but Spanish, Which in the Title of the *Catholicke King* amasses all Soveraigntie: As if all other Kings were his Viceroyes, and not God's, holding their Crownes in Fee from him, and not from that Supreme Power which hath said, *By me*

(Prov.8:15)
Kings rule.

I need not be coy in speaking it, since 'tis an Argument they daily maintaine, both with their Pens

[348] Juan de la Puente,
Chronista de la Mag^d
Catolica. Madrid . . . 1612

and Swords. They have not long since printed it, the King himselfe allowing the Presse; and not onely in America, but in all parts of Christendome (so farre as they can or dare), they avow this Doctrine by their Practice.

Suidas writes, the pride of Cleopatra swell'd so high that she would be call'd the *Queene of*

XI. For thine is the Kingdome, etc.

Queenes; And Curtius reports that Darius, the Persian Monarch, before he was vanquished by Alexander the Great, stil'd himselfe *King of Kings, and Kinsman of the Gods,* affording no Title to Alexander but of his servant. His pride and Ignorance of God (I confesse) might some way excuse his folly; but how I should excuse any Christian Prince that layes claime to an Universall Monarchy, I am yet to learn. David may command from Dan to Beersheba, or from the River to the Floud; but such an Extent of Dominion as includes all the Nations of the Earth, such an Expansion of Government as reaches from Sea to Sea, from Gibralter to the Mediterranean, from one point of Heaven to the other, is onely the Limit of Christ's Dominion, and the *Inheritance of the Son of God.* The whole Globe of the Earth, and all the severall Provinces contained therein, are too great a handfull to be grasped by any Palme but His, *Who is a great King above all Gods, and in whose hand are all the Corners of the Earth.* Tacitus, though an Heathen, would give Supremacie and singularitie of Rule to none but God—*Unum esse regnatorem omnium Deum,* was his Maxime. Nor, by the Rules of Christianitie, is universall Homage due to any but to Him alone, who claimes this honour, that *emoi kam psei pan gonu: Every knee shall bow to mee.* Therefore David concludes his Festivall Sacrifice with this Antheme: *Let the Heavens be glad, and the earth rejoyce, and let men say among the Nations, The Lord reigneth. For thine is the Kingdome.*

But Titles without Power make Authority ridiculous, and beget scorne, not reverence. They are but like Cities in a Map, where we onely travell over Names and Titles, not Countries. Therefore, to shew that God is not only *mighty in Word, but in Deed too;* That he is not only Powerfull in Voice and Name, but in Fact too; here is Authority joyn'd to his Scepter, and to the Latitude of Dominion the Prerogative of Power: *For thine is the Kingdome, and the Power.*

Well may our Prayers determine in this ascribing of power to God, when the first Prayers used in our Church beare this Confession in their Foreheads, and begin with this Attribute of Power, *Almighty.*

I have heard that Power belongeth unto God (saith David), And wee have seene the Declarations and Testimonies of that Power. It was that Mighty Power which first reduced the World out of that darke Confusion wherein it lay into a cleere and beautifull forme, and stamp'd the face of Method upon it when it was concluded in a rude Chaos. By that power were the Motions of the Heavens established; and by that same Power are the Species of Creatures moving upon the Earth conserved. By that Power were the elements extracted out of Nothing, and by that Power are they restrained to their Stations and Places.

The highest evidence of Earthly Power is the Power of Making Lawes, and the tying up of factious dispositions in an Obedience of doing whatsoever they command. But unto what an height is this Power elevated in God, who is the universall Law-giver, ruling them which rule us, by whose Decrees Nature and the Elements are governed, Life and Death administered?

A Story tels us that Canutus, sometimes King of this Land, sitting by the River's side at the comming in of the Tide, charged the Floud it should not presume to approach that stone whereon his feet rested. But the unruly Floud (disdaining to bee checkt by any command save God's, by whose ordinance it was allowed to make its usuall sallies from the Ocean, and then retire againe), notwithstanding his charge, wet his feet: Letting him see it was God only could give Lawes to the Water, saying to the Sea, *Thus farre and no farther shall thy proud waves come.* And whereas Homer fainingly tels us that the petty King of Ithaca, Ulysses, had the winds in a Bagge, to enlarge or shut up at his pleasure, wee are sure that it is onely the True God who hath the Winds in custody, which when He pleaseth *He brings out of his Treasures.*

In a word, *He hath the full exercise of Power,* both for the Dispensation and Execution of Lawes; The Portion of Shame or the Crowne of Glory, Judgement or Mercy, are the pay of his Exchequer: *In tua manu & potestate sunt misericordia & salus, mors & vita* ('Tis the Paraphrase of a devout Patriarch upon this place). He destroyes and Hee saves, He scatters abroad and collects againe, banishes and repeales, kils and makes alive, ruling the Grave by so high an hand, that when the first Death hath arrested these bodies of ours, Hee by his Power can Bale them, can recall the Breath

---

Quint. Curtius *Lib.2* [a]

Psal.2:8
[349]

Psal.95:3, 4

Rom.14:11
I Chron.16:31

[350] Luk.24:19

2.
And the Power

(Ps.62:11)

[351]

Job 38:11
[352]

(Jer.10:13)

Germani Patriarchæ Constantinop. *Expos. in orat. Dominic.*

which is fled, and transplant the defaced ruines of Nature out of that corruptible mould wherein they were buried into the Kingdome of Glory. For as the *Kingdome,* and the *Power,* so *The Glory is His.*

[353] 3. *And the Glory*
Psal.18:2
Luk.2:14

There is no Theme so conspicuous as the Glory of the Lord, Whose Anniverse the Heavens are (for *they declare his Glory*) and whose Trumpet the Tongue of Angels. *Gloria in altissimis* was the Antheme sung by the Angels: *Glory be to God on high.* That Glory was an argument which they found not on earth, but brought it along with them from Heaven. Nor doe they leave it here behind them: The Tenour of their Embassie is *Peace upon Earth* and *Grace* or *Good will to Men,* but *Glory only to God.*

[354]
1 Cor.3:21

Mat.6:29
1 Cor.1:31

What Monuments of Shame then doe those erect to themselves, and at how easie a rate doe they purchase confusion, who prize their owne deservings too much? What forbidden Altars doe they build, what high Places doe they set up for an Idolatrous worship, who Glorifie Dust and Ashes? Who, studying the Doxologie of Men in the most servile Postures of insinuation, are content to cast them-selves below the reputation of Men; and to promote their owne ends, make Advancement their Religion, and their Patron their God? *Let no man glory in men* (it was S. Paul's Lesson): no, not in the best of men, Princes. For to let us see that all our glorying, even in them, is but shame, our blessed Saviour so farre degrades the opinion of Salomon's Magnificence, that in his Gospell he preferres the Glory of the Lilly before his: And Hee that cloathes the Lillies, Crownes Kings. *Let him then that Glories, Glory in the Lord.* And let him that wrongs himselfe by Glorifying Men, at length doe God right by giving Him the Glory which is only due and peculiar unto Him.

Psal.115:1

[355]

King David (who had better right to take, than they to give), to the shame of Sycophants, modestly releases all his Claime or Title to Glory, conferring it wholly upon God: *Non nobis Domine, non nobis, sed Nomini tuo da Gloriam:* Not unto us, Lord, not unto us, but to thy Name give the Glory. For Heaven is the Sphere of glory, and God is the King of Glory, and Glory is the Prerogative of his Kingdome, which as it doth *Convenire soli,* so *Semper*—As it is *Only His,* so *Everlastingly His.* For thine is the Kingdome, the Power, and the glory, For ever.

4.
For ever
Psal.7:5

How loosely doe Honours sit on Men, when every disease shakes them off, and *Layes them in the Dust*? How miserable is the condition of all Earth's Glory, which hardly holds out a Life, but often dies before us, ravisht away by a frowne, or forfaited by a fault? Or if it doe last as long as the Owner's, with the Staffe of Office crackt and throwne into the Grave, is there buried with the Corps.

It is a wofull but fit difference to distinguish that specious Vanity which Man termes Glory from the Glory of God, which onely is true Glory, because onely Permanent. When the fashion of ours is as transitory as the fashion of the World, when it tastes the same frailty which our Bodies doe, even this, like a Lecture of Mortality, tels us that here all Glory is but Corruption; That either wee have none, or if any, it is included in our Hopes, respited and adjourned till that time when *This Corruptible shall put on Incorruption.*

[356]
1 Cor.15:54

But the Glory of God is an immortall Title, which Time cannot discolour, nor Age enfeeble; An unalterable Possession, which as He ever had, He hath now, and shall ever have. When all Motion shall cease, and the Time which measured that Motion shall be no more; when those great Lights in the Firmament, which successively watch the Jesses and observe the Journeyes of Time, by whose Kalendar wee compute the revolution of our owne Yeares and the expence of every Houre—When (I say) those Lights, like Dying Tapers, shall be eternally smothered and goe out, the Glory of the Lord shall shine forth, and make a fairer Light than ever the Sunne in the pride of his Meridian could cast: A Light which is preserved by His Presence, who is the true Light; A Light which can never be Eclipsed by the interposition of Darknesse and Sorrow; but shall continue, like that Glorious Essence which feeds it, *eis ton aiōnas*—*Thorow all Ages,* or *Thorow all Successions of Eternity* (for so the transcendent expression of our English hath it—*For ever and ever.* The one whereof referres to His *Being,* which *Ever was;* the other to His Duration, which *Ever shall be.*

[357]

Our Tenures here are suted and proportioned to our owne Being. They are Ours *Durante vita,*

XI. *For thine is the Kingdome, etc.*

whilest Life lasts, else they cannot properly be called ours, but another's. They are not Free-holds, but Farmes; Nor are wee Inheritors, but Tenants.

Is it not fit the great Landlord of Nature, who hath Leased unto us not onely the meanes to sustaine our Being but our Being also, should hold his Titles by a Tenure as lasting and as independant as we? Our Termes are bounded by a few yeares, but there is no scope of Time, no Terme that can hold any proportion with God, but *For ever and ever.* Eternity is God's Free-hold, and there is no Title worth his wearing which is not Eternall. *Thy Yeares are from everlasting, and the Scepter of thy Kingdome is an everlasting Scepter; Thy Power infinite, Thy Glory for ever and ever.* Which perpetuity concludes Him the Owner and Proprietary both in *The Kingdome, The Power,* and *The Glorie* which is here setled upon Him, and wherewith hee is invested, being put into a full possession with *Tuum est:* Thine is the Kingdome, &c. *(Ps.45:6)* [358]

The Complement we use with God is quite different from that we use to Men. In the shutting up of our Letters we commonly mention the Obligations we owe unto those wee write, professing how much and by how many Titles wee are Theirs. But here, in the close of our Prayers, we reward God out of his owne Inventorie, and, in the rehearsall of his Titles, professe unto Him how much is His: *Thine is the Kingdome, the Power, and the Glory.* 5. *Thine is, &c.*

And yet in this wee imply a Dedication, a Devoting of our selves to Him; For the ascribing of *Dominion* and *Power* to him imports the obedience and subjection and service which we owe Him. [359]

We can never in the way of thankfull Debtors owe him enough, who gave his Only Sonne a Ransome for us. We can never give Him too much Honour, who gave us all the Circumstances of our Being. Nay, such is our Poverty, we cannot give Him any Thing, but for a Gift are faine to tender Him a Repetition of His owne. Wee see by experience that it is no new thing for the bounty and munificence of God to pose us daily with new Blessings, or new Deliverances from Danger. But for us to present Him with any new forme of Gratitude is impossible. As in the old Legall Sacrifices, Offerings were made unto God of those Creatures which were His before (for so He claimes them, *The Beasts of the Field are mine*) and of those Fruits wherewith Hee had first enriched the Earth: So in this Evangelicall Sacrifice of Prayer and Thanksgiving, what wee offer unto Him is taken out of his owne Store. Psal.50:10

The Keyes of those Faculties and Organs wherewith wee praise Him are in His Custodie, The Heart that prayes is in His Hand, The Spirit which vocally interprets the Heart is in the disposal of His Will. And therefore, the Prophet David will not presume to enter upon the subject of His Praise without leave from Him: *Thou must open my lips, that my mouth may shew forth thy praise.* [360] Psal.51:15

O the vouchsafed grace of God! ('tis S. Augustine's exclamation). I did not buy the sacrifice, but received it from Thee; Twas not my Purchase, but thine owne Gift. Though God's love to Mankind cost Him deare, yet our Thanks to Him costs little, 'tis at a most cheape rate. Aug. *In Psal.49*

Such is his Bounty, and the riches of his Love to us, that He doth not onely finde the Sacrifice, but build the Altar too; Hee is not onely at the charge of the Offering, but of the Wood to dresse it. Hee bestowes the Holocaust, and Hee bestowes the Fewell. He obligeth us first, and then prompts us to a gratefull returne of that Obligation. Hee by his mercy gives us cause to praise Him, and Hee by the working of his Grace inspires us with a Duty and holy Zeale to ascribe this Praise. Thus wee pay God out of his owne Exchequer: We receive from Him not onely the matter of our Thanksgiving, but the Forme too; not only the Subject of our Gratitude, but the expression of that Gratitude. As the Favours we receive are His, so their Acknowledgement is his also. These Organs of our Bodies are His, and the Musicke they make is by Him. *The Praise wee yeeld Him is His owne* (saith S. Augustine). *Nay, Hee himselfe is His owne Praise,* saith the same Father in another place. [361] Aug. *In Psal.62* Idem *Soliloq. cap.10*

Since, then, all Titles of Possession thus meet and concenter themselves in God; Since the stile of his survay runs universally, and is Audited in a *Tuum est,* All is Thine: How miserable were wee, had wee no place to bee entred into this Audit? Since not onely the Dominion over all things, and Power and Glory is God's, but the meanes of rendring, the ability of conveying those Attributes [362] upon Him is given unto us by Him, what shame were it that we our selves should not accompany our owne Faculties? That wee, who entitle God to all his Attributes, should not be able to make any title to Him our selves? Certainly, in the intent of Christ, the Dedication of these Attributes and of our Prayers to God is lame on our parts, and imperfect, if we include not our selves in the Dedication, if wee are not able to say that as *the Power and the Glory is God's,* so we are His too.

(1 Cor.3:23)   S. Paul leaves the Corinthians upon this comfort, that *As Christ is God's, so they are Christ's.* And may that God, for His Christ's sake, grant unto us all that into this Account of God's Possession wee may cast our selves, and whilest wee utter this Doxology, *Thine is the Kingdome, and the Power, and the Glory,* may, in the assurance of our Faith, be able to say that wee our selves are *Thine*—That so, when wee shall sleepe in the Dust, by His Power wee may be raised up to the *Life of Glory* and established in *His everlasting Kingdome.*

[363]

6.
Amen.

Our deed is now finished and ready for the *Seale;* I must onely desire your helpe for the Impression of that Seale. It hath beene my Office, thorowout this whole Tract upon Christ's Prayer, onely to Chafe the Wax, to informe and mollifie, and prepare your Meditations by kindling a Religious zeale in you. My part is done, and I must now expect somewhat from you. To shew that your hearts went along with me in this holy exercise, to testifie your assent to the Dictates of Christ, that He spake no more to God for you then you would be ready to speake over againe for your selves, you must now adde your Suffrage, since the remainder lies on you. For as it is the Priest's duty to pray in the Temple, so 'tis the duty of the Congregation to say *Amen* to his Prayers.

[364]   I know some Writers of the Roman Church endevour to prove that None but the Priest should here say *Amen.* Indeed, to speake truth, in a Church where Prayer in an unknowne Tongue is practised and defended, where the People understand not what the Priest says, S. Paul thinks it no reason that in such a case their Devotion should exceed their Learning, or that they ought to say

1 Cor.14:16   *Amen*—*How shall the unlearned say Amen at thy giving thanks, seeing he understandeth not what thou sayest?* But in a Church where for the most part I hope we doe, or should, understand one

Psal.47:7   another; where as neere as wee can, wee follow the Psalmist's rule, *To praise God with understanding,* there is not colour nor reason to leave it onely to the Priest's Mouth: Seeing that in

Deut.27   Deuteronomie no lesse than Twelve times the Command is iterated, *Let all the People say Amen.*
Nehem.8:6   And in Nehemiah, when Ezra the Priest blessed the Lord, *All the People said Amen, Amen.*

[365]   It is then your worke. But since hee that offers at the Altar is a party with the Congregation and offers for himselfe too; Since the Priest in praying for others, prayes for himselfe (for wee say *Our* Father, and Forgive *us*); Since wee are not onely Embassadours from God for your sakes, but Heraulds too, I will by your patience survay this Seale, and Blazon the Coat which is engraven in it, and then leave it to be Affixed by you.

Hieron.*In Mat.*6   I doe not impose a new Name upon it, in stiling the *Amen* a Seale. S. Hierome cals it *Signaculum Orationis Dominicæ,* the Seale of the Lord's Prayer. *As a Seale is the confirmation of a Codicill:* so

Albinus Flaccus *De Divinis Offic.* p.78   Albinus Flaccus expresses it; And like a most Authenticke Signet, it hath remain'd unaltered, *retaining that Originall Stampe of Language which the mouth of God first put upon it.* S. Au-

Alexand.Hales *Part.*4:q.10 [366]   gustine gives the reason: There bee (saith hee) some Hebrew words which cannot be translated, as *Racha* and *Osanna;* the first whereof is the voice of Indignation, the last of Exultation. There bee others which wee might have translated, but yet *it was held fit by the Primitive Church, for the greater dignity and Authority of the words, to preserve them* in the Hebrew Garbe still, as *Alleluiah*

Aug.*De Doctr. Christ.*Lib.2:c.11 Vid. & Rabban. Maurum *De Instit.Cleric.*lib.1:cap.33 Tract in Johan.41:8[a]   and *Amen.* For which reason, the same Father, speaking of this word, by occasion of our Saviour's Asseveration (John 8.34) *Amen dico vobis* [Amen, I say unto you], sayes That in honour of it, neither the Greeke nor Latine Interpreter durst render it.

Tis certaine that *genoito, genoito,* in the conclusion of the 88. Psalme, and *Fiat* in the Latine, and *So be it* in our English might serve to expresse this *Amen.* But S. Augustine liked no translation of it, but it selfe.

Indeed, it cannot bee denied but that it must needs lose much weight being translated, in that no one word can expresse it. For though the Prolation of the word bee still the same, yet the meaning

XI. For thine is the Kingdome, etc.

varies with the use and according to the Acception in the Scripture. In the practice of the Jewes, *Amen* was a Note of Assent; nor was it used in their Synagogue at Prayers onely, but at the Sermons and expositions delivered by the Rabbines, to testifie that the people beleeved and assented to all which they taught. But the Schoolemen have gathered divers other acceptions of it in the Scripture. Sometimes it is taken *Nominaliter,* as a Name, signifying as much as *Verax* or *Veritas: Truth telling* or *Truth,* and so it is used Revel.3.14: *These things saith the Amen, the faithfull and true Witnesse.*

Sometimes it is taken *Adverbially,* and then it signifies as much as *Verè* or *Fideliter, Truely* or *Verily.* So it is used by our Saviour in the Gospell, by way of Asseveration: *Amen dico vobis— Verily, I say unto you.* In which sense, S. Bernard termes it *Verbum confirmationis,* The Word of Confirmation; And S. Augustine termes it our Saviour's oath.

Lastly, it is taken *Verbaliter,* Verbally, as it is an Hebrew word, importing as much as *Fiat: Let it be done* or *So bee it,* intimating *the Affection or Desire or Zeale of such as Pray:* Where the pronounced *Amen* is *Quasi Clausio,* the Close, or (in Saint Hierone's Phrase) the *Signet* with which our Prayers are Sealed up.

Indeed it is a Transcendent Seale which, like the Great Seale, commands or includes all other Seales. As our Prayers, so our Faith hath Seales too. The *Sacraments* are the Seales of our Faith. but this Seale of Prayer is the Seale also of the Sacraments. When wee desire those Sacraments may be effectuall to us, we testifie our desire by saying *Amen.* When, by those meanes Hee hath allowed, we either apply God to us or our selves to Him, wee conclude and strengthen the Application by an *Amen.* When we commend the Bodies of our deceased Brethren to Earth, *In hope of the Resurrection,* wee Seale up their Graves with *Amen.* And when we commend our owne Soules into the protection of God, we signe that Petition with the same *Amen.* In a Common wealth it would be thought a Forgery for a Party to seale his owne Pasport; but in a Church, 'tis Religion, and an Indulgence given by Christ, that each man may promote not only his Prayers, but his passage to Heaven, and contribute something to the Sealing of his owne Pasport.

I finde that Rabbi Jehudah thought the pronouncing of *Amen* so meritorious, that hee who said *Amen* in this World was worthy to say *Amen* in the Next. And others of the Rabbines esteemed it so effectuall, that being devoutly uttered, it would accelerate and hasten the time of their Redemption. For my part, I place no Merit in the Prolation or Sound of the word; but yet I account it such a strength to Prayer, and so fit an Attestation of the People's Zeale, that I must ever wonder wherefore the Church of Rome should make this *Amen* onely the Priest's Peculiar, shutting out the People for bearing any share in it; Or why they labour to give a reason that, like a Counter-verse, it ought to be pronounced in a soft single voice by the Priest, when the whole Congregation, like a full Quire and most fitly, should pronounce it: for so S. John reports, that hee *heard the Host of Heaven like the sound of many Waters, or like the voice of Thunder, crying Amen, Alleluiah.*

The Priest only must preach to the People, but the People may pray for themselves. Or if the Priest doe pray for the People, at least let the People say *Amen* to his Prayers. I shall never thinke he meanes fairely, or prayes with a good intent for mee, that usurpes both Priest and Clarke, and will not give me leave to say *Amen* for my selfe. I deny not that in the Church, the Priest's Prayers are more acceptable than the Congregation's, because he is the Mediator betwixt God and the People; Yet I will never beleeve but the Congregation's *Amen* is more obligatory, more effectuall than the Priest's. At the Siege of Jericho, the Priests' Trumpets shooke the Walls, but the Walls fell not downe till the *People shouted.* The saying of *Amen* is but the People's Acclamation, the joyfull shouting of the Congregation, in assurance of the Victory and successe of Prayer. *For by those that cry Amen, the Prayer is confirm'd* (saith S. Ambrose). Nay, *the Blessing which the Priest distributes is then confirm'd.* This was the opinion and practice of the Primitive Church; And some Writers of the Romane Church, handling purposely the *Order* of their Liturgie, hold it most fit to bee continued—So Amalarius Fortunatus, sometime Bishop of Trevere; so also Ivo Carnotensis Episcopus. But why summe I up humane Authorities, when God himselfe hath injoyned it? And

[367]
Vid.Buxdorf *De Synagog.Judaic. cap.1:pag.64*[a]

Gabr.Biel *Lect. 79 de Missa*

Bernard *Declamat mat.in illa verba*
Aug.*Tract.in Job 41;c.8*[a] [368]
Biel, loc.cit.

[369]

Buxdorf *De Synagog. Judaic. cap.5.pag.181*[a]

Alexander Hales *part.4.q.10*[a]

[370]

Revel.19:6.

Josh.6:20
[371]
Ambros.*In Epist. l.ad Corinth. 14:p.529.E.*
Id.*In Psal.40 pag.370b.*

De Ecclesiast. Offic.Li.3:ca.9;
Ivo Carnotens. *De Rebus Eccles. ser.pag.434* [a]

when He bids say *Amen,* let not the Authority of Rome silence you, but in obedience to his command and in assent to our Prayers, *Let all the people say, Amen.*

[372]   But yet Prayers are not Crown'd with their Effects unlesse God himselfe also say *Amen.* The People's *Amen* concludes the Prayer, expressing a desire to obtain, but God's *Amen* perfects it, by consummating that desire.

Let us therefore addresse our selves to Him, not only in our Prayers but for the successe of those Prayers, beseeching Him who at first pronounced a *Fiat* over the Worke of his Creation to repeat that *Fiat* over us, in accomplishing the Worke of our Redemption. *Dic verbum tantum: Lord, onely say the word,* and thy servants shall live. By the Power of thy *Word* thou didst set up a light in Darkenesse. Thou saidst, *Let there bee light, and it was made.* Gracious God, for thy mercie's sake, exercise that Act of Power upon us. When we shall be benighted in our Graves and shut up within the Region of Darkenesse, O Thou that art the *True Light,* suffer us not for ever *to sleepe in Death,* but grant that in Thy Kingdome, and in Thy Presence, wee may have the fruition of a *New Light.* That wee may *see Light in Thy Light,* and enjoy that Light by enjoying Thee who art that Light. That from thy Militant Church, wee may bee translated into thy Triumphant; That of Christians here, we may bee made Saints there; and finally exchange the *State of Grace* for a *Crowne of Glory* in Thy Kingdome, which shall know no End. Amen.

FINIS.

5
The Sermons to 1669

1640

Jerem.I.10
Behold I have this day set thee over the Nations, and over the Kingdomes; to Root out, and to pull down, to destroy and throw down, to build and to plant.

Did not the solemne comming up of your Tribes to this Place, and the publike preparation, loudly speake that Festivall we meet to celebrate, the very reading of this Text were Trumpet enough to proclaime the cause of your addresse and my appearing here.

I may begin my Sermon as David his Psalme: *I speake of the things which I have made touching the King;* and the *Hodie* [this day] in the Text applies my speech to the season: That God *who This Day set Him over us* warrants the occasion, and this Scripture gives me matter. [Psal.45:1] [2]

The words were spoken immediately to the Prophet Jeremy, a Sonne of Oyle by his Office, though not of him but improperly and figuratively, saith Saint Augustin. Jeremy then was the *Messenger*, not the Party, for which reason one Translation reads not *Constitui*, but *Legavi Te*.* Literally and Properly, they are meant of Christ, importing his Regall Power, and the Latitude of His Kingdome. *Not Jeremy, but the Lord Jesus,* saith S. Ambrose. Nor is He alone—St. Cyprian, St. Chrysostome, Victorinus and others agree with him. Which makes good St. Hierome's attestation: *Divers understand this Text of Christ's Person.* Nevertheless, as we draw Coppies without wrong to the Originall, so without injury to the sense of the Text or the Person of Christ, I shall apply the words to the *King*, who in respect of his Office and Domination upon Earth is Christ's Image and Deputy, the *Christus Domini,* the Lord's Annoynted. [Aug.lib.3: De Doctrina Christiana.Cap 11] [Ambros.*In Psal.43*] [Hieron. *Comment.in Jerem.1*] [3]

First therefore, I shall from hence trace this Soveraigne Power to the very Spring, discovering unto you the Author whose Ordinance Dominion is, who is *God Himselfe—Ego Constitui:* I have set, or I have Constituted. [Divis 1.]

Secondly, the Person Exalted, *Thee.* [2.]

Thirdly, the Extent of this Exaltation, *Over the Nations, and over the Kingdomes.* [3.]

Fourthly, the End or Exercise of His Power, which is twofold: [4.]

1. Destructive, to *Roote out* and to *pull downe,* to *Destroy* & to *throw down.*
2. Conservative, *To Build* and *To Plant.*

The *Ecce* here prefixt shall serve as an Herald to usher in my Discourse and Application:

Behold: And sure an Argument wherein God and the King are interessed will deserve an *Ecce.* Both these Persons meet in the Text, yet in that order, that the King may know his Dependance upon God, and the People their obedience to the King, even for this reason, because *God hath set him over them.* Where He comes priviledged by such an Author, and vested with such Authority, He will deserve not an *Ecce* alone, but an *Osanna* too: *Blessed be hee that commeth in the Name of the Lord.* For this *I* is the Lord—*I have set.* [4] Behold [(Mt 21:9)] I. I have set

Though you finde no Name subscribed, the Deed sufficiently declares the Author. And where the

---
*I have commissioned thee.

A SERMON
PREACHED
At St. PAVLS
March 27. 1640.

BEING
THE ANNIVERSARY
OF HIS *MAIESTIES*
HAPPY INAUGURATION
TO HIS *CROWNE*.

By HENRY KING, Deane of *Rochester*, and Residentiary of St. *Pauls*: One of His *Majesties* Chaplaines in Ordinary.

LONDON,
Printed by *Edward Griffin*. 1640.

Act is Eloquent, other denominations are of little use. Men are divided by their Tribes, and distinguished by their Titles; If God have any Name, it is to be read in his Attributes, the first of which is *His Power* and the effect of that Power—*Ego Constitui,* I have set thee up.

The Government of the Earth is in the hand of the Lord, and when Time is, He will set up a profitable Ruler over it, saith the sonne of Syrac. Heathens themselves were sensible of this truth. Homer termes Kings *diotrepheas basilêas** and Callimachus *ek de dion basilêes:* The Off-Spring of Jupiter. So Tacitus: *Principes imperium a Deo habent, eosque instar Dei esse:* Princes receive their Scepters from God, and are in His stead.

Doe they not appeare worse then Heathens who goe about to fetch the derivation of Kings from any other Pedigree then this? Those who either place *the power of making them* in the Pope, as doe the Pontificials; or *in the People,* as Buchanan: *Populo jus est, ut imperium cui vult deferat;* Or that joyne the People in Commission with God, abridging the Latitude of the Text and liberty of God's institutions: *God Institutes, the People constitute the King; God gives the Kingdome, the people deliver it; God elects, but the People confirme the Election* (A Distinction whose termes are contrary to the Text: 'Tis there *Constitui te*). If this be true, sure our Bibles are false, and our interpretation as erroneous as our Texts. Why doe not these Men, who in many things so neerely parallel the Jesuites, get leave from their Consistory, as the other from the Conclave, to frame an *Index Expurgatorius,* to expunge those places of Scripture which make against them? Blot out that of Daniel, *The most High ruleth in the Kingdome, and giveth it to whomsoever He will*—You heard, now, who said the People had right to bestow it where they listed. Blot out that of Moses, *Let the Lord God of the Spirits of all flesh appoint a man over the Congregation*—God's election is nothing, unlesse the People approve it. Lastly, Blot out that of Salomon, *By me Kings reigne*—These men have more wisely ordered the matter. And let Kings Themselves no more write *Dei Gratia* (which Rebuffus notes to be the just acknowledgement of His Power, who gave Them Theirs) since 'tis not so much *By the Grace of God,* as by the favour and Leave of the People.

It was ignorance of the first Cause which threw a Myst of blindnesse upon the World; which Myst, for all the Beames of Knowledge that have shone upon it, never since could cleare up. For it is a permanent Error in man-kind to mistake the Instruments and Secondary Agents in God's purposes for the Maine Efficient. It is so in this, where because in the setling or translation of Kingdomes, some Intermediate Actors are used, many ascribe these Effects to them, which are onely the worke of God. The Romans were wont variously to distinguish the derivation of their Empire: By Force (so Julius Cæsar was invested), By the Senate's Election (so Tiberius), By the Souldiers (so Severus), By Inheritance (so Octavius Augustus). But to what meanes soever they imputed their Emperours, were it Birth or Conquest, Election or Usurpation, 'tis God who gives the Title to Kingdomes by the First, and He also directs and permits it by the Last.

When the Israelites desired a King, they asked him of God, who first designed Him; and by a Law never to be reversed, reserved the Choice as a Prerogative peculiar to Himselfe—*Thou shalt make Him King, whom the Lord thy God shall choose over Thee;* so that if he come in by any other way, the Act is quarrell'd by the Prophet, and disclaimed by God himselfe: *They have set up a King, but not by me.* If by Succession, it is God who Regulates and prolongs that happy Line. Children are God's blessing to every private family; but an Heire to a Kingdome is His Blessing to a Land. Which Blessing is enlarged in the goodnesse of the Successour. Therefore when the good Emperour Marcus Aurelius perceived the ill inclination of his Sonne Commodus who was to succeed, he wish'd himselfe dead. But contrary to him, Hiram congratulates those who were sent from Judæa: *Blessed be the Lord God, who hath given unto David a wise Sonne over this mighty People.* And this was that Sonne whom David professes the Lord Himselfe had made choice of. *Of all my Sonnes (for the Lord hath given me many) He hath chosen Salomon to sit upon the Throne of the Kingdome of the Lord over Israel.* Nor onely in these Calmes of Peace, but in the Tempest of

---

*Rulers brought up by god.

222 THE SERMONS TO 1669

Warre, where the Sword hewes out a title to the Crowne, and the Robe of the Prince, instead of Purple, is Dyed in Blood—Even in this storme is God the Pilot, to guide all actions to His Ends.

In the passing away of the first Monarchies from the Assyrian to the Persian, His hand was set to the deed, visible upon the Wall, and legible in those fatall Characters which told Belshazzar that the Date of his Kingdome was numbred and finished. And truely, if you consider the power of Belshazzar, and the number of his tributary Princes, and the strength of Babylon his Metropolis, which was fenced with a treble Wall of great height, and the difficulties Cyrus encountered at the assault, being forced by many Channels and trenches to drain the River of Euphrates, that so he might approach the Walls which otherwise had beene inaccessible, you will perceive it was not an *Arme of Flesh*, but the Ordinance of God, which made Cyrus strong and successefull.

<small>Dan.5:26</small>
<small>[10]</small>
<small>2 Chro.32:8</small>
<small>Sr. Walter Rauleigh. *Hist.I* part:Lib.3.cap 3: pag.35</small>

Let all the Kings of the Earth, then, *Throw down their Scepters before this Maker of Kings*, and ascribe unto Him Their Kingdomes and their Power, for they are His: *Tuum est Regnum & Potentia**—'Tis part of the Doxology in Christ's prayer. Let them not reckon their Crownes the acquisition of their owne wisedome or strength, as Jacob told Joseph concerning his portion, *With my Sword, and with my Bow I tooke it;* But cry with that victorious Captaine of the Lord's Battailes: *The Sword of the Lord, and of Gedeon*—The Lord first, and then Gedeon. Gedeon may be the instrument, the hand to achieve; but God the Cause, God the Guider and Director of the Stroke.

<small>Gen.48:22</small>
<small>[11]</small>
<small>Judg.7:20</small>

And as the King casts downe His Crowne before the Lord, Let the People cast themselves down before the King. They that lift up their hands against Him in publike Rebellion, or their Tongues in murmur against his commands, or their Hearts in disobedient and discontented thoughts, are as ill Subjects to God as to the King. You need not aske, Whom have they resisted? St. Paul tels you, *They have resisted the Ordinance of God; for Non est potestas nisi a Deo*—He hath his power from God, His Office is God's Ordinance, His person dignified by Him too. *Constitui Te*—I have set Thee up: which is the King's Exaltation, my second point.

<small>Rom. 13:2 I.</small>
<small>2. *Thee*</small>
<small>[12]</small>

When our Saviour rebuked the unruly Wind and Sea, the Disciples asked with wonder, *Who is this* whom both Elements of Aire and Water obey? If any enquire who he is before whom God hath prostrated the obedience of his people, by whom he calmeth the uproare of the multitude *And Strivings of the people*, He can be no other then the Man whom the King of Kings was pleased to honour above all the rest. He may be greater then all the Rulers of the Earth, the *Lord Christ*, but lesse He cannot be then the *Lord's Annointed*. He may well be that *Lord unto whom the Lord said, sit Thou on my right hand, untill I make thine enemies thy foot-stoole* (for the Text naturally beares it) but meaner He cannot be then the *Man of God's right hand*, whom he hath set up and made so strong for Himself & for His purposes.

<small>Math.8:27</small>
<small>Psal.18:43</small>
<small>Psal.110.1</small>
<small>Psal.80:17</small>

It was an Argument of God's mercy and care of the World, that though the Apostacy of Mankind deserved in justice a finall dissolution, whereby all things might have reverted into their first Chaos, yet in the very Act of His displeasure, when He dissipated those who in the building of Babel cast up a Mound against Heaven and raised a worke to assault Him in his Throne, *He appointed a Ruler over every People when He divided the Nations*. Common-wealths without their Governor were like Ships without an Helme, in danger to strike upon the Sand or break upon the Rocks. The King is the State's Pilot, and His Law the Compasse. By Him are we kept safe from Enemies who by invasion might break in upon us from abroad, and by Him defended from Domesticke quarrels in which, by falling foule on one another, our Fortune might be broken into nothing.

<small>[13]</small>
<small>(Gen.11:7, 8)</small>
<small>Ecclus.17:17</small>

Sheep without a Shepheard, and Water without a Bank, and a Body without an Head are Emblemes of a State without a King. The King is the Head, the People the Body. He is the Shepheard, they the Sheep: Homer calls Menelaus *Poimina laōn*. And Moses beseeches God to *appoint a man over the Congregation, least they should be like Sheep without a Shepheard*. Lastly, as Saint John saith, *Aqua sunt populi:* The people are as an inundation of Water, like the waves for

<small>[14] Homer *Iliad*</small>
<small>Num.27:16</small>
<small>Rev.17:15</small>

---

*Thine is the Kingdom and the Power.

number and for noyse, and would resemble the wild disorder of a wrought Sea (for David joynes the *Noise of the waves, and the madnesse of the people* together), did not the King by his Authority limit their inconstant motion. So necessary is a King, even as Aire to our Breath—'Tis Calvin's expression, and a true one. The Prophet Jeremy calls Him *the Breath of our Nostrils.*

There is nothing which more clearely demonstrates the *God of Order* then the subordinate Government of the Kingdomes of the Earth. Nor doth any forme of Government come so neere His Owne, which is the Archetype, the first and best patterne of all others, as the Monarchall, when a state is governed by a King as sole Commander over all. For in this singularity of power, that person who is *eikōn empsuchos Theou,* the Lively Image of God, will some way represent the Unity of his Maker too. Therefore Gerson defines Dominion, that it is *a Soveraigne Rule committed to One,* Which Aristotle confesseth to be *the most Divine and Ancient kind of Gubernation.* Search the whole volume of holy Writ, from Moses to the Judges, and from them to the Kings, and tell me whether you finde more than One successively designed by God to be the Prince and Ruler of the people.

Indeed there is good naturall reason for it. Should the Account of time be regulated, not by the Sunne alone, who is the Prince and Monarch of the Skie, but by the joint Motion of the other Planets, which were a kind of Oligarchy; or by the Starres of the first Magnitude which are *Optimates Cæli:* the Peeres of Heaven, and were an Aristocracy; what disorder would then creep into our Kalendar? But how great would that Confusion prove, if those Gregarian sparks, those Plebeian lesser Starres which people the Skie, and onely glimmer by that Contribution of Light which they receive from the greater Luminaries, should have a predominant influence upon our Seasons? To prevent therefore such irregular mischief, the Creatour gave the rule of the Day to the Sun alone. And He who kindled that Glorious light in the firmament *Set up also the King,* to governe by the splendour of his Authority upon Earth, as being *the Light of our Israel* and God's Lieutenant; or (so Plato calls Him) as *God amongst Men.*

Nor onely amongst the people of God, but in all other Nations of the world was *the Authority at first singly invested in the King,* if you will believe Justin the Historian. And though Livy reports that the Romans disliked their Government under One, and thought they should do better to put the command of the Common-wealth from a King to a Senate, or to Consuls, yet (as Gregorius Tholosanus well observes) in a very short time they deerely repented the errour of their alteration. For not nine yeares after, upon the insurrection of Manlius Octavius, one of Tarquin's Race, they were forced to put the Government to one againe whom they stiled Dictatour, who was indeed a *Monarch for his time, freely and absolutely commanding all*—for so is his Office described by the writers of the Græcian affaires, as Gregor. Tholos. observes.

'Tis true that once, in the Carthaginian warre against Hannibal, the giddy multitude made two Dictatours, Minutius Rufus and Fabius Maximus. But upon the losse of that part of the Army which was led by Minutius (whose pride and rashnesse, by dividing himself from the counsels or help of his Colleague, hazarded the whole Common-wealth), they would have no more Dictatours then Fabius. Nor did they ever after ordaine more then one, even untill the time of Julius Cæsar, who retained the stile of perpetuall Dictatour, reducing the Roman Government according to the first forme into one Hand, onely exchanging the title of King into Emperour.

I adde no more of this: Plutarch tels us, that in perillous times nothing so much conduceth to the safety of a State then *That one only exercised a free, independent and uncontrol'd Authority over all* (so Gregor. Tholosanus renders him); Whereas commands depending upon divers votes beget distraction and ruine. And as this course prevents warre, so it best conserves peace—*Pacis interest omnem Potestatem ad unum transferri.** Indeed, if there be but one soule to informe the naturall body, why should there be more then one to rule the body of a State? In the predominance of the will or the phantasie, or the affections or the passions, above reason, which should be Soveraigne,

Psalm.65:7
Calv. *Instit.lib.4. cap.20*[a]
Lam.4:20

[15]

Gerson *Part. 2. de Origin. Jur. & leg.*

[16]

2 Sam.21:17
Plato *In Polit.*

Justin *Hist. lib.I*
[17] Livius *Dec.2:lib.1*

Gregor. Tholosan. *Syntag.jur. lib.47:ca.17 n.I*[a]

Plutarch *In Camillo*[b]

Polyb.*Hist.lib.3*
[18]
Plutarch *In Fabio Max.*

Plutarch *In Camillo*[b]
[19]
Tacit.*Hist: lib.I*

---

*It is important for peace that all power should be handed over to one man.

we see what a distracted Man is made. Is it not the same in a State, when phantastick or wilfull or turbulent spirits rise up to contradict their Prince and disturbe a Realme? I shut up this Point in the conclusion of Tacitus: *'Tis best to trust the care of the Kingdome to that one whom God hath appointed over it—I have set thee over the Nations, and over the Kingdomes*, which imports the Latitude of His Power, and is my third point.

Tacitus Annal.l.

3. *Over the Nations*
[20]

It was an old complaint, that ill Glosses corrupted good Lawes. Those perversions have long since crept into the Booke of God, and men's particular interests have distorted the Texts there to their owne practises. This Scripture hath not escaped the Rack of some Interpretations which would straine it to authorize an Universall Monarchy, and others who from this foundation would raise the Pope's Supremacy above Kings.

For the first, I deny not the words taken in their primitive meaning import an Universall Soveraignty; But it is in Him only whose *Inheritance is the Heathen*, whose title is King of Kings; that is, the Sonne of God, for *Hê basileia autou pantōn despozei*—His Kingdome ruleth over all. But to extend this to any sonne of Man is contrary to God's purpose and above man's capacity. When Nebuchadnezzar is termed *King of Kings*, 'tis is respect of the many Tributary Kings under him. And when Cyrus professeth *The Lord of Heaven and Earth had given him all the Kingdomes of the Earth, All* is taken Synecdochically, for the Greatest or the Most. So though Tidal be called *King of the Nations*, he was only King of the Scythians. But where this stile is left indefinite and absolute, it belongs onely to Christ.

Psal.2:8   Rev.19:16
Psal.103:19

Dan.2:37
Pererius In Dan.2
[21] *Ezra.1:2*
Gen.14:1

If, then, such a one as Salmander call himselfe Omnipotent, or the Emperour of Bisnega delight to be stiled *The God of great Provinces, Lord of the foure quarters of the Earth and of the Sea*; or the Persian, *Brother to the Sunne and Moone, Kinsman to the Starres*: or Solynan, the Turkish Emperour, *Lord of Lords,* I shall not much wonder: These are such who in their timpanous excrescent Titles imitate Him of whom the Spirit of God testifies: *A mouth was given Him which spake high Blasphemy*. But if any who should know Christ better and understand their owne limits are so excessive in their claimes, as if all the world were made for one alone (as Juan de Puente settles it upon the Catholick King), by assuming so much to themselves, they detract from Christ, usurping upon his right.

Drexel. Prodrom. Eter nit:cap.I

Revel.13:15
[22]

La convenienca ... Juan de la Puente Madrid:1612

I deny not divers Kingdomes and severall Nations may be united under one Scepter. It was a vaunt of the Romane Empire, and perhaps true enough, that *The rising and setting Sunne were the extent of their Territory in the length*. But God onely is that great King *in whose hand are all the corners of the Earth. The Sonne of Man is Sole Lord of the Princes of the Earth*: Unto Him *the Ancient of daies gives such Dominion and such a Kingdome, that all People, Nations and Languages, and all Powers serve and obey Him*.

Petrus Cunæus De Repub. Heb:L.I.cap.10
Psal.95:4
Revel.1:5
Dan.7:14, 27

For the other, that is the Pope's Supremacy, a thing not dream't of in the Churche's purer times: it is a pride ill comporting with the Mitre, and much mis-becomming Peter's Successour. If Christ disliked the strife for precedence amongst the disciples, determining the controversie so that he who made himself Least was by Him reputed Highest, we may well conclude that *Princeps Apostolorum*, Prince of the Apostles, was an attribute never begot in His purpose, nor form'd in his Schoole. In what Luciferian forge, then, may we believe that stile of *Princeps Regum*, Lord of Kings and Disposer of Kingdomes, was shaped? If the Master allow not his Apostles to quarrell amongst themselves for Place, can we thinke he likes that the Apostolicall See should justle with His Annoynted for the upper-hand? Whereas Pindarus could say that *eschaton exousin hoi basileuontes*: Kings are the Highest upon Earth; and a better Author, *God onely here is above the Emperor*.

[23]
Luk. 22:26

And yet He who is *Servus Servorum*—A Servant of Servants—in nothing but his Name, hath by his æquivocall practise long attempted the lifting up his Triple Mitre above the Crown (as Neptune once his Trident above Jupiter). And whensoever He lists to abuse the Throne by setting his owne

[24]

Chaire where that should stand, He will abuse Scripture to make it good. If He list to play at Football with Crownes, spurning them into what Gole he pleases (as once Celestin 4 settled the Crowne, and then kickt it off the Emperor Henry 6. head), He hath an *Omnia subjecisti pedibus ejus* for his warrant: Thou hast put all things under his feet. If He will make the neck of the King his foot-stoole, as Alexander 3. used the Emperour Frederick Barbarossa at Venice, he quotes the Psalme for it, *Thou shalt tread the yong Lion and the Dragon under thy feet*. If he desire to lift up his own Candlestick, made of the Alchymy of swelling Ambition and Avarice, wrought by the Jesuits, the best Chymists of the world, enchased and imbossed by the Canonists with titles of the richest Blasphemy which the tongue of men or divels could devise—*Dominus Deus noster Papa*, Our Lord God the Pope, & *Vice-God*: One who, in despite of God's Law, does what he lists—I say, if he desire to set his counterfet Candlestick higher then any of the Seven Golden Candlesticks, and then make his own dim Candle (whose modest light ought *To shine in good works before men*) blaze like a Comet, to outshine the lights of Earth, and vie with the Host of Heaven for Lustre, he can finde Text for that too: so did Innocent III, from God's creating Two Lights, one to rule the day, the other to rule the night; and blushes not to make Himself the Greater. So that whereas Christ, whose Vicar he calls himself, is content with the stile of *ho astêr ho prōinos*—*The Starre of the morning*—no proportion of light nor measure of brightnesse will serve as Emblem of his Power but the Sunne. Not to trouble you farther: if he desire to pare the Authority of Princes and make the King his Subject, He will, with Boniface 8. and John 22, pervert this very Text, *I have set Thee over the Nations and Kingdomes*.

The note is altered much since the daies of Gregory the great. He (as He acknowledgeth to Theotista, the Emperour Mauritius his sister) tooke his Bishoprick then as a Donative from the Emperour; He was pleased to make him so. Now in requitall, his Successour takes upon him to make the Emperour. Formerly, the Pope was wont to begin His letters to Kings with this salutation, *Salutem in eo per quem Reges regnant:* Health and safety be to you in Him by whom Kings reigne; now he salutes in his own Name, for he takes on him to dispose the Kingdome, and command the King. It was not so from the beginning: Aaron the High Priest never quarrelled with Moses for the place, but obeyed him in all things, as Prince and Ruler. And Salomon exercised his authority upon Abiathar, thrusting him from his Priest-hood and bestowing it upon Zadoc. Indeed the best Popes ever submitted to the Regall Authority; & one of them gives the reason, Eleutherius by name, who in an Epistle of his, written to King Lucius, sometimes King of this Island (which Epistle is recorded amongst the Lawes of Edward the Confessour), tells him, He was within his own Kingdome God's Vicar, set up with absolute power to governe the Person and the Place, Church as well as State: which is the just meaning of being Set over Nations and Kingdomes.

But much of your wonder concerning the Pope's Ambition will be taken off, when you shall know the Consistory to be a Competitour in the Canvase for Superiority above Kings: *As many as are Members of Christ, and of His Church, must subject themselves to the Consistorian Discipline,* neither Emperour nor Bishop excepted. And Beza is as zealous as he in the cause: *Who shall exclude Kings or Princes from this not Humane, but Divine domination of the Presbytery?*

Nay, some of this rigid Sect have gone so farre, that as the scornfull Bramble in the Parable of Jotham scratcht and contended with the Better Trees for the Kingdome, they make the people scramble with their Prince for priority, and carry it too—*Populus potior Rege*, And another: *The People greater and better then the King; The Law above the King, the People above the Law*. Reade they that list, they are the words of Buchanan. I know I may take up the Prophets word's in this particular: *I tell you a wonder, which many whilst they heare will not believe*. But it is an undenyable truth. Let the Allegations I have produced out of their owne Books testifie for me, that I slander them not. Whence you may plainly discerne, that these two jarring extreames, Papacy and Presbytery, whose faces stand contrary to each other, whose opinions are opposite as the sides of the Diameter, meet in this one Ecliptick line, to darken the Authority of God's Annointed—*To pluck*

Psal.8:6

Psal.91:13

[25] *Extravagant. Johan.xxii, Tit.14:verbo Declaremus. Theses Carassae dedicata Paulo Quinto vice-Deo Neapol.Excus: 1609*
Revel.I:12

Gen.I:16

Revel.22:16

[26]

Grego.*Espist.5*

Gratiam & Apostolicam Benedictionem.
[27]   1 Kings 2:35

Antiquit. Britannic: page.5 in Margine

Suecan.*De Disciplin. Eccles:p.456*
[28]

Beza De Presbyt. pag.124[a]

Judg.9:15
Jun.Brutus *Vindic.contra Tyrannos: quest.3* Buchanan.
de Iure regni [29]
Habac.1:5

Him down, and hold Him under whom God hath *set over Nations and Kingdomes, to Root out, and to pull down, to Destroy and throw down, to Build and to Plant;* which is the Exercise of his Regall Power, and my last part.

<small>To Root out, and put down, to Build, and to Plant. Dan.4:8 Psal.82:6.
[30] Livius li.:26

Ludovicus Vives</small>

When I consider the Majesty of a King, his spreading Titles (like Nebuchadnezzar's Tree, whose forehead toucht the Clouds) whose stile reaches Divinity, For God Himselfe hath said, *They are Gods*—When I consider the extent of his Command, and the subjects of His Power, I cannot but conclude with Livy, *Regnum res inter Deos hominesque pulcherrima:* A Kingdome is the most excellent thing in the eyes of God or men. But when I consider the disquiet, the frequent toyle and daily disturbance to which a King is submitted, I may with another vary the stile: *Dominion is nothing but a glorious trouble.* They that onely looke upon the glittering matter of a Diadem, and the Lustre of the Jewels set in it, may apprehend somewhat to delight the eye: but could they understand how many cares are lodged and concentred within the Pale and Circle of that Crowne, I may in the words of a great King say, They scarce would take it for the wearing, though it lay in their way. It was (no doubt) a sad Experience which wrung those words from Cæsar's mouth: when you would name a Masse of cares and crosses, *Cogita Cæsarem*—Think upon Cæsar.

<small>[31]

Micah.4:4
Jer.51:31</small>

We who are shrubs, and in the humble valley of private life shrowd our obscure heads, heare not the loud Tempests nor feele those incessant storms which beat upon the Cedar, whose exalted top raises him neerer to the lightening and rage of the upper Element. We who sit within our own thresholds and under our own Vines, are not sensible of every noise and danger which threatens a State. Post upon Post, and Messenger after Messenger run to advertise the King, and whosoever's Midnight is interrupted by the newes, Ours can complaine of no disturbance. We therefore who enjoy the blessing of His shelter, and reape the fruits of His Care whose trouble is to confirme our quiet, and whose broken sleeps, (as Epaminondas once told his Souldiers) are to procure our sounder rest—were there no command of God nor tie of Religion which should enjoyne us to obey and love Him whom He hath set over us, might thinke our selves bound to yield Him these duties, as largely merited in the paines He takes to support our good, and his continuall labour to effect that Peace which we more freely tast then He. I may justly use that speech which once the Poet to Augustus:

<small>[32]

Ovid. Trist.L.2.235
Job 5:7</small>

*Non tibi contingunt quæ gentibus otia præstas.**

Man is borne to labour, saith Job. The very Bread he eates is moulded with the toile of his hand, and macerated with the sweat of his brow. And truely, if we observe it, this bread of carefulnesse is served up to the King's Board as part of his Dyet. This Text will shew you of what graines it is made up, and with what labour kneaded; as if God had translated the First Man's Curse into the Best Man's Office. You have heard of *Swords broken into Plowshares, and Spears into Sithes.* I can from hence tell you of Spades and Pruning-hooks turned into Scepters. Adam's Husbandry is a Type of the King's Office. Adam was set to digge and dresse the ground; so is the King, to Roote out and to Plant, to cast down, and Build.

<small>Esai.2:4

Gen.3:23

[33]
Jerem.18:9</small>

Houses are indeed Epitomes of Kingdomes, and Gardens Models of Common-wealthes. When God speaks of a *Nation or Kingdome, to build and plant it,* the King is both his Over-seer and Actour. He is *architektōn megas:* like a faithful Architect, He builds up the walls of his Jerusalem, and repaires the breaches of Sion, that so he may secure all from the searching drifts of fraud, or gusts of open violence. Nor is He *Cementarius* onely, but in a sense *Hortulanus* too: His Office hath in it *Kēpourikon ti*—somewhat of the *dressing of a Garden* or husbanding ground. Let not the comparison seeme vile: God Himself accepts it. He is *geōrgos* (saith Christ), the Husbandman, and we *Theou Geōrgion,* His husbandry. He sowed us in the bed of Nature, and will reape us in Glory hereafter. He plants us in our severall vocations, and by the irrigation of His grace, quickens our Root, and our Leaf, our faith, and our works, which are the germination and fruit of that faith. Mary

<small>John 15:1
I Cor.3:9.</small>

---

*The peace which you give to the people does not extend to you.

Magdalen mistooke Christ for the Gardiner, and Saint Augustin commends her mistake. How can we dislike the figure in his Deputy the King, when God is here pleased to express His Office by Planting and plucking up by the Root?

[34]

The disorders of the people are the rubbish of a Land, their Vices like weeds: the Schismatick is a Thorne in the sides of the Church, the factious a Thistle in the State. He that desires to make a cleer and flourishing Common-wealth must cleanse the soile from such rank weeds, extirpe the Brambles, and lop off the seare boughs, else never can any Plantation of good Morality or Religion thrive.

I need not further pursue the Metaphor. These last words present unto your view the two Pillars upon which a Kingdome leanes, the Justice and Mercy of the King. The one in the conservation of good Plants, and cherishing such dispositions as are built for vertue to inhabit—These are the *Duo verba læta* [Two joyful words] (saith Saint Hierom)—The other in punishing the bad, expressed in *Quatuor Tristibus:* in foure sad words, though the Septuagint sets down but three.

Hieron. *Comment in Jerem.1:10* [35]

These *Quatuor Infausta* (for our Translation numbers them according to St. Hierom & the Chaldee Paraphrase), *Rooting out* and *pulling down,* and *destroying* and *throwing downe,* comprehend the Coercive power of Christ as King. For which cause expositors illustrate this place by the *Iron Rod* wherewith he bruiseth the Nations, and the *Sharp Sword* in the Revelation. This Coercive power hath he committed to his Deputy. And it is one of the flowers of the Crown peculiar to his Regall Office Naturally and Regularly exercised by the King: for by his master's warrant He beares the Sword, and, saith Saint Paul, *He beares it not in vaine.* Indeed He should beare it in vaine, did it either sleep in the Scabberd, through the slack execution of Lawes; or when it should strik[e], were it hindred and withheld by other hands, who as Judges of the King's Actions countermand that Authority which God intended as Absolute as it is Lawfull—Much more if, when it is drawne out, the edge should be turned against Him.

Psal.29   Revel.1:16

Rom.13:4

[36]

Arise O Sword, and smite my Shepheard, was the barbarous inhumanity used towards Christ, and (I confesse) oft-times since practised upon His Vicegerent. I doe not onely meane the Sword of Excommunication, more frequently used by the Bishop of Rome then his Crosyer (At which weapon, also, Knox and Buchanan have shewed themselves as cunning Fencers as he), but the Materiall, the Criminall Sword: And this defended as stiffely by those you scarcely would suspect—Men who, like the mutinous Israelites, upon all occasions of pretended discontent, cry downe Moses, and set up an Idoll made out of popular Votes and Contributions; Men who have found an arme to weild the Sword of Justice which God never appointed, in the mannage of which irregular Authority they have presumed to set the people on the Bench, and place the King at the Barre. Heare it justified by one of their own pennes: *when the King is cited by the People, the lesse is brought in question by the greater—Ecce iterum Buchananus, & est mihi sæpe vocandus Ad partes!** This is strange stuffe, which I know as much offends you (who are dutifully met, in the feare of God & in this Holy Place, to do Honor unto His Annoynted whom He hath set over you) to heare, as me to rehearse.

Zach.13:7

Exod.32:4

[37]

Buchanan.*De Jur.Regn.*
Juvenal
Satyr (4.1)

How much more ingenuously and mannerly do the Jesuits deale with Princes then these kinds of men? Suarius, in his Book written against our late learned Soveraigne: *Admit the King were made by the people* (as it is quite otherwise, He is constituted by God), *yet being made, he hath an absolute independant and unquestionable Authority over the People.* And Mariana thus writes: *The King is that Person unto whom God hath committed the charge and custody of the people*—A truth which ye have the more reason to value, since it comes from their pens whom you all know to have been none of the best friends to Soveraignty. But *Magna est veritas:* Great is the truth every where, and great this truth which extorts consent from these, and will evict it from all but such who, præposterous to God's order and method, will needs read this Text backward, turning the heeles to Heaven, the head to Earth, whiles they goe about to whelme the Kingdome over the King; and set

Suarius *Defens. Fid. Cathol.Lib.3: cap.3*
[38]
Johan.Mariana
De Rege & Reg. Inst.lib.1:cap.2
I Esdr.4:41

---

*Lo Buchanan [Crispinus] once more, and he must often be called to my side!

the Nations, that is, the people, above Him whom God hath set over them—*I have set Thee over Nations and Kingdomes.*

Application
[39] I have done with the Text, and should here end. But your expectation, and the duty I owe to this Day, require some just Commemoration from me. Here, therefore, my *Ecce* turns to you, who in your relation to the Text are concerned with the King. If I have hitherto spoken of a King, is he King for his own sake or for yours? No, the Text tels: he is *Super vos constitutus—He is set over you.* As God, then, hath given him the kingdome, so he hath given you the King *(Vobis datus est),* and in that gift, as he hath Crowned the King with a Crown of Gold, he hath Crowned you with a Garland of Peace. *There was a time, when there was no King in Israel:* would you know the Character of that time? *Every man did what was good in his own eyes.* No Law then, but Lust and Will the Rule of each one's Actions; Might, arm'd with injury and violence, made the weaker Subjects; and outrage was authorised by the power of the Actour. Think how beyond all expression miserable your case were, should the anger of God cause those times to revert upon you: When barbarous Rapes and horrid Massacres (cries wherewith your eares have never been acquainted) should sound in every corner of your City. Here then begin your thanks to God, that to prevent all these mischiefes, He hath given you a King.

Judg.17:6

[40]

And now, as God once said to Moses in the top of Mount Pisgah, let me say to you: *Lift up your eyes Westward, and Northward, and Southward, and Eastward.* Look upon any other parts of the World which are governed without a King; or where there is a King, yet so abridgd in his Authority that He is, as it were, in Wardship to a Senate or some such Supervisors—in Saint Paul's phrase, *Under Tutours and Governours*—and from the manifest inconveniences which Plurality of Rulers hath produced in the World (for They are a punishment to a Land), learn to prize your own happinesse under one Ruler, as he in Homer: *Eis Koiranos estō, Eis basileus;** and to pray that those may never be Masters of their will, who would subject either Him or you to their Tumultuous Parity.

Deut.3:27

Gal.4:2
Prov.28:2
Homer
Iliad.2
[41]

Look forth yet once more upon Kingdomes governed by formes Monarchall and Absolute as yours; and think whether *Talem Constituit*—whither God hath *set such a one* over them as over you. Whether the People (in David's words) are in such a case as you, free to the exercise of true Religion, and quietly enjoying every man his own; and from these steps you will finde cause abundant to raise the measure and to multiply the acts of your thankesgiving to Almighty God, and to say, *He hath not dealt so with any other Nation.* When, in the gratefull apprehension of these blessings, you have applied unto your selves what I have now said, I shall most properly apply all other circumstances of this Text both to the Day and to the Person in whose honour it is solemnized.

Psal.*144*:15

Psal.147:20

Luke 4:21   I may indeed justly take up the words of our Saviour in the Gospell, *This day is this Scripture fulfilled in your eares.*

[42] Dan.2:21   Fifteene yeares are now fully run out since God, who Taketh away and setteth up Kings, did with one hand both take from us and restore. He translated one King into his own Kingdome, & established another upon this Throne. Thus *Dominus dedit, Dominus abstulit:* The Lord gave, and the Lord tooke away; Blessed be the Name of the Lord. This very day was our Skie darkned, and by the setting of a Sunne ever Glorious and Memorable in his Race, an unnaturall mid-night threatned us even at Noone day, for then He fell. Yet I may truely say, *though that Light was taken from our eyes, no night ensued;* for a New Light, kindled out of His Ashes, began to shine upon us, and that *Stella de Jacob* in a good sense: That Starre of Jacob, who was risen long before and (though at some distance) sparkled in our hopes, now increasing in the proportion of his light, appeared, as he drew neere, a perfect Sunne in our Zodiack, Where ever since He hath happily [43] runne; and may he there long continue in Himself, and longer in His Posterity, even whilst the

Job I:21

---

*Let there be one ruler and let there be one king.

Sunne and Moon in the firmament continue their Motion and Light. That so this *Hodie* in my Text may beare towards Him some part of that signification which it doth to Christ his Master, whose yesterday and *today* is for ever.

This day hath God set Him up, and Over Nations and Kingdomes—literally so. Those who are well read in the Schoole of Honour, and have taken the Altitude of Princes' Titles, define foure Dukedomes to the making of a Kingdome, and foure Earledomes to each of them. How God hath magnified that sacred Person whom He hath set over you may be discerned in the number of His Realmes. Under His Scepter are Severall Kingdomes, and shall I say different Nations? Or rather, what more commends the skill and confirmes the greatnesse of the Builder, Two of Them by Union made One: According to that of the Prophet, *Faciam eos in gentem unam*—I will make them one Nation. How that Cement which combin'd them is now grown loose, or that distance appeares to make them look like Two againe, becomes not me to dispute. I will rather pray that He who is the Great Peace-maker may in his good time close the rupture, and as our Gracious Soveraigne hath by all meanes endeavoured their Re-uniting (in this according to the Text truely *Cementarius*), So, in the returne to their Obedience unto Him, They may be rendred One with Us againe.

Onely this, with much joy I must take leave to say: That whatever else occasions the difference, *Religion* cannot be the Cause. It was blasphemously spoken by Rabshakeh: *Let not thy God deceive thee in whom thou trustest*. In all Christian modesty I say to you, Let not any on whose trust you relie, Those who undertake to speak from God, deceive you by perswading This to be the Cause. I appeal to their own Conscience, if they dare be tryed by truth, whether in any One Fundamentall point our Church hath shrunk from the Orthodox Faith, or fallen neerer to Popery Now then at the first Reformation. Our *Sacraments* as then, so now administred, that no jealousie of Romish Superstition or slighting profanation can taint either Him that Gives, or those that Receive. Our *Ceremonies* the same, and Those much praised, and indeed admired, by learned Bucer, in his Censure passed upon the English Liturgy at the request of Archbishop Cranmer: And by Calvin earnestly commended to those English who fled to Frankeford, whom he exhorts to Conform. And as he perswades them to be lesse Rigid: *Vos ultra modum rigidos esse nolim*—so He professeth that himself would become more moderate, and if ever he lived to Print his works anew, correct those asperities which gave offence.

Lastly, our *Book of Common Prayer,* whose Forme, for the generall, is (according to Mr. Calvin's own Rule, in his epistle to the L. Protector of England) Setled and Constant: whose particular Matter by Bucer, Peter Martyr and other learned Divines who lived in the Time of the Reformation, was approved as a work beyond Exception, every way consonant to the Word of God. For which cause, he exhorts that *with all religious care it should be retained and vindicated from neglect*. This, I say, continues not varied from the second Service Book of King Edward VI but in some Two Circumstances, One in the *Litany,* where somewhat is left out; the Other in the *Communion,* where somewhat is added, as the Act before our own declares. And therein, Those very words, whose omission in the last Printed Service Books occasioned so much Cavill, are justly the same with King Edward the Sixth's Service Book of the first Edition.

If any doubt the truth of what I deliver, let their own Eye resolve them. It was St. Paul's commendation of the Bereans, that they took not things upon trust, but themselves searched to see if they were so indeed. I would faine commend their Example to you who, if you can be content to do so, you wil neither be misperswaded by any who for their own ends suggest apparant falshoods, nor prejudicate those who contradict them.

You see the Latitude of the King's Domination, considered in the Subjects *Nations* and *Kingdomes.* Will you see in what manner He hath exercised His Power over Them? And here I appeal to all: Under what King's Scepter hath been greater care taken to prevent Divisions and weed Faction out of the Church? Witnesse that *Declaration* of his Majesty, which banish'd those abstruse controversies concerning God's Decrees of Election or Reprobation from the Pulpit—Themes which onely filled the Hearers with scruples, and sent them home with feares—Teaching by it busie men to preach Christ (as they ought), not Themselves by venting their dangerous wit or Spleen. Or when hath more sedulitie been used to remove all scandalous Rubbish out of the State, which ill morality or lawlesse abuse of locall custome had contracted? When held *Distributive Justice* (which Plato terms *eruma poleōn,* the Prop of Kingdomes) a more equall Ballance, to give every man his owne? Or when hath *Criminall Justice* been tempered with more Mercy?

It was a just complaint of Dracoe's Laws in Lacedæmonia, that their Execution was as bloody as their Character, for they were written in Bloody Letters; And the Romans lamented the cruelty of those Tribunals where the cheape Proscription of Lives made the Judgment Seate little differ from a Shambles: *Poore men sould for shoos* (so the Prophet); Or as the Turks to this day sell heads, so many for an Asper. If there be (as I would hope otherwise) any such amongst us who make such low account of men's lives that they destroy where they might Build hopes of amendment, or *Pluck up by the Root,* where they need but pare the Leafe; If there by any who in discharge of such places are governed more by Custome then Conscience, who take dark Circumstance and lame surmise for Evidence, rashly giving Sentence, and as precipitately proceeding to Execution: Let their own Soules runne the fearefull hazzard of this Account. They learne it not from Him who placed them on the Tribunall, whose Sword hath seldome been wet with striking Offenders, and scarcelie unsheathed against those who brought themselves within the reach of His Coercive Justice. I may well apply that of Seneca: By practising so long upon his Patience, They have whetted and *provoked Him to a Severity, which He hath been most unwilling to put in Execution.*

Now, for the Conservative part of His Office, expressed in these Termes, *To Build, and to Plant:* whether you take Building *Materially* or *Morally,* in both these senses hath He been and still is a Glorious Builder. Nor will I carry you farre off for instance. As the Disciples to Christ concerning the Temple of Jerusalem, so let me say to you *ide, potapoi lithos:* See the Materialls for the re-edifying of this Mother Church, of which, should I say nothing, the Timber would cry, *Et Saxa loquentur*—and the very stones speake. Did any Eye within these few yeares hope to behold this neglected Temple (like Sion in her mournfull widowhood sitting in the Dust) trimmed up like a fresh Bride, Her wrinckled face, guttered with the teares of her decay and furrowed by the injurie of Time, made smooth againe, Her ragged garments changed into costly robes? Need I tell you who hath put upon her Beautie for Dust and Rubbish, and a face of Repaire for Ruine? Is it not the zeale of our most gracious Jehoash, who hath not onely (as King Jehoash) said: *Goe out into the Cities of Judah, and gather of all Israel money, to repaire the House of God,* but set them a patterne in His Own Munificence? Is it not His zeale, and the Care of his Pious Jehoida, the High Priest, who hath faithfully Stewarded the cheerfull *Contributions of the Princes and all the People,* and (what I mention to your Reputation) Your Benevolence, to the advancement of this *Good worke performed to God, and to His House?*

I can referre you to other Walls then These, of differing Matter, and quite another Station; whose *Foundations* are layed *not in the Hils,* (as the Psalmist spake of Jerusalem) but in the Floods. I doe not here crie out in the Poet's wonder, *Quanti montes volvuntur aquarum!*—what Hils of water rowle there? But what a Royall Navie (for Number and Burthen farre exceeding all which preceded Him) to bestride and mount the tops of those foaming Billowes? what Mountaines of Oake upon those Watery Mountaines! what Wooden Castles to keepe the Ocean in awe, like strong Walls and Bulwarks to repell those Adversaries who have long made this Kingdome the aime of their Ambition and Revenge!

It was the Grecians' Obloquie, indeed the Losse of the whole Empire, that at the Siege of Constantinople, they would not help their Emperour Constantinus Palæologus with mony, either to provide Ammunition or pay Souldiers to Man the Walls; by which defect that famous Citty was left to the pillage of Mahomet, and their incomparable wealth enriched the Turkes, a very small portion whereof timely afforded had saved all and rescued themselves from slavery. It will be much for your Honour that in succeeding Times, History may not have cause to report you men of such narrow hearts or Close hands. And let it be your present comfort that, like good Patriots for your Countrie's

1640

safety, you have contributed to the Building and Manning of those Wooden Wals, which unlesse they be able to keep off an Enemy, You flatter your selves in vaine to thinke that yours at home can doe it.

Finally, for his Morall Building, I may boldly affirme, That for all the vertues requisite to the making up of a most compleat Prince, and the Example of such a Life wherin the blackest fangs of detraction (though dared to speak their worst) can finde nothing to traduce or fasten on, No one (Consult your Chronicles)—I say, no One hath more fairely Edified then He whom God hath set over You. With how much truth may I apply to Him the Poet's Complement to Augustus: [54]

> *Urbs quoque Te, & rerum lassat tutela tuarum,*
> *Et Morum, similes quos cupis esse Tui.**

Ovid Trist: lib.2 (233–34)

He hath as Gloriously Reigned over you in His Example as in His Care, And to the whole World approved Himselfe *as Great a King in Vertue, as in Title:* In every particular making good that Rule, *Sit Exemplo major qui est authoritate Maximus.* Whether I looke on his Œconomick Relations as Husband, Father, or indeed as a good Man; Or whether I mention his solid Wisedome, and cleere Judgement, able to steere the Counsels and direct the most prudent Ministers of State in His Affaires; Or his undaunted Courage (for as God hath given Him a strong and Active Body, so He hath matcht it with as Active a Mind), not sparing to adventure His own Person where the safety of His People required, and Thus *Monstrat tolerare labores, Non jubet;* He hath not onely commanded others upon danger, but lead them on Himself; Or His excellent Moderation and Patience, not apt to be wrought into easie heate or rash effect of Passion; Or the Humility of His Disposition, made up of Titus his Affability, accessible to the meanest Suitors who come to solicit Him, and at all times more like a Father then a Master to those about Him; Or His singular Integrity, in which He may acquite Himselfe as righteous Samuel once did; *Beare record of me before the Lord: whom have I done wrong to, or whom have I hurt, or of whose hand have I received any Bribe to blind my Eyes?*—making His Justice, not His Power, the rule of what He doth. For *Nescit posse quod posse non debet:* He will not know the use of his Authority, but where Religion and Right make his Commands legitimate. [55]

I Sam.12:3

Let me not here omit the Regular distribution of his Time, for his Exercise, for his Meales: through the whole Course of his Life never guilty of the least intemperance. 'Tis that which Salomon holds worth the noting: *Blessed art thou, O Lord, when thy Princes eat in due season, for strength, not for excesse.* But above all (that indeed which crownes the rest), The Regularity of his Devotions, used by Him with such Reverence and Constancy that He hath made the Court Canonicall by His houres—Twise every Day, and openly, presenting Himselfe in God's Service, as if He meant by his owne practise to demonstrate before His Houshold a Text much like the Apostle's Rule, *He that will not Pray, let him not Eate.* [56]

Eccles.10:17

2 Thes.3:10

I am not to learne that in such Arguments as these, men's eares are commonly so obstructed with prejudice, Truth can hardly find Admittance. The supposed Ends of the Speaker or flattery of the Object are the ordinary excuses to divert their belief; But this must not prohibit me to speake, nor should it make you loth to heare. I doe not forget Where I am, or Whose Errand I deliver. This is no place to give Titles to Men, but to give Honour to God. Yet I must tell you, when there is so much Justice in the Cause, and so much Merit in the Person, and such an Opportunity as this to warrant, and my Conscience to beare Record, that (in the Attestation of Saint Paul) *I speake the truth in Christ, I lie not.* For 'tis not *Quod Audivimus,* but *Quod vidimus*†—I take not up on hearc-say: my owne Attendance hath long and often made me an Eye-witnesse, and I thanke God that I have [57]

Rom.9:1

---

*The city also wearies you, and the guardianship of your empire and of morality, which you wish to be like your own.
†What we have heard . . . What we have seen.

seene it. I say, for me on these termes to be silent were to prevaricate against the Truth; and for you not to desire to hear it, were to declare your selves most unthankfull to God, who hath blest you with so Religious and Just a King.

[58] I might adde a great deale more: But as the Person I speake of needs not, so all I can deliver falls short, and rather Darkens then Sets Him forth. I will therefore, in the last Place, for all the vertues His Example hath Planted amongst you, for His sincere endevours to continue (Like a true *Nursing Father of His Church*) the Religion planted in It, Exhort you to Pray that for our sins God deprive not us too soone of so rich a Blessing, by Taking Him away. For if there be any (as I am farre from the belief) who love not to heare Him praised, I hope they may well like to heare Him Pray'd for. Pray, therefore, *for the Life of the King and of his Sonnes:* Pray for *Him,* and for *His Plants,* The Pledges of our future Peace, That God will blesse Him in His Gracious Queene and Her happy Fruits, *In His Root* and in *His Branch,* In the *City* and in the *Field.* Let all who rise up against Him be *Covered with shame and ruine, But upon Himself, Let His Crown flourish*—O let it long flourish. [59] And when the sad Day comes wherein He must exchange This Kingdome for a Better, Let His Crown of Gold be changed into a *Crown of Glory.* Amen.

Esa.49.23.

Ezra 6:10

(Mal.4:1)
Deut.28:3 Psal.132:*18*

1661

A
SERMON
Preached at Whitehall
On the 29 of May,
Being the Happy Day of His Majesties
Inauguration and Birth

EZEK 21.27.
I will Overturn, Overturn, Overturn it, and it shall be no more, until he come whose Right it is, and I will give it him.

[2] Num.23:21 You will easily judge Thunder and Earthquakes improper Prologues to usher in such a Triumph as the Inauguration of a King. When Balaam in his Parable concerning Israel told Balak, *The shout of a King is amongst them,* sure, he meant not such boisterous Acclamations as This, whose noise disturbs the Upper Region, and affrights the Lower; But my excuse must be the common Say, that such Meteors as Thunder & Lightning usually clear a troubled Sky, and purge an ill-condition'd Ayr.

We have of late years suck'd in the unwholsome vapours of an Air tainted with Rebellion and Rapine, with ill Opinions and worse Actions, and therefore need the loudest Thunder to fright us into our lost Duties, and cleanse our Element, grown as degenerous as our selves.

Verse 26 I do not mistake the words in comparing them to thunder—*It is the voice of the Lord: Hæc dicit Jehovah.* 'Tis *he utters this voice, a mighty voice,* which *shakes the wilderness, and breaks the* Psal.29:5, 8 *Cedars of Lebanon;* which levels the Mountains to make them equal to the Vale; and beates the Towers, whose height threatned Heaven, to rubbish, untill they ly as low as their foundation. *The* [3] Nah.1:5 *mountains quake at him and the hills melt, and the Earth is burnt at His presence.*

2 King. 13:18 The dying Prophet Elisha was angry with the King of Israel, when he bid *him strike with the Arrows upon the ground,* that he strook only *Three times:* had he strook oftner, the Syrians had v.19 been quite overthrow'n. But this Artillery which stands mounted in my Text is sufficient to do the work intended. After these Three Overturns there needs no re-inforcing of the blow, nor is there any Subject left for further execution. The violent Hurrican, fiercest of whirlwinds, doth not more

A
SERMON

Preached at WHITE-HALL

On the 29th. of May,

Being the Happy Day of His Majesties Inauguration and Birth.

By HENRY L. Bp. of CHICHESTER.

Published by his Majesties Command.

LONDON,
Printed for *Henry Herringman* and are to be sold at his Shop in the Lower Walk in the New Exchange. 1661.

surely destroy all obstacles standing in the way, than these Three Overturns Remove that which obstructs His way who was to Come.

I know the History properly points at Zedekiah, who was that *wicked prophane Prince* (verse 25)
2 King.25:27. condemned to utter destruction: And at Jehoiachin, whose head was exalted by Evilmerodach upon the Abasement of the other's height.

[4] The Chaldee Paraphrase saith: As those words, *Take off the Crown,* threatned Zedekiah, so
V.21 *Remove the Diadem* threated Seraiah, the High Priest, *who was accordingly slain at Riblah*—This Diadem or *Cidaris* being an ornament worn on the Priest's head, and (as Hieron. writes) had the Name of God engraven upon it; As also you read (Wisd.18:24) *with thy Majesty graven upon the Diadem of his head.*

Yet this particular of my Text is Mystically interpreted of Christ, by whose Copy Kings hold their Right, *All Dominion being given to Him,* and from him derived upon His Vice-Gerents here in Earth.

And it may Prophetically and properly enough look on Zerubbabel, that excellent Prince, who was a Type of Christ too; whom, after a long interruption of the Regal Line, God raised up to *rebuild the walls of Hierusalem,* and *Repair the breaches of his Temple.* To which end he threatneth
Agge.2:3 an *Overthrow to the strength of Kingdoms* which should oppose his work of Restauration.

[5] I shall take the liberty, and that without violence to the words or distorsion of the sense, to apply them unto the happy occasion of *This Day,* and to reflect from hence upon the Calamities suffered under Those who sought to hinder It. Yet with no purpose to refresh the Memory either of Those Persons, or the Mischiefs by them Acted (which the Grace and Mercy of Him who was the greatest sufferer would have buried in an *Act of Perpetual Oblivion*), but in thankful duty to God, to commemorate the defeat of Their late unpardonable practices, who by Fraud Abjured, and by Force did all they could to keep out *Him who was to Come* from possessing his undoubted Right.

Division 1. So that this First Part of my Text is a Judgement threatned, not leaving untill That it threatens be utterly destroyed—*I will Overturn, Overturn, Overturn it, and it shall be no more.*

2. But this *Judgement* hath a Sequele of *Mercy,* and was intended only to make way for a greater
[6] Blessing in One who Comes after: which is an *He* eminent for His Personal endowments *(Until He Come),* And eminent for His Power, which is supported by Two such Pillars that it can never fail:
3. A successive Right of his own—*Until He Come whose Right it is.*
4. And then the hand of God, who establisheth this Right as His Donation: *And I will Give it Him.*

I.Part: *I will Overturn, &c.* I take the words in that Method wherein they ly: *I will Overturn, Overturn, Overturn.* The Greek, in stead of *Overturn,* reads *Adikian, Adikian, Adikian: Iniquity, Iniquity, Iniquity.* If you joyn them Both together, the Construction holds properly in relation to God's Justice, who will certainly by His revenge Overturn all Iniquity. And if you apply it to our own Condition, you must grant we have
Psal.55:9, 10 seen *Iniquity and violence and strife in the City,* and felt the bitter effects of them for many years. Nay, there was *Triplex Iniquitas:* Iniquity, Iniquity, Iniquity—one successive to the other, in the
[7] several variations of our Misery. And by the blessing of our Gratious God we have seen *Three Overturns,* like so many Batteries raised to destroy Each of them.

1. The First *Overturn* bent against the Tyranny of a single Person, who was the fatal Product of a Counsail more impious than the Means whereby he compassed his Bloudy ends. A strange Usurper, of whom I may truly say

Claudian
Nec bellua tetrior ulla est
Quam servi rabies in libera colla furentis:

Never was there Beast of that outragious Pride and Cruelty, who from a contemptible low condition was lifted so high as to trample upon the Laws and Necks of a (till then) Free people.

Psal.93:4 'Tis true, *The floods that then lifted up their voice—Vox Cataractarum:* Those *Tumultuous*
Psal.65:7 *waves,* and the *Madness of the People* in their unruly votes, Cryed quite contrary to God's Text. In

stead of *Take off: Set on* the Crown upon the head of usurpation, *Remove* the Diadem from Him who had only Right to wear it, adorn the Temples of a Tyrant. But *the Voice of God is mightier* (saith David). This Over-ruling voice cryes here against This tyrant, as *Profane* as Zedekiah at his worst—*bebelos kai anomos* (they are his Epithets)—and more wicked, for I find not Zedekiah's hand stain'd with half the Blood our Monster in his short Rule shed: I say, the same *voice cries from Heaven* which bid *Cut down the Tree* in Nebuchadnezzar's vision: *Take off the Crown,* dethrone the Usurper; and when He says the word, who can resist or countermand? [8] Vers.25

Dan.4:14

One wo is past: Our first *Overturn* hath cast down this aspiring Lucifer, causing *his Image* and remembrance *to vanish out of the City,* like a Night vision. So that we may ask *Quomodo cecidisti? How ar't Thou fallen? O how suddenly do'st Thou cast them down!*—such slippery footing hath all Greatness which is not warranted by the true Doner, but built on a Foundation of Blood. Psal.73:20

The next *Overturn* is against a Monster of more heads, A Complicated Tyranny under that Bed of Snakes which, Cut asunder formerly, Closed again in '59, Renewing their Cast skins with the old Practice to Tyrannise over their fellow Subjects, *According to the Trust reposed in them* (which was the word in fashion)—That Aggregate of Rulers, to whom no Name is proper but his who was the President of their Assembly, Legion, *For they were many*—A Medly compounded of all Trades, of all Professions, from the Soldier to the Mechanick Artizan; which in their Mixture resemble the Feet of Nebuchadnezzar's Image, Their whole design being supported like That, with *Iron* and *Clay:* The Miry Clay to shew the abject dirty Instruments engag'd in their new modell'd Rule, The Iron to enforce Obedience to it. At the Building of Babel all sorts of workmen were joyn'd: It was the same in this work of Confusion begun upon the Kingdom and the Church. In so Destructive a work these Operators were needful—'Twas fit that such men, who had before understood the use of the Hammer and the Ax, should be employ'd when Churches were to be demolished, and the *Carved work of our Temples* (as the Prophet complain'd) *Broken down with Axes and Hammers.* 2.

[9]

Mar.5:9

Dan.2:42
V.43
(Gen.11:1–9)

[10] Psal.74:6

But this unequal mixture overthrew the whole Frame of their design. The Sword, which for a time strengthned this lime building, deserting them, caus'd it to crumble into dust: As Cramps of Iron with-draw'n from a Rotten House make the ill-built Fabrick sink. And those examples of Insolence, which like the *Tail of the Dragon had cast down all our Stars,* both Those of the First Magnitude, the Peers, and Those who were Equal to Themselves yet joyn'd not in their horrid sense, were by the blessing of God and by His second *Overturn* Cast down themselves, becomming spectacles of reproach to all the world in those punishments which they deservedly suffered. Rev.12:4

There is but one *Overturn* more, and that, like the last breath and blast of a Storm when the violence is spent, ushers in a Calm. This I look on as bent against that Rising, little more than a year since, whose Spring and Head appeared in these parts, but the Stream was to be encreased in every County as they passed from this our Metropolis, whence their frantick Leaders set out, to the other Metropolis in the North—An attempt to hinder His Arrival who was expected, when His Foot was even upon the threshold ready to enter into his own, by an Army Collected from all Quarters of the Kingdom. Which design look'd at first with a dreadful aspect, like the *Ramm* in Daniel's vision, *Pushing Westward and Northward and Southward,* in each Part whereof some scatterings of the storm fell, until the Clouds which bare this Tympany vanished, almost without Noise, at the farewel of it. 3.

[11]

Dan.8:4

This, the prudent Counsailes of some Renowned Patriots, industrious to vindicate their oppressed Countrie's Liberty, and the valour of a Faithful General (who deservedly wears an Honor no man hath cause to envy), by crushing the New-threatning dangers as well as by suppressing the Old, opened so fair a way for His Arrival who was to come, that not a dropp of Blood was spilt to stain the Glory of His entrance, nor did any visible Face of danger appear to disturb his Peace being Come; For God sayes, he will *Overturn* whatsoever might withstand Him, *And it shall be no more.* [12]

Such an Approach as this discovers the hand which guided him to us, and deserves our loudest *Hosanna* to welcome Him, *Blessed is he that comes in the name of the Lord.* Psal.118.26

Those Others who went before Came in their own Name, meer Properties, Counterfaiting such

State as Actors on the Stage, whose Reign lasts no longer than the Scean. We had not for many years beheld the True Face of Majesty untill He came, who appears in the next circumstance of my Text.

You may please to note He is a single Person: *Eis koiranos estō, eis basileus*—here's no Plurality of Rulers. *Many Counsaillours* are the strength of a Kingdom, but more Princes than one, like many Suns in the Firmament, the certain ostents of destruction.

This *He* stands *kat' exochên,* as a note of eminence upon His Person and excellence upon His Endowments.

We find the First King of Israel was designed from the Goodliness of his Person: Saul was so, of whom I may say as Virgil of Turnus,

Et toto vertice supra est:

He was higher by the head than the rest of the People. *See* (saith Samuel when he presented Him) *whom the Lord hath Chosen, that there is none like to Him amongst all the People*—such a Stature and such a Person became a King. Petrus Cunæus writes *Not only Barbarous people, but the most Civilized attributed very much to the Presence and Stature and Majestick deportment of the Body; Thinking Those Capable of the highest atchievements who were endued with the best and Goodliest Shape.* Hieron. gives the reason: *The beauty of the Soul is consider'd by the features of the Body, which is the Soul's outward Garment.*

This made Samuel, sent to Annoint a King out of Jesse's house, when he saw Eliab, to beleeve him the man, for the Bravery of his Person; until God rectified his error, and pointed out David, who though not of the same Size and Pitch with his brother, was a *Goodly Person.* You will easily judge that, because, intending to combate Goliah, Saul *put his own Armour upon him,* which in a small Stature had been ridiculous to attempt.

In all the Histories I have read, I find not any Nation but one who best liked Persons ill-graced in their Bodies' lineaments for their Princes. Pedro Mexia puts this difference between the Gothes and the Saracens, That the Gothes desired a Prince of Tall Stature, The Saracens better approved one bedwarfed and of mean Features.

Generally, the Rule for Princes was the same which God appointed for the Priests: where Blemishes and Imperfections of the Body made the One incapable to serve at the Altar, The Other not so welcome to the Throne.

Our Third Richard's deformed Body and ill aspect made him look'd on as that Prodigy whom all fear'd, none lov'd. Therefore Socrates beleeved those could portend nothing but Mischief on whose Bodies Nature had set her Brand, and whose Aspect she had mark'd with cross ill-boding lines.

Now as the Outward Form of the Body makes a Candidate for a Kingdom, according to Aristotle—*Forma digna Imperio*—So the Endowments of the Mind compleat the Choice.

As Wisdom; This was the Cause of Joseph's advancement over Ægypt: *Can we find* (saith Pharaoh) *such a Man as this in whom is the spirit of God?* And it was Hiram's gratulation to Solomon, *Blessed be the Lord this day who hath given unto David a wise son to rule over this great People.*

Deliberation; Not rash in Action, nor unwilling to hear advice, but weighing each enterprise in the Scale of Counsail and Reason: *As it is a Prince's Prerogative that he cannot be Compell'd,* so 'tis his Misery not to be Counsaill'd.

Temperance; *Happy art thou O Land when thy Princes eat in due season for strength,* not admitting Disorder in their Meales.

Then Mildness and Sweetness and Affability in disposition; This made Titus the Emperour stil'd the Delight of Mankind, admir'd whilst he liv'd, and lamented in his death as the only darling of his Empire, born to oblige his whole People.

Personal valour; This mov'd Israel to elect Gideon for their Prince: *Come thou and Rule over us, Both Thou and thy Son and thy son's Son; for thou ha'st delivered us from the hand of Midian.*

Above all, Piety and Religion towards God; Josiah's singular Devotion and Zeal to God's service stand as Examples to render his Memory pretious through all Ages—To be a *Nursing Father of the Church* is one of the richest Jewels in a King's Crown.

Lastly, Nobility in his Extraction and Birth; *Happy ar't thou, O Land, when thy King is the son of Nobles*—so sayes the Preacher.

But when there are None of These, Neither Care of Religion nor Regard of Law, Neither Outward form Nor Inward Endowments, Neither Birth to dignify the Body Nor Vertue to ennoble the Mind—*Set thou a wicked man to rule over him:* This is the highest Calamity, the greatest Curse that can befall a Land. We have cause to say so, having by sad experience too lately felt the Mischief.

Be it spoken to the Honour of God and the Confession of a just Truth (far from any low purpose of Adulation, which neither befits my Office nor This Presence), we miss none of these Excellencies, these Vertues in that Royal Person whom God hath set over us. Each one's eye may inform any that doubt, in much of what I say, And the dayly experience of his scarcely pattern'd Goodness confirm the rest.

Whether I mention His constant Piety or love of Justice, His Active or Passive Fortitude, In all probations of a Daring Valour, who hath Outdone him? (Let Worcester be the witnesse.) And I am sure in the Trial of His Patience for many years none Could Out-suffer Him. 'Twas *Iugum portatum a Iuventute:* He hath been yoak'd to Necessities, and acquainted with Misfortune from his tender Age.

And for the Royalty of His Extraction, were I an Herald and not a Preacher, I might blazon It to the full, Proclaiming to all the World, That *He who is come to us* might Claim the Crown by His proper Merit, did it not Descend upon Him as His Undoubted Right.

It follows in the next words: *Whose Right it is.*

There be but *Two Great Rights* which you find mentioned in Scripture:
1. *Ius Primogeniturœ*, the Right of Primogeniture; 2. *Ius Regni*, the Right to a Kingdom.

In the first of these all Domination was originally founded; For the Elder Brother in his Tribe was *Princeps Familiœ*, the Prince of his Family. And not only the Excellence of Dignity which was his Birth-right, But the Inheritance is so fastned to Him as if God intended no separation, either by the Hatred or Affection of the Parent. The Text is most remarkable (and I wish all Parents would lay it to heart): *If a man have Two wives, one Beloved, and another Hated, and They have born him Children, both the Beloved and the Hated; And if the First-born son be hers that was Hated; Then it shall be when he maketh his sons to Inherit that which he hath, That he may not make the son of the Beloved First-born before the son of the Hated, which is indeed the First-born; But he shall acknowledge the son of the Hated for the First-born, by Giving him a double Portion of all that he hath; for he is the beginning of his strength, the Right of the First-born is his.*

Therefore, though the Law hath been overcurious to un-rivet this Birthright by God's & Man's Law entail'd upon the Elder, bringing in Feigned Persons & False Vouchees, and Formal Proclamations to devest It, I must only say thus much; *Sic non fuit ab initio* (as Christ said of Divorce)—*It was not so from the Beginning, but out of the hardness of men's hearts* did this Invention spring. How ill an Inheritance wrested from the Right heir to be plac'd upon another hath prosper'd, let the Example of so many unhappy families ruin'd upon this Accompt testify.

The second is *Ius Regni*, the Right to a Kingdom, which hath *Ius Divinum*—a Divine Right—for its warrant: *This receives such Authority from God, that the whole World cannot abrogate it.*

I do not only mean a Successive Right, but an Elective. I Confesse where Princes are Elected by their Subjects, the Government is not so Absolute, being oftimes clogg'd with Conditions, yet is the Right so firm that it can never be Reversed nor Reassumed by Those who first conferr'd it. Bellarmine is of a contrary Judgment when he saith, *although the People Actually transfer the Power upon the King, Yet Habitually They retein it in Themselves.* But this is Contradicted by a Persons of his own Party eminent for their Learning and famous for their Writings. Suarez plainly chargeth him with Falshood—*Non est simpliciter verum Regem pendere in sua potestate a Populo, etiamsi ab ipso eam acceperit**—And afterwards he very honestly and fairly Concludes: *When once a King is lawfully constituted, He hath Supreme Power over the People*. Again Royardus: *The People cannot withdraw their subjection from a lawful Prince*. Lastly, Franciscus a Victoria: In a Case like This (The Cardinals' Election of the Pope), *Those who Elect have not Authority over him whom they have Elected, but only an Authority to Apply that Dignity*—So sure and irrevocable is the Right of an Elective Prince.

But when the *Right of Succession* brings a King to his throne, This is of all others the Noblest, the Firmest, and Carry's the greatest mark of God's favour, both to the Present Prince, and to Those from whom he was Derived.

Succession to the Crown of Israel is by God promised to David as one of the Richest Temporal blessings He could give. He bids Nathan the Prophet tell him, *When thy dayes be fulfilled, and Thou shalt sleep with thy Fathers, I will set up Thy seed after Thee which shall proceed out of Thy bowels, And I will establish his Kingdome*. When God is angry with a Land, he cuts off the Line of Succession: *Write this man Childless;* He *quencheth his Light* and the Lustre of his Name, sending him to his last Bed *like a despised Lamp*, inglorious, and in the Dark, without any Heir to preserve either his Power or his Name.

When this Successive Right was interrupted, though by persons of the same Regal Line, what Tragedies ensued, and what Blood was spilt, let our own Chronicles resolve, from Richard the 2. to Henry 6.

It is the goodnesse of God to us, that we enjoy a Successive King: And it is the King's Glory, that He comes to us derived to His Crown through a Succession of Numerous Monarchs. To what Votes soever *Elective* Rulers ow[e] their Scepters, *Succession* is the Vote of God, who both declares the Right, and then Confirms it as his Donation. It follows in the last place:

And I will give it.

4. Crowns conferr'd by other hands sit loose and tottering upon the Head of such as wear them; *I will give it,* keeps Them fast.

This is the *Magna Charta* for Princes, The Great Charter by which Kings hold the Right to their Kingdoms: *By Me Kings Rule*. It is *God who sets up and pulls down, Giving the Kingdome unto whom He pleaseth*. Tertullian said well, *The Emperour is made by Him who made him Man before*. Even Heathens joyn'd in the confession of this Truth. The Greek Poet tells you, *Ek de Dios Basilêes;*† And Tacitus, more like a Christian than a Heathen: *Princes receive their Ruling Power from God and are in His Stead*.

Where are Those, then, who place the Right to Dispose Kingdoms in the Pope? As do his Sycophants the Canonists, who blush not to bestow the Style of God upon him—*Dominus Deus noster Papa*‡—That so He may have better colour to bestow the Other.

Or Those in another Extreme, who entitle the *People* to this Power, *Populo ius est ut Imperium cui vult deferat*.§ A strange Prodigy in opinion, not heard of until Those Men came into the World, who (as was falsly alleg'd of the Apostles at Thessalonica) *Turn'd the World upside down,* placing the Feet above the Head, and *Subjecting* the *Higher Powers,* contrary to the Rule of God, to the *People,* who by His Command ought to be subject unto Them.

I may apply Nazianzen's question to this purpose: *What madnesse is this to leave the Head and take Rules from the Feet?* He goes on, *It is præposterous to the Order of Nature when the Fountain is obstructed, and the Stream which borrows being from it holds full Course;* when the Sun loseth

---

*It is simply not true that the King depends for his power on the people, even though he received it from them.
†Kings are the offspring of the gods.
‡Our Lord God the Pope.
§It is the people's right to offer the power to whom they will.

his luster, and a dimme Star enlightned by it governs the World. *Male imperatur cum regit vulgus Duces,* cryes the Tragedian: It is a pittifull Kingdom where the People Rule the Prince. [26] Senec.*Trag.*

Chymists will tell you nothing can make Gold but the Great Elixar which Turns all it Toucheth: Doubtlesse the People's Power is a Metall of too low and Coarse Allay to produce a Crown. *Thou shalt set a Crown of Pure Gold upon His Head,* is God's Peculiar. Psal.21:3

When the rebellious Israelites in Moses' absence would needs make a God, That is a Leader or Ruler to go before them, They contributed their Earings to the carrying on that design; But the Effect and Issue of that Contribution was only a Calf. I beseech you remember, from all our Contributary Plate, from the silver Basin even to the smallest Bodkin, whether we had any Productions amongst us better than This. Exod.32:1 V.4

Certainly before Knox and Buchanan, and Junius Brutus, These Doctrines to Diminish Princes were never broached. One tells you, *The King hath no Propriety either in his Kingdome, or His Revenue.* Another quarrels Him for the upper-hand, scarcely grants him Precedence: If he do, 'tis all, And unlesse in Private, will not allow Him the Better Man. When he comes in Publick, *The People are his Better and much above him.* Again, *Though the King be Greater than any Particular Subject, Yet, he is Lesse than the whole People.* Again, *The People have the same Power over their King as the King hath over any single Man;* And again (take him for all) when the People call their King in question before them, *Minor ad Majorem in Ius vocatur:* the Lesser is Convented, Arraigned, Condemned by the Greater. Excellent stuff! From whence you may discern what hands lay'd the first foundation of our *High Courts of Justice.* Indeed, after all the Arts and Labour to assert this pretended Power of the People, after all the distorted Scriptures and Miss-apply'd Texts by Those *Sons of Bichri* who blew the First Trumpets of Sedition in our Israel—*Curse ye Meroz* &c. *And cursed be he that withholds his Sword from shedding Blood;* And *To your Tents O Israel we have no part in the son of Jesse,* with many like these—There was but one speeding uncontrollable Text to do Their Bloudy Business: *This is the Heir, come let us kill Him, and then the Inheritance* (the Right to dispose the Kingdom) *is ours.* [27] Junius Brutus *Vindiciae cont. Tyrannos, quæst. 3:p.136* Buchanan *De Iure Reg. apud Scotos* [a] Ibid. [28] (Judg. 5:23) Mat.21:38

I cannot without horrour mention it; And I pray God There be not too many amongst us who yet hold an Obedience not out of Conscience but Constraint or Outward Complyance, because They want opportunity to Resist.

This is the sense of a great Leader in his time, who, by occasion of that Text, *Put them in mind to be subject to Principalities,* replyes, It was good Politick advise St. Paul gave for that time—The Christians were few and poor, had no power to do otherwise, Nor were Ripe for any other purpose. I give you his own words.* Tit.3:1 [29] Buchanan *De Iure Reg.*

Strange kind of Men, who from such Principles as these scatter their Wildfire both from the Presse and Pulpit, to enflame their abused Hearers and Kindle that Combustion which by the Mercy of God hath been so newly quenched within this City, and indeed through the whole Kingdome (for it was a very diffusive Plott). And as it was one of the most Treacherous Designs wherewith these late Dayes of Mischief Teemed, so we have Cause to Multiply our Thanksgiving to God for the Timely Discovery and Defeat of it. The Apostle gives Them their proper Style, of *Filthy Dreamers,* Phanaticks and Enthusiasts *who despise Dominions, and speak evil of Dignities,* whether in the State or in the Church. If any thing of Order, or Decency, or Setled devotion be offered to Them, They Cry out *Popery* and *Superstition,* with as much Noise and as Little Sense as Demetrius with his Fellow Craft-men did upon Diana at Ephesus. And when you come to examine their dislike by sober Reason, They can give as little account as They: *The greater part whereof* (The Text tells you) Knew not what They ailed, *why They came together,* or why they made those hideous exclamations. [30] Jud. Ep:v.8 Act 19:24, 28 Vers.32

Men who decry the Pope, yet Cry up Themselves into an Authority as great as His, Not onely over the People but over the Prince; That declame against the present Government to introduce a

---

*Translated in the explanatory notes to this page.

240 THE SERMONS TO 1669

Judg.9:15 — Worse of their own—As Abimelech, who was the *Bramble* in Jotham's Parable, invited *All to Rest under his shadow,* which Could afford no Shelter but a Scratch—No Appeal lying from their
[31] *Protestat:* Jul.1638 *Proclam'd at Glasgow* — Irregular Consistories but to Themselves. (I need not tell you who Proclaimed Assemblies to be the supreme Judicatures in all Causes Ecclesiastical—some of those Heads are high enough now.) By which meanes They so entangle Those who fly to Their perplexed Judicatures for Relief that, like Sheep who in a Tempest run to the Bryar for Protection, They Return with a lost Fleece and a Torn skin.

Conclusion — But This is a Day of Good tidings, a Day of Comfort and Rejoycing. I will not therefore mingle any sharp Invective with it against Those who entertein it not with equal Duty or with the same affection as we do; Neither will I give a farther mention to These Discords which marr the Musick
Psal.118:24 — of this Day, A day of God's making—*Hic est Dies quem fecit Dominus.* Nay, *Hic est Dies in quo*
[32] — *Dominus fecit Regem:* This is the Day upon which God Made the King. This 29th. of May was the Happy Day of His Nativity:

> *Illa*
> *Sidus inocciduum perpetuumque dedit.**

On this Day did This Star arise in Our British Hæmisphere, who shines the brighter by this Concurrence, this addition to our Happinesse, That the *Inauguration to His Life* is now become the Solemn *Inauguration to His Crown.*

A Day wherein we meet to offer up our Thanks to God that *He is Come to His Throne whose*
1 Sam.9:20 — *Right it is;* And *Upon whom the Desire of All our Israel was set,* as Samuel told the first Annointed King.

To Offer up our hearty Prayers for the Continuance of this Triumph, That this Anniversary may long be celebrated by us; That the King may see a Revolution of many Sun-shines like This: And
[33] 2 Chron.35:25 — that as it was made a *solemn Decree* in *Israel* to keep an Annual Mourning for the slain Josiah, so it
Ester 9:24 — may passe among our Lawes to hold this Day, as once the Feast of Purim in Ester's time, in memory of our deliverance from a Servitude, nay from a Massacre, unto which we by Lot were destin'd.

Especially for the Deliverance of our Soveraign from the hands of a Bloody Haman, now pearched higher than the Gallows by Him prepared for others; And from the dangerous Votes of Those Miscreants who had Abjured His Right, to place it upon That *Barabbas,* who carries on him
Luc.23:19 — the perpetual Stamp of *Sedition and Murther.*

To blesse His Glorious Name that He hath preserv'd Him from forein Attempts laid to Destroy Him during His Exile, and undertaken by such whose neer Trust freed them from all suspect; As well as from Domestick Dangers after His Return.

[34] — To Blesse God who preserv'd Him that *He might Come;* And Blesse him again *That He is Come,* Given to the Hearty Desires of His Loyal People.

Ezra 6:10 — Finally, as Darius Commanded the Jews, To *Pray for the Life of the King.* And though at present I cannot say (as it there followes) *To Pray for the King's Sons,* Yet to Pray according to the Prospect our Hopes now have of that Happinesse, That He may have Sons to be the Subject of our Prayers in the future, as Himself this Day is.

That He may grow Old, Yet never superannated in His Prosperity and Comforts; That God would add many Years unto His Life, Yea, take from our years, who most gladly would spare them, to add unto His—

(Ovid.Fast 1.613)
> *De nostris Annis tibi Iupiter augeat Annos.*

---

*It gave a star which would never set and would last forever.

That we may account our felicity involved and wrapped up in His, As Alexander's Army confessed: *Omnes unius Spiritu vivere,* They were Spirited by Him. [35] Quint.Curtius

That as He is the *Breath of our Nostrills,* so we take Care that no unwholsome Vapours, no seditious Damps be raised to annoy His Peace or offend Him. Lamen. 4:20

That God would place Him, as He promised Zerubbabel, *As a Signet upon his right hand;* That He would own Him in all His undertakings, as He did Zerubbabel, that excellent Instrument of His Glory. Agge 2:23

What can I say more? Let me sum up all in that Eulogy, that Loyal Acclamation which Tertullian saies the Roman People used to their Emperour: *That God would Blesse Him with A Long Life, A Secure Empire, A Safe Palace, A Valiant Army, A Faithfull Counsail, A Contented People,* and (if it be possible) *Peace with all the World.* Tertullian *Apologet: cap.35* [36]

Let God Hear and Grant these our Prayers; And let Those want the Comforts of Life and benefit of Prayer themselves, who do not Cordially and with all Loyalty of Soul say *Amen* to this Prayer.

AMEN.

FINIS.

DUPPA

A
SERMON
Preached at the Funeral of the Right Reverend
Father in God
BRYAN,
Lord Bp. of *Winchester.*
At the Abby Church in *Westminster,*
April 24. 1662.

Pretious in the Sight of the Lord is the Death of His Saints. Psal.116.15

I need not tell you the occasion of our Meeting. The sad Object lying before your Ey declares that; And though He who is gone be principally concerned in drawing you to this House of Mourning, yet must ye not repute your selves wholly unconcern'd. The benefit will redound to you, who know by whom ye are told *how good it is to enter into it*—I wish ye may think so too. [2] Eccles. 7:2

I read of one Philoromus Gælata who was so much in love with Death, he liv'd some years in a Tomb to prepare Himself for it.

This Spectacle and this Discourse tends to this Preparation; So that I hope ye will not repent an hour's stay here with me.

The Grave is commonly as powerful an Oratour as the Pulpit, and by presenting the fears of an Ill Death instructs us in the Rules of a Good Life. My assurance is that as the winding Sheet fits every Body, by dilating or contracting it self to each one's size, so my discourse will suit it self to every Hearer. Like Philipp's Boy, it holds out to Youth a Skull, to Age a Coffin.

Who next amongst us is likely to fall into this low Centre may be doubtfull; 'Tis sure at one time or other we all must, And probably we shall not all of us a few dayes hence meet here again.

Therefore wheresoever that final Lot may chance to fall, whether on some Hearer, or on the Speaker, You will allow this Text a pious remembrancer to Those who stay behind, and an antidated valediction to those who next go hence. So then, as St. Paul told the Corinthians, *Whether it be I or You, so I Preach, and so Yee justly must believe,* That happy shall their condition be in the Next world, who after a Religious life dye well in This: [3] 1 Cor.15:11

For Precious in the sight of the Lord is the Death of His Saints.

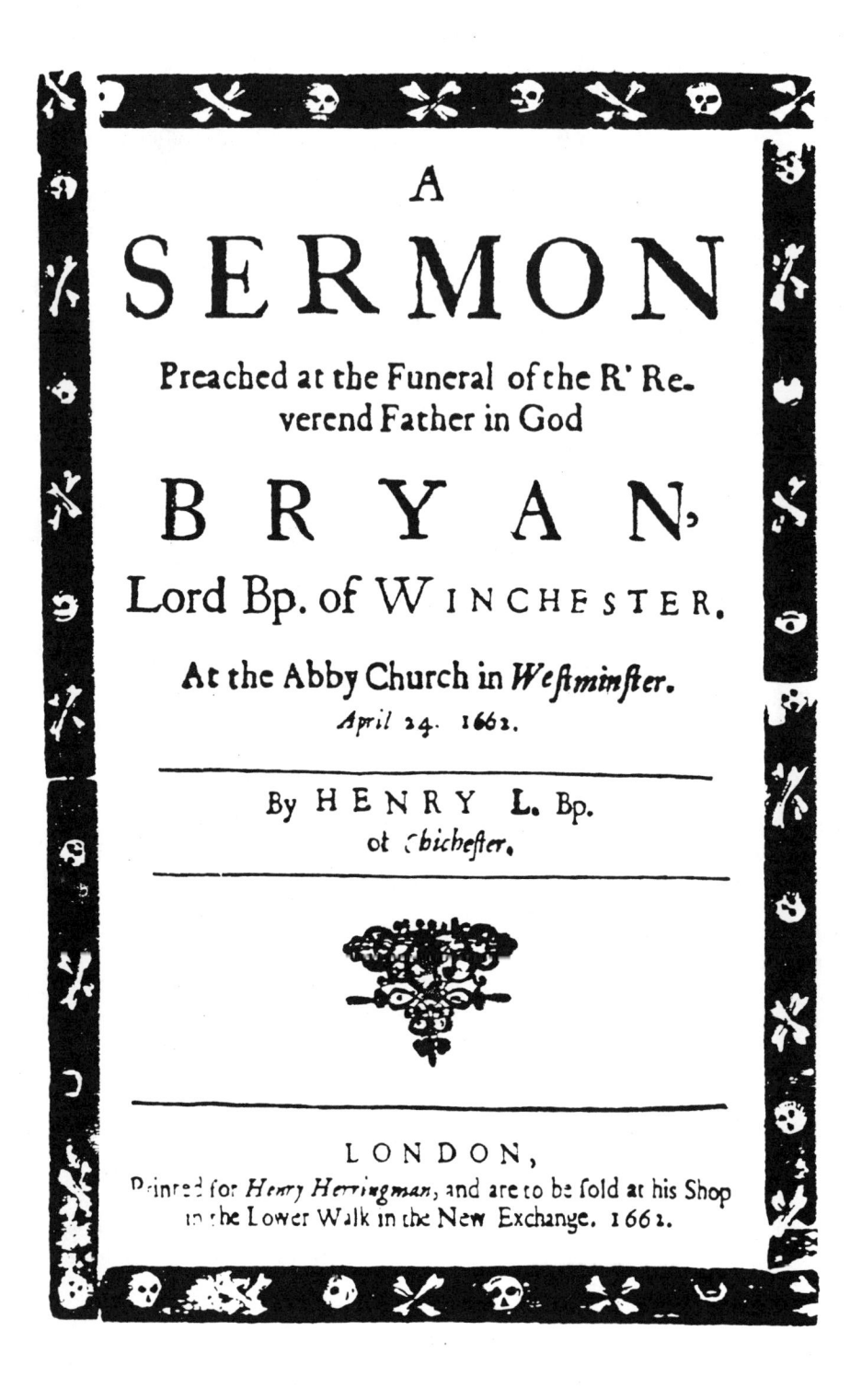

A
SERMON

Preached at the Funeral of the R^t Reverend Father in God

BRYAN,

Lord Bp. of WINCHESTER.

At the Abby Church in *Westminster*.
April 24. 1662.

By HENRY L. Bp.
of *Chichester*.

LONDON,
Printed for *Henry Herringman*, and are to be sold at his Shop
in the Lower Walk in the New Exchange. 1662.

I trouble you not with any Curious, but a Plain Division; The First Joint whereof is (that which disjoins Nature, and must Divide us from One another—Yea, makes a Division of us from Our selves, by Disuniting Soul and Body and taking asunder those Essential Parts by which we subsist): *Death*.

Division 1. *Death*

Then follows the Subject of our Funeral, *Sancti*. All are concluded under the Necessity of Dying: Men, the Best of Men, *Saints*.

2. *Saints*

Yet Thirdly, there is a mixture of Comfort to sweeten the Meditation of Death: It is *Mors Pretiosa*, Pretious:

[6] 3. *Pretious*

1. In that it puts an end to all Calamity.
2. Pretious for that Their Memory survives when They are gone.
3. Pretious in the Sight of Men, as being Honoured in their Exequies.

Lastly it is *Pretiosa in conspectu Dei:* Not Pretious only in the Ey and Estimation of the world, But *Precious in the Sight of the Lord*. He who sees all things is a Spectator of the Death of his Servants, and shews how dearly he values Them:

4. *In the Sight of the Lord*

1. By Avenging their Blood, if shed by violence in this world;
2. By Rewarding Them in the Next.

This is the Frame on which my ensuing Discourse is carried; whose Foundation you see is laid as low as the Grave.

I begin there where all must end, with *Death:* The full Period and Close of Nature—A Subject better defin'd by silence than speech, and sounds more pathetically from a Tomb than a Pulpit. The arguments of this place are (or should be) God and His Works; But amidst the whole Catalogue of those works of His we find not *Death:* A thing of so unblest a Being It cannot derive it self from His Hand and Facture who made All other things.

Pr. Part: *Death* [7]

Light was his Creature, Strook out and Kindled by his *Fiat Lux*—Let there be Light; And *Life* was inspired by His Powerful *Breath* who breathed *Spiraculum vitæ* into Man. But Darkness and Death are Children of other Parentage. God made no Privations to Smother His Works, No Extinguishers of Light or Nature, No Sickness to supplant Health, nor Infirmity to dissolve Strength. *The Generations of the World were healthful, and there was no Poison of destruction amongst them.* Darkness is but a defect of Light; and Death a Privation of Life, therefore none of His, *For God hath not made Death, neither hath He pleasure in the destruction of the living.*

Gen.1:3
Gen.2:7

Wis.1:14

Ver.13

If you would have Death's Pedigree, search not in God's Book of Creatures, amongst the Records of Life, but see the Annals of Sin. That and Sin were Twins nursed up together, engendred of two accursed Parents, the Serpent's Active Malice and Man's Disobedience. From hence do we derive this Monster, This Enemy to Nature and Opposite to God: For so it is.

[6a]

This demolisheth what He Builds: The goodly frame of Mankind is by Death ruined and layd in Earth. This Reverseth what He enacted, Marrs and unmakes all that He made before.

You see at what Breach Death enter'd, The Breach of God's Covenant. There the Inundation ran in, whose furious torrent will not be stopp'd until it hath overwhelm'd and cover'd the Universe.

From Adam did this Tyrant begin his dangerous Reign. On his Fall was Death's Throne erected; his Body became the first Stair of the Ascent; since which time he hath still raised that fatal Mound by heaping on it all the Bodies of his Children, *For in Adam we all dye.* His Fall maim'd and Creepled Posterity, which hath ever since complained of that bruise. The Earth yet groans under the barren Curse thrown upon it for Adam's sake, And *Every Creature groans with us also, travailing in pain unto this present.*

[7a] 1 Cor.15:22

Rom.8:22

Thus, as Ashur was the *Rod of God's vengeance* to scourge the rebellious Israelites, so Death became God's scourge to punish the Sin of Man: *Nescis quia pœna est, necesse esse ut moriamur?**

Esay 10:5

Aug.Ser.21 in Mat.

Here then you see, though Death were none of God's works, Yet it is over All His works. This

---

*Do you not know, that because it is the punishment, it is necessary that we shall die?

Thing of No being, this Privation, this Nothing, devours All things: For what is free from this Gangrene? What Plant doth not this Worm strike? What Elementary Body Animate or Inanimate is not subject to Corruption? Miserable experience shews that *Temples* are not privileg'd from ruine, Those *sheets of Lead* wherein the Dead sleep tast of Corruption:

Aug.Ser.17

[8]
Sunt et sua fata Sepulchris—
Tombs themselves have their Dying day; And those *Marble Quarryes* which stand over Princes moulder to dust as do the Bodies lying under them.

If then an inevitable Necessity of Death or some decay like it lies upon Metals and those solid Bodies which scarcely retain a Cause of Putrefaction within them, Certainly Man, whose complexion is not Stone nor his Ribbs Brass, must be better acquainted with Dust and Rottenness: *Say to Corruption thou art my Father, and to the worm Thou art my Mother and my Sister.* Yea, so far is He unable to bear off, by any Armour he can buckle on, the assaults of Death, That not *the Armour of the Apostle,* of more curious Temper and better proof than Steel—*The Shield of Faith and Brestplate of Righteousness,* which are able to resist *the fiery Darts of Satan*—can guard him from Death's Dart. For even the Best of Men, God's dearest Servants and Saints, are the subject of Death's triumph: It is *Mors Sanctorum,* the Death of Saints.

Job 17:14

Ephes.6:16

2. *Of Saints*

[9] *Psal.105*

That *Nolite tangere Christos meos*—Touch not mine Annointed—which encircles God's Servants, and like a Charm Exorcises all other dangers, cannot guard Them from this Fiend, Death. Moses his Body found a Champion to defend It from the Devil; He found no Champion to fight for Him against Death. The Decree is past and not to be reversed, *He must up to Mount Nebo and there Dye*.

Jud.epist. Ver.9
Deut.34.5

There is no Gluttony like Death. The greatest Practitioners in the School of Ryot have at length met a Surfet which hath done that nor Sea nor Land (Granges too narrow to serve their excess) could ever do, Choaked their boundless Appetite. But Death is a Glutton unacquainted with Surfet or Satiety; Of whom I may say, as the Scithian Embassadour once did to Alexander, *Satiety to Thee only serves to beget Hunger.* Not all the Gross Meals, the Grand Feasts which Warr or Pestilence have drest, could make Him say *it is Enough.* Not all those Messes in Revelation, *The Flesh of Kings and Captains, the flesh of Bond or Free men, Small and Great* (Provision sufficient for *all the Vultures invited to that Supper*) could make a Competent Meal for Death. Not all the Rarities of Nature, the choicest fruits the world affords, Youth gather'd in the Bud, and Beauty cropp'd in the flower, could satisfie Death's Palate; But after all these services, He must have a Feast of Saints cooked in all the barbarous fashions Tyranny and Cruel invention could devise. *They were Ston'd, were saw'n in sunder,* Rosted in the Fire, Broyl'd on Grid-irons, Flead, Torn in pieces, Brayed in Mortars—I have not memory nor language to recite this horrid Bill of Fare. Search the Histories of the Church and see it upon Record.

Q.Curt.

Revel.19.18
[10]
Ver.17

Heb.11.37

We should not grudge at this large Allowance made to Death, did He feed on Those that would not be missed amongst us, *Vulgares Animos*—trivial Soules—and *Frustra peritura cadavera:* Those unusefull burthens of the Earth, who only walk about and talk out their Time, having no profession but that of the Athenians, to *Hear and Tell News.*

Lucan
(7.730)
[11]
Act.17:21

Well were it for the world, did Death remove such unprofitable things as These, who like the *fruitless Tree* in the Gospel, *only cumber the Earth;* Did He only exenterate Nature, which at first hatch'd this devouring Cokatrice; and did not also eat through the Bowels of the Church, destroying those Holy Births which lye within her Womb.

(Lk 13:6, 7)

To our grief we must remember those heavy Stroaks have fallen thick upon us. You had one Famous Light, whose Learning and Exemplary Life shone brightly in the Orb of our English Church, extinguished very lately; And when that Earth which covered Him is scarcely made up, behold, here Another worthy follows, ready to take his final Lodging in the same Dust.

Dr Fern, Bp of West Chester

Thus doth this Tyrant double His Blow, depriving us of Two such incomparable Persons, that though you search their whole Order, and *Run through our Hierusalem with Lanterns* (as once the Prophet did), you shall not match again.

(Zephaniah 1:12)
[12]

Tune Duos una sævissima Vipera Cæna,
Tune Duos?—   Juvenal (6:640–41)

Let me play the Satyrist with Death: Cruel Viper as thou art, Could not *One* suffice thy ravenous appetite, but thou must have *Two* to gorge upon? I need not stay for the answer, I find it ready made there—*Septem, Septem, si forte fuissent:* were it possible to find out *Seven* more like Them, His dart is lifted up, as ready now to strike as He was then.

We have cause (God knows) too much to lament these great Losses in such a barren Time as ours, which produceth very few Saints; And where Good men are thinly found: Like the shaking of the Olive Tree, which amongst many Leaves yield perhaps here and there a Berry; Knowing that *Ten Righteous Persons* (if so many may be found) are able to beat off a *Showr of Vengeance and Fire* not less violent than that which fell on Sodom and Gomorrah. Nay, One Aaron is authorized to stand in the Gapp betwixt an Offended God and a Sinfull People.   Gen.18:32 [13]

Indeed the World is now in its Dotage, Creepled and Bed-rid, In the last and worst Age: So that had it not some few sound Crutches to support it, some few Pillars not eaten in by the vices of the Time, nor Canker'd by those Opinions which madly fly about (not only to the disfiguring our Churche's Decency and Order, but the shaking and undermining even Her Fundamental Truths), It could not subsist. Whensoever then a Good man dyes, a Shore of the declining world is taken away, and a *Pillar of the Church,* threatning a Ruine to that part where the Stay was broken out.   Greg.Nazianz. *Ora.in Laud. Patris*

It is our best Course therefore to strengthen our remaining Stayes by our Prayers; Knowing that the Devil's malice is ever planted against our Best Fortifications, assaulting Those most hotly who stand in the Breach.

For he doth not wound us blindly or by chance, but by Election and Judgement. So doth his Agent Death cull out the Best, Garbling the Race of Men, and Commonly leave the refuse—*Mors optima rapit, deterrima relinquit*—Making us know to our grief that of Hieron. to be most true: Sinners are the proper inhabitants here, Saints only sojourn in the world—*I am a Stranger and a Sojourner as all my Fathers were.*   [14]   Psal.39:12

They who justly consider how many Hundreds of Men yield one Saint, How many years Religiously spent are required for His probation, and How many Virtues go to the Making up of a Saint: They who Consider again how hard a thing it is to Pair and fellow Goodness when Death hath mis-matched it, and how unequally the successions of Virtue are preserv'd amongst us, who seldome inherit any thing of our Fore-fathers' worth, but only their Imperfections and Infirmities— They, I say, who in all these unfortunate consequences justly apprehend the loss of Good men, will not blame us to set that value upon their Death at which Sorrow and Affection deservedly prizes Them, Confessing that *Sanctorum Mors Pretiosa:* Their death is Pretious.   [15]

Pretious indeed: For how ill soever the bargain proves on our parts, it is good to Them: as in a hard Purchase, what the Buyer loses the Seller gets. 'Tis *Mors pretiosa* to Them in an other Capacity, That gainful sense the Apostle means: *Mors Lucrum—Death is their Advantage,* whereby They gain an end to those Miseries Life exposed and the World's converse cast upon Them, and may seal their valediction to both in those words of the Poet: 3. *Pretious*   Phil.1:21

Finitis gaude tot mihi Morte malis.*   Ovid. *Lib.3, Trist.El.3:*(56)

Hear how St. Bernard exalts Death's Market, and raiseth the Price of it: *Pretiosa plane tanquam finis Laborum, tanquam Victoriæ consummatio, tanquam vitæ Janua, tanquam perfectæ Securitatis ingressus:†* It is Pretious, as being an Antidote against all Infirmity. Though the Potion hath some bitterness—*O Mors, quam amara!*—The effect is sweet: He who takes it down, in that draught takes his everlasting *Quietus.* Though the infected Air spreads new diseases over the World,   [16] Ecclus 41:1

---

*Rejoice that so many evils are ended for me through death.
†Such clearly precious things as the end of toil, the achievement of victory, the door of life, the entrance to perfect freedom from cares.

that infection pierces not so low as the Grave, such an Armour of proof are five feet of Earth. It is a Pretious Receipt for Sleep beyond all the Opiate or Mandragoras Physick can prescribe. He who is lodg'd in Earth lies in an Inner Chamber which Noise cannot disturb: The wars of the Elements are not heard in that Quarter, The Wind contesting with the Wave, Nor the Breach of Waters, Nor the Tongue of Thunder. None of these can dispossess them of that slumber which only the Archangel's Trump shall waken, Nor any other way disturb their quiet habitation, upon whose door the Characters of Eternal Peace are engraven: *Write, Blessed are Those that dy in the Lord* (so saith the Spirit), *for they finally rest from their Labours.*

Revel.14:13

[17]

How Pretious the death of Saints is, all from hence must graunt, who from the sense of Pain can understand the benefit of Ease, Or from the miseries of war are instructed in the Blessings of Peace, And from the World's perpetual disquiet have learnt what price they ought to set upon an endless Rest: This meerly concerns Themselves.

There be other differences which continue Their value unto us when They are gone. First, the *Honour due to their Memory* after Death, which distinguisheth Persons of Desert from Those of no Consideration.

Eccles.3:19
Psal.49:10

The whole circumference of natural Being meets in one Centre. *That which befalleth the sons of Men befalleth Beasts; as the one dieth so dieth the other* (saith the Preacher), And *Wise Men Dy as well as Fools,* But yet, in this Fatal Heraldry there are differences to discriminate the Elder and the Younger house. Tacitus will tell you, *Death which is equal to all is distinguished by the honour shewed to the Deceased, or the neglect to them when gone.* Thus did the Romans distinguish their Two Emperours, Augustus and Tiberius, the Successor in his Empire though not in his Virtues: Augustus They Deified, but their hate to Tiberius was such, They would have His Memory survive no where unless in Hell. Such is the fate of wicked ones, to be forgotten, and *such honour have the Saints,* to Live in their Posteritie's remembrance.

Tacit.*Annal: lib.1* [18]

Sueton.*in Tiberio*
Psal.149:9
Tacitus

Esai.*14*:19, 20

(2 Kings 9:10)
[19]

Which Honour is by a Second evidence demonstrated in their *Exequies.* The Prophet could not threaten a greater Curse than to be cast out as unworthy of the Rites of Burial: Paricides and Traitors, Murtherers of Parents or Murtherers of Princes, who are our Civil Parents of the whole Kingdom, were thus used amongst the Heathen: *Mê thakês ton athapton—let them ly unburied;* And *ea kusi kurma genesthai—let Dogs eat their Flesh* upon earth, as they did Jezabel's, and Fowls of Prey devour their Carcasses when hanging in the Air. So God tells the King of Babylon: *Thou art cast out like an abominable Branch, Thou shalt not be joined with them in Burial.*

Origen *Contr. Cels:lib.3*

True it is that Heraclitus is Charg'd by Origen That He did think a Dead Body not worth a Grave or Rites of Burial, but to be cast out to the Frost of the Night and Heat of the Day as a contemptible Relick, eternally lost in its separation from the Soul.

Hieron.*lib.3. contra Vigilant.*

So Hieron. chargeth Vigilantius as one wedded to the superstition of the Samaritan and Jew, who reputed the Bodies of the Dead unclean Things, reproaching the Cœmeteries & Consecrated Ground wherein they are lay'd as follies to be laught at, and terming Those who Buried Them, *Traders in dust and Idolaters of Dead Men's Bones.*

Against the Oxford answer 1602 to the Ministers Petition (I Tim.3) [20]
Vid. *Their Answer to Gifford* 1591
Act.8:2

The Brownists in their Apology come as neer These I have named as may be, Affirming *Burial* to be no Ecclesiastical Action, because not named by Timothy among the *Ministerial duties.*

Barrow and Greenwood take it at bownd from Them, and ask where it was made an Eccle siastical duty, or why to be performed in Hallowed Ground, as if we had no Fields. They forgot (it seems) *Devout men carried Stephen to His Burial.*

And I must tell you, our Preciser sort of late have run in the same line; They would by no means endure the Body to come within the Church, but it must be left without in the Church-yard. Nor would They use in Committing the Corps to Earth any word or Ceremony, but put it into the Ground as one would bury the meanest Creature that lay Dead. Let me ask without offence, what doth this differ from the Curse denounced by the Prophet against Jehojakim, *The Burial of an Ass?*

Jer.26:19

Aug. *De Civ. Dei lib.11:c.13*

S. Augustin teaches Them more Civility if They would learn: *The Bodies of Dead Christians are not to be thus slightly and Contemptibly cast into the Earth.*

Tender and soft Conscienc'd men as They are, who *strain at Gnats and swallow Camels.* They made no scruple to Preach up the Highest Rebellion in the State, & Fowlest Disorder in the Church, that any Age ever knew; Yet their umbrageous Phantasies startle now at any thing of Decency & Order—As if Popery were obtruded in that *Sign,* which hath no other meaning but to signify to the world that *we are not ashamed of the Cross of Christ crucified,* or Antichrist lurked under that Innocent habit used in the Ministerial Office. [21] Mat.23:24 / Liturgy in Publick Baptism

But I am upon a Theam of Burial due to Christians, and in Christian Charity I would Bury these weaknesses too, if They be so—or not, rather, Obstinacies—only putting Them in mind, There cannot be too much Dignity given to the Body, when Dead, which Living was *a Temple of the Holy Ghost:* That Body which Christ assumed when He took our Flesh; That Body In which and For which He Died, paying the price of his unvaluable Blood to redeem it; Lastly, That Body which He will hereafter Glorify and *make it Like unto His own Glorious and Incorruptible Body.* (1 Cor. 6:19) / Philip.3:1

Sure, if the Prophet tells you with sorrow That it pitty'd all Eies to see the ruins of decay'd Sion, and that the *dust and rubbish of it was priz'd and favour'd* by them, Let none disvalue the Bodies of Saints demolished by Death, which are more Considerable than the Stones of Sion in her greatest beauty. But rather let it be a motive in the Honour of their Funeral Rites to declare how Pretious their Death is in the sight of Men, when the Text assures you that it is *Pretious in the sight of God.* [22] Psal.102:14 / 4. In the sight of God

Should man's ingratitude lose the Remembrance of Those who in their time have best deserved in the World, Yet God is not as Man, to forget His Servants. They need no Monument to preserve nor Epitaphe to innoble them, who live in God's Remembrance. The Memorial and Name *of the wicked Men perisheth* like the Dung, and rotts faster than their Corrupted Bodies, but *the Just shall be had in everlasting Memory.* Psal.9:5 / Psal.111:6

There can be no greater motive for Christians to live well, than to think *Deus videt*—God is a spectator of all their Actions whilst They live here. Nor can there be a greater terrour to any who by Violence deprive them of that life, Than to consider He is the Avenger of his Servants and Saints. So the Price He puts upon them is in *Rewarding* Them in the next world, and *Avenging* Their Blood in This. [23] Senec.

Yet I must tell you, this speculation of God's Vengeance upon their Destroyers, if taken by our own Perspective, may deceive us. As God doth not alwaies at first Call hear our Prayers when we Invoke His Mercy, but takes His own Time to perform what we desire; So He doth not ever, when we implore His Justice, let loose His Thunder to strike Those Men of Blood to whom His severest vengeance is due. *Thou God to whom vengeance belongeth, shew Thy self,* is the Prophet's excitation of Him; And yet for all this Cry He tells you in another place, God makes *as if he heard not.* Yea, though he hath pronounced that *the Blood-thirsty and deceitful should not live out half their dayes,* we have seen the Gray-hair'd Murtherer finish a large Account of Time and number many years, Nay, dye in his Bed; when those who deserv'd to be Canoniz'd for Saints and Martyrs have dy'd upon the Scaffold. 1. He Avengeth / Psal.94:1 / (Is.48:8) / [24] Psal.55:23

If These men dy the Common death of all men, then the Lord hath not sent me (saith Moses) with some indignation, in the case of Korah and his fellow Conspirators. Num.16:29

O Beloved! Yee must neither misdoubt us who preach the Certainty of God's Judgments, If in Your Ey these Judgments fall not on Them so soon or so severe as you expect: Much less must you misjudge God Himself, either from the delay of His Vengeance, or by permitting them to enjoy Augustus his *Euthanasia,* a quiet and Calm Death. Sueton.

We are no competent Judges of God's motion to Revenge, no more than of the Means by which he doth accomplish it.

God says *Their foot shall slide in due time,* But then he asks, *who shall appoint Me the time?* If He strikes not presently, we must not think Him slow or forgetfull: *The Lord is not slack as some men count Slackness.* [25] Deut.32:35 / Jer. 50:44 / 2 Pet.3:9

Or if He permits any notorious Offenders to finish their dayes by a Natural Death in their Bed, do we know *Qualem in conscientia sustinent Gehennam?*—What hard contests, what sharp Conflicts, what Hell their Consciences endure?

When God threatens *He will cast Jesabel upon a Bed,* Think you this done in favour of Her, who seduced His servants *to commit Fornication?* No, but to revenge Her Adulteries upon the very Bed whereon she committed them.

So when He suffers the fowlest Assasinates to dy in their Bed, it is not always Mercy, but rather as if He hanged Them at their Own Door, making those very Beds on which *they proudly stretcht themselves,* and where They contrived their Hellish Machinations, the Place of Execution and Torment to Them.

For my part, I shall ever reckon these inverted forms of Justice among the Prodigies which Christ predicted of the Last and worst Times, *When the Stars should fall from heaven, the Sun be darkned, the Moon turn'd to Blood.*

How many *Stars* in the Sphear of the Church (for those Lights are Stars in the Spirit's compellation) have since these unhappy times been darkned? How many Nobles have been strook off by violent Death, who are Stars in the Orb of the Kingdom? How hath the *Moon* languished under Her Eclipse—Queens mourned in Widdowhood and Exile? Nay (which is a Portent greater than that) how hath the most *Glorious Sun* which ever shone in the Firmament of our English Throne been *turn'd to Blood?*

It was a Bloody Time wherein we liv'd of late; and sure, it was believ'd the New Modell'd State could not thrive unless, like the Vine, Blood were powr'd at the Root of it. Tertullian tells us the heathen Persecutions gave the President: who, if the Seasons prov'd unkindly, or the Aspect of Heaven frown'd on them in ill weather, If they suffer'd Famine or Pestilence, If their Designs miscarried by Land, or their Adventures by Sea, they ran down to the Amphitheater, crying, *Christiani ad Leones:* Some Christians must be sacrifized to the Teeth of Beasts, to mend those Mischiefs.

You may remember how some Seducèd People were incited to run down with Tumultuous Petitions and Confused Clamours for Justice upon Delinquents; Alleging their Trade was improsperous for lack of execution done upon Delinquents.

When they had prevayl'd, and by Gross prevarication (*Law and no Law:* Laws made for that purpose, then Abrogated when the Turn was serv'd)—when (I say) by these Juggles they had got off some of the wisest Heads in the State, and Highest in the Church; Nay, when they had struck the *Vena basilica,* emptying the Blood of the Principal Veyn which gave Life and Spirit to the whole Kingdome; how well those abused People have thriv'd and the Trades improv'd, Themselves feel to their utter undoing, and we all see.

God grant this Unvaluable, this Guiltless, this yet unexpiated Blood, with many Thousands besides shed since the last eruption of our Civil War, be not charg'd upon the Heads of every one of us who survive.

It is the Positive Law of God, *He who sheddeth Man's Blood, by Man shall his Blood be shed.* And I know not what Power upon Earth can dispense with it. If there be any who frame excuse, or by Sophistry and False Reason endeavour to Palliate the Crime, let them take heed lest they pluck down the Guilt upon Themselves.

This *Loud crying Sin* will not easily be silenced: The Tongue of Blood is never hoarce by long crying. *I have heard the Voyce of thy Brother Abel's Blood crying to me from the Ground* (saith God), and *This Blood* (though shed so many hundred years past) *Cryes still.* Indeed how can it be otherwise? *He who Bottles every Tear shed* in sorrow or contrition, and who numbers every drop of water distilled from the Eyes of His servants, shall He not much more keep a Tale of every Drop of Blood? Certainly he will, and in His Calculation each Drop hath its just value, to bring a fearfull recompence upon the Heads of all their Murtherers.

Surely I have seen yesterday the Blood of Naboth, and the Blood of His sons, and I will Requite Thee (saith the Lord). 'Tis an Asseveration: *He sees to Pity It,* and *He sees to Revenge it* upon all the House of Ahab. It is ever in *Conspectu eius:* In his sight—*So precious is the death of His*

Saints. He puts a price upon Their Loss in His *Revenge,* and He puts a price upon Their Virtues in His Reward.

You see how God looks down upon His servants, with what Aspect He beholds their Sufferings here; They must now look up to *Him from whence cometh their Salvation.* The Apostle directs their Eye, *Looking up to Jesus the Authour and Finisher of our Faith, who for the Joy set before Him endured the Cross,* &c.

There needs no better *Reward* than to be in *Conspectu Domini,* In God's sight: *In Thy sight, and in Thy Presence there is fulness of Joy for evermore.* The Pain of the Cross was eas'd to that poor dying Man Hanging upon it, in the promise of his Saviour, *Hodie mecum eris*—Thou shalt be where I am. Those who can summ up the Sorrows of a Miserable Life may best collect the Blessings of the Life to come.

It were a vain thing for us on Earth to attempt the defining of those Joyes in Heaven which be *Arrêta* and *Agnōsta: Eye hath not seen, nor Tongue can utter, nor Heart conceive Them.*

This onely is the dictate of our Faith and best Evidence of Those unseen Joyes, That the *Beatifica Visio, The Sight of God,* will both recompence all the Crosses laid on us, and supply all the Comforts which we wanted upon Earth—*That Blessed Vision,* whereby we shall see God, not under the *Dim Cloud of His Promises,* but in the Clear Light, the *Performance of His Reward.*

We must know, for all this, there is *chasma mega—A Great Gulph*—betwixt our expected Bliss and us; Perhaps *A Red Sea* and a *Terrible Wilderness* are enterpos'd, and must be passed through before we can arrive at the *Land of Promise.* Happy shall Those be who are nor afraid to wade through a Red Sea discolour'd by their own Blood, if God's Honour or His Cause require it; nor faint in the apprehension of a Wilde Great Desert, if He think good to lay that tedious probation upon their Patience. Let this assurance Cheer both Their and Our dejected Spirits: we shall undoubtedly receive the Reward, *if we Faint not;* And what contempt soever we endure in the Eyes of Men, we shall finde a full Reparation *In the sight of God.*

I have done with the Text. And now, according to the Custome of a Funeral, You will expect I should say somewhat concerning the Subject of it.

I confess My self an ill Herald, and unversed in These Displays, It being the first time which brought me to perform this Office for the Dead; And if God so pleas'd, I wish from my Soul I might have missed it now.

I cannot but remember, at this time was a Twelvemonth, in the Highest Celebrity which our English Court can Boast, the *Solemn Feast of St. George* held at Windsor, His Infirmity Forced Him, by Particular Licence and Approbation of His Soveraign, to Depute me to That Office which in That place properly belong'd to Him.

I little thought that, in a Mournfull Solemnity where Himself became the Subject, I should the following Year, and the very next Day after that Triumph, be Deputed to this Last Service at His Grave.

But thus you see how Joyes and Sorrows by course exercise their several Jurisdictions over us, And how the Greatest Triumph Earth affords is attended at the Heels by such a Gastly follower as Death.

That I heartily Lov'd, and from the converse of many younger years Valued the Owner of that Dead Relick lying before me, is a real Truth. For that cause Ye therefore must not expect any large Panegyricks from me, lest happily Yee might think He needed them.

Though Praise be a fit Gloss set upon Desert, there is danger, at least suspicion, in the excess: As unskilfull Painters, by laying on too much Varnish, dead the Colours and marr the Piece they would set off. Indeed, in any Mournfull Arguments, Invention is commonly most free where with least interest and Concern it looks upon the Object. Passion or Affection mingling with them render it too serious for any Rhetorick but Sorrow. This I profess to be my Case; And if it would not betray more of the weaker Sex than is fit for me to own, I could make good the words of St. Augustine, *Potius libet flere quam aliquid dicere:* My Eyes could easily prove more fluent than my Tongue.

[34] Yet lest Ye fail of all Ye look for, As the Evening Sun immediately before his Set Unites and, in some short flashes, casts forth his Beams, before he bury them in that Cloud wherein he Sets, I will briefly summ upp the Passages of His Life even from his Youth, which was His Sun-rise, unto the Declination of His Age, which brought Him to this Bed of Darkness.

He was Born of Worthy and Virtuous Parents.

His Education was in This Famous School, In This very College, where He was admitted a King's Scholar of that Noble Foundation, which hath sent out so many Excellent Proficients in Learning to each University—For Both those Fair Rivers doth this Spring, by contributing some Supplies to Them annually, feed.

Here, He had the greatest Dignity which the School could afford put upon Him, to be the *Pædonomus* at Christmas, *Lord of His Fellow-Scholars:* Which Title was a pledge and presage that [35] from a Lord in Jeast, He should in His riper Age become One in Earnest.

From Hence He was translated by Election to Christ's-Church in Oxford: where having run through some Offices in the College, conferr'd both as Rewards and Trials upon the best Deservers, He was remov'd to All-souls; and when His Degree and Time made Him capable of Publick Employment, Chosen Proctour of the University.

After the taking His Degree of Doctor, in some few years He was by His Royal Master (whose Chaplain He had been) made Dean of Christ-Church, so becoming Head of that College into which He was first admitted Student.

The more Publick Office of Vice-chancellour was then cast upon Him by that Martyr'd Archbishop, who well understood the Universitie's advantage from so deserving a Substitute.

These Offices he supply'd with such Ability and Integrity, That His Gracious Master thought Him [36] worthy to receive the Greatest Trust He possibly Could plant in Him, To be the Tutour and Educator of our Sovereign in His Minority, together with His Princely Brother.

This Trust brought on Him the Honour of a Bishoprick for His Reward, first Chichester, then Salisbury. Thus being lifted up Two Ascents by the bounty of His Old Master, He was easily raised to the Third by His Present Sovereign, The Bishoprick of Winchester, in which He became Ex Officio *Prelate of the Garter.* That Honour, being always annexed to This Office, He so well Became That None before Him Did, nor Any who follow can Better. For He was every way Qualified, both in the Comeliness of His Person, and the Gracefulness of His Deportment, and the Excellency of His Parts: All which Capacities rendred Him worthy the service of a Court, and Prov.22.29 every way *fit to stand before Princes.*

He had this happiness, That from the very First Relation to those Tender years of His Gracious [37] Soveraign, during His Care and Tuition of Him, He held the same Degree and Station in His Favour; which never abated in the least measure, but continued to His Death.

And as He was ever acceptable to the presence of His Master whilst able to make His approaches to the Court, So when Infirmity (which confin'd Him to His Chamber) render'd Him fit onely to be visited, He wanted not those Royal Visits made to Him by His Lord. Who though He could not say, (Mt.8.7) as Christ to the Centurion imploring His Goodness to His sick servant: *Ego veniens sanabo: I will* *Ego veniens* *come in presence to perform His Cure;* Yet He perform'd the First part, *He came*—not seldome neither, both to see Him in His weakness, and to comfort Him amidst His pains.

2 King.13:14 I must not omit to tell you, As once the King of Israel came to see the Dying Prophet Elisha that he might take his Farewell, and with that Farewell a Blessing from One he never should see again: [38] So did a Better King than He, the *King of our Israel,* repair to This dying Prelate a few hours before His Expiration, not onely to See, but to require a Benediction from Him at Parting; which in the lowest Posture of Humility He besought. And let me tell you (not to Flatter Him), amongst His other Virtues, never was there a more affable Sweetness or less Pride in so great a Prince. Both which He fairly expressed, when Kneeling down at the Bed-side, He begg'd His last Blessing,

which He like Jacob on His Death-Bed (and now *as Dim-sighted* as Jacob), with one Hand laid upon His Master's Head and the other lifted up to Heaven, He with a most Passionate Zeal Bestowed. And I Hope and Pray that, like the Last Blessing of Old Jacob pronounced over His Princely Son Judah, It shall remain in all Glorious Successes confirmed to Him: *That unto Him the People may be Gathered* in all Loyalty, never seduc'd again to Run after the Seditious Trumpet of Those *Sons of Bichri* who in these late Years usurped His Scepter: *That His Hand may bee upon the Neck of His implacable Enemies,* whom no Acts of favour or Indulgent Clemency can Reconcile: And lastly, *that the Scepter may not depart from Him and from His Royal Tribe untill Shiloh come.* Gen. 48:10
Gen. 49:10
2 Sam. 20:1 [39]
Gen. 49 Vers. 8
Verse 9

I have very little more to say; Onely tell you, in addition to His former Honour, He was dignified with the Office of High Almoner, being intrusted with the bestowing His Majestie's Charity: which like a faithful Steward, He so justly dispensed, That in evidence of His Integrity He Copy'd out that Office in his own Practice, Not only in His Legacies to Christ-Church in Oxford and to Alsoules, to the Churches of Salisbury, of Chichester, and Winchester, But to a Famous Almehouse erected at His peculiar charge in Richmond, the place of His retirement, which stands a Conspicuous Monument and Memorial of Him whilst the World lasts. 'Tis well when our Good deeds follow us, but much better when they goe before. In works of Charity perform'd whilst we live here, we are God's immediate Almoners; what is done when we are Gone is more properly Our Executors' than Ours. They are happy who by any hand bestow their Almes, but it is more honour and better satisfaction when Our Charity needs no Executor but the Doner's Hand to dispense, nor overseer but His own Eye. [40]

From His Charity, you will easily Calculate His other Virtues. His Bounty was alwaies eminent according to His ability; And when He came to be owner of a large and full Fortune He so well practis'd St. Paul's Lesson, *A Bishop must be given to Hospitality,* that in His generous way of living, to His own and the Honour of His whole Order, He demonstrated That his Heart was no way undersiz'd or too Narrow for His Fortune; Nor did He since His Advancement study the sordid Art of Gain, but rather how He might nobly Spend and Lay out what He got. 1 Tim. 3:2

His Disposition was most free & open, His Heart without close Angles or oblique Corners; And in His long Relation to the Court had never studied that first Principle of the Court Grammar, To speak one way and mean Another—*Ubique sentires Illum hoc affici quod loquebatur,** As Erasmus said of St. Augustine. [41] Erasmus *De August.*

His Learning was Great and General, and as Nicephorus Gregoras said of One, He was *Mousaion zōon,* A walking Library. His Gifts in Preaching elegant and very excellent, yet not intended to delight the Eare, but to inform the Conscience. And I heartily wish Those elaborate Peeces of Devotion may not die with Him, but in their Publication remain amongst His other Legacyes bequeathed to the World.

I may apply to Him that Eulogy which Nazianzen bestowes upon His Father: He was *alwaies so faithfull to God in the service of His Church,* wherein He liv'd, that He never receded from His first Principles in any slackness either toward Hir Doctrine or Hir Discipline. Insomuch that His Sacred Majesty, desirous to preserve the Succession of His English Church, & sensible of His Bishops' Decay, Most whereof were Dead & Those Few who remain not likely to last long, was pleas'd to commit this Trust principally to His Solicitation. In discharge whereof how industrious He was, some who yet live know, and none better than My self, who was His only associate in several travels undertaken to bring it to effect. Greg. Nazianzen *Orat. in Laudem Patris* [42]

'Tis true, divers waies were propounded, yet all found dangerous, Under the Inquisition we then liv'd, both to the Undertakers and the Actors.

His Majesty, therefore, at last thought of a safer & more certain Expedient, to call over to Him Two of the remayning Bishops, who joyned to a worthy Prælate residing with Him in his Exile Bp. Bramhall, now L. Primate of Armach

---

*At every point, you felt he fulfilled in himself what he said.

might Canonically Consecrate some of Those eminently deserving Divines who then attended Him—Thus Preserving the Order in a Few, untill God gave opportunity to fill up the Other Vacancies.

[43] Rom.11:*13*

This desire was, by a trusty Messenger sent over by His Majesty, communicated only to Five, whereof (I shall *not Magnifie my Office* to say) My self was One, who in the integrity of my Conscience can profess that, in the willing acceptance of this Summons, I never declin'd any hazard when I might doe the King my Master or the Church Service. But great Age and greater Infirmity denying the concurrence of any One of the Rest (though otherwise most ready), that designe fell: And God hath in the Miraculous Restoration of His Sacred Majesty Restor'd the Church to that Luster wherein (blessed be His Name) you now see it.

He in whose presence I here stand bears me record, I mention not these Circumstances to any other End than my Soveraign's Honour; For it is not fit so meritorious an Act should be conceal'd and smothered, but that all might take notice how Carefull He was to Preserve and Support the Church, at that Time when in His Exil'd condition He could not well Support Himself.

[44] (Lk.2.29)

To conclude; This worthy Person now gone before us often professed to Mee, that He desired only Two Blessings in this world, and then He should cheerfully sing His *Nunc Dimittis,* Depart in Peace; To see the King His Gratious Master's Return unto His Throne, And the Churche's happy Restitution to Hir Rights.

Psal.90:10

God gave Him the desire of His Lipps: He liv'd to see Both, And, in a good old Age, full of Dayes, having compleated *Seaventy and three yeares* (which is above the Standard of Humane Life in Moses his Calculation) with some few dayes over, He exchanged His Painful Life for an everlasting Rest; Leaving His Virtues to bee Imitated by Those that can, And His Loss to be Lamented by All who are left behind.

God for his Mercie's sake grant Our *Death may be so Pretious in His sight,* That when the Eyes which see us now must see us no more, We may with These Eyes of Ours Æternally see Our Redeemer in His Kingdome. Amen.

FINIS.

VISITATION

A
SERMON
Preached at a
VISITATION, &c.

Tit.2.1. *But speak Thou the things which become Sound Doctrine.*

This Text is a short View of the Priest's Duty, made up into a Monition or Directory;

In which you have

1. The *Person* admonished, *Thou.*

[2]

2. The *Advise,* which contains in that one word Both his *Commission* and his *Charge, Speak.*

3. The *Matter* of his Discourse, *Things.*

4. The *Form* of it, *Which become.*

5. The *End* unto which all Circumstances are intended, *Sound Doctrine.*

1. The Person, Thou

Each Minister is an *Apostle* sent out to Preach the Gospel of Peace, *Apostellomenos.*

In what better Language therefore can I speak to Ministers, than in the words of an Apostle?

Nay, he is *Episcopus Animarum,* a kind of *Bishop* set over the *Souls* committed to his Charge. What fitter Compellation therefore can I find for you, than that which was addressed to Titus, the first Bishop of Crete?

If St. Paul thought it not unneedful to advertize Him who was advanced to that high place of Government in the Church, ye cannot think it an Impertinent Custom which thus assembles and

A

SERMON

Preached at *Lewis* in the Dioceſs of

CHICHESTER,

By the

Lord Bp of CHICHESTER,

At His

VISITATION

Held there, *Octob.* 8. 1662.

LONDON,

Printed for *Henry Herringman*, and are to be ſold at his Shop in the Lower Walk of the *New-Exchange*. 1663.

[3] adviseth you, for the discharge of that Duty which concerneth All who have any Share or Title to the Ministry.

We are slack and dull by Nature, therefore need Admonition to quicken us.

The most active Ambassador betwixt Prince and Prince might sometimes need a Letter of Advise to refresh his Memory; Much more we, who are Embassadors sent to treat betwixt God and his People.

Some there are so well-conceited of themselves that they disdain Admonition, as Upbraider of Defect in them.

The Bishop of Rome, when he is *in Cathedra*, thinks himself Inerrable, and by his Place can neither need Advise nor Exhortation. But St. Augustine, a better Bishop than he, though not of so large a Diocese, writing to Auxilius, a Bishop also, touching a Rash Excommunication passed upon Classicianus and his Family, desires him not to take ill Advise from his hand: *Think not that because we are Bishops we cannot do amiss, or are exempted from receiving their Advise, who fairly admonish us of our Duties.*

Aug.*Epist.7*:

[4]

Hieron.*Lib. 1: Ep.51*

2 Pet.1: 12, 13

(Eph.4:20)

Theophilus Alexandrinus, writing to Hieron, tells Him *The best men are subject to Error and Infirmity, therefore want Remembrancers to put them in mind of their Defects. I will not be negligent to put you always in remembrance, though ye be stablished in the present truth.* Far be it from any, then, who have rightly *learned Christ,* to spurn against the Word of Exhortation when seasonably uttered, or to think meanly of that Office which Christ entrusted to the holy Ghost.

[5] Jn. 14:26

He told his Disciples, when he promised to send the Comforter, that amongst many other blessings, *He would be their Remembrancer, shewing them all these things: suggerendo*—by quickning their Memory, and bringing his Sayings back to their knowledge.

Ignat.*Epist. ad Trallens.*

So that Exhortation or Admonition doth not upbraid the Infirmity of the Man or Slack performance of his Duty, but rather animate him to go on in what he hath well undertaken. As Ignatius told the Trallenses, *I strengthen you by my Admonitions.*

August. *Epist.81*

And St. Augustine told Eudoxius, *I write not to Chide or Find fault, but rather to Commend, and desire you to do what you do.*

Indeed, he who Exhorts and Admonisheth what should be done is so far from Diminishing or Disparaging, that he rather Dignifies him whom he Admonisheth.

A Remembrancer is but an Index, which refers to a man's own Abilities, telling him how Able he is, and how Willing he ought to be in discharge of the Duty required from him:

[6]
Ovid.*Trist. Lib.5: Eleg.15*

Qui monet ut facias quæ iam facis, ipse monendo
Laudat, & hortatu comprobat acta suo.

In this Sense and Style doth St. Paul excite Titus, who was a Bishop, and in this sense do I excite you. Here onely is the difference: St. Paul spake to Titus as *one* who stood for *all Crete;* I, in his words, speak to *all you* as One.

Ephes.4:3
V.5,6
Judg.20:1
Act.2:1

It were ill Grammar but worse Divinity to consider Those that should be of One Spirit, knit fastest *In vinculo pacis*—*In the bond of peace*—whose Office is to preach a Religion consisting of Unity: *One God, One Faith, One Baptism,* As a Multitude; Or to speak unto Them who in the Service of God's Church should go together (as Israel to the Battel against Gibeah) *As one man,* in the Plural. We are met here in *One place,* And I hope *Homothumadon, with one mind,* as the Apostles on the day of Pentecost; why should not I then speak to you as *One?*

[7]

Such Meetings as these are unto the People Exemplary Sermons, and Instances of that Brotherly Agreement and Union which we Preach.

Ill men have their Combinations, and Factious men have their Conventicles, but these (St Augustine says) *Unitatem faciunt contra Unitatem:* Unite and band themselves to break this Union, and so become a Conspiracy rather than an Union.

Tertull. *Apologet: cap.40*

Onely good men properly have their *Union.* When good men are Congregated and met to good ends, you cannot call that Assembly a Factious Conventicle, but a Council.

Visitation

May we all conspire as happily in *Doctrine,* and in Endeavour to settle the Divisions in our Church, as we do in *Place;* And then, as by the Act of a Synod, we shall establish that Canon which bids us be of *one Mind, as our Father is one.* (Jn 17:21)

This Union is an happy Qualification, and makes us capable to discharge the Duty of Apostles. [8] When the Spirit fell upon them in Tongues, 'twas when They were in One place and met with One Mind. These Capacities fit us for the receiving of the Holy Ghost in Tongues, and then for the Exercise of Those Tongues: Loquere In—Speak Thou.

Which implies both a *Commission* and a *Charge*. 2. *Speak*

If it be Treason in Embassadors to forge their Message or Treat without Letters of Credence, by 1. *Commission* what name shall I style their Insolent Usurpation who enter upon this high Calling without Commission?

The Ministery was not an Office Rashly Instituted, Therefore ought not to be Unadvisedly Undertaken.

In the 6 of Esay, you find God in a Deliberation what Prophet to choose: *Whom shall I send?* 'Tis Isa.6:8 true, too, that Esay there obediently offers himself to the Task: *Send me,* and is accepted. But before his setting forth He has his Mission, *Go and say unto the People.* Vers. 9

The Reason is given by St. Paul. *No man taketh this Honor to himself, but he who is called of* [9] *God, as was Aaron.* Nay (saith he) Christ took not to Himself this Honor, to be made the High Heb.5:4 priest, But He who said to Him, *Thou art my Son, This day begat I thee,* Gave it to him. Vers.5

I fear there be some Straglers in our Church, who, as they speak what Christ and his Apostles ne'r taught, so they have done what they did not—I mean, Invested themselves in the Ministerial Function before Lawfully Ordained, and Run on God's Errand before he sent them.

Of which sort were Those Obscure men Hierom speaks of, *Qui de cavernis cellularum damnant* Hieron.*Lib.* *orbem*—who from their dark Corners and close Angles, wherein they lurk, breathe out the *1: Ep.55* Sentence of Damnation against all that are not of their Opinion and Sect.

Would that unruly violence which transports them stop a little at the book of Jeremy, They should find their giddy zeal waited on by as much rebuke and danger as the false Prophets, who are [10] first Degraded, and then Cursed: God disclames their service, *I have not sent them, neither did I* Jer.14:14, 15 *command them, neither spake unto them;* And after, condemns them to Sword and Famin.

I am sure that Prophet was so tender of himself in this particular, That lest he might be suspected for an Intruder upon his Office, He makes a voluntary protestation, *He had not thrust in himself for* Jer.17:16 *a Pastor.*

So St. Paul, before he delivers any message by his Pen to the Corinthians, opens his Commis- 1 Cor.1:1 sion: *Vocatus ad Apostolatum—Paul, called to be an Apostle* of Jesus Christ by the will of God.

Nor doth he keep it back from Timothy, but shews it, although he required it not: *Whereunto I am* 2 Tim.1:11 *appointed a Preacher.*

The Minister is *Sagitta electa,* a *chosen Shaft* drawn from the Quiver of God. An Arrow doth not Esa.49:2 flie of it self, unless sent from the Bow by that hand which fits it to the String. How disordered then [11] must their motion needs be, who leap out of the Quiver, and fly without their Mission?

St. Paul doth not onely ask why any should do this, but how they should perform the scope of this Message: *Quomodo prædicabunt nisi missi? How shall they preach unless they be sent?* Rom.10:15

The Apostles never spake with power until they had received the holy Ghost, And then see how St. Peter's first Sermon, like a sharp Sword, peirces to the quick: *The Hearers were pricked to the* Act.2:37 *heart, and said to the Apostles, Men and brethren, what shall we do?*

Those who preach without this Spirit may preach the dead Letter, or rather not *Prædicare* but *Sonare,* not Preach but make a noise.

We are perswaded, that in the Lawful Ordination in our Church, the *Spirit of God* is imparted in those words, *Accipite Spiritum Sanctum: Receive the holy Ghost.* Nor must we judge them Ministers who want these Seals of Ordination to their Patent.

God touched the lips of Esay; And Ezekiel must have remained still dumb, had not the hand of [12] Esa.6:7; Ezek.33:22 God opened his mouth. Christ our Blessed Saviour signed the Apostles' Commission in his Gospel,

Matt.28:19 *Go out and preach to all Nations;* But he sealed not that Commission until the day of Pentecost, wherein He gave the Holy Ghost as the Seal of his love and favour to them.

Those Preachers who have this Hand to their Patent, and this Seal to their Commission, can, onely, call themselves Preachers.

When they have this warrant, it will not onely be seasonable to speak but necessary, For their Commission then becomes a Charge, and this *Loquere,* speak Thou, is not so much a License as a Mandat.

2. *Their Charge*

There was no Vessel of the Sanctuary but had its peculiar use. There is no Priest but is, or should be, a Sanctuary, like it holy, and furnished like it.

[13] I know my Heart is my Portable Oratory, but if my Tongue be tied up to the Roof of my mouth, I am onely a Chapell without the Service, and an Altar without the Sacrifice.

Psal.148 The Praise and glory of God is a Stock entrusted to the world, Every Creature hath a Talent from this Treasury, and with it drives this pretious Trade. Therefore David musters up the Elements, as well as the Bodies formed out of them, and will have every Letter in the Creator's Alphabet, as well as the Words made out of those Letters, to *Praise God.*

Shall every Creature in his way, and every Beast in his Dialect, Praise God, And shall the world's Interpreter, Man, be mute? If God will not dispence with this want of service in those Creatures which want Speech, how can he, whom alone he hath made Vocal, excuse his silence? Where is the Tribute of the Tongue due but from him who is endued with Organs of speech? Or where is speech [14] significant, as when the Tongue is prompted by a knowing heart? The Prophet says that *the Lips of* Mal.2:7 *the Priest preserve knowledge:* And therefore Speech, as it is most profitable, so most warrantable from Him. He who *lets not down his Pitcher into this Well,* As he refused now to draw water for the Thirsty's relief, so he must hereafter look to thirst, for his punishment.

The first thing Christ did when he came to Jacob's well was to ask the courtesie of the Samaritan's Joh.4:7 pitcher, *Give me water.* And Abraham's servant concluded, from the ready letting down of Gen.24:21 Rebekkah's Pitcher into the well, that God was with his Errand.

God's Messages are like refreshing Dews to a barren and thirsty Land. There is none, then, that derives himself from Christ, who is not as liberal of his Comforts as Christ of his *Living waters* Rev.22:17 when he proclames *Qui sitit veniat—Let every one that thirsts come.*

God grant our Wells never want these Waters, nor that the Wells prove so illiberal to deny them.

[15] When Fountains of knowledge restrain their waters, not pouring out by the Tongue, which is the Conduit of speech, to fill the Cisterns—I mean, the ears and hearts of the Congregation—that dearth threatens drought to the Fountain it self.

Eccles.3:7 The Preacher says, *There is a time to speak, and a time to be silent.*

But the Apostle brings not the Minister within the compass of this Interpretation; No time must 2 Tim.4:2 silence him, no respite, no privation of speech, but he *must preach in season and out of season.* Or if he do make any pause in this service, it must be onely Caution must stop him, not Silence. *Sit* Gregor. *Pastoral.part.2: cap.4* *Rector discretus in silentio, utilis in verbo, ne aut tacenda proferat aut proferenda reticescat,** is Gregory's Rule.

There is no Law bids him repress his words, But both the Law of God and the Law of Reason bids him weigh them before he speaks.

Psal.39:1 When David resolves upon his *Dixi Custodiam* [I said, I will take heed], St. Ambrose glosses [16] Ambros. upon it, *He doth not silence, but bridle his tongue from offence.*
Offic.11:3
Esa.58:1 The Prophet's Charge was the same, *Clama ne cesses—Cry and cease not, lift up thy voice like a Trumpet;* so must a Preacher, who is *Salpigx Apostolike—*an Apostolical Trump; And he must Chrysost. remember that whosoever shall give an account for an idle word, must render it also for a slothful Homil.ad silence (St. Ambrose tells Him).
Pop. Antioch

---

*Let the master be discreet in his silence, profitable in his words, lest either he speak out what should be kept silent or keep silent what should be spoken.

If Hierom in his Epistle to Damasus approves that speech of Damasus for good, That held reading without making use of it onely a studious Sleep, or rather a learned Lethargy; sure I may term a speechless Calling such a sleep which is next of kin to Death. *Silent folly is better than concealed wisdom* (saith the Son of Syrach), and safer it is never to have known anything, than to lock up that gift of knowledge in the breast, and either wilfully lose the Key of that Cabinet, or let it, for lack of use, Rust in neglect and sloath.

Well did St. Bernard call the Ministry *A fearful and weighty task, which would make an Angel shrink under it*. Indeed it is as full of danger as of burthen. *The Lips are the Soul's snare*, and ofttimes words are like nets to ensnare the speaker.

So that which to other men is onely a single danger, is doubled to us: We are in equal hazard to betray our selves by silence, as by our speech; And our not speaking contracts as certain ruine to us as our speech.

Miserable streight wherein our Calling is concluded! We can neither speak safely, nor yet with safety hold our peace. When we speak, every hearer is a Judge, to arraign, or censure, or traduce our meaning; And when we speak not, God threatens to condemn us. Yet we must on, Resolving with our selves that though it be sometimes Offensive to speak, 'tis ever Dangerous to hold our peace, for *There is a necessity laid on me, Wo to me if I preach not*.

Where speaking is so needful, there can be no greater sin than silence, nor Solæcism than to speak vainly; To prevent which, the next Circumstances direct both *What* and *How* to speak: *Speak Thou the Things*.

When the Voice bade the Prophet Cry, It there directs him what he should Cry: 'Twas the same Spirit which commanded the Prophet there to write, and the Apostle here to speak; And he who gave Authority to his Calling, teacheth him to give weight to his words.

As Judgment is the Ballast of Wit, so Matter of Words. A Vessel at Sea which bears more Sail than Ballast is ever apt to over-set: so they whose Phantasie is stronger than their Religion, whose words more full of sound than devout sense, for want of just poise lose their own Adventure, and endanger others.

There is a great deal of difference between *legein* and *lalein*, to Speak and to Prate: The one hath Reason on its side, The other onely Noise.

The first part of the Preacher's care must therefore be to avoid that Scoff which Lactantius gives those idle Philosophers, *Multa loquuntur nihil dicunt*: who though they spake much, yet they said nothing, because nothing to purpose.

Words are excellent tinctures, so that like Metalls in the Alembeck they have their just fixation; else, like unclosed Distillations, They breathe out in Fume.

In our Alchimy, wherein we labour to make Gold out of Clay, and by perswasions to prepare that Earth which we bear about us for final glory, The subject we undertake must fix our words, else we do but *beat the air*, forming those empty shadows which vanish as they appear and expire with the voice which delivered them.

This were to assail the Auditory *Verbis tinnulis & emendicatis*—with tinkling words. Those who affect them are ill husbands for the Church, instead of Corn, onely sowing Chaff, and instead of Devotion, Words—truly, *Semini-verbii* (as Gregory calls them), Sowers of words—whose fruit, like that in the Parable, perisheth for want of Root.

It teacheth not farther than the Ear, but as it springeth up in the present delight of the hearers, so it vanisheth with their Applause (as Isidor Peleusiot).

Such as these may be good Grammarians, not good Preachers, good Criticks, not good Apostles.

Christ told Peter, when admitted his Disciple, *That He should from thenceforth catch men*. But the Commendation of Those I speak of is that they are at best *lexithêres*, Hunters of words.

To say no more, As our Religion consists not in *Saying*, but *Doing*, so the subject of those who are Agents of the Establishment of Religion must not be words, but matter.

Though Philosophy might allow the divided Sects of nominals and Reals, Divinity owns none but

Hieron.*Lib.1: Epist.28*

Ecclus.41:15
[17]

Prov.18:7

[18]
1 Cor. 9: 16, 17

3. *Things*
Esa.40:6

[19]

[20]
Hier.*Lib*.1; *Ep*.55
Gregor.*Pastor. part.2:cap.4*
(Mt.13:21)

Isidor.Peleus. *Lib.1:Ep.62*
Luc.5:10

[21] Isidor.Pelus. *Lib.2.Ep.101*

Reals—Men so sincere, and real, and material in their Discourses, That *speak Things*. Yet Bodies are allowed their Shadows, nor doth Divinity disprove a Dress of Decent Circumstance. Therefore it follows, *Loquere quæ decent—Speak things which become*.

4. *Which become*   To apparel our Discourses in more Ceremony than becomes the subject, or to use none at all, are Extremes alike culpable.

To put upon a small body more clothes than it can bear is to smoother our Conceptions, and stifle the Argument we preach with multiplicity of words; yet to put on None at all were to establish the Heresie of the Adamites in the Pulpit, and to dogmatize Nakedness. Good matter clad in very thin or ill words is one of the strangest, most mishapen things that may be.

[22]

Adam knew not He was naked until he had eaten of the Tree of Knowledge, and then his Knowledge made him ashamed of his Nakedness. Ignorance may without blushing walk naked; for darkness needs no Mantle, and night is Covering to it self. But knowing Arguments sent abroad without a decent apparel, like Tapers set up in sluttish Candlesticks, bear Light about them onely to shame the Author.

Words are the Interpreters, nay, the Robes of Knowledge, without which it will not appear unto the world, and being best clad is most amiable.

Knowledge in its own disposition is very coy and reserved, like the nice Venetian, who never shews Hirself undress'd. If it be presented naked, not cloathed in fit words, It is so bashful, or so disdainful, that it hides it self from every Apprehension.

[23]   For mine own part, I never liked him who serv'd up more Sauce than Meat, more Words than Matter, or Wit than Religion. But yet I have ever thought Choise Matter ill dress'd like good Meat ill Cook'd, which neither credits the Bidder nor pleases the Guest.

Truth is the Pulpit's object, Decency the Attire of Truth: yet as I would not speak all truths, so neither apparel the truth I speak in every dress. An Egyptian Mantle or a Babylonish Garment were sin to an Israelite.

As every Light Tune would not go well with the Grave Dorick Harp, so every Dialect would not fit the Church. That Language which commends the Stage would misbecome the Pulpit: Light conceits or flashes of unseason'd wit prophane that holy ground. And again, that bitter Style which in a Declamation were an ingenious Satyre, translated into a Sermon might prove a Libel.

That Rule which St Paul gave the Church must be well observed in the Pulpit, *Let all things be done decently and in order.*

1 Cor.14:40

[24]   If you ask by what Rule we must measure this Decency, Surely not by Theirs who condemn or laugh at all the world who are not in their fashion. Decency was never measured by Singularity or Affectation.

Many have been more factiously proud and phantastical, and therefore more ridiculous, in an affected Plainness, than others in their studied Curiosity.

Greg.Nazianz. *Orat.29*[b]   Hierom says, *Superba Rusticitas* was the garb of some of his time, who had nothing but a *rude Insolence* to bear out their want of Knowledge, for Ignorance and Boldness commonly go together.

The most unexcepted and safe Rule of *Decency* is Religious discretion, When God's Messages want neither fit Ornament to set them forth, nor Integrity to apply them. I have it from the Prophet Psal.93:5   David: This is that *Beauty* He loves and *Holiness* that He commends, when he tells you, both these conjoyning *become the House of the Lord.*

[25]   For those therefore who quarrel with Learned Elaborate Sermons, And are so Umbragious to boggle at any thing which is not presented to them in their Mother-Tongue, Who give Sentence against a Preacher for a Latine Sentence or Authority out of a Father alleged in a Sermon, I shall truly pity them, for that they disallow what St. Paul in his practice justifi'd.

Hinkelman *Error Anabaptism. cap.2: Error.1,&2.*   Though that Anabaptistical spirit that reigns amongst many in these latter days, dares affirm: *Those who in our Universities and Schools study Divinity grasp onely the Dead Letter, attain not the Quickning Spirit, and therefore cannot be Ministers of the New Testament, who are styled by St. Paul Ministers, not of the Letter, but the Spirit;* Yet they may see that St. Paul Himself (whom they dare not deny to be a Minister of the New Testament) makes use of Human Learning, and cites some Verses out of Epimenides, Aratus, and Menander; which shewed that He had studied the Greek Poets, as Moses the Learning of the Egyptians, and Daniel the Wisdom of the Caldeans, supposing Religion to receive much advantage by the study of Human Learning. [26]

For which cause, Petrus Cunæus writes that the Old Levites challenged as their right an universal knowledge of all Laws and all Sciences, Humane or Divine. *Petrus Cunæus De Repub. Hebr. lib.2:cap.9*

Indeed St Augustine invites us to the reading of Ethnick Authors upon this motive, That they were Usurpers and unjust Possessors of Knowledge, whereof Christians onely could make the best use. [27]

This apprehension caused Porphyrius (as Eusebius tells) to complain of Origen: That he had robb'd the Greek Philosophers of their Treasure, to enrich his own Religion. Therefore Julian the Apostate, observing the great advantage Christians made by reading the Works of those Learned Heathens who in many things were by Them confounded, and wounded by their own Pens, peremptorily forbad all Christians the use or study of Human Authors. *Euseb. Hist. Eccles.lib.6: cap.13*

Socrat. Hist. Eccles.lib.3: cap.10

How well doth this suit the humor of our late Levites (quite differing from those Elder by me alleged) who account Ignorance a mark of the Spirit, and none so fit for the Ministry as those who never took Degree in the Schools?

I shall not trouble my self or you with more words in this Argument, but onely say, If there be any who so much dote upon their lack of Learning, accounting it an Holy Ignorance to know nothing which belongs to worldly Science; If there be any so wedded to their sudden Conceptions or præcipitate Barbarism that they cry down all Learning or Elegance in Pulpits; Or imagine that the spirit of Elocution speaks best from the worst Interpreters (As if God's Messages could be delivered in too good Language)—God forgive them. [28]

I have heard a woe denounced against *those that do the work of the Lord negligently,* but never against any who perform it with too much care. *Jer.48:10*

Erasmus well said, *Eloquentiam non pugnare cum simplicitate Religionis*: Eloquence is not inconsistent with Religion.

And Severus Sulpitius gratulated the accurate and elegant Style of St Augustine, as an improver of that devout Subject whereon he treated. Nay, St Ambrose is said to have converted St Augustine, then a Manichee, to the Christian Faith by his great Eloquence; which wrought so powerfully, when he onely out of curiosity went to hear Him at Millain, that taken by the bait of his Elocution, this great Champion was drawn into the Net of the Church. *Aug.Epist 37:6*

[29]

Nor is this strange; As St Paul told the Corinthians *That he had taken them by deceit,* so ofttimes it falls out that the Preacher's Eloquence by perswasion wins the Auditory to the Confession of some Truths, which plain reason or force of Argument could not before evince. *2 Cor.12:16*

'Tis true, David says *The King's Daughter is all glorious within,* and yet in that place she is presented in *Garments embroidered, and wrought with the needle.* Indeed it had been an unsuitable, mismatched Beauty, had not Her outward Ornaments held some proportion with Her inward Perfections. *Psal.45:14*

I apply it thus: Good Matter and sound Doctrine were unfashionable Virtues, if not set out so as *Becomes Sound Doctrine.*

This is our Issue and your Fruit, That Fruit whose Leaves, under which it grows, are our Words. For this cause is *Paul a Planter, Apollos a Waterer,* that the Congregation may gather the Blessings of this Husbandry. [30] 5. *Sound Doctrine.* (*1 Cor.3:6*)

And as the Tree whereon it grows hath many Branches, so the Fruit hath many Species, even so many as there be Virtues, Moral or Theological.

This is the Treasure for which we dig, whose Mine is the Scripture, whose Mint the Church, whose Stamp Christ Himself, By whose Impression in our Baptism we are coined, and become Current Christians.

As every Vein of Ore hath a Test to try it, so this hath a Touch-stone joyned to the Metall, which

260 THE SERMONS TO 1669

<small>Jam.1:27</small> warrants both the Value and the Truth. St James defines *Pure Religion* by Charity and Cleanness, *To keep ones self unspotted from the world.* And whatsoever conduceth to This is that sound Doctrine St Paul here means.

<small>[31] Ephes.2:20</small>
<small>1 Cor.3:11</small> This is that Christian Building whose Foundation is *Christ and his Apostles.* The Religion which stands not on these Bases is weak and false; the Apostle testifying, *Aliud fundamentum nemo ponit*—The saving Truth never had any foundation but this.

<small>Psal.40:8</small> This is the Genealogy of Faith, whose extraction is the Sacred Scripture, That Volume which reveals Him who *came to do the Will of God,* and instructs us to conform our Lives according to that Revealed Will.

<small>Eccles. 12:13</small> This Book hath too many Leaves now to read over; but if you will have the Analysis and sum of all, the Preacher hath gathered it: *Let us he[a]re the Conclusion of the whole matter: Fear God, and keep his Commandements.* He who teacheth this Lesson teacheth *Sound Doctrine,* And he who Learns it throughly hath all we can Teach.

<small>(1 Sam:20)</small> To speak beyond this I cannot. I may with Jonathan *shoot Wide, or Short, or Over,* and by that a little better direct your aim, not inform you better. I may dissolve this Mass, or melt this Ingot, to
<small>[32]</small> make it more portable; but I cannot alter the Metall, or put any better Stamp upon it than *Doctrina sana,* Sound Doctrine.

<small>1. Pure</small> This Doctrine therefore is *Sound,* that is *Pure,* not adulterated with Fables or mingled with Traditions which have imbased Religion, and brought down the price of Truth in all those parts of Christendome where this false Coin is current, this Counterfeit Stuff vendable, And their Practice
<small>Matth.15:9</small> allow'd who teach for Sound Doctrine *Commandments of Men.*

<small>Psal 12:6</small> The Doctrine of Christ is refined from this Dross: Hear it from the Psalmist, *Thy words are pure, like silver seven times tried in the fire.*

<small>1 Pet.2:2</small> This is that *Adolon gala,* Sincere milk, which the Children of God suck from the Breast of the Church their Mother.

<small>2. Wholesome</small>
<small>2 Tim.2.13</small>
<small>Jer.6:14</small> Or *Sound,* that is *Wholesome, logos hugiainōn,* A word which heals the Soul, yet not so as the Prophet complains of those Mountebanks, who *heal the hurts of the people with sweet words.*
<small>[33]</small> Popular Flatteries, distilling from Sermons, fall down upon the Congregation like Mill-dews, whose unwholesome sweetness corrupts the Pasture, and Rots those who feed upon it. This
<small>Psal.141:5</small> Doctrine is no suppling Plaister, no *Balm to break the head with smiles;* No Reteining Divinity, which takes Pension to serve any one's humour or is content to wait upon the Phantasie of the Patron, but free and open; whose End is not to delight the Times, or serve Turns, but to Cure the Men.

<small>3. Entire</small> Or *Sound,* that is, *Entire,* spun out of an even Thred, which hath no Cross Opinions interwoven, no Party-colour'd skeins of Faction, no coarse Woollen made out of gross Fleeces shear'd from the Flock of Rome, No Relicks nor wonder-working Rags torn from any Shrine, and then patched to that White Robe of Truth which was the first Garment Christ gave his Spouse, and hath ever since been the Church's Livery.

<small>[34]</small> Such ill-fashion'd Attire puts Her forth, as for Her Penance, in a dy'd Coat, and cloathes Her in that motly Habit which makes Her ridiculous to the Christian world.

<small>4. Plain</small> Or *Sound,* that is *Plain* and *Perspicuous,* not muffled up in dark Conclusions. The old Proverb tells us, *Via Plana est Via Sana:* the Plain way is the Sound way, And for sure, the Plainest Religion is the soundest, as in Heraldry the Plainest Coat the best.

Wheresoever you find Obscure subtilties thrown over Truth, it is to be fear'd that Curtain is hung before it for no good purpose, but meerly to disguise somewhat which the Inventor could wish the world might not know.

As the *true Church is seated on a Mount,* where it cannot be hid, so it is built, like Drusus his house, All Window, That by Her Tenets, as so many Casements, Each devout Eye may look clearly through, and freely survey the simplicity of the Fabrick.

<small>5. Firm</small> Or *Sound,* that is, *Firm:* firm at the Foundation, and smoothly laid. The most firm Figure and

Base for Building is the Plain. A Complete Geometrical Building admits no Stones but what are hewn from the Rock, and Squared. If the Foundation be rugged or uneven, full of pointed Scruples and craggy Doubts, the Building must needs lean on one side; And if once it leans, it will be an hard matter by any new devised Distinction to skrew it up, or set it right again. [35]

When Curiosities are applyed to underlay a mis-treading foot, they commonly cast it more awry.

Or *Sound*, that is, *Solid* at the heart; And commonly the most solid is still most plain. I know the Knotty piece of Wood is hard, but that Hardness inclines to Brittleness, which doth not prove it *sound*, but hard to work upon. But the heart of Oak, as it is most sound and durable, so most smooth. This soundness and this Plainess makes it both apt for Building, and promise Strength. 6. *Solid*

Knots tied upon a Cord were devis'd for a scourge to Torture, not for strength. Hard and Intricate Riddles in Divinity have no use but to rack the Brain, Not to Inform but to Pose the Understanding. [36]

To deliver my full meaning, The *Plain, Positive, Catechestical Doctrine of the Church,* as it is most Easie and Familiar, so most Sound and Orthodox.

How many, by over-bold searches after the Abstruse Mysteries of Faith and Hid Decrees of God, have quite blinded themselves, and perplexed others?

How many, in seeking to solve unnecessary scruples, have raised doubts and tied knots in many a Conscience, which they are not able to untie again?

How many have accounted it their glory to Trade in subtil Questions, and preach Polemicks to the People, when they might have Edified themselves and their Congregations better by a Catechism than a Controversie?

I have lived and shall die in this Opinion, That there can be no greater danger to a setled Church, than Liberty to dispute and call in question the Points and Articles of an Established Religion. [37]

I grant, Disputes amongst the Learn'd are sometimes useful Triturations, which by the Flail of Argument separate Truth from Error; But the pressing of those Arguments in the Pulpit, in Popular Congregations, oft-times suspend Religion, and make weak Apprehensions stagger from their first Conclusions.

The Reason is Evident; for when Arguments are press'd, and Objections for the Other urged, That which is most plausible sways the Hearer, and commonly carries the Cause.

Nothing therefore could more conduce to the Peace of the Church and Confirmation of Religion, than the laying Controversies asleep and silencing Disputes, which hang so many doubts upon the Cause that, like wrong Biasses, they draw men from the Mark.

'Tis piety to Believe what were not safe to Question; And besides, men would want cunning to suspect the Truth of their Religion, who never heard Objections fram'd against it. [38]

Those who are put to wade unto the Articles of their Faith through Disputes and Logick sometimes ingulph themselves in Depths which drown, but often strike on Rocks which break them into Irresolution. St. Paul, therefore, steers us from this rocky Coast: *Put away vain Questions, knowing that they engender strife.* These are *logoi plêthunontes mataiotêta*—The fomenters of vain Curiosity: *Multam in disputando habentia vanitatem** (so the Vulgar reads). 2 Tim.2:23

Eccles.6:11

Positive Divinity contains abundantly enough for the satisfaction of the Knowledge and salvation of the Soul. A little Logick serves a Christian, And a man may go to Heaven without quaint Distinctions. *Without Controversie, great is the mystery of godliness, which is God manifested in the flesh, justified in the spirit, seen of Angels, preached unto the Gentiles, Believed on in the world, and taken up into Glory.* 1 Tim.3:16

[39]

This is the Scheme of Christian Religion, the Scale of Faith, whose Mysteries, though great, yet *without Controversie* or Dispute: The Original is *homologoumenōs,* Confessedly.

He therefore who loves God, *and Believes in Him whom he hath sent, Christ Jesus;* He who is able to distinguish Conversation which may corrupt his Manners and Opinions, which may corrupt his Faith; He who makes Faith his *Major,* Greatest Proposition, and a Religious fruit of that Faith Joh.17:3

---
*Having much vanity in disputation.

exhibited in the Actions of his Life his *Minor* Proposition; He who Syllogizes in this Figure, this perfect form of Living, and then Concludes according to these Premises—I mean, Ends according to this Beginning—hath Logick sufficient to save his Soul, and School-divinity enough to bring himself to Heaven.

[40] 7. *Sano modo*

I must yet add one Condition more, necessarily required to *sound Doctrine,* That it be delivered *Sano modo, In sound terms:* That there be not onely no Contradiction *In Terminis;* That the terms be not onely not Repugnant to the Truth of the Position—but not Ambiguous or Innovated, so as they either darken or distort the meaning of it.

Concil. Carthag. 4: Can.1

For which Reason, the Councell of Carthage appointed that at the Consecration of a Bishop, one part of the Examination should be, *If in the first place he assert the Doctrine of Faith in plain words and simple terms.* An Old truth presented in New terms hath oft-times raised new Senses and another Construction, And so by a varied delivery made it suspected. Error hath many faces, Truth possesseth no shape but one.

For a man to keep within this Circle, that he speaks nothing Contrary to *sound Doctrine,* or nothing but what may be reduced to It, Is safe Descretion, but not *sound Religion.* Policy, or cold Neutrality, use to lie at this Guard.

[41]

Esse Directè & esse Reductivè in Prædicamento are Two things in Logick: That which may be Reducible to a Prædicament is *Oblique,* or Collateral, not *Directly* in it; Nor can we call what is Reducible, Direct Truth. Sound Doctrine conveyed in Dubious or Indirect Phrase, is not sound Doctrine, but lame and crazy. The best that can be said of It, 'Tis *Doctrina sana, non sano modo*— Sound Doctrine delivered in unsound sick Terms; which like infected cloathes, Infect the Body that wears them.

Aeneas Gazdus *pag.14*

Axitheus tells Theophrastus, *Hosê tōn logōn hê machê tosautê tōn dogmatōn planê**. There is much Error in those Discourses which are delivered in doubtful, or different, or unsound Phrase.

2 Tim.1:13
[42]

St. Paul requires Soundness as well in the Form as in the Matter of Doctrine, Therefore he writes to Timothy thus, *Formam habe sanorum verborum: Hold the form of sound words,* (so the new Translation); Or as the Greek, *Haputupōsin eche tōn hugiainontōn logōn,* which another renders, *Keep the true Pattern of the wholesome words*—That is, *Deliver sound Doctrine in sound words.*

Conclusion

To wind up all—It is Magalian's useful Application, and shall be Mine—St. Hierom interprets this soundness of Doctrine in *Truth of Learning confirm'd by Integrity of Life.*

Tit.2:7

For which cause St Paul, more fully interpreting this Charge, bids Titus *shew himself a Pattern of good works.*

Example is the most powerful Sermon, and a Blameless Life the best Comment upon the Text of Christ.

Nilus Paræn. 11

It was the advice of Nilus Martyr, *logō tên aretên didaske, ergō de autên kêrutte;†* And justly, for he perswades strongest whose Life is as Eloquent as his Tongue, preaching in his Conversation no less than in his Words.

Tit.2:8

This indeed is sound Doctrine, and (as the Apostle styles it) *sound speech that cannot be condemned.*

[43]

This is the End of our Sermons, this is the Fruit of your Patience. For this cause we preach, and the People hear, That by the Rule of sound Doctrine they may rectifie their Crooked lives.

1 Tim 1:9, 10.

All sin is an Obliquity, and the habit of Vice—*Prophaneness, Adultery, Murther, Lying &c.—are contrary to sound Doctrine.*

Whatsoever therefore teacheth the Unmarried Continence, the Married Chastity, Children Obedience to their Parents, Subjects Loyalty towards their Sovereign; Whatsoever teacheth the Afflicted Patience, the Happy Temperance, the Faithful Perseverance, and all sorts of People Charity, is *Doctrina sana,* That *sound Doctrine* which we must preach, the Congregation learn.

---

*Who will believe me when I speak if by my life they see I do not believe myself?
†Teach virtue by words but preach it by deeds.

When St Paul had delivered his perfect Charge to Timothy, He concludes with *Hæc doce & exhortare—These things teach and exhort.* I cannot make a better close than to exhort you to Receive what we are commanded to Teach.

1 Tim. 6:7

These Lessons digested into a Religious practice, will approve the Teachers of the Congregation *True Disciples of Christ,* and you *not Hearers onely of the Law, but Doers of it.*

[44]
Jam.1:22

When we have taken this Degree in Faith, it will derive on Us the Reward of Labourers, on You the Reward of the Righteous; Which the Righteous Lord will in due time give us for His Dear Son's sake: To Whom, with the Blessed Spirit, the Assurer of this Mercy to us, Be all Honor, and Glory, and Thanksgiving for ever: *AMEN.*

COMMEMORATION OF CHARLES I, KING AND MARTYR

A
SERMON
Preached the 30th of January at White-Hall
1664

2 Chron.35: Vers. 24, 25:
And all Judah and Jerusalem mourned for Josiah.
And Jeremiah lamented for Josiah, and all the Singing-men and the Singing-women spake of Josiah in their Lamentations to this Day, and made them an Ordinance in Israel; and behold they are written in the Lamentations.

We are met in the House of Mourning, and I wish that Text of the Preacher, *It is better to enter into it than the House of Mirth,* may prove as acceptable to you as it is proper to the occasion.

Eccles. 7:2

In compliance wherewith, my Text, in every part of it from Top to Bottom, is hung about with Blacks, to suit the just and solemn Mourning of this Day: *A Day wherein the Lord hath called for Weeping, and Mourning, and Girding with Sackcloth.*

[4]

Esa.22:12

Yet not long since, This very Day, recorded in bloody Letters, was reckoned the first Day in our unhappy Kalendar, A Day of *Liberty and Restauration* to the whole Kingdom.

Behold Joy and Gladness (as it follows in the Prophet), *slaying Oxen, and killing Sheep, eating Flesh and drinking Wine,* in their large Thanksgiving Dinners and Solemn Feasts. What *Liberty,* no Man could tell, unless *a Liberty to the Sword,* to Rapine, and to Plunder, A liberty to profess all Religions except the Right, and exercise any Law but That which was Prescribed.

Ver.13

Jer.34:17

May I not too truly apply to This Day the words of Hezekiah? *This is a Day of Trouble, of Rebuke, and of Blasphemy:* Trouble to the whole Nation, Eternal Rebuke to the Actors, Blasphemy and Reproach to the Protestant Religion, so stained by the Fact wrought on it that all the Waters which environ our Island can never wash it out. For where was it ever known that such a King was Murthered by the Sword of Justice, and Pretence of Religion gave aim to the Assasinate's Blow? When Those who, by their Office, were to Preach Peace, became the Trumpets of Rebellion; when every Pulpit was made a Sconce, from whence no Platform shot more frequent Fire than their *Tongues did bitter Words,* against the Church, and against Him who was the Nursing Father of It.

Esa.37:3
[5]

Psal.64:3

For this Cause, so much of our Sorrow as can be spared from our greater Obsequies may be allowed to lament this Scandal to the best Reformed Church of England, when we find those Men acting by their sharp Principles who desir'd to be accounted most opposite to Them, Both assuming the Title of *Sacerdotes Reformati,* Reformed and Reforming Priests.

Pap:Massonius
Vit.
Pauli 4ti
[6]

Yet need we not much wonder, since in all Ages no Rebellion brake out which had not the stamp of Religion to make it currant. Florus tells us, the Civil Disturbances of Rome borrowed from hence

A SERMON

Preached the 30th of *January* at White-Hall, 1 6 6 4.

Being the Anniverſary Commemoration of

K. Charls the I,

Martyr'd on that Day.

By *Henry King* Lord Biſhop of CHICHESTER.

Printed by His MAJESTIES Command.

LONDON,
Printed for *Henry Herringman*, and are to be Sold at his Shop in the Lower walk of the *New-Exchange*. 1665.

Commemoration of Charles I, King and Martyr

their Colour, and had their Flamens (who were their Priests) to blow them up. In our own Kingdome, Wat Tyler and Jack Straw had one Ball, a Priest, to plead for their Rising in the Pulpit.

And Littestar, the Dyar of Norwich, who took upon Him the Title of *King of Commons* (Suprest and Hang'd by Spenser the noble Bishop there), had his Chaplains too.

The French History tells us the furious Crys of Boucher, Guarren, Fruardent, with others (Thirteen in number), All Chaplains to the Duke of Guise, in all their pulpits tearmed Charls the Ninth, their King, a Tyrant, and Favourer of Hereticks; Insomuch that the seduced Parisians changed their wonted Acclamations of *God Save the King,* to *God Save the Guise,* Head of the Catholick League and Patron of Religion: The Tragical issue whereof was the Massacre of so many Protestants, and shortly after, the Death of the King—A sad Glass to shew the Rise of our late Distempers here, where praying for the King was prohibited by Order, And (I speak upon knowledge) in some places, none admitted to the Communion but those who fought against Him. [7]

Not to trouble you further, John Knox and others were Chaplains in the Scottish Rebellion in which the Archbishop was murther'd, the Churches demolished, and the Queen forced to fly.

And if any doubt who were the Chaplains to make our People stumble in their Duties, to sollicit our own and the Churche's troubles, If nothing appears under Smictymnus his Mask, Archer and Lemuel Tuke (who acted open-faced, without their Vizors) may sufficiently declare: The one whereof Preach'd it *lawful to resist the King,* The other *to kill Him.*

These, and many more like these, were the Prologue to that cruel Tragedy on this Day acted, And Chaplains to that general Mischief which the whole Kingdome then groaned under. [8]

And I dare boldly affirm, upon what Clod of Earth, in what Field soever, the sharp Battels were fought, the Sparring Blows were made in the Pulpit.

If this Repetition be unpleasing, I beg pardon. It so little pleases me, That from my Soul I wish there never had been cause to give it mention, or make it any part in the luckless Subject of our History.

Yet since our Saviour excus'd the Ointment expended on Him by the Woman and would not have it forgot, as being *done to bury Him,* I hope I may have leave to reflect a little upon those *Dead flies* whose onely aim was to *corrupt the sweet Ointment of* our Josiah's Name, which is like *Ointment poured out,* perfuming all places with the Example and Memory of his Virtues. Mat.26:12, 13

For what the Woman did to Christ in Piety, they did in Malice, to bury Him too—at least, to Antidate his Funeral by burying His precious Fame, his good Name, before the fatal Stroak which brought his Body to the grave. [9]

Our Text's Subject is Josiah's Funeral, *They mourned for Josiah;*   1.

Where you have the general Train of Mourners, *All Judah and Jerusalem;*   2.

Then the Particular: The Prophet Jeremiah *lamented* for Josiah; *The Singing-men, and Singing-women spake of Josiah in their Lamentations to this Day;*   3.

The perpetuation of this solemn Mourning: *And made them an Ordinance in Israel;*   4.

The Record kept of Them: *Behold, they are written in the Lamentations.*   5.

When we mention Josiah, we mention the best Prince that ever sate upon the Throne of Judah: *One who did right in the sight of the Lord, and walked in all the ways of David his Father;* One not less zealous for the House of the Lord than for the Service in it; For he caused the Temple to be Repaired, *and the Law of God diligently to be Read in it.* 1. Subject: Josiah. 2 Kings 22:2 [10] cap.22:3

Yea, so great was His desire to restore the Temple to its former Lustre, *That he took down all those Houses joyning to the House of God,* which either Defiled, or Defamed it by their Neighbourhood. 2 Kings 23:7

But that Josiah is not my scope.

My scene must here change from Judea to Great Brittain, from Judah's King to our Own, who fell under worse hands than Pharaoh Necho. (2 Chron.35) Vers.21

He fairly warned Josiah, and persuaded him to decline the Fight wherein God's Ordinance, which sent him against Euphrates, made his Arm too strong to be resisted. 2 Chron 35: 20, 21

But our Pharaoh Necho and his Complices did all they could, by false Oaths and Flatteries, to bring their Master within the Reach of their Blow, *and take the Anointed of the Lord in their Pits.*

A Fact so horrid, that it is easier to bewail in Tears than utter in Words.

Indeed, the grateful Duty to a Dead Master, and the Allegeance to such a King, make all expressions I can use too narrow for the Argument; upbraiding my Inabilities with that practical truth: *Nothing is more difficult than to match so great a Sorrow with Language equal to it.*

So that with Nazianzen, upon an occasion somewhat like this, I might wish another Jeremy in my stead, who onely was able to frame *a Lamentation proportionable to the cause,* and invent a Threne worthy of his excellent Pen, and of the Subject, The Piety of our Josiah being not Inferiour to that Elder Josiah, and his Moral virtues every way equal.

So great and meritorious a Person as Josiah is not to be narrowed by the common Expressions of a bewailing Tongue, nor will any Rhetorick suffice, unless assisted and supplied, where Words fall short, by the number of the Mourners, as here it was: *All Judah, Jerusalem, &c.*

Nothing is so Natural as to Lament the dead. *Man goeth to his long home, and the Mourners go about the Streets:*

Mæsta phalanx Teucrique sequuntur.

The Stoicks, indeed, by their rigid precepts labour'd to seal up the fountains of our Eyes, pronouncing it unmanly for our Sex to melt in Tears. Ennius was of the same humour: He would have *no weeping at his Grave, nor Funeral solemnity.* Nay, Ludovicus Cortusius Patavinus, by his last Will, forbad Mourning for him, and because he would have no shew of a Funeral, he ordered that the Black Monks, habited like Mourners, should not be invited to his Burial. But Solon, wiser than all three, thought his Memory disparaged if he deserv'd so little of Lacedæmon that none were found to bewail his Loss: His words were *Mêde moi aklaustos thanatos peloi.* He did expect some Tears dropt over his Hearse, and some Train of Mourners to attend him to his Funeral Pile.

They are miserable Men who go out of the world as it were in the Dark, neither miss'd nor bewail'd by any.

Josiah, you see, had many, *All Judah and Jerusalem.* A less proportion of Mourners would not suit his Funeral.

When Masters of private Families Dye, those in the Houshold are Mourners by Custom. But when the *Pater Patriæ,* the common Father of the Kingdom, the Lord Paramount and Master of us all, Dyes, the whole Confluence of the People, by an universal Summons, are call'd together as sharers in the Solemnity.

When our Saviour was Born, there was a general Tax went from Augustus to be levied through the World. Which Tax was but a concurrent shadow of the universal Homage due to the New Born King, whose Empire extended not over Judea onely, but the whole World, as *King of Kings, and Lord of Lords.*

And sure, when soever his great Vice-gerents leave the World, it is fit that their Death, which is (as one calls it) *Fatalis Nativitas,* a Fatal Birth, should be Solemnized by a Tribute of Tears levied upon the whole Kingdom.

If that Tyrant John Basiliwick, D[uke] of Muscovy, exacted *Phialas sudore plenas,* a Tribute of Sweat wip'd from his Subjects' brows, and kept in Glasses and Bottles for him to see; sure, a good Prince dying may expect a Subsidy of Tears Bottl'd up and Sorrow kept in store, to weep bitterly for such a Loss.

It is held an usual Duty at the King's Coronation to bring Contributary wood to make a Bonfire. 'Tis then (*Ratione Contrariorum* [By the reason of contraries]) an equal Duty, when He is uncrowned by Death, to bring some Contributary water falling from our eyes to Quench that fire again.

Nicephorus Gregoras writes, that in their *Næmia,* those mournful Exequies for the Emperour, the People wished the whole River of Nilus drawn up into their Eyes, that so they might raise a Mourning proportionable to the Loss. And at the Burial of Titus, the Mourning was so general That (as Eutropius expresseth it) *All sorts of men thought themselves concern'd in that Pretious Loss,* Lamenting as disconsolate Orphans deprived of their Father. *Lib.10*

[15] *Eutropius in Tito*

Nay, Barbarians themselves who had been conquer'd by the Sword of Germanicus did bear their share in the sorrow for his Death.

I know Buchanan, whose study was to diminish Princes and contract their Grandeur, tells us that a *King, though he be better and greater than any particular Subject, yet He is less than the whole Aggregate and Multitude of His Subjects.*

Buchanan *De jure Regni apud Scotos*

But a Text more authentick than his tells us, in the Person of King David: *Thou art better than ten Thousands of us,* which you must not take for a confin'd number: *of so many,* but Indefinite, nay Infinite—the Originall is *Muriadas* [Myriads].

2 Sam.18:3

So here you see the King set in skale with the whole Kingdom, for *All Judah and Jerusalem mourned for Josiah.*

Which transcendent Lamentation grew into a Proverb, *Like the mourning of Hadadrimmon in the vally of Megiddo.* (Where, give me leave to tell you, Though Abulensis thought this Hadadrimmon a person, then King of Syria, in whose assistance Josiah engag'd against Pharaoh Necho, who therefore, in gratitude, bewailed his death so excessively that it became Proverbiall; Yet Baronius will have Hadadrimmon to be only the place where Josiah fell.)

[16] Zach.12:11

Baron.*Annal.*

This Rite of mourning had Josiah; And though our own Josiah deserved no less then He, and had it from all that understood His value, yet at the time of his cutting off, it was reputed so great a crime to express any shew of sorrow for Him, that a mourning suit was look'd on as the Livery of a Malignant, and an affront to the State, nay, Libell upon the Murtherers.

My selfe knew some assaulted meerly for their Habit, and hardly escaping with life.

By which you see the misery of Judæa, under his Captivity, translated to England, where *Ne fletus quidem gratuitus:* It was dangerous to mourn, and men were forc'd to fine for their sorrow expressed at the murder of our unparalleled Josiah.

[17] Hieron. *In Sophoniam*

The Large and numerous Train which attend the Funeral shew the Greatness of the Person, but the Quality of the Mourners speak his Vertue and Merit: It did so here, when the Prophet Jeremiah lamented for Josiah.

3. The Prophet Jeremiah lamented, &c.

The better the Persons are that attend, the greater is the honour done to the Dead. When *Christ wept* at the Grave of Lazarus, the Jews look'd on it as a special Evidence of his affection, *See how he loved him.* And though Saul deserv'd not such an honour from Samuel, having so oft revolted from the command of God sent by that Great Prophet, yet was it the demonstration of a scarcely paralleled Love that *Samuel mourned for Saul all his Days,* and this before his Death.

John 11:35

(1 Sam 15:35)

That the Prophet Jeremiah did no less for Josiah, the Threnes and Lamentations by him left to Posterity shew, divers whereof were particularly applicable to him, telling the World how well this excellent Prince deserv'd, *Like whom there never was any before, neither succeeded any to equal him.*

[18]

1 King.13:12

That the Subject of our Funeral this Day solemnized was as meritorious as Josiah, I speak not in the custom of those who, in their funeral Sermons, oft times bely the Dead, atributing Vertues to them whereof, whilest they liv'd, they were not guilty. But my own knowledge, confirm'd by an attendance upon him for many years, makes me confidently rise to this Superlative.

The Hebrews make Jeremiah Chief Mourner—*Maxime lugebat*—which was partly out of Pitty, for that he ran upon a Danger wherof he was forewarn'd—indeed forbidden to encounter Pharaoh Necho, as Justin Martyr infers. But especially in remembrance of His Vertue and Piety: His singular love to God's Service and care of the Temple, both in adorning it, and ordering the Provision for the Priests.

[19]

That our Gratious Josiah took as great care to preserve the Churche's Patrimony and protect the Priestly Office against those Sacrilegious Harpies who make the spoil of both their aim, let the charge given to his Treators at Uxbridge testifie, with several other expressions in his Declarations.

Therefore Jeremiah and the Schools of the Prophets had reason to lament: *Discipulorum inter jubeo plorare catervos;*

<small>Zach.12:*13*</small> And the House of Levi had cause to Mourne Apart;

<small>Joel 2:17</small> And *Florent Sacerdotes*—Let the Priests weep *betwixt the Porch and the Altar.*

Many whereof, when He was cut off, had neither maintenance from the Altar at which they served, nor so much as a Porch to shelter their unhoused heads from the injury of the weather.

<small>Amos 8:3</small> The loss of such a Patron might justly cause the whole Church to *Lament, To turn the Songs of*
<small>[20] Vers.10</small> *the Temple into Howlings,* to change our Anthems into Dirges and *Ditties of Lamentation,* as it did
<small>*The Singing Men and Singing Women made mention of Him, spake of Josiah in their lamentations.*</small> in Josiah's dayes, when the *Singing Men and Singing Women spake of Josiah in their Lamentations.*

What strange Contrarieties doth Nature and Custom put betwixt our Beginning and our End! When we come into the World, Tears and Lamentation are our Prologue: *The first Voice I uttered*
<small>Wisd.7:3</small> *was Crying, as all others use.* But at our going hence, Musick Ushers us to our Grave. When I consider the truth of that saying, *Musica in luctu importuna:* Musick in a time of mourning is an importunity, both unwelcome and unseasonable: May I not justly wonder what use the *Singing Men and Singing Women had at Funerals?* Might we not say, as God doth, *Take from me the noise*
<small>Amos.5:23</small> *of your Songs, I will not hear the Melody,* &c?

<small>[21]</small> Sure those who feel the weight and know the apprehension of a just grief, raised from a deserving Cause, need no Helpers to improve it. And yet in all Ages, and in all places, there have been such. The Romans had their *Præficas* (*Tanquam in hoc ipsum Præfectas,* saith one), who like Counter-
<small>Jerem.9:17</small> verse led to the Chorus in their Dirges for the Dead. And Jeremy the Prophet bids *Call for the Mourning Women Skilful to Lament.*

'Tis true, Their Funeral Songs were first invented by Symonides in Greece. But besides these,
<small>Scaliger</small> they had *Organa Thênetika,* Instruments used at Funerals, according to the Quality of the Person who dyed: For meaner People, *Tibias,* Pipes; for the Noble, Trumpets.

<small>Math.9:23</small> When Jairus his Daughter lay dead, the Text tells you there were *Minstrels,* who were put out by our Saviour. The Reason given by the Jews for coming to those places was that by their sad Tones, they might work upon the Affections and encrease the Mourning. We in our practice have none but
<small>[22]</small> Bells for the Common sort, and Trumpets for the Prince.

And surely it is not merely conceit, that though they are the same Bells which Ring at a Coronation and at a Funeral, yet our Passion, intent upon the Subject, believes they sound more sad and heavy for this Last than for the first.

'Tis just so in the Trumpet, whose shril and Lofty Sounds give spirit to a Triumph, but at their Master's Hearse, their dull and hoarser Accents plainly seem to groan.

Yet this is not all: However the Hebrew reads the *Singing Men and Singing Women,* the Greek hath it *Archontes kai Archousai:* The Nobles of either Sex. And justly might they so do.

Ammianus Marcellinus, bewailing the death of the Emperor, says, *His Fall did warne all those*
<small>[23]</small> *who were in the next station of honour below him* That Their condition, when He was shaken, could
<small>Zach.11:2</small> not be long secure. *Ululat Abies quia cecidit Cedrus*—Well might the Firr-tree Lament, being of lower growth, when the Lofty Cedar fell. It was a Prophetick warning given by our excellent Josiah, when He found some of His Nobles cool and stagger'd in their Duty towards Him: They themselves would one day find the mischief, nor must look to retain their Lustre long, when He their Great Luminary was Eclipsed, *Per quem Nobiles Nobiliores facti;** As when the Fountain of Honour was diminished, the Streams deriv'd from it must needs fail. He, I say, gave them This Prophetick warning, and some of them found it verified.

For when the proud Levellers of that time took the confidence to invite the Peers to quit their

---

*By whom the nobles are made more noble.

Station, and sit with them in the House of Commons, Upon a Contest betwixt a very mean Person and a great Peer, one of the most Insolent of the Party, to whom Complaint was made, scornfully answered: He hoped to see the time That a faithful blue Apron should be as good as a Blue Ribbon. [24]

Therefore most justly *Plorent Proceres:* Let the Peers mourn, no less than the Priests. Both which have Reason *to speak of Josiah to this Day in their Lamentations.*

To perpetuate the Memory of which Solemn Lamentation, That neither the Person nor the occasion should be unremembered,

They made them an Ordinance in Israel.   4. And made them an Ordinance &c.

We have know'n many Ordinances in our late wicked Times, to carry on the War and prosecute the Life of our Josiah. 'Tis well we have here one Ordinance to bewail the Facts and Repent our selves.

The Prophet David calls the grave the *Land of forgetfulness,* where we forget and are forgotten; Psal.88:12
And elsewhere He Complains, *I am forgot as a Dead man out of mind.* But Josiah found a [25] Psal.31:*12*
Preservative to keep his memory alive after Death.

As the Daughters of Israel by an established custom yearly bewail'd the Daughter of Jephtha, so Judg..11:40
did the surviving Israelites Lament Josiah, and so we our late *Martyr'd Soveraign.* The Children of the Captivity had their solemn weeping in the fifth moneth; we have ours in the first. Zach.7:3

It was the Old fashion at Funerals, when they committed the Body to the Earth, to Salute and take their sad farewell of the Deceased Party at once; we shall not need to do that, nor yet bespeak our Incomparable Josiah as Virgil did the Brave and Noble Pallas:

Salve æternum mihi maxime Palla   (Aen.11.97, 98)
Æternumque vale.

O thou who wert as eminent for thy goodness, as great in thy Titles, Receive our last Valediction in the Tears of us who are left behind. Here is an Ordinance to keep Thee Fresher than all the spices which Embalm thy Body.

Nicephorus writes that in Chabda, a City in India, when the Husband dyed, the wife was a [26]
perpetuall Mourner at his Grave. Should we follow the Son of Syrach's rule, to *Weep for our Loss* Niceph. Calixto *Lib.8.Cap.38*
as he is worthy, we should never give over, never be out of Mourning, But truely say, (Ecclus.38:*17*)

Vigilantque mei sine fine dolores.*

A story tells us, that at Zeilan in Asia, the Inhabitants believe Adam and Eve to have wept three Purchas *Pilgrims.Asia:*
hundred years for their Murthered Son Abel; from whose Tears a purifying water sprang wherein *lib.5.cap.17*
Pilgrims washed.

I dare not say what a Torrent shall grow from our Sorrow for so Inexpressible a Loss; but the Duration of it shall, if the World lasts so long, Treble this Account of Time.

The Apostle sayes, *Abel, though Dead, speakes yet:* so doth our Dead Soveraign speak this Day Heb. 11:4
from every Pulpit, nor will the Voice of his Blood be silenced whilst there is a Tongue to proclaim or Memory to retain it.

And as the famous Ægyptian Synophanes, having lost his Son, *Statuam dolori consecravit:* [27]
Consecrated to Sorrow a Pillar, to stand as his Monument; so in our Ordinance, for the perpetuating of this day (though other Tomb or Statute He hath none), we raise a Column to the memory of his Pretious Name, which malice cannot stain or Time decay.

And for an Inscription upon this Pillar, the sighs of a whole Land shall be Recorded, and the Lamentation of a people never worthy of such a Prince.

Bajazet the second, in token of his Sorrow for his son, wrote his Letters in Black Paper with *Turkish*
white Characters. We need not put our grief into such Phantastick Dress as he did, seeing our Loss *History p.476*

---

*And my sorrows are endlessly awake.

is more nobly writ, in Mourning Hearts and Thoughts suitable to the Occasion: All which endorsed upon our Looks, and bound together, are sufficient to make a Volume large as Ezekiel's, *written within and without with Lamentations and Mournings and Wo.*

Ezek.2:10

[28]
5. *Written in the Lamentations*

Unto these, the Last clause in the Text seems to refer you: *Behold, they are written in the Lamentations.*

What Lamentations for Josiah these are, I dispute not: Some believe They were not those extant in the end of Jeremie's Prophecy, at least not all of them, but fram'd purposely for him, though lost by the injury of Time, or neglect of such who ought to have preserved them.

Sure I am we can never want matter of Lamentation for our unparallel'd Josiah: Our Annual Sorrow, not apt to grow barren by continuance, will prompt us to New forms suitable to their Argument.

First, whil'st we consider the *Person,* Endowed with all the Vertues and perfections which might adorn a Prince.

Secondly, when we reflect not onely upon his Loss, but upon the manner of it and the *Circumstances of his Death,* sufficient to wring out Tears from marble.

Whil'st we consider his *Vertues,* I may truely pronounce, Never did any sit upon the English Throne who could in all perfections match Him.

[29]

As Niceph. Gregoras of the Emperour, so may I of Him: *I cannot recount all his Vertues,* and without prævarication I dare omit none which I know.

His Religion was so constant in the practice of it, That not all the Glories of the Court, exhibited in their most solemn Revels and Masques, could divert, nor His Journies of Recreation, when He came home wet and weary, could interrupt it: I am able to give signal instances in both.

His Temperance never stained by any excess of Meat or Drink.

His Chastity never tempted to those Wandrings which Beauty invites. Let his profession made to some of his Royal Branches, the Night before his Death, witness that.

Jan.29.1648/9

His strength of Reason and Acuteness of Judgment the Conference in the Ile of Wight testifies, which was manag'd Chiefly by himself against all the Knot of Divines (so they are call'd) there combin'd to oppose him; who, when They neither had Ingenuity to submit to his Reasons, nor any Arguments of their own to convince Him, Those weak Opponents left Him with this Complement: That they wished such a Pen, in the hand of such Abilities, might ever be imploy'd in a Subject worthy of it.

[30]

The same was evidenced before, in his Entercourse at New-Castle with Mr. Hinderson; who of an Antagonist in Dispute prov'd a Convert, and upon His Death-bed not only confessed the rare Endowments of his Royal Master, but left it as a Legatory Charge to his Countrey-men, That they should value Him as a Jewel whose worth they hitherto understood not; Withall professing, That he believed him no whit inferiour to the Best of all the Kings in Judah.

Nay, I dare be bold to affirm, without Partiality or Assentation, That all the vertues which singly adorned Every one of them were United and conjoined in Him:

[31] Claudian
(*Stilicho 1*)

————*Sparguntur in Omnes,*
In te mista fluunt.

For the Excellency of *His Pen,* let me refer any to the Declarations sent to the Parliament, and his Answers to theirs; which whosoever judicially weighs, will find his wrote by so Masterly a Hand, that in respect of theirs, they look'd like Tintarit's or Holben's Pieces compared to a Painter of Signs.

Hieron.

Odi istam quadrante dignam Eloquentiam:* so little weight did Those pension'd Scriblers hold, compared to him.

---

*I hate this fine eloquence worth a mere farthing.

And truely, that Cardinal of France did not Him more Right or himself Honour in any thing, than in that *Emblem* (said to be his) wherein a single hand was decipher'd holding a Great Pen, and an infinite Number of lesser Pens held up against it; which verified in Him the old saying which you shall find mention'd in Aullus Gellius, *Unus Cato mihi pro centum Millibus, et Plato instar omnium.** One like him might stand against an hundred thousand. Peruse his *Cabbinet*, for the opening whereof a Commitee of Picklocks was appointed; who, after a Studious Search, and long fumbling about it, discover'd nothing but what was visible to the whole Kingdom, *His Resolution to adhere to the Protestant Religion, and constant affection to His Royal Consort, That Excellent Lady:* Who never refus'd Trouble Abroad, nor fear'd Danger at Home, when she might any way assist Him in his Distress. [32]

Which was plainly seen, when at one Time her Return from Holland was welcom'd by a Bullet shot from the mouth of a Cannon: And at another time, putting to Sea, She had a Chase Peece sent after Her for a farewel.

All which hazards then, and Afflictions since when exiled from Her Own, she suffer'd like that Undaunted Queen Zenobia, with so much Magnanimity and such high Resolution as became the Daughter of Her Great Father Henry the fourth.

And I heartily wish Her Story may be particularly transmitted to Posterity, that the Example of so Peerless a Wife and the Barbarous usage she underwent may never be forgot. [33]

Where give we leave to say, Though the Rifling this Cabbinet prov'd one of the highest Honours, as well to the Owner as to Her, yet was it, by Those whose Valour was always less than their Spight, intended a Brand of Eternal Defamation. Nor ever can the Actors acquite Themselves from the baseness of the Action, whereof a Noble Enemy Would never have been Guilty.

When there was hot war betwixt Philip, King of Macedon, and the Thebanes, whose Scouts had intercepted some Letters which pass'd betwixt the King and his Queen Olympia, Mother to Alexander the Great: without Violating the seals, They sent them back, holding it an unmanly insolence to pry into the written passages betwixt Man and Wife.

But why do I mention the demeanour of a Noble Enemy, compar'd to those who in all their Actings (I say in all) declar'd that They never understood the Rules either of humanity or Honour? [34]

And as they us'd the Cabbinet, so did they that Incomparable Jewel found in it too, *Our Blessed King's Portraiture,* Which those infamous Raylours whom the Proud Faction kept in pay went about to persuade the world was none of His. Did not the Papers, all writ by his own hand, refute that Libel, Look upon the Matter, and you may Conclude None but the Heart of a King Enlarg'd by God could Indite It. And if you consider the Style, *Loquela prodit:*† No Pen I ever knew, either then, or since, but *His own,* could write It.

One of them, and indeed the most Malicious in the Pack, who calls himself *Iconoclastes,* so shamelessly rails That, as St. Paul said to Simon Magnus, so might I to him: *Thou art in the Gall of Bitterness.* And as the Apostle charged Elymas the Sorcerer for *Mischief* and *perverting the Truth;* so it is very memorable This Wretch had the fate of Elymas, *Strook with Blindness* to his Death. Acts 8:23

Act 13:10

There is mention'd in the Prophet *Scriptura Ezekiæ;* The writing of Hezekiah. What this was I will not dispute; But sure I am, Our Hezekiah hath left the written Account of *His Solitude and Sufferings* upon so firm a record, that the Incomparable Author needs no Monument but his Book. That is, in Nazianzen's Phrase *empnoê stêlê*, a Living column. [35]
Esa.38:9

Gregor.Nazianz. *Orat.in Laudem Basilii*

Nor needs he any sheet of Lead to enwrap Him: His own precious Sheets will preserve Him, And cause admiring Posterity to look upon Him as a Second *Ecclesiastes,* sadly preaching to the world the Misery of Mankind and the vanity of all humane Glories, verify'd in the Greatest of Men, and in the Best of Princes.

If the Loss of so Excellent a Person as this may justly raise our Lamentation, The Manner and Circumstance which brought Him to His End must needs encrease it.

---

*One Cato has for me the worth of a hundred thousand, and Plato more than all.
†The language reveals it.

To parallel which unhappy Passages I never found any History, Divine or Humane, excepting only the History of His Great Master's sufferings under the Jews.

[36] In his Meditations upon Death at Carisbrook, He tells the world: *As he had leisure enough, so cause more than enough, to Meditate and prepare for Death, knowing there were but few steps between the Prisons and Graves of Princes.*

pag.146 And els-where He professeth it his Greatest Comfort, *That he had the Honour to imitate his Saviour's Example in suffering for Righteousness, though obscured by the fowlest charges of Tyranny and Injustice.* How did he Rejoice and bless God, on that very day which was to Him his last on Earth, when from that worthy Prælate who had leave then to attend him, he understood that Chapter of Mathew the Seven and Twentieth, which is the History of our Saviour's Passion, was not chosen by him to suit his purpose, but was the proper Lesson appointed by the Rubrick and order of the Church for the Morning Service? I say, how did he rejoyce That his own sufferings held such Conformity with his Saviour's, unto whom in very few hours he was ready to resign Himself?

[37] Indeed, whil'st I recount the steps and passages which carri'd Him to His Grave, There is scarcely any Circumstance of our Blessed Saviour's Passion (with Humility and Duty be it spoken) unto which his carry'd not some resemblance.

Luk.23:18 The Clamour of the Jews upon the First *(Away with him)*, and the Tumultuous Exclamations of an enraged People upon the Last.

Joh.18:14 Caiaphas' Prophecy upon the First: That *one must dye for the People;*

And Cromwell's Profession, heard to fall from him at Childerly, near Cambridge, when he was in the Armie's Power, against the Last: *It was not fit that Man should live.*

The Tampering with Judas to Betray him, I draw not into the Parallel: I must not say *he was Betray'd*, but Parted with, He was. And yet, the High Price set upon him carries this Excuse— perhaps as those who expose Land to Sale in a very high demand, unto which they believe the purchaser would not rise, do in effect deny the Sale; so I hope this Price, which they could not expect might be easily laid down, shewed a desire to Keep Him still Themselvs.

[38] Yet when this was done, and His implacable Enemies had his Person in their power, Though they wanted not Will to Destroy him, They wanted a colour for their Murtherous Purpose.

Luk.23:4, 14 When Christ was brought to Pilate by the Jews, and He plainly told them *he found no fault in him*, They reply'd *they had a Law, and by That Law, he was to Die.*

Mensuraque Juris Vis erat
Psal.94:20, 21 But in this case Our Jews had no Law. The Law was yet to make, and the Heads of the proud Faction, laid together, resolv'd to erect a-new One of Cassius his Tribunals, and write the Law thereby enacted like Dracoe's, in Blood: I mean their *High Court of Justice,* Whose Character the Psalmist gives you—*They imagine mischief as a Law. They gather them together against the Soul of the Righteous, and condemn the Innocent Blood.*

But this brought not their design to effect. *Quomodo te torques, O Malitia*—O Malice, how dost thou torture thy brain? Now they have invented a Law, They cannot find a Judge to Execute It.

[39] The Office is tendered to all the Robe here left behind. Amongst whom (I speak it to their Reputation, and the Counterballance of many errours which might be imputed during the distempers) not one was found to accept the Office; All of them leaving it to the Law-makers themselves,

Joh.18:31 and saying in effect (as Pilate to the Jews): *Take ye him, and Judge him according to your own Law.*

Untill a Man at last appear'd, capacitated only by his Ignorance and Impudence. This wretch,
1 Sam.22:18 Commissioned by them as Doeg the Edomite was by Saul for the Murther of Ahimelech: *Fall thou upon him,* undertook the cruel Task.

And truely, in the Manage of that foul Business, Pilate shew'd himself the more Civil Person; Indeed, the Better Christian.

Pilate, upon the Evidence given in by the Jews (to shew that nothing alledged by them convinc'd
Mat.27:24 his Judgment), *Took Water and washed his hands,* professing *he was Guiltless of the Blood of that*
[40] *Just Person.* But that Purple Radamanth profest Nothing should satisfie him But to wash his hands in His Soveraign's Blood.

Besides, when Our Saviour stood silent amidst the Clamorous Accusations of the Jews, Pilate invited the Prisoner to speak, *Answerest thou nothing?* &c. But this Barbarous Wretch, who sate in Pilate's place, denyed his soveraign the Liberty of answering for himself; *Sir, I must interrupt you, you may not be permitted to speak of Law or Reason* (Alas, these were not the Rules of their proceeding). *The Authority of the People is Superiour here, and* (whatever God says to the Contrary) *you are now Subordinate and Subject to Them.* Joh.19:10
Marc.15:4

This was the sence of that Reverend Præsident's speech in this Case, though contrary to Pilate's, who was the Præsident and Præfect of Judæa.

Let me proceed in my Parallel. If the *Mocks and Derisions* of the Souldiers added to the sufferings of Christ, Ours did the same to Their King, using Acts of the highest Scorn, even to the Interrupting his private Devotions, and words (if possible) worse than their Actions, *Spitting in his face,* as in His Master's, from rotten unwholsome mouths, not worthy to be named here. Mat.27:29
[41]

Mat.26:67

Nay, upon the Day when that fatal Sentence was pronounced: To sever the Wisest and Best Head in His Three Kingdomes from His Body, a wretched miscreant, whose best education was from the Dray-cart, then sitting as one of the Judges (in which ungratious Pack there were few of better breeding) had the Impudence to say unto him, *Now, Stroaker, cure thy self:* Alluding to those Miraculous Cures performed by the *Regal Touch;* which mock was equivalent to that of the Jews:

He saved others, Himself He could not save. Mat.27:42
Luk.23:*35*

I have but one more, Their Obstinacy and Impenitence for the Murther committed; which appears when it was moved, in the House wherein they sate, that the Names of all those Regicides who had the confidence to condemn their Soveraign might in all places for which They serv'd be engraven in Plates of Brass, that Posterity might never forget such renowned Patriotts. Poor deceived Men! As if that sinful Act of theirs were not, like the Sin of Judah, *engraven with a Pen of Iron,* to be recorded at their Final Account. [42]

Jer.17:1

I beseech you now judge, what doth this Impudence of Theirs differ from the Cry of the Impœnitent Jews, *His Blood be upon us, and upon our Children?* Mat.27:25

And truly, I speak it with much Christian Sorrow, It hath been observed That not One of those Men who Murthered Him, at the time of his Execution did express the least pœnitent Remorse for the Bloody Fact by Them committed.

Whether, then, our Jewish Sanedrim, Our High Court of Justice, did not in all particulars at least match the Jews, if not exceed them, Let the World judge.

Nor indeed know I any thing which might conclude them Not Jews, But that They wanted the Seal of their Cursed Covenant—I mean That Circumcision which the Law of Moses, and the Law of the Land, appoints for such horrid Murderers. [43]

Think not, I beseech you, That I come to whet the Sword of Justice, or sharpen the Ax: my Office is rather to blunt it.

My intent of coming to this place is to invite Mourners fit for such a Funeral; as all *Judah and Jerusalem for the first Josiah,* so *The whole Kingdom and the City* for the Celebration of our Own Josiah's exequies.

For All are involved in the misery of this Day. In one kind or other all were Contributors unto it: Not only Those who voted in the Cursed sentence, But Those who voted their Commission to Sit; All Those who by their Raised Forces abetted the Bloody Fact; All Those who approv'd it when it was Done; All Those who did not endeavour to hinder it, if they had Power: Lastly, All Those who do not heartily detest the Bloody Fact, and bewail the Person taken from us with a Lamentation worthy so Irreparable a Loss. [44]

Well may I say to the whole Kingdom, as Christ to the Women who followed Him, Lamenting, to his Cross: *Daughters of Jerusalem, weep not for me, but weep for your selves.* So may I bid the Sons and Daughters of Our Jerusalem *weep,* not so much for *Him,* as for your *selves and for your Children:* Who All, more or less, were instrumental in the Tragedy of this Day. Luk.23:28

All Ages. Old and Young: With sorrow must we remember the time when Old men, who needed a

Staff to under prop them, Ty'd to their Swords, with feeble Knees knocking one against the other faster than the Drum beat, to shew their good will to the Cause went tottering about the Streets. Nay, Young Boys, as if they had been taught to suck in Their Parents' Rebellion with their Milk, march'd up and down in a warlike manner.

[45] All Conditions and Professions, whether of Law or Gospel: What the First did, too many can well remember; And what the Last did, This whole City yet rings of. Nay, in that Sphere where I am plac'd, I dare affirm no Romance yields Example of more Lunatick prancks than some play'd, who transform'd themselvs from Ministers to Captains and Colonels.

Esa.2:4   A strange Metamorphosis! We read in Esay of *Swords converted into Plow-Shares* and *Spears into Sithes:* But, till of late, never heard of *Ink-horns* converted into *Bandileres,* and *Pens* into *Pistols.*

And as all Conditions, so all Sexes concurred in the production of this mischief.

We had a Maiden Troop, rais'd and maintained by their Contribution who went under that Style: Nay, in that City which my self have best reason to know, A Band of Women, led by One who took upon Her the Office and Title of a Captain, with Drums beating and Colours flying, marched daily through the Streets.

[46] And to shew This Sex is almost as good for Fortification as for Fight, at that time when in These very Streets the Drum, by a Ridiculous and Scandalous Beat, call'd together Men of the Spade and Mattock, to go dig in the Works cast up to keep out their King, some Ladies, to express their Zeal to the Cause, appear'd upon the Ramparts, and set their hands, not accustomed to such Tasks, unto the Spade.

Prov.31:13, 19   That vertuous Woman whom Solomon, in his Character, describes, dealeth in *Wool and Flax,* not Iron; And layes *Her hand to the Distaff,* not the Spade.

Wherefore, upon this occasion, I cannot but remember that when our Late Master was told divers Ladies wish'd ill to his Cause, He reply'd, He was confident no Woman of Vertue and Honour would be against Him.

I do not summon *These Daughters of Jerusalem* to weep at this Funeral—Tears Dropt from such Eyes upon this Glorious Dust would dishonour it. Nor am I so skilful an Herald as to tell where to [47] Rank these Ladies for the Cause, unless with the Chaplains for the Covenant: Let them *weep together,* and lament the several Scandals by either of them brought, by the One upon Their Sex, by the Other upon their Function.

Zephaniah 3:18   I come hither (in the Prophet Zephanie's Phrase) *to gather them that are Sorrowful for the Solemn Assemblies,* The *Fasts* and *long winded Exercises,* intended only to draw on That Mischief
Ibid.   which we *This Day bewail,* And unto *whom the Reproach of these Transactions is a Burthen:* Such as These whom I have mentioned have work enough *To weep for Themselves.* As indeed we all have,
Mal.2:13   and To *Cover the Altar with our Tears.*

Nor is it our Duty to weep only, but to Pray.

Jer.31:9   The Prophet bids us come *with weeping and Supplications.*

In the first to Lament our own Sins, which were contributors to this Irreparable Loss: In the Last to Deprecate the future Miseries which, upon the Account of His Blood, hang over this Nation.

[48]   When the Lamenter cries *The Crown is Fallen,* He goes on, *Wo unto us for we have Sinned.*
Lam.5:16   'Tis true that, sometimes, *Plectuntur Achivi*—The People are punished for the Prince's fault: As
(Horace Ep.1.2.14)   at David's Numbering the People, The Sheep died for the Shepherd's Offence—*Quid Oves istæ?*
(Ps.74:1)   cryes David.

But Samuel tells Israel, when God had given them a King, *If they continued in Their Obedience,*
1 Sam.12:14   *not rebelling against his Command,* They should Enjoy their King: *But if ye shall do wickedly, ye*
Vers.25   *shall be consumed, both ye and your King.*

I can therefore impute to None but our selves The Loss of Our King. For Those many Crying Sins of the Land was Our Glorious Sun Darkned at the Height of His Life's Noon and His

Spreading Beams quenched in His own Blood, According to that Threat from God by His Prophet Amos: *I will cause the Sun to go down at Noon, and Darken the Earth in the Clear Day.* Amos.8:9 [49]

We have therefore Just Cause to Pray that the Happy Light sprang from the Loins of our Late Buried Sun may long continue His Lustre, not lessened by our unthankfulness, nor darkned by Our Sins.

That, according to the Example of so unparallel'd a Parent, He may continue a Patron of the Protestant Religion, and Protectour of the Liberties of His Subjects—As, Blessed be God, He doth.

Lastly, That as He happily Inherits His Kingdoms, so He may Inherit His Vertues too: But that those Vertues may never be Put to that Cruel Bloody Test unto which the Piety and Patience of His Martyr'd Father were, this Day sixteen years, Put.

That God, who hath Power to grant and Will to assent when He is faithfully supplicated, Accept our humble Supplications for His Beloved Son's sake, our Gratious Intercessour.

AMEN.

Explanatory Notes

1621

St. Paul's Cross, 25 November 1621 (registered at Stationers' Hall, 14 December 1621). Introduction, pp. 16–17; Keynes, *Bibliography* 53–56; Hannah, *Poems and Psalms,* xv–xxii. This sermon is the only one in which the biblical text was printed within brackets in the original. The errata (p. [L3ᵛ]) have been incorporated into the text, but see second note to p. 66.

63, *one of Hers:* Queen Anne valued Bishop John King highly. Henry King's will names "that greate gilte Bason in forme of a Rose with the Ewer and a pair of Flaggons suteable to itt lefte perticulerly to mee as the guift of Queene Anne to my Father, with her Armes upon them, with an Injunction that they might be transmitted to posterity as an evidence of her gratious favour to him." There were also two great silver flagons with her arms, two large silver fruit dishes "cutt with six lesser of the same Kinde," twelve gilt plates inscribed "A. R.," and another New Year's gift of a gilt basin and ewer, "parte of my Father's Legacie lefte to me upon the same desire."

one degree from a Defender of the Faith: heir to the King, whose hereditary title this was, from Henry VIII's time.

may that heart want the prayers: a sentiment repeated by King in *ELP.* 160, in *1661.* 241 and the poem "Upon the King's Happy Returne from Scotland" (Crum, *Poems,* 82):

> And may that Soule the Churche's blessing want,
> May his Content be short, his Comfort scant;
> Whose Bosome Altar does no Incense burne,
> In thankfull Sacrifice for Your Returne.

65, *the poore Asse:* Erasmus, *Adagia* (Hanover, 1617), 147.

66, *eare:* a pun on the archaic meaning of the word *to plough.*

Belus: King has confused Belus with his son Danaus, King of Argos, forty-nine of whose fifty daughters were punished in hell for murdering their husbands on their wedding nights, by having to fill vessels full of holes with water.

The word that I told you: the list of errata instructs that the new Authorized Version, "The word that I said unto you," replaces this translation here and at original pages [11] and [18] (pp. 67, 68).

66–67, *Memory:* cf. *Lent 1,* memory as a cabinet, man's forgetfulness of God's goodness (p. 116, etc). King's ultimate source is the appendix *De memoria and reminiscentia* of Aristotle's *De Anima.*

Samson: Judg. 17:25, "when their hearts were merry . . . they said, Call for Samson, that he may make us sport."

first dish: City Guild feasts are still preceded by a visit to the Guild Church—for instance, the Elder Brethren of Trinity House process to St. Olave's, Hart Street before their Trinity Monday feast.

preaching were become as necessary: evidently particularly topical, for the previous week, on 17 November, John Chamberlain had written to Carleton: "Yt seems we grow into a superstitious opinion of sermons as the Papists do of the masse that nothing can be done without them" (Chamberlain, *Letters* 2.408).

68, *the other in the Sea:* the Armada, as in Donne, *Sermons* 2.238, a passage on memory to which King is probably indebted here and also in *Lent 1,* cf. *Spital,* 111.

new streames of blood: cf. *ELP,* 158.

69, *beads:* i.e., the rosary.

he preaches best: cf. *Visitation* 262.

Ashdod: city of the heathen Philistines.

Funguntur: Horace has "fungat." This (like "Monitoribus *asperi*" for "asper," p. 70) is an example of King's custom of adapting the grammar of his quotations to fit that of his own sentence—chief cause of what appear to be his many *mis*quotations.

Remember thy Creator: the text of *Lent 1*, which develops the thought suggested here; cf. also Donne's Valediction sermon (2.238) on the same text.

70, *Monitoribus asperi:* See note to p. 69, Funguntur. King wrongly attributes this to Juvenal.

Looke up to Heaven: cf. *Lent 1*, 117; *Lent 2*, 129.

insolent Spaniard: King may have been able to read De La Puente (cited also in *ELP* 212 and *1640* 224) in Spanish. His poems "Madam Gabrina" and "The Defence" are prefixed by Spanish tags (Crum, *Poems*, 144–45).

71, *two Catholique Lights:* The Pope and the King of Spain.

Chirographum lethale, the deadly Indenture: cf. *ELP* 161—"Death's bond" (Col. 2:14). I have been unable to trace the source of this Latin translation, see my introduction, "King's Reading." For similarly unidentified Latin biblical quotations, see second note to p. 80 below.

72, *build his nest:* the same connection is made by Bishop John King in his sermon on the death of Archbishop Piers (*Jonas,* 670).

he gave away our Land: to Philip II, who failed, however, to take possession of it with his Armada.

73, the hunt metaphor in relation to Christ is developed more fully in *Spital,* 105.

Mare nos repellit . . . : Bede, *Historia Ecclesiastica Gentis Anglorum* 1.13 (under A.D. 731). Bede is quoting a letter written to Rome by the Britons, preserved by the earliest British historian, Gildas, a Welsh monk (ca. 516–47).

74, *Paracelsians:* from Paracelsus, one of the first Greek physicians.

Vena basilica (marg.): cf. *Duppa,* 248 and "A Deepe Groane," lines 93–94 (Crum, *Poems,* 113), "the rich Basilick veine."

75, *Canon . . . Nature:* as his bishop, as well as his father.

the woman in the Wildernesse: Rev. 12:13, cf. *Lent 2,* 130.

Rerum irrecuperabilium: Walther, *Proverbia* 2.4.87a.

mendacia: Walther, *Proverbia* 2.8.208.

Snow-ball: There is a further reference to snow at p. 77; both were perhaps suggested by the "fowle weather" in late November that lasted until early December 1621, described in Chamberlain's letters (2.413): "I do not remember such a sharpe weeke" (414); "I am forced to write in my gloves, a thing I never used nor practised before" (416).

76, *Parsons:* Robert Parsons or Persons (1546–1610), a Catholic convert and with Edmund Campion co-superior of the Jesuit mission in England. He held that Catholics owed allegiance only to the pope and not to the English monarch.

no name: The English Protestant's Plea had been anonymous; this was also a time of particularly high feeling against the Jesuits, who had been proselytising widely.

St Omer's . . . Doway: the English Catholic seminaries in Normandy.

stolne away: the accusation of the Jews, to disprove the Resurrection.

Seeds-men: this pun on the literal meaning of "seminary" seems first to have appeared in Burleigh's Proclamation of 1591 against "Seedmen of seditious seminaries, priests and Jesuits," given in full in appendix 1 of Robert Southwell's *An Humble Supplicacion to her Majesty,* ed. R. C. Bald (Cambridge, 1953), 61; I owe this reference to Dr. Nancy Pollard Brown.

disavowed for a Sonne: the long Latin marginal quotation from Schulkenkius here omitted makes the various accusations summarized by King. Thomas Preston's real name was Roger Widdrington.

76–77, *Non novi hominem:* St. Peter's denial of Christ (Matthew 26.72). The text of Preston's "Examination" by the Archbishop of Canterbury (the day before the sermon was registered for publication at Stationers' Hall), affixed to most copies of this sermon (see Keynes, *Bibliography,* 54), gives his reply to his questioners that he "was never in company where the said *Doctor King* late Lord Bishop of London was . . . neither did he ever (to his knowledge) see the said Bishop in any place whatsoever, nor could have knowne him from another man."

77, *Three Conversions:* Robert Parsons, *A Treatise of Three Conversions of England from Paganisme to Christian Religion. The First under the Apostles in the first age after Christ. The Second under Pope Eleutherius and K. Lucius, in the second age . . . The Third, under Pope Gregory the Great, and K. Ethelbert in the sixth age . . . by N.D.* (1603).

Life of St. Francis: the fourteenth century *Liber Conformitatum Vitae Beati Francisci ad vitam Jesu Christo,* written by Bartolomeo Albizzi in 1385 (a printed edition of which [Bonn, 1620] is at Chichester), draws detailed comparisons between events in the lives of St. Francis and Christ. The Royalists compared King

Charles I's martyrdom with Christ's passion in similar fashion; see *Commemoration* 272-73. King himself compares his father's sufferings to Christ's, pp. 79-80 below.

Garnet's strawe: Henry Garnet, an earlier superior of the Jesuit mission in England, was executed on 3 May 1606, for not revealing his prior knowledge of the Gunpowder Plot. His canonisation was sought because, when his severed head was thrown into a basket of straw, a blood-stained ear of wheat leapt out into the hands of a bystander; after a few days, it was seen to carry the image of a crowned child's face. (The straw was long preserved by the Jesuits at Liège.)

Our Lady of Loretto: the house inhabited by the Holy Family at Nazareth is said to have been miraculously transported by angels to Loreto, near Ancona in Italy, in 1295; the first written reference to this origin of the shrine dates from 1470.

Calvino-Turcismus: id est. Calvinisticae Perfidiae (1597), by William Reynolds, strongly criticized the Protestants' position, comparing them to the infidel Turks. It provoked various replies, including William Barlow's *Defence of the Protestant Religion*.

Golden Legend: a favourite compendium of the saints by Jacobus de Voragine. Caxton printed it in English about 1483. Its historical unreliability was condemned as early as the sixteenth century, by Ludovico Vives and Melchior Cano among others.

the Dogge at Nile, Topsell, *Historie* 143.40.

Saunders (etc): Roman Catholic controversialists, the first two also English converts.

Arch-priest: the title given to the superior of the English mission. King perhaps intends to insinuate that Robert Parsons was the author.

Surveyour: an allusion to Matthew Kellison's *A Survey of the New Religion, detecting many grosse absurdities which it implieth* (1603). For Kellison, see my introduction, 16; he was also the disseminator of the Nag's Head Tavern scandal at the Reformation, discrediting the validity of Archbishop Parker's consecration.

seven-headed city: i.e., Rome, with its seven hills.

78, *the Psalmist:* The original marginal reference is to Psalm *14,* the numbering in some Latin editions, though not the official Clementine Vulgate.

all his Sonnes: see my introduction p. 16.

(marg), *B[ps]:* i.e., Thomas Morton, Arthur Lake, Nicholas Felton.

Archbishop of Canterbury: George Abbot, remembered for accidentally shooting a keeper dead whilst hunting, in the summer after Bishop King's death.

his last Testament: apart from punctuation and spelling, and plural nouns where *1621* has "hand" and "passage," this is the exact text of the will, PRO: Prerogative Court of Canterbury wills, 35 Dale.

79, *so long did he observe:* the will was witnessed on 5 March, but he did not die until 30 March.

the curtains: enclosing his four-poster bed.

80, *Resurgam:* see my introduction, 30, and note 65.

Cupit dissolvi: this translation is neither from the Clementine Vulgate nor King's own version, however, cf. second note to p. 71. It is also used by Bishop John King, Thomas Morton, John Donne, and Joseph Hall, like others of King's Latin quotations, notably 2 Timothy 2:12.

81, *most Honourable friends:* a copy of the sermon inscribed by King to John, Earl of Bridgewater (now in York Minster Library) suggests he may have been among them. Robert Burton records that his copy (now at Christ Church) was also "ex dono Authoris" (Mr. H. J. R. Wing, Assistant Librarian, kindly told me this).

some abler pen: this was eventually Henry Mason, prebendary of St. Paul's, rector of St. Andrew Undershaft, former chaplain to Bishop John, and donor of several books in Henry King's library inscribed not only to him but to his youngest brother William (at dates between 1619 and 1632). Mason's *New Art of Lying, Covered by Jesuites under the Vaile of Equivocation* (1624) singles out the originally anonymous writer of yet another version of the story, *The Bishop of London's Legacie* (for which he is the only evidence for a first edition shortly after Henry's sermon, in 1622), as the most shameless example of equivocation. In the second edition of 1623 Mason (pp. 75 and 82) echoes Henry King's sermon, "hee [George Musket, the author]is contented to owne his own abortive brat."

82, *Sosias:* Amphitryon's servant in Plautus's play of that name, whose features Mercury borrows when Jupiter takes Amphitryon's form.

Every wood will not make a Mercury: i.e., his statue, which should be of box wood. A saying of Pythagoras: not every mind is capable of being trained as a scholar's.

EXPLANATORY NOTES

ACT SERMON

St. Mary the Virgin, Oxford, 10 July 1625. Introduction 17–18, 40–41 and 48–50; Keynes, *Bibliography*, 58–62. The Act Sunday at Oxford came between the Saturday and the Monday debates on which degrees were awarded. The two preachers at Morning and Evening Prayer in the University Church were chosen from the new doctors of divinity. On this occasion, Henry King preached the Matins sermon, which he entitled "David's Enlargement"; John King's title in the afternoon was "David's Strait." (His style is more forceful than Henry's, and his quotations are not only in Greek and Latin, but also in Hebrew; his printed sermon is ten pages longer than Henry's.) The two were published together at Oxford by the University printer. On the close parallels between Henry's sermon and one of Donne's, see Introduction, 49. Some of the more striking verbal similarities between King and Donne, and King and Hooker, are indicated here.

The printing of this sermon differs from the rest in its single-line spacing and its heavier italicisation and capitalisation, common features of other contemporary Oxford publications. It is also given a literary running-title, like only two other sermons, *Spital* and *1640*.

82: The text is from the Authorised Version of the Bible. Donne uses the previous verse, Ps. 32.4, together with this one, as the text of the third of his "8 Sermons on the Penitential Psalms" (*Sermons* 9.296–315), preached at St. Paul's and dated tentatively by Evelyn Simpson as Advent 1624 or Lent 1625. Donne's "course" is in fact on Psalm 32 only, traditionally the penitential psalm against pride. Donne calls this part of his text "the Sacrament of Confession."

83, *He sayes he will confesse:* "His saying he would doe it, that is, his meaning to doe it, was the very doing of it" (Donne, *Sermons* 9.304).

the Act onely crownes him: here and subsequently, King puns on the occasion of his preaching (cf. *determine*, the technical word for successfully concluding the debating exercises for a degree). Though Donne also speaks of "the two Acts, *David's* Act and *God's* Act" (p. 297), his occasion does not provide the same point.

St Augustine sayes: Donne seems to have this passage from St. Augustine in mind when he speaks of the branches full of fruit (p. 298).

It is a Deliberation: "a word that implies both Deliberation, and Resolution, and Execution too" (Donne, *Sermons* 9.297, cf. also 303).

86, *one Translation of ours:* the Genevan or "Breeches" Bible, with Calvinist commentary, cf. also p. 94.

87, *like a monument of shame:* cf. Donne, *Sermons* 9.306: "sealed up in that monument."

As if it meant to crush out: the torture "peine forte et dure," by which the felon was crushed to death, cf. Donne, *Sermons* 9.307. "God doth not keep the Conscience of man upon the wrack, in a continuall torture and stretching," with which, again, cf. "a racking or torturing the conscience" below (where King's reference is to Cassander).

vomitus sordium: cf. Donne, *Sermons* 9.304, "It is but a homely Metaphor, but it is a wholesome, and a usefull one, *Confessio vomitus.*" Both writers cite Origen as their source.

being put to his Oathe: as with the Jesuit Garnet's previous knowledge of the Gunpowder Plot, see 1621, 77 note.

I doe not here derogate: King's view here resembles Hooker's (*Works* 3.48, etc.), Donne's, and also Francis White's, Dean of Carlisle, printed in the previous year. "The difference then between the Papals and us in this question is not about the thing itself, considered without abuses, but concerning the manner and also the obligation and necessity thereof" (*A Reply to Jesuit Fisher's Answer to Certain Questions propounded by His Most Gracious Majesty King James* [London, 1624], in More and Cross, *Anglicanism*, 514).

88, *Councell at Florence:* 1439–42, a session of the Council seeking reunion with the Greek Church, which was hoping for support against the Turks, who were nearing Constantinople. This and the Council of Trent (p. 92 below) also were cited in Hooker's arguments.

sometimes, a private Confession: cf. "this holy ease of discharging their heavy spirits," etc., Donne, *Sermons* 9.310.

when our Saviour cleansed the Leper: the same incident is used to a different end by Donne, *Sermons* 9.314.

St. Jerome's: for this whole paragraph, cf. Hooker, *Works* 3.86, who cites the same passage from Peter Lombard.

89, *The Greeke is:* Donne quotes this in Latin, *Sermons* 9.298 (see introduction, 51), a possible argument that his sermon came first and King was showing off his knowledge of Greek.

'Tis true: could in that case be in reply to Donne's habitual self-denunciation.

90, *Sinne is a loud argument:* cf. Joseph Hall in a Whitehall sermon, 8 August 1624(?): "There is no sin, that is dumb: there is none, that whispers: every one is vocal, loud, clamorous to solicit heaven for vengeance." (Hall, *Works* 5.210).

Explanatory Notes

91, *Wilt thou not confesse thy riots:* cf. Donne, *Sermons* 9.300, and contrast 310–11.

Though thy great sinnes: perhaps answering Donne, *Sermons* 9.310–11

Take heed, therefore, how thou underratest any sinne: cf Donne, *Sermons* 9.301: "But we hide greater sins with lesser," etc.

Marcus Eremita: the marginal reference suggests that for Marcus and Nilus Martyr, King is using the anthology (or "library"—"*Bibliotheca*") of Greek and Latin fathers compiled by Margarinus de la Bigne, see appendix 1. The "subtle net" is used again in *Spital,* 106—Donne has a similar net in *Sermons* 9.301.

Adam: Donne's lengthier reference to this is in a different context, *Sermons* 9.307.

blame the Planets: cf. *ELP,* 67 and (for God as responsible for evil), Donne, *Sermons,* 9.298.

92, *Laterane Councill:* the fourth, 1215.

Trent Council: the seventh session (3 March 1547), called to combat the rise of Protestantism in Europe. All seven sacraments were defined and Christ's institution of each defended.

Thou art not to confesse: the passage from Chrysostom is quoted in full by Hooker, *Works* 3.54 and there linked with the text of this sermon.

This is God's prerogative: cf. Hooker, *Works,* 3.85. "As for the ministerial sentence of private absolution, it can be no more than a declaration of what God hath done."

93, *a thing past in graunt:* cf. Donne, *Sermons* 9.312. "Thou hadst already forgiven the iniquity, and the punishment of my sin."

94, *Nor yet doth he:* cf. Hooker, *Works* 3.71: "They imagine . . . that when God doth remit sin and the punishment eternal thereunto belonging, he reserveth the torments of hell-fire to be nevertheless endured for a time."

If he do lay a crosse: "and for this World, what calamities and tribulations soever fall upon us, after these Confessions and Remissions, they have not the nature of punishments, but they are Fatherly Corrections, and Medicinall assistances, against relapses" (Donne, *Sermons* 9.313); cf. also, "so if it please God to lay punishment on them whose sins he hath forgiven, yet is not this done for any destructive end of wasting and eating them out . . . there is nothing meant to the sufferer but furtherance of all happiness, now in grace, and hereafter in glory" (Hooker, *Works* 3.61).

95, *in the last day:* "God keeps nothing in his minde against the last day" (Donne, *Sermons* 9.313).

no Arrerages: "From hence they hold God satisfied for such arrearages as men behind in accompt discharge not by other means" (Hooker, *Works* 3.72)

SPITAL SERMON

Preached from the outdoor pulpit at St Mary's Hospital, Bishopsgate, Easter Monday (18 April) 1626. Introduction, 18–19; Keynes, *Bibliography,* 62.

97, *Pythian Oracle:* the priestess of Apollo at Delphi delivered the god's answers to enquirers. (Pythagoras' name means "mouth of the oracle.")

an Imprecation: cf. also *1621,* 68, *ELP,* 158.

98, *a devout violence:* cf. *ELP,* 139.

Tetragrammaton: the four-lettered word for God in Hebrew, usually rendered Yahweh or Jehovah. In *ELP,* 157–58, King develops this theme further in relation to familiarity over naming God in church.

99, *vast subject of God's mercy:* cf. *Act,* 95.

100, *the whole Trinitie:* cf. the similar discussion in *ELP,* 147–48.

100–101, *six severall payments:* two years later, Joseph Hall, in a 1628 Lent sermon at Whitehall, also refers to the six blood-lettings of Christ (Hall, *Works,* 5.336–37), presumably from a common (patristic?) source.

his hands and feet: introduction, 47.

his witnes: the writer of St. John's Gospel (Jn 19:35).

103, *thy Saviour hath so tamed:* cf. Herbert's poem "Death," which King may have known (see note to *ELP,* 139):

> But since our Saviour's death did put some bloud
> Into thy face;
> Thou art grown fair and full of grace,
> Much in request, much sought for as a good.
>
> (*Poems,* 186 13–16)

EXPLANATORY NOTES

104, *Happy misfortune:* in the great mediaeval "Exultet" sequence of the Easter Eve ceremonies, "O felix culpa" refers to Adam's fall.

105, *this same Hunter:* cf. *1621*, 73.

that Crie was at fault: the hounds had been put on the wrong scent.

Iniquitie with Cords: cf. King's poem "The Woes of Esay," lines 75–77 (Crum, *Poems,* 138):

> Woe unto those that draw Iniquity
> With cordes: and by a vaine security
> Lengthen the sinfull trace;

emergent Occasions: possibly a phrase in current contemporary use, but certainly used by Donne in his *Devotions upon Emergent Occasions* (1624).

106–107: Charity was a traditional theme of Spital sermons, which were attended by representatives of the four Royal hospitals and the children of Christ's Hospital.

Bridewels: The original Bridewell was built as a royal palace for Henry VIII opposite Blackfriars (a plaque marks the site in New Bridge Street), but was given by Edward VI to the Corporation of London as a house of correction for the poor and idle.

Bethelem: founded in 1247 as a priory, but from the end of the fourteenth century a hospital for the insane. In King's time it lay immediately north of the present Liverpool Street Station. He was preaching from its open-air pulpit.

Pesthouse: near St. Giles-in-the-Fields. The idea of isolation for infectious disease was established in Elizabeth I's reign.

107, *the golden body of that Saint:* cf. Jonson's *Volpone* 1.1.2: "Open the shrine, that I may see my saint."

Apples of Gomorrah: none are mentioned in the Bible—perhaps a confusion with the grapes of Sodom, which are "grapes of gall, their clusters are bitter" (Deut. 32:32).

108, *the Dogstar:* Sirius, the brightest star, whose influence was supposed to cause great heat and pestilence.

a rick: the Genevan translation.

Empires have their Periods: the division into four successive empires or civilisations was developed by the historian Sleidanus (Philippson) in *De Quattuor Summis Imperiis,* a copy of which (Strasbourg, 1544) is at Chichester.

109, *these two last Visitations:* i.e., 1603 (the year Queen Elizabeth—"Deborah"—died) and 1625 (the death of James I—"Solomon").

Josiah: a similar parallel was later drawn between Josiah and Charles I after his execution, cf. *Commemoration,* 265–67.

Manes: Manichaeus, who gave his name to the heresy that God and the Devil have equal power in the world.

110, *that Church:* the Roman.

distribute them amongst the Saints: a practice also criticised in *ELP,* 151.

111, *Never did any People:* Joseph Hall in "A Holy Panegyric," preached for James I's Accession Day in 1613, starts from the same point, in a lengthy, more vehemently anti-papal, consideration of England's deliverances: "And, if any nation under heaven could either parallel or second Israel in the FAVOURS of God, this poor little Island of ours is it" (Hall, *Works* 5.89).

When Spaine rose up: the Armada, 1588.

the Breath of his rebuke: the motto on Queen Elizabeth's famous Armada jewel (now in the Victoria and Albert Museum, London) reads in translation: "God blew and they were scattered."

some English Jesuited Pioners: the Gunpowder Plot, 5 November 1605.

112, *the Sanguine Crosse:* a red cross chalked on the door of houses sealed up with their infected inhabitants within.

Death's Computation: the weekly Bills of Mortality that published the number of dead in each London parish, with the manner of their death.

Funestos etc.: King wrongly attributes this to Virgil, *Georgics* 3.

113, *the Joyes it leads to:* cf. *Duppa,* 245–6 and Donne's sonnet "Death, be not proud," lines 5–8:

> From rest and sleepe, which but thy pictures bee,
> Much pleasure, then from thee, much more must flow,
> And soonest our best men with thee doe goe,
> Rest of their bones, and soules deliverie.
>   (Grierson, *Poems* 1.326)

Explanatory Notes

Lent 1

Whitehall, 3 March 1625/26. Introduction, 18 and 48–49; Keynes, *Bibliography* 64.

116, *Bernard hath it:* Donne quotes from this same passage, in translation, in a sermon on Ps. 38:3 (*Sermons* 2.72–73), dated about 1624/25—unlike King, he does not specify its location.

it cannot impaire: cf. King's poem 'Madam Gabrina' (Crum, *Poems*, 145):

> When old age shall raze
> Or Sicknes ruine many a good Face,
> Thy choice cannot impaire (lines 41–43)

117, *that hee that runs:* the Authorised Version and other contemporary translations read "he may run that readeth it"; King's translation alters the meaning.

Dracoe's lawes: "whose execution was as bloody as their character" (*1640*, 230). Draco, an Athenian legislator of the seventh century B.C., aimed to replace private vengeance by severe public justice.

Vexatio dat intellectum: proverbial, used also in *ELP*, 168—King's is the form cited by Walther (*Proverbia* 2.5.77a). Donne quotes it as: "afflictio dabit intellectum" (*Sermons* 2.354)

the dust of the diamond: cf. King's poem on Donne's death (Crum, *Poems* 77), written five years later, in 1631:

> So Jewellers no Art, or Mettall trust
> To forme the Diamond, but the Diamond's Dust.   (lines 57–58)

a Revelation of God: cf. Joseph Hall, *The Remedy of Profaneness* (1637). "There is nothing, that we can see, which doth not put us in mind of God: what creature is there, wherein we do not espy some footsteps of a Deity? every herb, flower, leaf, in our garden; every bird and fly, in the air; every ant and worm, in the ground; every spider, in our window; speaks the omnipotence and infinite wisdom of their Creator: (Hall, *Works* 6.322). To Donne, the Book of Creatures is the third book of life, after those in the Revelation (listing the elect) and the Scriptures (*Essayes in Divinity*, 7–8).

Not all the curtaines of night etc.: cf. the passage in *Act*, 90, beginning "Thinkst thou, by drawing a curtain about thy bed," used by Fraser Mitchell to compare with Donne's style (introduction, 40–41).

118, *the Elephant:* Topsell, *Historie*, 196. "They avoid cleare water, loathing to see their owne shadow therein." Hall had used this parallel in *Meditations and Vowes*, 1605 (Hall, *Works* 2.4).

119, *the Philosopher:* Aristotle.

the report of a Feast: King uses this analogy twice subsequently—in *Lent 2*, 128, and in the poem "Silence" (Crum, *Poems*, 159, dated by her 1630–33).

> Was ever stomach that lack't meat
> Nourish't by what another eat?   (lines 7–8)

Mine . . . Thine: King develops this idea to a contrary conclusion in *ELP*, 148–49 (where he again calls the Lord's Prayer "the master-piece of prayer"); Donne regards these words, "mine" and "thine", as a disease to which even contemplative men are subject (*Essayes in Divinity*, 32).

120, *the Cinque Ports of his Senses:* see introduction, note 74, and cf. *ELP*, 190. The Cinque Ports were originally five ancient privileged seaports that furnished the navy: Hastings, Sandwich, Dover, Romney, and Hythe, to which were later added Rye and Winchilsea.

the Wiseman: Solomon, supposed writer of the Book of Proverbs and the Apocryphal Book of Wisdom.

shall be forgotten by him: Three months later, while King's sermon was still in manuscript, Donne makes the same reference in his sermon of 21 June 1626. "It is never impertinent to repeat *S. Augustine's* words . . . God begins a dying man's condemnation at this, that as he forgot God in his life, so he shall forget himselfe at his death" (*Sermons* 7.214).

122, *Dog-starre:* see *Spital*, 108 and note.

Memory in the hinder part of the head: cf. Donne: "Though the Memory be placed in the hindermost part of the brain, defer not thou thy remembering to the hindermost part of thy life" (*Sermons* 2.235).

123, *best computed by Daies.* cf. King's poem "An Exequy," lines 19–20 (Crum, *Poems*, 69):

> So I compute the weary howres
> With Sighes dissolved into Showres.

This whole section is full of word-echoes of "An Exequy."

Stylo veteri: the old style Julian calendar remained in use in England until 1762, but the new style Gregorian calendar was used on the continent from 1582.

our whole terme is bounded (etc): cf. "An Exequy," lines 95–100:

> Each Minute is a short Degree
> And e'ry Howre a stepp towards Thee.
> At Night when I betake to rest,
> Next Morne I rise neerer my West
> Of Life, almost by eight Howres' sayle,
> Then when Sleep breath'd his drowsy gale.

Thus doth Time incessantly feed on us: Ovid's famous phrase, "tempus edax rerum," *Metamorphoses* 15.234.

124, *my sinnes repent themselves of mee:* a paraphrase of St. Ambrose, *De Poenitentia* 3, also quoted by Hooker, *Works* 3.53.

the Vigill and Eve of our last Festivall: an echo of Donne, "A Nocturnall upon S. *Lucies* day":

> Since shee enjoyes her long nights festivall,
> Let mee prepare towards her, and let mee call
> This houre her Vigill, and her Eve.
>
> (Grierson, *Poems* 1.45, lines 42–44)

125, *not creepe:* cf. "An Exequy":

> How lazily Time creepes about
> To one that mournes. (Crum, *Poems*, 69.16–17)

declineth: the Geneva version, following the Vulgate. The Authorized Version has "goeth away."

feather us: the same image is used at the end of *Lent 2*, 134.

Our Bodies will sleepe: cf. "An Exequy," lines 57–60:

> Then wee shall rise,
> And view our selves with cleerer eyes
> In that calme Region, where no Night
> Can hide us from each other's sight.

Contrast Donne's balder use of the concept, to introduce a theological statement on the light of grace and the light of glory: "There shall be no night, no need of candle nor of sun, for the Lord shall give them light, and they shall reign for ever and ever" (*Sermons* 2.358).

their Fruition as Immortall as their Joyes: cf. *ELP,* 175: "a fruition of Joyes, which shall there beginne but never end."

Lent 2

Whitehall, 20 February 1626/7. Introduction, 18; Keynes, *Bibliography* 64.

128, *the Historie of a Medicine:* see *Lent 1,* 119 note.

129, *ere it be Noone with us:* cf. "An Exequy," lines 23–26:

> Thy Sett
> This Eve of blacknes did begett,
> Who was my Day, (though overcast
> Before thou hadst thy Noon-tide past)

Man . . . points upwards: cf. a probably earlier passage in *ELP* 173 and note): "Man's exalted straight forme bids him looke up, inviting his Contemplation to things above." I detect an echo here of *Hamlet* (2.2.223), a suggestion reinforced by other possible memories of the same play below, the mole working underground (cf. 1.5.162), and see note to p. 131.

his bright Sunne of Metals, Gold: cf. Ben Jonson, *Volpone* (1.1.10–11).

130, *the Prophet:* David, traditionally the writer of the Psalms and therefore of King's text.

True as the Turtle: i.e. dove.

Explanatory Notes

131, *pamper'd in ease and Ryot, like ranke soiles:* an echo of Hamlet's soliloquy (*Hamlet*, act 1, sc.2), particularly lines 137–39:

> 'tis an unweeded garden,
> That grows to seed; things rank and gross in nature
> Possess it merely.

Sure the World: Joseph Hall attributes this "the world grows old" theme to Gerson, whom King had been using in *Lent 1*, 124.

the Philosopher: Aristotle, cf. *Lent 1*, 119.

I desire to bee dissolved: cf. *1621*, 80, note.

132, *within the circle of a Crowne:* a set piece owing much to speeches in Shakespeare's historical plays, for instance *Richard II* (2.1.100, 3.2.160, 4.1.191), *2 Henry IV* (2.1.1–31), *3 Henry VI* (2.5.1).

133, *as the Prophet David does:* a mystical meaning, despite King's claim on page 125, "I take it Literally."

An Exposition upon the Lord's Prayer

A course of sermons preached at St Paul's, ca. 1623–28. Introduction, 19–20, 31–40; Keynes, *Bibliography* 64–70. Printed 1628; 2nd edition, 1634 (two impressions).

135, *that (since confessed) scandall:* see *1621* and notes.

that excellent Meditation: King James wrote a short Calvinist *Meditation upon the Lord's Prayer* (*Meditation*), dedicated to Buckingham and printed in his *Works*, 571–99. King's remarks on the Brownists and on extempore prayer owe something to this, but more importantly, each section follows as its scheme James's brief summary of the clauses of the prayer, presumably what King means by "tooke life from" (dedicatory epistle). King also uses in different contexts some of James's phrases and Latin tags in the *Meditation*, much as he develops words from Donne's writings (see my introduction, 50, and notes to *Act*, *Lent 1* and *ELP III*.

ELP I

137, *conformations:* "confirmations," 1628.

most beneficiall: "most perfect, useful and comfortable," *Meditation*, 574.

138, *the Pelagian:* Pelagius, a fourth-century British monk writing in Rome, formulated the heresy that people could win salvation by their own efforts: God's grace was not necessary.

139, *our Engine of Battery . . . with (though not against) the Almighty:* cf. George Herbert, "Prayer" (Herbert, *Poems*, 51, lines 5–6).

> Engine against th'Almightie, sinners towre,
> Reversed thunder, Christ-side-piercing spear

The passages have a common origin in St. Ambrose, but "though not against" suggests King may have known this poem in manuscript (Herbert's poems were first printed in 1633), see my preface, note 4.

140 (marg.), *Luc. 11:1:* added 1634.

conceived and borne at the same instant: "they will have a thing both conceived and borne at once, contrary to nature," *Meditation*, 575.

in the Pulpit at the end of their Prayers: The Lord's Prayer was enjoined by canon before the sermon.

extemporall: "extemporary," 1628.

141, *safe:* 1628; "false," 1634.

tell God somewhat . . . .: "tell God a thing hee knew not before," 1628.

the Wiseman: Solomon; see *Lent 1*, 120, note.

142, *Septies in die:* cf. *Meditation*, 584. *Qui stat videat ne cadat* (below) occurs at p. 591 of the *Meditation*, and *a maiore ad minus* (p. 149 below) at p. 583.

143, *hearty Prayer:* "prayers," 1628.

last everlasting: probably an echo of Donne's "The Anniversarie," lines 9–10 (Grierson, *Poems* 1.24): "But truly keepes his first, last, everlasting day."

to life: "to a life," 1628.

EXPLANATORY NOTES

ELP II

the Curtaine: frequently used to protect pictures at this time; cf. Olivia in *Twelfth Night*, Act 1, sc. 5: "We will draw the curtain and show you the picture," and Hall, *Works*, 5.407: "If we meet with a curious picture . . . we keep it choicely and set a store by it, either locking it up in a sure cupboard, or gracing it with a gilded frame and with a fair curtain."

144: *stricter:* "strict" 1628. The long Latin passage omitted after the words: "the fierie darts of Satan," merely gives the sense of the preceding clause and like other such passages (cf. p. 196, from Biel), would seem to have been added for publication.

the rate of a man's life: the biblical span allotted to man is three score and ten years; see Donne's elaborate disquisition on the number *seventy* (*Essayes in Divinity*, 60). If this is not a misprint for "seventy," the biblical span of life, King is probably thinking of the Seven Ages of Man.

string with their Beads: i.e. using the rosary as an aid to prayer. King James inveighs vehemently against this practice, linking it to the heathen's vain repetitions (*Meditation*, 597).

145, *The Brownists:* Congregationalists, followers of Robert Browne (ca. 1550–1633), a Puritan separatist who with his Norwich congregation set up a spiritual democracy in Amsterdam, though he was eventually ordained into the Church of England.

Incarnate Starres: cf. *Duppa*, 248.

Quintessence: the language of alchemy, which King uses again at pp. 185, 200, and 202, and in *1640, 1661*, and *Visitation*.

147, *And let mee tell those men . . . acceptable both to God and Men:* cf. *Visitation*, 258–59.

Pia rusticitas: quoted again at *Visitation*, 258, and cf. "To my honour'd friend Mr George Sandys" (1638), Crum, *Poems*, 91–92.

> Men who a Rustick Plainnesse so affect
> They think God served best by their Neglect . . .

Christ's mercy: added 1634.

purchased: "repurchased," 1628

148, *Meum and Tuum:* King uses these words to reach a different conclusion *Lent 1*, 119, see note.

a God of the valleyes: an allusion to 1 Kings 20:28, cf. also *ELP*, 160, and Donne, *Sermons* 6.228 (4 March 1624/5). "God is the God of the Mountains, as well as of the Valleyes: Great and small are equall, and equally nothing in his sight." Since King's sermon precedes the reference to 1623 in section IV (see introduction, 19), almost certainly it came earlier than Donne's.

150, *we are only privations:* cf. Donne's *Essayes in Divinity*, meditation 30, on "Nothing," and lines 16–37 of his "Nocturnall upon St *Lucies* Day" (to which poem King also appears to allude in *Lent 1*, 124), particularly lines 16–18.

> From dull privations, and leane emptinesse:
> He ruin'd mee, and I am re-begot
> Of absence, darknesse, death; things which are not . . .

and

> If I were any beast . . .
> But I am None;

(lines 32, 37)

ELP III

151, *the most successfull Warriour:* King David, still in the seventeenth century regarded as the author of the Psalms.

153, *Gesner:* Conrad Gesner's unnatural natural history, *Historia Animalia*, was the source of Topsell's *A Historie of Four-footed Beastes*.

the Tree of Porphyry: a traditional diagram in logic setting out a definition of humankind and its attributes. (Porphyry [ca. 233–304 A.D.] was an anti-Christian Platonic philosopher).

Hinnibilis: cf. Topsell, *Historie*, 330: "Concerning the voice of Horsses, the Latines call him *Hinnitum*."

the Names which men bear: See introduction, 19. The subject matter of this section suggests King knew

Explanatory Notes

Donne's *Essayes in Divinity,* book 1, part 2: "Of the Name of God" (pp. 23–25) and book 2, "Of Men's Names" (pp. 43–47); though the examples and the development of the theme by the two writers differ. King shows a gentle humour here, absent in Donne.

154, *Martial:* the quotation is actually "Sed tu barbara nomen habet sordida," and King's reference, "Lib. 1, Epig. 149," does not exist in any edition I have seen.

154, *John 23:* not an error—during the papal schism, the profligate, greedy antipope John 23 was elected in 1410. He called the council of Constance (1414–17), but on threat of excommunication, fled from it in disguise. He was immediately deposed.

Sapiens (etc): recorded as a proverb in H. P. Jones, *A Dictionary of Foreign Phrases and Classical Quotations* (Edinburgh, 1923). The phrase was also used as a motto by the Ingolstadt publisher Adam Sartorius. Among Henry King's books is a tract by the Jesuit Gretser (*Antitortor Bellarminianus* or *Tonsura Gordiana* [1611]) with Sartorius's device of wisdom standing on a globe in a country setting and this motto.

155, *Eudæmon Johannes:* ("Cretensis")—the pseudonym used by the Cretan Jesuit André Heureux, who died in 1625, and was therefore probably still alive when this sermon was written.

witnesses: i.e., godparents ("gossips") at the baptism, whose names commonly were given to the child.

(marg.), *Sentent.:* almost certainly a misprint for "Senens," i.e., "of Sienna"; see appendix 1.

156, *infirme:* 1628; 1634 has the obviously incorrect "infinite."

157, *Tetragrammaton:* see *Spital,* 98, note.

the Day of Expiation: The Jewish Day of Atonement.

ELP IV

Most of King's quotations and references in this section are from the Bible.

159, *Sicca morte:* cf. *1621,* 74, that has a similar passage on the Jesuits.

the Best of that ranke: James I.

160 (marg.): 1628 reads: "The Prince his return from Spaine," and omits the date, suggesting it was still fresh in his hearers' minds at the time he preached.

the Continent. Prince Charles paid what was supposed to be a secret visit to Spain in 1623 to meet his intended bride, the Infanta, a Roman Catholic. The match floundered over religious differences, to the undisguised delight of the English, who lighted street bonfires in celebration on Charles's return (see below, "his Bonfire").

our Jacob: a popular contemporary identification—the Latin for "James" is "Jacobus."

Jordan: the River Tweed, crossed by King James I on his way to take up the English throne in 1603.

these Kingdomes: Scotland and England.

out of date: though this passage must have been strengthened for publication four years later in 1628, its structure suggests that the sermon was preached no later than 1624 and certainly, from King's previous remarks, before James's death in March 1625.

above five thousand yeares: Ussher's *Annales Veteris et Novi Testamenti,* setting the date of Creation at 4004 B.C. and challenging the estimates of Eusebius and others, was not published until the 1650s; the idea may have been generally current, but King knew Ussher well enough to send him his translation of the Psalms for comment in 1651, and may already by this date have known of his conclusions.

Nor let it seeme uncharitable: see *1621,* 63, third note.

161, *as neere Heaven:* King's will of 1653 (PRO: Prerogative Court of Canterbury wills, Coke 136) returns to this passage from Jerome: "I shalbe as nere heaven at Jerusalem as here in England, being assured that noe distance of place can seperate me from the Love of my redeemer."

fourth of Matthew: corrected in 1634 from "third" in 1628.

Capitall Mannor: cf. George Herbert, "Redemption" (line 5): "In Heaven at his manour I him sought," and note to p. 139.

Chyrographum Lethale: see *1621,* 71 note.

fright treason: cf. *Hamlet,* 4.5.123–25:

> There's such divinity does hedge a king,
> That treason can but peep to what it would.

See introduction, 53

falling: "falling flat," 1628.

162, *the keyes:* of the Kingdom of Heaven: symbol of the power to bind and loose from sin given to Peter by Christ (Mt. 20:19) and traditionally the emblem used for both St. Peter and the Papacy.

his Impost upon the Bordelli: tax on the brothels owned by the Vatican, a notorious scandal used by critics of the Papacy.

164, *the Legend:* see *1621,* 77, note.

Chrysostome: the omitted marginal quotation from Chrysostom is in Latin; he is also quoted in the text in Latin in *ELP VI,* 182. This bears out my conclusion in the introduction that King acquired the Greek text, which he quotes more frequently, at a later date, and that the many marginal Greek quotations from Chrysostom unaccompanied by a reference to his name in the text were added for publication.

166, *O that I had wings:* the text of *Lent 2,* where King again uses the parable of the Foolish Virgins and hawking imagery (as above).

ELP V

167, *necessity:* according to Lancelot Andrewes, it was the use of this controversial theological term in the Lambeth articles of 1595 that prevented their general acceptance as canons for the Church of England.

Prisoners: cf. "An Essay on Death and a Prison," lines 15–22 (Crum, *Poems,* 139–40). King would remember that (for instance) in 1618, according to contemporary custom, Lady Roos, as a noblewoman, was under house arrest in his father's episcopal palace before her trial. He seems here, however, to have in mind particularly the Tower, where Raleigh, for whom he wrote an epitaph, and the Earl of Northumberland were held prisoner, since the next paragraph must refer to the Tower menagerie, the only one of the kind in seventeenth-century England.

168, *the Master of the Sentences:* Peter Lombard, whose *Sententia* has just been quoted (and clumsily inserted into the syntax of King's sentence, cf. second note to p. 164 above).

one Predicament: (see glossary) the phrase "on earth as it is in Heaven."

Oft times we wish abundance: the words on human loss here and pp. 172–73, and the poignant passage at p. 175, suggest that this is the sermon composed closest to the death of King's wife in January 1624. Like the two Lent sermons, it echoes "An Exequy" in thought, though perhaps the fact that there are fewer verbal similarities here, and that King entertains the idea that human beings will rebel against losing those whom they love, supports my contention (see notes to Lent sermons) that the poem and those sermons come later than this, after more tranquil reflection.

Vexatio: see *Lent 1,* 117, note.

before age hath reacht his mid-way: cf. "An Exequy," line 26: "Before thou hadst thy Noon-tide past."

169 (marg.), *2 part:* 1628; omitted 1634.

an impossibility: cf. King James, *Meditation,* 580.

the Definition . . . the definition: (logic) the sense is not clear.

the Arminian: King James takes issue with the same view, p. 581. Jakob Arminius (Hermandzoon), Dutch theologian and reformer, challenged Calvin's views on free will and election and influenced more liberal European protestants. His teaching was condemned at the Synod of Dort, 1619. His name came to signify those who held a sacramental view of religion, in contrast to "Calvinist."

171 (marg.), *Levit. 5:7:* King's location is wrong; perhaps he meant Lev. 16:34.

our Letany: not the Prayer Book litany as such but the response to the Ten Commandments, read before the Communion Service.

172, *Bias:* (fl. ca. B.C. 566) one of the Seven Wise Men of Greece, born at Priene which, Valerius Maximus relates, he saved from ruin.

173, *all the Sailes Devotion can beare:* cf. this passage with "An Exequy," lines 101–4 (Crum, *Poems,* 71):

> Thus from the Sunne my Bottome steares,
> And my Daye's Compasse downward beares.
> Nor labour I to stemme the Tide,
> Through which to Thee I swiftly glide.

(marg.), *Biel:* 1628; omitted 1634.

ELP VI

178, *the first roome in our thoughts:* cf. *Lent 1,* 122. This passage, and more particularly the consideration of

Explanatory Notes

"this day" (pp. 182–184 below) bears close verbal resemblance both to *Lent 1* and Donne's Valediction sermon.

179, *have it signifie all kinds of meat:* "signifies all sort of food," *Meditation,* 582.

banishes all Husbandry: this passage suggests Burgundy's speech on the devastation of war (*Henry V,* 5.2.23–67).

180, *both because:* King does not complete the syntax here.

our wastefull excesse: cf. Sir Epicure Mammon's speech in Jonson's *Alchemist* (2.2.72–87): "My meat shall all come in in Indian shells"; the sentiment is common in classical writers and the Fathers.

181, *God's hot indignation:* cf. "The Woes of Esay," lines 51–52 (Crum, *Poems,* 137):

> Therfore God's vengefull ire
> Glowes on his People . . .

The "Joyning of house to house," (below), is the first of the "Woes of Esay" (lines 1–18).

183, *This Day:* cf. *Lent 1,* 122.

Counterpart: the client's part of an indenture.

all the numerous distributions of Time: this passage occurred almost verbatim at *Lent 1,* 123–24, where it is preceded by a reference to the rich man in the Gospel, as above, *Stulte,* etc.

ELP VII

184, *Earth is but as the Center:* Like most of his contemporaries before the Restoration, King retains a pre-Copernican view of the universe; see introduction, "King's Reading."

those 1022. stars: the estimate in the Ptolemaic catalogue, rejected by Donne: "how weake a stomack to digest knowledge, or how strong and misgovern'd faith against common sense hath he, that is content to rest in their number of 1022 Stars?" (*Essayes in Divinity,* 34)

the Astronomer: Ptolemy (as reported by Aristotle).

185–86, the original pagination duplicates p. 221, but corrects itself at p. 224.

186, *Wherein I purpose not:* Cf. *Act,* 88–89. There are many echoes of that sermon throughout this section of *ELP.*

In the practise of our Law: cf. *Act* 89–90.

187 *(For so he enforces):* a long Latin quotation from Augustine ("Ergo iustus es . . . Debita nostra"), unlikely to have been in the sermon as preached, is here omitted.

188, *Thus it raises up:* an echo of the Prayer Book Litany: "That it may please thee to strengthen such as do stand . . . and to raise up them that fall."

189, *Mortall and Veniall:* cf. *Act,* 90–91.

Saith Hieron,: the marginal reference, with a quotation from the original Latin, was also added in 1634.

whose least drop had beene enough: possibly recalling the final speech of Marlowe's Faustus,

> See, see where Christ's blood streams in the firmament!
> One drop would save my soul, half a drop
>
> (sc. 19, 146–47)

Cf. the passage on hell-fire in Donne's Valediction Sermon: "no means in our selves, to derive one drop of Christ's blood upon us" (*Sermons* 2.239).

190, *the Five Ports:* Cinque Ports, cf. *Lent 1,* 120 note and introduction, note 74.

a Chaine long enough: cf. "The Woes of Esay,"lines 77–79 (Crum, *Poems,* 138):

> Till their owne Chayne
> Of many linkes, form'd by laborious paine,
> Doe pull them into Hell.

it surely takes leave: as Riches does in *Everyman*—such morality plays would have been familiar to King from his youth.

191, the customary "Amen" is not printed after this sermon, perhaps because King's text is resumed in the next.

290 EXPLANATORY NOTES

ELP VIII

S. Augustine's beginning: a long Latin quotation ("Debitor sum . . . devotus est Debitor") is omitted (the passage is marked in King's Chichester copy of St. Augustine).

the Contagion which lately dispersed us: the 1625 plague, the worst before the Great Plague of 1666, see *Spital* and notes.

by other service interrupted: presumably as Archdeacon of Colchester and chaplain to the King—the "course" of sermons covers several years. Joseph Hall refers to a year elapsing between his two Court sermons on the theme of "The Impress of God" (Hall, *Works* 5.56). King may, however, mean that he was one of the small number of clergy who remained in London to minister to the sick.

Counterpart: see note to 183; this is part of an extended metaphor relating to bonds (192).

our Forefather: Adam.

192, *though Nature's Deed be cancelled:* cf. *Macbeth* (3.2.48) and introduction, 53.

Anabaptists . . . Family of Love: the inward-looking charity of these sects is ridiculed by Jonson in the characters of Ananias and Tribulation Wholesome in *The Alchemist*.

193, *those whom the Exchange cals Good men:* cf. *The Merchant of Venice* (1.3.12) and introduction, 53.

194, *Pandects:* a mediaeval legal compilation: a section of the *Corpus Iuris Civilis*.

196, *made no reply:* cf. *1621*, 75: "The injury is no injury if not apprehended (saith one)." King evidently has now found his reference.

thy Atturney will: this suggests a well-known contemporary joke, perhaps related to the dispute over a cloak not returned, found in contemporary manuscript miscellanies either in a letter from the owner, a young lawyer Thomas Roberts, or in a pair of poems "on a cloak," purporting to be from Roberts and from the delinquent, William Bond. Donne had already used the same joke in a sermon preached at Lincoln's Inn about 1618 (*Sermons* 2.154). "Yf any man will sue thee at law for thy coate, let him have thy cloake too, for if thine adversary have it not, thine advocate will." Even if Donne is King's only source, he uses him (as usual) to carry the point a step further: "And since thou art sure to lose it both ways," etc.

Sunne go downe: the marginal reference to Luke was added in 1634, when one to Matthew (1628) was omitted.

ELP IX

197, *his Penman:* Moses, who was supposed to have written the first five books of the Old Testament under divine guidance.

198, *Cereus* (etc): wrongly attributed by King to "Juvenal."

199, *The Devill, to effect his ends:* cf. *Hamlet* (2.2.637–39).

> The spirit that I have seen
> May be the devil; and the devil hath power
> To assume a pleasing shape;

201, *S. Augustine's words:* these have already been used, on p. 199.

At which lucklesse period he leaves them: a habitual ending in contemporary character writing, of which the whole paragraph is reminiscent (cf. for instance Sir Thomas Overbury's character of "A Whore" (1632 ed., sig. H4 + 1): "and there I leave her"—see introduction, 53.

ELP X

204, *Wee first grow familiar:* a frequent theme in King's poems. For this section, see particularly "An Elegy occasioned by Sicknesse," Crum, *Poems*, 174–77 and "The Dirge," 177–78.

205, *Youth is a hot Fever:* cf. *Lent 1*, 120, 121, etc.

each Sinne bears a Whip: there is no such actual emblem illustration in the better-known collections. The closest are the figure of Vice in Alciati (an edition of his emblems [Lyons, 1547] is in the Chichester catalogue), Punishment with a birch in her hand, beating the back of the sinner (Vaenius, *Emblemata Horatiana* [Antwerp, 1607], and Repentance, in Peacham's *Minerva Britannia* (1612), 46:

> One hand a fish, the other birch doth beare
> Wherewith her body she doth oft chastize. . . .

Explanatory Notes

206, *Amorite . . . Hittite:* Canaanite (and therefore heathen) tribes conquered by the Israelites. Bishop John King made this same joke in his sermon on the death of Archbishop Piers (*Jonas* 669), to which Henry is frequently indebted in his own anti-Roman Catholic writing.

ELP XI

211, *the Latine Copies:* the Roman Catholic Church omitted this doxology from the Lord's Prayer, for the reasons King suggests, until after Vatican II in 1963–65.

Syriacke: Aramaic, the language Christ would have spoken in first-century Palestine.

his credit: i.e., Calvin's.

212, *first Mover:* (philosophy) the Creator who set everything in motion.

the Catholicke King: see *1621*, 71 and note.

213, *the first Prayers:* in the three principal Prayer Book services, Holy Communion, Morning Prayer, and Evening Prayer, the first word of the first prayer is "Almighty."

Letting him see: Canute was actually demonstrating to his courtiers what he himself already recognised; King's mistake may be due to a quick reading of the slightly confusing account in Thomas of Walsingham's Chronicle (which he cites in 1626, in *Spital*).

214, *it is a wofull but fit difference:* this passage and that beginning "O the vouchsafed grace of God" on p. 215 were printed in the anthology *From the Fathers to the Church* (ed. Bro. Kenneth, C.G.A., London: Collins, 1983: 266–67 & 58–59).

215, *finde the Sacrifice:* referring to Gen. 22:6–13, Abraham's intended sacrifice of Isaac. He provided the altar, but God provided the ram as a substitute.

unknowne Tongue: i.e., Latin.

216, *How shall the unlearned say Amen:* cf. King James, *Meditation,* 597: "those ignorants can never say *Amen* to their owne prayer which they understand not."

1640

St. Paul's, 27 March 1640. Introduction, 21–22 and 37; Keynes, *Bibliography* 70–73, Cardwell, *Synodalia* 1.380–94; Tyacke, *Anti-Calvinists,* 238–43. The use of Greek and Latin quotation in the text is heavier here than usual. The general use of "then" and "whither" for "than" and "whether" may reflect the usage of the manuscript behind the printed text.

219, *Sonne of Oyle:* two types of men were set apart in Israel by anointing, kings and priests.

one Translation: the Latin gloss in Arias Montanus, *Biblia Hebraica* (the 1609 edition of which is at Chichester).

Literally and Properly: The address to Jeremiah was in fact the *literal* meaning of the text; the *figurative* (improper) meaning is that whereby Christ was foreshadowed.

the Author: cf. Canon 1: "The most high and sacred order of kings is of divine right, being the ordinance of God himself" (Cardwell, *Synodalia* 1. 389).

221, *sonne of Syrac:* traditionally the writer of the Apocryphal book Ecclesiasticus.

Tacitus: one of several references in this sermon (see also 227–28) that are repeated at *1661*, 238–39 (where "sceptres" here is translated "ruling powers").

the Pope . . . the People: cf. Canon 1: "For any person to set up . . . any independent coactive power, either papal or popular, is to undermine their great royal office" (Cardwell, *Synodalia* 1. 390).

Buchanan: the edition noted in the margin is still at Chichester, marked by King at the passage quoted here, and the additional ones used in *1661*.

Consistory . . . Conclave: i.e. the Geneva court of discipline, and the Roman Catholic College of Cardinals.

Blot out that of Daniel: this and the texts that follow are all "express texts" from Canon 1; see introduction, 21.

222, *Whom have they resisted?:* cf. Canon 1: "and though they do not invade, but only resist, St Paul tells them plainly they shall receive to themselves damnation" (Rom. 13.2) (Cardwell, *Synodalia* 1. 390.91).

He appointed a Ruler: "A supreme power is given to this most excellent order by God himself in the Scriptures, which is, that kings should rule and command in their several dominions all persons of what rank or estate soever . . . and that they should restrain and punish with the temporal sword all stubborn and wicked doers" (Cardwell, *Synodalia* 1. 389–90).

EXPLANATORY NOTES

he is the Shepheard: probably a deliberate echo of James I's 1603 speech to the Commons (quoted Berman, *Henry King,* 58): "I am the Head and [all the whole Isle] is my Body; I am the Shepherd, and it is my flocke."

224, *the Persian:* an example cited by Bishop John King in his funeral sermon for Archbishop Piers (*Jonas* 669–70).

Triple Mitre . . . Trident: intended as an irreverent parallel.

226, *We who are shrubs,* etc.: cf. Donne, *Essayes in Divinity,* 66: "if thou beest not a Cedar to help towards a palace . . . yet thou art a shrub to shelter a lambe, or feed a bird."

bound to yield Him these duties: cf. Canon 1: "For as it is the duty of the subjects to supply their king [with tribute, custom, aid, etc.], so is it part of the kingly office to support his subjects in the property and freedom of their estates" (Cardwell, *Synodalia* 1. 391). This and the passage preceding echo George Morley's elegy on King James I, frequently copied into verse miscellanies, and into the Stoughton manuscript with King's own poems by one of his amanuenses (Hobbs, *SM* 87–88).

> Death's iron hand hath clos'd those Eyes
> Which were, at once, three Kingdom's spies,
> Both to foresee, and to prevent
> Dangers, as soone as they were meant.
> That Head, whose waking Braine alone
> Wrought all men's Quiett but its owne,
> Now lyes at Rest: O let him have
> The Peace he leant us, to his Grave . . .
>   For two and twenty yeares long care . . .
>   For his stolne sleep only by snatch . . .

Epaminondas: famous Theban general renowned for his love of truth, who defeated the Spartans at Leuctra in 371 B.C.

First Man's Curse: "Cursed is the ground because of you; in toil you shall eat of it all the days of your life" (Gen. 3:17).

227, *our Translation:* the Authorised Version. For most of the sermon, however, King uses the Geneva Bible, which with its Calvinist gloss was preferred by the hearers he hopes to convince.

228, *præposterous:* a favourite word with King; cf. "An Exequy," lines 21–22 (Crum, *Poems,* 69).

> Nor wonder if my time goe thus
> Backward and most præposterous.

should here end: (another 20 pages follow).

cries wherewith your eares, etc.: ironic, in view of the war to come; cf. also p. 232. Hall has a somewhat similar but more graphic passage in his "Panegyric" Accession Day sermon for James I (Hall, *Works,* 5.94), to which this sermon bears other similarities, such as its views on monarchy.

Starre of Jacob: cf. *ELP,* 160 note.

229, *shall I say different Nations?:* England and Scotland (joined by James I of England and VI of Scotland), Wales and Ireland. Perhaps King meant to echo Captain Macmorris, the Irishman in *Henry V* (5.3.2): "My nation? What is my nation?"

Cement . . . grown loose: in 1639, Scottish discontent had given rise to the abortive Bishops' War, to be followed in the summer of 1640 by a further English campaign against Scotland.

our Ceremonies the same: cf. Charles I's preamble to the 1640 Canons: "the said rites and ceremonies, which are now so much quarrelled at, were not only approved of, and used by those learned and godly divines, to whom at the time of reformation under king Edward the Sixth, the compiling of the book of Common Prayer was committed . . . but also again taken up by this whole church under queen Elizabeth" (Cardwell, *Synodalia* 1. 382).

One in the Litany: Elizabeth I's Prayer Book (1559) omitted the words: "From the tyranny of the Byshop of Rome, and all hys detestable enormities, from all false doctrine and heresye. . . ."

the Other in the Communion: "and take and eate this, in remembrance that Christ died for thee, feede on him in thine heart by faith with thanksgevynge. . . . And drinke this in remembrance that Christes bloude was shedde for thee, and be thankful."

before our own: i.e., Prayer Book.

whose omission: in the administering of the bread and wine, Charles I's Prayer Book (1637), like Edward

VIth's 1549 one, omits the first half of the words in the books of Elizabeth I and James I: "The bodie of our Lord Jesus Christ, which was geven for the, preserve thy body and soul into everlastinge life. . . . The bloud of our Lord Jesus Christ which was shedd for the, preserve thy body and soule into everlastinge life."

so much Cavill: by the Parliamentary committee to examine the Prayer Book (consisting of lay peers and moderate divines such as Matthew Wren, James Ussher, and Robert Sanderson).

that Declaration: Charles I's order in 1627 against preaching or writing on controversial matters in religion; see Cardwell, *Synodalia* 1.170.

230, *Dracoe's laws:* see *Lent 1*, 117 and note.

Sword . . . scarcelie unsheathed: glancing at Charles's unwillingness to consent to Strafford's execution.

Pluck up by the Root: this, and the wish on p. 232 that God will bless the King "in his root, and in his branch," suggest that long before the Root and Branch petition of December 1640, calling for the abolition of bishops, this phrase from Malachi was in the air.

See the Materialls: the architect Inigo Jones had designed a neo-classical portico for St. Paul's, paid for by King Charles (see below: "set them a pattern"), and was constructing a classical outer shell for the decaying, old, gothic cathedral. The timbers for the current restoration were evidently stored within sight of the pulpit and the congregation—the Paul's Cross sermon had been moved inside the church in 1633; cf. p. 227: "in this Holy Place."

Jehoash . . . Jehoida: Charles I and Archbishop Laud. One of the charges against Laud, when he was imprisoned in December of this same year and later impeached, was that he used the heavy fines in the Court of High Commission for this restoration, and removed houses next to the cathedral and the church of St. Gregory at its west end.

other Walls then These. ships' sides. In 1637, King had been one of several poets to salute in verse the launching of the great naval vessel *Sovereign of the Seas* (Crum, *Poems*, 92)

231, *you have contributed:* by the unpopular Ship Money Tax; King brings history to its defence.

adventure His own Person: Charles had led the army at York in the Scottish campaign of 1639.

Titus: Roman emperor, A.D. 79–81; after a dissolute youth, he became a much-loved ruler (cf. *1661*, 236, "the delight of mankind")

the Regularity of his Devotions: King had commented on this as early as the first year of Charles's reign; *Lent 1*, 121.

232, *in His Root,* etc.: see note on p. 230. The reference to Deuteronomy is in the context of curses changed to blessings.

1661

Whitehall, 29 May 1661 (Charles II's thirty-second birthday); reprinted 1713.
Introduction, 26–27; Keynes, *Bibliography*, 75–76; Hutton, *The Restoration;* V. Wedgwood *Trial of Charles I.*
Upper Region: air; earth being the lower region.

234, *the History:* the literal meaning; cf. *Lent 2*, 128, "Though David be the Historie, Man is the Morall."

Copy: i.e., copyhold.

Act of Perpetual Oblivion: The Bill of Indemnity and Oblivion, which was brought before Parliament, 14 May 1660, just after the King was proclaimed, and passed 29 August, pardoned all concerned in the late trouble except those regicides (signatories of Charles I's death warrant) who had not surrendered. All but seven of these already had been pardoned by the Declaration of Breda, 1659.

a single Person: Oliver Cromwell.

a Counsail: the Council of State created by the Rump Parliament to fulfill the executive and advisory functions of the abolished Privy Council.

a contemptible low condition: poetic licence—Cromwell was actually an East Anglian squire. As Protector, he became virtually a constitutional monarch, though he refused the crown.

235, *his Image:* before the King's return, Cromwell's coat of arms and all other traces of his rule were removed from public places, by order of Parliament. Pepys notes that as early as 17 March, "all the States' arms in the fleet" were replaced with the Royal Arms (*Diary* 1.133–34).

Closed again in '59: The Rump Parliament, "interrupted" in 1653, was recalled in January, 1659, and again in May.

the Sword . . . deserting them: the Army who, angered at losing control of Parliament, forcibly "interrupted" it again in 13 October. In December, however, General Monk opposed his colleagues Fleetwood and Lambert, and supported its recall as a move towards bringing back the King.

those punishments: ten unrepentant regicides had been hung, drawn, and quartered in October 1660.

that Rising: on 10 April, Lambert, the cavalry commander who had put down Sir George Booth's Royalist rebellion in 1659, escaped from the Tower, where he had subsequently been imprisoned by the Council of State, and rallied forces in several places, in a fanatical rising against the King's recall. Sir Richard Ingoldsby captured him and his principal supporters, without a fight, on 22 April near Daventry, and the rest fled without bloodshed. (King's account is more vivid than that in Pepys, *Diary* 1:109, 111, 114).

the other Metropolis: York.

This, the prudent Counsailes: "Thus" perhaps provides a more grammatical reading.

a Faithful General: George Monk, who welcomed Charles II at Dover. On May 26, three days before this sermon, Monk and Montague had received the "honour" of the Garter. Pepys points out that only James I's favourite Buckingham had previously received this honour *before* being created a peer (Pepys, *Diary* 1.161). Monk was subsequently created Duke of Albemarle and Montague Earl of Sandwich.

Those Others: Oliver and his son Richard Cromwell.

236, *no Plurality of Rulers:* cf. *1640*, 222–24.

the Endowments of the Mind: cf. King's praise of Charles I in *1640*.

Titus: cf. *1640*, 231.

237, *Worcester:* 3 September 1651, the battle that ended Charles II's earlier abortive attempt to regain the throne with Scots help. (He evaded capture by hiding in an oak tree at Boscobel, Shropshire—the "Royal Oak.")

the Law hath been overcurious: presumably the laws made during the Commonwealth to dispossess Royalist heirs in place of younger Parliamentarian members of the family, but see introduction, n. 53.

it can never be Reversed: cf. Hooker, *Works* 3.350.

Suarez: cf. *1640*, 227: "Suarius"—the translation is slightly altered; cf. the quotations and references here with *1640*, 221, and second note.

238 (margin), *Callimachus:* cf. *1640*, 221, "the Off-Spring of Jupiter."

Tacitus: ibid. Either King is using his old sermon because he has not yet recovered his books, or he has these quotations together in a commonplace-book collection.

Dominus Deus, etc.: quoted and translated *1640*, 225.

Buchanan: ibid. and note.

placing the Feet above the Head: cf. *1640*, 227.

239, *all our Contributory Plate:* much of the silver and plate of the whole country was melted for coinage by both sides.

Buchanan: cf. *1640*, 221 and note.

Curse ye Meroz: Stephen Marshall, the "SM" of SMECTYMNUUS (see 265, note), "author" of Presbyterian anti-monarchist commemoration pamphlets, preached on this text before Parliament at St. Margaret's, Westminster, on 23 February 1642, as Queen Henrietta Maria left for France. His sermon was printed as *Meroz Cursed.* "To your tents, O Israel" was the title on the paper thrown into Charles I's carriage as he drove into the city of London, seeking the five members of Parliament, the "birds" who had "flown" from the House of Commons on 4 January 1642.

I give you his own words: Finge ad Christianos . . . tum Romae erat. In translation, they read: "Imagine that someone from among our Doctors is writing to Christians under Turkish rule—I mean, to men poor in their possessions, humbled in spirit, unarmed and few in number, exposed to every injury on all sides. What other advice could he give, I ask, than what Paul gave to the church which was then at Rome?"

their Wildfire: cf. King's "Elegy on Sir Charls Lucas, and Sir George Lisle," lines 125–26 (Crum, *Poems*, 104):

> they proclaim
> The Kingdom by their Wild-fire set on flame

that Combustion: White's Plot, December 1660.

Popery and Superstition: King is perhaps thinking in particular of Richard Baxter, at this time vociferously leading the nonconformist objections to the Anglican liturgy at the Savoy Conference, which had reopened on 4 May.

240, *Jotham's Parable:* contrast *1640*, 225.

Explanatory Notes 295

(marg.), *Glasgow:* the Glasgow Assembly did not meet until 21 November of that year. King seems to confuse it with a similar protestation made in July 1638, at Edinburgh, against the King's declaration on the use of the canons and service book.

high enough now: on 4 December 1660, the bodies of the chief regicides were exhumed and hung in their shrouds in Westminster Hall; their skulls were stuck on poles.

hold this Day: Convocation had just drafted the new services (traditionally believed to have been formulated by Brian Duppa) for the King's Accession Day, and for the commemoration of the execution of Charles I.

Haman: Colonel Bradshaw, President of the Assembly at Charles I's trial; see *Commemoration,* 272–73.

Barabbas: Cromwell.

the Prospect our Hopes now have: Charles II's betrothal to Catherine of Braganza had been announced to Parliament on 8 May.

De nostris Annis: a very free adaptation of Ovid, which reads:

> Et quodcumque sua Imperator auget ope
> Augeat imperium nostris ducis, augeat annos.

241, *let Those want the Comforts of Life:* cf. *1621,* 63 and third note.

DUPPA

Westminster Abbey, 24 April 1662. Introduction, 27–28; Keynes, *Bibliography* 76. For the life of Brian Duppa (1589–1662), see *The Correspondence of Bishop Brian Duppa.*

242, *I read:* I can find no reference either to Philoromus Gælata or to Philip's boy. Philip of Macedon did indeed have repeated to him every time he gave an audience the sentence "Philip, Philip, remember thou art mortal"; but the references here sounds more like an emblem, a version of that found in Henry Peacham's *Minerva Britannia* (1612), p. 8, where a disembodied arm holding out a skull is linked to Philip:

> And Phillip dayly causèd one to say
> Oh king, remember that thou art but clay.

an hour's stay: evidently the contemporary preaching length; cf. Donne, *Sermons* 6.64: "these four steps . . . will be our quarter clock, for this houres exercise."

243, *Joint . . . disjoins:* though King has just disclaimed a "curious" division, he provides a more elaborate plan, with more witty metaphysical wordplay, than in any other sermon.

Period and Close: i.e. "end of sentence" and "end of musical phrase."

The page numbers [6] and [7] are duplicated in the originals.

Death's Pedigree: not the traditional one as in Milton's *Paradise Lost* 2.781–87 (derived from Jas. 1:15).

244, *Thing of No being:* cf. *ELP,* 150, note.

unusefull burthens: Lucan, *Pharsalia* 7.730, "viles animas perituraque frustra." King either adapts the Latin or remembers it incorrectly. He had used it previously in *1621,* 77. The idea of this passage also lies behind "An Exequy," line 12 (Crum, *Poems,* 69): "I Languish out, not Live the Day."

(marg.), *Dr Fern:* Henry Ferne (1602–62), consecrated at the Restoration as Bishop of Chester, after stoutly defending the lawful Church in England during the Interregnum.

245, *Aaron:* contrast *ELP,* 139: the rhythm here is less striking.

Mors optima rapit: Walther, *Proverbia* 2.2.89a.

246, *He who is lodg'd in Earth:* see introduction, 27, and Spital, 113.

(marg.) *the Oxford answer:* the Millenary or Humble Petition (1603) from leading Calvinist divines asked that the Church of England should be further reformed in the direction of Calvinism in such matters as theology, the abolition of ritual, and the centrality of preaching (which implied a resident clergy). The Oxford answer was from the Vice-Chancellor, proctors, doctors and Heads of Houses, who rightly saw this as an attack on their nonparochial status and use of livings to augment their slender stipends. Two "answers" to the Answer survive; see C. M. Dent, *Protestant Reformers in Elizabethan Oxford* (Oxford, 1983), 163.

Brownists: see *ELP,* 145, note.

Ministerial duties: listed by St. Paul in his first letter to Timothy (3:1–13), from which passages are appointed for reading at the Prayer Book ordination services.

Barrow and Greenwood: Henry Barrow (ca. 1550–93), a strict Puritan imprisoned by Archbishop Whitgift, whose writings from the Tower, printed in Holland, led to his execution, with his fellow prisoner John Greenwood, a Separatist. Barrow went further than Browne: he considered no church order necessary.

(marg.), *Gifford:* William Gifford, a Papist, edited Stapleton's *Speculum Pravitatis Hæreticæ* (London, 1580) and was held responsible for the view there expressed that heretics had no religion.

247, *Tender and soft Conscienc'd men:* The Army initiated several demands for liberty of religion for "tender consciences" during the Interregnum.

that Sign: the cross made on the forehead in baptism: the words are from the Prayer Book baptismal service.

They need no Monument: echoing the Latin epitaph, probably composed by Henry King (and translated by his brother John, see Crum, *Poems,* 242), that hung near Bishop John King's tomb in St. Paul's.

let loose His Thunder: cf. "An Elegy upon the most Incomparable King Charls the First," lines 231–33 (Crum, *Poems,* 124):

> O God! canst Thou these prophanations like?
> If not, why is thy Thunder slow to strike
> The cursed Authors?

Gray-haird Murtherer: Cromwell died in his bed, in contrast to Charles I; this whole passage refers to the troubles just past.

248, *inverted forms of Justice:* for all this passage, cf. "Elegy," lines 515–20:

> But He whose Trump proclaims, Revenge is Mine,
> Bids us our Sorrow by our Hope confine,
> And reconcile our Reason to our Faith,
> Which in thy Ruine such Conclusions hath;
> It dares Conclude, God does not keep His Word
> If Zimri dye in Peace that slew his Lord.

those Lights are Stars: from Gregory Nazianzen, cf. *ELP,* 145: "they are Incarnate Starres."

New Modell'd State: Cromwell's army was known as the New Model Army.

Vena Basilica: cf. *1621,* 74 (marg.), note.

249, *the first time:* see introduction, n. 54.

The very next Day: St. George's Day is 23 April; King was preaching on 24 April.

250, *This Famous School:* Westminster, which still has closed scholarships to Christ Church, Oxford, and Trinity College, Cambridge.

this Spring: of the Muses. King may have had in mind the title of a famous Commonwealth collection of poems supposedly by scholars of both universities, Abraham Wright's *Parnassus Biceps* (London: 1656). The phrase had been used as early as 8 June 1653 by the subdean of Christ Church in the fulsome dedication to Cromwell of a sermon preached at St. Mary the Virgin, Oxford, printed as *Ramus Olivae (The Olive Branch).*

Pædonomus: this annually elected Lord of Misrule presided over the school revels, surrounded by guards with halberds. He was dressed in black silk with gold lace and silver buttons, and a cloak of "ritch taffata of carnation in graine" (Lawrence Tanner, *Westminster School* [London, 1934], 9).

Royal Master: Charles I.

Martyr'd Archbishop: Laud, executed 1645, who had been Chancellor of the University of Oxford.

Tutour and Educator: from 1638 to 1641.

251, *first Principle of the Court Grammar:* echoing King's elegy on Richard, Earl of Dorset, whose chaplains both Duppa and he had been (Crum *Poems,* 67–68).

Those elaborate Peeces of Devotion: like King's, however, Duppa's sermons were not collected and published after his death. He was saved from a similar oblivion to King's by the publication of his correspondence this century.

252, *a trusty Messenger:* Eleazor Duncon, see introduction, 24.

to any other End: King is nevertheless excusing himself, in face of criticism of the bishops' dilatoriness, see introduction, loc. cit.

Nunc Dimittis: Lk. 2.29–32: "Now lettest thou thy servant depart in peace" (one of the canticles at Evensong in the Prayer Book), a phrase used in this connection by Duppa himself in his letters. Cf. also Sir Justinian Isham to him on the eve of the Restoration: "Mee thinks I see your Lordship welcoming your King with teares of joy, and even ready with old Simeon to say *nunc dimittis,* etc." (*Duppa,* 182).

Visitation

St. Michael's, Lewes, Sussex, 8 October 1662 (printed 1663—the errata at the end have been incorporated in the text). Introduction, 28–29, 36–38, Keynes, *Bibliography,* 8. *Articles of Visitation and Enquiry . . . within the Diocess of Chichester* (London, 1662).

Sound Doctrine: cf. King's *Articles of Visitation* 3.12: "Doth he in his Sermons preach sound Doctrine, tending to the edification of the people in the knowledge and faith of Jesus Christ, and obedient to God's holy Commandments?"

Directory: the word would recall to his hearers the Directory of 1645, the alternative service book prescribed during the Interregnum.

254, *The Bishop of Rome:* King is establishing here his own dislike of popery for the benefit of his nonconforming clergy, who expected all bishops to be tainted with it.

the Trallenses: The Greek here omitted is from the corrupt version of St. Ignatius's epistles current in western Christendom before Ussher printed, at Oxford in 1644 from a manuscript found in England, a more correct version, in a parallel text (copy in the Chichester Library).

255, *Rashly Instituted:* an allusion to the Prayer Book description of marriage: "an honourable estate, instituted of God . . . and therefore is not by any to be enterprised, nor taken in hand, unadvisedly, lightly or wantonly."

258, *Adamites:* nudists.

the nice Venetian: Venetian courtesans of the time were notorious; cf. Lady Would-Be's ingenuous desire to imitate them and Mosca's ruse to get rid of her (Ben Jonson, *Volpone* 3:5).

Superba Rusticitas: Jerome, Epistle ad Tranquillum, cf. *ELP,* 147 note.

quarrel with Learned Elaborate Sermons: cf. *ELP,* 146–47.

260, *the true Church is seated on a Mount:* cf. Donne, *Satire* 3.79–81:

> On a huge hill,
> Cragged, and steep, Truth stands, and hee that will
> Reach her, about must, and about must goe;
>
> (Grierson, *Poems,* I.157)

(cf. also below, "craggy doubts").

261, *his Major, Greatest Proposition:* in the next two paragraphs and below, King picks up "a little logic serves a Christian" (above) and continues in the vocabulary of logic.

262, *like infected cloathes:* cf. *Spital,* 113.

Commemoration of Charles I

Whitehall, 30 January 1664/5. Introduction, 29–30; Keynes *Bibliography,* 81; Wedgwood, *King's War* and *Trial of Charles I;* Lockyer, *Trial of Charles I.*

263, *the first Day:* i.e., of the Commonwealth.

all Religions except the Right: the 1653 Instrument of Government and Cromwell's subsequent ordinances allowed toleration for all forms of religion except Papacy and orthodox Anglicanism.

265, *Wat Tyler . . . Littestar:* the same examples are used in "An Elegy on Sir Charls Lucas, and Sir George Lisle," shot at Colchester in 1648 (Crum, *Poems,* 106), first printed in the second edition of King's poems, (about November 1664, two months before the sermon was preached). The verse text refers only to "The Butcher Cade, Wat Tyler and Jack Straw" (line 164), but the long marginal reference, no doubt fresh in King's mind and possibly added for publication, names Littestar, with much other historical detail that King acknowledges to be from "Speed," i.e., John Speed, *A Chronicle of England* (1614).

the Massacre: of St. Bartholomew, 24 August 1572.

the Queen: Mary of Guise, after the Edinburgh riots, 1558. No archbishop was murdered, but the Bishop of Galloway died of the shock.

Smictymnus: if the spelling is King's and not the typesetter's, he evidently did not realise that Smectymnuus, "author" of a series of Presbyterian pamphlets against monarchy, derived from the initials of the writers, who were preachers Stephen Marshall, Edward Calamy, Thomas Young, Matthew Newcomen, and William Spurstow.

Archer: John Archer, preacher at All Hallows, Lombard Street, a Fifth Monarchy man. He also argued, in *The Personal Reigne of Christ Upon Earth* (London, 1642), p. 52, that Christ would "swallow up all kingly power" and "come and throw down all their Thrones." He was answered in an attack by Joseph Hall, *The Revelation Unrevealed* (1650).

Lemuel Tuke: Tuke, vicar of Gresley in the diocese of Peterborough, was suspended in 1635 for refusing to read the Book of Sports, and frequently in trouble for Puritan practices thereafter until 1642, when he became Lecturer to the parish of Rayne and later that of Steeple, in Essex, and a Congregationalist. In 1658, he was made curate of Sutton in Ashfield, Nottinghamshire, and though ejected at the Restoration, "Old Mr Tuke" evidently presided over a local nonconformist conventicle until his death in 1670 (see A. G. Matthews, *Calamy Revised,* Oxford: Clarendon Press, 1934). King's reason for singling out Tuke may be personal: he was probably involved in the local petition against Emmanuel Uty, King's former curate at Chigwell, Essex, brought before the House of Commons on 8 January 1641: Uty was subsequently deprived for "Arminian practices" (*The Journal of Sir Simonds D'Ewes,* ed. W. Notestein, New Haven: Yale University Press, 1923, p. 232).

our Josiah: Josiah was the model of a good King of Israel; the parallel became a commonplace in Royalist writings at the time of Charles I's execution; cf. also King's "Elegy upon the most Incomparable King Charls the First" (Crum, *Poems,* 117–32), first printed as his in *Poems* (1664), which has many close parallels to this sermon. (Though dated "March 11. 1648," on the strength of a marginal reference to a book printed in 1659, Margaret Crum (p. 214) suggested it was not completed, for anonymous publication later that year, until after that date)

the Temple . . . those Houses joyning: see *1640,* 230 and note on "Jehoida," and the "Elegy," lines 43–46 (Crum, *Poems,* 118).

266, *false Oaths and Flatteries:* expressed more strongly in the "Elegy" (lines 389–90):

> Till on pretence of safety Cromwels wile
> Had juggl'd Him into the Fatal Isle

Even Marvell, Cromwell's Latin secretary, suggests that Parliament and Cromwell manoeuvred Charles into the wrong by encouraging his attempts at escape; cf. "An Horatian Ode upon Cromwel's return from Ireland," lines 50–53):

> He wove a Net of such a Scope
> That Charles himself might chase
> To Caresbrooks narrow case

Solon: (d. 558 B.C.) lawgiver and one of the Seven Wise Men of Athens.

John Basiliwick: Ivan the Terrible, Duke of Moscow.

267, *Næmia:* probably "naenia" is intended, funeral poems sung in primitive times at Rome, though the Nemean Games in Greece were also held originally for funerals.

Germanicus: grandson of Augustus and general of the army of the Rhine; poisoned by Tiberias through jealousy.

(marg.), *1 Kings:* King wrongly refers to "2 King 15:25."

268, *charge . . . at Uxbridge:* the peace negotiations of Jan.–Feb. 1645, the "last chance of a treaty that was not a surrender" (Wedgwood, *King's War,* 394). The treaty failed because Charles stood firm on episcopacy, on Ireland, and his authority over the army.

shelter their unhoused heads: an echo of the storm scene in *King Lear* (3.2) and of *Timon of Athens* (4.3); King may also remember how Bruno Ryves, Dean of Chichester, was turned out at night with his family and took shelter under hedgerows until the Earl of Arundel offered them shelter (Walker, *Sufferings,* 12).

stagger'd in their Duty: another memory of *King Lear:* Goneril's instructions to her servants (1.3) and Lear's reactions to their treatment of him (2.4).

This Prophetick warning: in the King's farewell to the Parliamentary Commissioners at Newport, Isle of Wight, when that treaty failed in 1648. "My Lords, you cannot but know that, in my fall and ruin, you see your own, and that also near you" (Wedgwood, *Trial,* 37).

269, *a very mean Person:* probably John Lilburne, leader of the Levellers, who campaigned for popular rights in government, and attacked the House of Lords (in particular the Earl of Manchester) in June 1646, for which he was imprisoned in the Tower.

blue Apron . . . Blue Ribbon: the apprentice's garb and the Order of the Garter ribbon.

in the first: 30 January, the day of Charles I's execution.

Son of Syrach: see *1640,* 221, note.

Explanatory Notes

270, *to some of his Royal Branches:* the Prince of Wales (in a letter from his father, printed with the *Eikon Basilike*), and Princess Elizabeth and Prince Richard—his interview with them at Whitehall is printed in *Reliquiae Sacrae Carolinae* (London, 1650).

Conference in the Ile of Wight: at Newport. Bod. MS Jones 47, fols. 146–7, is a copy of "His Majestys Answer to the Bills and Propositions presented to him at Carisbrook Castle . . . Decemb: 24, 1647," in the hand of one of King's amanuenses (the late Margaret Crum kindly drew my attention to this).

Mr Hinderson: Alexander Henderson, a Scottish Presbyterian minister, was set the task of converting Charles to that form of church government by the Scottish army, while he was their captive at Newcastle. Henderson was so shaken by the King's integrity, though in his eyes the views he held were wrong, that he retired exhausted to Edinburgh to die, 16 August 1646 (Wedgwood, *King's War*, 552).

Sparguntur in Omnes: quoted in the margin of the "Elegy" beside lines 51–52 (Crum, *Poems,* 119), where he translates it:

> In whom all Vertues we concentred see
> Which 'mongst the best of them divided be.

Tintarit's or Holben's pieces: the painters Tintoretto and Holbein: there are frequent references to portrait painting in the sermons, see introduction, "Imagery."

pensioned Scriblers: no doubt in particular John Milton, Cromwell's Latin secretary (see p. 271, note on *Iconoclastes*) and his assistant and successor, Andrew Marvell.

271, *Cardinal of France:* Mazarin.

his Cabbinet: Robert Hammond carried out the opening at Carisbrook, see King's epigram on the subject, Crum, *Poems,* 101. Probably also a reference to the publication by the Parliamentarians of Charles's damaging correspondence with the Queen and others, captured at the battle of Naseby, *The Kings Cabinet Opened* (London, 1645), an action commonly contrasted, as here, with the magnanimity of the Thebans towards Philip of Macedon.

That Excellent Lady: Henrietta Maria had returned to England at the Restoration. She held great state at Somerset House, given her by her son, Charles II, and died the same year as Henry King, 1669.

one Time . . . another time: in 1643, when returning with Admiral van Tromp, she was shot at by armed Newcastle colliers off Bridlington Bay; in 1644, her ship (also Dutch) was chased by a Parliamentary one as she left Falmouth.

Zenobia: (from Palmyra) third-century queen of the whole East; the Emperor Aurelian spared her for her bravery in opposing him.

Henry the fourth: of France.

Our Blessed King's Portraiture: the subtitle of *Eikon Basilike*—"*in his Solitude and his Sufferings,*" see introduction, 30 and note 61.

Iconoclastes: the title ("breaker of the image" or *eikon*) of Milton's official refutation of the book in October 1649. He claimed it cleared the cause rather than the King, and that one prayer was lifted verbatim from Sidney's *Arcadia;* he had already defended the people's rule in *The Tenure of Kings and Magistrates* (13 February).

Blindness to his Death: Elymas's blindness was only "for a season": King may have heard the rumour of Milton's death; see introduction, note 60.

his Meditations upon Death: King's page references for *Eikon Basilike* are to *The Workes of King Charles the Martyr,* printed by James Flesher for R. Royston (1662). (The copy of the *Eikon* among King's books at Chichester is in Latin.)

272, *that worthy Prælate:* William Juxon, Bishop of London (the incident is recorded in Thomas Herbert's memoirs), see Wedgwood, *Trial,* 205–6.

Conformity with his Saviour's: On 2 Feb. 1649, *A Handkerchief for Loyal Mourners,* unlicensed and anonymously printed, related the King's sufferings to Christ's in the manner of late mediaeval accounts that compared details of the life of St. Francis to Christ's. On 4 Feb., the Sunday following the execution, Bishop Warner of Rochester preached on Christ's Passion and the implicit parallels were plain to his congregation. Many Royalist preachers followed his example.

the High Price: the sum paid to the Scots was actually payment (long overdue) for their soldiers, but as they handed over the King at the time they received it, the parallel was soon drawn.

Cassius: not Julius Caesar's, but a tribune of the people, who competed for the consulship with Cicero. He made laws diminishing the influence of the Roman patricians.

the Robe: (synechdoche) the Bench of Judges.

a Man at last appeared: John Bradshaw, previously Judge of the Court of Sheriffs in London, then Chief Justice of Chester. In the intentional absence of any senior member of the Bench, he was elected President of the illegally constituted High Court of Justice to try the King.

Radamanth: one of the three judges of the Underworld in Greek mythology.

273, *Sir, I must interrupt you:* King quotes almost verbatim from the popular account of the trial printed by Gilbert Mabott day by day as it occurred: *A Perfect Narrative of the Proceedings of the High Court of Justice in the Tryal of the King* (London, 1649).

Spitting in his face: Augustine Garland, the regicide, was accused of this action at the Restoration, but it was disallowed. Herbert describes the soldiers at Whitehall, also, deliberately breathing their tobacco over the King, which he wiped away.

Regal Touch: the monarch's "touching" for scrofula, a custom that lasted to the end of Queen Anne's reign (1714). The "wretched miscreant" is probably Colonel Thomas Pride, who worked in a brewer's yard in his youth, though the same was also said of Colonel John Okey.

All Ages, Old and Young: King's picture is complemented by a vivid Parliamentarian one in Marvell's "Ode upon Cromwel's return from Ireland," lines 1–2, 5–8:

> The forward Youth that would appear
> Must now forsake his *Muses* dear . . .
> 'Tis time to leave the Books in dust,
> And oyl th'unused Armours rust,
> Removing from the Wall
> The Corselet of the Hall

274, *that Sphere where I am plac'd:* the Church. Hugh Peter and Philip Nye were the most notorious chaplains to the Army. Another was Francis Cheynell, intruded into King's parish of Petworth.

no Romance: perhaps in particular *Don Quixote*.

that city: Chichester. King is the only source for this incident.

as good for Fortification: in the autumn campaign of 1642, women worked with men to build the defences of London (Wedgwood, *King's War*, 131).

divers ladies: the best known was the Countess of Carlisle, who from being a Royalist and friend of Strafford, became a spy at Court for Pym.

275, *Patron of the Protestant Religion:* Charles II's toleration of Papists was viewed with suspicion. King is cooler here towards him than in *1661*.

Appendix 1: Index of Sources Used by King with Notes on Less Familiar Authors

The editions cited are those from the Chichester catalogue sufficiently early to have been used by King.

*Denotes a volume still present at Chichester.

ABULENSIS (ALONSO TOSTADO) [ca. 1400–1455]: Bishop of Avila 1449, present at Council of Basle; commentator on historical books of Old Testament: *Commemoration* 267

ACOSTA, JOSE [1539–1600]: Superior and historian of Spanish Jesuits in Peru: *ELP X* 208

AENEAS OF GAZA (GAZDUS) [ca. fifth century]: Neoplatonist turned Christian; wrote *Theophrastus*, on relation between body and soul. *Visitation* 262

ALEXANDER AB ALEXANDRO [d. 328]: Bishop of Alexandria, succeeded by Athanasius; leading part in Council of Nicaea and putting down Arian schism. "*Dier. General.*": *Spital* 109

ALEXANDER OF HALES (HALENSIS) [ca. 1170–1245]: taught Bonaventure and Aquinas at Paris. *Postillae in universa Biblia*, Part 4: *ELP I* 137, 139; *II* 144, 145, 148, 150; *III* 157; *VI* 178, 180; *VII* 185; *IX* 196; *XI* 199, 200, 212, 217

ALBINUS FLACCUS (ALCUIN) [735–804]: The Renaissance appears to have confused Alcuin with Albinus, who helped Bede with the *Historia Ecclesia*. Alcuin was born in York; became tutor and adviser to Charlemagne; Abbot of Tours, where he established a famous school and library. *De Divinis Officiis*, Rome 1591: *ELP XI* 212

AMALARIUS FORTUNATUS [ca. 809–56]: Bishop of Trier. King apparently confuses him with AMALARIUS OF METZ [ca. 780–850] liturgical scholar and pupil of Alcuin, who wrote *De Ecclesiasticis Officiis*: *ELP XI* 217

AMBROSE, ST. [ca. 339–397]: *Opera, 3 vols, Basle. 1567; Opera*, Paris 1549 [King's own copy, signed and annotated: sold at Sotheby's 1949 for £4]: *Act* 87, 93; *Spital* 98; *ELP II* 146, 149; *III* 156; *VI* 179; *X* 204; *De Abraham: ELP IX* 202; *In Epistolas: ELP XI* 217; *De Officiis: Act* 83; *Spital* 107; *Lent 2* 124; *ELP I* 141; *II* 150; *VIII* 193; *Visitation* 256; *De Poenitentia: Spital*, 105; *Lent 1*, 124; *In Psalmos: Spital*, 106; *1640*, 214; *De Sacramentis: ELP II* 150; *XI* 210; *De Virginibus: Lent 1* 124; *Lent 2* 129, 133; *ELP I* 143; *III* 157; Sermons: *Spital* 104; *Lent 2* 130, 133; *ELP I* 139

AMMIANUS MARCELLINUS [b. 330]: of Antioch; continued *History* of Tacitus: "Paris 1544": *Commemoration* 268

ANTIQUITATES BRITANNICAE: (ed. by Abp Matthew Parker[?]) *Hanover 1605: *1640* 225

APULEIUS, LUCIUS [fl. 155]: Silver Latin author. *ELP VI* 181

AQUINAS, ST. THOMAS [ca. 1225–74]: *Summa Theologica*, Antwerp, 1585; Paris, 1607; *Opuscula*, Venice, 1587. *Act* 95, *Spital* 103, 106; *Secunda secundae: ELP I* 137, 142; *III* 152, 156; *VII* 185; *IX* 201; *X* 205, 208; *XI* 210

ARETIUS, BENEDICT [ca. 1505–74]: Swiss Hellenist, botanist and theologian. *Problemata Theologica*, Lausanne 1578; *Problemata Theologiae*, Geneva 1617: *III* 153

ARIAS MONTANUS, BENEDICTUS [1527–98]: Learned Spanish monk of the order of St James; edited great Polyglot Bible for Philip II. *Biblia Interlinearis*, Geneva 1609: *1640* 219; *De arcano: ELP III* 156, 158

ARISTOTLE [384–22 B.C.]: *Opera omnia*, Basle, 1563; *De Anima* lib.3, Graec.Lat. Juli Pacii interp. Hanover, 1611; *Idem*, Frankfurt, 1596; *Natural. Auscult.* . . . cum Comment. Analyt. Juli Pacii, Frankfurt, 1596. *Lent 1* 119, 121; *1640* 223; (*1661* 236); *De Caelo: ELP II* 150; *Metaphysics: Spital* 103; *Physics: Lent 1* 123

ATHANASIUS, ST. [ca. 296–373]: *Spital* 103

ATHENAEUS [fl. ca. 200 A.D.]: of Naucratis, Greek author of the *Deipnosophistai (Sophists at Dinner)*, anecdotal conversations of twenty-three learned men dining together at Rome. *1621* 80

AUGUSTINE, ST., OF HIPPO [354–430] King's most quoted author: *Opera, 7 vols Paris, 1555; *Adversus Julianum*, Paris, 1616. *1621* 70, 74, 76; *ELP I* 141; *VI* 178–9; *VII* 186; *IX* 197, 201; *Duppa* 250; *Confessions* (Cologne, 1629): *Lent 1* 123; *ELP II* 147; *De Bono perseverantiae: ELP I* 137; *V* 174; *De Civitate Dei: 1621*

78; *ELP I* 138; *II* 144; *VIII* 195; *IX* 201; *X* 207; *Duppa* 246; *De Doctrina Christiana: ELP XI* 212; *1640* 214; *Enchiridion: ELP V* 170; *IX* 198; *Epistolae: ELP I* 141; *VII* 187; *XI* 215; *De Haeresibus ELP V* 170; Sermons: *1621* 69, 72; *Act* 83, 89; *Spital* 103; *Lent 1* 123; *ELP I* passim; *II* passim; *III* 154, 157, 158; *V* 172, 173; *VI* 175, 181, 182; *VII* 187, 188, 190; *VIII* 193, 194, 196; *IX* 198–9, 202; *Duppa* 243; *Soliloq.: ELP XI* 315; *Tractatus in John: ELP XI* 212; *De Trinitate: ELP V* 168

AULUS GELLIUS [early second century]: Silver Latin essayist: *Noctes Atticae*, useful for its quotations from lost authors. *Commemoration* 270

BALDUS (PIETRO BALDO DE BALDI) [1327–140′]: renowned professor of canon and civil law at Perugia and Bologna. *ELP IV* 162

BARONIUS, CAESARO [1538–1607]: Italian cardinal; Oratorian, friend and follower of St Philip Neri. **Annales Ecclesiastici* 10 vols. Cologne 1609: *1621* 68; *Commemoration* 267

BASIL, ST. [ca. 330–79]: brother of St Gregory of Nyssa and Doctor of the Eastern church. *Act* 90; *Lent 1* 117; *ELP V* 173; *VIII* 195; *IX* 197; *XI* 212

BELLARMINE, ST. ROBERT [1542–1621]: Italian cardinal and Jesuit, Archbishop of Capua; professor of theology at Louvain and Rome. *Disputationes*, 2 vols, Venice 1603 (*vol 1: Donne's copy): *ELP X* 207–8; *1661* 237

BEDE, THE VENERABLE [ca. 673–735]: *ELP X* 208

BERNARD, ST., OF CLAIRVAUX [1090–1153]: *Opera*, Paris 1561; *Paris 1632 (available for *Visitation* only); *Operum Flores*, Lyons 1579: *Act* 94, 104; *ELP II* 147; *VI* 180, 181; *XI* 201, 202; *Duppa* 245; *Visitation* 257; *Meditationes: Lent 1* 117; *In Psalmos: Spital* 105, 108; Sermons: *Lent 1* 116, 118; *ELP VII* 187–8; *IX* 197

BEZA, THEODORE [1519–1605] (see also JUNIUS BRUTUS): French friend and disciple of Calvin; translator and commentator on New Testament. *1621* 75; *De Presbyt.: 1640* 225

BIBLIOTHECA PATRUM GRAECO-LATINORUM, TOM.I: [probably collection by Margarinus de la Bigne (1573–1641), *Bibliothecae veterum patrum, seu scriptorum ecclesiasticorum: Tom.1. graeco-lat.* [which contains Marcus Eremita here quoted]: *Act* 91

BIEL, GABRIEL [ca. 1420–95]: Scholastic philosopher and theologian; professor at Tübingen University, which he helped to found; later joined Brethren of the Common Life. *Expositio Canonae Missae: Act* 91; *Lent 1* 123; *ELP I* 141; *II* passim; *III* 152; *V* 169; *VI* 180, 183; *VII* 185–86; *IX* 196; *XI* 198, 201, 217

BOLSECK, HIERONYMUS [d. 1584]: Carmelite friar at Paris who became a Protestant, but challenged Luther's teaching and returned to the Roman church; author of hostile lives of Beza and Calvin: *1621* 75

BOETHIUS, ANICIUS MANLIUS SEVERINUS [ca. 480–524]: Latin Christian theologian and philosopher. *De Consolatione [Philosophiae]*, 1562; *Lent 2* 129

BONAVENTURE, ST. [Giovanni di Fidenza 1221–74]: Franciscan theologian; Seraphic Doctor of the Church. *Act* 88; *ELP X* 206

BOSQUIER, PHILIPPE [1561–1636]: Flemish Franciscan at Paris, Rome and Flanders. *Ara Coeli* and *Philippicae*, Douai 1606: *ELP IX* 200

BOTERUS, GIOVANNI [1540–1617]: Italian theologian and man of letters; left Jesuits to become Charles Borromeo's secretary; at his death became Minister to the French King. *De originis urbium: Spital* 108

BOZIUS, TOMASO [d. 1610]: Oratorian, of Rome. *De Iure divin, et natural.*, Rome 1600. *De signis ecclesiae: 1621* 75

BRADWARDINE, THOMAS [ca. 1290–1349]: Archbishop of Canterbury; famous mathematician (named in Chaucer and Dante). *De Causa Dei: ELP V* 170

BRULEFER, ETIENNE [1st half fifteenth century—ca. 1500]: Franciscan doctor of theology, taught at Paris; became Strict Observant, founded monastery in Brittany; commentator on St Bonaventure and Duns Scotus. *Distinctiones: ELP IX* 198; [= "Brukser," *ELP X* 206, marg.?]

BUCER, MARTIN [1491–1551]: originally Dominican; became Lutheran divine; attempted to mediate between Luther and Zwingli, whom he succeeded as leader of South German and Swiss protestants; 1549: Regius Professor of Divinity at Cambridge. **Gratulatio de Restitutione Religionis in Anglia*, 1548: *1640* 229

BUCHANAN, GEORGE [1506–82]: Scottish (Latin) poet; tutor to James I. **Histor. Scotica. Rerum* Edinburgh 1583, bound with *De iure Regni apud Scotos: 1640* 221, 225, 227; *1661* 238–39; *Commemoration* 267

BULLINGER, JOHANN HEINRICH [1504–75]: Swiss reformer influenced by Luther, Melancthon and Zwingli, whom he succeeded as chief pastor of Zurich; entertained English Marian exiles. *Sermones* (Zurich, 1567): *Act* 88

BUXTORF, JOHANN [1564–1629]: German Hebrew scholar. *Synagoga Judaica: ELP XI* 213, 217

BZOVIUS, ABRAHAM [1567–1637]: Polish Dominican, Prior of Cracow; taught in Rome; continued Baronius's *Annales* with vols 13–21: *1621* 73

CAJETANUS, TOMASO DE VIO [1469–1534]: Italian Dominican humanist; General of order and Cardinal; chosen to plead with Luther; translated Bible. *Spital* 101; *In Mt.: ELP II* 151; *III* 152, 158; *VII* 184; *VIII* 195

CALLIMACHUS [b. ca. 310 B.C.]: learned Alexandrian poet, critic and bibliographer. *1640* 220; *1661* 238

CALVIN, JEAN [1509–64]: *Opuscula*, 1563; **in 5 Libr. Mosis*, Geneva, 1602 (and 6 other Old Testament vols); *In Epistolas*, Geneva 1610. *Spital* 111; *ELP II* 146; **Epist. et Respons.* (Geneva 1575): *1640* 229; *Harmon. in Mat.6: 1621* 73; *VIII* 195, *XI* 210; *Institutiones: 1640* 223

CAMERARIUS, JOACHIM [1500–1574]: German classical scholar, friend and biographer of Melancthon; ecumenical reformer; helped draw up Confession of Augsburg, reorganise universities of Tübingen and Leipzig. "*Historic. Meditat.*": *ELP VIII* 194

CANO, MELCHIOR [1509–60]: Spanish Dominican; professor of theology at Salamanca, worked to restore patristic learning; at Council of Trent; supported Philip II against Pope and Jesuits. *Loci Theologici: 1621* 81

CARRANZA, BARTOLOMEO [1503–76]: Spanish Dominican canonist and archbishop; in England for marriage of Mary Tudor. **Summa Conciliorum et Pontific.*, [Lyons] 1600 (heavily annotated by King): *ELP I* 140; *VII* 140

CARTWRIGHT, THOMAS [1535–1603]: Cambridge Puritan divine; exiled in Geneva during reigns of Mary and Elizabeth; died before Hampton Court Conference for which he had drawn up Millenary Petition. *ELP I* 141; *XI* 210

CASSANDER, GEORG [1513–66]: ecumenical Catholic theologian; taught at Louvain, Bruges and Ghent; wrote for Emperor Ferdinand I. *Act* 87, 89; *ELP IX* 198

CASSIODORUS, FLAVIUS MAGNUS AURELIUS [ca. 485–580]: Roman author and monk; helped preserve classical learning through Dark Ages; his books of Imperial edicts and decrees became the model for mediaeval chanceries. *Lent 2* 125

CASTRO, ALPHONSO A [1494–1558]: Spanish Franciscan friar; Archbishop of Compostella; present at Council of Trent. *Adversus Omnes Haereses* Lib. 14, 1534: *ELP I* 137, 140 ("Oratio"); *V* 170; *VII* 188

CHALCONDYL, NICOLAS [fl.1470]: historian of the Turks and the Greek empire. *1640* 230

CHEMNITIUS, MARTIN [1522–86]: German Lutheran theologian and polemicist; attacked Council of Trent. **Harmonia Evangel[iae]*, Frankfurt 1615: *ELP XI* 210; **Examen Concilii Trident.*, Frankfurt 1578: *ELP X* 207, 208

CHRYSOSTOM, ST. JOHN [ca. 347–407]: *Opera Latina*, 5 vols, Basle 1539. *Spital* 105; *In Mt.: 1621* 69; *ELP I* 141; *II* 147, 149, 151; *III* 152, 158; *IV* 164; *V* 174; *VI* 182; *IX* 201; *XI* 211–12; *Homilies; Act* 92; *ELP III* 154; *XI* 211; *Visitation* 256

CICERO, MARCUS TULLIUS (TULLY) [106–43 B.C.]: *Paradoxes: ELP V* 172

CLAUDIAN [fl. 395–404]: Greek poet from Alexandria writing at Rome; epic on wars with Goths. *Poemata* Lyons 1589; *cum notis Barthii*, Hanover 1612; Amsterdam 1630: *1661* 234; *Commemoration* 270

COCHLAEUS (DOBENECK), JOHANN [1479–1552]: canon of Mainz, Meissen and Breslau; humanist, bitterly opposed to scholasticism, disliked by both sides; tried to prevent Tyndale printing his English New Testament at Cologne. *1621* 75

CONIMBRENSES: group of Jesuit writers at Coimbra University in Portugal, who produced famous Latin editions of Aristotle. *in 3 lib. de Anima*, Venice, 1602; *Comment. in 4 lib. de Coelo*, Cologne 1600 and 1602: *ELP VII 184*

CRABBE, PIERRE [1470–1554]: Belgian Franciscan. *Concilia* 3 vols, Cologne 1551 (4th vol. of Councils added by Surius, q.v.): *ELP VIII* 194

CUNAEUS (VAN DER KUN) PIETER [1586–1636]: Dutch lawyer and antiquarian. *De Republica Hebraeorum: 1640* 224; *1661* 236; *Visitation* 259

CURTIUS, QUINTUS RUFUS [temp. Claudius or Vespasian]: Latin romantic historian of Alexander the Great. *Historia*, Paris 1543: *ELP XI 213; 1661* 241; *Duppa* 244

CYPRIAN, ST. [d. 258]: **Opera*, Paris 1607; *1621* 75; *Lent 1* 120; *De Oratione Dominica: ELP I* 141; *II* 144, 145; *V* 171, 174; *VII* 187; *IX* 199

CYRIL OF ALEXANDRIA, ST. [d. 444]: *Glaphyra: Spital* 111

DAMASCENE, ST. JOHN [ca. 675–ca. 749]: *ELP III* 156; *V* 168

DE DOMINIS, MARCO ANTONIO. See SPALATENS

DE LA PUENTE, JUAN: Dominican; wrote at request of Spanish King *La Conveniencia de las dos Monarquias Catolicas de la Iglesia Romana y las del Imperio Espano* [1612]: *1621* 70; *ELP XI* 212; *1640* 224

DIONYSIUS THE CARTHUSIAN [1402–71]: German theologian and mystic, biblical commentator. *In Mathaeum Evangelistam et Epistolas Pauli* Cologne 1538: *ELP I* 139; *X* 209; *1661* 236

DOROTHEUS, ST. [sixth century]: Palestinian ascetical writer and monk, Archimandrite of the monastery he founded near Gaza. *Doctrinae: Act* 89, 90

DREXEL, HIEREMIAS [1581–1638]: Jesuit ascetic and neoplatonist; preacher to Maximilian of Bavaria. *Prodromus Eternitatis: 1640* 224; *Commemoration* 266

DRUSIUS (VAN DER DRIESCHE), JOHANN [1550–1616]: Dutch Protestant refugee; professor of oriental languages at Leyden, then at Oxford; Biblical commentator. *ELP III* 156

ECKIUS, JOHANN MAIER [1486–1543]: German theological professor at Ingolstadt, humanist, antischolastic; organised Catholic opposition to Luther; German dialect translation of Bible. *Enchiridion,* Cologne 1567: *Act* 88; *ELP X* 207, 208

ELIAS CRETENSIS [eighth century]: Bishop of Gortyna and Metropolitan of Crete. At 2nd Council of Nicaea 787. Traditionally author of commentary or *Scholia* on Gregory of Nazianzen. *Act* 87

ENNIUS [d. 169 B.C.]: tragedian and first Latin epic poet; his *Annals* sometimes quoted by Virgil without acknowledgement. *Commemoration* 266

EPIPHANIUS, ST. [ca. 315–403]: Palestinian, founded monastery in Judaea; Bishop of Salamis; upheld teaching of Council of Nicaea on heretics. **Opera Graeca et Latina* 2 vols. Paris 1622: *Spital* 109

ERASMUS, DESIDERIUS (ca. 1466–1536): *ELP XI* 211; *Duppa* 251; *Visitation* 259

EUSEBIUS (ca. 260–ca. 340): "Father of Church history". Eusebius, Socrates, etc, *Historiae Latinae Ecclesiae,* Basle 1570: *Spital* 112; *ELP III* 151; *X* 206; *Visitation* 259

EUTHYMIUS ZIGABENUS [early twelfth century]: monk and theologian at Constantinople; fundamentalist Biblical commentator. *Act* 94; *Spital* 108

EURIPIDES [ca. 480–406 B.C.]: *Lent 2* 130

EUTROPIUS [temp. Emperor Valens, 364–78]: wrote abstract of history of Rome for Emperor. *1640* 221; *Commemoration* 267

EVAGRIUS SCHOLASTICUS [ca. 536–600]: Syrian laywer and historian, continued the *Ecclesiastical History* of Eusebius. *Spital* 108, 112

FAZELLUS, TOMASO [1498–1585]: historian of Sicily. *ELP X* 207

FENESTELLA [d. 20 A.D.]: Roman authority on ancient history and customs from Annals. *1640* 221

FISHER, JOHN. See ROFFENSIS

FLORUS, LUCIUS PUBLIUS ANNAEUS [temp. Trajan and Hadrian]: historian of Rome, developing the work of Livy. *Commemoration* 263

FORTUNATUS. See AMALARIUS FORTUNATUS

FULGENTIUS, ST. [468–533]: Roman civil servant, then monk; became Bishop of Ruspa; knew Greek. *Opera,* Basle *1599: Act* 92

GALATINUS, PETRUS [d. 1539]: Franciscan, converted Jew; *De Arcanis Catholicae Veritatis,* Frankfurt 1602: *Spital* 100; *ELP III* 156

GERHARDT, JOHANN [1582–1637]: German Lutheran systematic theologian; biblical commentator. *Aphorismi Sacri: ELP I* 138, 143

GERMANUS, ST. [ca. 634–ca. 733]: Patriarch of Constantinople; mystical interpreter of the Bible. *Exposit. in Orat. Dominic.: ELP XI* 212

GERSON, JEAN LE CHARLIER [1363–1429]: Augustinian Chancellor of university of Paris; extreme Nominalist; mystical teaching; believed author of *Imitation of Christ* until nineteenth century. *Opera: 1621* 82; *Lent 1* 124; *ELP IV* 164; *VII* 185; *1640* 223

GORRANUS, NICOLAS [ca. 1230–95]: French Dominican theologian, New Testament commentator. *Comment. in 4 Evangel.,* Antwerp 1617: *ELP II* 144

GREGORY NAZIANZEN ST. [329–389]: *Opera,* 2 vols. Paris 1609–11. *Orationes: 1621* 65, 69; *Spital* 103; *ELP II* 145; *V* 171; *1661* 239; *Duppa* 245, 251; *Visitation* 258; *Commemoration* 266, 271

GREGORY THE GREAT (MAGNUS), ST., POPE [ca. 540–604]: *1621* 76; ELP II 150; *De Cura Pastoralis* (London 1629): *Visitation* 256, 257; *Moralia: ELP X* 205; Dialogues: *ELP X* 208; Epistles: *1640* 225; *ELP IX* 200

GREGORY, PIERRE THOLOSSANUS [1540–1617]; French lawyer and politician; opposed Jesuits and Council of Trent. *Syntagma Iuris Universali: ELP XI* 212; *1640* 223, 229

HALENSIS. See ALEXANDER OF HALES

HIEROM, HIERON[IMUS]. See JEROME, ST.

HILARY, ST., OF POITIERS [ca. 315–67]. *Opera,* Basle 1570; *Spital* 106; *Lent 2* 125

HINKELMANN, PETER [1571–1622]: theologian and philosopher from Rostock. *Anabaptisti Errores,* Rostock 1613: *Visitation* 258

HIPPOCRATES [b. ca. 460 B.C.]: *ELP VI* 181

HOLINSHED, RAPHAEL [d. 1580]: came to London early in Elizabeth's reign; chronicler of English history much used by Shakespeare and other dramatists. *1621* 66

HOMER [ca. ninth century B.C.]: *Ilias* (in the Latin of Laurentius Vallens, Geneva 1510): *1640* 222, 228; *1661* 236; *Odyssey; 1621* 77, 80; *ELP X* 207

HORACE, HORAT[IUS] (QUINTUS HORATIUS FLACCUS) [65–8 B.C.]: "cum notis Lambini" (no date or place); "Horatii, Juvenalis, Persii cum Senecae Tragediis" (no date or place). Ars Poetica: *1621* 69; *ELP VII* 188; Odes: *Lent 1* 124; Satires: *Lent 2* 128; *ELP V* 172

HUGO CARDINALIS (HUGH OF ST. CHER) [ca. 1200–63]: Dominican, taught law at Paris; cardinal and papal legate to Germany; wrote first biblical concordance. *Postilla in 4 Evang.* Paris 1545: *1621* 74; *Lent 2* 131; *In Mt.: ELP I* 140; *II* 144; *VII* 191; *VIII* 195

IGNATIUS OF ANTIOCH, ST. [ca. 35–ca. 107]: *Polycarpi et Ignatii Epistolae* (Oxford 1644): *Visitation* 254

ISIDORE OF PELUSIUM [d. ca. 450]: abbot; opposed heretic Nestorius. *1621* 69; *Spital* 104; *ELP III* 156; *V* 174; *IX* 201; *Visitation* 257

ISYCHIUS (HESYCHIUS) [fl. ca. 300]: of Jerusalem, biblical textual critic. *Spital* 110

IVO OF CHARTRES, ST. (CARNOTENSIS) [ca. 1040–1116]: most learned canonist of his age. *De rebus ecclesiasticis: ELP XI* 217

JEROME, ST. (HIERON) [ca. 342–420]: *Opera,* 5 vols. Paris 1609. *Spital* 103; *Lent 2* 125; *1661* 236; *Commemoration* 267, 270; *Epistolae Selectae,* (Paris 1603): *1621* 68, 77, 78; *Act* 94; *Lent 2* 133; *ELP I* 139; *II* 147; *III* 158; *IV* 161; *V* 173; *VII* 185, 189; *Visitation* passim; *Contra Vigilantium: ELP IX* 198, 200; *Duppa* 246; *In Mt.: Act* 88, 89; *ELP I* 141; *VI* 184; *XI* 216

JUNIUS BRUTUS, STEPHANUS (Pseudonym of Theodore Bèze, q.v..): *Vindiciae contra Tyrannos* (printed 1579; bound with Machiavelli 1580): *1640* 221; *1661* 239

JUSTIN MARTYR, ST. [ca. 100–ca. 165]: *Spital* 101–2, 103; *Commemoration* 267

JUSTINUS (JUSTIN THE HISTORIAN) [second or third century]: Latin abridger of the universal history of Trogus Pompeius. *Historia* 1481 and 1543: *1640* 223

JUVENAL [ca. 60/70–ca. 128]: (bound with Horace, q.v.) Satires: *1621* 68, 70, 72, 77; *Act* 87, 90; *Spital* 107; *ELP II* 143; *IV* 159, 162; *V* 168, *IX* 198; *1640* 227; *1661* 245

LACTANTIUS [ca. 240–ca. 320]: *Opera,* Antwerp 1539; *Basle 1563; "1613." De origine erroris: Spital* 110; *ELP III* 155, 156; *X* 210; *Visitation* 257

LEO THE GREAT, ST. (POPE) [d. 461]: *Opera,* Paris 1614. Sermons: *Act* 90; *Spital* 98, 101, 102, 104; *ELP VI* 182; *VII* 187; *VIII* 195

LINDANUS, WILHELM DAMASUS [1525–88]: Bishop of Roermond, contemporary of Bellarmine, counter-Reformer. *Dialogismi: 1621* 75

LIPSIUS, JUSTUS [1547–1606]: great Belgian humanist, revived Stoicism; studied and taught at Louvain, etc. *Civilis Doctrina,* Leyden 1589. "Polit. Praefat.": *1661* 236

LIVY (TITUS LIVIUS) [59 B.C.–17 A.D.]: *1640* 223, 226

LOMBARD, PETER [ca. 1100–60]: taught at Paris; biblical commentator, using Greek Fathers as well as Latin; "Quadripart. volum. S. Theolog.". *Sententiae* ("Master of the Sentences"): *Act* 89; *Spital* 104; *ELP II* 150; *V* 168, 170; *IX* 197, 199; *X* 205

LORICHIUS, GERHARDT [fl. 1540]: German Protestant preacher who turned Catholic; biblical commentator: *Institutiones Catholicae: ELP X* 207–8

LORINUS, JEAN [1559–1634]: French Jesuit; biblical and Aristotelian commentator. *Commentatio in Psalmos,* 3 vols, Cologne 1619. "The Syriack" bible: *Act* 88; *Spital* 98, 102, 108; *Lent 2* 125

LUCAN [36–65]: *Poemata,* Paris 1545; "1593" (Plantin). *Pharsalia: 1621* 77; *ELP VI* 180–81; *Duppa* 244

LUTHER, MARTIN [1483–1546]: *Opera,* 7 vols. Wittenburg 1582: *ELP I* 139; *In Galat.: Lent 1* 119

LYRA, NICHOLAS OF [1270–1340]: French Franciscan, professor of theology at the Sorbonne; his fundamentalist biblical commentary was the first to be printed. *Glossa Ordinaria,* Parts 3 & 5: *ELP II* 144; *VII* 188

LYRINENSIS, ST. VINCENT [d. before 450]: monk of Lérins; semi-Pelagian, opposed to St. Augustine; *Commonitorium* supports authority of Scripture against tradition. *ELP IX* 201–202

MAGALIAN, COSMAS [b. ca. 1566; fl. ca. 1610]: Portuguese commentator on Aristotle and professor of theology at Coimbra. *Visitation* 262

MALDONATUS, JOHANNES [1534–93]: Spanish Jesuit, Professor at the Sorbonne; revived Catholic theology; commentator on Gospels. **Comment. 4ʳ Evang.,* Lyons 1617: *ELP XI* 210

MARCUS EREMITA [fl. ca. 400]: hermit, pupil of Chrysostom, perhaps abbot of Ancyra; ascetical writer on fasting and penitence. *Act* 91; *Spital* 105

MARIANA, JUAN [1536–1624]: Spanish Jesuit theologian; prepared to accept tyrannicide to remove oppressive rulers. *De Rege et Regis Institution.* Mainz 1605: *1640* 227

MARLORATUS, AUGUSTIN [1506–63]: French Protestant theologian; translated New Testament into French. *Act* 83, 90, 94; *Spital* 111

MARTIAL [40–104]: "ex Offic. Plantiana," 1606; *Epigrammata,* ed. Ramirez de Prada, Paris 1607. *1621* 66, 68, 77; *ELP III* 154

MASSONUS, JEAN PAPIRIUS [1544–1611]: French Jesuit historian; taught, became lawyer, then librarian to Chevalier de Chiverny. **Vitae de Episcop. Roman.* Paris 1586: *Commemoration* 263

MINUTIUS FELIX [second or third century]: African author of an elegant Latin defence of Christianity, *Octavius: 1621* 75; *ELP I* 142; *III* 155, 156; *VI* 181

MONTAIGNE, MICHEL DE [1533–92]: French nobleman, inventor of the essay genre. *ELP III* 154

NICEPHORUS CALLIXTUS XANTHOPULUS [fourteenth century]: Byzantine Church historian. **Historia Latina,* Frankfurt 1588: *Commemoration* 267, 269

NICEPHORUS GREGORAS [ca. 1295–ca. 1359]: Byzantine historian; *History of Constantinople* printed with Nicetas and Chalcondyl. *Duppa* 251; *Commemoration* 270

NILUS MARTYR [d. ca. 430?]: the Renaissance seems to have confused two Niluses, the fourth-century Egyptian bishop martyred under Maximian, and the writer, a disciple of Chrysostom at Constantinople, influential for his letters and writings on monasticism. *Act* 90; *Visitation* 262

OLAF THE GREAT (MAGNUS) [969–1000]: *ELP X* 207–8

ORIGEN [ca. 185–ca. 254]: Homilies: *Act* 87, 89; *ELP IX* 197, 201; *X* 207; *Contra Celsium: Duppa* 246

ORTELIUS, ABRAHAM [1527–98]: greatest geographer of his age after Mercator; of German parentage, lived in Antwerp, travelled widely. *Theatrum Orbis Terrarum: ELP X* 208

OVID [43 B.C.–18 A.D.]: *Epistolae cum notis Bermani,* 1607; *Opera,* Amsterdam 1630; *Fasti, Tristia etc.,* Antwerp 1587: *Act* 86; *ELP X* 207; *1640* 226; (*1661* 240); *Duppa* 231, 245; *Visitation* 254

PEDRO DI MEXIA: Spanish chronicler of France and the Roman emperors. *1661* 236

PERERIUS, BENEDICTO [1535–1610]: Spanish Jesuit; taught theology and philosophy at Rome. *Selectae Disputationes in sacris scripturis,* Ingolstadt 1601; *Opera Theologica* Cologne 1620: *1640* 167

PERSIUS [34–62]: bound with Horace, q.v. *ELP V* 167

PETRARCH, FRANCESCO [1304–74]: **Opera,* Basle 1581; **De remediis utriusque Fortunae,* Lyons 1577: *Spital* 113

PETRONIUS ARBITER [d. 85]: Silver Latin poet; King translated five epigrams (Crum, *Poems,* 156–57). "1614": *ELP I* 138; *X* 204

PETRUS ALIACUS (D'AILLY) [1350–1420]: nominalist; Chancellor of univ. of Paris. *ELP II* 145

PHILOSTRATUS [second to third century A.D.]: One of four members of a Lemnos family responsible for several Greek writings that include *Lives of the Sophists* and *Letters* (influential rhetorical exercises). *Spital* 112

PINDAR [b. 522 or 518 B.C.]: Odes: *Lent 2* 131; *ELP IV* 159; *1640* 224

Appendix 1

PLATINA, BARTOLOMEO [1421–81]: Vatican librarian under Sixtus IV. *Vitae Pontificorum, Cologne 1626: *1621* 73

PLATO [427–348 B.C.]: *Opera Graeca,* Basle 1556: *Lent 1* 115; *ELP X* 206; *1640* 223, 230

PLINY (THE ELDER) [ca. 23–79]: *Spital* 109

PLUTARCH [ca. 46–120]: *ELP IV*.162; *IX* 202; *1640* 223

POLYBIUS [ca. 202–120 B.C.]: Greek historian of the rise of Rome. *1640* 223

POSTELLUS, GUILLIAUME [d. 1581]: brilliantly learned, long-lived professor of languages at Paris, travelled the east searching for manuscripts; friend of humanist Daniel Bomberg in Venice (1537); joined Jesuits at Rome (1543) but his visions, astrology and other eccentric and heretical beliefs caused St. Ignatius to dismiss him (1545). After imprisonment by the Inquisition, he returned to Paris (1559) to prove the French king's right to be universal monarch, as the descendant of Japhet (no doubt the book cited by King belongs to this period). *Victory of Women: Spital* 110

PRESTON, THOMAS (alias of ROGER WIDDRINGTON) [d. 1640]: supposed convertor of Bishop John King to Roman faith (introduction, 16); joined Benedictine order (1590) and English mission (1603); expelled from England 1613; returned, imprisoned in the Clink, Southwark; having accepted James I's Oath of Allegiance, later submitted to Rome in the matter and died in prison. *Appellation: 1621* 76

PURCHASE, SAMUEL [ca. 1575–1626]: rector of St. Martin's, Ludgate, chaplain to Bishop John King; travel writer. *Pilgrims: ELP III* 153; *X* 208; *Commemoration* 269

RABANUS MAURUS [ca. 784–856]: one of the greatest theologians of his age, educated under Alcuin—"praeceptor Germaniae"; biblical commentaries with mystical interpretation. *De clericorum institutione: ELP XI* 212

RALEIGH, SIR WALTER [ca. 1552–1618]: King wrote an elegy for him (Crum, *Poems,* 66). *History of the World: 1640* 222

REBUFFUS, PIERRE [1500–57]: learned lawyer from southwest France practicing in Paris; ordained priest 1547. *1640* 221

RICHARD OF ST. VICTOR [d. 1173]: native of Britain, mystic and theologian teaching in France. *Act* 89

RIVIUS, JOHANNUS [ca. 1553–ca. 1595]: physician and classicist at Leipzig. *Opera* Basle 1582: *De Superstit.: Spital* 111

ROFFENSIS (JOHN FISHER, BISHOP OF ROCHESTER) [1469–1535]: Chancellor of Cambridge, first Lady Margaret Professor of Divinity; friend and patron of Erasmus; executed for refusing to accept Henry VIII's divorce. *ELP X.*207

ROYARD (Oudenarde), JEAN [d. 1547]: of Bruges; Franciscan, sermon writer (considered "phonix" of his order). *Homiliae,* 1538. *Dominic. in Advent.: 1661* 238

SA, EMMANUEL [1530–96]: Portuguese Jesuit: biblical commentator. *Aphorismi,* Cologne 1612: *ELP X* 208

SALMERON, ALPHONSO [1516–85]: Spanish Jesuit (founder member); biblical commentator. *Comment. in Evang. & Act. Apost.,* 5 vols. Cologne: *ELP VII* 186, 188, 190; *VIII* 194

SANDYS, GEORGE [1578–1644] Son of Archbishop Edwin Sandys; Gentleman of the Privy Chamber, Treasurer of Virginia Company; poet (King wrote commendatory verses to his *Paraphrase upon the Divine Poems,* 1638: Crum, *Poems,* 89–92), traveller. *Relation of a Journey: Spital* 109

SCALIGER, JULIUS CAESAR [1484–1558]: humanist, antagonist of Erasmus; first grammar on scientific principles: *De causis linguae latinae,* 1580: *Commemoration* 68

SENECA, LUCIUS ANNAEUS [ca. 4 B.C.–65 A.D.]: *Opera,* Basle 1590 (in Reading University Library, signed by King and dated "1610"); *cum notis Lipsii,* Antwerp 1615; *Tragediae,* Amsterdam 1624. *Act* 90, 91, 92, 93; *Spital* 99, 112; *Lent 1* 118, 121, 123; *ELP I* 142; *Epistles: 1621* 71; *Lent 2* 128, 133; *Duppa* 247; *De Beneficiis: ELP VI* 177, 183; *De Consolatione ad Polybium: ELP V* 172; *Commemoration* 266; *Tragedies: 1621* 74; *ELP IX* 199; *1661* 239

SEXTUS SENENSIS (SISTO OF SIENA) [1520–69]: Jew converted to Christianity, became celebrated Dominican preacher. *ELP III* 156, 157

SOCRATES SCHOLASTICUS [ca. 380–450]: of Constantia; Greek Church historian, continued Eusebius to 439. *Historiae Latinae,* Basle 1570: *Visitation* 259

SOHN, GEORG [1551–1589]: Reformed theologian at Marburg. *De Cultu Dei: Spital* 111

SOLINUS, CAIUS JULIUS [ca. 230?]: Roman geographer.* "*Polyhistor. cum notis Camertis*" (Vienna 1620): *Spital* 108

SOTO, DOMINIC A [1494–1560]: Dominican; professor of philosophy at Alcala, succeeded Cano as theology professor at Salamanca; accompanied Emperor Charles V to Council of Trent; commentator on Aristotle and Peter Lombard. *In 4 lib. Sentent.: ELP X* 208

SOTO, PEDRO DE [1495–1563]: Dominican (brother of above?); lectured at Salamanca, co-founder of University of Dillingen; Pius IV's theologian at Council of Trent; invited by Cardinal Pole to lecture at Oxford in the 1550s. *ELP X* 208

SPALATENS (DE DOMINIS, MARCO ANTONIO [1566–1624]): Italian theology professor who left the Jesuit order and became Bishop of Spalato; joined Church of England, made Dean of Windsor and Master of the Savoy; reconciled to Rome, but imprisoned by Inquisition. **De Republica Ecclesiastic.* pars 3, Hanover 1622: *1640* 229

STAPLETON, THOMAS [1538–98]: English Catholic convert; controversialist, particularly on relation of Papacy to temporal powers; helped to found English College at Douai; taught at Louvain. *ELP III* 155; *VIII* 195

STEPHANUS (ESTIENNE), HENRI [1531–98]: scholar, author, editor and printer, grandson of Henri, founder of the famous printing firm, first in Paris and later in Geneva. *Apologia Herodoti: Spital* 111

STOW, JOHN [1525–1605]: chronicler of England and of London. *Annals: Spital* 108, 112

SUARIUS (SUAREZ), FRANCISCO [1548–1617]: Spanish Jesuit, taught theology at Salamanca, etc.; commentary on *Summa* which reconciled Aquinas with Duns Scotus. *Defensio Fidei Catholici: 1640* 227; *1661* 237

SUECANUS: Protestant reformer. *De Discip. Eccles.: 1640* 225

SUETONIUS (CAIUS SUETONIUS TRANQUILLUS) [ca. 70–ca. 160]: *De Vita Caesarum: ELP IV* 160; *Duppa* 246, 247

SUIDAS [ca. 1000]: supposedly a Greek lexicographer (the name means "fortress *or* armoury of information"). *ELP XI* 212

SURIUS, LAURENT [1522–1578]: bitterly antiprotestant pupil of Peter Canisius at Cologne; joined order of St Bruno. Continued Lippomann's biographies of the saints and Crabbe's history of the Councils. **Concilia,* 4 vols, Cologne 1567: *ELP X* 207

SYMMACHUS, QUINTUS AURELIUS [345–405]: Roman noble, administrator and orator; opposed by St. Ambrose. *Spital* 107

TACITUS [ca. 55–ca. 117]: *Annales (Historiae): 1640* 220, 223, 224; *1661* 238; *Duppa* 246

TERTULLIAN [ca. 160–ca. 220]: African Church father; educated as lawyer at Rome, returned to Carthage on conversion to Christianity. First apologist to write in Latin: his rugged style became the anti-Ciceronian model. **Opera, cum notis Pamelii,* Cologne 1617. *1621* 75, 77; *Spital* 103; *Apologeticum: ELP X* 209; *1661* 238–41; *Duppa* 248; *Visitation* 254; *De Anima: Lent I* 115; *De Oratione· FLP I* 141; *II* 144, 145, 151; *IV* 165; *V* 172; *VII* 186, 189, *IX* 198

THEOPHYLACT [eleventh century]: Archbishop of Bulgaria; pupil of Michael Psellus and tutor to Emperor Michael VII's son; biblical commentator in tradition of Chrysostom. "In Evangel. Latin.," Basle 1554; **Comment. in Scti Pauli Epistol. Grae. Lat.,* London 1636. *1621* 78; *ELP VIII* 195; *IX* 200–201

THUCYDIDES [ca. 460–ca. 400 B.C.]: "Historia Latina." *Spital* 109

TOSTATUS. see ABULENSIS

TULLY. see CICERO

VATABLUS ARIAS, FRANCISCO [d. 1547]: French Hebraist at Paris; biblical commentator; Protestants tried to claim him as theirs. *Lent 2* 125

VERGIL, POLYDORE [ca. 1470–ca. 1555]: Italian historian from Urbino; naturalised Englishman, prebendary of various cathedrals, including St Paul's; Archdeacon of Wells; returned to Italy 1581. *Helin. Geog.: ELP III* 154

VICTORIA, FRANCISCO DE/A [ca. 1485–1546]: Spanish Dominican scholastic theologian and humanist; taught at Paris and Salamanca (first theology professor there), substituted Aquinas for Peter Lombard; "Father of International Law." *Act* 87; *1661* 237, 238

VICTORINUS, C. MARIUS [fourth century A.D.]: Roman grammarian, rhetorician, polemicist and neoplatonic philosopher from Africa who influenced St. Augustine's conversion; writer of New Testament and literary commentaries. *1640* 219

VIRGIL (PUBLIUS VERGILIUS MARO) [70–19 B.C.]: "ex edit. Stephan," 1549; "cum notis Manutii"; "Amsterdam 1628." *Aeneid: Lent 2* 130; *ELP X* 207; *1661* 236; *Commemoration* 266, 269

VIVES, LODOVICO [1492–1540]: Spanish philosopher and theologian; under threat of Inquisition, fled to Paris and England; became professor of theology at Oxford. *Meditationes* Lyons 1558: *ELP III* 157; *1640* 226

VOLATERRANUS, RAPHAEL MAEFFEIUS [ca. 1450–1522]: learned man of letters at Rome. *Spital* 112

WALSINGHAM, THOMAS OF [d. ca. 1422]: monk of St Alban's abbey and historian. *Histor. Anglic.: Spital* 108, 112

WEEMSE (WEMYSS), JOHN [ca. 1579–1636]: Scottish divine who became a prebendary of Durham; friend of Bishop John King. *Christian. Synagog.: ELP III* 153

ZANCHIUS, HIERONIMO [1516–90] Italian canon regular, pupil of Peter Martyr; taught theology at Heidelberg. *Opera*, 3 vols, 1613. *De Natura Dei: ELP III* 156–57; *V* 168

Appendix 2: A Chronology of King's Life

16 Jan. 1592	Baptised Worminghall, Bucks (grandfather Philip King's home). Father John Archdeacon of Nottingham, chaplain to Archbishop of York, John Piers.
ca. 1596	Thame School (founded by Lord Williams, maternal great-uncle).
ca. 1601	Westminster School.
1605	Father becomes Dean of Christ Church, Oxford.
1606	Latin lines printed in *Charitates Oxonienses* for visit of Christian IV of Denmark to Oxford.
1608	Elected to Christ Church.
20 Jan. 1609	Matriculated.
19 June 1611	Bachelor of arts degree.
8 Sept.	Father consecrated Bishop of London.
6 Nov. 1612	Death of Prince Henry: "Elegy"; Latin elegy in Oxford tribute *Iusta Oxoniensium*.
1613	Latin verses in Oxford collection *Lusus Palatini* for marriage of Princess Elizabeth and Elector Palatinate; also in *Iusta Funebria* on death of Sir Thomas Bodley.
3 Apr. 1614	Death of Dr. John Spenser, President of Corpus Christi, Oxford: father's friend. Latin elegy (for hearse?).
7 Jul.	Master of arts degree.
Sept.	Death of future wife's father, Robert Berkeley of Ulcombe, Kent.
23 Jan. 1615	Father ordains John Donne deacon and priest.
11 July	Will of Anne Berkeley's guardian, Mrs. Lloyd, widow of Principal of Jesus College, Oxford, proved: this and Robert Berkeley's will disputed till 13 June 1616.
1616	Ordination(?).
24 Jan.	Prebendary of St. Pancras; Rector of Chigwell, Essex (curate: Emmanuel Uty).
10 July	Leaves Oxford. Marriage to Anne Berkeley before Dec. 21 (Chamberlain, *Letters* 2.44).
1617	Archdeacon of Colchester. Latin verses in Oxford collection *Iacobi Ara*, for King James's return from Scotland.
5 Nov.	First sermon, at Paul's Cross. Birth of first child, John(?) (died before Dec. 1619).
29 Oct. 1618	Execution of Sir Walter Raleigh: "Elegy."
18 Nov.	Rector of Fulham (curate Thomas Howells).
3 Mar. 1619	Death of father's patron, Queen Anne: Latin verses in Oxford tribute *Annae Funebria*.
19 Apr.	Donne's Valediction sermon at Lincoln's Inn.
6 June	Member of Lincoln's Inn by special admission.
9 Dec.	Second son John baptised.
26 Mar. 1620	Bishop John preaches at St. Paul's before King to inaugurate Royal Commission on fabric. Henry appointed a commissioner.
30 Mar. 1621	Death of Bishop John: "Elegy" (or later?).
3 Apr.	Daughter Anne baptised.
26 Aug.	Barton Holiday's "Technogamia" acted before King at Woodstock: brothers William and Philip King in cast: "To his Freinds of Christ Church."
22 Nov.	John Donne installed Dean of St. Paul's.

Appendix 2

25 Nov.	Preaches Paul's Cross sermon refuting father's apostasy: printed 1621.
	Richard Argall dedicates to Henry *The Song of Songs Metaphrased, Part I*.
3 Jan. 1622	Daughter Anne buried.
4 Apr.	Son Henry baptised.
6 Oct. 1623	Son Philip baptised. Prince Charles returns from Spain.
Nov. (end)	Visits Donne daily during serious illness: appointed his executor.
24 Jan. 1624	Wife Anne buried in St. Paul's, in Bishop King's tomb: "Exequy."
	Leases Vicarage House, near west end of St. Paul's.
3 Mar.	Installed canon of Christ Church by proxy.
28 Mar.	Death of Richard, third Earl of Dorset: Henry his chaplain: "Epitaph."
	Year of first acquaintance with Izaak Walton, Donne's parishioner at St. Dunstan's(?).
27 Mar. 1625	Death of James I: already King's Chaplain—Latin verses in Oxford tribute *Parentalia*.
19 May	Degrees of bachelor of divinity and doctor of divinity: an Oxford representative at clergy Convocation.
10 July	Act-Sunday sermon at St. Mary the Virgin, Oxford.
	Member of the Court of High Commisson.
	Henry Mason dedicates to Henry *Christian Humiliation or a Treatise on Fasting*.
2 Feb. 1626	Coronation of Charles I.
3 Mar.	Preaches Lent sermon at Whitehall (printed 1627).
10 Apr.	Preaches Easter Monday Spital sermon (printed).
20 Feb. 1627	Preaches Lent sermon at Whitehall (printed).
	Probable year of Giles Farnaby's dedication to Henry of *The Psalms of David, to fower parts for Viols and Voyce* (Pennsylvania University English manuscript 29).
25 Jan. 1628	Son Philip buried.
	An Exposition Upon the Lord's Prayer.
30 March	Signatory to letter from shareholders of Guiana company.
30 Jun.	Copy of Henry Spelman's *Glossarium* given by author to King.
25 Jul.	William Laud becomes Bishop of London.
Jan.(?) 1630	Writes "Anniverse," six years after wife's death.
29 May	Birth of Prince Charles: "By occasion of the young Prince his happy Birth."
28 Mar. 1631	Donne on deathbed gives Henry his sermon notes.
31 Mar.	Donne dies. Henry and John Mountford executors. Henry commissions Donne's memorial statue in St. Paul's. Writes "Upon the Death of my ever Desired Freind" (printed with *Deaths Duell*, 1632).
1632	"Tell me you starres" printed by William Porter in *Madrigals and Ayres*.
6 Nov.	Swedish King Gustavus Adolphus killed at Lutzen: "Elegy" (printed in *Swedish Intelligencer*, 1633).
20 Jul. 1633	Charles I's return from Scotland.: "Upon the King's happy Returne."
Aug.	Laud Archbishop of Canterbury.
3 Nov.	With John Mountford, gives evidence to Royal Commission for repairing St. Paul's.
	Last appearance on Court of High Commission.
1634	*An Exposition Upon the Lord's Prayer*, second edition, two impressions.
Nov.	Rent paid to George Aungier for property near Guildford in Surrey.
30 Sept. 1635	Uncle Philip's will proved: Henry executor.
8 Jun. 1636	Henry Blount's "Voyage into the Levant" entered in Stationers' Register: commendatory poem by King.
3 Feb. 1637	James Howell's letter to "Mr. Thomas W." of the Temple about poems by Henry, his brothers and sisters.
6 Aug.	Ben Jonson dies: contributes to Duppa's tribute *Jonsonus Virbius*.
13 Oct.	The *Sovereign of the Seas* launched at Chatham: "A Salutation of His Majestye's Shipp."
16 Dec.	Son John matriculates at Christ Church.

APPENDIX 2

1638	Commendatory verses for folio edition of George Sandys' *A Paraphrase Upon the Divine Poems.*
	Gives Bible and Book of Common Prayer to Christ Church. Commissions buildings there under terms of uncle Philip King's will.
24 Aug.	Death of Lady Anne Rich: contributes to memorial collection by John Gauden (Rich's chaplain) (Bodleian MS Eng. misc. e.262).
11 Nov.	Designated by Order in Council to read sermon notes of dissident George Walker, with Dean of St. Paul's and Dr. Mountford.
2 Jan. 1639	Brother John buried at Christ Church.
6 Feb.	Installed as Dean of Rochester.
13 Dec.	Letter to Richard Powell of Forest Hill (Hannah, *Poems and Psalms*, 38–39.)
27 Mar. 1640	Paul's Cross Accession Day sermon (printed).
22 May	As Dean, present at Convocation that produced Laudian Canons.
	"Sic Vita" printed in *Poems by Francis Beaumont, Gent*.
9 Jul.	Mrs. Kirk, lady-in-waiting, daughter of Sir Robert Killigrew, buried in Abbey: "Elegy."
12 Oct.	Elected Bishop of Chichester.
16 Jan. 1642	Rector of Petworth (curate Oliver Whitby).
6 Feb.	Consecrated bishop.
15 May	Takes part in consecration of Ralph Brownrigg.
29 Dec.	Chichester falls to Sir William Waller. Henry escapes to Shere via Petworth.
April 1643	Deprived of rents, goods, and library by John Downes and William Cawley.
27 June	Henry's sequestration ordered in Commons.
14 Jul.	Queen arrives at Oxford: "To the Queen at Oxford."
30 Aug.	Brother-in-law Edward Holt buried at Oxford: "Elegy."
3 Oct.	Henry's petition to delay sequestration refused.
28 Oct.	Petition to Lords, through Northumberland (owner of Petworth House) accepted, but without effect.
1645	Parliament in Oxford. Probably among bishops present even though they could not sit.
ca. May	Son John seduces Elizabeth Oughtred at Shere.
2 Nov.	Henry refuses to appear before two members of Parliament at Richard Onslow's house about the matter.
1646	Death of cousin George Duncombe of Albury.
20 Feb.	At Blakesware, home of nephew John, near Sir Ralph Sadler.
14 Sept.	Death of Earl of Essex: "On the Earl of Essex."
	Three lyrics printed in *The Academy of Compliments*.
1647	Henry, with most of his brothers and sisters and their children, at the "college" in Lady Salter's house at Richings, near Slough.
ca. March	"Epigram" on Colonel Robert Hammond's searching Charles I's papers at Carisbrook.
17 June	Son John given permission to proceed master of arts.
	Elegy on Richard, Earl of Dorset, printed in corrupt version in *Certain Elegant Poems written by Dr. Corbet*.
26 Aug. 1648	Execution of Sir Charles Lucas and Sir George Lisle at Colchester: "Elegy" written after October 29.
30 Jan. 1649	Execution of Charles I.
9 Feb.	Buried at nearby Windsor. "A Deepe Groane" (if King's).
11 Mar.	Writes "From my sad retirement" (printed 1659).
16 May.	"Deepe Groane" printed in *Monumentum Regale,* and *Reliquium Sacrae* (1650).
7 Jan. 1651	*Psalms of David* licensed for printing.
	Some of books probably sold in London with those of the Dean and Chapter of Chichester.
30 Oct.	Letter from Langley to Ussher with *Psalms of David*.
14 Jul. 1653	Makes will "in perfect health."
1654	*Psalms of David,* second edition.

29 Nov.	Anne, Lady Stanhope, Northumberland's daughter, buried at Petworth: "Elegy."
	Two lyrics printed in *The Harmony of the Muses*.
ca. May 1655	Eleazor Duncan consults with five bishops, including King, about possibility of consecrating new bishops on continent.
June	Duncon's letter to Hyde about King holding ordinations.
22 Jan. 1656	Letter from Hitcham to Edward Bysshe about St. Paul's.
	"When first the Magick" printed in *Choice Drollery*, and five poems in *Parnassus Biceps*.
11 Mar. 1657	*Poems, Elegies, Paradoxes and Sonnets* registered with Stationers' Company.
15 Jun.	Death of Lady Katherine Cholmondeley, Countess of Leinster.
	Writes "Elegy" included in Bodleian MS Eng. poet. e.30.
30 Dec.	Living two miles from Stoke [Poges, Bucks] (letter from William Dillingham to Sancroft).
1658	Translation of Henry's Latin epitaph by father's tomb printed in Dugdale's *History of St Paul's Cathedral*.
	"Prethee turn that Face away" printed in *Wit's Interpreter*.
17 Nov.	Sister Dorothy Hubert dies.
1659	Elegy on King Charles, "From my sad Retirement," revised and printed.
	"Prethee turn that Face away" printed in Playford's *Select Ayres and Dialogues*.
8 Jul. 1660	Preaches at Whitehall (unprinted: Pepys disliked sermon).
Jul.–Aug.	Named for archbishopric of York: appoints chaplains.
14 Aug.	Resigns prebendal stall at St. Paul's to brother Philip.
2 Sept.	Frewen appointed to York.
29 Sept.	Francis Cheynell evicted from Henry's rectory of Petworth.
28 Oct.	Assists at the consecration of four new bishops.
	Signs testimonial of loyalty for Richard Busby, head of Westminster School.
20 Nov.	Bishops readmitted to House of Lords: regular attendance.
21 Apr.(?) 1661	Preaches St. George's Day sermon at Windsor in place of Duppa (unprinted).
29 May	Preaches at Whitehall for anniversary of King's return (printed).
	Elegy on Prince Henry printed in *Le Prince d'Amour*.
24 Apr. 1662	Preaches Duppa's funeral sermon in Westminster Abbey (printed).
8 Oct.	Preaches Visitation Sermon at Lewes (printed).
	Included in Fuller's *Worthies*, with his elegy on his father.
Jan. (end) 1663	Death of John Donne the younger, who bequeathed those of his father's papers in Henry's hands to Izaak Walton's son.
	Payne Fisher dedicates James Howell's poems to Henry.
8 Mar.	Preaches Lent sermon at Whitehall (heard by Pepys: unprinted).
	"Exequy" printed in *A Crew of kind London Gossips*; "Prethee turn" in *Recreations for Ingenious Headpieces*; "A Penitentiall Hymn" in Gifford's *Divine Services*.
9 Feb. 1664	Thomas Chadwell arrested by the Lords for speaking against Henry: discharged at his "special instance."
	2nd issue of *Poems*, with four additional ones.
13 Nov.(?)	Writes about Hooker to Walton (printed in Walton's *Life*.)
	Sets up restoration fund for Chichester Cathedral.
	Contributes to restoration of Oxford Music School.
30 Jan. 1665	Preaches at Whitehall on anniversary of Charles I's execution (printed).
	Presents silver almsdish and patten to Petworth church.
Jan. 1666	Francis Tryon, old friend, dies: Henry executor of will.
4 Mar.	Lent preacher at Whitehall (sermon unprinted).
23 Mar.	Letter to Archbishop Sheldon about Francis Challoner.
12 Jul.	Visitation sermon at Lewes, recorded by Giles Moore (unprinted).
	Gives silver flagon (dated 1640) to Petworth church.
4 Mar. 1667	Death of brother Philip, at Langley
3 Feb. 1668 } 23 Jul. } 16 Aug. }	Letters to Sheldon about Thomas Wilkinson.

21 Feb. 1669	Son Henry dies.
28 Feb.	Preaches Lent sermon at Whitehall (heard by Evelyn: unprinted).
8 Sept.	Preaches at Triennial Visitation at Lewes (unprinted).
30 Sept.	Dies at Chichester.
8 Oct.	Buried in south choir of cathedral.

Glossary of Words Unfamiliar or Changed in Meaning

abatements (to make)	to settle account
abrogated	done away with
advertise	admonish
antedate	anticipate
assentation	obsequious agreement
atrophy	wasting away of the body
attachment	an arrest
bandileros	bandoliers: musket cartridges
bangle [verb]	(hawking) beat about instead of making for quarry
barritors	continual inciters of suits or quarrels in disturbance of the peace: an offence punishable by fine or imprisonment
bates	abates
begin	i.e., to speak
blacks	mourning clothes
blazon	(heraldry) describe a coat of arms
bottom	vessel, boat
bray	pound small
burse	meeting-place (originally of merchants)
calenture	tropical fever
canon, (canonical)	an ecclesiastical law
cast [verb]	find guilty, convict
cautelous (cautelously)	cautious, crafty
character	symbol in writing
cheap [noun]	bargain
chorography	art of delineating a region on a map
chyle	white milky fluid created by the action of the pancreatic juice and the bile on the chyme (semi-fluid matter into which food is converted).
climacteric	critical period
collect	short prayer in the liturgy
compact [verb]	join tightly together
cognisance	badge
conclude	overcome in argument
concoct, concoction	digest, digestion
confer	compare
contemn	scorn
convented	brought together
coranto	news sheet
corsive	corrosive
cosenage	cheating
course, by	by turn
creepled	crippled
curtesie	favour

315

dark	obscure
demised	(legal) transferred
depravations	corruptions
desperate	hopeless
determine	conclude (literally of exercises for degree): maintain a thesis
difference	(heraldic) alteration or addition to coat of arms to distinguish junior member or branch of a house
dilassation	i.e., dilatation (OED), stretching
dilation	expansion (cf. above)
discruciation	torture
distinctions	categories
donatives	gifts
dogmatise	to deliver as a dogma
doxology	short formula of praise (to God)
draw, (drew)	track by the scent
edify [intransitive verb]	to profit spiritually or mentally
either	or else
elevatum	(ecclesiastical) elevation of the bread and wine at the mass after their consecration
empirick	unscientific quack practising medicine (originally, physician in classical times drawing rules of practice from experience only)
engine	(military), i.e., of battery
ephemerides	daily journal
escheat	confiscate or forfeit
essence	a fifth element distinct from the other four; or (alchemy) a distillation of the essential properties of matter
evince	triumphantly overcome
evict	draw out
excite	urge on
exenterate	disembowel
facture	making
fine for	(legal) pay entrance fine for
fix, (fixation)	(alchemy) make stable, involatile
flead	flayed
fore, fores	(apparently) principle meeting place, from Latin *forum* (not in *OED*, unless "course of affair")
freebooters	those who plunder others
frowardly	perversely
garbling	sorting out the best in
give on, upon	make an assault
glass	i.e., perspective glass (q.v.)
grange	large barn
gregarian	belonging to the common sort
gubernation	the act of governing
gyres	rings
gyves	shackles
haggards	untamed female hawks
have upon	(of execution) carry out

Glossary of Words Unfamiliar or Changed in Meaning

heteroclite	person who deviates from the rule
history	a relation of incidents
horseleech	leech (medical)
humorous	affected by the four humours of the body; sanguine, phlegmatic, choleric, melancholic
husbandry	careful housekeeping
imp [noun]	young shoot (metaphor), young child (without pejorative meaning)
[verb]	to graft
impeccable	exempt from sin
impetrate	obtain by asking
impost	tax
inchoation	beginning
indagation	investigation
indifferent, (indifferency)	impartial
informes [verb]	shapes, moulds
ingeniously	openly
inned	accommodated at an inn
integrals	(philosophy) component parts
interested (to be)	have a share
jealous	fearful, suspicious
jesses	(apparently) stage of journey (*ELP XI*—variant of "gest"?) *OED:* straps attached to hawk's leg to bring it back while flying—metaphor, constraint?
journeyman	one qualified in a trade who works for a day's wages
label	strip of parchment attached to a document
lackey [verb]	wait upon
lading [noun]	loading, i.e., load
lay	make to contribute
let	hindrance
lesson	piece of music
lie at guard	(a position of defence)
list [verb]	like, wish
macerated	softened by cooking (tenderised in liquid)
mandragora	mandrake (a narcotic)
marish	marsh
mere, merely	true, absolutely, only
messes [transitive verb]	courses of food
mess	to feed
miscensure	condemn
mollify	soften
momentany	transitory, passing
mystery	trade
nice	precise, fastidious
nominal	(logic) existing in name only
nonage	legal infancy, immaturity
novelist	seeker out of novelties
object [verb]	place before the eyes

obliquity	fault
obloquy	speech against
omer	Hebrew measure of capacity
onus	(legal) debit or charge
ostent	a sign or portent
parget	decorative plaster work
party	part
pater-noster	"Our Father,": i.e., the Lord's Prayer (Latin)
peccants	offenders
peculiar [noun]	special area of jurisdiction
period	full stop, end
perspective	optical instrument for viewing objects
pharos	lighthouse
phlebotomy	the cutting open a vein to let blood flow
plagiaries	kidnappers
port	port-hole
pose [verb]	present
predicament	(logic) what is stated or asserted about a subject
prejudicate	judge beforehand
preposterous	back to front
prescribe upon	make a claim on
president	precedent
pretend	claim
prevent	anticipate, go before
projector	speculator
prolation	utterance
proscription	condemning to death
puny [noun]	(legal) junior, lesser
put . . . upon	entrust or commit to verdict
quames	qualms
querries	equerries
quietus	discharge or release
quietus est	Latin: "it is discharged"
quit rents	(legal) rents in lieu of service
race [verb]	raze, erase
reals	(logic) actuals
recite	quote
reduce	lead back
remembrancer	officer who reminds public figures of important matters
reversion	buying succession of office while another still holds it
scale	ladder
scandalize	make a public scandal of, discredit
sconce	stand for a torch
seare	withered
seizen	(legal) possession of freehold
shifts	ingenious devices
staple	market

statute	statue (late Middle English)
success	fortunes
sudden	rash, not thought out
suit	(legal) suing in a court of law, petitioning
suit fine	(legal) fine for non-attendance in court
supersedeas	something which acts as a check
synecdochically	using part for the whole
talent	weight of lead
tetter	pustular eruption of the skin
threne [noun]	lament (Greek)
timpanous	resounding
tincture	(alchemy) supposed spiritual principle whose quality can be infused into material things
train	trail of gunpowder
travell	travail, work
triturations	flailings
tropical	metaphorical
umbrageous	suspicious, shady
unclosed	(alchemy) uncovered
unvalued, unvaluable	beyond value
vaunt	vanguard
vicegerent	deputy ruler
view, at the	by sight (opposite: at a distance)
ward	lock
warrant	assurance
wild-fire	highly inflammable substances thrown in warfare
worms	serpents
zanies	buffoons, simpletons

Bibliography

Aubrey, John. *Brief Lives*. Edited by O. L. Dick. London: Secker and Warburg, 1949.
Atterbury, Francis. *Sermons on Several Occasions*. London, 1734.
Aylmer, G. E., ed. *The Interregnum: The Quest for Settlement*. London: Macmillan, 1972.
Baildon, W. P., ed. *The Records of the Honourable Society of Lincoln's Inn: The Black Books*. 4 vols. London, 1897–1902.
Bald, R. C. *John Donne: A Life*. Oxford: Clarendon Press, 1970.
Berman, Ronald. *Henry King and the Seventeenth Century*. London: Chatto and Windus, 1965.
Bernard, John. *The Life and Death of the Most Reverend and Learned Father of Our Church. Dr. James Usher . . . Published in a Sermon at his Funeral . . . And now re-viewed with some other Enlargements*. London, 1656.
Blench, J. W. *Preaching in England in the late 15th and 16th Centuries*. Oxford: Clarendon Press, 1964.
Blencowe, R. W. "Paxhill and its neighbourhood." *SAC* 11, 1859.
Bosher, R. S. *The Making of the Restoration Settlement 1642–62*. 2nd ed. London: Dacre Press, 1957.
Browne, Thomas. *The Works of Sir Thomas Browne*. Edited by G. L. Keynes. 6 vols. Cambridge: University Press, 1928–31.
Cardwell, Edward, ed. *Synodalia*. 2 vols. Oxford: Oxford University Press, 1842.
Chamberlain, John. *The Letters of John Chamberlain*. Edited by N. E. McClure. 2 vols. Philadelphia: American Philosophical Society, 1939.
Collinson, Patrick. *The Religion of Protestants*. Oxford: Clarendon Press, 1982.
Cross, Claire. *Church and People 1450–1660*. London: Fontana, 1976.
Davies, Horton. *Like Angels from a Cloud*. San Marino, Calif.: Huntington Library, 1986.
Donne, John. *The Sermons of John Donne*. Edited by G. R. Potter and E. M. Simpson. 10 vols. Berkeley: University of California Press, 1953–62.
———. *Essayes in Divinity*. Edited by E. M. Simpson. Oxford: Clarendon Press, 1952.
Donne, John. *John Donne: The Elegies & The Songs & Sonnets*. Edited by Helen Gardner. Oxford: Clarendon Press, 1952.
Donne, John. *The Poems of John Donne*. Edited by H. J. C. Grierson. 2 vols. Oxford: Oxford University Press, 1912.
Duppa, Bishop Brian. *The Correspondence of Bishop Brian Duppa and Sir Justinian Isham*. Edited by Sir Giles Isham. Northamptonshire Record Society, 17 (1955).
Evelyn, John. *The Diary of John Evelyn*. Edited by E. S. de Beer. 3 vols. Oxford: Clarendon Press, 1955.
Fuller, Thomas. *The Church-History of Britain*. London, 1655.
———. *The History of the Worthies of England*. London, 1662.
Green, I. M. *The Re-establishment of the Church of England 1660–66*. Oxford: Oxford University Press, 1978.
Hall, Joseph. *The Works of Joseph Hall, D.D.* Edited by Peter Hall. 12 vols. A new edition, revised and corrected. Oxford: D. A. Tallboys, 1837.
Hamper, W. *Life, Diary, and Correspondence of William Dugdale*. London, 1827.
Herbert, George. *The Poems of George Herbert*. Edited by F. E. Hutchinson. Oxford: Clarendon Press, 1941.
Hobbs, M. "An edition of the Stoughton manuscript, an early seventeenth-century poetry collection in private hands connected with Henry King and Oxford." Ph.D. diss., University of London, 1973.
———. "More Books from the Library of John Donne." *The Book Collector* 29 (1980): 590–92.
———. "'To a most dear friend'—Donne's Bellarmine." *Review of English Studies* NS 32 (1981): 435–38.
———. "Henry King, John Donne, and the Refounding of Chichester Cathedral Library." *The Book Collector* 30 (1984): 189–205.

———. "Henry King: 'A Pale Imitation of Donne'?" *Notes and Queries* NS 32 (1985): 78–82.

———. "The Restoration Correspondence of Bishop Henry King." *SAC* 125 (1987): 139–53.

———. *The Stoughton Manuscript*. London: Scolar Press, 1990.

Hooker, Richard. *The Works of Richard Hooker*. Edited by John Keble. 3 vols. 3rd ed. Oxford: Oxford University Press, 1845.

Hutton, Ronald. *The Restoration*. Oxford: Clarendon Press, 1985.

Ingamells, John. *The English Episcopal Portrait*. London: Paul Mellon Centre for Studies in British Art, 1981.

James I. *The Works of . . . King James I*. Edited by Richard Montague. London, 1616.

Kendall, R. T. *Calvin and English Calvinism to 1649*. Oxford: Oxford University Press, 1979.

Kennett, White. *A Register and Chronicle, Ecclesiastical and Civil*. London, 1728.

Keynes, G. L. *A Bibliography of Dr John Donne*. 4th ed. Oxford: Clarendon Press, 1973.

———. *A Bibliography of Henry King, D.D., Bishop of Chichester*. London: Douglas Cleverdon, 1977.

King, Henry. *Poems and Psalms by Henry King D.D*. Edited by John Hannah. London: William Pickering, 1843.

King, Henry. *The Poems of Bishop Henry King*. Edited by John Sparrow. London: Nonesuch Press, 1925.

King, Henry. *The Poems of Henry King, Bishop of Chichester*. Edited by Margaret Crum. Oxford: Clarendon Press, 1965.

King, Bishop John. *Lectures upon Jonas*. 2nd ed. London, 1619.

King, Peter. "The Episcopate during the Civil Wars 1642–9." *English Historical Review* 83 (1968): 523–48.

Laud, William. *The Works of William Laud*. Edited by W. Scott. 7 vols. *Library of Anglo-Catholic Theology*. Oxford: J. H. Parker, 1847–60.

Lockyer, Roger, ed. *The Trial of Charles I*. London: Folio Society, 1974.

McAdoo, Henry. *The Spirit of Anglicanism: A Study of Anglican Theological Method in the Seventeenth Century*. London: A. and C. Black, 1965

Maclure, Millar. *The Paul's Cross Sermons 1534–1642*. Toronto: Toronto University Press, 1958.

Malcolm, Noel. *Marco Antonio de Dominis . . . Venetian, Anglican, Ecumenist, and Relapsed Heretic*. London: Strickland and Scott Academic Publications, 1984.

Mason, Lawrence. "The Life and Works of Henry King." *Transactions of the Connecticut Academy of Arts and Sciences* 18 (1913): 227–89.

Mason, T. A. *Serving God and Mammon: William Juxon, 1582–1642*. Newark: University of Delaware Press, 1985.

Mitchell, W. Fraser. *English Pulpit Oratory from Andrewes to Tillotson: A Study of its Literary Aspects*. London: S. P. C. K., 1932.

Moore, Giles. *The Journal of Giles Moore*. Edited by Ruth Bird. SRS 68, 1971.

More, P. E., and F. L. Cross. *Anglicanism: The Thought and Practice of the Church of England, Illustrated from the Religious Literature of the Seventeenth Century*. London: S. P. C. K., 1957.

Morrill, John, ed. *Reactions to the English Civil War 1642–49*. London: Macmillan, 1982.

Packer, J. W. *The Transformation of Anglicanism, 1643–1660*. Manchester: Manchester University Press, 1969.

Parr, Richard. *The Life of the most reverend father in God . . . James Usher, Archbishop of Armagh*. London, 1688.

Pepys, Samuel. *The Diary of Samuel Pepys*. Edited by R. C. Latham and W. Matthews. 11 vols. London: George Bell, 1970–82.

Russell, Conrad, ed. *Origins of the English Civil War*. London: Macmillan, 1973.

Shirley, F. J. *Richard Hooker and Contemporary Political Ideas*. London: S. P. C. K., 1949.

Simpson, Evelyn M. *The Prose Works of John Donne*. 2nd ed. Oxford: Clarendon Press, 1948.

Simpson, Percy. "The Bodleian Manuscripts of Henry King." *The Bodleian Quarterly Record* 5 (1952–53): 324–40.

———. "John and Henry King: A Correction." *The Bodleian Library Record* 4 (1952–53): 208–9.

Smith, Harold. *The Ecclesiastical History of Essex under the Long Parliament and Commonwealth*. Colchester: Benham and Co., 1932.

———. "John Donne and Contemporary Preachers." *Essays and Studies* 16 (1930): 157–58.

Sutch, Victor D. *Gilbert Sheldon, Architect of Anglican Survival, 1640–75*. The Hague: M. Nijhoff, 1973.

Topsell, Edward. *A Historie of Four-footed Beastes*. London, 1607.

Tyacke, Nicholas. *Anti-Calvinists*. Oxford: Clarendon Press, 1987.

Walker, John. *An Attempt towards . . . an Account of the Numbers and Sufferings of the Clergy of the Church of England*. 2 vols. London, 1714.

Walther, Hans. *Proverbia Sententiaque Latinatis Medii Aevi*. 9 vols. Carmina Medii Aevi Posterioris Latina 2. Göttingen, 1963–86.

Walton, Izaak. *The Lives of Dr John Donne, Sir Henry Wotton, Mr Richard Hooker, Mr George Herbert*. 3rd ed. (1st collected ed.), London, 1670.

Wedgwood, C. V. *The King's War*. London: William Collins, 1958.

———. *The Trial of Charles I*. London: William Collins, 1964.

Williamson, George. *The Senecan Amble*. Chicago: University of Chicago Press, 1951.

Wilson, A. N. *The Life of John Milton*. Oxford: Clarendon Press, 1983.

Wood, Anthony. *Athenae Oxonienses*. 2 vols. Oxford, 1713.

Index to the Sermons

Abbreviations used: met. = metaphorical use; person. = personification. A number in italic type signifies the use of a paraphrase only of the actual name; square brackets surround another form of the name also found in the text. For names of King's authorities, see appendix 1.

Aaron, 139, 202, 225, 245
Abarim, Mount (range), 69, 165. *See also* Nebo; Pisgah
Abbot, George (archbishop of Canterbury), *78*
Abel, 148, 248, 269
Abiathar (high priest), 225
Abimelech, 240
Abraham, 118, 154, 188; bosom of, 113; and Isaac (met.), 214; and Lot, 148, 182; servant of, 256; and Sodom, 93, 146
Absolon, 125
Absolution, 92–93, 94, *186*
Abulensis. *See* Alexander of Hales
Achan, 208
Achitophel, 125, 154
Actaeon, 104
Act of Oblivion [Perpetual], 234
Adam [our Forefather, the first husband]: creation and fall, 91, 110, 120, 150, 192, 226, 258; disobedience, 161, 198, 199–200; results of Fall, 132, 167, 177, 187, 191; traditions about, 102, 269
Adamites, 258
Adversity, 94, 98, 122, 127–29, 132, 168–69, 172–73, 175, 204–5
Aesculapius, 110
Africa [Affricke], 153
Age, old, 115, 120–21, 122, 124–25, 205, 252
Ahab, 125; house of, 248
Ahimelech, 272
Ai, 208
Ajax, 144
Alchemy, 239; (met.) 145, 150, 200, 257
Alc(h)oran, 207
Alexander III (pope), 225
Alexander VI (pope), 73
Alexander of Hales, 148, 267
Alexander the Great, 69, 162, 213, 241, 244, 271
Alexandria, 112, 171
All Souls' College, Oxford, 250, 251
Almaricus, 209
Amaleck, 139
Amaziah, 70
Ambition, 129
Ambrose, St., 259
Amen, meaning of, 216–18
America, 212; South, 207
Amorite, 206

Amos, 70
Anabaptists, 192; Anabaptistical, 258
Ananias (cheater), 90
Ananias (messenger to Saul), 125
Anastasius II (pope), 73
Ancient of days (God), 177
Angels: fall of, 104; (met.) heaven, 173
Anger, 196, 201, 205
Anne (James I's queen), *63*
Antichrist, 72, 162, 247
Apollonia, St., 111
Apollonia Geria, 194
Apollos, 121, 259
Arabia, 161; Arabian triumphs, 193
Aratus, 259
Archer, John, 265
Arians, 74, 75
Aristotle [the Philosopher, the Astronomer], 77, 119, 121, 123, 153
Ark, 130; of the Covenant, 169
Armada [fatall Crescent], 68; [Spain's fleet], 111
Arminian, the, 169
Army (political party), 235
Arphad, King of, 67
Ashdod, (met.) 69
Ashur, 203, 243
Assyrians, 99, 222
Astrology, 154. *See also* Planets
Athanasius, St., 75
Atheist, an Italian, 67
Atlantes, 153
Atlas, 127, 175
Augustine, St., 77, 178–79, 207, 254, 259
Augustus, emperor Octavius Caesar, 221, 246, 247, 266; in Ovid, 226, 231
Authorised Version. *See* Bible
Auxilius, Bishop, 254
Avernus, Lake, 108
Axitheus, 262

Babel, Tower of, 72, 86, 222, 235; (met.) 111, 202
Babylon, 108, 222; King of, 246; Babylonish, 258
Bajazet(h) II, 269
Balaam, 232
Balak, 232
Ball, John, 265
Baptism, sacrament of, 105, 259; names in, 154–55

Barabbas, 77. *See* Cromwell, Oliver
Barbary, 109
Baronius, Cardinal Cesare, 68
Barrow, Henry, 246
Basiliwick, John [Ivan], Duke of Moscow, 266
Beersheba, 165, 213
Belshazzar, 222
Belus, 66
Benedict VIII (pope), 154
Bereans, 229
Bethel, 70
Bethel(eh)em Hospital, 106
Bethulia, 99
Beza, Theodore, 75, 225
Bias, 172
Bible, translations of: Authorised Version, 214, 227, 262; Geneva, 86, *94*, 140; Junius and Tremellius, 113; Rhemist Testament, 110, 171, 180, 208; Septuagint, 83, 89, 95, 98, 107, 166, 211, 227, 268; Vulgate (St. Jerome), 94, 137, 180, *211*, 261. *See also* Scriptures
Bichri, sons of, 155; (met.) 239, 251
Bishop of Rome, 227, 254. *See also* Pope
Bishops, role of, 78, 251, 252–54, 262
Bisnega, Emperor of, 224
Blasphemy, 68, 97–98, 158
Body: human, 175; politic, *see* Common wealth
Bolsec, Jerome, 75, 77
Bonaventura, St., 206
Boucher, 265
Bradshaw, John, *272–73;* as Rhadamanthus, 272
Bridewell, 106
Britain, Great. *See* England
Brownists, 145, 246
Brutus, 72, 202
Bucer, Martin, 75, 229
Buchanan, George, 227, 239, 267
Burial: Church of England, 80; Jewish view, 217; Nonconformist view, 266–70; Samaritan view, 246–47

Caelestius, 202
Caiaphas, 77, 272
Cain, 148
Cairo, 108
Caldecott, Matthew, 79 (marg.)
Calf, Golden, 239; (met.) 72, 227
Calvary, Mount, 73, 91, 101, 105
Calvin, John, 75, 76, 195, 229
Calvino-turcismus, 77
Canaan, 179; Canaanite, 203
Canonists, 162, 225
Canterbury, Archbishop of. *See* Abbot, George
Canute, 213
Cardinal of France. *See* Mazarin
Carisbrook (Isle of Wight), 272
Carthaginians, 74, 223
Cartwright, William, 141
Cassius, 202; (tribune) 272
Castriot, George [Scander Beg], 148

Catadupes, 65
Cathari, 188, 193, 204
Catholic King. *See* Spain, King of
Catholic League, 265
Cedron. *See* Kedron
Celestine IV (pope), 73, 224
Ceremonies (ceremonial), 211, 229; puritan dislike of, 158, 246; sign of cross, 247
Chabda (India), 585
Chaldeans, 229, 562
Chaldee Paraphrase (of the Bible), 95, 108, 132, 150, 234
Chaos, 70, 213, 222. *See also* Creation, the
Charles I: as prince, 63, 159–60; as king, 115, 135, 250; and the Church, 229, 268; character and achievements, 228–32, 270–71, 275; devotion, *121,* 270, 272; trial and death, compared with Christ's, 272–73; as King Hezekiah, 271; as Josiah, 265–66, 267, 268; as Ecclesiastes [the Preacher], 271
Charles II: care for Church in his exile, 251–52; relationship with tutor, 250–51; Restoration, 235–36, 240–41, 252, 275; right to throne, 237
Charles V (Holy Roman emperor), 88
Charles IX (king of France), 254
Chichester, 250, 251; in civil war, 274
Childerley (near Cambridge), 272
China, 153
Christ. *See* Jesus
Christ Church (Oxford), 250, 251
Church, the: mystical body of, 149, 182; six ages of, 188; unity of, 255; whole (true), 148, 164, 260
Church of England: church lands, 107; in civil wars and Interregnum, 235, 264, 251–52, 263, 265; compared with the Roman Catholic Church, 174; mission, 165, 213; ordinations, 255; and the Reformers, 229; threats to, 201–2, 263; times of service, 79, 143; use of vernacular, 164, 216
Cinque [Five] Ports, 106, 119, 190
City. *See* London
Civil war, incidents in, 235, 239, 248, 265, 267, 268–69, 273–74
Classicianus, 254
Cleopatra, 212
Cleop(h)as, 102
Cluet, Richard [(Bishop John King's) chaplain], 79–80
Cochlaeus, Johann, 77
Commodus, 221
Common Prayer, Book of [our Liturgy]: confession in, 79, 87, 92; of Edward VI, 229; of 1637, *229;* prayers in, 140, 213, 229; quoted, 92, *104,* 149, 171, *247;* Reformers on, 229
Commons, House of, 269
Common wealth [Body politic], 108, 148–49, 182, 222, 226–27
Communion, Holy [Sacrament]: frequency of, 181; malignants barred from, 265; origin, 105; puritan lack of reverence, 158; seals of faith, 157, 217; service of, 79, 229; value of sacraments, 179–80, 187–88

Compostella, 151
Conclave of Cardinals, 92, 159, 162, 221
Confession, 87–90, 92–93
Conscience, 90
Consistory (Genevan), 221, 225; (met.) 240
Constantine (emperor), 151
Constantinople, 108, 230
Constantius Paleologus (emperor), 230
Contagion. *See* Plague
Conventicles, 65, 140, 254
Council of State, 234
Councils of the Church: Basil (Basle), 207; Florence, 88, 207; Lateran Council, 92; Milan, 188; Toledo, 140; Trent, 92, 206, 207, 208
Cranmer, Archbishop, 229
Creation, the, 70, 97, 100, 119. *See also* Chaos
Creatures, Book of, 97, 118, 243, *256*
Crete, 252, 254
Cromwell, Oliver, 234–35, 272; as Barabbas, 240; as Haman, 240; as Lucifer, 235; as Pharaoh Necho, 266
Cross, sign of. *See* Ceremonies
Croton[e], 109
Cyrus, 68, 222, 224

Dalila, 67, 224
Damasus, 257
Dan, 165, 213
Daniel, 259
Darius, 213, 240
David: and Goliath, **99**, 236; as king, 141, 213, 221, 236, 238; against Saul, 125; numbering the people, 109, 274; as Psalmist, 83, 86, 125–34, 146, 178, 214; the keys of David, 93, 103, 113, 140
Dead Sea, 108; (met.) 133
Death, 114, 124, 131–32, 204, 241, 245–46; (person.) 102, 111–12, 113, 243–45
Deborah. *See* Elizabeth I, Queen
De La Puente, Juan, 70
Deluge. *See* Flood
Demetrius (of Ephesus), 208, 239
Devil (Satan): author of lies, 76, 197; cause of the Fall, 97, 100, 116, 198; fowler, 91, 105; great thief, 67; hunter (foe): of Christ, 74, 105; of man, 104, 106; man's accuser, 89; serpent, 70, 73, 104; tempter: of Christ, 72, 161; of man, 105, 199, 201, 202; of Job, 199–200; the Devil's agents: Death, 245; Pelagius, 138; his combat with Christ, 101–2. *See also* Lucifer; Prince of Darkness
Diana (goddess), 208, 239
Dinah, 130
Dives, 210
Doeg, 272
Dog star, 108
Dove, the, 130–31, 133
Doway (Douai, Normandy), 76, 77
Draco, laws of, 117, 230, 272
Drunkenness, 67, 68, 167, 201, 205
Drusus, 260

Duppa, Bishop Brian, 249–52
Durandus, 208

Earth: the world (contrasted with heaven), 160–63, 169, 173–74, 184–85; earth's glory, 168–69, 212, 214–15; the ground, 102–3, 109, 129, 174, 207, 246; smallness of, 184; (astron.) 117, 174, 176; (person.) 100, 177, 245. *See also* Creatures, book of
Easter, 95; Greek, 103
Eden, Garden of, 149
Edom (Ishmael), 153
Edward the Confessor, laws of, 225
Egypt [Aegypt] (Egyptians, Pharaoh): bubonic plague in, 108, 109; Christ's flight into, 73, 105; clothing, 258; desert fathers in, 141; exodus from, 99, 102, 112, 203; Israelites in, 101, 105; Joseph in, 170, 178, 236; language, 153; passover, 112; plagues, 74, 75, 101. *See also* Nile
Eikon Basilike [*Our Blessed King's Portraiture*], 271–72
Election and reprobation, 138, 160, 167, 169, 171, 229
Elements, the four, 70, 145, 180, 205, 213
Eleutherius (pope), 225
Eliab, 236
Elias. *See* Elijah; Elisha
Elijah [Eliah, Elias], 80, 94, 125, 140, 205
Elisha [Elias], 80, 95, 144, 182, 203, 232, 250
Elizabeth I, Queen, 99; as Deborah, 109
Elymas, 271
Emath, King of, 67
Empirick, 200
England [Great Brittain]: British Isles, *229;* delivered from foreign troubles, 111, 160; earlier rebellions in, 265; nearness to Heaven, 161; the Pope and, 72. *See also* Law, English
Epaminondas, 226
Ephemerides, 70, 176
Ephesus, 208, 239
Ephraim, 78
Epimenides, 259
Epyrots, 148
Equality under God, 149
Erasmus, 459, 460, 545, 563
Esau, 148, 204
Esther, 153, 240
Eteocles, 148
E(æ)tna, Mount, 91, 207
Eudaemon, Johannes, 155
Eudoxius, 254
Eugenius (pope), 88
Euphrates, 222, 265
Europe, 108
Eve [Evah, the Woman], 73, *100*, 190, *192*, 269
Evilmerodach, 234
Exchange (the Royal), 193
Extortion, 106–7, 181–82, 188, 193, 194
Ezekiah. *See* Hezekiah
Ezekiel, 255, 270
Ezra, 216

Fabius Maximus, 223
Faith: aids to, 102, 187, 103, 202, 226, 262–63; Christ's teaching on, 141, 260; eye of, 165; goal of, 133, 175; mysteries of, 261; related to reason, 212, 263; rule of, 157; sacraments as aids to, 157, 217; saving, 113, 119, 152, 203; (belief), 173
Family of Love, 192, 209
Fear, 204
Felix (governor), 123
Felton, Nicholas (bishop of Ely), 78, *80*
Fern, Henry (bishop of Chester), 244
Festus, 98
Fiery furnace, 99
First Cause: God the creator, 97, 168; (philos.) 119, 150, 177, 212, 221
Flood, 93, 98
Francis, St., life of, 71
Frankfurt [Frankeford], 229
Frederick Barbarossa (emperor), 225
Free will, 167–69
French History, the, 265
Fruardent (Feuardent), François, 265

Gad, 109
Gadarenes, 73
Garden. *See* Eden; Gethsemane
Garnet, Henry, 77
Garter, Order of, 250; ribbon of (blue), 269; St. George's Day service, 249
Gehazi, 188
Gehenna (Hell), 207, 209
General, a faithful. *See* Monk, George
Geneva (Bible). *See* Bible
Germanicus, 160, 267
Gesner, Conrad, 321
Gethsemane, Garden of: arrest in, 66, 161; Christ's agony in, 86, 91, 101, 141, 172; disciples in, 139
Gibeah, 254
Gibeon, 128, 174
Gibraltar, 213
Gideon [Gedeon], 99, 113, 222, 236
Gilead, Balm of, 210
Gloss (mediaeval, of Bible), 71, 125, 139, 142, 147, 149, 152, 174, 188, 190, 201
Gluttony (excess), 106, 108–81, 186, 205, 244
God: nature of, 149–50; attributes of: glory, 163–66, 203, 213–15; forgiveness, 186; grace, 94, 138, 159, 164, 165, 187, 215, 226; prevenient grace, 138, 202; justice, 234, 247–49; mercy: (theology of), 93–95, 98–99, 124, 169, 210; (examples of), 99, 104, 105, 112, 160, 196, 222, 247; saving mercy, 110, 189; contrasted with man's mercy, 148, 176, 195; power, 105, 117–18, 213, 221; God not author of sin, 92, 197–98, 199, 201; before Time, 122, 150, 156–57, 214; man's chief end, 152; no name for, 155–56; prescience, 199; will of God: revealed, 167–69; secret, 167–70, 169, 215, 260; instruments of, 109–10. *See also* First cause; Order, God of
Golgotha, 101
Goliath, 99, 236

Gomorrah, 107, 245
Good Friday, 79, 174
Gorgon, 99
Goths, 236
Greece, ancient, 109, 112, 268
Greek Church, 88, 103, 207, 211
Greek History, the, 193
Greeks (modern), 153, 230
Greenwood, John, 246
Gregory the Great, St., 225
Guarren, 265
Guise, Duke of, 265
Gunpowder Plot, 111

Habbakuk, 76
Hadradrimmon, Valley of, 109, 267
Haman. *See* Cromwell, Oliver
Hannibal, 223
Heaven: (astron.) 117, 176, 184–85; contrasted with the world, 129, 160–61, 169, 173–75, 209; hosts of, 165; nature of, 150; as resting place, 133–34
Hebrew language (scriptures in), 100, 108, 179, 211, 216, 268
Heckelburg (Norway), 207
Heckla (Iceland), 207
Hell, 92, 190, 207, 209–10; power of, 149
Henderson [Hinderson], Alexander, 270
Henrietta Maria (Charles I's queen), 232, 271
Henry IV (king of France), 271
Henry VI, King, 238
Henry VI (emperor), 225
Heraclitus, 246
Herod, King, 73, 105
Hezekiah [Ezekiah], 70, 77, 174, 263
Hiera (Vulcanean islands), 207
High Court of Justice, 239, 272, 273
Hippocrates, 109
Hippolitus, 154
Hiram, 221, 236
Hittites, 206
Holbe(i)n, Hans, 270
Holland, 271
Holofernes, 99
Holy Writ. *See* Scriptures
Homer, 77
House of Commons. *See* Commons, House of
Humours, the four, 201, 205
Hunters, 104
Hur, 139, 202
Hus, John, 171

Iconoclastes (John Milton), 271
Index Expurgatorius, 221
Innocent III (pope), 225
Isaac, 153
Isaiah [Esay], 255
Is(h)mael, 104, 153
Isis, 65
Isle of Wight, 270
Israel (Israelites): in Egypt, 101, 102, 112; exodus,

103, 203; in wilderness, 139, 142, 184; gathering manna, 66, 180, 182; rebelling against God, 93, 227, 239, 243; in Canaan, 254; clothing laws, 258; reverence for Tetragrammaton, 98, 157; kings, reason for, 228; kings of, chosen by God, 221, 236, 240, 274
Israel (Jacob), 153
Ithaca, 213
Ivan the Terrible. *See* Basiliwick, John

Jacob: in Egypt, 123, 178, 222; and Esau, 148; vision, 133; wrestling, 119, 139; deathbed, 250; Jacob's Well, 256. *See also* James I
Jael, 99
Jairus, 268
James, Duke of York, *250*
James I, [our late learned sovereign], 63, *71*, 135, 227, 228; as Jacob, 160, *228;* as Solomon, 109
Jane (saviour of women), 110
Jehoash, 230
Jehoiachin, 234, 246
Jehoida, 230
Jehudah, Rabbi, 217
Jepthah, daughter of, 188, 269
Jeraboam, 70, 154
Jeremiah [Jeremy], 219, 265, 267; Lamentations of Jeremiah, 265, 270
Jericho, 217
Jerusalem, 143, 161; Christ's entry into, 72; the prophet bewailing, 127; stoning prophets, 69; (met.) 69, 226; New Jerusalem, 166. *See also* Sion
Jesse, 236
Jesuits, 75, 157, 225; causing death of princes, 73, 74, 11, 159; Jesuit polemicists, 76, 221, 227
Jesus Christ: nativity, 73, 103; flight into Egypt, 73, 105; circumcision, 101, 155; tempted by Devil, 161, 201; Sermon on Mount, 179; calming storm, 196, 204; centurion's servant, 250; cleansing leper, 88; feeding the multitude, 179; meets madman among the tombs, 74, 235 (met.); Samaritan woman, 256; woman taken in adultery, 88; woman and precious ointment, 265; entry into Jerusalem, 72; money-changers in the Temple, 193; washing disciples' feet, 72; agony in the Garden, *see* Gethsemane; arrest and trial, 76, 161, 272-73; scourging and crowning with thorns, 101, 105, 110; to women of Jerusalem, 273; crucifixion (passion), 68, 73, 101-2, 110, 127, 172, 174; pardon to dying thief, 124, 183, 196, 249; side-piercing 101, 105; wounds, 101; wounded afresh by sins, 68, 91, 189; watch over sepulchre, 76; resurrection 102, 151; as king, 227; second Adam, 161; parables told by: foolish virgins, 133, 165; (met.) 143, 210; labourers in vineyard, 125; Pharisee and publican, 139, 187; rich man and barns, 123, 183; strong man armed, 67, 143; talents, 189
Jews: persecution of Christ, 73, 74, 105, 117, 118, 164, 272; still expecting kingdom, 160; at Crucifixion, 101; at Resurrection, 102; use of amen, 217; funeral music, 268; ritual cleanliness (burials), 246

Jezebel, 148, 154, 246, 248
Job, 70, 97, 199-200
John, St. (apostle), 80, 151
John Baptist, 140, 165, 166
John XXII (pope), 225
John XXIII (antipope), 154
Jonah [Jonas], 122, 142, 204
Jonathan, 99, 260
Jordan, river, 144; (met.) 142, 160
Joseph, 71, 222, 236
Joshua, 174, 179
Josiah, 109, 237, 240, 265, 270. *See also* Charles I
Jotham, parable by, 111, 225, 240
Judah, 251; (land), 70, 105, 221, 265, 266
Judas, 105, 154
Judas Maccabaeus, 99, 208
Judith, 99
Julian the Apostate (emperor), 259
Julius Caesar, 202, 221, 223, 226
Julius II (pope), 162
Junius Brutus, 239
Jupiter, 224
Justification: by faith, 119; by works [merit], 169, 188, 201
Justin Martyr, 168

Kedar, tents of, 183
Kedron (Cedron), brook, 91
Kellison, Matthew, 77
King, Bishop John (father), 63, 75-81, 135; death, 78-81; tomb, 80; will, 77
King, John (brother), 79, 82
King, Philip (uncle), 79 (marg.)
Kingship, 71, 161-63, 219-22, 226-28; kings God's deputies, 161, 212, 219; qualities of ruler, 236-37; right of inheritance, 237-38
King's Waste, 107
Knox, John, 227, 239, 265
Korah, 247
Koran. *See* Alcoran

Lacedemonia, 193, 230, 266
Lake, Arthur, Bishop of Bath and Wells, *78*
Lambert's rising. *See* Rising
Lamech, 104
Language, 84-86
Laodicea, church of, 177
Last day (day of judgment): Christ's coming at, 165-66; punishment on, 95, 98, 204, 205-9; rewards of, 113-14, 133-34; trumpet at, 162
Lateran Council. *See* Councils of the Church
Latins. *See* Roman Catholic Church
Laud, William, Archbishop of Canterbury [martyred], 250; as Jehoida, 230
Law, English, 87, 148, 186, 189, 194, 196, 230; during civil wars, 237, 240, 269, 272
Lazarus, 106, 267
Legend, the Golden, 77, 164
Legion, 74, 235
Leo X (pope), 73

Levellers, 268
Leviathan, 163
Levites: (Old Testament), 259, 263; (met.) 259
Lewis. *See* Louis
Liberius (pope), 73
Licurgus, 193
Light, 218, 243
Lipara, 207
Littestar, Geoffrey, 265
Liturgy, our. *See* Common Prayer, Book of
Locris, 109
Logic (logicians), 70, 191–92, 261–62
London, City of [this our city], 65, 78, 171–72, 193, 228, 235; charity in, 106–7; City guilds, 67; civil wars in, 239, 274; extortion in, 106–7; plague in, 95, 108, 111–13
Lord Protector (Somerset), 229
Lord's Prayer: nature of, 143–45, 152, 185, 211; addressed to whole Trinity, 147; compared to a letter, 145–46, 210; [masterpiece of prayer], 119, 143; not for reprobates, 148, 193
Loretto, Our Lady of, 77, 151
Lot, 148, 182
Louis, St., 111
Lucifer, 154, 194; fall of, 93
Lucius (king of Britain), 225
Ludovicus Cortusius Patavinus, 266
Luke, St. (apostle), 180, 189, 211
Lust, 67, 106, 190, 201, 205
Luther, Martin, 75, 76, 119, 139, 171

Mahomet, 230
Man (generic): as created, 71, 120, 175, 226; character of, 83, 116–17, 118, 129, 190–91, 196; disobedience, 116; Fall of, 100, 104, 115–16, 197–98; human relationships, 191–92; made in God's image, 97, 173, 195, 203, 212, 256; microcosm of universe, 70, 169; transitoriness, 123, 130; unwilling charity, 175, 182; man's will, 164, 167–69, 172, 174. *See also* Adam
Manes, 109, 192
Manlius Octavius, 223
Manna, 66, 179
Marcus Aurelius (emperor), 221
Marius (emperor), 161
Martin, Sir Henry, 79 (marg.)
Martyrs, 74–75
Mary Magdalene, St., 119, 226–27, *265*
Mary of Guise, *265*
Masters and servants, 71
Matthew, St. (apostle), 180, 189
Maundy Thursday, 174
Mauritius (emperor), 225
Maximinus (emperor), 112
Mazarin, Jules [Cardinal of France], 271
Mediterranean sea, 213
Megiddo, 267
Memory, 66–67, 69, 117–18, 122
Menander, 259
Menelaus, 222

Mercury, 82; (planet) 91; (met.), 76
Mercy Seat, 95, 98
Meroz, 239
Messor, 109
Methusaleh, 154
Milan [Millain], 259. *See also* Councils of the Church
Milton, John, *271*
Minerva, 143
Minutius Rufus, 223
Monarchy, 223–24, 228, 236; first monarchies, 222; universal monarchy, 162–63, 212–13, 224
Monk, George [faithful General], 235
Morton, Thomas, Bishop of Coventry and Lichfield, *78, 80*
Moses: 67, 153, 247, 259; and Aaron, 139, 202, 225; and the exodus, 259; and the golden calf, 239; with God, 146, 158, 169, 173; on Mount Abarim, 69, 77, 165, 228, 244; Pentateuch, author of, 179; praying, 141
Music, 70, 141, 265
Mutability, 67, 123, 131, 169, 183, 212
Mystical interpretations of Scripture, 125, 179, 234. *See also* Types, Old Testament

Naaman, 144
Nabal, 182
Naboth, 148, 248
Names, 153–55; God's names, 155–57; Puritan names, 155
Nathan, 94, 238
Nature: external, 70, 109, 176, 188, 197; human, 120, 175, 204, 226; (person.), 177, 180, 181, 236
Navy, Royal, 230
Nebo, Mount, 244. *See also* Abarim
Nebuchadnezzar, 129, 224, 226, 233
Necho (pharoah), 265, 267
Neptune, 224
Newcastle, 270
Nicodemus, 125
Nile, river [Nilus], 65, 76, 109, 145, 267
Nimrod, 104
Nineveh, 93
Noah, 130, 188
North[erne] Sea, 111
Norwich, 265
Norimberg (Nuremburg), 88
Nunneries, 130

Octavius. *See* Augustus
Oecolampadius, 75
Olympia (queen), 271
Olympus, mount, 72
Omer (measure), 180
Omer, St. (Normandy), 76
Oracle, Pythian, 97
Order: in creation, 70, 213; God of, 146, 178, 223; in the heavens, 223; in religion, 146, 178, 239, 258; at resurrection, 113, 177
Ordination, 255–56
Origen, 207, 209, 259

Ovid, 77
Oxford, university of, 250

Paedonomus, 250
Palestine, 161
Pallas, 269
Pandects, 194
Papacy, 225
Papists. *See* Roman Catholic Church
Parables. *See* Jesus Christ
Parisians, 265
Parliament, 71; Rump, 235. *See also* Commons, House of; Peers
Parsons, Robert, 76, 77
Passover, 95; Paschal Lamb, 112
Patroclus, 77
Paul, St., 77, 150; and Apollos, 121, 259; conversion of, 125; and Felix, 123; and Festus, 98; at Ephesus, 208; in the Epistles, 255, 252, 255; as Saul, 73, 153
Peers (House of Lords), 269–70
Pelagius, Pelagians, 138, 170, 171, 202
Pentateuch, 179
Pentecost, 255, 256
People, power of, 221, 222, 225, 238–40
Pericles, 196
Persecution, 74–75, 248
Perseus, 99
Persia, 109, 222; emperor of, 224; laws of, 167; Persians, 69
Pesthouse, 106
Pestilence. *See* Plague
Peter, St. (apostle), 76, 80, 107, 152, 255, 257
Peter Abelard (Abailardus), 170
Peter Martyr, 229
Petionius, 208
Phaeton, 129
Pharoah, 101, 103. *See also* Necho
Philip of Macedon, 271; Philip's boy, 241
Philistines, 67
Philoromus Gaelata, 241
Philosophy (philosophers), 109, 206, 257, 259
Phydias, 143
Pilate, Pontius, 272–73
Pilgrimage, 161, 208
Pisgah, mount, 228. *See also* Abarim
Plague, 108, 109–10, 111–13, 191
Planets, 144, 174, 223; influence of, 91–92, 109, 167
Plato, 115
Pleiades, 97, 144
Pliny, 153
Polynises, 148
Pompey, 67
Pontificians [Pontificials], 155, 208, 221. *See also* Roman Catholic Church
Pope: indulgences [remitting sins], 94, 193, 194, 208; infallibility, 254; making kings, 162, 221, 238; pride of place, 72–73, 93, 162, 224–25. *See also* Bishop of Rome
Popery, puritan fear of, 155, 229, 239, 247. *See* Roman Catholic Church

Porphyry, 153, 259
Practical Christianity, 68–69, 83, 142, 174, 262–63
Prayer: advice on, 141–43; *amen*, use of, 217; Christ's example, 137; definitions of, 133, 139–40; extempore, 140–41, 147; intercession, 149, 204; meditation, 150–51; necessity of, 137–39, 158–59, 171, 182–83, 203, 210, 245; not sufficient alone, 166, 177; of thanksgiving, 138, 160; unanswered, 247. *See also* Lord's Prayer
Preaching [God's Word]: printed sermons, 82; as propaganda, 159, 229–30, 239, 260–261, 263–65, 274; preacher as example, 69; unlearned preachers, 65–66, 147, 258–59; value of, 65, 179, 181, 256–63
Presbytery [Presbyterianism], 225
Priamus, 154
Priene, 172
Priests, role of, 93, 216, 217, 263. *See also* Confession; Ordination
Primitive Church, 65, 73, 90, 216, 217
Prince of Darkness, 190
Prometheus, 209
Protestant religion, 80, 174, 263, 271, 275
Prudentius, 208
Purgatory, 94, 206–8
Purim, feast of, 240
Pythagoras, 96

Rabbis [Rabbines], 156, 217
Rabshakeh, 229
Reason: intellect (as opposed to man's nature), 104, 120, 128, 164, 174, 211; contrasted with faith, 195, 208, 212, 256
Rebecca, 256
Red Sea, crossing of, 99; (met.) 91, 249
Redemption [salvation], 68, 100–101, 110–11, 113, 147, 160, 161, 191
Reformation, the, 229
Regicides, *273*
Rehaboam, 122
R(h)adamanth. *See* Bradshaw, John
Rhemists, 180
Rialto, 193
Riblah, 233
Richard II, 238
Richard III, 236
Riches (wealth), 106, 186, 190
Richmond (Surrey), 251
Rising, (Lambert's), *235, 239*
Roche, St., 111
Roman Catholic Church: equivocation, 77, 82; lack of charity, 174, 194; lucrative or superstitious practices criticised, 69, 110–11, 151, 155, 208–9; proselytising, 75, 80–81; theology criticised, 87–89, 90, 167, 169, 188, 189–90, 216, 217–18. *See also* Pope; Popery
Rome, ancient, 74, 109, 110–11, 155, 193; civil wars, 263; funeral music, 268; persecutions, 248; Roman Empire, 224; rulers of, 221, 223, 241, 246; tribunals, 230
Romulus, 155

Sacraments. *See* Baptism; Communion, Holy
Sacrilege, 107
St. Paul's cathedral (London), *230*
Saints: invocation of, 110–11, 151, 155; persecution of, 74–75, 244–45; relics of, 260; shrines of, 151, 157; value to Church, 157, 244–46, 247
Salisbury (Wilts), 250, 251
Salmander, 224
Salomon. *See* Solomon
Salvation. *See* Redemption
Samaria, 72, 203; Samaritan view of dead, 246; Samaritan woman, 256
Samson, 67, 102
Samuel, 236, 240, 267, 274
Saracens, 236
Satan. *See* Devil
Saturn (planet), 91
Saul (king of Israel), 125, 236, 236, 267, 272; armour, 69
Saul. *See* Paul, St.
Saunders, Nicholas, 77
Scander Beg. *See* Castriot, George
Schoolmen: opinions cited, 122, 156, 169, 179, 185, 198, 217; criticised, 163, 187, 200
Scottish Rebellion (1568), 265
Scriptures [Holy Writ]: contradictory, 178, 198; distortion of, 208, 224, 225, 227, 239; not enough alone, 174; Roman Catholic attitude to, 164; value of, 88, 147, 164, 223, 259
Scythians, 224; ambassador, 244
Seal, the Great, 217
Sebastian, St., 111
Seneca [wise heathen], 172
Separatists, 130, 140
Sepulchre, Holy (Jerusalem), 151, 161
Seraiah (high priest), 233
Sergius II (pope), 154; Sergius IV (pope), 73
Serpent. *See* Devil
Seven, perfection of, 144
Severus (emperor), 194, 221
Severus Sulpitius, 259
Shiloh, 251
Simon Magus, 271
Sin: definitions of, 86–87, 90–91, 129, 262; God's forgiveness for, 93–95, 100, 187; mortal, 74, 86–87, 90–92, 104, 105, 113, 124, 204, 209; original, 133, 167, *187;* responsibility for, 197–98; traditional deadly sins, 105–6, 129, 167, 205; (person.) 205, 243; venial, 90–91, 189–90, 208
Sion, 143, 226, 247. *See also* Jerusalem
Sisera, 99
Slander, 108
Smictymnus (Smectymnuus), 265
Socrates, 153, 236
Sodom, 93, 109, 146, 245
Solomon: building the Temple, 120, 143, 152; glory of, 214; regal authority of, 225; wisdom of, 152, 154, 178, 236
Solon, 193, 266
Solynan (Suliman, emperor of Turkey), 224

Sosias, 82
Soul, the, 116, 119, 168, 175, 178; after death, 78, 125, 129, 132; food of, 179
Spain, King of, 71, 72, 212, 224
Spenser, Bishop Henry de, 265
Spital, 106
Stapleton, Thomas, 195
Stephen, St., 73, 80, 154, 246
Stoics, 266
Straw, Jack, 265
Susannah, 83
Swearing. *See* Blasphemy
Symonides, 268
Synophanes, 269
Syrac(h), son of (the Preacher), 221, 257, 269
Syria: king of, 73; Syrians, 232
Syricius (pope), 73

Tacitus, 213
Tartarus, 207
Telemachus, 80
Temple, the (Jerusalem): built by Solomon, 120, 143; dedication of, 152; in New Testament, 230; (met.) 158; rebuilding, 234, 265
Tempter. *See* Devil
Tetragrammaton, 98, 157
Thebans, 271
Themistocles, 116
Theophilus Alexandrinus, 254
Theophrastus, 262
Theotista, 225
Thessalonica, 238
Thiatira, church of, 106
Thomas, St. (apostle), 119
Three Conversions, The, 77
Tiberius (emperor), 221, 246
Tidal, 224
Tierra del Fuego, 207
Time: obscures memory, 67; speed at which, passes, 123–24, 129, 165, 183–84. *See also* God
Timothy, 246, 252
Tintarit (Tintoretto), 270
Tithes, 107
Titus (bishop of Crete), 252, 254, 262
Titus (emperor), 236, 237
Touching for the King's Evil, 273
Trallenses, 254
Trinity, the, 100, 116, 147, 149, 156; human faculties as image of, 156
Troglodytes, 153
Trojan horse, 105
Tuke, Lemuel, 265
Turks, 148, 230; Turkish emperor, 224; Turkish history, 269
Turnus, 236
Tyler, Wat, 265
Types, Old Testament, 100, 130, 226, 234. *See also* Mystical interpretations of Scripture
Tyre, daughters of, 131

Ulpian, 194
Ulysses, *80*, 213
Universe. *See* Order
Uriah, 94
Uxbridge, treaty of, 268
Uzzah, 169

Valentine, St., 111
Venice, 225; nice Venetian, the (courtesan), 258
Venus (planet), 91
Vespasian (emperor), 161
Vigilantius, 246
Virgin Mary, Blessed, 100, 103, 211
Vulcanean islands, 207

Westminster School, 250
Wiclif, John, 171

Winchester (Hants), 250, 251
Windsor, 249
Woman in the wilderness, 130
Women preachers, 65
Worcester, battle of, 237
World. *See* Earth

York, 235
Youth, 120–21, 122, 205

Zadok (high priest), 225
Zedekiah, 78, 234, 235
Zeilan (Asia), 269
Zenobia (queen), 271
Zerubbabel, 233, 241
Ziph, wilderness of, 125
Zodiac, 77; (met.) 174, 229

General Index

Numbers in parentheses indicate which note within a grouping of notes is being referenced.

Abbot, Archbishop George, 17, 33, 279 n.78(4)
Acts (parliamentary): of Oblivion, 293 n.234(3); of Uniformity, 28
Addison, Launcelot, 55 n.4
Albury (Surrey), 16, 23
All Souls' College, Oxford, 26
Ambrose, St.: King's references to, 44, 52
Anabaptists, 35
Andrewes, Bishop Lancelot, 32, 39, 57 n.87; sermon style, 9, 42, 45, 47
Anne of Denmark, Queen: gift to Bishop John King, 277 n.63
Aristotle: *De Anima*, 277 n.66–67; "just ruler," 27, 29
Armada, 19, 50
Arminians (Arminianism), 21, 37, 57 n.82; common English characteristics, 33–34, 35, 36, 38–39
Articles of religion, Thirty-nine, 56 n.71
Arundel, Thomas Howard, Earl of, 23
Atterbury, Bishop Francis, 29
Aubrey, John: *Brief Lives*, 53 n.82
Augustine, St.: King's references to, 52
Aungier, George, 16

Bacon, Francis, 46
Baillie, Robert, 25
Baptism. *See* Sacraments
Barrow, Bishop Isaac, 54 n.14
Baxter, Richard, 295 n.239(7)
Bede, the Venerable: *Ecclesiastical History*, 278 n.73(2)
Berkeley, Anne. *See* King, Anne (wife)
Berman, Ronald: *Henry King*, 15, 21, 41, 47
Bernard, Nicholas: funeral sermon for Ussher, 27, 29, 56 n.59
Beza, Theodore (Junius Brutus): *Vindiciae*, 21
Bible: Apocrypha, 36; Chaldee paraphrase, 51; commentators on, 51; mystical interpretation of, 42–43, 48; the Psalms, 51; in relation to the sacraments, 39–40; translations of: Authorised Version, 29, 46, 50; Douai-Rhemist, 40, 46, 51; English, 50; Geneva, 50, 52; polyglot bibles, 25, 51; Septuagint, 51; untraced Latin version, 51; Vulgate, 51
Bishops: in civil wars and interregnum, 22, 23, 31, 33, 54 n.27; guardians of the faith, 38; order of, 28, 37–38; pastoral role, 28, 38; sequestered, 23
Blakesware (Herts), 23
Blount, Henry: *Voyage into the Levant*, 47
Bodleian Library, Oxford: King's poems in, 56 n.54; King's sermons in, 11; other manuscripts in: Fell papers, 15, 57 n.99; Walker papers, 15
Bosher, R. S.: *Restoration Settlement*, 23, 24, 26, 54 n.26
Bradshaw, John, 300 n.272(6)
Braganza, Catherine of, 56 n.53, 295 n.240(7)
Bramhall, Bishop John, 28
Bridgewater, John, Earl of, 279 n.81
Brown, Robert, 45
Browne, Thomas, 9, 18, 50, 53, 54 n.12, 57 n.87
Brownists, 35, 286 n.145
Brownrigg, Bishop Ralph, 24, 31, 36, 40, 57 n.78
Buchanan, George: *De iure Regni apud Scotos*, 21, 24, 50
Burleigh, Robert: Proclamation (1591), 278 n.76(5)
Burton, Edward, 25, 55 n.54
Burton, Robert, 50, 53, 278 n.81
Bush, Douglas: *Oxford History of English Literature*, 41
Bysshe, Edward, 54 n.22

Calamy, Edward, 22, 298 n.265(4)
Calvin, John, 34, 35, 36
Calvinism (Calvinists): antipapist, 35, 36; concepts of: godly pastor: 38; godly prince, 22; moderate, 10, 21, 31, 33, 35, 39; preaching, 28, 42, 43; strict, 32, 33, 34, 38, 39
Cambridge Platonists, 32
Canons. *See* Laudian canons
Carlisle, Lucy, Countess of, 300 n.274(5)
Cawley, John 24
Cawley, William (father of John, regicide), 23, 24
Ceremonies, church, 36–37
Challoner, Francis, 29
Chamberlain, John: *Letters*, 16, 277 n.67(4), 278 n.75(5)
Charles I, 26; Spanish Expedition, 19, 287 n.160(2); marriage, 18; and Laudian canons, 21; and army, 23; and Parliament, 21–22; appointment of bishops, 33; imprisonment, 30; trial, 30; execution, **106 n.59; burial, 23–24; annual commemoration of, 29; character, 22, 27, 29; as type of Josiah, 29;** of Christ, 30, *See also Eikon Basilike*
Charles II: abroad, 24–25, 26, 27; character, 27, 28, 30; ecclesiastical policy, 25–26; restoration, 27; son by Lucy Walters, 56 n.53
Chichester: bishop's palace, 23; cathedral, 31; cathedral library, 10, 20, 23, 24, 31; diocese, 25, 28, 29, 30, 55 n.45; war and siege, 14, 21, 23

General Index

Chillingworth, William: *Religion of Protestants*, 39
Cholmondley, Lady Katherine, 56 n.54
Christ Church, Oxford, 15, 27, 34
Chrysostom, St. John, 44, 52
Church of England: central position in, 10, 18, 31–32, 36, 38, 40; before civil wars, 21, 32; in Interregnum, 24, 25, 38, 297 n.263(2); at Restoration, 26, 28; church government matters, 28, 39; claim to be catholic and apostolic, 24, 33, 34, 35, 38; confession in, 18, 35, 39; joint ordinations, 28; as reformed, 22, 35, 52; services of, 19
Civil war and Interregnum period: research on, 9, 22, 23, 25, 54 nn. 26 and 27
Clarendon, Edward Hyde, Earl of, 22, 25, 26
Clergy: role of, 28–29, 38; in Interregnum, 22, 23, 24, 25, 54 n.33
Commonplace books: King's own, 18, 26, 27, 46; commonplace verse miscellanies, 16, 49, 53
Common Prayer, Book of: Edward VI's, Reformers on, 22, 36; Elizabeth's I's, 293 n.229(4); Charles I's, 293 n.229(7); apostolicity of, 39; parliamentary Committee to examine, 293 n.229(8); confession in, 35; moderate clergy's devotion to, 36; ordination in, 15, 24, 28, 38; psalms in, 51; allusions to, 289 n.188, 297 n.255
Conant, Malachy, 29
Confession and absolution. *See* Church of England; Common Prayer, Book of; King, Henry; Roman Catholic Church
Convocation (of clergy), 21, 28, 54 n.24; ordering Restoration services, 295 n.240(4)
Cosin, Bishop John, 33, 35, 40
Councils of the Church, 52
Court, the. *See* Whitehall
Coverdale, Bishop Matthew: translation of Psalms, 51
Crofts, James, 56 n.53
Cromwell, Oliver, 24, 30, 38, 56 n.59, 294 nn.234(5) and 235
Cross, Claire, 54 n.33
Crum, Margaret: *Poems of Henry King*, 10, 20, 54 n.29, 56 n.58

Danaus, king of Argos, 277 n.66(2)
Davies, Horton: *Like Angels*, 12 n.5, 25, 41, 50, 52, 57 n.74
De Dominis, Bishop Marco Antonio, 35, 37, 50
Dillingham, William, 25
Divine Right of Kings, 21, 26–27, 29, 37
Doctrines of the Church: election and reprobation, 32, 33–34; freewill and predestination, 33, 34; justification, 33–34; original sin and the fall of man, 33, 34; prevenient grace, 32, 33, 34; redemption, 33
Donne, John: legal training, 15; Egerton's secretary, 48; incorporated at Oxford, 48; ordination by Bishop John King, 15, 48; benefices: Sevenoaks (Kent), 48; St. Dunstan's in the West (London), 19, 56 n.54; Dean of St. Paul's, 16, 38, 46, 52, 57 n.76, 58 n.114; prebendal psalms, 58 n.114; friendships: with Henry King, 15, 17, 48; with George Herbert, **17, 53; death, 20; will,** 20
—books owned by, 10, 20, 24, 47, 48, 50; marginal markings in, 20; reading compared with King's, 51–53
—poems: printing of, 20; quoted: *Death be not proud*, 283 n.113; *A Nocturnall*, 284 n.124(2), 286 n.150; *The Anniversarie*, 286 n.143(2); *Satire 3*, 297 n.260
—sermons: manuscripts of, 16, 48; physical characteristics of, 17, 42, 44; preaching: style compared with King's, 9, 11 n.1, 40–41, 42, 43, 45, 47, 48, 49, 50, 284 n.125(4); length, 54 n.14; delivery, 44; sources compared, 17–18, 32, 51–52, 53, 54 n.14; lack of Greek, 58 n.115; themes shared with King: confession 17–18; monarchy 37, 57 n.81; order 37; repentance, 18, 37; Roman Catholic Church 17–18, 35
—sermons (individual works): Spital sermon, (*Sermons* 4, no. 3): 54 n.14; on the plague, 15 Jan. 1626 (*Sermons*, 6.212): 19; on 32nd psalm (*Sermons*, 9.216–315); 17–18, 41, 49, 280–81; Valediction (*Sermons*, 2.235–49): 16, 18, 48–50, 278 nn. 68 and **69(5), 289 nn.** 178 and **189(3), 283–84;** *1.86:* 45; *2.72:* 283 n. *117(3); 2.154:* 290 n.196(2); *6.228:* 286 n.148(2); *7.214:* 283 n.120(3); *7.305:* 54 n.12; *8.119:* 37; *8.191:* 43; *9.152:* 36; *XXVI sermons*, 48; *LXXX sermons*, 49; *Sapientia Clamans*, 48
—works, other: *Devotions upon Emergent Occasions*, 282 n.105(3): *Essayes in Divinity*, 50, 283 nn. 117(5) and 119(3), 286 nn. 144(2) and 150, 287 n.153(4), 289 n.184(2), 292 n.226
Donne, John, the younger, 49
Dorset, Richard Sackville, third earl of, 23, 27, 48
Dort, Synod of, 33
Douai (Normandy), 16
Downes, John, 23
Drama, contemporary English texts of, 44, 53
Duncombe, George (cousin), 23, 53 n.2, 55 n.49
Duncon, Eleazor, 24, 55 n.49
Duppa, Bishop Brian, 23, 24–25, 26, 27, 28, 30; correspondence, 54 n.33, 55 n.42; King's funeral sermon for, 27–28; Restoration Prayer Book services, 295 n.240(4); sermons, 297 n.251(2)
Dutton, Anne. *See* King, Anne (sis.)

Earle, Bishop John, 26, 56 n.61
Egerton, Sir Thomas, 48
Eikon Basilike (Charles I), 30, 56 n.61
Eliot, T. S., 10
Emblems, 291 n.205(2), 295 n.242
English Protestant's Plea, The, 16
Evelyn, John: *Diary*, 22, 30

Falkland, Lucius Carey, Viscount, 26
Family of Love, 35
Fathers of the early Church, 20, 29, 31, 45, 49, 51–52
Felton, Bishop Nicholas, 33
Frank, Mark, 32, 40, 41, 57 n.87
Frewen, Archbishop Accepted, 24, 25, 26, 55 n.48

Fuller, Thomas, 9, 18; *Church History,* 31
Fulman, William: manuscripts of, 15
Funeral sermons, 27, 56 n.54

Gardner, Dame Helen, 20
Gauden, Bishop John, 28, 30, 56 n.61
Gesner, Conrad, 43
Glanvill, Bishop Joseph, 46
Gloucester, Richard, Duke of, 29, 56 n.53
God: attributes of: forgiveness, 18; glory, 20, 32, 43, 47; mercy, 32, 33, 34; will of, 20
Great Tew group, 26
Green, I. M.: *Re-establishment,* 25, 26, 54 n.28, 55 n.69
Grindal, Archbishop, 33
Guildford, Surrey 23
Gunpowder Plot, 16, 19

Hacket, Bishop John, 40
Hales, John, 23, 31, 32, 33, 54 n.33, 56 n.69
Hall, Bishop Joseph: moderate Calvinist, 31, 32, 34; **at Synod of Dort, 33; Bishop of Exeter, 19; out of favour, 20; in Interregnum, 24**
—sermons: preaching style, 9, 42, 45, 47; printed sermons, 27; punctuation, use of, 44; sources used, 51, 52; style compared with King's, 10, 19, 20, 42, 45, 47; themes shared with King: monarchy, 37; order, 37; preachers, 36; the Roman Catholic Church, 35; Presbyterians, 104 n.49; views on Court sermons, 101 n.27
—works: *Art of Divine Meditation,* 20, 32; *Episcopacy by Divine Right,* 21; *An Holy Panegyric,* 36, 37, 282 n.111, 292 n.225(3); *The Impress,* 290 n.191(4); *The Remedy,* 283 n.117(5); *The Revelation Unrevealed,* 298 n.265(5); other sermons: on the plague, 19, 280 n.90, 281 n.100–101, 285 n.131(2), 286 n.143(4)
Hamlet. See Shakespeare
Hammond, Henry, 25, 26, 39, 54 n.33, 55 n.48, 58 n.116
Handkerchief for Loyal Mourners, A, 299 n.272(2)
Hannah, John, 15
Hanoverian succession, 16, 27
Henrietta Maria, Queen, 18, 299 n.271(3) and (4)
Henry V, Henry VIII. See Shakespeare
Herbert, George, 11 n.4, 17, 31, 42; poems, 50, 53; quoted: *Death,* 282 n.103; *Prayer,* 285 n.139; *Redemption,* 287 n.161(3)
Herringman, Henry, 55, 56 n.51
High Commission, Court of, 20
Hitcham (Bucks), 23
Holinshed, Raphael: *Chronicle,* 51
Holt, Elizabeth. See King, Elizabeth (sis.)
Hooker, Richard: *Of Ecclesiastical Polity:* influence on King, 10, 17–18, 49, 52; shared themes: monarchy, 21, 27, order, 37; style compared, 46; friend of Henry King's father, 56 n.61; references, 294 n.237(3), 280–81
Hubert, Dorothy. See King, Dorothy (sis.)
Huguenots, 21

Hutton, Ronald: *Restoration,* 54 n.26
Hyde, Edward. See Clarendon, Earl of

Iconoclastes (John Milton), 30
Independants, 29
Inns of Court, 16
Interregnum, research on, 22, 54 nn. 26 and 27
Intruded ministers, 28, 29
Isham, Sir Justinian, 25, 55 n.42, 297 n.252(3)

James I: at Christ Church play, 34; first speech to Parliament, 22; injunctions to preachers (1622), 21; instructs King to vindicate father, 16; death, 19; *Meditation upon the Lord's Prayer,* 135, 285 n.131(2), 285–91
Jerome, St., 52
Jesuits, 35
Jonson, Ben, 58 n.121; elegies for, 27, 50; plays: *Alchemist,* 289 n.180(2), 290 n.192(2); *Volpone,* 53, 282 n.107(7), 285 n.129(3), 297 n.258(2); *Works* 113 n.127
Junius Brutus. See Beza, Theodore
Juxon, Archbishop William: London articles, 37–38; in office, 26, 28, 39, 57 n.82

Keckermann, Bartholomew: *Rhetoricae Ecclesiae,* 42
Kellison, Matthew, 16
Kennett, Bishop White: *Register,* 18, 29, 40
Keynes, Sir Geoffrey: *Henry King, a Bibliography,* 11, 15; *John Donne, a Bibliography,* 20
King, Anne (sis.): m. Richard Dutton, 23
King, Anne (née Berkeley) (wife), 15; death, 17, 32
King, Dorothy (sis.): m. Richard Hubert, 23, 54 n.33
King, Elizabeth (sis.): m. Edward Holt, 16, 23; m. Sir John Millington, 55 n.45
King, Henry: early life and education, 15; father and Hooker, 58 n.118; ordination, 15, 48; marriage 15; admitted to Lincoln's Inn, 16; residentiary prebendary of St. Paul's, 16, 36, 51, 58 n.114; Archdeacon of Colchester, 15, 16, 57 n.82; wife's death, 17, 32; canon of Christ Church, 15; Royal chaplain, 15, 29; chaplain to Richard, Earl of Dorset, 27, 48; commercial and legal transactions, 23, 25; executor of Donne's will, 20; of uncle Philip King's will, 16; Court of High Commission, 20; Dean of Rochester, 21; Bishop of Chichester, 15, 22, 28, 30; at siege of Chichester, 23, 24; sequestration, 23; during wars and Interregnum, 23–25; "college" at Richings, 23; ordinations, 15, 24, 25, 29, 55 n.45; projected crossing to continent, 24; named as Archbishop of York, 25–26; relinquishes St. Paul's canonry, 25; appointing chaplains, 25; in diocese, 25; Visitations 28–29, 30, 32; in House of Lords, 55 n.50; at Court, 26; death, 30; memorial, 30–31; coat of arms 58 n.107; will, 23, 24, 33, 54 n.31, 277 n.63, 287 n.161; portraits 58 n.108; books owned by, 20, 24, 27, 47, 50, 51, 52, 91–94, 97: autograph notes in, 24, 51; reading compared with Donne's, 51–53; friendships with: Donne, 15, 17, 48; Brian Duppa, 24–25, 27;

correspondence with: Gilbert Sheldon, 10, 26, 29, 30; Izaak Walton, 17; love of music, 18, 20; "middleness," 10, 17–18, 31–32, 34, 35, 36, 37, 39–40; teaching on prayer, 20; reputation as preacher, 16, 18, 40–41; audiences, 18, 19, 21, 24, 49
—poems, 16, 20, 23, 58 n.121; manuscripts of, 10, 11, 16, 20, 44, 54 n.17, 59; first printed, 16, 56 n.51; **second edition, 29, 55 n.34, 298 n.265;** *On Death and a Prison,* **288 n.167(2);** *A Deepe Groane,* 278 n.74(2); *A Dirge,* 290 n.204; *An Elegy occasioned by sickness,* 290 n.204; elegies: *On King Charles I,* 24, 28, 29, 55 n.34, 296 nn.247(4) and 248, 298 nn.265(7) and 266, 299 n.270(4); *On Dr Donne,* 283 n.117(4); *On Richard, Earl of Dorset,* 296 n.251; *On Bishop John King,* 17; *On Sir Charles Lucas & Sir George Lisle,* 29, 55 n.34, 295 n.239(5), 297 n.265; *Epigrams,* 53; *An Exequy* 17, 32, 284, 288 n.173, 292 n.228, 295 n.244(2); *Upon the King's Happy Return,* 277 n.63(3); *Madam Gabrina,* 283 n.116; *Silence,* 283 n.119(2); *A Salutation of His Majesty's Ship The Sovereign,* 293 n.230(5); *To Henry Blount,* 47; *To His Friends at Christ Church,* 34; *To George Sandys,* 286 n.147(2); *The Woes of Esay* 39, 282 n.105(3), 289 nn.181 and 190(2)
—*Psalms,* translation of, 25, 55 n.40
—*Sermons:* printing of, 19, 29, 43–44; length of, 18, 27, 43, 44, 57 n.99; structure 41–44; physical characteristics, 11, 59; marginal references, 17, 22, 24, 31, 42, 43, 44, 49, 60; additions for publication, 43, editions of, 16; unprinted sermons, 16, 21, 27, 29, 30, 40; sermon manuscripts, 26, 78–79
—*Sermons* (individual works): *1621,* 16–17, 19, 36, 37, 38, 39, 43; *Act,* 17–18, 36, 38, 40, 49; *Spital,* 18–19, 27, 34, 37, 39, 40; *Lent 1,* 17, 18, 48–49; *Lent 2,* 17, 18; *1640,* 21–22, 35, 36, 37, 50; *1661,* 26–27, 35, 36, 37, 56 n.53; second edition, 16, 27; *Duppa* 18, 23, 24–25, 27–28, 36, 38, 40, 50; *Visitation,* 28–29, 36, 38, 46; *Commemoration,* 23, 28, 29–30, 107 n.65
—*Exposition upon the Lord's Prayer,* 31–40; other references, 9, 16, 17, 19–20, 25, 31, 33, 40, 51, 53, 44; second edition, 16, 20, 44
—recurrent themes: adversity, 17, 18, 20; Book of Creatures, 18, 47; extempore prayer, 36; extortion, 19, 23; extremes of opinion, 19, 25, 32, 36, 46; memory, 17, 48, 49; mercy of God, 32; mutability, 17, 18; order (hierarchy), 17, 21, 37, 38; resurrection and after-life, 17, 32; sin, repentance and forgiveness, 18, 20; swearing and excess, 34; youth and age, 18. *See below,* views on
—sources, 17, 44, 50–53; biblical, 20, 22, 43, 46, 50–51; biblical commentators, 20, 42, 51–52; Fathers, 20, 31, 41, 44, 45, 48, 52; Schoolmen, 20, 52; unpuritan, 36; Catholic theologians, 52; Protestant reformers, 35, 52; classical writers, 36, 43, 44, 46, 52; classical legend, 19, 43; English writers, 53
—style, 9–10, 16, 17, 18, 19–20, 22, 27, 28–30, 44–48; use of "characters," proverbs and emblems, 46; perorations, 18, 31, 34, 43; rhetorical devices, 18, 43, 45–46; use of commonplace book (set themes), 18, 20, 26, 27, 46; vocabulary, 44–45; Greek and Latin quotations, 18, 29, 29, 44, 45, 51, 59; use of Hebrew, 51; use of Bible, 19, 20, 21, 22, 43, 46; use of Spanish, 278 n.70(3); imagery, 19, 27, 40, 47–48, 50; legal imagery, 16, 20, 47–48; metaphysical qualities (conceits), 19, 27, 41, 45, 47, 49; mystical interpretations, 42; moral interpretation, 43; typology, 43; style compared with: Donne's, 9, 40–41, 42, 43, 45, 47, 49, 50; with Hall's, 10, 19, 42, 45, 47; influence of father, 16, 31, 35
—views on: alchemy, 53; astrology, 53; bible's relation to sacraments, 39–40; biblical translation, 40, 46, 51; bishops, 38; Book of Common Prayer, 36; Church of England, 31–32, 35, 38; ceremonies, 36–37; church property, 39; confession, 17–18, 35, 36, 38–39; equality, 39; extempore prayer, 36; mathematics, 53; medicine, 53; monarchy, 21–22, 26–27, 37; ordination, 28, 38–39, 43; papacy, 16–17, 18, 35, 37; people, rule by the, 21; practical divinity, 31, 32, 34, 40; preaching 17, 28–29, 36, 38–39, 43, 46; priestly role, 28, 38; reason and faith, 32–33; sacraments: baptism, 36, Holy Communion, 39; science, 53. *See also* Doctrines of the Church; Jesuits; Monarchy; Papists; Popes; Puritans
King, Henry (2nd son), 16, 23
King, Bishop John (father): Bishop of London, 48; chaplain to Egerton, 48; Dean of Christ Church, Oxford and vice-chancellor, 48; ordains Donne, 15; Queen Anne's gift, 277 n.63; reported conversion, 16; illness and death, 17, 33; memorial, 30, 56 n.65, 296 n.247(3); will, 279 n.78(5); portrait, 58 n.107; as godly pastor, 38; influence on Henry, 16, 31, 35; marginal references, 50; sermon style, 42; strict calvinism, 30, 31, 33, 36; unpuritan sources, 36, 51; *Lectures upon Jonas,* 20; sermon for Archbishop Piers, 278 n.72, 291 n.206, 292 n.224
King, John (bro.), 15, 16, 17, 57 n.99, 58 n.108; translated father's epitaph, 296 n.247(3)
King, John (nephew), 23
King, John (son): bequest to Chichester cathedral library, 20, 24; seduction of Oughtred's daughter, 16, 23
King, Philip (bro.), 23, 25
King, Philip, the Auditor (uncle), 16, 48
King Lear. See Shakespeare
King's Cabinet Opened, The (1645), 299 n.271(2)
Knole (Kent), 48

Lake, Bishop Arthur, 33
Langley (Berks), 23, 54 n.33
Latitudinarians, 40
Laud, Archbishop William, 20–21, 31, 37, 39, 57 nn.82 and 99, 293 n.230(4)
Laudian canons, 21, 291 nn.219(4) and 221(3), 292 nn.222 and 226(2), 229(3)
Laudians, 26, 27, 39. *See also* Arminians
Lawrence, Dr., 23
Lectures upon Jonas. See King, Bishop John
Lewes (Sussex), 28
Lilburne, John, 229 n.269(1)

GENERAL INDEX

Lincoln's Inn, 16
Lisle, Sir George, 29
London, city of: commerce, 19; guild feasts, 277 n.67(2); Lord Mayor and Corporation, 18; musical and literary circles in, 20
Lords, House of. *See* Parliament
Lord's Prayer: commentators on, 20; omission of, 36

Mabbott, Gilbert: *A Perfect Narrative*, 30, 300 n.273
Macbeth. *See* Shakespeare
Maclure, Millar: *The Paul's Cross Sermons*, 16, 41
Magdalen College, Oxford, 26
Mariana, Juan, 21
Marlowe, Christopher: *Dr Faustus*, 289 n.189(3)
Marriott, Richard, 56 n.51
Marshall, Stephen, 294 n.239(3), 298 n.265(4)
Martyn, William, 57 n.78
Marvell, Andrew, 56 n.60; *On Cromwell's Return from Ireland*, 298 n.266, 299 n.270(6), 300 n.273(4)
Mason, Henry, 279 n.81(2)
Mason, Lawrence, 15
Mason, T. A.: *Serving God and Mammon*, 39, 57 n.82
Massingham, H. J., 40
Matthews, Archbishop Tobie, 37
Mediaeval church, 35, 39; commentators, 51
Medici, Cosimo de, 58 n.116
Millenary petition, 296 n.246(2)
Millington, Elizabeth. *See* King, Elizabeth
Milton, John, 30, 35, 53, 56 n.70; *Iconoclastes*, 30, 299 n.271 (8); *Paradise Lost*, 30
Mitchell, W. Frazer: *English Pulpit Oratory*, 10, 40–41, 48, 50, 57 n.93
Monarchy. *See* King, Henry; views on
Monk, General George, 294 n.235(3) and (8)
Montague, Bishop Richard, 54 n.29; *A New Gagg*, 33
Montaigne, Michel de: *Essais*, 18, 53
Moore, Giles, 28, 30
More and Cross: *Anglicanism*, 11, 31
Morley, Bishop George, 26; elegy on James I quoted, 292 n.226(2)
Morrill, John: *Reactions*, 33
Morton, Bishop Thomas, 33, 37, 50, 52, 58 n.119
Mountfort, John, 20, 23
Mystics, continental, 32

Neile, Bishop Richard, 31
Newick (East Sussex), 55 n.45
Nicholas, Edward, 25, 33, 55 n.45
North, Roger, 54 n.17
Northumberland, Algernon, tenth earl of, 23

Oakes, Sam, 29
Order. *See* King, Henry: views on
Ordination. *See* Common Prayer, Book of; King, Henry: views on
Oughtred, Elizabeth, 16, 32
Outghtred, William (father), 16, 23, 53 n.2
Overall, John, 39, 52
Overbury, Sir Thomas: *Character of a Wife*, 53
Oxford, University of: answers to the Millenary petition, 296 n.246(2); Charles I and Parliament at, 18; melting down of college plate, 26; sermons printed at, 49; statutes, 15; University Church of St. Mary the Virgin, 17. *See also* All Souls' College; Christ Church; Magdalen College

Papists, 16, 32, 35, 40, 52. *See also* Roman Catholic Church
Parliament: and Charles I, 21–22; in Oxford, 17; House of Commons, flight of five MPs from, 294 n.239(3); House of Lords, Bishops expelled from, 15; Henry King active in, 55 n.50, 58 n.107; Rump Parliament, 294 n.235(2); Short Parliament, 21, 54 n.24; of 1603, 22; of 1624, 33
Parliamentarians, 23, 27, 29
Paul's Cross pulpit, sermons at, 16, 21, 22, 43, 57 n.99, 293 n.230(3)
People, rule by. *See* King, Henry: views on
Pepys, Samuel, 22, 26, 29, 40; quoted, 294 n.235(1) and (5)
Perkins, William, 33
Personal Reign of Christ, The (John Archer), 298 n.265(5)
Petworth (Sussex), 23, 29, 54 n.29
Piers Plowman, 19
Plague, 17, 18–19, 37
Pliny, 43
Popery, suspicion of, 33, 36
Popes, 16–18; Papal supremacy attacked, 16–17, 35, 37
Prayer Book. *See* Common Prayer, Book of
Presbyterians, 25, 28, 29, 37
Preston, Thomas, 16
Prideaux, Bishop John, 31
Priests. *See* Clergy
Primitive (early) church, 31, 35, 39
Purchase, Samuel: *Pilgrims*, 47
Puritans: bishops appointed to please, 22, 33; in civil wars and interregnum, 28; dislike of learning, 29, 52; hypocrisy, 35–36, 39, 40; manners in church, 36; the name, 34; preachers, 17; sermon seekers, 22; spirituality, 32, 34
Purgatory, 35
Pye, Sir Robert, 58 n.116

Reformers, continental, 22, 35, 36, 51, 52
Regicides, 28, 294 n.235(4), 295 n.240(3), 300 n.273(2)
Restoration, 24, 25–30; service of thanksgiving for, 26
Reynolds, Bishop Edward, 28, 55 n.45
Richings Park (Bucks), 23, 54 n.33
Richmond (Surrey), 24, 54 n.42
Roe, Sir Thomas, 20
Roman Catholic Church: auricular confession, 17–18, 35, 36, 38; clergy, 35; 37; lucrative or superstitious practices, 35; place of Bible and tradition, 40; religious life, 35; spiritual writers, 32, 34, 35; venial sin, 35. *See also* Jesuits, Papists; Popery
Rome, ancient, 35
Root and Branch petition, 293 n.268(2)

General Index

Royalists: devotion to executed king, 22, 30; sufferings, 27, 28; uprisings, 24
Royal Navy, 22
Ruddy, Christopher, 57 n.76
Ryves, Dean Bruno, 23, 298 n.268(2)

Sacraments: baptism, 36, 38; Holy Communion, 39; in relation to the Bible, 39–40
St. Paul's cathedral, London: administrative chapter, 19, 48; Deanery, 52; deans' books, 16; Philip King (uncle) auditor of, 15; prebendal duties, 19, 36, 51; property leases, 23; restoration of, 22, 293 n.230(3) and (4); St. Pancras prebend, 39, 51; Vicaridge House, 16. *See also* Paul's Cross
Salter, Lady, 23
Sancroft, Archbishop William, 36
Sanderson, Bishop Robert, 25
Sapientia Clamans, 48
Scottish Assemblies, 295 n.240(2)
Schoolmen (mediaeval), 20, 51–52
Seneca, 46, 52, 58 n.120
Separatists, 35
Septuagint. *See* Bible
Shakespeare, William: plays, 18, 46, 50, 53; *Hamlet*, 37, 53, 285 nn. 129(2) and 131; 288 n.161(5), 290 n.199; *Henry V*, 289 n.179(2), 292 n.229; *Henry VIII*, 127; *King Lear*, 53, 298 n.268(2) and (3); *Macbeth*, 53, 290 n.192; *Merchant of Venice*, 53, 290 n.193; First folio, 58 n.121
Sheldon, Archbishop Gilbert, 25, 26, 29, 30, 54 n.33, 55 nn. 42 and 44
Shere (Surrey), 23
Ship Money, 22, 293 n.231
Ships' chaplains, 29
Shirley, F. J.: *Richard Hooker*, 56 n.61
Shirley, James: *The Triumphs of Peace*, 22
Simpson, Evelyn, 9, 17, 48, 52
Simpson, Percy, 15
Sleidanus: *De Quattuor Imperiis*, 282 n.108(3)
Smectymnuus, 298 n.265(4)
Smith, Humphrey, 36, 57 n.76
Sotheby's, 16
Sparrow, John: *Poems of Henry King*, 40
Spelman, Sir Henry, 20, 54 n.17
Spital sermons, 18, 43, 54 n.14
Stanhope, Lady, 30
Staninough, Mr., 58 n.116
Stapleton, Thomas, 35
State, Council of, 294 n.234(5)

Stationers' Hall, 16, 21
Stow, John: *Annals*, 51
Stretton, Richard, 29
Subject's Sorrow, The (Brown, Robert), 29–30
Sutch, Victor: *Gilbert Sheldon*, 54 n.27, 55 n.39

Taylor, Bishop Jeremy, 31, 57 n.87
Thame (Oxon): Lord Williams' school, 15
Thomas, Lambrook, 55 n.45
Topsell, Edward: *Historie*, 43
Tuke, Lemuel, 30

Ussher, Archbishop James: antipapist, 35; Barnard's funeral sermon for, 27, 29, 56 n.59; recipient of King's *Psalms*, 25; writings, 44, 287 n.160

Verse miscellany manuscripts. *See* Commonplace books
Visitation articles, 28
Voluntarists, 33
Vulgate. *See* Bible

Walker, Anthony: *True Account of the Author, A*, 30
Walker, John: *Sufferings*, 22, 54 n.33
Waller, Sir William, 23
Walters, Lucy, 56 n.53
Walton, Bishop Brian: polyglot Bible, 25
Walton, Izaak: King's letter to, 17, 58 n.118; *Lives*, 11 n.4, 20, 22, 23
Warner, Bishop Robert, 58 n.45, 300 n.272(2)
Westminster Abbey: Duppa's funeral service at, 27; service of thanksgiving in, 26
Westminster School, 15, 28, 48, 51, 53
White, Dr. Francis, 57 n.75
Whitehall (Court), 34, 49; sermons at, 18, 21, 26, 29, 30, 49, 55 n.48
White's Plot, 295 n.239(6)
Wilkinson, Thomas, 55 n.44
Williamson, George: *Senecan Amble*, 41, 57 n.76
Windsor (Berks), 23; Garter Day service at, 27
Winiffe, Bishop George, 31
Wood, Antony, 22, 25, 28, 34, 54 n.33
Wright, Abraham, 40; *Parnassus Biceps*, 296 n.250(2)
Wykes, John, 21

Yates, Frances, 9
York, 26; York Gospels, 26
York, James, Duke of, 30